PHYSICS

A course for GCSE

Cambridge University Press
Cambridge
New York   New Rochelle
Melbourne   Sydney

Acknowledgements

Our thanks to Mrs V. Head, Mrs M. Rose and Mrs M. Steel who typed the final manuscript. We also wish to thank Mr C. Sawyer, B.Sc.(Eng.) and Mr J. A. Timney, Ph.D., for reading parts of the manuscript and for their valuable comments and suggestions. We are particularly indebted to Mr J. W. Noakes B.Sc. M.Inst.P. AIL who supplied some original questions for use at the end of some of the chapters.

G.R. and S.H.

Acknowledgement is made to the following Examination Boards for permission to reprint questions from their past papers:

Associated Examining Board	(AEB)
Joint Matriculation Board	(JMB)
London & East Anglian Group	(L & EAG)
Northern Examining Association	(NEA)
North West Regional Examinations Board	(NWREB)
Oxford and Cambridge Schools Examinations Board	(O & C)
Oxford Delegacy of Local Examinations	(O)
Southern Universities Joint Board	(S)
University of Cambridge Local Examinations Syndicate	(C)
University of London Schools Examinations Board	(L)
Welsh Joint Education Committee	(W)
West Yorkshire and Lindsay Regional Examinations Board	
	(WY & LREB)

The Examination Boards accept no responsibility whatsoever for the accuracy of the answers given.

Acknowledgement is made to the following for permission to reproduce the photographs used in this book:

Page 30 (top): Space Frontiers/Daily Telegraph Colour Library, (bottom) Mr C. Sawyer. 37: Department of Metallurgy and Materials Science, University of Cambridge. 40: Ray Hamilton/ Camera Press London. 45: Nike. 110: Clive Lloyd/Barnabys. 129: British Coal. 140, 232, 234: Griffin and George. 208: Sinclair Stammers/Science Photo Library. 209: Richard Wolf UK Ltd. 235 (top): Photograph from the Hale Observatories. 235 (bottom): University of Manchester, Jodrell Bank. 358 (left, centre): David Redfern, (right) Topham.

Cover photograph: Paul Brierley

Preface

This book is designed specifically for students preparing for the GCSE examinations in Physics. It covers fully the syllabuses of all five of the GCSE examining groups or associations. The student will need to select the topics which suit their own particular syllabus.

As experienced examiners, we have for many years been concerned at the overall quality of the answers to basic physics questions. This book tries to remove the inaccuracies, misconceptions, misunderstandings, lack of precision and poor presentation of answers which unfortunately have been all too common in the past.

In each chapter there are worked examples so that the student can learn good practice in tackling numerical problems. A number of exercises are included for students to test themselves. Each chapter has a good selection of actual examination questions which will further test understanding.

Physics is an experimental science and therefore students should engage in as much practical work as is possible. Full details of many practical experiments are given throughout the book. There is a systematic and logical approach to both theory and practical work. The comprehensive index at the end of the book will enable the student to find any topic easily and quickly.

Gilbert Rowell
Sidney Herbert
July 1986

Published by the Press Syndicate of the University of Cambridge
The Pitt Building, Trumpington Street, Cambridge CB2 1RP
32 East 57th Street, New York, NY 10022, USA
10 Stamford Road, Oakleigh, Melbourne 3166, Australia

© G. Rowell and S. Herbert 1987

First published 1987
Reprinted with corrections 1987

Printed in Great Britain by Ebenezer Baylis & Son, The Trinity Press, Worcester and London

British Library cataloguing in publication data
Rowell, Gilbert
  Physics : a course for GCSE
  1. Physics
  I. Title II. Herbert, Sidney
  530   QC23

ISBN 0 521 27128 2

DP

Contents

Introduction

0.1 Experimentation

Experimentation is a necessary and essential part of the study of Physics. To perform an experiment successfully, you must have a clear understanding of the logical steps to be undertaken, have the manipulative skills, judgement and patience needed to make a systematic collection of readings and, finally, be able to calculate the result from the figures or data collected. When you have performed the experiment successfully you still have to present a written account of it in as neat and concise a way as possible. This account is usually formulated under sub-headings such as *Title, Diagram, Method, Results, Calculation* or *Graph*, and *Conclusion*. In each of the experiments described in this book, the *Diagram* and *Table of results* are emphasised in each experiment. When you perform an experiment you should make certain that, before you leave the laboratory, you have written neatly in a practical notebook both an accurately drawn, clearly labelled diagram and a list of *all* the measurements you took. Armed with these two vital pieces of information you could, if necessary, complete the parts of the account that belong under the other sub-headings at home.

The mistakes most commonly made when drawing or writing material under the sub-headings *Diagrams* and *Table of results* are described below.

(a) Diagrams

The three diagrams in Fig. 0.1 all show the apparatus used in testing Hooke's Law for a spring (see p.34).

It should be obvious why Fig. 0.1(a) is useless. But why is Fig. 0.1(c) preferable to Fig. 0.1(b)? Diagrams that have been drawn freehand, without the aid of instruments, look untidy and slovenly. Diagrams should always be drawn neatly with the aid of pencil, ruler, set-square, compass, protractor, geoliner, etc. and the labels added to the completed diagram with a line pointing to the actual component of the assembled apparatus.

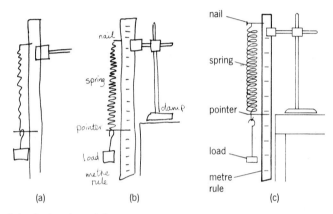

0.1   *Bad and good diagrams*

(b) Table of results

Some pupils write down experimental readings on scraps of paper and then find these figures meaningless when writing the account of the experiment. To avoid this confusion, all measurements should be carefully recorded in a table of results set out in either (i) headed columns or (ii) numbered rows.

Table 0.1   **Typical results for a Hooke's Law experiment**

Load L/N	Pointer reading/cm		Average pointer reading/mm	Extension e/mm	Show calculations
	Loading	*Unloading*			
0	40.0	40.0	400	0.0	$400 - 400 = \quad 0$
0.5	42.2	42.2	422	22.0	$422 - 400 = \quad 22$
1.0	44.3	44.5	444	44.0	$444 - 400 = \quad 44$
1.5	46.6	46.6	466	66.0	$466 - 400 = \quad 66$
2.0	48.8	48.8	488	88.0	$488 - 400 = \quad 88$
2.5	51.0	51.0	510	110.0	$510 - 400 = 110$
3.0	53.2	53.2	532	132.0	$532 - 400 = 132$

Table 0.2 Recording using numbered rows

			Show calculations
1. Original length of tube	$l =$	501.0 mm	
2. First micrometer reading	$s_1 =$	10.6 mm	
3. Second micrometer reading	$s_2 =$	11.3 mm	
4. Increase in length of tube	$(s_2 - s_1) =$	0.7 mm	$11.3 - 10.6 = 0.7$
5. Original temperature of tube	$\theta_1 =$	19.0 °C	
6. Final temperature of tube	$\theta_2 =$	100.0 °C	
7. Increase in temperature	$(\theta_2 - \theta_1) =$	81.0 K	$100 - 19 = 81$

Headed columns: First write out the headings, then 'box' them in to form a table. All the readings are entered *as they are taken* so that the completed table looks similar to Table 0.1.

The headings must include the units in which each quantity is measured. If the load L is equal to 0.5 N, then it follows from load $L = 0.5$ N that load $L/N = 0.5$ is the method of expressing the number 0.5. Hence, if each heading shows the quantity divided by its unit then the numbers only need to be entered in the columns.

Numbered rows: The results obtained during an experiment to measure the linear expansivity of copper are given in Table 0.2 as an example of this method of recording.

The numbering is optional, but each row must be set down logically and on a separate line. Notice that the appropriate symbols and units are entered for each quantity measured. Ensure that there is sufficient space on the right of the equals sign to enter readings as shown in the final table above. Notice that the results are listed so that the calculation is made easy, namely, the two micrometer readings are on lines 2 and 3 although they were not necessarily the second and third measurements taken. Always list all the actual readings taken. Never do subtractions in your head and then write down the answer only. If lines 2 and 3 are not recorded it is impossible to check the correctness of line 4.

0.2 Performing and recording the experiment

When the instructions have been read carefully, the apparatus assembled as shown in the diagram, the correctly labelled diagram drawn and the results table set out you are ready to perform the experiment itself. Each measurement or reading taken should be entered immediately into the prepared results table. It may be advisable to write these results in pencil at first, and then ink them in if the calculation works out successfully.

Written accounts of experiments should always follow a general pattern which may be laid down by your teacher. The following example shows a scheme that is often used:

Title: To test Hooke's Law for a helical spring.

Explanation: Hooke's Law states that, provided the elastic limit is not exceeded, the extension e of the spring is directly proportional to the load L applied to it.

Diagram: The line diagram (or isometric/oblique projection view) should be accurately drawn and correctly labelled, as in Fig. 0.1(c).

Method: The detailed step-by-step account of how the experiment was performed should be written in the past tense. It should include enough information so that another person, unfamiliar with the experiment, could read the account and be able to perform the experiment successfully. Any special precautions, or additional steps taken to improve the working of the apparatus should be included in the method. Thus the method should be an accurate, chronological account of what was done and how it was done. An example of the *Method* for the Hooke's Law experiment now follows.

The apparatus was set up as shown in the diagram. Before any load L was added, the position of the pointer on the rule was noted and recorded. This position acts as an arbitrary zero. A load of 0.5 N was attached to the end of the spring. The load oscillated for a while but it was allowed to come to rest before the new position of the pointer was noted and recorded in the table of results. Loads of 0.5 N were added until the total load was 3.0 N and, after coming to rest in its steady position, the reading of the pointer was noted for each value of the load. Then the load was removed in equal steps of 0.5 N and the steady pointer readings noted and recorded. The average position of the pointer reading for each load was calculated by adding together the loading and unloading readings and dividing by two. The extension e of the spring was calculated for each load by subtracting the zero load reading of the pointer from the average position of the pointer for each load.

A graph of load L against extension e was plotted and a straight-line graph through the origin confirms that e is directly proportional to L.

Results: The table of results has been discussed in detail on p.1.

Calculations: All mathematical calculations must be shown in full in your practical notebook; preferably alongside, or near, the results table so that the working out may be checked by your teacher. In Physics, almost all quantities have units and it is a very common mistake to omit these units from calculations. The appropriate unit should always be quoted in the final result. If there is no unit, as for example in refractive index, mechanical advantage or velocity ratio, then it is a good idea to include the note 'no units'.

Graph: Graphs will become more and more important as you progress from this level to higher levels of study in Physics. Sound basic training at these early stages is essential for any future work that you may pursue. Figure 0.2(a) shows the recommended method of labelling graphs so that they are seen as mathematical devices dealing with numbers only. This is achieved from a reading such as $p = 1.0 \times 10^5$ Pa which gives $p/\text{Pa} = 1.0 \times 10^5$. Thus if the quantity involved is divided by its unit when written on the axis of a graph, numbers alone may be written on the axes. Since the SI symbols of p and V represent pressure and volume respectively, it is not strictly necessary to include the words 'pressure' and 'volume' also (Fig. 0.2b) as they are implied by the symbols. However, in this book the words will be written alongside the SI symbols to help you to become familiar with the meaning of the various symbols. When you understand the symbols you can leave out the words if you wish.

Up to this level it is permissible to use multiples or sub-multiples of SI units and even non-SI units if it will simplify the numbers used on the graph. Thus the graph in Fig. 0.2(b) would be an acceptable alternative to Fig. 0.2(a) since 100 kPa and 50 cm^3 are easier numbers to work with than 1.0×10^5 Pa and 50×10^{-6} m^3, which maintain basic SI units. The use of a **sketch graph**, i.e. one that shows the relationship between two quantities without involving numbers, is also recommended. Fig. 0.2(c) shows an example of a sketch graph illustrating that the resistance R of a wire is directly proportional to the length l of the wire. Note that the axes are labelled 'resistance' and 'length', the names of the two quantities involved. Symbols R and l, and units are not used. As an exercise, draw a sketch graph of pressure p against volume V for a fixed mass of gas at constant temperature.

In this book we also recommend that a title and the values of the scales used are added to those graphs dealing with experimental or numerical data. Here we

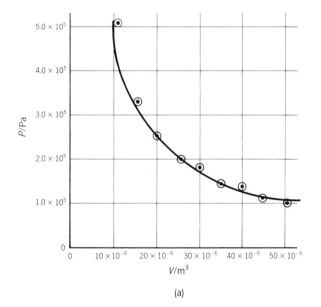

(a)

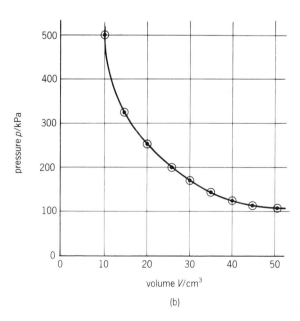

(b)

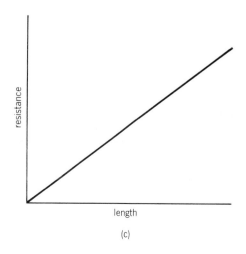

(c)

0.2   Presentation of graphs

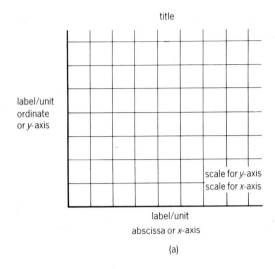

title

label/unit
ordinate
or *y*-axis

scale for *y*-axis
scale for *x*-axis

label/unit

abscissa or *x*-axis

(a)

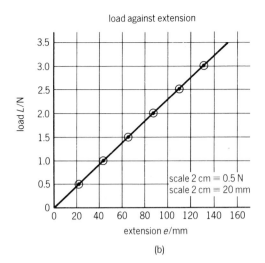

load against extension

load *L*/N

scale 2 cm ≡ 0.5 N
scale 2 cm ≡ 20 mm

extension *e*/mm

(b)

0.3   *Titles, labels, units and scales for graphs*

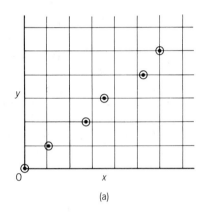

y

0   *x*

(a)

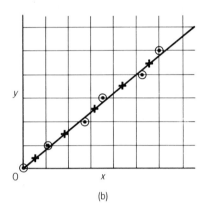

y

0   *x*

(b)

0.4   *Drawing the best straight line*

recommend that every graph (see Fig. 0.3a) should have

(a) a title;
(b) both axes labelled;
(c) units of the quantity on each axis;
(d) scales being used on each axis;
(e) points plotted with crosses (× or +) or with dot and circle ⊙.

The graph in Fig. 0.3(b) is drawn from the results of the Hooke's Law experiment given on p.1. Extreme care is needed to plot the points accurately. The plotted points must be 'joined' with a single straight line or a continuous curve. The graph should cover as much of the area of the graph paper as possible. This requires a sensible choice of scale for each axis. It is unlikely that points plotted from real experimental results will *all* lie on a straight line (or smooth curve) due to errors, so try to produce a straight line (or smooth curve) which passes through as many of the plotted points as possible or which leaves an equal distribution of points on either side. A useful way of achieving a balanced graph of this type is shown in Fig. 0.4. Suppose you have to draw the best straight line through the *six* points marked in Fig. 0.4(a). Simply

mark (in a different colour or notation) the mid-point for each pair of plotted points. These **five** mid-points are marked with a + in Fig. 0.4(b). The mid-points usually lie very nearly on a straight line. Therefore, joining the **five** mid-points in Fig. 0.4(b) with a straight line gives the best straight line through the original six points. Should the mid-points not lie on a reasonably straight line, the procedure can be repeated to obtain mid-points of the mid-points, and so on, until a straight line is achieved.

An alternative method of dealing quickly with points which do not all lie on a perfect straight line uses a narrow strip of clear plastic with a straight-edge (e.g. a piece of clear Perspex 30 cm × 2 cm). Position the plastic over the points, as shown in Fig. 0.5, so that they are visually equally distributed above and below the straight-edge. This is possible because you can see the points below the straight-edge through the clear plastic. Then draw a straight line along the straight-edge.

Figure 0.5 also shows another difficulty commonly encountered when drawing a graph, namely, what to do about point P which lies well outside the range of the straight line through the other five points. In this case you should treat point P as an error and not

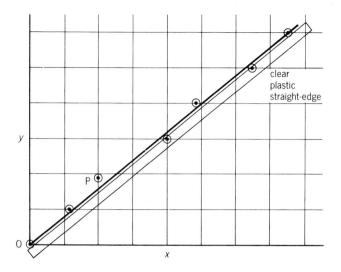

0.5 Alternative method of drawing the best straight line

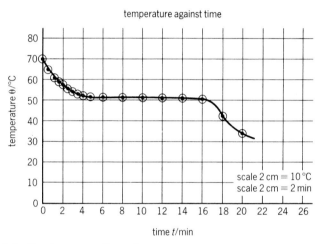

temperature against time

scale 2 cm ≡ 10 °C
scale 2 cm ≡ 2 min

time *t*/min

0.6 Drawing a smooth continuous curve

include it when drawing the straight line but instead find out why this point was in error. To find out why P is in error,

(a) check that the point was plotted correctly;
(b) check the calculations for computing P;
(c) check the apparatus;
(d) if possible, repeat the measurements which gave the point P.

Curves should be drawn with a French curve or a plastic strip which can be bent into any shape required. A friend can hold the bent strip in position while you draw round its outline. The final curve should be smooth and continuous, as shown in Fig. 0.6.

Conclusion: State and display prominently any conclusions you draw from the experiment. Be honest when writing the account and conclusion. Do not contrive to produce the expected answer, particularly if the results and technique do not justify it. If when you calculate the result you realise that it is not the accurate value you tried to measure, your teacher will be able to tell you whether the result is

(a) acceptable within the limits of experimental error;
(b) due to an experimental error; or
(c) due to a mathematical error.

Practical experiments can be interesting and stimulating, particularly if they are performed successfully.

0.3 Gradient or slope

When you have plotted a graph, you are often required to determine the gradient (or slope) of the straight line or of the curve at a given point.

To determine the gradient of a straight-line graph

The straight-line graph in Fig. 0.7 plots potential difference V against current I for a resistor at constant temperature. **The gradient (slope) of the line is the tangent of the angle θ which the line makes with the horizontal**; i.e. tan θ in Fig. 0.7. In this case the gradient of the line gives the resistance of the resistor.

To determine the gradient, construct a right-angled triangle anywhere on the line so that the line forms the hypotenuse. Make the triangle as large as possible to ensure greater accuracy.

$$\text{gradient} = \tan \theta$$
$$= \frac{AB}{BC}$$
$$= \frac{(2.4 - 0.4)}{(1.2 - 0.2)} \frac{V}{A}$$
$$= \frac{2.0}{1.0} \Omega$$
$$\text{gradient} = 2.0 \ \Omega$$

So the resistance of the resistor is 2.0 Ω. The y-values of points A (2.4) and B (0.4) have to be read from the y-axis; a rule placed parallel to the x-axis at the points A and B will help evaluate these correctly. Note also that the unit from the y-axis (V) has been written with the numbers. Likewise, the x-values of points B (1.2) and C (0.2) have to be read from the x-axis with the aid of a rule placed parallel to the y-axis; here the unit from the x-axis (A) has been included. B and C have to be chosen carefully and deliberately such that BC=1.0; an easy number by which to divide. By introducing the units V and A and combining them as V A^{-1} the gradient (slope) of the line gives the resistance R of the resistor in ohms (Ω). When dealing with physical quantities it is important to quote the unit; this method of attaching units to the numbers taken from a graph enables this to be achieved.

Another useful piece of information can be obtained from the intercept of a straight-line graph with the y- or x-axis. The use of intercepts can be illustrated using a graph of reciprocal *u* (1/*u*) against reciprocal *v* (1/*v*)

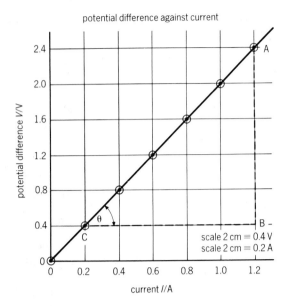

0.7 To determine the gradient (slope) of a straight-line graph

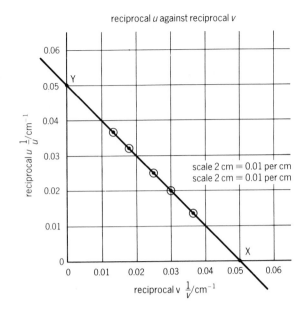

0.8 Using intercepts to determine the gradient of a straight-line graph

for a converging (convex) lens of focal length f. The formula linking u, v and f is $1/u + 1/v = 1/f$ which when re-arranged gives $1/u = -1/v + 1/f$. When compared with the general equation of a straight line $y = mx + c$ the intercept c is equivalent to $1/f$. In this example the intercept on either axis is equivalent to $1/f$.

In Fig. 0.8 the intercept with the y-axis is at OY $= 0.05$ cm^{-1} and with the x-axis is at OX $= 0.05$ cm^{-1}.

$$\text{intercept } c = \frac{1}{f}$$

$$f = \frac{1}{c}$$

$$f = \frac{1}{0.05} \quad \frac{1}{\text{cm}^{-1}}$$

$$f = \frac{100}{5.0} \text{ cm}$$

$$f = +20 \text{ cm}$$

Note that in this example the straight line slopes downwards to the right and hence the gradient (slope) of the line is **negative**.

To determine the gradient at a point P on a curve

First the tangent to the curve at point P must be constructed (see Fig. 0.9). Stand a plane mirror vertically across the curve so that the silvered surface is directly on top of P. Rotate the mirror on a vertical axis through P until the curve in front of the mirror appears continuous with those seen *in* the mirror and behind the mirror. Without moving the mirror, draw a straight line along its back (silvered) edge, through the point P. This line is the **normal** to the curve at the point P. Now construct a line perpendicular to the normal. This line is the required tangent to the curve

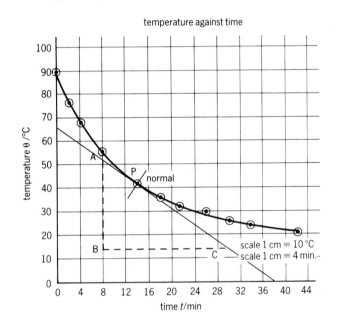

0.9 Gradient at a point on a curve

at P. Note that the gradient (or slope) of the tangent at P is negative (see Fig. 0.9) and can be calculated as follows:

$$\text{gradient (slope)} = \frac{\text{AB}}{\text{BC}}$$

$$= \frac{(52 - 16)}{(8 - 28)} \quad \frac{°\text{C}}{\text{min}}$$

$$= \frac{36}{-20} °\text{C min}^{-1}$$

$$\text{gradient (slope)} = -1.8 °\text{C min}^{-1}$$

Note that by labelling the triangle ABC correctly the negative sign of the gradient (slope) emerges from the calculation.

0.4 Solution to problems

Another aspect of Physics which deserves attention is the solution of problems. At the end of each chapter, exercises and calculations are given to test your knowledge and understanding of the Physics you have learned. Here is a general method of approaching numerical problems.

1. Draw a 'sketch' diagram wherever possible.
2. Copy down the numerical information given in the question.
3. Write down the relevant formula.
4. Substitute the given values into the formula.
5. Calculate the answer, remembering to show all steps in the working out and giving the correct units for your final answer.

To illustrate this approach consider the following example.

Example

An object is accelerated uniformly from rest at $6\,\mathrm{m\,s^{-2}}$. Calculate (a) the velocity v after 10 s, (b) the distance s travelled during 10 s.

$$u = 0\,\mathrm{m\,s^{-2}} \quad\quad s$$

sketch diagram

$$a = 6\,\mathrm{m\,s^{-2}} \quad t = 10\,\mathrm{s}$$

$u = 0\,\mathrm{m\,s^{-2}}\ (\text{rest}) \quad v = ? \quad a = 6\,\mathrm{m\,s^{-2}}$
$t = 10\,\mathrm{s} \quad s = ?$ information

(a) $v = u + at$ formula
$\quad v = 0 + 6\,\mathrm{m\,s^{-2}} \times 10\,\mathrm{s}$ substitute
$\quad v = 60\,\mathrm{m\,s^{-1}}$ calculate

(b) $s = ut + \frac{1}{2}at^2$ formula
$\quad s = 0 \times 10 + \frac{1}{2} \times 6\,\mathrm{m\,s^{-2}} \times (10)^2\,\mathrm{(s)}^2$ substitute
$\quad s = 0 + 3 \times 100\,\mathrm{m\,s^{-2} \times s^2}$ calculate
$\quad s = 300\,\mathrm{m}$ note units in answer

Questions

Q1 In an experiment to measure the average thickness of a sheet of paper, a pupil measures the thickness t of several numbers of sheets n and obtains the following results:

thickness t/mm	11.0	21.5	32.0	43.0	54.0	64.0
number of sheets n	10	20	30	40	50	60

Plot a graph of thickness t against number of sheets n and hence calculate the average thickness of a single sheet of paper. From the graph find the thickness of 80 sheets of paper.

Q2 A boy measures the circumference c and diameter d of various circles. His results are shown in the table below.

circumference c/cm	3.2	6.3	12.6	15.7	19.0
diameter d/cm	1.0	2.0	4.0	5.0	6.0

Plot a graph of circumference c against diameter d and determine the gradient (slope) of the straight line.

Q3 To find the average mass of a £1 coin a girl finds the mass m of various numbers n of the coins. Her results are shown in the table below.

number of coins n	10	15	20	25	50
mass m/g	96	143	189	238	475

Plot a graph of mass m against number of coins n and find the average mass of one coin. From the graph find the mass of 38 £1 coins.

Q4 The mass m of several volumes V of the same material is measured and recorded in the table.

mass m/kg	0.25	0.50	0.75	1.00	1.25	1.50
volume V/m³	0.5	1.0	1.5	2.0	2.5	3.0

Plot a graph of mass m against volume V and determine the gradient (slope) of the straight line.

Q5 Plot a graph of velocity v against time t for the values given in the table below.

velocity v/m s^{-1}	10	15	20	25	30	35
time t/s	0	2	4	6	8	10

Determine the gradient (slope) of the straight line.

Q6 A coil of wire has a resistance R which varies with temperature θ as shown in the table below. Plot a graph of resistance R against temperature θ.

resistance R/Ω	5.5	6.0	6.4	6.9	7.4	8.0
temperature θ/°C	10	20	30	40	50	60

What is the resistance of the coil at 0°C? At what temperature does the coil have a resistance of 7 Ω? Find the gradient (slope) of the straight line.

Q7 The table below gives seven pairs of readings of velocity v and time t. One pair of values does not lie on the straight line which passes through the other six points.

velocity v/m s^{-1}	5.5	16.0	21.0	30.0	35.0	42.0	50.0
time t/s	0.7	2.1	2.8	4.2	4.6	5.5	6.5

Plot a graph of velocity v against time t and find (a) the point which should *not* be used when drawing a straight line graph; (b) the velocity when $t = 0$; and (c) the time when the velocity is $25\,\mathrm{m\,s^{-1}}$.

Q8 A 10 m plank of wood marked off in equal intervals of 1 m is inclined to a vertical wall as shown. For each of the first six marks on the plank the vertical height h and the horizontal distance d are recorded in the table of results below.

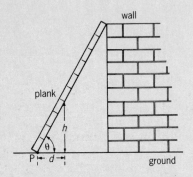

vertical height h/m	0.87	1.73	2.60	3.46	4.33	5.19
horizontal distance d/m	0.50	1.00	1.50	2.00	2.50	3.00

Plot a graph of the vertical height h against horizontal distance d and from the graph find (a) the height of the wall; (b) the distance of P from the base of the wall; (c) the angle of inclination θ of the plank with the ground.

Q9 A large mass is released, from rest, from a height 100 m above the ground. Its height h above the ground is measured at various times t from its release and recorded in the table below.

height h/m	100	95	80	55	20	10
time t/s	0	1	2	3	4	4.2

Plot a graph of height h against time t and draw a smooth curve through the points. Find the time taken for the mass to reach the ground. Construct the tangent to the point (2,80) and find the gradient (slope) of the line at this point.

Q10 The results in the table below are for height h and (time)^2 t^2 for the mass in Q9.

height h/m	100	95	80	55	20	10
(time)^2 t^2/s^2	0	1	4	9	16	18

Plot a graph of height h against (time)^2 t^2 and find the gradient (slope) of the straight line.

Q11 The area A of a rectangle is given by $A = l \times b$ where $l =$ length and $b =$ breadth of the rectangle. The following values of l and b give an area of 36 m^2.

length l/m	18	12	8	4	3	2
breadth b/m	2	3	4.5	9	12	18
$\dfrac{1}{\text{breadth } b}$/m^{-1}	0.50	0.33	0.22	0.11	0.085	0.055

Using the same scale for both axes plot a graph of length l against breadth b and draw a smooth curve through the points. On the same graph draw a straight line $b = l$ (at 45°) through the origin. The point where this line meets the curve gives the length L of the side of the square which has the same area as the rectangle. Find the length L from the graph. Draw another graph; this time of length l against reciprocal breadth (l/b) and show it is a straight line through the origin. Calculate the slope (gradient) of the straight line.

Q12 The two liquids used in an experiment involving balancing columns of liquids in a U-tube are oil and water. The height of the oil h_o and the height of the water h_w above a common level are recorded in the table below.

height of oil h_o/cm	10.0	12.0	14.0	16.0	18.0	20.0
height of water h_w/cm	8.0	9.5	11.4	12.8	14.6	16.2

Plot a graph of height h_w against height of oil h_o and find the gradient (slope) of the straight line.

Q13 When a resistor R is connected across the terminals of a cell the potential difference V across the resistor varies as the value of R is changed. The results in the table below show the values of $1/V$ and $1/R$.

$\dfrac{1}{\text{potential difference } V}$/V^{-1}	2.0	1.6	1.3	1.1	1.0	0.89
$\dfrac{1}{\text{resistance } R}$/$\Omega^{-1}$	1.0	0.7	0.5	0.3	0.25	0.16

Plot a graph of $1/V$ against $1/R$ and find the value of $1/R$ when $1/V = 0$

Q14 What is the difference between a sketch graph and a normal graph? Draw a sketch graph of your answers to Q1, Q5, Q9 and Q10.

Q15 A man buys 100 ball-bearings which are all nominally the same size. How would you suggest that he finds (a) the average mass of 1 ball-bearing, (b) the average diameter of the ball-bearings; and (c) an accurate value for the diameter of one of the ball bearings. (Assume a micrometer screw-gauge is used to measure the diameter of the ball-bearings.)

Q16 In a 'Hooke's Law' experiment a rubber band is used in place of the spiral spring. The results table is shown below.

Load/N	0	0.5	1.0	1.5	2.0	2.5
Extension/cm	0	1.0	2.4	4.1	6.4	10.0

(a) Plot a graph of Load against extension and show that the rubber band does *not* obey Hooke's Law; (b) Sketch, on your graph, the curve you might expect to obtain from a set of readings for extension obtained as the load is reduced from 2.5 N to 0 N; (c) The rubber band is replaced by one of stiffer rubber. Using the same graph, sketch the curve you might expect for the new rubber band.

1 Forces

1.1 Introducing forces

If someone describes an object by saying 'It is red', many different objects fit the description, e.g. a red post box, bus, rose, scarf, dress, ball, etc. If the description is expanded to 'It is red and round', you will perhaps imagine a red ball, apple, frisbee or a tomato. You cannot be certain what 'it' really is unless you have some additional information describing 'it' in more detail. Suppose 'it' is next described as 'Red, round and edible', you will probably choose 'apple' or 'tomato' from the objects mentioned already but you may think of alternatives. However, suppose you are given an apple and asked 'What is it?' The answer is simple, 'it' is an apple; you have seen, felt and tasted an apple and know instinctively what it is. Someone who has detailed experience of an apple can imagine what an apple looks like and what it tastes like. However, consider how difficult it would be to describe what an apple is to someone who has never seen or tasted an apple. No words of description can ever really completely convey the delights of an apple. The best thing to do is to give an apple to the person and so reveal all!

Now think about a 'force'. What is it? No one has seen, tasted or felt a force, although you may have felt or seen the *effects* of a force. Your teacher cannot open a cupboard and bring out a 'force' for you to see and touch. How can a 'force' be explained to the whole class so that you all imagine the same thing? It can only be done by describing what happens when a 'force' is applied to some real object. The description must be very clear so that you will each give the same meaning to the term. The concept of a force is very difficult, but it must be mastered because forces occur throughout the different branches of physics.

Gravitational force

A ball released from eye-level can be observed to fall with increasing velocity (i.e. it accelerates) until it hits the ground. How can this downward acceleration of the free-falling ball be explained? The Earth exerts a gravitational force called the **force of gravity** (or weight) on the ball. Whatever it is that is responsible for accelerating the ball, or any other object, is called a **force** or, more correctly, an **unbalanced force**. The force of gravity is an example of a force acting at a distance, i.e. it acts even when the ball is not in contact with the Earth. If you see an object accelerating – either speeding up or slowing down – then you must conclude that an unbalanced force is acting on it. In addition you can deduce that the unbalanced force acts in the direction the object moves in as it speeds up, and acts in the opposite direction to the motion of the object as it slows down. At this stage, it seems tempting to suggest that any moving object is moving under the action of an unbalanced force. However, this would be quite wrong. An object can only move with **uniform velocity** (constant speed in a straight line) when there is *no* net force acting on it, that is, when the forces acting on the object are **balanced**. If an unbalanced force is applied, the object must speed up, slow down or change its direction of motion. If the object neither speeds up nor slows down and continues its motion in a straight line then there can be no resultant force acting on it. **To accelerate a body from rest an unbalanced force is needed and the increase in velocity will continue as long as the force is applied.** However, when the accelerating force is removed the body will continue with the velocity it has at the moment when the force is removed.

Frictional force

In real life an object which is moving over a horizontal surface does not continue with constant velocity when the accelerating force is removed. Instead the object slows down and eventually stops. The deceleration is caused by a **frictional force** between the object and the surface on which it travels. A frictional force always acts to oppose the motion of an object over a surface and is an example of a **contact force**.

Contact and non-contact forces

Examples of contact forces are frictional forces, normal reaction forces, tensions and forces in collisions. Forces at a distance (non-contact forces) include gravitational forces of attraction between two masses, electrical forces of attraction (or repulsion) between two electrically charged objects and magnetic forces of attraction (or repulsion) between two magnetised objects or a magnetised object and a

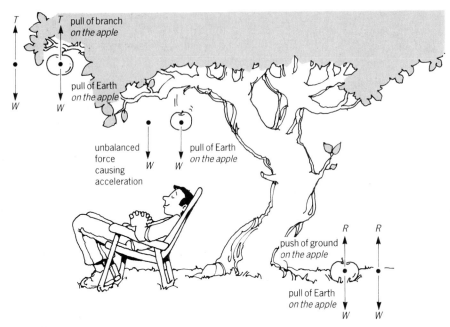

magnetic material. In general, forces at a distance

(a) are equal and opposite;
(b) depend upon the distance between the two 'objects';
(c) depend upon the medium between the two 'objects' for electrical and magnetic forces but not gravitational forces.

It is important to remember that motion alone is not proof that an unbalanced force is acting. Only acceleration, deceleration or a change of direction of motion is proof of an unbalanced force. Therefore, **force is that which *changes* the velocity (speed in a straight line) of an object.** When two or more forces act on a body in such a way that their effects cancel, we say that there is no **resultant** force or there is zero unbalanced force. If there is no *change* in the object's velocity (i.e. no acceleration) then no *resultant* force is acting. Note that this means that the object is at rest and remains at rest or moves with uniform velocity.

1.2   Main types of force

There are three types of force:

(a) gravitational forces,
(b) electromagnetic forces,
(c) nuclear forces.

Gravitational forces

Figure 1.1 shows a gravitational force acting on three apples: one attached to the tree, one falling freely and one at rest on the ground. It also illustrates the distinction between contact forces and forces at a distance (non-contact forces). The apple attached to the tree has a force called the 'weight of the apple'

acting on it; this is a non-contact force caused by the pull (attraction) of the Earth. (There is also an equal and opposite non-contact force due to the apple attracting the Earth, but the effect of this pull on the Earth is so small it can be neglected.) The weight W of the apple causes the apple to exert a pull P on the branch of the tree; the value of P is equal to W. The pull P of the apple on the branch is a contact force and the branch exerts an equal and opposite pull T on the apple. This **reaction force** T is equal in value to P which is in turn equal to W.

Free-body force diagram

In Physics it is often necessary to consider the effects of the forces on a single body. It is essential that all the forces acting on the chosen body are included and it is helpful to understand what other objects or bodies exert these forces.

Consider the apple on the branch of the tree. The forces acting on it are W and T, so the stationary apple and its forces can be represented by a single point from which an upward vertical force T and a downward vertical force W are drawn. This is shown alongside the apple in Fig. 1.1 and is known as a **free-body force diagram. A separate free-body force diagram should be drawn on every occasion for each object.** Note that in Fig. 1.1 the phrase '*on the apple*' appears in the description of both forces T and W; the force P which acts *on the branch* is not included in the diagram. Convention calls upward forces positive ($+$) and downward forces negative ($-$). The lengths of the lines that represent the forces could indicate their relative magnitudes.

Now consider the free-falling apple which is about to hit the boy sitting under the tree. There is an unbalanced force (the weight W) acting on the apple which causes it to accelerate towards the ground. This (non-contact) force is represented by a downward vertical force W acting at a point which represents the apple. Since the apple is above the ground it has potential (or stored) energy; this energy is converted into kinetic energy ($\frac{1}{2}mv^2$) as the apple falls – as the boy will soon find out when the apple hits him on the head!

Finally consider the third apple which is resting on the ground. At first sight, the forces shown in the diagram look the same as those on the first apple. However, closer inspection shows that the weight W of the apple causes the apple to exert a downward push P on the ground and so the ground exerts an equal and upward push R on the apple. For the apple to remain at rest (**in equilibrium**), the downward pull W of the Earth must balance the upward push R of the ground since these are the only two forces acting on the apple. Note that the push of the ground on this apple and the pull of the branch on the first apple both act through the centre of gravity of the apple, and the direction of the force is the same in both cases but the forces themselves act on opposite sides of the apple.

Magnetic forces

Consider a powerful magnet supported by a hand (see Fig. 1.2a). The forces acting on the magnet are (a) the pull of the hand P, (b) the pull of the Earth W. When the magnet is held stationary, $P - W = 0$, i.e. there is zero unbalanced force. However, if the magnet is moved to a position above an iron nail resting on a bench (Fig. 1.2b), the forces on the magnet alter very slightly. This is due to an additional small force f, the attraction of the nail (magnetic material) on the magnet. For a stationary magnet, $P_1 - W - f = 0$.

Now consider the forces acting on the nail at rest on the bench; they are the pull of the Earth w on the nail (its weight), the pull of the magnet f on the nail and the push of the table R on the nail. Hence $R + f - w = 0$ and on this occasion the reaction force R is *not* numerically equal to w: $R = w - f$. As f is exerting an upward pull on the nail, the push R need not be as large as if no magnet were present.

As the magnet is lowered the force of attraction increases from f to F_1, when the nail will jump (accelerate) off the bench and stick to the magnet. Now consider the nail in motion on its way up to the magnet. As the nail is accelerating upwards there must be an unbalanced (resultant) force acting vertically upwards. The free-body force diagram shows two forces F_1 and w acting on the nail. Clearly F_1 must be greater than w and the resultant force $(F_1 - w)$ gives the mass m of the nail an acceleration a. This also illustrates that the magnetic force of attraction increases as the distance between the magnet and the nail decreases. In fact, the force varies as the reciprocal of the square of the distance ($F_1 \propto 1/(\text{distance})^2$). As soon as the nail is no longer in contact with the bench, the bench cannot push on the nail and hence the reaction force R disappears.

Finally, consider the case when the nail is firmly stuck to the magnet. The nail is physically as close to the magnet as it can get, thus the magnetic force of attraction is at its greatest (F_2). Note the distance between the nail and the point at which the magnet acts is not zero because the magnetic pole is a short distance inside the magnet. The forces acting on the nail are now (a) F_2 (a non-contact force), the pull of the magnet on the nail, (b) the reaction r, the push of the magnet on the nail due to a contact force and (c) w, the weight or pull of the Earth on the nail. For

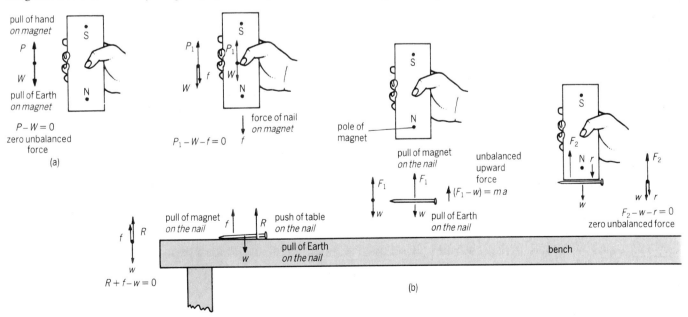

1.2 Magnetic forces. The free-body force diagram alongside each object shows only the forces acting on that object.

equilibrium, $F_2 - w - r = 0$, i.e. zero unbalanced force. The reaction force r is a measure of the force holding the nail to the magnet and a force F slightly greater than $r = (F_2 - w)$ is needed to pull the nail vertically downwards. If the magnet is powerful F_2 can be quite large and so $(F_2 - w)$ can be quite high. A strong pull will then be needed to pull the nail vertically downwards. Note that in this case the reaction force r is downwards; when the nail was on the bench the reaction force R acted upwards.

If the nail is slid *horizontally* away from the magnet it can be removed easily. Only two horizontal forces act on the nail: the horizontal pull X on the nail and the frictional force Y (a contact force) between the nail and the surface of the magnet. The frictional force Y is relatively small and therefore the slightly greater force X required to overcome Y is also comparatively small.

Exercise 1.1

Draw the free-body force diagram for the nail being pulled away from the magnet and explain why force X is greater than force Y.

Note *Vertical* forces do not affect the *horizontal* movement because $F_2 - w - r = 0$ and a force cannot act at right angles to itself.

Electrical forces

Two identical metal-coated pith balls are suspended from a rod so that their distance apart can be adjusted. In Fig. 1.3(a) the balls are shown in equilibrium a short distance apart. There are two forces W and T on each ball which are equal and opposite and act through the same point. W, the weight, is the downward pull of the Earth on the ball; T is the upward pull of the string on the ball and is called the **tension** in the string. When each ball is in equilibrium $T - W = 0$.

The tension in a string can be briefly explained here. Consider the string to be under the action of two forces: (a) the downward force of the ball on the string and (b) the upward force of the rod on the string. These two outward forces are trying to stretch the string. In turn, the string applies forces to the ball and the rod to try to prevent itself from being stretched. These forces will be the force of the string on the ball and the force of the string on the rod. The pairs of forces exerted at the ball and at the rod will be equal and opposite. Since the equilibrium of the ball alone is being considered here, only that force T which is exerted by the string on the ball is used.

Another point worth noting is the presence of an extremely small gravitational force of attraction $F = G\,(m_1 m_2 / r^2)$ between the masses of the two balls. However, for small masses the value of this force is so small that it is ignored. But if one mass m is the mass

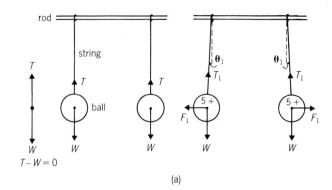

(a)

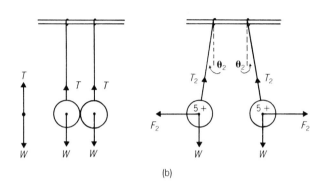

(b)

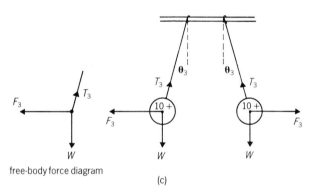

free-body force diagram

(c)

1.3 Electrical forces

of the Earth, the force F on a mass m_2 is significant and is equal to the weight of m_2.

If small positive charges ($+5$ units) are given to both balls then the balls move apart slightly due to the electrical **force of repulsion** F_1. The supporting string will be inclined at a small angle θ_1 to the vertical as a result of the three forces W, F_1 and T_1 acting on each ball. The non-contact forces W and F_1 make the ball exert a downward pull on the string at an angle θ_1 to the vertical. An equal and opposite upward pull T_1 of the string on the ball keeps the ball in equilibrium. So W and F_1 must have a resultant force which is equal and opposite to T_1 and acts in the same straight line as T_1.

Note In Chapter 7 (p.87) you will find out how to work with three forces which are not acting in the same straight line.

In Fig. 1.3(b) the strings have been moved closer together so that the uncharged balls are touching.

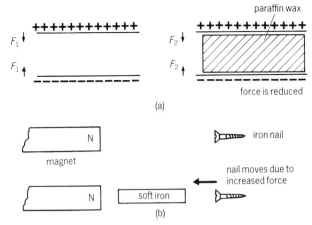

paraffin wax

F_1 ++++++++++

F_2 +++++++++++

F_1 ‾‾‾‾‾‾‾‾‾‾

F_2 ‾‾‾‾‾‾‾‾‾‾

force is reduced

(a)

N

magnet

iron nail

nail moves due to
increased force

N   soft iron

(b)

1.4 *Effect of the medium on forces*

When +5 units of charge are given to each they repel each other with a force F_2 greater than F_1, as is shown by the increased angle of deflection θ_2 of the strings. So if the distance between the two charges is reduced the force of repulsion between them increases. If the charge on each ball is increased to +10 units (Fig. 1.3c) the angle of inclination of the strings increases still further to θ_3, showing that the force also increases as the charge increases. As before, the forces F_3, W and T_3 (shown in the free-force body diagram) must be in equilibrium.

These demonstrations show that the electrical force of repulsion F between two charged objects increases as the distance d between the charges decreases and as the magnitude of the charge Q increases ($F \propto Q_1Q_2/d^2$). Simple demonstrations to show how the force depends on the medium between two charged (or magnetised) objects are shown in Fig. 1.4. In Fig. 1.4(a) two oppositely charged metal plates are shown attracting each other with a force F_1. When a slab of paraffin wax is inserted between the plates the force of attraction is reduced to F_2. Figure 1.4(b) shows a nail just far enough away from the N-pole of the magnet for it not to move towards the magnet. If a piece of wood is placed between the nail and the magnet the nail remains where it is. However, if a piece of soft iron is placed between the magnet and the nail the force of attraction is increased and the nail moves towards the piece of soft iron.

Since all objects have mass they will, at or near the Earth's surface, be subjected to the force of gravity (called the weight of the object) and should fall unless they have reached the ground or another object in their path. If an object is at rest above or on the surface of the earth then at least two forces must be acting on the

object, its weight acting vertically downwards and at least one force acting upwards to produce a net (resultant) force equal in size to the downward force and which acts in the same straight line. The object will have no resultant force acting on it; hence it can remain at rest when there is zero unbalanced force acting on it.

Nuclear forces

Nuclear forces are short-range forces binding the nucleus of an atom together, and are beyond the scope of this book.

1.3 Work and energy

Another important concept which permeates the whole of physics is **energy**. Like a force, it cannot be seen or touched itself; however its effects are obvious. Whatever energy might be, these effects must lead us to say that energy is responsible for what we see happening. **Energy is the capacity or ability to do work**. In Physics, **work** is a highly specialized term which needs explanation.

Work

Work is said to be done if **an unbalanced force moves its point of application through a distance measured in the direction of the force**. The work done is calculated from the product of the force and the distance moved *in the direction* of the force, i.e. work done = force × distance moved in the direction of the force. From this definition, no work is done if the distance moved in the direction of the force is zero.

The girl in Fig. 1.5(a) is pushing with all her force on a brick wall which does not move. She uses a lot of energy in her muscles but no work is done on the wall because the 'distance moved' by the wall is zero. Now consider the farmer (Fig. 1.5b) who is carrying a sack of potatoes steadily along a level ground. Here no work is done on the potatoes because the force on them in the direction of motion is zero. The downward vertical force known as the weight W of the sack is balanced by the upward push P of the farmer's arms on the sack. Hence the resultant vertical force is zero. The motion is in a horizontal direction which is perpendicular to the direction of the forces. Since no force acts in the horizontal direction, no work is done in the Physical sense although it would be very difficult to persuade the farmer that he has done no work!

Centripetal force

Movement along the line of action of the force must take place for work to have been done by that force. The force that is acting is not always obvious; for example a bob on the end of a string whirling round in

---

Exercise 1.2

How would the forces of repulsion in Fig. 1.3 be affected if a slab of paraffin wax were inserted between the charged balls?

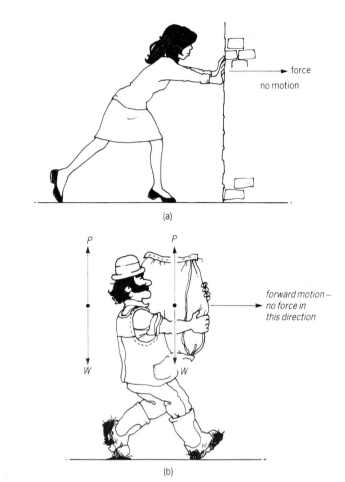

(a)

(b)

1.5 Examples of no work being done

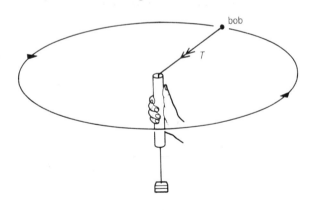

1.6 Centripetal force

a horizontal circle (see Fig. 1.6) does so because it is subjected to a **centripetal** (centre-seeking) force *T*. The velocity of the bob is constantly changing, so it must be being accelerated. (Although the speed of the bob is constant, its direction changes as it travels along its circular path.) Since it is being accelerated there must be a force causing this acceleration. This force is the centripetal force. The motion of the bob is everywhere at right angles to the direction of the force: that is, the distance moved by the force measured in the direction of the force is zero. Hence the centripetal force is said to do *no* work in moving the bob in a horizontal circle.

This shows that it is essential to consider movement *only* in the direction of the applied force when dealing with the term 'work'.

Energy

A body that is capable of doing work is said to possess energy. Energy is classified in many different forms, such as **potential** energy (energy of state or position as in a compressed spring or an object held above the ground, e.g. a pile driver), **kinetic** energy (energy due to motion), **chemical** energy, **heat** (internal) energy, **light** energy, **sound** energy, **electrical** energy, **magnetic** energy, **gravitational** energy and **nuclear** energy. Energy can be converted from one form to another or, more correctly, from one form to several other forms of energy. For example, electrical energy supplied to a filament lamp is converted to internal energy which appears as heat energy, light energy, plus other forms of energy.

1.4 Molecules and atoms

All matter can be classified under one, or more, of the three **states of matter**: solid, liquid and gas. All matter consists of molecules or atoms in various states of energy.

Molecules

A **molecule** of a substance is the smallest particle of the substance which can exist under normal circumstances and still retain all the properties of the substance.

A general figure for the thickness *t* of a molecule is of the order of 1×10^{-9} m. It is very difficult to visualize a value as small as 10^{-9} m; it means that one thousand million molecules placed side by side would stretch across a one-metre rule. One thousand million is also almost impossible to imagine; it approximately represents the total population of India, China or the USA and the USSR.

A molecule can be made up of a group of even smaller particles called **atoms**, for example, a molecule of hydrogen (gas) consists of two hydrogen atoms which are joined together. Molecules can consist of a single atom as in the rare gas argon, of two similar atoms joined together as in the case of oxygen gas, or of a small group of atoms joined as in the case of water which consists of one oxygen atom linked with two hydrogen atoms. Very large groups of atoms can also link together to form polymers, etc.

Atoms

Atoms themselves are thought to consist of three basic particles: **protons, neutrons** and **electrons**. (Many other atomic and subatomic particles are thought to exist but are beyond the scope of this book.) A model

Investigation 1.1 To estimate the size of a molecule

Make up a solution of oleic acid in alcohol of known concentration by volume $1/C$, for example, 1 part in 1000 cm^3. Using this solution fill a 1 cm^3 graduated dropping pipette and find the number of drops contained in 1 cm^3 of the solution. Count the number of drops in 1 cm^3 several times and calculate the average number n of drops in 1 cm^3. Hence the average volume occupied by one drop is $1/n$ cm^3. The volume of oleic acid in one drop is $1/C \times 1/n$ cm^3.

Fill a large clean tray almost to the brim with water and lightly dust the surface with lycopodium powder. Holding the dropping pipette just above the water surface, carefully deposit one drop of the solution onto the centre of the water surface. The oleic acid and alcohol mixture lowers the surface tension of the water and so the lycopodium powder is drawn outwards towards the sides of the tray. The alcohol evaporates leaving a permanent patch of oleic acid of area A cm^2. Measure, with a metre rule, across the clear patch in two directions at right angles and either treat the area as a square or rectangle or calculate an average 'radius' and treat the area as a circle. Since only an order of magnitude is being attempted for the molecular thickness, a rough estimate of the area of the clear patch will be accurate enough. If the volume V of the oleic acid spreads to its *maximum* area its thickness would be at a minimum. This is theoretically a molecular thickness t.

$$V = At$$
$$t = \frac{V}{A}$$
$$t = \frac{1}{C} \times \frac{1}{n} \times \frac{1}{A} \text{ cm}$$

An alternative method for measuring the size of the drop of liquid is to place it near a graticule (fine scale) and view both through a magnifying lens while you measure the diameter d of the drop. The volume V of the drop can be calculated from $V = \frac{4}{3}\pi r^3$ where r is the radius of the drop.

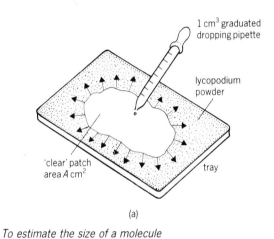

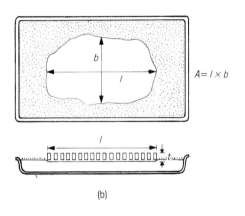

(a) (b)

1.7   To estimate the size of a molecule

of an atom can be imagined to contain a tiny core called a **nucleus** in which protons and neutrons are held together by nuclear forces; surrounding the nucleus are electrons in orbits, like the planets revolving round the Sun. Each proton carries a positive charge equal in size to the electrical charge on an electron but opposite in sign, hence electrons carry negative charges. Neutrons are neutral or uncharged. The particles forming the nucleus, i.e. the protons and neutrons, are collectively known as **nucleons**. The mass of an electron is 9.1×10^{-31} kg, an incredibly small mass. A very small force exerted on an electron can accelerate it to fantastically high speeds. The mass of a proton is almost the same as the mass of a neutron and each is about 1840 times the mass of an electron. Thus the mass of an atom is almost entirely concentrated in the nucleus of the atom, and the mass of an atom is almost equal to the mass of its nucleus, i.e. the sum of the masses of the nucleons (protons plus neutrons) which make up the nucleus.

Typical figures for the diameter of a nucleus and the diameter of an atom are 10^{-14} m and 10^{-10} m

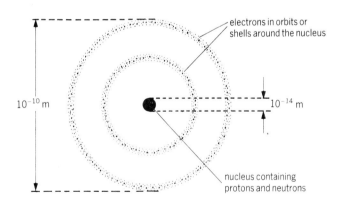

1.8   The structure of the atom

respectively (Fig. 1.8), which means that the diameter of an atom is about 10 000 times the diameter of the nucleus. Hydrogen is the smallest atom known (see Fig. 1.9a) and is also the only atom which does not have a neutron in its nucleus. Some idea of the relative scale of the nucleus and the electron in a hydrogen atom is given by the following: if London represents the proton then the electron would orbit through

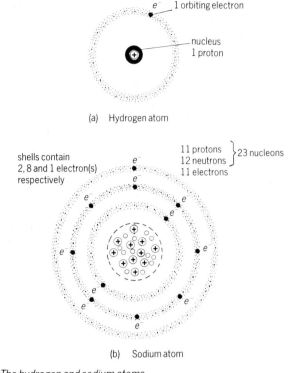

(a) Hydrogen atom

shells contain
2, 8 and 1 electron(s)
respectively

11 protons
12 neutrons } 23 nucleons
11 electrons

(b) Sodium atom

1.9 The hydrogen and sodium atoms
⊕: *proton;* ○: *neutron;* e⁻: *electron*

Newcastle and Paris, with nothing in the space in between. Hence the 'atom' is largely empty space.

In a neutral atom there must be an equal number of protons and electrons so that the electrical charges cancel out. Figure 1.9(b) shows a neutral sodium atom with its electrons arranged in **shells**. If a neutral atom were to lose an electron the remaining portion of the atom, called an **ion**, would appear to have a single positive charge. An ion is any charged particle, usually consisting of an atom (or group of atoms), which has either lost or gained one or more electrons. Electrons, being negatively charged particles, are themselves negative ions.

1.5   Solids, liquids and gases

Solids

The **kinetic theory of matter** proposes that all matter is composed of minute particles (molecules, atoms or ions) held together by **intermolecular forces**. In solids these forces are strong enough to hold the molecules together and so give the solid its rigid shape and form. Molecules in a solid alternately attract and repel one another and so vibrate about a fixed mean position;

Investigation 1.2   To demonstrate the random motion of molecules in liquids and gases

Shine a very bright lamp onto a glass (or Perspex) rod. This, acts as a lens to focus the light onto the centre of the glass cell shown in Fig. 1.10(a). Focus a microscope on a point just above the base of the cell so that only a slight adjustment will be needed later when the cell is filled. To investigate liquid molecular movement, place some water with graphite particles suspended in it in the cell (Fig. 1.10b); to investigate gas molecular

movement place smoke particles from a burning straw in the cell and put a cover plate on top to seal the smoke and air into the cell (Fig. 1.10c). Now adjust the microscope slightly until you can see very bright specks against a grey background; it may take a minute or so for the eye to adjust so that it can see these bright specks.

The particles of graphite (or smoke) scatter (reflect) the light shining on them and so appear as bright points of light darting about in a random or erratic motion. Note that the graphite (or smoke) particles are much larger than the water (or air) molecules. The particles can be seen by the light they scatter but the molecules themselves are too small to be seen.

The irregular movement of the visible particles (of graphite or smoke) is explained as being due to an *uneven* bombardment of the particles by the invisible molecules of water (or air). Fig. 1.10(d) illustrates how particles of just the right size can be subjected to an unbalanced force due to an uneven bombardment of the particle by the molecules.

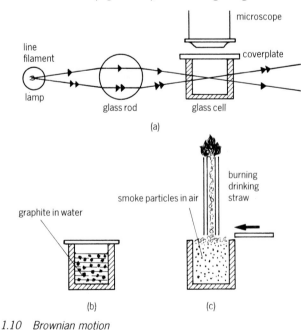

(a)

(b)   (c)

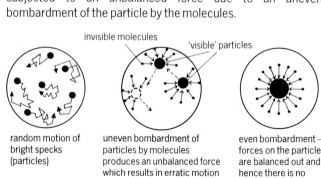

random motion of bright specks (particles)

uneven bombardment of particles by molecules produces an unbalanced force which results in erratic motion

even bombardment – forces on the particle are balanced out and hence there is no motion

1.10 Brownian motion

they do not move through the body of the solid. As the temperature rises the vibrations become larger and the separation of the molecules increases slightly.

Liquids

The intermolecular forces in liquids are less strong than in solids and thus the liquid takes the shape of the container which holds it. Liquid molecules also vibrate but since they move more freely than solid molecules at the same temperature they move at quite high speeds throughout the body of the liquid. Molecules in a liquid are slightly further apart than in a solid.

Gases

In gases the intermolecular forces are much weaker and the molecules are free to take up any space which is available to them. Molecules of a gas are moving randomly and at quite high speeds (400 m s^{-1}) at normal temperature and pressure. Molecules in a gas are about ten times further apart than molecules in the other two states under ordinary conditions. A consequence of this molecular movement is that gases mix very easily.

Diffusion

If a bottle of perfume is opened in one corner of a room the scent can very soon be detected throughout the whole room. This spread or movement of the scent molecules is known as **diffusion**. Diffusion also occurs in liquids, where it takes much longer (days as opposed to minutes). It is not noticeable in solids because it takes many years for a very small layer of the substance to diffuse. The kinetic theory of matter can be used to explain the pressure exerted by a gas on a container in terms of molecules colliding with the walls of the container (see p.139). It can also be inferred that the average speed of the molecules increases when the temperature rises. This can explain how solids, liquids and gases expand when heated, and why pressure of a gas increases when it is heated at constant volume. The kinetic theory was originally developed for gases and the assumptions are given in Chapter 11. Diffusion has important applications in the body, e.g. oxygen diffuses from the alveoli (air sacs) into the blood capillaries in the lungs; carbon dioxide diffuses from the blood capillaries to the alveoli in the lungs; digested food diffuses from the small intestines into the blood capillaries of the villi.

Brownian motion

The random, haphazard motion of small particles in a container (see Fig. 1.10) is known as **Brownian motion**. It can be explained by imagining that invisible molecules are bombarding the visible particles.

Investigation 1.3   To illustrate diffusion in liquids

Place a layer of deep blue copper(II) sulphate solution in a tall beaker and allow it to settle. Copper(II) sulphate is a salt which ionises completely when placed in water into copper Cu^{2+} ions and sulphate SO_4^{2-} ions; the Cu^{2+} ions are responsible for the blue colour. Then carefully pipette a layer of water onto the copper(II) sulphate layer. Cover the beaker with a filter paper and leave it undisturbed for several days.

Initially the water layer floats on top of the copper(II) sulphate solution (Fig. 1.11a) because it is less dense. The boundary line very soon disappears and after a few days the solution becomes a homogeneous pale blue colour (Fig. 1.11b).

This intermingling can be explained by describing the molecules of water and the copper and sulphate ions as moving randomly in all directions. After a few days the molecules and ions have all completely intermixed and so the blue colour becomes paler. The two liquids are said to diffuse into each other.

Diffusion is the differential movement of molecules (or ions) from a region of high concentration to a region of lower concentration. There is a greater movement of water molecules from the water layer into the copper sulphate layer because it has a greater concentration of water molecules than the copper sulphate solution. Likewise, there is a greater movement of ions from the copper sulphate layer into the water layer because of the greater concentration.

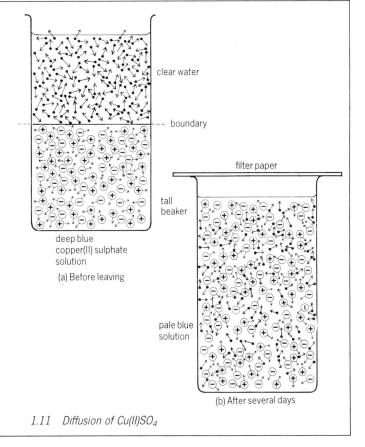

clear water

boundary

filter paper

tall beaker

deep blue copper(II) sulphate solution

(a) Before leaving

pale blue solution

(b) After several days

1.11   Diffusion of Cu(II)SO₄

Investigation 1.4   To illustrate diffusion in gases

A gas jar of brown bromine gas and a jar of air are placed, separated by a cover plate, **in a fume cupboard**. The cover plate is removed so that the two open ends of the jars are in contact. The bromine gas spreads (diffuses) rapidly into the air to produce a uniform paler brown colour in both jars. Fig. 1.12(a) shows the molecules of bromine and air in the gas jars moving rapidly and freely and taking up the space available to them.

When the space available to the molecules is increased (Fig. 1.12b), the bromine molecules transfer to the space that held

the air at a greater rate than they return because of their initial high concentration in the left-hand jar. Likewise the air molecules transfer to the space that held the bromine at a greater rate than they return to the air space because of their initial high concentration in the right-hand jar. The way that the two gases intermix within seconds demonstrates that the molecules are moving rapidly.

Performing the demonstration with the two gas jars held horizontally rather than vertically reduces the possibility of mixing taking place because of the different densities of the gases. (A less dense gas would rise into a more dense gas.)

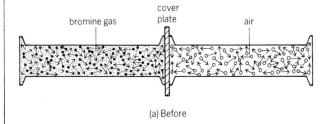

(a) Before

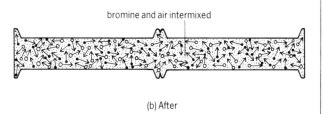

(b) After

1.12   Diffusion of bromine gas. This experiment is performed in a fume cupboard

Questions

Q1 Gamboge particles suspended in water are observed, when viewed through a microscope, to move about in a random haphazard manner. This demonstrates

    A Brownian motion **B** Conduction **C** Convection
    D Diffusion **E** Osmosis

Q2 The size of a molecule is of the order of
    A 1×10^{-1} mm **B** 1×10^{-3} mm **C** 1×10^{-6} mm
    D 1×10^{-9} mm **E** 1×10^{-12} mm

Q3 The size of the nucleus of an atom is of the order of
    A 1×10^{-6} m **B** 1×10^{-8} m **C** 1×10^{-10} m
    D 1×10^{-12} m **E** 1×10^{-14} m

Q4 Which of the following describes particles in a solid at room temperature?
    A Close together and stationary
    B Close together and vibrating
    C Close together and moving around at random
    D Far apart and stationary
    E Far apart and moving around at random   *(L & EAG)*

Q5 Draw simple sketch diagrams and alongside these, the free-body force diagrams associated with each of the following:
    (a) a book resting on a table;
    (b) a child sitting at rest on a swing;
    (c) a parachutist free falling from an aircraft;
    (d) a parachutist descending steadily after his parachute has opened;
    (e) a sledge sliding down a gentle slope;
    (f) a piece of dust on a record revolving at a constant speed. In each case, state whether or not the 'body' is subjected to an unbalanced force and if so, state the direction of the force.

Q6 A given atom is made up of **three** types of particle. Name (i) the three particles, (ii) the particle with the smallest mass, (iii) the particle which has no electric charge. *(W)*

Q7 (a) Describe the differences between solids, liquids and gases in terms of (i) the arrangement of molecules throughout the bulk of the material, (ii) the separation of the molecules and (iii) the motion of the molecules.
    (JMB part question)

Q8 A drop of oil of volume 0.010 cm³ is allowed to fall on some clean water in a dish and it spreads to form a circle of radius 14 cm. Estimate the upper limit of the diameter of an oil molecule.
    In such an experiment describe (a) what is done in order that the circle may be clearly visible, (b) what apparatus is used and any precautions that are taken.   *(L)*

Q9 In an experiment to estimate the size of a molecule, a drop of olive oil, of volume 0.12 mm³, was placed on a clean water surface. The oil spread into a patch of area 60×10^3 mm². Use these figures to estimate the size of a molecule of olive oil pointing out any assumption you make.   *(O & C)*

Q10 100 identical drops of oil, of density 800 kg/m³, are found to have a total mass of 2×10^{-4} kg. One of these drops is placed on a large clean water surface and it spreads to form a uniform film of area 0.2 m².
    (a) What is the mass of one drop?
    (b) What is the volume of one drop?
    (c) What is the thickness of the film?
    (d) If a second oil drop of the same mass were placed on the film, what would you expect the new area of the film to be?   *(O)*

Q11 A spherical drop of oil of diameter 1.0 mm is placed on the surface of some water upon which a fine powder has been shaken. The oil drop spreads out until it forms a patch of area 0.05 m². A second drop of the same size is then placed on the surface, and the patch increases in area to 0.10 m². Suggest an explanation for the effect of the second drop. From these results, make a rough estimate of the size of an oil molecule. (Use $\pi \approx 3$.)

(O & C part question)

Q12 (a) Explain why when a small quantity of oil is on the surface of water, the oil spreads to form a continuous film.

(b) (i) Explain briefly **one** reason for believing that the thinnest films are one molecule thick. (ii) Describe fully a laboratory experiment which would enable you to estimate an upper limit for the diameter of an oil molecule.

(c) Give a short account of an experiment which demonstrates Brownian motion of smoke particles in air. Explain how we can deduce from these observations that the molecules of a gas are in continual random motion. *(O)*

Q13 In an experiment to determine the size of molecules of olive oil, a small drop of the oil, of measured volume, was placed on a water surface which had previously been cleaned and dusted lightly with fine powder. The effect observed was that a patch, which was clear of powder, formed around the point where the drop had been placed and grew rapidly to a certain size at which it remained stable, as illustrated in the diagrams.

(a) Explain why the clear patch appeared and grew initially.

powdered surface

appearance of surface after drop placed at A

(b) Explain why the clear patch did not grow large enough to cover the whole water surface.

(c) How would the measurements be made to obtain a value for the approximate diameter of the final, stable, clear patch?

(d) The approximate diameter of the final, stable, clear patch was measured and found to be 0.20 m. Assuming the patch to be circular, estimate its area.

(e) Describe how the volume of the drop of oil could have been measured, including in your description how the volume would be calculated from any measurements made.

(f) Given that the volume of the drop was, in fact, 1.7×10^{-10} m³, calculate a value for the size of a molecule of olive oil.

(g) Explain one important assumption you have made in calculating your answer to part (f).

(h) State, with reasons, whether or not your answer in part (f) is a maximum or a minimum value of the size of an olive oil molecule. *(O & C)*

Q14

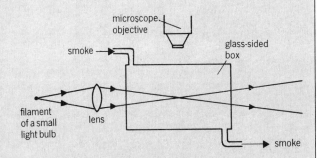

(a) In the figure above the microcope is focussed on point A at the centre of the glass-sided box. This box contains smoke-laden air. State what the observer sees in the field of view of the microscope when the box is strongly illuminated from the left-hand side. Give an explanation of his observations. What deduction can be made regarding the structure of gases from what is seen through the microscope? What change would you expect in the observations as the contents of the glass box were cooled to 0 K (if such a thing were possible)?

(b) A burette with a very fine jet, containing a pure, oily compound, is adjusted so that tiny drops of the substance slowly break from the jet. When one of these droplets of oil is added to a tray of water, the surface of which has been dusted with talc, a clear circular patch grows from the point where the droplet struck the water and, after a few seconds, the size of the patch remains stationary, its diameter now being 30 cm.

Why do the particles of talc move away from the point where the oil droplet struck the water? Why does the patch stop growing after a short while?

Assuming that the oil droplet is spherical and its radius is 0.30 mm, calculate the thickness of the oily patch on the surface of the water in the tray. (The area of a circle $= \pi r^2$, the formula for the volume of a sphere $= \frac{4}{3}\pi r^3$, where r is the radius.) How can the diameter of such tiny droplets used in the experiment be measured with accuracy? What information regarding the size of the molecules of the oily substance can be gained if the size of the droplets issuing from the jet can be measured? *(C)*

Q15 When a mixture of smoke and air is suitably illuminated and viewed through a microscope small bright specks are seen to be moving in a jerky, random fashion.

(a) What are the bright specks?

(b) Why do they move?

(c) What change, or changes, in their motion would you observe if the mixture were warmed?

(O & C part question)

2 Units, measurement and density

2.1 SI units

Scientists all over the world would like to work with a consistent and coherent system of units. Following the Conférence Générale des Poids et Mesures (CGPM) in 1968, agreement on an international system of units, Système International d'Unités (shortened to 'SI units'), was reached. The system uses seven base units and all other units are derived from these base units by multiplying or dividing one unit by another without introducing numerical factors. In the SI system each physical quantity has only one unit, which can be either a base unit or a unit derived from base units. For convenience of working, multiples and sub-multiples of units are allowed and can be obtained by adding the approved prefix to the unit being used. The seven base units are: **metre, kilogram, second, ampere, kelvin, candela** and **mole** (see Table 2.1). The candela is a unit of luminous intensity which is not required at this level and will not be used in this book. The mole is defined as the amount of substance of a system which contains as many elementary entities as there are atoms in 0.012 kilogram of carbon-12. When the mole is used, the elementary entities (which may be atoms, molecules, ions, electrons, other particles or specified groups of such particles) must be specified. The mole is more important in the study of Chemistry than in Physics but it will be met in electrolysis (Chapter 26). The other five units are used extensively in Physics, as are the many derived units that result from combinations of the five base units.

In this chapter the three base units of length, mass and time are introduced; those of current and temperature will be dealt with in Chapters 25 and 13.

In the SI system the base unit of length or distance measurement is the **metre**. This is defined as 'the length equal to 1 650 763.73 wavelengths in vacuum corresponding to the transition between the levels $2p_{10}$ and $5d_5$ of the krypton-86 atom'. This means that the distance called one metre can be 'easily' reproduced by scientists all around the world with great precision and accuracy. However, the appropriate use of a metre rule, vernier callipers or micrometer screw gauge, depending on the length to be measured and the accuracy required, will normally suffice for the work in this book.

The SI base unit of mass is the **kilogram**. It is defined as a mass equal to the mass of the international prototype of the kilogram. (This prototype is in the custody of the Bureau International des Poids et Mesures at Sèvres near Paris, France.) This base unit is the one unit which is *not* defined in terms of reproducible measurements of physical phenomena. Hence each country must have a *copy* of the international prototype kilogram. Again, the accuracy required in this text will be achieved by the correct use of an appropriate balance.

In SI the base unit of time is the **second**. It is defined as 'the duration of 9 192 631 770 periods of radiation corresponding to the transition between the two hyperfine levels of the ground state of the caesium-133 atom'. Again, this degree of accuracy will not be needed at this level and a stopclock, stopwatch or electronic timer will suffice.

Note In this text the printing of symbols for units and quantities will follow the recommendations in the ASE publication *SI Units, Signs, Symbols and Abbreviations for use in School Science, (3rd edition, 1985).*

Prefixes for SI units

The prefixes in Table 2.2 may be used to indicate decimal multiples or sub-multiples of both base and derived units. The prefix should be used so that, normally, the numeric part of the quantity will lie between 0.1 and 1000. The prefixes used with 'kilogram' are anomalous for an SI base unit since they are added to the word 'gram' (1×10^{-3} kg) but it is self-evident how fractions and multiples of the kilogram should be expressed.

Table 2.1   Names and symbols for base SI units

Physical quantity	Name of SI base unit	Symbol for unit
length	metre	m
mass	kilogram	kg
time	second	s
electric current	ampere	A
thermodynamic temperature	kelvin	K
luminous intensity	candela	cd
amount of substance	mole	mol

Table 2.2 Prefixes for use with SI units

Sub-multiple	Prefix	Symbol
10^{-1}	deci	d
10^{-2}	centi	c
10^{-3}	milli	m
10^{-6}	micro	μ
10^{-9}	nano	n
10^{-12}	pico	p
10^{-15}	femto	f
10^{-18}	atto	a

Multiple	Prefix	Symbol
10^{1}	deca	da
10^{2}	hecto	h
10^{3}	kilo	k
10^{6}	mega	M
10^{9}	giga	G
10^{12}	tera	T
10^{15}	peta	P
10^{18}	exa	E

Other units in use

Certain other units which are not part of the SI system are recognised as likely to be used in appropriate contexts. They are given in Table 2.3.

The CGPM (1964) has accepted 'litre' as an alternative name for the cubic decimetre but recommends that it should not be used to express results of high precision. The advantages in the coherence of SI units, especially when performing calculations, may be lost when litre and millilitre are used in preference to cubic decimetre and cubic centimetre since the relationship to the coherent unit is lost.

Table 2.3 Units exactly defined in terms of SI units

Physical quantity	Name of unit	Symbol for unit	Definition of unit
time	minute	min	60 s
time	hour	h	60 min = 3600 s
time	day	d	24 h = 86 400 s
angle	degree	°	$(\pi/180)$ rad
angle	minute	′	$(\pi/10800)$ rad
angle	second	″	$(\pi/648\,000)$ rad
volume	litre	l, L	10^{-3} m^3 = dm^3
mass	tonne	t	10^3 kg = Mg
pressure	bar	bar	10^5 Pa

2.2 Area and volume

Investigation 2.1 Using the units

Measure the length l, breadth b and thickness t of the top of a table in your laboratory. For lengths greater than about 15 cm, a metre (or half-metre) rule calibrated in mm will give reasonable accuracy. For example, for a table-top of length l = 108.0 cm and breadth b = 92.6 cm the metre rule gives an accuracy of about 0.1%, roughly 1 part in 1000. The surface or working **area** A of the table-top is given by $A = lb$. Hence A = (108.0) cm $\times$ (92.6) cm or A = (1.08) m $\times$ (0.926) m, so A = 10 000.8 cm^2 or A = 1.000 08 m^2. Note that when the numbers are multiplied to give A there are six significant figures in the 'answer', which is an 'accuracy' of 0.001%, roughly 1 part in 1 000 000. Since the original measurements for l and b were only accurate to 1 part in 1000, this level of accuracy is not right. The answer for A should be expressed as 10 000 cm^2 or 1.000 m^2, i.e. to an accuracy of 1 part in 1000. This calculation presents a slight dilemma; should we work in cm or m? In calculating the area A it seems that using metres (giving 1.000 m^2) is more useful.

metre rule reading to 1 mm

2.1 *Measurement of length and breadth using a metre rule*

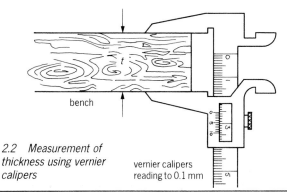

2.2 *Measurement of thickness using vernier calipers*

vernier calipers reading to 0.1 mm

continued

Investigation 2.1 continued

Now find the **volume** V of the table-top. This can be determined from $V = A t$ where A = area just measured and t = thickness of the table-top. Suppose the thickness t = 2.5 cm. The accuracy of this measurement using a metre rule is 1 part in 25 (or 40 parts in 1000), thus it is forty times less accurate than the other two measurements, about 4.0%. Vernier callipers (Fig. 2.2) could measure the thickness t = 2.51 cm, i.e. to 1 part in 250 or 4 parts in 1000, which gives a much greater degree of accuracy.

Hence the volume V of the table-top is given by V = (1.00) m^2 × 0.0251 m, V = 0.0251 m^3. (The '1' in the 'answer' implies an accuracy of 1 part in 251 which is about 4 parts in 1000. This is similar to the total error in the three measurements: $1 + 1 + 4 = 6$ parts in 1000).

2.3 Mass

How could the mass of the table-top be determined? One method is to rip the top off the table and place it on a balance to read its mass in kg or g, but this is not a sensible method. If the volume V is known and the **density ρ** of the material from which the table-top is made is found from tables of constants the mass m can be calculated from $m = \rho V$. Suppose the table-top is made of a hardwood of density $\rho = 650$ kg m^{-3}. Then the mass m of the table-top would be $m = (0.0251)$ m^3 × (650) kg m^{-3} = 16.9 kg. This method is very useful for quantity surveyors who need to estimate the quantity of all the different materials which will be needed to build a house or block of flats etc. **The mass of a substance is the quantity of matter contained in the substance.** It is measured in kilogram (kg) using a balance. Mass is a physical quantity which does not vary with an object's position on or above the Earth. An astronaut who has a mass of 75 kg on Earth also has a mass of 75 kg on the Moon or in orbit around the Earth or the Moon. The physical make-up of the astronaut does not alter as he moves about, therefore his mass is the same wherever he is.

2.4 Density

Density is defined as mass per unit volume, and is usually symbolised by ρ (rho).

$$\rho = \frac{\text{mass}}{\text{volume}} \frac{m}{V}$$

also $m = \rho V$ and $V = m/\rho$. The 'triangle' shown below may help you to recall the transposition of the formula. Cover up the symbol for the quantity you are trying to find; the remaining two letters show how these two quantities should be combined, e.g. covering V gives m/ρ.

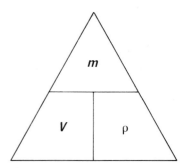

To find the density of a substance, the mass m and volume V of the substance must be determined as accurately as possible. Finding the mass of a substance, whether it be in solid, liquid or gaseous form, is comparatively easy using a balance and, where necessary, a suitable container. However, determining the volume of the substance is not so easy and therefore the method used depends on the shape and state of the substance involved.

The SI unit of mass is the kilogram and the unit of volume is the cubic metre, thus the SI unit of density is kilogram per cubic metre (kg m^{-3}). However, using a cubic metre of most solids (except perhaps expanded polystyrene!) is impracticable. In a laboratory the sizes of the solids are likely to be such that their masses are less than one kilogram. Hence it will be much more practical to measure the mass in gram and the volume in cubic centimetre so that the density has a unit of gram per cubic centimetre (g cm^{-3}). This can, if required, be converted into the correct SI unit of kg m^{-3} by using the multiplying factor 1000.

$$\frac{1 \text{ kg}}{1 \text{ m}^3} \equiv \frac{1000}{(100)^3} \frac{\text{g}}{\text{cm}^3}$$

$$1 \frac{\text{kg}}{\text{m}^3} \equiv \frac{1}{1000} \frac{\text{g}}{\text{cm}^3}$$

hence g cm^{-3} $\equiv 1000 \times$ kg m^{-3}.

Aluminium has a density of 2.7 g m^{-3}, or 2.7 × 1000 × kg m^{-3} = 2700 kg m^{-3}.

Density of solids

Solids can be divided into two categories: (a) regularly shaped solids and (b) irregularly shaped solids. In either case the mass is determined by placing the solid on a suitable balance and noting the mass m in gram.

Note This book will try to eliminate the misuse of the verb 'to weigh' by using the phrase 'find the mass of' when mass is being determined. Unfortunately 'mass' and 'weight' are often wrongly interchanged. However, they do *not* mean the same thing, and you must make sure that you grasp the fundamental difference between these two quantities. Mass is the *quantity of matter* contained in an object and is measured in kg, while the weight of the object is the *force* exerted on it by the Earth and is measured in newton (N).

Investigation 2.2 To find the density of regularly shaped solids

The volume V of a cuboid shape (Fig. 2.3a) can be calculated from $V = lbh$ by measuring the length l, breadth b and height h using a half-metre rule. The volume V of a cylinder (Fig. 2.3b) can be calculated from $V = \frac{1}{4}\pi d^2 h$ by taking measurements of the diameter d and height h using vernier callipers. The volume V of a sphere (Fig. 2.3c) can be calculated from $V = \frac{4}{3}\pi r^3$ by using a micrometer screw gauge to take measurements of the diameter d from which $r = d/2$. Find the mass m of each of the shapes using a balance. Fig. 2.4 shows examples of balances typically found in Physics laboratories. The spring balance which can be used to find the mass or weight of an object will be dealt with later (see p.35).

For each solid shape in turn, the density ρ can be calculated from $\rho = m/V$ and will be in $g\,cm^{-3}$. These can then be converted to the SI unit $kg\,m^{-3}$ by multiplying by 1000 and adding the new unit.

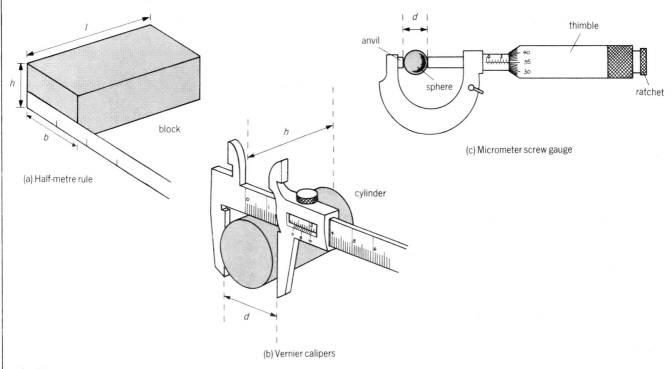

(a) Half-metre rule

(b) Vernier calipers

(c) Micrometer screw gauge

2.3 Measuring instruments

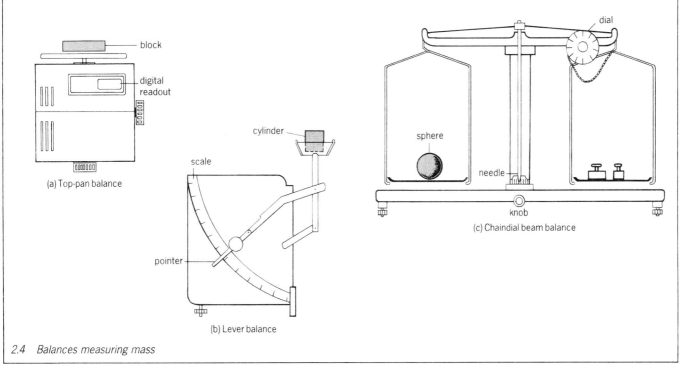

(a) Top-pan balance

(b) Lever balance

(c) Chaindial beam balance

2.4 Balances measuring mass

Investigation 2.3   To find the density of irregularly shaped solids

As the name implies, the volume of these solids cannot be calculated directly by taking measurements of length. Some other method of finding the volume V, e.g. by displacement, must be used instead. The examples of irregularly shaped solids which illustrate the methods employed are a stone, which is denser than water, and a cork, which is less dense than water.

The stone Partly fill with water a measuring cylinder which will admit the stone (Fig. 2.5a). Note the volume V_1 of the water in the measuring cylinder and record it in cm³ rather than ml. It is sensible to preset the original volume V_1 to a round whole number, say 20 or 30 cm³, to make the later subtraction easier. Find the mass m of the stone using a balance. Then tie a piece of thread to the stone and so lower it gently into the water until the stone is *completely* submerged. (Why do you think thread is used rather than string?) The level of the water rises to indicate a volume V_2 which you can read off the measuring cylinder. This volume is the volume of the water plus that of the stone. Hence the volume V of the stone is given by $V = (V_2 - V_1)$.

Note The volume of water used is unchanged but the stone now takes up space that was occupied by the water and so the level of the water rises.

The density ρ of the stone can be calculated from

$$\rho = \frac{m}{V} = \frac{m}{(V_2 - V_1)}$$

This method will only work for solids which do not dissolve in water. If a soluble solid is immersed in water the level of the water hardly rises at all. The molecules of the solid are small enough to fit into the 'spaces' between the water molecules. If a water-soluble substance is used then a liquid other than water must be used to find its volume.

The cork When finding the volume of a solid that floats, e.g. a cork, a sinker must be attached to ensure that both the cork and sinker are completely submerged. Fill an Eureka can with water and allow it to overflow so that the level of the water in the can is exactly at the level of the spout (Fig. 2.5b) and place a measuring cylinder under the spout. Then tie a thread to the sinker and lower it gently into the water so that it is completely submerged. The volume V_1 of the sinker will cause an equal volume of water to overflow into the measuring cylinder. The volume V_1 of water in the measuring cylinder is equal to the volume of the sinker. Next find the mass m of the cork using a balance. Tie the cork and sinker together with thread and lower the pair of solids into the water in the can. Water again overflows from the spout into the measuring cylinder, due this time to the additional volume of the cork. The volume V_2 of water in the measuring cylinder represents the volume of the cork and the sinker. The volume V of the cork is calculated from $V = (V_2 - V_1)$. Hence the density ρ of the cork is

$$\rho = \frac{m}{V} = \frac{m}{(V_2 - V_1)}$$

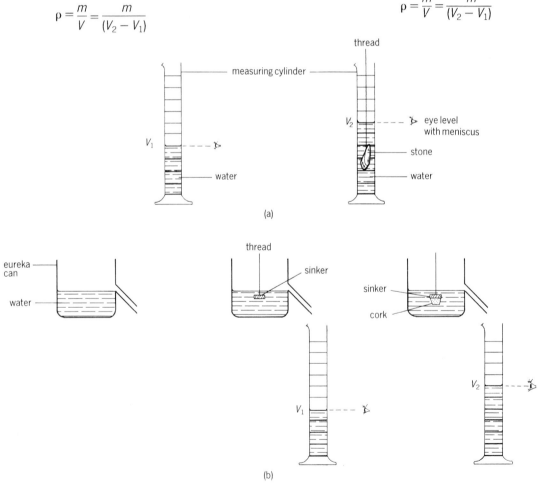

2.5   *Measuring the volume of an irregularly shaped object*

Clearly the volumes of cork and sinker could have been found using a measuring cylinder, provided the cork and sinker fit into the cylinder.

Density of liquids

The densities of most liquids lie in the range 0.7 to 1.3 g cm^{-3} (700 to 1300 kg m^{-3}) but mercury is a particularly striking exception; because it is a liquid metal its density, 13.6 g cm^{-3} (13 600 kg m^{-3}), is rather high.

Density of a gas

To find the density of a gas it is necessary to measure its mass m and volume V. However, it is not easy to

---

Investigation 2.4   To find the density of a liquid

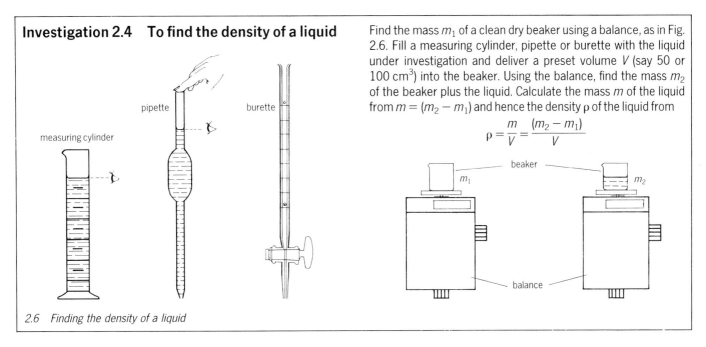

pipette

burette

measuring cylinder

2.6   Finding the density of a liquid

Find the mass m_1 of a clean dry beaker using a balance, as in Fig. 2.6. Fill a measuring cylinder, pipette or burette with the liquid under investigation and deliver a preset volume V (say 50 or 100 cm^3) into the beaker. Using the balance, find the mass m_2 of the beaker plus the liquid. Calculate the mass m of the liquid from $m = (m_2 - m_1)$ and hence the density ρ of the liquid from

$$\rho = \frac{m}{V} = \frac{(m_2 - m_1)}{V}$$

beaker

m_1

m_2

balance

Investigation 2.5   To find the density of air

Although air is a mixture of gases it will serve to demonstrate the principle involved in the experiment.

Fit a thick-walled, 1 litre flask with a rubber bung and a short piece of pressure tubing fitted with a Hoffman clip (Fig. 2.7). The 'empty' flask is not, in fact, empty but is full of air at the pressure and temperature of the laboratory. Using a balance find the mass m_1 of the flask with its attachments. Connect the pressure tubing to a good quality vacuum pump. Then switch on the pump and allow it to evacuate the flask for several minutes. Tighten the clip *before* switching off the pump and disconnecting the tubing from the pump. Since the flask is now almost empty, its mass will be less than before by an amount which represents the mass m of the air removed. Using a balance find the new mass m_2 of the flask with its attachments after the air has been removed. Calculate the mass m of the air removed from $m = (m_1 - m_2)$.

Note   The mass m of 1 litre of air is only about 1.3 g therefore the balance should be able to give readings accurate to 0.01 g.

The next task is to measure the volume V of the air which has been removed. This is done by allowing water to fill the space which was occupied by the air. Fill a sink with water and push the tubing attached to the flask below the water surface. Water will rush into the flask when you loosen the clip. The reason for this is that 'no' air inside the flask means there is 'no' air pressure inside the flask. Atmospheric pressure acting on the surface of the water in the sink forces the water into the empty flask. Water will flow into the flask until it is almost completely full but a small

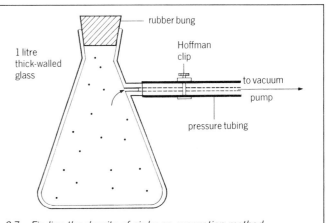

rubber bung

1 litre thick-walled glass

Hoffman clip

to vacuum pump

pressure tubing

2.7   Finding the density of air by an evacuation method

bubble (of air) will remain. This shows that the vacuum pump was unable to remove *all* of the air. The volume of the water in the flask represents the volume V of the air which was removed. Carefully dry the outside of the flask and find the mass m_3 of the flask plus water using a balance. Hence the mass m_w of the water is given by $m_w = (m_3 - m_2)$. Since 1 g water occupies 1 cm^3, the mass m_w of water in gram also gives the volume V in cm^3. Alternatively, the water can be poured into a measuring cylinder and the volume V noted in this way. Calculate the density ρ of air from

$$\rho = \frac{m}{V} = \frac{(m_1 - m_2)}{V}$$

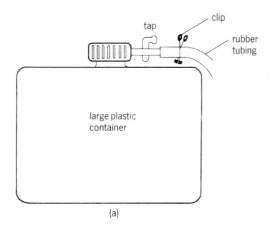

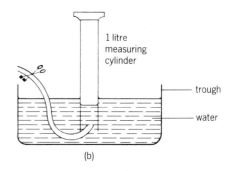

2.8   *Finding the density of air using a pressurised container*

measure either of these quantities with any degree of accuracy. The mass of 1000 cm³ of air is only about 1.3 g, and so a large volume of the gas should be measured. Since a 'large' volume of gas must be kept in a 'large' container, the mass of such a container is likely to swamp the mass of the gas that it contains unless a really accurate balance is used. A lever or beam balance will not do here; a top-pan balance which gives readings to 0.01 g and whose upper limit can give the mass of the container must be used.

It is important in this experiment to record the atmospheric pressure and the temperature of the air in the laboratory. An increase (or decrease) in the pressure exerted on a gas decreases (or increases) its volume. So although the mass of the gas remains constant its volume varies according to the pressure exerted on it. Likewise, an increase (or decrease) in the temperature of a gas causes an increase (or decrease) in its volume. Again the mass remains constant but the volume varies with temperature. Since the volume of a gas varies in this way the density ρ = mass/volume will also vary with pressure and temperature. If the same experiment is performed on different days or in different places you will almost certainly get different results. It is therefore essential that your answer for the density of air is quoted with its corresponding pressure and temperature. It can then be reduced to a value measured at standard temperature and pressure (s.t.p.) and compared with values given in tables of constants.

Note   This experiment can be dangerous and will normally be demonstrated by a teacher who will place a safety screen between your class and the flask. In Chapter 4 the crushing effect of atmospheric pressure on an evacuated tin can will show the considerable force which can be exerted by the atmosphere. In investigation 2.6 air and its resulting pressure were removed from the flask. The external pressure will crush (implode) the flask if its walls are not thick enough to withstand the very large forces exerted on it. Needless to say, the flask should be inspected very carefully for any flaws or cracks before the investigation and if these are found or suspected the flask must not be used.

If a good quality vacuum pump is not available an alternative experiment using a large (40 litre) plastic container is possible (see Fig. 2.8). Extra air is forced into the container using a bicycle pump or a foot pump. This additional air will ensure that the pressure inside the container is greater than atmospheric pressure. The mass m_1 of the container with extra air in it is found using a top-pan balance. Some of the extra air is slowly released into an upturned measuring cylinder filled with water and standing in a large dish of water. Attempts should be made to release exactly 2 litre of air from the container. When the volume V of the released air has been determined the mass m_2 of the container and its residual air is found using the balance. The mass m of the air released is calculated

Table 2.4   Some typical densities at s.t.p.

Substance	$\rho/(kg\ m^{-3})$	density/$(g\ cm^{-3})$
aluminium	2700	2.7
copper	8930	8.93
gold	19 300	19.3
iron	7860	7.86
lead	11 300	11.3
mercury	13 600	13.6
osmium	22 480	22.48
platinum	21 400	21.4
silver	10 500	10.5
zinc	7100	7.1
ice (at 0 °C)	920	0.92
cork	240	0.24
glass	2500	2.5
wood	400–800	0.4–0.8
turpentine	840	0.84
water	1000	1.0
air	1.293	0.001 293
carbon dioxide	1.977	0.001 977
oxygen	1.429	0.001 429
hydrogen	0.0899	0.000 899

from $m = (m_1 - m_2)$. Calculate the density ρ of air from

$$\rho = \frac{m}{V} = \frac{(m_1 - m_2)}{V}$$

Again the pressure and temperature of the air in the laboratory should be recorded. It should be noted that the pressure on the air collected over water is atmospheric pressure plus the pressure exerted by the column of water in the dish and hence is a value slightly above that of atmospheric pressure.

The effects of temperature and pressure changes

Changes in pressure exert little or no significant influence on the volume of solids and liquids. However, temperature increases cause most solids and liquids to expand. If the volume of a substance increases, the density of that substance will decrease because its mass remains unaltered. The expansion of solids is usually exceedingly small and is normally ignored. However, the expansion of liquids is comparatively greater and changes in density can be detected. In fact, convection currents (see p.130) in liquids and gases are a direct result of changes in density caused by changes in temperature.

The **upthrust** in liquids depends upon the density of the liquid. As the density of a liquid varies with temperature this must be taken into account when, e.g. ships are sailing from hot climates to cold climates or vice versa. Unless appropriate action is taken the ship floats lower in warmer water than in cooler water because warm water is less dense than cold water.

Questions

Q1 The prefix *kilo* means a factor of 10^3. The prefix *milli* means
  A 10^{-9} **B** 10^{-6}
  C 10^{-3} **D** 10^6
  E 10^9

Q2 Which of the following properties of a solid would change if it were transported from the Earth to the Moon?
  A mass   **B** volume
  C density   **D** weight
  E surface area

Q3 Put the following substances in order from that with the lowest density to that with the highest density:
  1 ice, 2 mercury, 3 steam, 4 water.
  A 1–4–2–3   **B** 1–4–3–2
  C 3–1–4–2   **D** 3–4–1–2
  E 4–3–1–2   (L)

Q4 A room is 4 m long, 2.5 m wide and 2 m high. If the density of air in the room is $1.3 \ \text{kg m}^{-3}$ then the mass of air, in kg, in the room is
  A 0.065 **B** 3.8 **C** 6.5 **D** 15 **E** 26   (L)

Q5

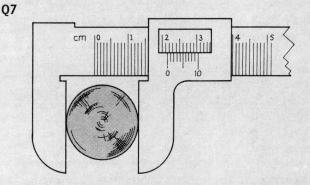

Block 1: 1000 kg, 1 m × 1 m × 1 m
Block 2: 4000 kg, 2 m × 2 m × 2 m
Block 3: 16 000 kg, 2 m × 2 m × 2 m

The diagram shows the mass and dimensions of three rectangular blocks. Calculate the density of the material of each block. Which one of the following statements is correct?
  A The blocks all have the same density.
  B Block 3 has twice the density of blocks 1 and 2.
  C Block 1 has the same density as block 3.
  D Block 3 has half the density of blocks 1 and 2.
  E The blocks all have different densities.   (JMB)

Q6 A measuring cylinder contains $8 \ \text{cm}^3$ water. A small piece of brass of mass 24 g is lowered carefully into the measuring cylinder so that it is completely submerged. If the density of brass is $8 \ \text{g cm}^{-3}$, the new reading of the level of water in the cylinder is
  A $5 \ \text{cm}^3$ **B** $8\frac{1}{3} \ \text{cm}^3$
  C $11 \ \text{cm}^3$ **D** $32 \ \text{cm}^3$
  E $40 \ \text{cm}^3$

Q7

The diagram shows vernier calipers being used to determine the diameter of a cylindrical rod. What is the reading shown by the calipers?   *(O & C part question)*

Q8

The diagrams show vernier calipers used to determine the diameter of a cylindrical rod. The first diagram shows that the calipers have a zero error. What is this zero error and what is the reading of the calipers for the diameter? What is the correct value for the diameter taken from these readings?   *(O & C part question)*

Q9 Write down the micrometer screw gauge readings shown in the figures below.

How many complete revolutions of the thimble correspond to a 1 mm movement in (a), (b) and (c)?

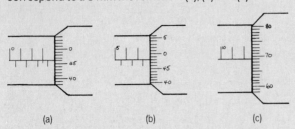

(a)   (b)   (c)

Q10 (a) What is meant by the density of a substance? State consistent units in which the various quantities you have mentioned could be measured.

(b) A tin containing 5000 cm^3 of paint has a mass of 7.0 kg.

(i) If the mass of the empty tin, including the lid, is 0.5 kg calculate the density of the paint.

(ii) If the tin is made of a metal which has a density of 7800 kg m^{-3} calculate the volume of metal used to make the tin and the lid. *(JMB)*

Q11

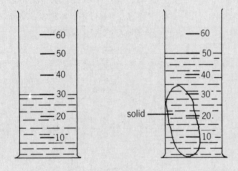

solid

The diagrams show a cylinder, graduated in cm^3, containing water, before and after an irregularly-shaped piece of metal is placed in the cylinder. The mass of the solid is 170 g. Determine the density of the solid. *(O & C)*

Q12 (a) The pitch of the screw of a micrometer screw gauge is 0.50 mm. When this micrometer is used to determine the diameter of a wire, the screw is turned back through $4\frac{1}{2}$ turns from the closed position. What is the diameter of the wire? A pupil says that the micrometer has a zero error to be added. How would you verify this?

(b) A measuring cylinder contains 50.0 cm^3 of a light oil at 0 °C. When a lump of dried ice is placed in the oil the total volume is 72.0 cm^3. After all the ice has melted the total volume is 70.0 cm^3. Determine the density of ice. (Take the density of water as 1.0 g cm^{-3}.) Why is a light oil used in this experiment rather than water at 0 °C? *(O & C)*

Q13 When salt is added to water the resulting solution is called brine. If 56 g of salt is added to 1000 cm^3 of water calculate the density of brine. (Assume the density of water is 1 g cm^{-3}.) What other assumption must be made in this calculation?

Q14 Copy and complete the table below by inserting the missing values.

Substance	Mass/g	Volume/cm^3	Density/g cm^{-3}	ρ/kg m^{-3}
Aluminium	27	10	2.7	2700
Lead	114	10		
Copper	120	15		
Mercury	1360	100		
Wood		250		500
Gold		5	19.4	
Oil	80		0.8	
Air	24			1.2

Q15 Describe experiments to determine the densities of
(a) a solid, such as wood;
(b) a liquid, such as glycerol;
(c) air.

Q16 A measuring cylinder contains 60 cm^3 of water. An iron block 6 cm in length is completely immersed in the water, and the reading on the cylinder is found to increase to 81 cm^3.
(a) Calculate the average cross sectional area of the block.
(b) If the density of iron is 7.9 g cm^{-3} calculate the mass of the block. State **two** precautions you would take when obtaining a reading from the measuring cylinder. *(C)*

Q17 A rectangular shaped aquarium with base measuring 0.40 m × 0.20 m and height 0.20 m is filled with water to a depth of 0.15 m. Calculate the volume of water in the aquarium. What is the mass of this water? (Density of water = 1000 kg m^{-3}.) 1.92 kg of ornamental gravel is spread on the base of the tank and the water level rises to a height of 0.16 m. Calculate the volume of the gravel and hence find its density.

Q18 The average density of the Earth is 5500 kg m^{-3}. Assuming the Earth to be a sphere of radius 6.4 × 10^6 m calculate the mass of the Earth. (Take $\pi \approx 3$.)

Q19

clip

to vacuum pump

flask

The diagram illustrates the apparatus for an experiment in which the density of air is to be determined.
(a) Describe briefly how the volume of the flask could be measured.
(b) List the readings which must be taken before the mass of air in the flask can be calculated.
(c) During the determination it is necessary to remove all the air from the flask. How does the experimenter know that this has been done?
(d) It is usual to measure the atmospheric pressure and also the room temperature when determining the density of air but not when determining the density of a solid. Why is this necessary? *(L part question)*

3　More about forces

3.1　Gravity on Earth

Force is the push or pull of one body on another causing an acceleration. In SI units it is measured in newton (N). Every object has mass and is thus pulled towards the Earth by gravitational attraction. When an object is released from a 'short' distance above the Earth it accelerates to the ground with a constant acceleration known as the **acceleration of free fall** g. In general,

an unbalanced force F acting on a mass m causes the mass to move with an acceleration a where $F = ma$.

The unit of force is $kg\,m\,s^{-2}$ which is known as N (newton).

When a body is falling freely the value of the acceleration is g and the force acting on the body, known as the weight W, is given by $W = mg$. The weight of a given mass will vary if the value of g varies. In fact, slight variations of g can be measured at different places on the Earth's surface. Two factors affect the value of g:

(a) the shape of the Earth,
(b) the rotation of the Earth.

First consider the Earth as a stationary sphere (see Fig. 3.1a). The force of attraction F between the Earth (mass M) and the object (mass m) is given by

$$F = \frac{G\,M\,m}{r^2}$$

where r is the radius of the Earth. The constant G is known as the **universal gravitational constant** and is exceedingly small in value. When r is constant the force $F = \text{constant} \times m$. The pull of the Earth on the mass m is the weight $W = mg$ and comparison of the equations gives $g = \text{constant}\,(GM/r^2)$. The pull of the Earth on the mass m causes it to accelerate

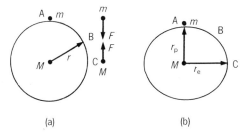

(a)　　　　　　　　　(b)

3.1　Gravitational attraction

'downwards' with a value of g which is constant at all points A, B, C and elsewhere on the Earth's surface (Fig. 3.1b). A free-body force diagram also shows that the pull of the mass m on the Earth acts in the opposite direction to that of the weight. However, the mass M of the Earth is so large that the 'upward' acceleration a' given by $F = Ma'$ is insignificant and so is ignored. The Earth is not a perfect sphere: the radius at the pole r_p is less than the radius at the equator r_e. This means that the force of attraction at the pole $F_p = G\,M\,m/r_p^2$ is greater than that at the equator $F_e = G\,M\,m/r_e^2$ for a mass m. Therefore the acceleration of free fall g_p at the pole is greater than the acceleration of free fall g_e at the equator. The value of g varies with latitude due to the variation in radius of the Earth.

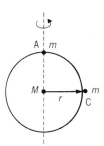

3.2　Variation of g with latitude

As you know, the Earth is not stationary, it spins on its axis completing one revolution each day as well as orbiting round the Sun in one year. Treating the Earth as a uniform sphere for simplicity, consider the mass m at the pole A and the equator C (see Fig. 3.2). In one day the mass at A turns through $360°$ on the spot while the mass at C covers a distance of $2\pi r$. A force is needed to keep the mass at C in its circular orbit. This centripetal force is given by mv^2/r where v is the speed of the mass in its orbit. The total gravitational force at C, $F = G\,M\,m/r^2$ has to do two jobs:

(a) provide the force to keep the mass in circular motion,
(b) use the remaining force to accelerate the mass towards the Earth.

Thus $F = (mv^2/r) + mg_e$ at the equator while $F = mg_p$ at the pole. This means $mg_e < mg_p$, i.e. $g_e < g_p$, hence g varies with latitude as the orbit varies in radius from r at C to zero at A.

It is interesting to speculate what would happen if

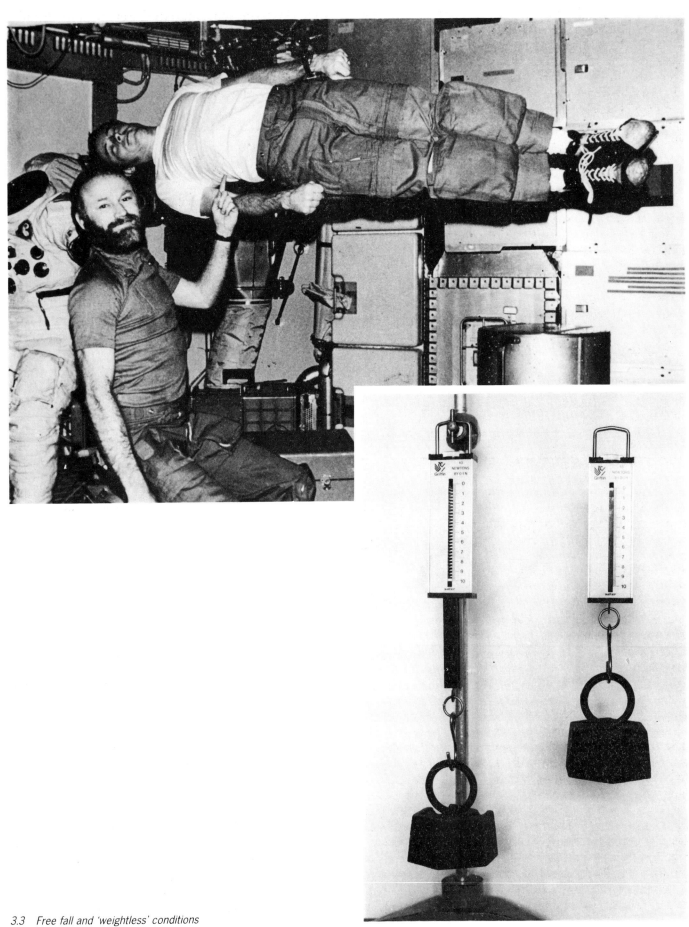

3.3 Free fall and 'weightless' conditions

the rotation of the Earth were to increase until the centripetal force on the mass at the equator $mv^2/r = F = GMm/r^2$. The total gravitational force would be used solely to keep the mass at C in circular orbit and there would be no force left to accelerate the mass towards the Earth. Any further increase in the speed of rotation of the Earth would let the mass 'float' off into space. However, if a piece of the Earth (a spacecraft) with astronauts on board is blasted to a height R above the centre of the Earth with a speed v such that $mv^2/R^2 = F = GMm/R^2$, the spacecraft will orbit the Earth in apparently weightless conditions.

Accurate measurements of the acceleration of free fall g show that g varies with latitude as shown in Table 3.1. Hence it follows that the weight of a given mass varies over the surface of the Earth from a maximum at latitude 90° to a minimum at latitude 0°.

Table 3.1   Measurements of g at different latitudes

Latitude/degrees	$g/m\ s^{-2}$
0	9.7804
15	9.7838
30	9.7933
45	9.8062
60	9.8191
75	9.8286
90	9.8321

At this level it is usual to ignore the slight variations in g and use an average value of 9.81 m s^{-2}. To simplify calculations g is often taken as the nearest whole number, i.e. 10 m s^{-2}, and so the pull of the Earth on 1 kilogram mass, i.e. its weight, is taken as 10 N. Most public examination boards use $g = 10$ m s^{-2} or 10 N kg^{-1} to try to simplify the candidates' calculations. However, you should always check carefully the value of g quoted on the front of the examination paper. In this book also, the value of g is taken to be 10 m s^{-2} or 10 N kg^{-1}.

3.2   'Weightlessness'

The value of g decreases with increase in height above the Earth. This means that the weight of a given mass (the pull of the Earth on the mass), decreases as its height above the Earth increases. As an object leaves the Earth and travels towards the Moon it reaches a point where the small pull the Earth exerts on it is exactly equal to the pull on the Moon. This point, where the two gravitational forces are equal and opposite, is called a **neutral (null) point**.

When a spaceship is orbiting the Earth there must be a force directed towards the centre of the circular orbit which keeps the spaceship circling at the same altitude. The pull of the Earth on the spaceship at this height just equals the centripetal force required to maintain circular motion. This means that the spaceship, and the objects and astronauts inside it, *appear* to be 'weightless'. However, the Earth is still exerting a pull on the spacecraft and its contents. The spacecraft and its contents have a weight mg' where g' is value of the acceleration of free fall at the height of the spacecraft. The weight (force) is 'small' at this height because g' is comparatively small, but it is just sufficient to prevent the spacecraft from hurtling off into space, i.e. it keeps it in circular motion. The objects and astronauts inside the spacecraft must also experience a pull to keep them in orbit around the Earth; this is provided by their 'weight'. Within the framework of the moving spacecraft the objects and the astronauts *appear* to weigh nothing; they experience what is called 'weightlessness'. Unfortunately this is rather ambiguous because it wrongly suggests that the astronauts etc. do not have any weight. The term is used because if an object is attached to a spring balance in a spaceship orbiting the Earth, the balance will register zero since the object does not exert a force on the spring of the balance. Thus it *appears* to weigh nothing.

An object attached to a spring balance can in certain circumstances produce a zero reading in a school laboratory. For example, if the spring balance with the object attached is released from a height and allowed to fall freely to the floor the spring balance will register zero while it is falling. The object is moving with an acceleration equal to the acceleration produced on it by the pull of the Earth and so it will not exert a force on other objects moving with it. Therefore the spring balance registers zero and the object appears to have no weight. However, the pull of the Earth on the object (which has been defined as its weight) is necessary to keep the object moving towards the floor. An orbiting spacecraft is in a similar state of free fall but, because of the orbital speed and its height above the Earth, it is 'falling' in such a way that it follows the curvature of the Earth. It never gets any closer to the Earth because the Earth's surface has simultaneously 'fallen' away from the spacecraft.

Note   Some textbooks define weight as 'the force exerted by an object on something which supports the object', e.g. the force exerted by an object on a spring balance is called its 'weight'. This definition leads to different conclusions about weightlessness – an object really can be weightless! In contrast, the definition of weight as the pull of the Earth on the object means that weight W, given by $W = mg$, can only be zero if $m = 0$. Since all objects have mass and g cannot be zero except at a theoretical distance of infinity, W must always have some value no matter how small that value may be. This weight (force) may all be 'used up' in performing some task so that the pull of the Earth on the object does *not* cause the object to exert a force on another object, e.g. a spring balance, which is supporting it. The spring balance then gives a zero reading and we say the object *appears* to be 'weightless'. Using the definition of weight given in this book it is incorrect to say the object is weightless; it must be carefully stressed that it only *appears* to be 'weightless'. (The stress on the word *appears* and the inverted commas around 'weightless' indicate that the word is not being used literally.)

Fig. 3.3(a) shows a mass attached to a spring balance registering zero on the scale as both fall freely to the floor in a laboratory while Fig. 3.3(b) shows an astronaut 'floating' freely in a spacecraft orbiting the Earth. Both *appear* to be 'weightless'.

3.3 Newton's First Law of Motion

Isaac Newton (1642–1727) studied the motion of objects and formulated three laws of motion. These are discussed more fully in Chapter 6.
(**Note** The statements are not expressed in the words that Newton used.)

The First Law

Every object which is at rest will remain at rest unless an unbalanced external force is applied to it. Also an object which is moving at uniform speed in a straight line will continue to do so unless an unbalanced external force is applied to it.

The first statement above is common experience for everyone. For example, if you leave a book on the bench then it will stay in the same position until someone moves it; i.e. they apply a force to it. If the book is not in the place where you left it then the only sensible conclusion is that someone 'pushed' or 'pulled' it into its new position.

The second statement is not quite as obvious as the first. When you see an object moving in a straight line, for example along a bench in the laboratory, it does not continue to move at the same speed, but always slows down and eventually stops. This can be reasoned as follows. It takes a force to make a stationary object move, so it should also take a force to make a moving object slow down and stop. Hence if a moving object is observed to slow down and stop you can conclude that a force has made this happen. This force is mainly the frictional force between the moving object and the surface over which it is moving. Since the frictional (contact) force between an object and the surface on which it travels cannot be completely eliminated, and moreover, the air exerts a 'drag' force on an object pushing its way through the air which also slows it down, it is very difficult to demonstrate the truth of this second statement. However, if frictional forces are reduced as much as possible, it can be shown that an object travelling at a given speed goes much further than it would when normal frictional forces exist. For example, an ice hockey puck shoved along a wooden floor will slow down due to the frictional force between the puck and the wood. If the same force is given to the same puck on an ice rink it will slide a much greater distance on the ice due to the reduced frictional force.

In the laboratory, the effect of reducing friction on a moving object can be demonstrated using a linear air track as shown in Fig. 3.4. If the metal rider is given a gentle push when the air supply is switched off, it will travel only a short distance before coming to rest. However, when the air supply is switched on the rider will hover just above the track supported on a 'cushion' of air. If the rider is now given the same gentle push it will travel the whole length of the track and will even, if rubber bands are stretched across each end of the track, rebound and cover the length of the

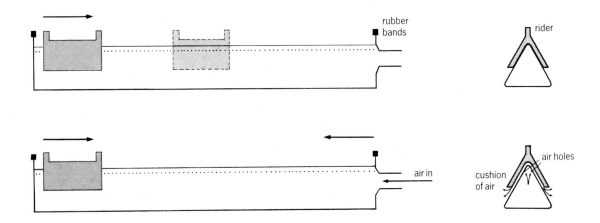

3.4 Riding on a cushion of air

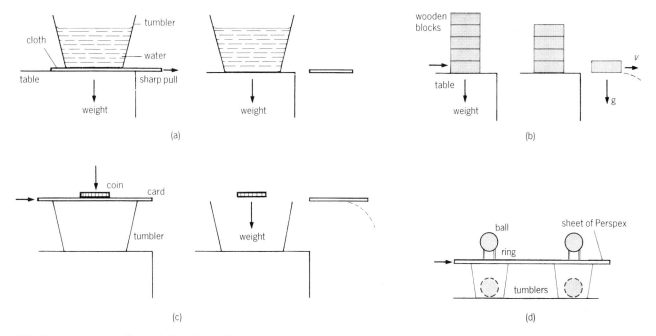

track several times. Since in this case the retarding forces are reduced, the rider moves for a much longer time. In theory, if there were no retarding forces acting on a moving object, the object would continue to move at a steady speed in a straight line. Therefore any object moving with uniform (steady) speed in a straight line must have no resultant force acting on it. If an unbalanced force were acting on the object it would either speed up, slow down or change its direction of motion. In fact Newton's First Law describes what a force 'does', i.e. it changes the velocity of an object.

Inertia

There are some interesting party tricks which demonstrate that a body will remain at rest unless acted upon by an unbalanced force. Figure 3.5 shows four examples of a horizontal force having little or no effect on vertical forces.

Trick 1 Place a tumbler partly filled with water on a seamless cloth on a table. Then remove the cloth without touching the glass or spilling the water. (If the cloth is given a quick, sharp 'downward' pull the horizontal force between the cloth and the base of the tumbler is not strong enough and does not act long enough to move the tumbler horizontally. Suddenly the cloth is removed and the tumbler drops vertically onto the table due to its weight.)

Note The tumbler will tip over or be pulled off the end of the table if an upward tug or a slow pull is exerted on the cloth. It is therefore advisable to practise with an empty tumbler until you have found the right type of force to apply to the cloth.)

Trick 2 Stand a pile of wooden blocks on a table. Then remove the lower block without touching the others. (Give it a sharp horizontal hit with a stick. The bottom block moves quickly so that any horizontal force between it and the one above will not move the rest of the pile in a horizontal direction. Once the lower block has been removed the weight of the other blocks makes them 'fall' vertically onto the table.)

Trick 3 Place a coin on a stiff piece of card resting on a tumbler that is standing on a table. Then get the coin into the tumbler without touching it. (Give the card a sharp horizontal flick with a finger so that it shoots away allowing the coin to drop vertically into the tumbler due to its weight.)

Trick 4 Rest a rectangular Perspex sheet with its corners on four tumblers (Fig. 3.5d). Place a ball supported on a narrow ring directly above each tumbler. Remove the Perspex so that each ball falls into the tumbler beneath. With the flat of your hand apply a short, sharp, horizontal force to the edge of the sheet. With practice, you will be able to push the sheet out from between the rings and tumblers.

In each of these four tricks there is a reluctance of the object to change what it is doing. If it is at rest it tends to remain at rest; if it is moving it tends to continue moving. The property of an object which resists a change in its motion is called **inertia**. Clearly the bigger the mass of the object the more difficult it is either to move it when it is at rest or to stop it when it is moving, and therefore the greater is its inertia. Hence the mass of an object is a measure of its inertia (i.e. the ratio between force applied and acceleration produced). This is a better definition of mass than saying it is the quantity of matter in the object.

3.4 Elasticity

Forces applied to an object can not only move the object, they can also deform its shape. You can mould a piece of plasticene or clay into any shape you wish simply by applying a force with your hands. Once the force is removed the plasticene or clay will remain in its new shape. Other materials behave differently when subjected to a force which is later removed. If you squeeze a balloon, football or tennis ball in your hands it will change its shape but it will recover its shape as soon as the force is removed (see Fig. 3.6). A rubber band can be stretched by pulling on it but it will return to its original size when the force is removed. A coiled spring can be extended by pulling on it or compressed by pushing on it.

Which materials are **elastic**? Basically, any substance which recovers its original shape and size when the force has been removed after it has been stretched, compressed, bent or twisted. Elastic substances are not only rubber and rubber compounds. Metals, especially steel, are quite elastic. A wooden rule can be bent into an arc and will straighten out when the force is removed. However, if the rule is bent too far it will snap. There is a limit to the applied force from which the material will recover when the force is removed. This limit, which is different for each substance, is known as the **elastic limit**.

Investigation 3.1   To discover the relationship between applied force and extension

Set up the apparatus as shown in Fig. 3.7(a). Fix a pin to the lower end of the spring to act as a pointer and record the position of the pointer on tne metre rule when no force is applied. This arbitrary zero position should be checked at the end of the experiment to ensure that the maximum force applied to the spring did not exceed the elastic limit. Attach a weight hanger (which applies a known force F to the spring) to the lower end of the spring. When the spring stops oscillating record the new position of the pointer. The difference in the two readings gives the extension e which can be recorded in mm. Add slotted weights of, say, 0.5 N to the hanger (also of weight 0.5 N) so that the force can be increased from 0 to 3 N in equal steps of 0.5 N. As you add each weight to the spring note the reading of the steady pointer on the metre rule. It is good practical technique also to take the pointer readings as the weights are removed so that an average pointer reading can be used to calculate the extension of the spring.

Table 3.2   Table of results for investigation 3.1

Force F/N	Pointer reading/mm Loading	Unloading	Mean reading/mm	Extension e/mm	$\dfrac{e}{F}\dfrac{mm}{N}$
0				0	—
0.5					
1.0					
1.5					
2.0					
2.5					
3.0					

The results can be tabulated as shown in Table 3.2. A calculation of the ratio $e : F$ should show it to be constant within the limits of experimental error. Similarly, the graph of extension e against force F (Fig. 3.7b) should be a straight-line graph passing through the origin. This demonstrates that e is directly proportional to F. Any unknown force can be deduced from the extension it causes on the spring by reading it from the graph, provided it lies within the range of the graph.

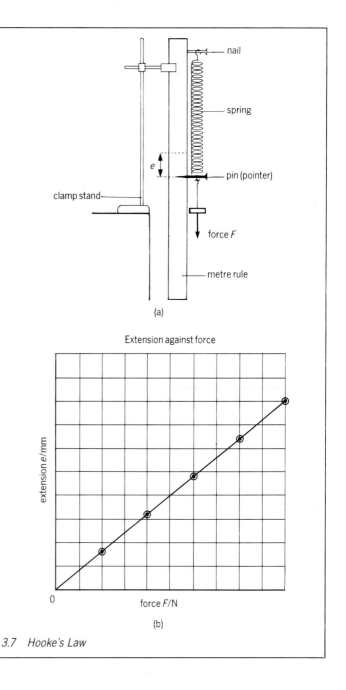

(a)

Extension against force

extension e/mm

force F/N

0

(b)

3.7 Hooke's Law

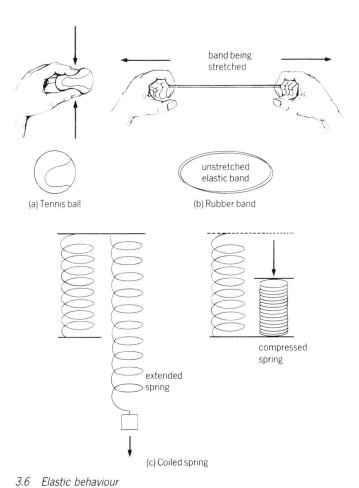

band being stretched

(a) Tennis ball

unstretched elastic band

(b) Rubber band

extended spring

compressed spring

(c) Coiled spring

3.6 Elastic behaviour

Hooke's Law for a spring

The relationship between the extension in a helical spring and the applied force was first investigated by Robert Hooke and is known as **Hooke's Law**. Hooke's Law states that **for a helical spring or other elastic material, the extension e is directly proportional to the applied force F, provided the elastic limit is not exceeded**. The elastic limit is the point at which the spring or other material becomes permanently deformed. For forces applied up to the elastic limit the spring returns to its original length or shape when the force is removed.

Spring balance

A very important practical application of this law is seen in the **spring balance** (Fig. 3.8). This is a compact version of the apparatus used in the investigation above. The spring and its pointer are assembled in a casing which has a suitable scale calibrated on it. The zero of the pointer can be adjusted. The balance has a hanger from which to support it and a hook on which to hang the object to be weighed.

Suppose an object is hung on the balance. The pull of the Earth on the object causes the object to pull on the spring with a force equal to its weight; the force registered on the spring balance is the weight W of the object. When you have to **weigh** an object, i.e. measure the force of gravity acting on the object, you should use a spring balance. You may well find spring balances in your laboratory which are calibrated in gram or kilogram, i.e. in units of mass rather than force. Since the weight W of an object of mass m is given by $W = mg$ and $W = \text{constant} \times e$ for the spring,

$$mg = \text{constant} \times e$$

$$\text{hence} \quad m = \frac{\text{constant}}{g} \times e$$

Thus at a given place, i.e. for constant g, m is proportional to e. Therefore masses can be *compared* using a spring balance. If the spring balance is used to weigh an object of mass m in two different places, the value of g in those locations may differ. This would produce two different weights $W_1 = mg_1$ and $W_2 = mg_2$. At the first place $m = W_1/g_1$ and at the second place of using the balance $m = W_2/g_2$. From this you can see that to obtain masses using a spring balance the force W_2 must be divided by g_2, the *local* value of the acceleration of free fall. It would be simpler to use a top-pan balance or a beam balance!

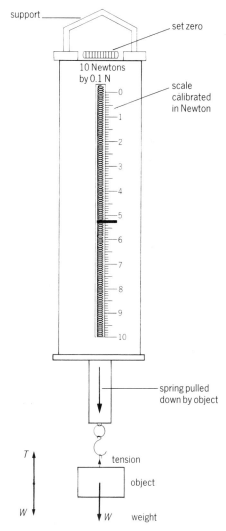

support

set zero

10 Newtons by 0.1 N

scale calibrated in Newton

spring pulled down by object

T

tension

object

W

W weight

3.8 A spring balance measuring weight

Investigation 3.2 To investigate the effect of increasing forces on a metal

Clamp one end of a two to three metre length of fine copper wire (32 SWG or similar) and pass it over a smooth pulley wheel, as in Fig. 3.9. Attach a 0.5 N weight hanger to the other end of the wire to keep it taut. Then attach a pointer to the wire so that it is close to a millimetre scale. Add various weights, to the weight hanger in, say, steps of 0.5 N and note the extension for each load. In this investigation you can load the wire to its elastic limit and beyond until the wire snaps.

A graph of load against extension for a similar wire will look like the graph in Fig. 3.10. Between O and E the relationship between load and extension is linear and is in accordance with Hooke's Law. Between E and B the relationship is non-linear, the wire recovers its shape when the load is removed but has a permanent extension. At Y, the **yield point**, the wire 'runs' and large extensions occur even without an increase in the load. At S the wire snaps.

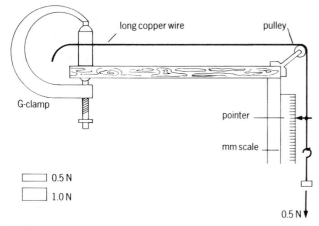

3.9 Hooke's Law and beyond for a wire

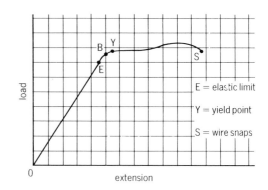

E = elastic limit

Y = yield point

S = wire snaps

3.10 Extension for loads beyond the elastic limit for a wire

The behaviour of the wire can be explained in terms of molecular theory. Figure 3.11 shows a simplified version of how the force between two molecules varies with the distance between their nuclei. At one molecular diameter apart the electrical forces are balanced, hence the resultant force is zero. Molecules in the metal wire are vibrating about a mean position of one molecular diameter for a given temperature. If the molecules move any closer together then a strong force of repulsion pushes them apart. This is why it is difficult to compress a solid. Alternatively, if the molecules move further than one molecular diameter apart then a force of attraction pulls them closer together, hence the difficulty in stretching a wire.

When a stretching force is applied to the wire the molecules are pulled further apart and the force of attraction between the molecules increases and equals the stretching force. If the stretching force is removed the internal molecular forces of attraction bring the wire back to its original shape. However, the force of attraction is only able to act over a short range, so that when the extension is greater than, e.g. Y in Fig. 3.10, the layers of molecules (or atoms) slip over each other and a permanent change occurs in the internal structure of the wire. The deformation is said to be **plastic** and unloading the wire does not restore the wire to its original length.

A machine called a **tensometer** can be used to stretch a short, thick metal rod until it snaps. As extremely large forces are applied the metal begins to narrow at the centre (see Fig. 3.12).

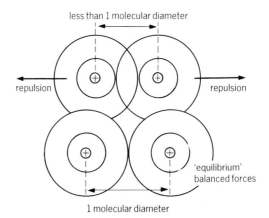

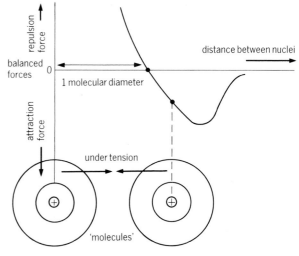

3.11 Attractive and repulsive intermolecular forces

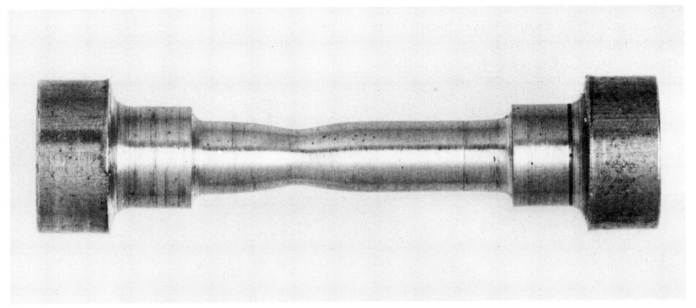

3.12 'Necking' of a thick metal bar under stress

3.5 Forces in liquids

Now let us move from forces in solids to forces in liquids. If a solid is placed into a liquid the solid will push the liquid out of its path with the result that the liquid will push back on the solid. This is an example of Newton's Third law of motion which states **'action and reaction are equal and opposite'**. The upward force exerted by liquids on objects placed in the liquid is known as the **upthrust**. Upthrust acts on a body in a liquid even if the body is resting on some support such as the bottom of a vessel, provided the space between the body and the support is not evacuated. A marble dropped into water in a beaker will sink to the bottom of the beaker as in Fig. 3.13(a). The forces acting on the marble are its weight W, the upthrust U of the water and the reaction R of the base of the beaker; $W = R + U$. A marble resting in a hole in the container will not have an upthrust acting on it. This time the downward forces on the marble are its weight W and the weight w of the liquid above it pressing the marble into the hole. The total reaction on the edges of the hole $R_2 = W + w$, which is much greater than the reaction R in the beaker where $R = W - U$.

Archimedes' Principle

Consider a cork which is pushed under the surface of some water in a beaker (Fig. 3.14). The forces acting

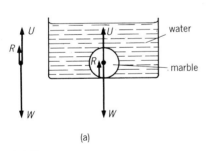

(a)

3.13 Upthrust and sinking

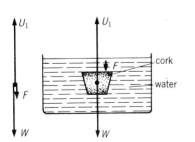

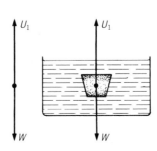

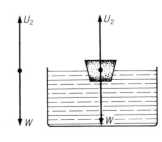

3.14 Upthrust and floating

on the cork are its weight W and the push P of the finger downwards plus an upthrust U_1 due to the water. When the cork is stationary $W + P = U_1$. Since $U_1 > W$, a resultant upward force of $(U_1 - W)$ will cause the cork to accelerate upwards when the finger is removed. Eventually the cork will come to rest partly submerged in the water when $U_2 = W$, i.e. when the upthrust is equal to the weight of the cork.

Archimedes investigated upthrust and discovered the relationship known as **Archimedes' Principle**. This states that '**if a body is totally or partially immersed in a fluid (gas or liquid) the fluid exerts an upthrust which is equal to the weight of the fluid displaced**'.
Note Archimedes' Principle is concerned with *forces* and should therefore be investigated using spring balances.

Investigation 3.3 To test Archimedes' Principle

The apparatus shown in Fig. 3.15 can be used. Suspend a solid, e.g. a block of metal, by a fine thread from a spring balance. Record the weight W_1 of the solid. The solid used should give an extension which is near to the maximum for the balance. Fill a Eureka can with water to the level of the spout and collect and remove any surplus water that overflows. Place a clean, dry empty beaker on a compression spring balance and record its weight w_1. Then carefully lower the solid, still attached to the balance, into the Eureka can so that part of it is immersed in water.

Although the weight W_1 of the solid has not changed the reading W_2 on the spring balance shows an *apparent* decrease in weight. This apparent loss in weight is due to an upward force, the upthrust U_1, acting on the solid as the solid pushes the water aside. Clearly the upthrust $U = W_1 - W_2$ where W_1 is the weight of the solid and W_2 is the apparent weight of the solid partly immersed in water. At the same time the water displaced by the solid overflows and is collected in the beaker standing on the compression balance. The reading on this balance will increase from w_1 to w_2. The weight of the water displaced is calculated from $(w_2 - w_1)$. Within the limits of experimental error, $U_1 = (W_1 - W_2)$ should be found to be equal to $(w_2 - w_1)$.

Continue the experiment by lowering the solid further so that it is completely immersed in the water. Read its apparent weight

W_3 from the spring balance and hence calculate the new upthrust $U_2 = (W_1 - W_3)$. It is important not to let the solid touch the sides or bottom of the Eureka can as this would lead to errors in the weighings. The reading on the compression balance will increase to w_3 as more water is displaced. Again the new weight of water displaced $(w_3 - w_1)$ should equal the upthrust $U_2 = (W_1 - W_3)$. You can record your readings by copying and completing the following table of results.

weight of solid	$W_1 =$	N
apparent weight of solid when partially immersed	$W_2 =$	N
apparent loss in weight or upthrust U_1	$(W_1 - W_2) =$	N
weight of empty beaker	$w_1 =$	N
weight of beaker plus water	$w_2 =$	N
weight of water displaced	$(w_2 - w_1) =$	N
apparent weight of solid when totally immersed	$W_3 =$	N
apparent loss in weight or upthrust U_2	$(W_1 - W_3) =$	N
weight of beaker plus extra water	$w_3 =$	N
weight of extra water displaced	$(w_3 - w_1) =$	N

Repeat the experiment with the same solid but using a different liquid, e.g. cooking oil. The readings W_1 and w_1 will remain unchanged but the other readings will be different because the density of the liquid is not the same as the density of water. However, you should still find that $(W_1 - W_2') = (w_2' - w_1)$ and $(W_1 - W_3') = (w_3' - w_1)$, where the dash signs denote weighings involving the second liquid.

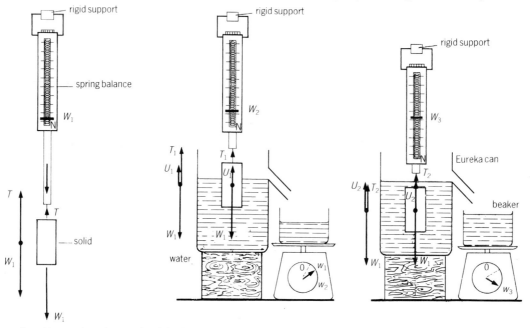

3.15 *To show upthrust is equal to the weight of the liquid displaced*

3.6 Upthrust

Upthrust in liquids

It is well known that certain solids, e.g. cork and wood, float in water while others, such as glass, stone and metals, sink in water. What is the property of the solid and the liquid which determines whether or not the solid will sink? The deciding factor is the ratio of the density of the solid to the density of the liquid. If the solid is more dense than the liquid its mass is more tightly packed into a given volume. Hence the liquid it displaces weighs less than the solid and so the upthrust is also less than the weight of the solid. Therefore there is an unbalanced downward force $(W - U) = $ (weight $-$ upthrust) acting on the solid and it sinks.

Note The acceleration of the solid when sinking through water will be less than the acceleration of free fall (see Fig. 3.16a). However, the water offers little resistance to a solid moving through it and so the solid accelerates quite quickly.

If a steel ball-bearing is dropped through a sticky liquid such as glycerol the events are quite different (Fig. 3.16b). When the ball is first dropped into the liquid it accelerates; the viscous drag force F exerted by the glycerol on the ball increases with the speed of the ball, until this force and the upthrust are equal to the weight. When the forces balance the ball is moving and therefore it will continue to travel with uniform speed known as the **terminal speed**. The terminal

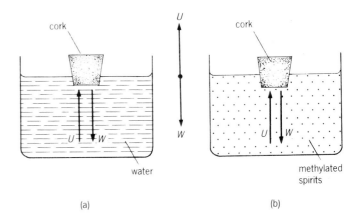

3.17 *The same object sinks to different depths in different liquids*

speed can always be reached under the right conditions, e.g. raindrops falling from a great height reach their terminal speed when the upthrust and the air resistance force combined equal the weight of the droplet.

When the density of the solid is less than the density of the liquid the liquid can always provide an upthrust equal to the weight of the object. Consider a cork floating first in water and then in methylated spirits (Fig. 3.17). The cork settles into a position of equilibrium in both liquids but more of the cork is immersed in the meths than in the water. The density of meths is less than that of water and, since it is the weight of the volume of liquid displaced by the cork which is the value of the upthrust, a greater volume of the less dense meths has to be displaced in order to provide an upthrust equal to the weight of the cork. Hence the cork sinks deeper in the meths.

Not only can less dense solids float on liquids, less dense liquids can float on more dense liquids as long as the two liquids do not mix. Some examples are water floating on mercury, turpentine floating on water, vinegar floating on oil.

Objects made from dense materials can also float, e.g. ships made of steel float on water yet the density of the steel is much greater than that of water. This is possible because the average density of the whole ship is less than that of water. Since the average density is the mass of the ship divided by the volume of the ship including the air spaces, the ship will float if the air spaces are large enough. It is interesting to note that the density of sea water is greater than that of fresh water and so a ship with a given load floats higher out of the water when at sea than it does in rivers supplied with fresh water. Furthermore, warm sea water is less dense than cold sea water so that the loaded ship will float lower in warmer waters. When a ship is being loaded the climate of the seas through which it will travel must be taken into account. Various levels or lines marked on the side of the ship indicate the safe loading levels for these various water densities.

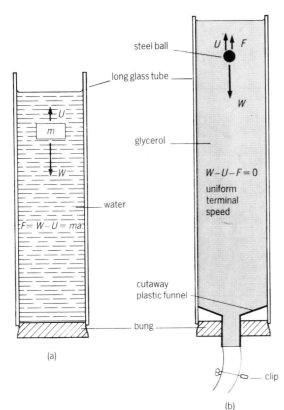

3.16 *Terminal speed*

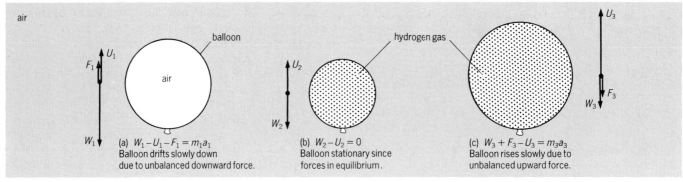

air

U_1 balloon

F_1

air

W_1

(a) $W_1 - U_1 - F_1 = m_1a_1$
Balloon drifts slowly down
due to unbalanced downward force.

U_2

W_2

(b) $W_2 - U_2 = 0$
Balloon stationary since
forces in equilibrium.

hydrogen gas

U_3

F_3

W_3

(c) $W_3 + F_3 - U_3 = m_3a_3$
Balloon rises slowly due to
unbalanced upward force.

3.18   Upthrust in air

Upthrust in gases

Upthrust is not confined to liquids; it can also occur in gases. For example, hot-air balloons, hydrogen-filled balloons, airships etc. all float or even rise in air due to the upthrust produced when the object displaces a large volume of air whose weight is equal to or greater than that of the object. Consider a balloon blown up with air, as in Fig. 3.18(a). The weight of the air inside the balloon and the balloon fabric will always be greater than the weight of the air which the balloon displaces since the volume of air displaced is approximately equal to the volume of air inside the balloon and the balloon fabric is more dense than air. Therefore the upthrust U_1 is less than the weight W_1 and the resultant unbalanced downward force on the balloon causes it to drift slowly downwards. There is also a 'frictional' drag force F (air resistance), caused by the large surface area pushing the air aside as it moves down, which helps to slow down the descent of the balloon. The free-body force diagram leads to the equation

$$W_1 - U_1 - F_1 = ma_1$$

i.e. there is a 'small' unbalanced force causing the balloon to 'accelerate' downwards quite slowly. Now consider the same balloon filled with hydrogen gas (which is less dense than air). When inflated to a certain volume (Fig. 3.18b) the balloon has the free-body force $W_2 - U_2 = 0$. The upthrust U_2 balances the weight W_2 and the balloon is in equilibrium, i.e. with zero unbalanced force. This happens because the weight of the air displaced by the balloon U_2 equals the weight of the less dense hydrogen filling the balloon *plus* the weight of the balloon fabric W_2. If the balloon is further inflated with hydrogen gas (Fig. 3.18c) its weight increases to W_3 because it contains more hydrogen. However, its volume is also greater and so the volume of air it displaces is greater. The weight of the displaced air is equal to the upthrust U_3 and is greater than W_3. The resultant unbalanced upward force makes the balloon rise and as it does so the air resistance to its motion F_3 acts downwards. The free-body force diagram gives $W_3 + F_3 - U_3 = m_3a_3$, therefore the balloon 'accelerates' slowly upwards.

3.19   Hot air balloons

Exercise 3.1

Explain why a hot-air balloon can rise when carrying people and materials in a basket. How can the balloon be made to descend? Draw a free-body force diagram in each case to show why the balloon rises or descends.

3.7   Principle of Flotation

The Principle of Flotation states that **a floating object displaces its own weight of the fluid in which it floats.**

Investigation 3.4 To test the Principle of Flotation

A simple test of the Principle of Flotation can be performed using the apparatus shown in Fig. 3.20. Fill a large Eureka can with water to the level of the spout; allow any excess water to flow into the sink. Place a compression balance under the spout of the can so that any water which is displaced will be collected in the balance's pan. Hang a large test-tube from a spring balance by a thread tied to its rim and load it with lead shot until its weight W is, say, 0.5 N. Then gently lower the loaded test tube into the water in the Eureka can. The weight w of the displaced water can be read directly from the compression balance. As you increase the weight of the loaded test tube by adding 0.5 N amounts of lead shot (effectively 50 g masses) the tube will sink deeper; so more water will be displaced and be recorded on the compression balance. You can load the tube until it either touches the bottom of the can or cannot hold any more lead shot. Use a table of results like the one below to record the readings. In all cases you should find that the pair of values of W and w are equal.

weight of loaded test tube W/N	0.5	1.0	1.5	2.0
weight of water displaced w/N				

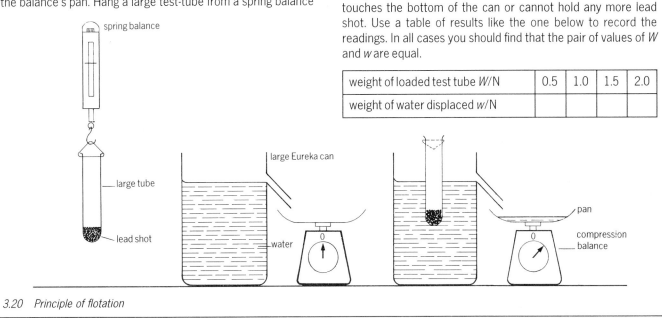

3.20 Principle of flotation

Hydrometers

A useful instrument in which the Principle of Flotation is applied is the **constant weight hydrometer** which floats at different levels in liquids of different densities. One form of this hydrometer is shown in Fig. 3.21. The hydrometer sinks in the liquid until the weight of the liquid displaced is equal to the weight of the hydrometer. The hydrometer is calibrated to measure the density of the liquid in kg m^{-3}. It floats upright because the bulb is weighted with lead shot. The narrow stem gives greater sensitivity to the readings.

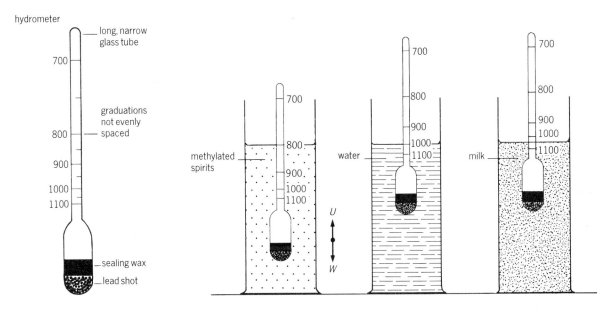

3.21 Hydrometers

Another form of hydrometer (Fig. 3.22) must be used when only a small amount of the liquid is available, e.g. when testing the density of the acid in a car battery. The tubing is placed in the acid, as in Fig. 3.20(a), and the rubber bulb is squeezed to expel air from the system and so reduce the pressure of the air inside the glass container. When the bulb is released (Fig. 3.30b) the atmospheric pressure forces the acid up into the container where the hydrometer floats in the acid. The level of the acid on the hydrometer scale is a measure of the density of the acid. This should be 1250 kg m^{-3} if the battery is fully charged. A reading of 1180 kg m^{-3} indicates that the battery is fully discharged and in urgent need of recharging. In breweries hydrometers are used to measure the relative density of the beers. Using a suitable hydrometer, milk and wine can be tested to make sure they have not been diluted with water.

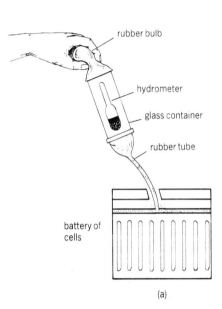
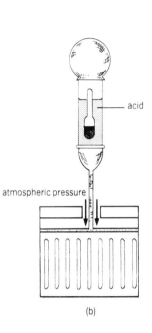
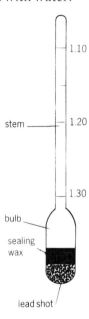

(a)   (b)

3.22 Hydrometer for testing the acid in a car battery

Questions

Q1 An unbalanced force F acting on a mass m causes it to move with an acceleration a. Which formula gives the correct relationship between F, m and a?

A $F = m + a$ **B** $m = F/a$ **C** $F = m/a$

D $a = m/F$ **E** $a = Fm$

Q2 A 2 N load causes a 10 cm extension of a spring. When two such identical springs are joined end-to-end to form one continuous spring and a load of 4 N is applied the new extension is

A 5 cm   **B** 10 cm   **C** 20 cm

D 30 cm   **E** 40 cm

Q3 A small tube closed at one end floats upright in a liquid with about half the length of the tube immersed in the liquid. Which one of the following changes will NOT cause the tube to sink lower in the liquid?

A The density of the liquid is reduced.

B A small mass is placed inside the tube.

C Atmospheric pressure is increased.

D The liquid is heated.

E A cork is put into the top of the tube.

Q4 A beaker of water, weighing 10.8 N, rests on a compression balance. A block of metal, weighing 4.32 N and volume 0.000 06 m^3, supported by a string is lowered into the water so that it is fully submerged but not touching the beaker. The compression balance will now read

A 10.2 N   **B** 10.8 N   **C** 11.4 N

D 14.52 N   **E** 15.12 N

Q5 A small satellite S moves with constant speed in a circular path around the Earth. Show on a simple sketch the directions of the velocity and acceleration of S at some instant. How does the force on S depend on

(a) the mass of the Earth,

(b) the distance from S to the Earth's centre?   *(S)*

Q6 Describe briefly how the length of a light spiral spring changes when the spring is stretched by a force which is gradually increased in magnitude. Would you expect the same comments to apply to a straight steel wire as it is stretched?   *(S)*

Q7 How would you demonstrate that, within some elastic limit, a metal, such as copper, is perfectly elastic? Describe briefly what is observed if the elastic limit is exceeded.

(L part question)

Q8 The given table shows the extensions, x, of an elastic cord when it is subjected to a series of forces, F.

force, F/N	1.1	2.0	3.0	3.7	4.7	5.3
extension, x/m	0.13	0.25	0.37	0.45	0.60	0.74

Plot the graph of FORCE against EXTENSION and use the graph to estimate

(a) the range of loads (forces) for which Hooke's Law is obeyed, and

(b) the extra force required to cause the extension of the cord to increase from 0.3 m to 0.5 m.

Q9 In a laboratory experiment a lump of metal is hung on the end of a vertical spring which has its upper end fixed. Would you expect the extension of the spring to be different if the experiment is repeated

(a) at the top of a tall tower,

(b) on the surface of the Moon? Give reasons for your answers, naming the scientists associated with any physical laws to which you refer. *(S part question)*

Q10 For a light coiled spring which obeys Hooke's Law, a tension of 160 N would produce an extension of 72 mm. The spring is hung vertically from a fixed support, and a mass of 12 kg is attached to the lower end.

(a) Calculate the extension of the spring.

(b) The mass is now pulled down a further distance of 18 mm and then released. What is the resultant force acting on it immediately after release, and what is the acceleration produced? *(O part question)*

Q11 Describe how you would obtain, as accurately as possible, a series of readings for the load and corresponding extension of a spiral spring.

A student obtained the following readings:

load/N	0	1	2	3	4	5	6
length of spring/cm	10.0	11.5	13.0	14.5	16.0	18.5	24.0

Using these results, plot a graph of load against extension and estimate the load beyond which Hooke's Law is no longer obeyed.

The spring is at rest with a mass of 0.2 kg on its lower end. It is then further extended by a finger exerting a vertical force of 0.5 N. Draw a diagram showing the forces acting on the mass in this position, giving the values of the forces.

Describe the motion of the mass when the finger is removed. Make your description as precise as possible, by giving distances. State the position where the kinetic energy of the mass will be greatest. *(L)*

Q12 A light spring which obeys Hooke's Law is hung from a beam. The lower end carries a pointer which is against the 50 mm mark on a vertical scale when the spring has no load, and which moves to the 130 mm mark when a load of 20 N is carried by the spring.

(a) What load would extend the spring by 1 mm?

(b) Where on the scale would the pointer be when the load was 10 N?

(c) When the load is replaced by one of 12 N, what is the pull exerted on the spring by the beam? Explain.

(d) Draw a graph of extension against load for the spring.

(e) Calculate the energy stored in the spring when it is stretched by a load of 20 N. *(O)*

Q13 A light helical spring hangs vertically with its upper end fixed. A light pointer, attached to its lower end, can be used to take readings on a vertical scale when masses of various sizes are attached to the lower end of the spring. The following table gives the scale readings of the pointer for different attached masses:

mass attached /kg	0	0.2	0.4	0.6	0.8
scale reading /mm	120	126	132	138	144

(a) Make a table showing corresponding values of the force on the spring in newtons and its resulting extension in metres.

(b) Plot a graph of force (*y*-axis) against extension (*x*-axis).

(c) State Hooke's Law. Are the readings for this spring consistent with it? Explain.

(d) Use your graph to find the force that produces an extension of 15 mm and the energy stored in the spring at this extension.

(e) The spring is loaded with a 0.4 kg mass. This is pulled down 3 mm below its equilibrium position and then released. Explain what happens as fully as you can. *(O)*

Q14 A block of length 20 cm, uniform cross-section area 4 cm², and density 1.25 g cm⁻³ is suspended from a spring balance and fully immersed in a liquid of density 0.8 g cm⁻³.

(a) Calculate the mass of the block.

(b) Calculate the weight of the block.

(c) What would be the reading on the spring balance if the block were half immersed in the liquid? *(AEB)*

Q15 State the Principle of Archimedes and describe an experiment which demonstrates the principle.

A hot air balloon is tethered to the ground on a windless day. The envelope of the balloon contains 1200 m³ of hot air of density 0.8 kg m⁻³. The mass of the balloon (not including the hot air) is 400 kg. The density of the surrounding air is 1.3 kg m⁻³.

(a) Explain why the balloon would rise if it were not tethered.

(b) Calculate the tension in the rope holding the balloon to the ground.

(c) Calculate the acceleration with which the balloon begins to rise when released. *(O & C)*

Q16 State the Principle of Archimedes and describe an experiment which may be performed to verify it.

A large lump of ice floats in a beaker of water. Explain what happens to the level of the water in the beaker as the ice slowly melts. *(W)*

Q17 A disc of cork floats in water. When a lump of metal is placed on the top surface of the cork the cork moves downwards but remains floating. Explain this in terms of the forces acting. When the same lump of metal is attached firmly to the bottom surface of the disc, with the metal completely submerged in the water, the downward movement of the cork is less than when the metal was attached to the top surface. Why is this? *(C)*

4 Pressure

4.1 Definition of pressure

Pressure is the normal (i.e. perpendicular) force acting on unit area:

$$\text{pressure } p = \frac{\text{normal force}}{\text{area on which force acts}} = \frac{F}{A}$$

(See Fig. 4.1a). The SI unit of pressure is N/m² which is known as the pascal Pa.

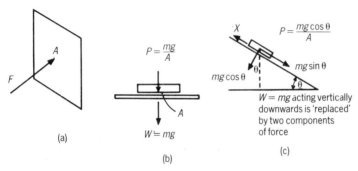

4.1   Pressure is normal force per unit area

The force which a solid object exerts on the surface which supports it is equal in value to the object's weight $W = mg$ N. If the supporting surface is horizontal and the area of contact between the solid and the surface is A m² as in Fig. 4.1(b), the pressure p exerted by the solid on the surface is given by $p = W/A = mg/A$ Pa. However, if the supporting surface is inclined at an angle θ to the horizontal as in Fig. 4.1(c), the pressure on the surface is now $mg\cos\theta/A$ Pa because the component of the weight W acting normally to the surface is $mg \cos \theta$. In fact Fig. 4.1(c) can be used to show that the pressure the object exerts

---

Example

A block weighing 1200 N rests on an area of 4 m². Calculate the pressure exerted by the block on the surface which supports it.

$$p = ?   \quad F = 1200 \text{ N} \quad A = 4 \text{ m}^2$$

$$p = \frac{F}{A}$$

$$p = \frac{1200}{4} \quad \frac{\text{N}}{\text{m}^2}$$

$$p = 300 \text{ Pa}$$

---

on the surface varies from mg/A to zero as the angle θ varies from 0 ° to 90 °; when $\theta = 0$ ° the weight W is normal to the surface while when $\theta = 90$ ° the surface is vertical. In this latter case the solid falls vertically without pressing on the surface.

The pressure exerted on a surface is sometimes known as a **stress** and results in a **strain**. If the supporting surface is not strong enough to withstand this strain it may alter its shape drastically or even fracture. For example, the man in Fig. 4.2 wishes to cross a gap but has only a thin plank of wood to use as a bridge. He knows that if he walks on the plank it will bend to such an extent that it will just snap. This will be caused by the pressure exerted by his weight on the plank. The pressure $p = W/a$ where W is his weight and a is the area of his shoes in contact with the plank. Can the man cross the gap safely? If he lies down on the plank and 'pulls' himself slowly across it may be possible for him to reach the other side safely because his weight W will be 'spread' over a larger surface area of contact A and hence the pressure $p = F/A$ he exerts will be reduced. This reduced pressure may be small enough not to strain the plank to breaking point. Similarly, if you are unfortunate enough to be caught on thin ice on a pond you should lie down flat to 'spread' your weight over as large an area as possible to reduce the pressure. To rescue someone in this position lay down a ladder or wide plank on the ice and tell the person to crawl along it to safety. Certain animals which live in sandy or soft, muddy regions have 'large' feet so that their weight is distributed over a large area. Hence the pressure they exert on the ground is such that they do not sink too deeply into the sand or mud. Snow shoes enable people to walk over soft snow without sinking too deeply into it. Spacecraft which have landed on the Moon and on planets have all been fitted with large-area pads on their feet to prevent them sinking too far into the unknown surfaces.

Tanks, bulldozers and other heavy mechanical equipment are fitted with caterpillar tracks which consist of large flat surfaces punctuated with short spikes. If the vehicle were supported by the spikes alone the pressure would be enormous due to the very small area of contact (Fig. 4.3a). This enormous pressure makes spikes penetrate the surface to give good grip and traction while allowing the vehicle's weight to be supported on an area of contact equal to the large flat area of the track. Therefore the vehicle will sink only a little way into the supporting surface as shown in Fig. 4.3(b). Other examples include spiked running shoes and football boots.

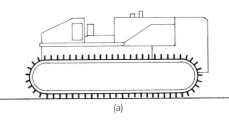

(a)

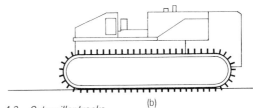

(b)

4.3   Caterpillar tracks

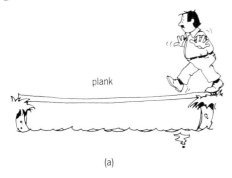

plank

(a)

(b)

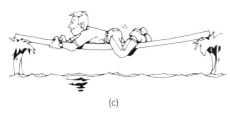

(c)

4.2   Distribution of weight over a greater area gives less pressure

Spiked running shoe

Example

A man wants to make a garden path using slabs of concrete measuring 1 m × 0.8 m × 0.1 m and weighing 1920 N. These slabs are too heavy to lift and place in position so it is usual for each one to be turned on edge and 'walked' to the area where it is required. The pressure which the slab exerts on the soil varies from 2400 Pa to 24 000 Pa according to the area of the face in contact with the soil. Indeed when the slab is being turned on a corner the pressure is even greater and the slab will sink quite deeply into the soil.

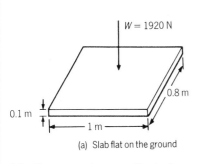

(a)   Slab flat on the ground

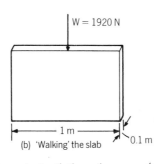

(b)   'Walking' the slab

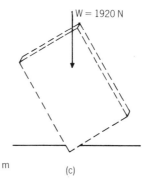

(c)

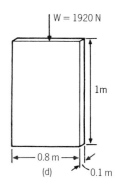

(d)

4.4   Pressure varies according to the area in contact with the soil.
(a) The slab is flat on the ground: $p = F/A = 1920 \text{ N}/0.8 \text{ m}^2 = 2400$ Pa.
(b) Walking the slab: $p = F/A = 1920 \text{ N}/0.1 \text{ m}^2 = 19\,200$ Pa.
(c) Turning the corner.
(d) On the next side: $p = F/A = 1920 \text{ N}/0.08 \text{ m}^2 = 24\,000$ Pa.

4.2 Molecular theory of pressure

In solids

Pressure exerted by a solid on a supporting surface can be explained in terms of molecular interaction between the molecules of the two substances involved. When two solid surfaces are being forced together the vibrations of the molecules cause an overlap of the electron clouds surrounding adjacent molecules at the region of contact and hence a mutual repulsion force is set up. The closer the surfaces come into contact the greater the repulsive force produced. Since molecules in a solid vibrate about a fixed mean position the *net* bombarding force due to the motion of the molecules is negligible. The pull of the Earth on the mass of the solid is responsible for the force which presses the solid onto the supporting surface. This forces the contact layers of molecules closer together than their equilibrium distance, and so causes an electromagnetic repulsive force to be set up between the different types of molecules (see Fig. 4.5). The weight of the solid is responsible for the solid exerting a force equal to its weight on the surface. Hence the pressure exerted by a solid resting on a horizontal surface is calculated by dividing weight by the surface area of contact.

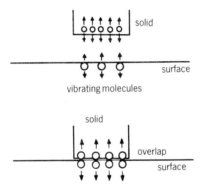

4.5   Pressure on a molecular scale

In gases

The pressure exerted by the weight of a solid resting on a horizontal surface contrasts sharply with the way a gas exerts a pressure on the walls of its container. Here the actual weight of the molecules plays very little part; the molecular bombardment of the walls by the energetic molecules is responsible for the pressure. When a gas molecule approaches very close to the wall of the container the molecules of the container repel the approaching molecules, changing their momentum (see Fig. 4.6). From Newton's Third Law (see p.76) it follows that the approaching molecules must exert an equal and opposite force on the wall of the container. Since a momentum *change* takes place the force is given by the *rate* of change of momentum (see p.73). Very large numbers of molecules travelling

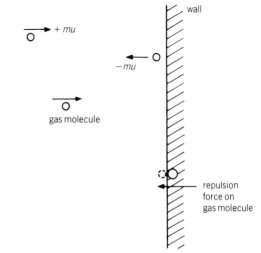

4.6   Pressure exerted by gases

at relatively high speeds are involved, and so the force exerted can be quite high. Thus the molecular bombardment of the walls of the container exerts quite considerable pressure.

The pressure due to the Earth's atmosphere (atmospheric pressure) used to be considered due to the weight of the air in a column extending several hundred kilometre upwards, acting on unit area. Consider a metal can open to the atmosphere as in Fig. 4.7(a). The atmospheric pressure will be the same inside and outside this can. If the screw cap is replaced and tightened so that the air inside the can is sealed from the atmosphere (Fig. 4.7b) the pressure of the gas inside the can is still atmospheric pressure but is clearly no longer due to the weight of the column of air above it. The pressure the trapped gas is exerting must be due to the molecular bombardment of the walls because the weight of the air in the can is of the order of 0.02 N for a surface area of say 0.5 m^2. This suggests a pressure of 0.02 N/0.5 m^2 = 0.04 Pa which is much less than the value of atmospheric pressure (about 100 000 Pa).

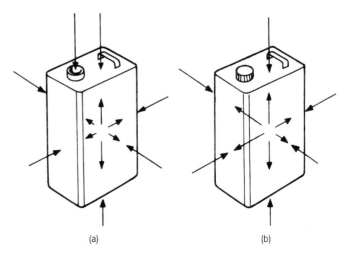

4.7   Atmospheric pressure in open and closed cans

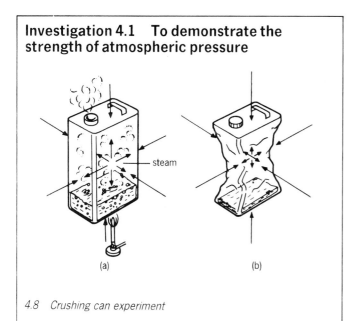
The steam inside the can has condensed into a very small volume of water, leaving a partial vacuum behind, and the number of molecules per unit volume is considerably reduced. Since the temperature in the can has been reduced the speed of the molecules is also lower. Both effects reduce the pressure inside the can. Any residual air molecules and water vapour molecules cannot exert a pressure equal to the external atmospheric pressure. Hence the greater external pressure crushes the can. The large pressure difference on opposite sides of the walls of the can results in a very large unbalanced force acting inwards.

There are some useful applications of a pressure difference across a surface, e.g. the rubber sucker, drinking straw and pipette. When the moistened concave surface of the rubber sucker (Fig. 4.9a) is pressed against a flat surface the air between the two surfaces is squeezed out, leaving the pressure in the enclosed space much reduced. The external atmospheric pressure acting on the sucker forces the sucker against the flat surface. Figure 4.9(b) shows a child sucking out the air inside a straw. The pressure p_2 of the air that remains in the straw is less than the atmospheric pressure p_0 pressing down on the surface of the liquid outside the straw. Therefore the liquid is forced up the straw and into the child's mouth. The pressure p_1 at the bottom of the straw is greater than atmospheric pressure p_0.

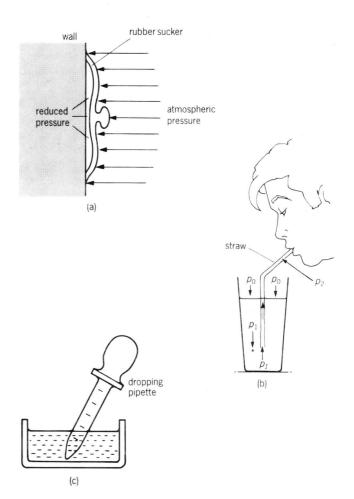

4.9 Applications of atmospheric pressure: (a) a sucker; (b) drinking through a straw; (c) a dropping pipette

Exercise 4.1

Explain how squeezing and releasing the bulb of the dropping pipette in Fig. 4.9(c) will fill that pipette.

In liquids

Pressure in liquids is different from that in both solids and gases. In a liquid the forces holding the molecules together are not strong enough to give the liquid a rigid shape and so the liquid must be held in a container. The molecules in a liquid do move around inside the liquid and 'collide' with the walls of the container. Although the movement of liquid molecules is slower than the movement of gas molecules there are many more molecules per unit volume in a liquid than in a gas. As with solids, the weight of the liquid molecules pushes down on the base of the container, and this vertical force acts to give a pressure on any horizontal surface in the liquid. But unlike solids, a liquid also exerts a pressure on the 'vertical' walls of the container. Internal stresses are set up in the liquid by external forces, and these allow the pressure in a liquid

47

to be transmitted in all directions. The solid surface needed to contain a liquid must exert a force on that liquid; this force is equal and opposite to the force exerted by the liquid on the containing surface. The force exerted by the liquid is called the **thrust** and is perpendicular to the surface.

(**Note** If the thrust acted at an angle to the surface then the opposing force of the surface on the liquid would have a component parallel to the surface of the liquid. This unbalanced force would make the liquid move relative to the surface. When the liquid is at rest in a container no such motion takes place, therefore no such unbalanced force is present. Only a force perpendicular to the surface can have no component parallel to that surface. Thus for any shape of surface in a liquid at rest the thrust of the liquid will be normal (perpendicular) to the surface.)

4.3   The effects of pressure in a liquid

Consider a very small area within a liquid at rest. The fluid will exert a thrust on this area, creating a pressure of thrust divided by area. If the area is so small as to be almost nil the pressure on it is known as the **pressure at a point** in the liquid. Note that pressure (defined as the *normal* thrust (force) per unit area of a surface presented *normally* to the force) is a scalar rather than a vector quantity.

Note Pressure acts equally in all directions and pressures can be added algebraically.

It is important to realise that the pressure at a point in a liquid is dependent only on the *vertical* depth of the point. It follows that the pressure at all points on the same horizontal level in a liquid must be the same. Another important fact is that pressure at a point in a liquid (or indeed a gas) acts equally in all directions. Consider a section of liquid of cross-sectional area A depth h and weight W with its upper surface subject to atmosphere pressure p_0 and the lower surface to pressure p (Fig. 4.11a). For this imaginary section of liquid to remain in equilibrium there must be no unbalanced vertical force acting on it. Thus $F_0 + W = F$. The thrust of the liquid is a force equal to its weight $W = mg = V \rho g$ where ρ = density and V = volume of the liquid. Since the volume V is $h \times A$ it follows that $W = hA\rho g$. Hence

$$p_0 A + hA\rho g = p A$$
$$p_0 + h\rho g = p.$$

Thus $p - p_0 = \Delta p = h\rho g$, i.e. the difference in pressure Δp between two horizontal levels in a liquid of given density ρ and at a place where the acceleration of free fall is g depends on the *vertical* distance h between these two levels. Since the area does not appear anywhere in the pressure equation $\Delta p = h\rho g$, the pressure in a liquid is independent of the cross-sectional area and hence the 'shape' of the liquid.

The pressure p_1 at depth h_1 is the same at all points on the same horizontal level (Fig. 4.11b). Since no liquid flows horizontally when the liquid is at rest there can be no unbalanced force in the horizontal direction. Consider a horizontal section of liquid as shown. The forces $p_1 A_1$ on the equal areas A_1 at each

---

Investigation 4.2   To show that pressure in a liquid at rest increases with depth

Fill a tall cylinder with three equal-sized outlets (see Fig. 4.10) with water from a running tap. Position three beakers to catch the water. Then remove the corks from the outlets. Water from the outlet 3 is thrust further horizontally than that from outlet 2 which in turn goes further than that from outlet 1. This shows that the pressure is greater at the deeper point in the liquid. The volume of water collected from the jets also increases with the depth of the outlet.

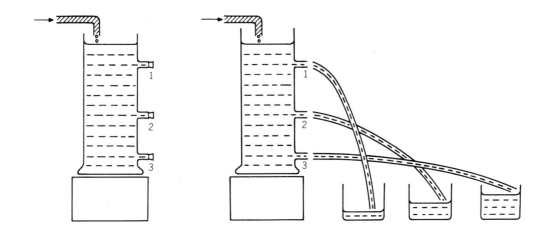

4.10   *Pressure in a liquid increases with depth*

48

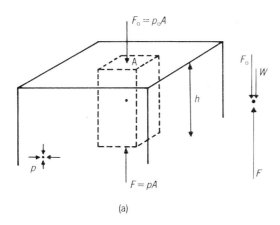

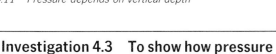

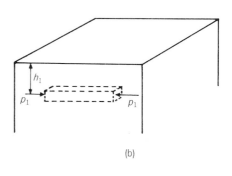

4.11   *Pressure depends on vertical depth*

Investigation 4.3   To show how pressure varies with depth

Suspend a loaded wooden block on a spring balance. First weigh the block in air using the spring balance and record its weight W_1 (see Fig. 4.12a). Then find the apparent weight W_2 when the base of the block is at a measured depth h below the surface of the liquid (Fig. 4.12b). The apparent loss in weight $\Delta W = W_1 - W_2$ is due to the difference between the thrusts on the top and bottom horizontal surfaces of the block and is $h\rho gA$ where $A =$ base area of the block. Record several readings of ΔW for different values of h. Since $\Delta W = h\rho gA$ or $\Delta p = \Delta W/A = h\rho g$, a graph of apparent change in weight ΔW plotted against the depth of the base in the liquid h will give a straight line through the origin.

Repeat the experiment for different liquids with the block immersed to the same depth each time. You can then show the direct proportionality of pressure Δp ($\Delta W/A$) and density ρ by plotting a graph of ΔW against ρ.

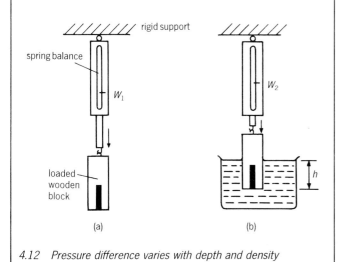

4.12   *Pressure difference varies with depth and density*

Exercise 4.2

Draw sketch graphs to show the relationship between (a) ΔW and h and (b) Δp and ρ.

end face of the section of liquid must be equal and opposite. Liquids are incompressible but will flow and hence occupy the space available. Thus they exert a pressure equally in all directions. The number of molecules per unit volume is constant in a solid and in a liquid but this is not so for a gas. Hence gases are easy to compress but solids and liquids are not.

A liquid must always come to rest in a container with its upper surface horizontal, since this is the only way the pressure at all points at the same vertical depth from the surface of the liquid can remain constant. In the rectangular tank in Fig. 4.13(a) it is easy to see that the depth of water h must be the same for all parts of the container and that the pressure $p_3 > p_2 > p_1$. What is not so easy to understand is that if the liquid is

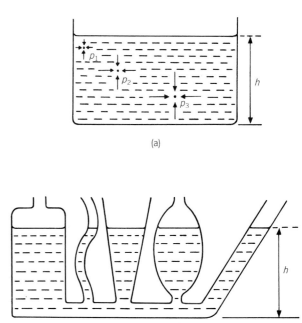

4.13   *Pressure is independent of cross-sectional area*

49

contained in several interconnecting vessels of different shapes as in Fig. 4.13(b) the surface of the liquid is horizontal and in all cases at the same *vertical* height h above the base. Pressure in a liquid is independent of the cross-sectional area and therefore the shape of the vessel. If the pressure at the surface of a liquid is atmospheric pressure p_0, as is often the case, and the pressure p_1 at a point which is h_1 deep in a liquid of density ρ then the total pressure at the point is $p_1 = p_0 + h_1\rho g$.

Investigation 4.4 To measure the pressure in the laboratory gas supply

Bend a piece of plastic (or glass) tubing into a U-shape and clip it to a board. A small quantity of liquid put into the U-tube will settle as shown in Fig. 4.14(a). Since atmospheric pressure p_0 is pressing down on both open limbs, the surface of the liquid must be at the same horizontal level in both limbs. Connect the tube to the gas supply in the laboratory and turn on the tap. The surface levels will change to those in Fig. 4.14(b).

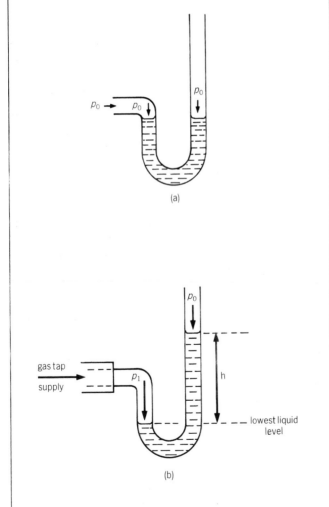

4.14   Manometer to measure the excess pressure of the gas supply

---

4.4   Measuring pressure differences

Manometer

A manometer is a useful instrument for measuring pressure differences. It consists of a U-tube containing a suitable liquid; i.e. a low-density liquid (such as oil) when measuring small pressure differences and a high-density liquid (such as mercury) for large pressure differences.

The pressure p_1 of the gas supply is greater than atmospheric pressure p_0 (otherwise gas would not come out from the pipe when the tap is turned on) and this pressure is transmitted to the liquid in the left-hand limb of the tube. This forces the liquid round the tube into the right-hand limb until there is a 'head' of liquid h above the lowest surface level. Equating pressures at this level gives $p_1 = h\rho g + p_0$ and so the excess pressure of the gas above the atmospheric pressure is given by $\Delta p = p_1 - p_0 = h\rho g$.

The long narrow tube and the wide dish in Fig. 4.16(a) can be considered as the two 'limbs' of a manometer with the mercury forming the connection between the two limbs. With the long tube open to the atmosphere the mercury is at the same horizontal level both inside and outside the tube. Atmospheric

---

Exercise 4.3

Copy and complete the diagrams in Fig. 4.15 to show what happens to the liquid in the manometer when it is connected to a container which holds air at a pressure p_2 less than atmospheric pressure. Write down an equation which describes the final state of the liquid in the tube.

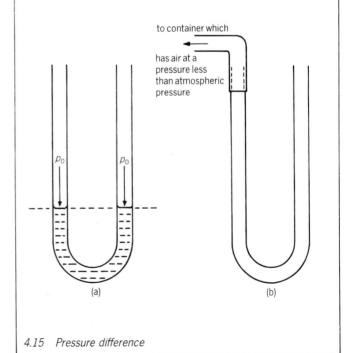

4.15   Pressure difference

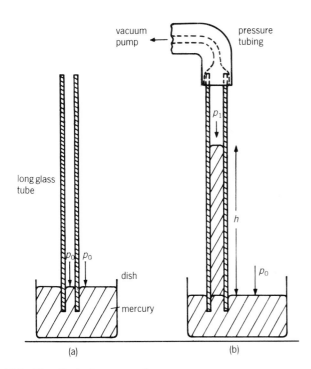

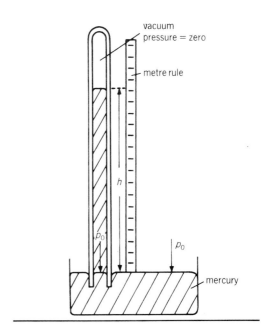

4.16 *The effect of pressure changes on mercury*

4.17 *Simple barometer*

pressure p_0 acts equally on the mercury in the tube and in the dish. If the top of the tube is connected by pressure tubing to a good vacuum pump, air can be removed from the tube causing a drop in pressure to p_1. The pressure on the mercury surface in the dish is still p_0, which is greater than p_1, and so the mercury is forced into the tube (Fig. 4.16b). Equating pressures at the lowest mercury level gives $p_1 + h\rho g = p_0$, i.e. the pressure of the residual gas plus the pressure due to the column of mercury is equal to the atmospheric pressure. If all the air were removed from the tube p_1 would be zero and the equation would become $h\rho g = p_0$, i.e. atmospheric pressure supports a column of mercury of vertical height h.

Barometers

A simple mercury barometer can be made using a thick-walled tube one metre long which is sealed at one end (Fig. 4.17). Mercury is carefully poured into the tube and any air bubbles trapped in the mercury are removed by covering the open end with a thumb and inverting the tube several times. (**Note** Mercury is poisonous — the thumb must be washed afterwards!) The tube is then filled completely with mercury and the open end of the tube sealed with a thumb while it is inverted into the wider vessel. The thumb is removed when the end of the tube is below the surface of the mercury in the 'reservoir' vessel. Since the pressure exerted by the column of mercury in the full length of the tube is greater than atmospheric pressure p_0 some mercury will run out of the tube into the reservoir. The space left at the top of the tube

contains 'no air' and hence no pressure is exerted in this region. The mercury will stop flowing when the pressure at the lowest horizontal level is the same both inside and outside the tube, i.e. when the mercury level inside the tube is at a *vertical* height h such that $h\rho g = p_0$ (atmospheric pressure). **Standard atmospheric pressure** is defined to be 101 325 Pa.

Pressure is often quoted in height, or head, of a column of liquid; standard atmospheric pressure is roughly 0.76 m of mercury (Hg).

Note m, cm or mm of mercury are *not* SI units of pressure.

Atmospheric pressure can also be measured using an aneroid barometer, see p.139. The bar is a unit of pressure. Pressures on meteorological charts are given in millibars. 1 millibar = 10^{-3} bar. 1 bar = 10^5 Pa. Normal atmospheric pressure = 1013 millibar but it is also = 1.013×10^5 N m^{-2} (Pa).

Example

Calculate atmospheric pressure in Pa when a mercury barometer supports a column of mercury 76 cm high. (Density of mercury = 13 600 kg m^{-3}.)

$\Delta p = ?$ $\quad h = 0.76\,\text{m}$ $\quad \rho = 13\,600\,\text{kg m}^{-3}$ $\quad g = 10\,\text{m s}^{-2}$

$\Delta p = h\rho g$

$\quad = 0.76\,\text{m} \times 13\,600\,\text{kg m}^{-3} \times 10\,\text{m s}^{-2}$

$\quad = 0.76 \times 13\,600 \times 10\,\text{kg m}^{-1}\,\text{s}^{-2}$

$\quad = 103\,360\,\text{N m}^{-2}$ $\qquad$ (since kg m s^{-2} = N)

$\Delta p = 103\,360\,\text{Pa}$

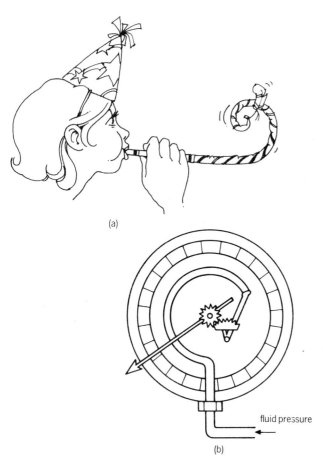

4.18　*Principle of the Bourdon pressure gauge*

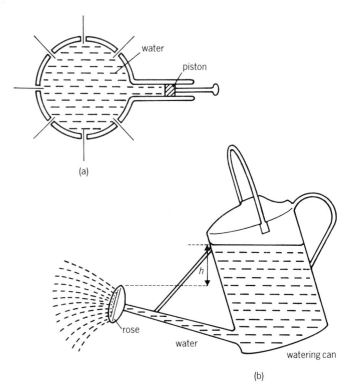

4.19　*Pressure is transmitted equally throughout liquids*

Bourdon pressure gauge

Pressure of liquids and gases can be measured using a Bourdon pressure gauge. This works like the toy squeaker which uncurls when blown (Fig. 4.18a). In a Bourdon gauge (see Fig. 4.18b) an oval-shaped metal tube tries to straighten out when a fluid pressure is applied and this rotates a pointer over a suitable scale. Oil pressure gauges in cars and the gauges fitted to gas cylinders are of this type.

4.5　Transmission of pressure

Liquids are incompressible, i.e. their volume cannot be reduced by the application of pressure. Therefore if pressure is applied to a liquid at one point it will be transmitted throughout the liquid. Pascal's Principle states that **pressure applied to an enclosed liquid is transmitted to every part of the liquid, whatever the shape of the liquid.** This can be demonstrated using the glass vessel shown in Fig. 4.19(a). When a force is applied to the piston the pressure exerted on the water is transmitted equally throughout the water so that the water issues from each hole with equal force. Another example of the equal transmission of pressure is given by water flowing from the holes in the rose of a watering can (Fig. 4.19b). The pressure head h in the

watering can causes the water to flow out. A pressure head is also most important for the supply of water to our homes. Water held in a high reservoir is fed along pipes to houses at lower levels (see Fig. 4.20). Why do you think it is necessary for a water pump to be fitted in the multistorey building but not in the two-storey house?

Hydraulic machines

The transmission of pressure is made use of in hydraulic machines where a small force applied at one point is made to exert a much larger force at some other point. In Fig. 4.21(a) the force F_1 is applied to a piston of area A_1 and an increase in pressure $p = F_1/A_1$ is transmitted throughout the liquid. Thus an upward pressure of p is applied to the larger piston of area A_2 which results in an upward force of $p \times A_2$. Therefore this piston is capable of supporting a force $F_2 = p \times A_2 = F_1 A_2/A_1$, assuming there is no loss of efficiency due to leakage of liquid around the pistons. Thus the applied force F_1 has been increased by a factor of A_2/A_1. This arrangement of pistons is a machine with a **mechanical advantage,** under perfect conditions, of A_2/A_1 (see p.107). A practical application of this principle is the hydraulic jack used for raising motor cars (Fig. 4.21b). The effort is applied via a simple lever which increases the mechanical advantage of the machine. Valve V_1 prevents the liquid running back when the effort is released; valve V_2 allows more liquid to flow from the reservoir as the car is raised to ensure that the system is completely filled with liquid at all

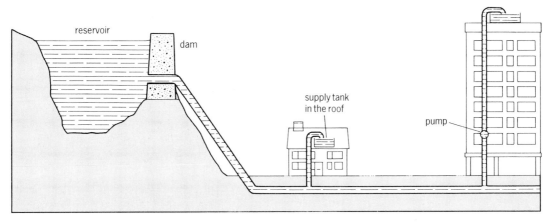

4.20 Water supply system

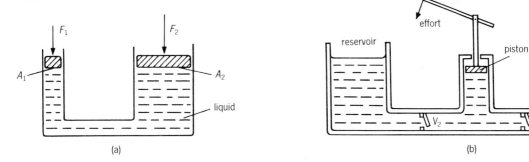

(a)

(b)

4.21 Hydraulic lift using the transmission of pressure

times. A third valve (not shown in the diagram) lets the liquid return to the reservoir so that the pressure can be released and the car lowered to its original position. Special self-sealing washers are fitted between the pistons and the cylinder walls to reduce leakage of liquid around the pistons. A hydraulic fork-lift truck uses the same principle. In a hydraulic press a rigid plate is fixed above the larger piston and enormous forces can be exerted between them, e.g. pressing steel sheets into car-body shapes.

Car braking system

Modern cars often have disc brakes on the front wheels and drum brakes on the rear wheels, both being operated by hydraulic pressure. Foot pressure on the brake pedal is transmitted via levers to the piston in the master cylinder and so increases the pressure in the brake fluid. This increase in pressure is transmitted equally and simultaneously to all four wheels (Fig. 4.22 shows only one side of the car.) The increase in

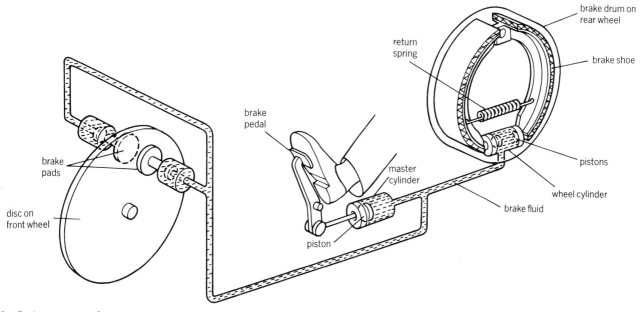

4.22 Braking system of a car

pressure forces the pistons in the wheel cylinder to move the brake shoes outward against the rotating drum, hence slowing down the rear wheels. At the same time the pistons at the front force the brake pads inwards against a rotating disc to slow down the front wheels. When the foot pressure is released the return spring pulls the brake shoes clear of the drum, at the same time returning the brake fluid to the cylinder.

4.6 Pumps

The movement of fluids and gases is achieved by some form of pump. Doctors inject vital drugs into patients using a hypodermic needle. When the tight-fitting piston is drawn back along the barrel the pressure in the barrel is reduced and atmospheric pressure drives the liquid in (see Fig. 4.23a). When the piston is forced down again it drives the liquid out of the small nozzle under great pressure (Fig. 4.23b).

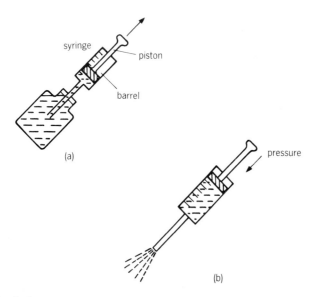

4.23   Syringe

Bicycle pump

Another pump in common use is the bicycle pump for inflating tyres. As the pump handle is pushed in, air trapped between the washer and the end of the pump is compressed (Fig. 4.24a). As the volume it occupies is reduced the air molecules, although moving at the same speed, hit the walls more often. This increase in the rate of bombardment increases the pressure p_1 inside the pump. When p_1 is greater than the pressure in the tyre p_2, the rubber tube around the tyre valve is forced open and air at the higher pressure enters the tyre (Fig. 4.24b). When the pump handle is pulled out the volume of the residual air at the end of the barrel is expanded and its pressure decreases. The pressure inside the tyre is much greater than that in the barrel

so the rubber tube is forced against the valve and prevents air escaping from the tyre. When the pressure p' of the air remaining at the bottom of the barrel is less than the atmospheric pressure p_0 on the 'open' side of the washer, air flows past the washer. Once the barrel is refilled with air the whole process can be repeated. In practice the mechanical compression of the gas produces a heating effect and the barrel can get quite hot after just a few strokes.

Just as adding air to the tyre increases the pressure of the air inside the tyre, so removing air from a container will reduce the pressure inside it. If the washer in the bicycle pump is changed round (reversed) then the pump can be used as a vacuum pump.

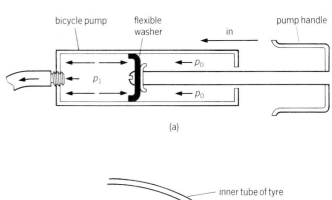

(a)

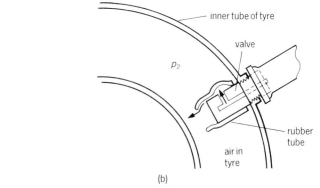

(b)

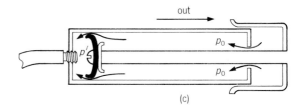

(c)

4.24   Bicycle pump and tyre valve

Exercise 4.4

Draw a diagram similar to Fig. 4.24 but with the washer reversed and explain, in terms of pressure, how air is extracted from a container.

4.7 The siphon

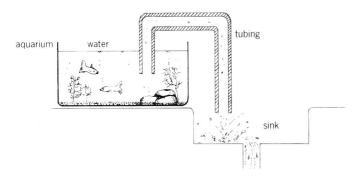

4.25 Siphon

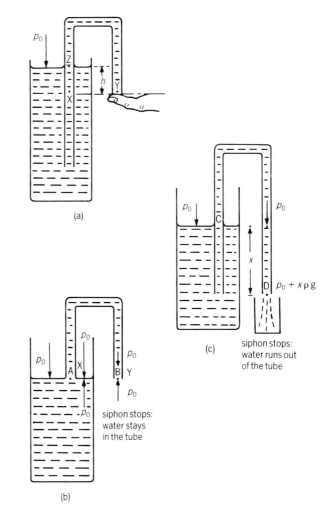

4.26 Principle of the siphon

A siphon is a very useful way of transferring liquids from one container to another, e.g. when emptying water from an aquarium (fish tank). When filled with water, even a small tank can be too heavy to lift to pour the water out. The water can be siphoned out by using a tube filled with water. One end of the tube must be placed in the tank below the surface of the water and the other end must be lower than the level of the water in the tank. The tube may be filled with water by sealing one end with a finger while water is poured in until it is full. Then both ends are closed while one end is dipped into the water in the tank and the other end placed in a container below the water level in the tank. Alternatively, the tube can be positioned in the tank as shown in Fig. 4.25 and air sucked out, reducing the pressure of the air remaining in the tube. Atmospheric pressure acting on the surface of the water in the tank will drive water into the tube, and once the level of the water in the right-hand limb of the tube is below the level of the water in the tank the flow of water will continue.

To understand how the siphon works, first consider the static conditions shown in Fig. 2.26(a). A finger is sealing the end Y of the tube. Since pressure in a liquid at a given horizontal level is equal

$$\text{pressure at X} = \text{pressure at Y}.$$

The pressure at $X = p_0 + h\rho g$, where p_0 is the pressure at the surface of the liquid (here atmospheric pressure) and h is the depth of X below the surface of a liquid of density ρ. Therefore the pressure of the water at Y acting on the finger is also $p_0 + h\rho g$. If the finger is removed the downward pressure at Y due to the water is $p_0 + h\rho g$ and the upward pressure at Y due to atmospheric pressure is p_0. An excess pressure of $(p_0 + h\rho g) - p_0 = h\rho g$ acts downwards and so the water flows out of the tube. Once the water has begun to move the equation of hydrostatic pressures is no longer valid. Instead there is a decrease in pressure along the 'length' of the tube. Even the horizontal part of the tube has a pressure gradient across it due to the need to overcome the viscosity force of the moving water, hence the pressure decreases from one end of the tube to the other. Water continues to flow until the level of the water in the tank reaches the level of the 'open' end of the tube (Fig. 4.26b). Water remains in the tube and is now stationary therefore the hydrostatic pressures can be equated. The pressure at X is p_0 downwards and so at Y is also p_0 downwards. Externally a pressure of p_0 acts upwards at the surface at Y and the atmospheric pressure p_0 is transmitted through the water to act upwards at X. At both points X and Y the pressures are equal; there is no pressure difference and hence no flow of liquid. The siphon can be restarted either by pouring water into the tank to raise the level of the water surface above the end Y, or by lowering the end Y below the level of the surface of the water in the tank. Clearly the important factor is the *difference* in the levels of the water in the tank and the 'open' end of the tube.

Now consider a siphon working as shown in Fig. 4.26(c). This time the siphon stops working when the level of water in the tank reaches the end C of the tube. If a finger were placed at D just to hold the water stationary, the pressures could be equated. The pressure at C is p_0; that at D is $p_0 + x\rho g$. When the water level in the tank drops just below C both ends of the tube are open to atmospheric pressure. At C the pressures are equal and opposite while at D the net downward pressure is $(p_0 + x\rho g) - p_0 = x\rho g$. This time the water runs out of the tube and the siphon can only be restarted by refilling the tube.

From the theory above it appears that atmospheric pressure p_0 plays no part in the action of the siphon. Hence a siphon ought to work in a vacuum, and this has been achieved for pure liquids. However, in liquids which contain dissolved gases, for example water containing dissolved air, atmospheric pressure does help to prevent the water from breaking up into lengths separated by air bubbles by preventing the dissolved air from expanding.

The theory also suggests that the action of the siphon is independent of the height of the bend in the tube above the water level in the tank. A mercury siphon has been reported to work in a vacuum when the top of the tube was 100 cm above the mercury in the reservoir. Since the normal barometric height of mercury is 76 cm, the presence or absence of atmospheric pressure seems to have no effect as long as the pressures are equal on the surface of the liquid and at the open end of the tube.

An alternative explanation of the action of the siphon compares the 'column' of water in the tube (ZY, AB and CD in Figs. 4.26(a), (b) and (c) respectively) to a chain hanging over a pulley as in Fig. 4.27. When the length of unsupported chain is longer on one side of the pulley than the other the weight of the chain pulls the chain off the pulley in the direction shown. If links ZX attached to the 'short' end of the chain are being 'supported' in equilibrium, these will be pulled up and over the pulley as the other end falls. If the length of unsupported chain on either side of the pulley is equal the chain is in equilibrium and there is no movement (Fig. 4.27b). If the chain is longer on one side of the pulley than on the other (Fig. 4.27c) the

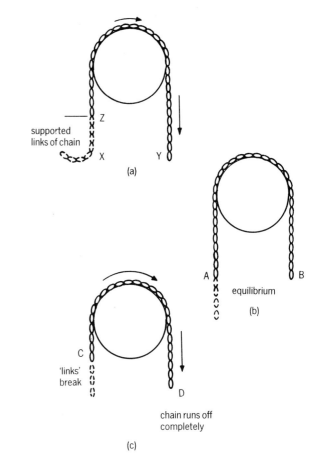

4.27 Chain model of the siphon

chain will run completely off the pulley and would have to be repositioned to start the demonstration again.

The movement of the chain depends on the strength of the links which make up the chain. If one link breaks the chain will separate. It is believed that the cohesion forces between the water molecules hold the water together in a continuous chain while the water is moving. Atmospheric pressure plays no part in the chain model either, so the 'model' should work even in a vacuum.

Questions

Q1 What is the pressure, in pascals, in a liquid of density $1000\ kg\ m^{-3}$, 10 m below the surface? (Acceleration of free fall = $10\ m\ s^{-2}$.)

 A $\dfrac{1}{1000}$ **B** $\dfrac{1}{10}$ **C** 10 **D** 1000 **E** 100 000

Q2 Which of the following statements about the pressure at a point in a liquid is NOT correct?
The pressure at a point in a liquid
 A acts equally in all directions.
 B increases with increasing depth.
 C is greater vertically than horizontally.
 D increases with increasing density.
 E varies with the value of the acceleration of free-fall.

Q3 A cubical tank of side 2 m is evacuated of air on a day when atmospheric pressure is 10^5 Pa. The crushing force exerted by the atmosphere on the tank is
 A 4×10^5 N **B** 8×10^5 N **C** 12×10^5 N
 D 16×10^5 N **E** 24×10^5 N

Q4 Which of the following is NOT appropriate for use in the construction of a mercury barometer?
 A A glass tube 700 mm long.
 B A glass tube having a bore of 5 mm.
 C A glass tube having walls 3 mm thick.
 D A glass tube sealed at one end.
 E A supply of distilled mercury. (L)

Q5 How can a sensitive barometer be used to estimate the height of a mountain? A barometer reads 75.5 cm of mercury at the foot of a mountain and 65.5 cm of mercury at the top of the mountain. Estimate the height of the mountain, in metres, assuming the density of mercury is 13 600 kg m^{-3} and the average density of air is 1.25 kg m^{-3}.

Q6 You are provided with the apparatus listed below. A manometer (U-tube with both ends open). Flexible tubing. Retort stand and clamp. A millimetre scale.
(i) Draw a diagram showing how you would arrange this apparatus in order to measure the excess pressure of the gas supply in the laboratory.
(ii) Name a suitable liquid for use in the manometer.
(iii) State the measurements you would take.
(iv) Show how you would use the measurements to calculate the excess pressure, in Pa (N m^{-2}).   *(AEB)*

Q7 A glass U-tube with open ends is partly filled with water and is clamped in a vertical position. One end of the tube is connected to the laboratory gas supply. Draw a diagram to show the final water levels and indicate clearly what measurement is required to calculate the pressure of the gas supply; state the formula necessary for this calculation.
   (S)

Q8

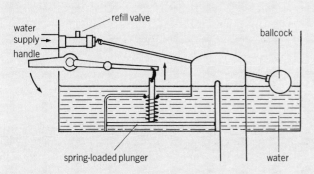

A common form of siphon used in the home is the one found in a lavatory cistern. Explain how when the handle is operated a piston lifts the water into the siphon tube and empties most of the water out of the system. Explain the action of the valve which controls the flow of water from the supply into the cistern with the aid of the floating ballcock.

Q9 Describe the apparatus you need in order to construct a simple mercury barometer. How is such a barometer made? How would the barometric height be affected
(a) if there was a marked rise in temperature, the atmospheric pressure remaining the same;
(b) if the barometer was taken to the bottom of a deep quarry, the temperature there being the same as at the surface;
(c) if the barometer was slowly tilted to an angle of about 45° with the vertical?
   On a day when the barometric height is 735 mm of mercury, what would the pressure of the atmosphere be in newton per square metre (Pa)? Briefly describe how the principle upon which an aneroid barometer works differs from that of a mercury barometer. (Density of mercury = 13 600 kg m^{-3}.)
   (C)

Q10 (a) Describe a simple experiment you would perform to demonstrate that the pressure in a liquid increases with depth.

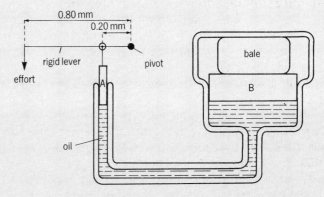

(b) The diagram shows a simple hydraulic press used to compress a bale. By means of a rigid lever, a vertical force is applied directly to a piston A, of cross-sectional area 0.002 m^2. The pressure on the liquid due to the movement of A is transmitted through the oil filling the vessel to a well-fitting piston B, of cross-sectional area 0.30 m^2.
(i) Using the figures shown in the diagram, calculate the force applied to piston A when an effort of 40 N is applied to the end of the lever.
(ii) What is the pressure exerted on the oil by the force applied to A?
(iii) What is the pressure exerted on B?
(iv) Calculate the force exerted on B.
(v) Determine the velocity ratio of the press.   *(O & C)*

Q11

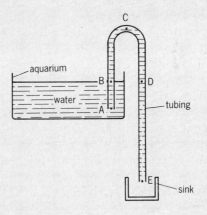

The diagram show how to empty the contents of a large aquarium into a low-lying sink using a piece of polythene tubing.
(a) Describe what must be done with the tubing before the emptying process will start.
(b) Soon after the aquarium begins to empty, the lower end is momentarily blocked by placing a finger at end E. Compare the pressure in the water inside the tube at each of the five points A, B, C, D and E with that of the atmosphere.
(c) Explain why water flows through the tube from A to E.
   (L)

5 Speed, velocity and acceleration

5.1 Speed

The speed of an object is its **distance moved per unit time.**

$$\text{speed} = \frac{\text{distance moved}}{\text{time taken}} \quad \frac{\text{m}}{\text{s}} (\text{m s}^{-1})$$

However, this definition applies only to an object which is moving steadily during the 'time taken' of the quotient. When the object is not moving at a constant speed then the quotient distance moved/time taken gives the *average* speed and therefore it is better to write

$$\text{average speed} = \frac{\text{distance moved}}{\text{time taken}}$$

The average speed is usually more useful than the actual speed.

Example

If a body moves a distance of 10 m in 5 s then

$$\text{average speed} = \frac{\text{distance moved}}{\text{time taken}} = \frac{10}{5} \frac{\text{m}}{\text{s}}$$
$$= 2\,\text{m s}^{-1}$$

When the body covers the distance of 10 m moving steadily throughout the 5 s the average speed is 2 m s^{-1}. This average speed is also the actual speed at every instant during the five seconds.

A body moving a distance of 5 m in 2 s, resting for 1 s and moving a further distance of 5 m in 2 s will also have an average speed of 2 m s^{-1}.

In this second example the actual speed is clearly not the same as the average speed; for one second of the time the body has zero speed. Thus to calculate the distance moved by a body it would be better to employ the equation

$$\text{distance moved} = \text{average speed} \times \text{time taken}$$
$$\text{m} = \text{m s}^{-1} \times \text{s}$$

5.2 Velocity

The velocity of an object is its **displacement per unit time.**

$$\text{velocity} = \frac{\text{displacement}}{\text{time}} \quad \frac{\text{m}}{\text{s}} (\text{m s}^{-1})$$

in the direction of the displacement. **Displacement** is distance measured in a straight line and in a specified direction. Velocity is a **vector quantity**, that is, one which requires both magnitude and direction for its complete specification and is therefore different from speed, a **scalar quantity** for which only the magnitude is important. When the velocity in a particular direction is constant (uniform) then

$$\text{total displacement} = \text{velocity} \times \text{time} \quad \text{m s}^{-1} \times \text{s}$$

in the direction of the velocity. If the velocity is non-uniform then the displacement can be calculated from

$$\text{displacement} = \frac{\text{average}}{\text{velocity}} \times \frac{\text{time in the}}{\text{specified direction}}$$

Non-uniform velocity requires that an acceleration has taken place.

5.3 Acceleration

The acceleration of an object is its **change in velocity per unit time.**

$$\text{acceleration} = \frac{\text{change in velocity}}{\text{time taken}} \quad \frac{\text{m s}^{-1}}{\text{s}} (\text{m s}^{-2})$$

in the direction of the change. Acceleration is also a vector quantity and both the magnitude and direction of the acceleration must be specified. Note that an object moving with uniform velocity has zero acceleration because there is no *change* in velocity. Uniform acceleration requires that the velocity changes regularly (uniformly) with time.

Example

If the velocity of an object is initially u m s^{-1} due east and it increases steadily to v m s^{-1} in a time t s the acceleration a can be calculated from

$$a = \frac{(v - u)}{t} \quad \frac{\text{m s}^{-1}}{\text{s}} (\text{m s}^{-2}) \text{ due east}$$

The conventional notation, followed in this book, is to use s to represent the displacement, u to represent the initial velocity, v to represent the velocity at time t, and a to represent the acceleration at time t.

Example

A car travelling at a velocity 10 m s^{-1} due north speeds up uniformly to a velocity of 25 m s^{-1} in 5 s. Calculate the acceleration of the car during these five seconds.

Let the direction of motion of the car, due north, be taken as the positive (+) direction.

$u = +10\,\mathrm{m\,s}^{-1}$ $v = +10\,\mathrm{m\,s}^{-1}$ $t = 5\,\mathrm{s}$ $a = ?$

$a = \dfrac{v - u}{t}$

$a = \dfrac{(+25) - (+10)}{5}\;\dfrac{\mathrm{m\,s}^{-1}}{\mathrm{s}}$

$a = \dfrac{25 - 10}{5}\,\mathrm{m\,s}^{-2}$

$a = \dfrac{15}{5}\,\mathrm{m\,s}^{-2}$

$a = +3\,\mathrm{m\,s}^{-2}$ due north (+)

$v = +25\,\mathrm{m\,s}^{-1}$ $t_2 = 5\,\mathrm{s}$
$u = +10\,\mathrm{m\,s}^{-1}$ $t_1 = 0\,\mathrm{s}$

Example

A car travelling at a velocity 25 m s^{-1} due west slows down uniformly to a velocity of 5 m s^{-1} due west in 10 s. Calculate the acceleration of the car during these ten seconds.

Let the direction of motion of the car, due west, be taken as the positive direction.

$u = +25\,\mathrm{m\,s}^{-1}$ $v = +5\,\mathrm{m\,s}^{-1}$ $t = 10\,\mathrm{s}$ $a = ?$

$a = \dfrac{v - u}{t}$

$a = \dfrac{(+5) - (+25)}{10}\;\dfrac{\mathrm{m\,s}^{-1}}{\mathrm{s}}$

$a = \dfrac{5 - 25}{10}\,\mathrm{m\,s}^{-2}$

$a = \dfrac{-20}{10}\,\mathrm{m\,s}^{-2}$

$a = -2\,\mathrm{m\,s}^{-2}$

$v = +5\,\mathrm{m\,s}^{-1}$ $u = +25\,\mathrm{m\,s}^{-1}$
$t_2 = 10\,\mathrm{s}$ $t_1 = 0\,\mathrm{s}$

Example

A ball is thrown vertically upwards with a velocity of 20 m s^{-1} and after 4 s returns to the same position with a velocity of 20 m s^{-1} downwards. Calculate the acceleration of the ball during these four seconds.

Let the direction of the upward velocity be taken as the positive direction.

$u = +20\,\mathrm{m\,s}^{-1}$ $v = -20\,\mathrm{m\,s}^{-1}$ $t = 4\,\mathrm{s}$ $a = ?$

$a = \dfrac{v - u}{t}$

$a = \dfrac{(-20) - (20)}{4}\;\dfrac{\mathrm{m\,s}^{-1}}{\mathrm{s}}$

$a = \dfrac{-20 - 20}{4}\,\mathrm{m\,s}^{-2}$

$a = \dfrac{-40}{4}\,\mathrm{m\,s}^{-2}$

$u = +20\,\mathrm{m\,s}^{-1}$ $v = -20\,\mathrm{m\,s}^{-1}$
$t_1 = 0\,\mathrm{s}$ $t_2 = 4\,\mathrm{s}$

$a = -10\,\mathrm{m\,s}^{-2}$

The ball accelerates vertically downwards.

Example

Calculate the weight of a 1 kilogram mass.

$m = 1\,\mathrm{kg}$ $g = 10\,\mathrm{m\,s}^{-2}$ $W = ?$

$W = m \times g$

$W = 1\,\mathrm{kg} \times 10\,\mathrm{m\,s}^{-2}$

$W = 10\,\mathrm{kg\,m\,s}^{-2}$

$W = 10\,\mathrm{N}$ acting downwards

Note The negative sign means that the acceleration is in the opposite direction to the chosen positive direction of the velocity. In this case it is also known as **retardation** or **deceleration**.

Being able to calculate the uniform acceleration of a body is useful because the force F acting on a mass m can be calculated from $F = m \times a$. The units of force are kg m s^{-2}, or more simply N (newton). An important force is the force of gravity or pull of the Earth acting on an object (see p.29). The pull of the Earth on an object is called the **weight** of the object. If an object of mass m is released from a short distance above the Earth it accelerates downwards at the acceleration of free fall g. Hence the pull of the Earth known as the weight of the object is calculated from weight $W = m \times g$ N. The acceleration of free fall g close to the Earth's surface has an average value of 9.8 m s^{-2} and to simplify calculations this is often approximated to 10.0 m s^{-2}. **Note** The force known as the weight of the object acts on the object whether it is moving or stationary.

Since force and weight are vector quantities they require both magnitude and direction for their complete specification. If in the force equation $F = ma$, $a = 0$ then $m \times 0 = 0$, thus the force is zero. Zero acceleration could mean either that the body is stationary (has no velocity) or that it is travelling with uniform velocity (has no *change* in its velocity). Thus a body at rest or travelling with uniform velocity has no net force acting upon it (i.e. has zero unbalanced force). Movement is not evidence of a force; only acceleration indicates the action of a force.

5.4 Equations of motion

Calculations involving the displacement, velocity, acceleration and time of motion of a moving body use the **equations of motion**. These equations are derived from the definitions of average velocity and acceleration.

For a body undergoing uniform acceleration,

$$\text{average velocity} = \frac{(u + v)}{2} \qquad (1)$$

$$\text{acceleration} = \frac{(v - u)}{t} \qquad (2)$$

displacement = average velocity × time

$$s = \frac{(u + v)}{2} \times t \qquad (3)$$

From equation 3

$$a = \frac{v - u}{t}$$

$$at = v - u \qquad (4)$$

$$u + at = v$$

$$v = u + at \qquad (5)$$

From equation 3, $(v + u) = 2s/t$, and from equation 4 $(v - u) = at$. Multiplying these equations together gives

$$(v + u) \times (v - u) = \frac{2s}{t} \times at$$

$$v^2 - u^2 = 2\,a\,s$$

$$v^2 = u^2 + 2\,a\,s \qquad (6)$$

Substituting equation 5, $v = u + at$, in equation 3,

$$s = \frac{(u + v)}{2} \times t$$

$$s = \frac{(u + u + at)}{2} \times t$$

$$s = \frac{(2u + at)}{2} \times t$$

$$s = \frac{2\,ut + at^2}{2}$$

$$s = ut + \tfrac{1}{2} at^2 \qquad (7)$$

These four equations should be memorised and used when solving problems.

$$s = \frac{(u + v)}{2} t \qquad\qquad v = u + at$$

$$s = ut + \tfrac{1}{2} at^2 \qquad\qquad v^2 = u^2 + 2as$$

For a body travelling with uniform velocity, $v = u$ and $a = 0$, so these four equations reduce to $s = ut$.

Example

A rocket is uniformly accelerated from rest to a speed of 960 m s^{-1} in $1\tfrac{2}{3}$ minutes. Calculate the distance travelled.

$1\tfrac{2}{3}\,\text{min} = 100\,\text{s} \quad s = ? \quad u = 0\,\text{m s}^{-1} \quad v = 960\,\text{m s}^{-1}$
$t = 100\,\text{s}$

$$s = \frac{(u + v)}{2} t$$

$$s = \frac{(0 + 960)}{2}\,\text{m s}^{-1} \times 100\,\text{s}$$

$$s = \frac{960}{2} \times 100\,\text{m s}^{-1} \times \text{s}$$

$$s = 480 \times 100\,\text{m}$$

$$s = 48\,000\,\text{m}$$

Example

A bicycle rider accelerates from rest to a velocity of 36 km h^{-1} in 10 s. Calculate the acceleration of the rider assuming that he travels along a straight track.

$$36\,\text{km h}^{-1} \equiv \frac{36 \times 1000}{60 \times 60}\,\text{m s}^{-1} = 36 \times \frac{10}{36}\,\text{m s}^{-1} = 10\,\text{m s}^{-1}$$

$u = 0\,\text{m s}^{-1} \quad v = 10\,\text{m s}^{-1} \quad a = ? \quad t = 10\,\text{s}$

$$v = u + at$$

$$10\,\text{m s}^{-1} = 0 + a\,10\,\text{s}$$

$$10\,a\,\text{s} = 10\,\text{m s}^{-1}$$

$$a = \frac{10\,\text{m s}^{-1}}{10\,\text{s}}$$

$$a = +1\,\text{m s}^{-2}$$

Example

A motor car is uniformly decelerated from 90 km h^{-1} to 18 km h^{-1} in a time of 10 s. Calculate the acceleration.

$$90\,\text{km h}^{-1} \equiv 90 \times 1000/60 \times 60\,\text{m s}^{-1}$$
$$= 90 \times 10/36\,\text{m s}^{-1} = 25\,\text{m s}^{-1}$$
$$18\,\text{km h}^{-1} \equiv 18 \times 1000/60 \times 60\,\text{m s}^{-1}$$
$$= 18 \times 10/36\,\text{m s}^{-1} = 5\,\text{m s}^{-1}$$

$u = 25\,\text{m s}^{-1} \quad v = 5\,\text{m s}^{-1} \quad a = ? \quad t = 10\,\text{s}$

$$v = u + at$$

$$5\,\text{m s}^{-1} = 25\,\text{m s}^{-1} + a\,10\,\text{s}$$

$$5\,\text{m s}^{-1} - 25\,\text{m s}^{-1} = 10\,a\,\text{s}$$

$$-20\,\text{m s}^{-2} = 10\,a$$

$$10\,a = -20\,\text{m s}^{-2}$$

$$a = -\frac{20}{10}\,\text{m s}^{-2}$$

$$a = -2\,\text{m s}^{-1}$$

This calculation can be simplified by first rearranging the equation of motion:

$$a = \frac{v - u}{t}$$

$$a = \frac{5 - 25}{10}\,\frac{\text{m s}^{-1}}{\text{s}}$$

$$a = \frac{-20}{10}\,\text{m s}^{-2}$$

$$a = -2\,\text{m s}^{-2}$$

Example

A particle travelling due east at 2 m s^{-1} is uniformly accelerated at 5 m s^{-2} for 4 s. Calculate the displacement of the particle.

$s = ? \quad u = 2\,\text{m s}^{-1} \quad t = 4\,\text{s} \quad a = 5\,\text{m s}^{-2}$

$$s = ut + \tfrac{1}{2} at^2$$

$$s = 2\,\text{m s}^{-1} \times 4\,\text{s} + \tfrac{1}{2}5\,\text{m s}^{-2} \times 4^2\,\text{s}^2$$

$$s = 2 \times 4\,\text{m s}^{-1} \times \text{s} + \tfrac{1}{2}5 \times 16\,\text{m s}^{-2} \times \text{s}^2$$

$$s = 8\,\text{m} + 5 \times 8\,\text{m}$$

$$s = 8 + 40\,\text{m}$$

$$s = +48\,\text{m (due east)}$$

Example

Calculate the velocity of a ball after 4 s if it is initially travelling vertically downwards at $5\,\mathrm{m\,s^{-1}}$. Assume $g = 10\,\mathrm{m\,s^{-2}}$.

Let the direction vertically downwards be taken as the positive (+) direction.

$u = +5\,\mathrm{m\,s^{-1}} \quad v = ? \quad a = +10\,\mathrm{m\,s^{-2}} \quad t = 4\,\mathrm{s}$

$v = u + at$

$v = 5\,\mathrm{m\,s^{-1}} + 10\,\mathrm{m\,s^{-2}} \times 4\,\mathrm{s}$

$v = 5\,\mathrm{m\,s^{-1}} + 10 \times 4\,\mathrm{m\,s^{-2}} \times \mathrm{s}$

$v = 5\,\mathrm{m\,s^{-1}} + 40\,\mathrm{m\,s^{-1}}$

$v = +45\,\mathrm{m\,s^{-1}} \text{ (vertically downwards)}$

Example

A boulder is sliding down a slope with a uniform acceleration of $3\,\mathrm{m\,s^{-2}}$. If its starting velocity was $2\,\mathrm{m\,s^{-1}}$, calculate its velocity after it has slid 10 m down the slope.

$s = 10\,\mathrm{m} \quad u = 2\,\mathrm{m\,s^{-1}} \quad v = ? \quad a = 3\,\mathrm{m\,s^{-2}}$

$v^2 = u^2 + 2as$

$v^2 = 2^2\,(\mathrm{m\,s^{-1}})^2 + 2 \times 3\,\mathrm{m\,s^{-2}} \times 10\,\mathrm{m}$

$v^2 = 4\,(\mathrm{m\,s^{-1}})^2 + 6 \times 10\,(\mathrm{m\,s^{-1}})^2$

$v^2 = 4\,(\mathrm{m\,s^{-1}})^2 + 60\,(\mathrm{m\,s^{-1}})^2$

$v^2 = 64\,(\mathrm{m\,s^{-1}})^2$

$v = +8\,\mathrm{m\,s^{-1}} \text{ down the slope}$

5.5 Motion graphs and their interpretation

An alternative method of solving dynamics problems is to represent the motion of the body graphically. The following graphs, which illustrate the motion of various particles, emphasise the vector nature of displacement, velocity and acceleration.

A stationary particle at a displacement *x* from the observer (Fig. 5.1)

Note that the displacement–time graph (Fig. 5.1a) could be represented by the solid line or the dotted line depending on which direction is taken as the positive direction. If the scalar quantities of distance travelled, speed and rate of change of speed du/dt had been plotted instead of the vector quantities then only the positive quadrant of the graph need be shown, as in Fig. 5.2.

A particle moving with uniform velocity in a stated direction (Fig. 5.3)

As before, the equivalent distance–time, speed–time and rate of change of speed–time graphs would be the positive quadrants of those in Fig. 5.3 on p.62.

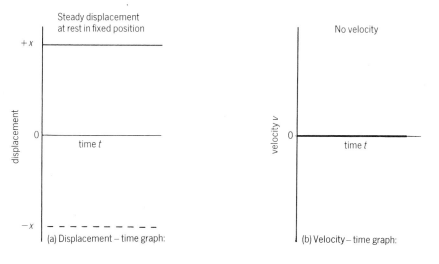

(a) Displacement – time graph:

(b) Velocity – time graph:

(c) Acceleration – time graph:

5.1 *Motion graphs for a stationary object at a displacement x from the observer*

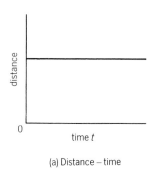

(a) Distance – time

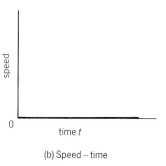

(b) Speed – time

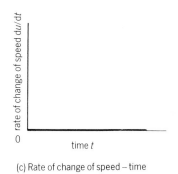

(c) Rate of change of speed – time

5.2 *Scalar graphs for a stationary object at a fixed distance from the observer*

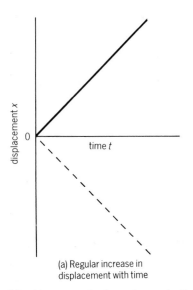

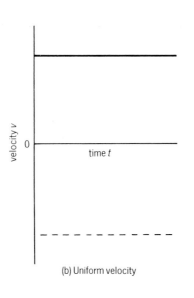

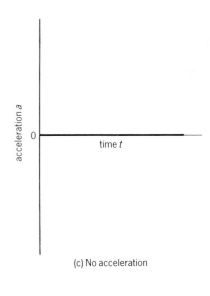

(a) Regular increase in
displacement with time

(b) Uniform velocity

(c) No acceleration

5.3   Motion graphs for uniform velocity

A particle moving with uniform acceleration in a stated direction (Fig. 5.4)

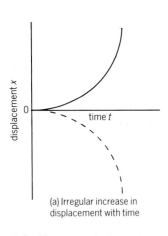

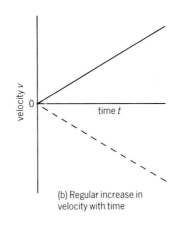

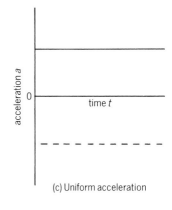

(a) Irregular increase in
displacement with time

(b) Regular increase in
velocity with time

(c) Uniform acceleration

5.4   Motion graphs for uniform acceleration

Example

A ball is released from rest from the top of a cliff. Taking the top of the cliff as the reference (zero) level and upwards as the positive direction, the motion graphs are as shown in Fig. 5.5. The corresponding graphs of the scalar quantities are given in Fig. 5.6. Note that they are quite different from the motion graphs.

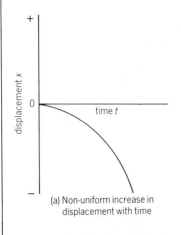

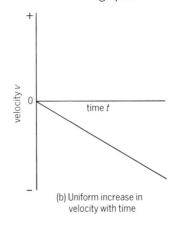

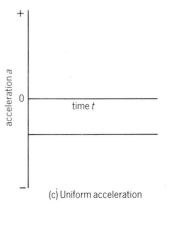

(a) Non-uniform increase in
displacement with time

(b) Uniform increase in
velocity with time

(c) Uniform acceleration

5.5   Motion graphs for a ball released from rest from the top of a cliff

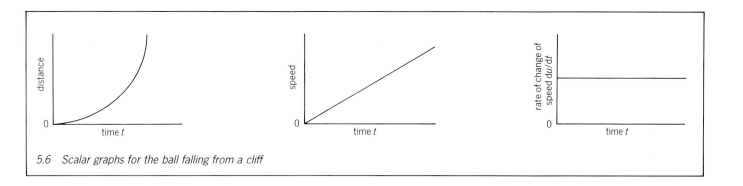

5.6 Scalar graphs for the ball falling from a cliff

Example

A ball thrown vertically upwards with a velocity u from the top of a cliff of height h falls to the beach below. This time, let us take the beach as the reference (zero) level and, as before, upwards as the positive direction. The motion graphs are shown in Fig. 5.7 and the three corresponding graphs using scalar quantities are given in Fig. 5.8.

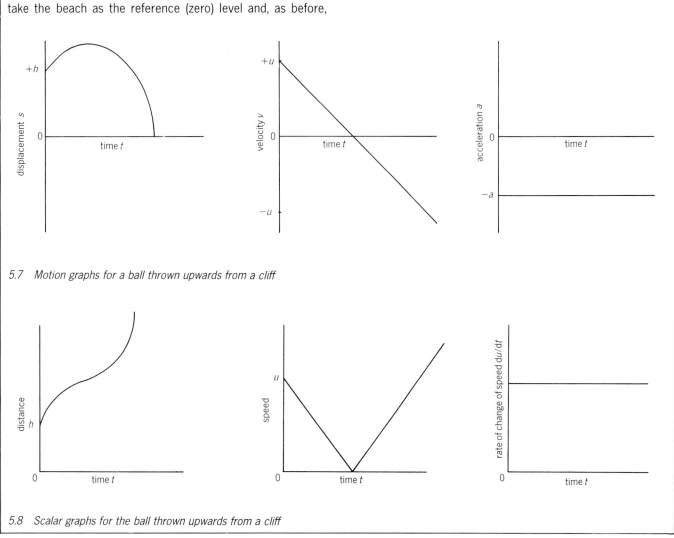

5.7 Motion graphs for a ball thrown upwards from a cliff

5.8 Scalar graphs for the ball thrown upwards from a cliff

Exercise 5.1

What would be the appearance of the displacement–time graph if, instead of the top of the cliff, the ground level had been taken as the reference (zero) level?

It should now be clear that plotting the vector quantities (displacement, velocity and acceleration) against time on a graph gives more useful information than using the corresponding scalar quantities.

5.6 Solving equations with motion graphs

Some quantities which can be determined from displacement–time and velocity–time graphs are (a) velocity, (b) displacement and (c) acceleration.

(a) To determine velocity from a displacement–time graph

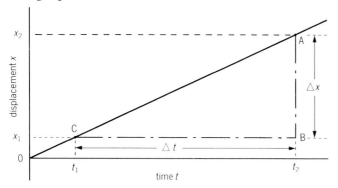

5.9   Calculating velocity from a displacement–time graph

From Fig. 5.9:

slope (gradient) of the line $= \dfrac{AB}{BC}$

$$= \frac{x_2 - x_1}{t_2 - t_1}$$

$$= \frac{\Delta x}{\Delta t} \equiv \text{velocity}$$

Thus the velocity is determined from the slope (gradient) of the line of a displacement–time graph.

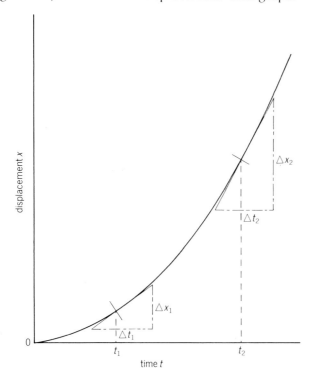

5.10   Graph showing increasing velocity

In Fig. 5.10 the slope (gradient) at various points on the curve shows that the velocity is increasing.

At t_1 the velocity $= \dfrac{\Delta x_1}{\Delta t_1} = v_1$

At t_2 the velocity $= \dfrac{\Delta x_2}{\Delta t_2} = v_2$

and from the graph you can see that velocity v_2 is greater than velocity v_1.

(b) To determine displacement from a velocity–time graph

(i) Uniform velocity   It follows from the definition of uniform velocity that the displacement x of a body travelling with a uniform velocity u_1 after time t_1 is $x = u_1 t_1$.

Example

Calculate the area of the shaded region shown on the graph in Fig. 5.11.

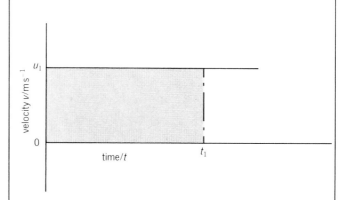

5.11   Calculating displacement from a velocity–time graph

area $=$ height $\times$ length

$= u_1 \, \text{m s}^{-1} \times t_1 \, \text{s}$

$= u_1 t_1 \, \text{m s}^{-1} \, \text{s}$

$= u_1 t_1 \, \text{m}$

Thus the area bounded by the line, the perpendicular at t_1 and the x- and y-axes gives the displacement of the moving particle.

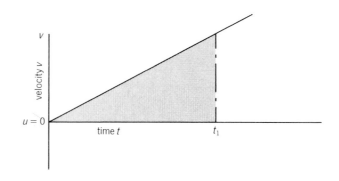

5.12   Calculating displacement from a graph for uniform acceleration

(ii) Uniform acceleration   The shaded area in Fig. 5.12 is given by

$$\text{area} = \tfrac{1}{2} \times \text{base} \times \text{perpendicular height}$$
$$= \tfrac{1}{2} t_1 \, \text{s} \times v \, \text{ms}^{-1}$$
$$= \tfrac{1}{2} v t_1 \, \text{m} \cancel{\text{s}} \cancel{\text{s}}$$
$$= \tfrac{1}{2} v t_1 \, \text{m} \equiv \text{displacement}$$

This is consistent with displacement $x = \tfrac{1}{2}(u + v)t = \tfrac{1}{2}(0 + v)t_1 = \tfrac{1}{2}v t_1$ from the formula on p.60.

An interesting example of the difference between vector velocity and scalar speed is illustrated in the following worked example.

Example

A car decelerates uniformly from 20 m s^{-1} to rest in 4 s, then reverses with uniform acceleration back to its original starting point, also in 4 s.

From the velocity–time graph (Fig. 5.13a)

$$\text{area} = \frac{1}{2}(+20) \times 4 + \frac{1}{2}(-20) \times 4$$
$$= 10 \times 4 - 10 \times 4$$
$$= 40 - 40$$
$$\text{displacement} = 0 \, \text{m}$$
$$\text{average velocity} = \frac{\text{displacement}}{\text{time}}$$
$$= \frac{0}{8} \frac{\text{m}}{\text{s}}$$
$$= 0 \, \text{ms}^{-1}$$

From the speed–time graph (Fig. 5.13b)

$$\text{area} = \frac{1}{2}(20 \times 4) + \frac{1}{2}(20 \times 4)$$
$$= 10 \times 4 + 10 \times 4$$
$$= 40 + 40$$
$$\text{distance} = 80 \, \text{m}$$
$$\text{average speed} = \frac{\text{distance}}{\text{time}}$$
$$= \frac{80}{8} \frac{\text{m}}{\text{s}}$$
$$= 10 \, \text{ms}^{-1}$$

Clearly, its displacement after 8 s is zero (it is back at its starting point) but nevertheless it has travelled a distance of 80 m. Its average velocity is zero but its average speed is 10 m s^{-1} as shown by the graphs in Fig. 5.13.

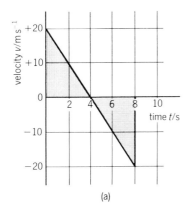

(a)

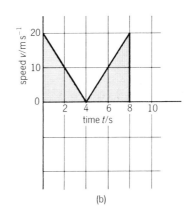

(b)

5.13   *Calculating (a) displacement from a velocity–time graph; (b) distance from a speed–time graph*

Example

The graph in Fig. 5.14 represents the velocity of a body during the first 30 seconds of its motion. Determine the displacement of the body after 30 seconds.

Method 1 The area of a trapezium is calculated from half the sum of the parallel sides multiplied by the perpendicular distance between the parallel sides.

$$\begin{aligned}
\text{area} &= \tfrac{1}{2}(30\,\text{s} + 10\,\text{s}) \times 20\,\text{m s}^{-1} \\
&= \tfrac{1}{2}40\,\text{s} \times 20\,\text{m s}^{-1} \\
&= \tfrac{1}{2}40 \times 20\,\text{m s}^{-1} \times \text{s} \\
&= 20 \times 20\,\text{m} \\
&= 400\,\text{m}
\end{aligned}$$

Thus the displacement is 400 m in the direction of the velocity.

Method 2 The given area can be divided up into simpler areas such as a triangle, a rectangle and a triangle (see the dotted lines on the graph).

$$\begin{aligned}
\text{total area} &= \text{area}_1 + \text{area}_2 + \text{area}_3 \\
&= \tfrac{1}{2}10\,\text{s} \times 20\,\text{m s}^{-1} + 10\,\text{s} \times 20\,\text{m s}^{-1} \\
&\quad + \tfrac{1}{2}10\,\text{s} \times 20\,\text{m s}^{-1} \\
&= 5 \times 20\,\text{m} + 200\,\text{m} + 5 \times 20\,\text{m} \\
&= 100\,\text{m} + 200\,\text{m} + 100\,\text{m} \\
&= 400\,\text{m}
\end{aligned}$$

Thus the displacement is 400 m in the direction of the velocity.

Method 3 The given area can be determined by 'counting squares'. Each square on the graph in Fig. 5.15 represents an area of $5\,\text{m s}^{-1} \times 5\,\text{s} = 25\,\text{m}$ and hence a displacement of 25 m.

First count the number of complete squares; here there are 12 squares numbered 1–12. Then *estimate* how many complete squares can be formed from the part squares; here there are 4 squares numbered 13–16. Thus the total number of squares is $12 + 4 = 16$.

> 1 square represents a displacement of 25 m.
> 16 squares represent a displacement of $16 \times 25\,\text{m}$
> $= 400\,\text{m}$.

Thus the displacement is 400 m in the direction of the velocity.

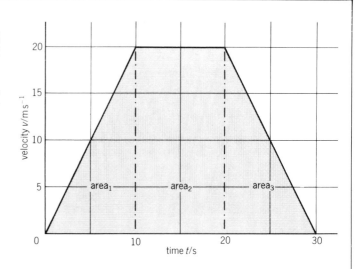

5.14   *Calculating the area under the graph*

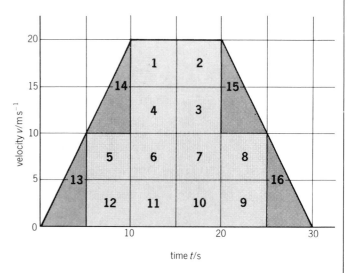

5.15   *Finding the area under the graph by counting squares*

(c) To determine acceleration from a velocity–time graph (Fig. 5.16)

From Fig. 5.16, slope (gradient) of the line

$$\begin{aligned}
&= \frac{\text{AB}}{\text{CD}} \\
&= \frac{u_2 - u_1}{t_2 - t_1} \\
&= \frac{\Delta u}{\Delta t} \equiv \text{acceleration}
\end{aligned}$$

Thus the acceleration can be determined from the slope (gradient) of the line of a velocity–time graph. The velocity–time graph for a body travelling with non-uniform acceleration would be a curve and the slope (gradient) at points on the curve would give the

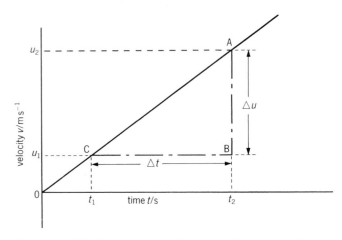

5.16   *Calculating the acceleration from a velocity–time graph*

instantaneous acceleration at these times. If you look at Fig. 5.14 you can see that the body accelerates from rest to a velocity of 20 m s^{-1} in the first 10 s, moves for the next 10 s at a uniform velocity of 20 m s^{-1} and then decelerates to rest in the final 10 s.

Acceleration from 0 s to 10 s

$$\text{acceleration} \equiv \text{slope (gradient) of the line}$$
$$= \frac{20 - 0}{10 - 0} \frac{\text{m s}^{-1}}{\text{s}}$$
$$= \frac{20}{10} \text{m s}^{-2}$$
$$= +2 \text{ m s}^{-2} \text{ in the direction}$$
of the velocity

Acceleration from 10 s to 20 s

$$\text{acceleration} \equiv \text{slope (gradient) of the line}$$
$$= \frac{20 - 20}{20 - 10} \frac{\text{m s}^{-1}}{\text{s}}$$
$$= 0 \text{ m s}^{-2}$$

Acceleration from 20 s to 30 s

$$\text{acceleration} \equiv \text{slope (gradient) of the line}$$
$$= \frac{0 - 20}{30 - 20} \frac{\text{m s}^{-1}}{\text{s}}$$
$$= -\frac{20}{10} \text{m s}^{-2}$$
$$= -2 \text{ m s}^{-2}$$

So the body decelerates, or accelerates in the negative direction in the last 10 s.

5.7 Practical methods of determining velocity and acceleration

One way to determine the velocity or acceleration of a moving object is to time the motion of the object, with a stopwatch or electronic timer, over measured distances along its path. The distance travelled divided by the time taken is the average speed (or velocity if it is moving in a straight line) for each of the time intervals involved. Acceleration can then be calculated from the *difference* in the velocities calculated for two different places along the object's path divided by the time interval between these two places.

Another method of determining velocity or acceleration is to attach **ticker-tape** to the moving object. The moving object then pulls the tape 'through' the ticker-tape timer unit as shown in Fig. 5.17. This unit makes a steel strip vibrate 50 times per second and mark a black dot on a white strip of paper moving under a carbon paper disc. Each successive pair of dots represents a time interval of 1/50 s (0.02 s) no matter how far apart these dots may be. The measured distance between any two successive dots is the distance the object has moved in 0.02 s. Therefore the tape records both the distance moved and the time taken and so enables speed or velocity to be calculated.

The tape can be cut into strips and stuck on graph paper to make a chart. Each strip should cover the same time interval, e.g. ten spaces representing 0.2 s. The length of the first tape is the distance travelled in 0.2 s and thus the average speed (or velocity) over that

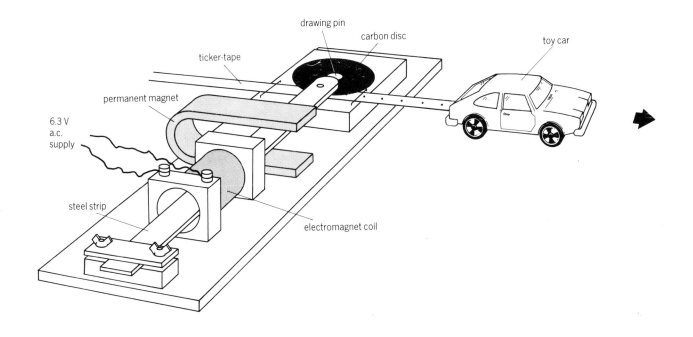

5.17 Ticker-tape timer

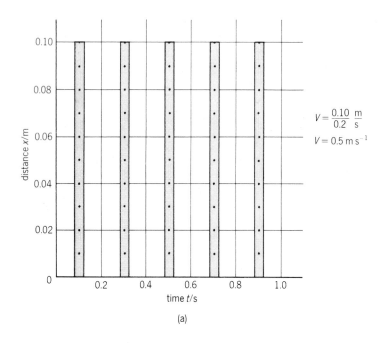

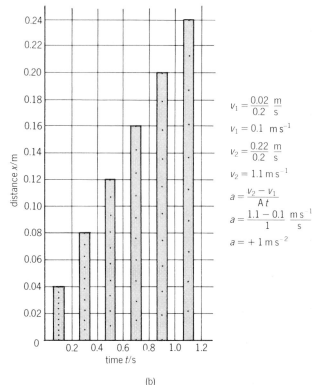

$$v = \frac{0.10}{0.2} \frac{m}{s}$$
$$v = 0.5 \, m\,s^{-1}$$

$$v_1 = \frac{0.02}{0.2} \frac{m}{s}$$
$$v_1 = 0.1 \, m\,s^{-1}$$
$$v_2 = \frac{0.22}{0.2} \frac{m}{s}$$
$$v_2 = 1.1 \, m\,s^{-1}$$
$$a = \frac{v_2 - v_1}{\Delta t}$$
$$a = \frac{1.1 - 0.1}{1} \frac{m\,s^{-1}}{s}$$
$$a = +1 \, m\,s^{-2}$$

5.18 Ticker-tape charts of (a) uniform velocity; (b) uniform acceleration

(b)

distance is calculated from the length of the tape divided by 0.2 s. Figure 5.18(a) illustrates uniform velocity where

$$v = \frac{0.10 \, m}{0.2 \, s}$$
$$v = 0.5 \, m\,s^{-1}$$

In Fig. 5.18(b) uniform acceleration is shown:

$$v_1 = \frac{0.02 \, m}{0.2 \, s}$$
$$v_1 = 0.1 \, m\,s^{-1}$$
$$v_2 = \frac{0.22 \, m}{0.2 \, s}$$
$$v_2 = 1.1 \, m\,s^{-1}$$
$$a = \frac{v_2 - v_1}{\Delta t}$$
$$a = \frac{1.1 - 0.1}{1} \frac{m\,s^{-1}}{s}$$
$$a = +1 \, m\,s^{-2}$$

Thus the charts show uniform velocity of 0.5 m s^{-1} and uniform acceleration of 1.0 m s^{-2} respectively.

5.8 Acceleration of free fall *g*

An important acceleration which affects our daily lives is the **acceleration of free fall** *g*. This is the acceleration with which all objects fall when released from a 'short' distance above the Earth's surface, and is constant for all objects regardless of their mass. Sometimes this

does not appear to be true for all objects; e.g. you would expect a lump of lead and a sheet of paper released together about 2 m above the floor to reach the floor together. They do not. The explanation is that the 'large' surface area of the relatively light piece of paper enables air resistance and Archimedes' upthrust to exert an appreciable retarding effect on the paper. The air resistance is almost solely responsible for the retardation as the upthrust is very small indeed. Hence the piece of paper flutters down more slowly than the lump of lead, which is hardly retarded at all.

Exercise 5.2

If a coin and a feather are placed inside a long, sealed glass tube from which almost all the air has been removed, the coin and the feather will fall simultaneously when the tube is inverted. However, if the coin and the feather are released together and allowed to fall freely in air the coin will hit the ground first. Explain why the feather reaches the ground some time after the coin.

Exercise 5.3

On a Moon walk an American astronaut released a hammer and a feather together and they were both seen to hit the Moon's surface at the same time. Explain why they both hit the Moon's surface simultaneously. The demonstration in the second question showed that objects accelerate at a constant rate on the Moon also. However, it must be pointed out that the acceleration of free fall on the Moon is only about one-sixth of the acceleration of free fall on Earth.

Investigation 5.1 To find the acceleration of free fall g by timing the direct fall of a steel ball

Using the equation of motion $s = ut + \frac{1}{2}gt^2$ and noting that when the ball is released from rest $u = 0 \text{ m s}^{-1}$, the equation becomes $s = \frac{1}{2}gt^2$.

$$s = \tfrac{1}{2}gt^2$$
$$2s = gt^2$$
$$\frac{2s}{t^2} = g$$

The value of g can be determined from $g = 2s/t^2 \text{ m s}^{-2}$.

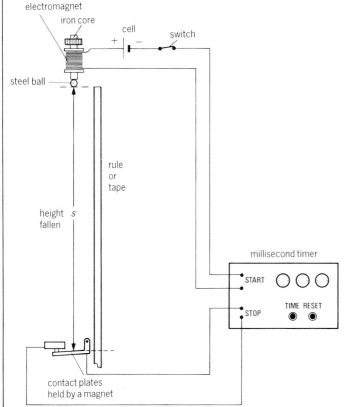

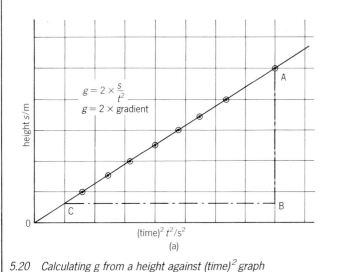

5.19 *Measuring the acceleration of free fall by direct timing*

Set up the apparatus as shown in Fig. 5.19. Check that, with the switch closed, the steel ball is *just* held by the core of the electromagnet and when the switch is opened again the ball is released immediately. Opening the switch should also start the timer; when the ball hits the contact plates, these should open and switch off the timer. Measure the height fallen s by the steel ball from the base of the ball to the top of the hinged plate with a rule or a tape measure. Make s as large as possible and choose sensible values such as 2.0 m, 1.75 m, 1.5 m, 1.25 m and 1.0 m. For each value of s take four measurements of the time taken for the ball to fall freely. Calculate the average time t for each set of four measurements for each height s. Set out a table of results as shown in Table 5.1.

Table 5.1 Table of results for investigation 5.1

Height fallen s/m	Timings /s				Average time t/s	t^2/s^2	$g = \dfrac{2s}{t^2}$/ m s^{-2}
	1	2	3	4			

Calculate the value of g from $g = 2s/t^2$ for each pair of values of s and t and calculate the average value of g from your results. Alternatively, plot a graph of s against t^2 (see Fig. 5.20) and find g from $g = 2 \times$ gradient.

Note The graph of s against t is a curve; a straight-line graph is obtained only if s is plotted against t^2.

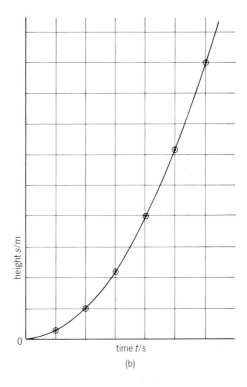

5.20 *Calculating g from a height against (time)^2 graph*

Investigation 5.2 To find the acceleration of free fall *g* using a simple pendulum

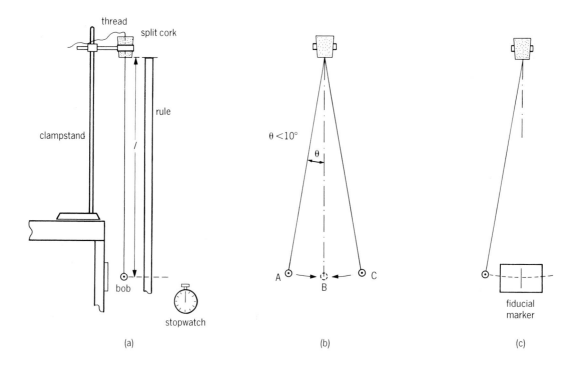

5.22 Measuring the acceleration of free fall by the simple pendulum method

The period *T* (time for one complete oscillation) for a simple pendulum is related to the length *l* of the pendulum by the relationship $T = 2\pi\sqrt{(l/g)}$ where *g* is the acceleration of free fall.

$$T = 2\pi\sqrt{\frac{l}{g}}$$

$$T^2 = 4\pi^2\frac{l}{g}$$

$$gT^2 = 4\pi^2 l$$

$$g = 4\pi^2\frac{l}{T^2}$$

The value of *g* can be determined from $g = 4\pi^2 l/T^2$.

Set up the apparatus as shown in Fig. 5.21(a). With a tape measure or a rule measure the length *l* of the simple pendulum from the base of the split cork to the centre of the bob. Make *l* as large as possible and choose sensible values such as 2.0 m, 1.75 m, 1.5 m, 1.25 m and 1.0 m.

In this experiment it is important that the amplitude of swing θ should be small, i.e. less than 10° so that the motion of the bob is approximately simple harmonic motion and the relationship $T = 2\pi\sqrt{(l/g)}$ applies. Before taking timings of the oscillations, set the pendulum bob swinging, with small amplitude, and observe the rhythm of the swing. You could use a count-down method to start and stop the stopwatch, i.e. count five, four, three, two, one, zero and start the watch on the count of zero. Continue the count from zero to one through ten and stop the watch when ten is reached. The timings of the oscillations may be taken with

reference to either the extreme ends of the swing A and C (Fig. 5.21b) or the central position B. It is more accurate to use the position B. A line drawn on a piece of card can act as a fiducial marker to indicate this position B (Fig. 5.21c). It is important to note that the period *T* depends neither on the amplitude of swing, provided the amplitude is small, nor on the mass of the bob.

For each value of the length *l* take at least two measurements of the time for *n* complete oscillations. The number of oscillations *n* may be 10, 20 or 50 depending on (a) the length of the pendulum used and (b) whether the timing apparatus available is a stopwatch or a stopclock. When a stopwatch reading to 0.1 s is used with the length of the pendulum in the range 1.0–2.0 m then 10 oscillations give reasonably accurate

Table 5.2 Table of results for investigation 5.2

Length *l*/m	Timing for 10 oscillations /s		Average time *t*/s	Period *T*/s	T^2/s²	$g = 4\pi^2\dfrac{l}{T^2}$/m s^{-2}
	1	2				

70

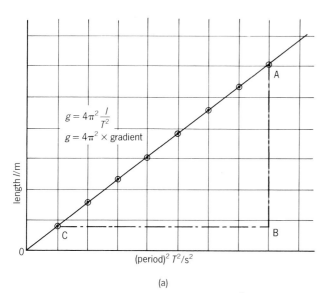

$$g = 4\pi^2 \frac{l}{T^2}$$

$$g = 4\pi^2 \times \text{gradient}$$

(a)

5.23   *Calculating g from a length against (period)^2 graph*

results. Assuming $n = 10$, the average time for the 10 oscillations is calculated for each value of l. Set out a table of results like that in Table 5.2.

If the timing for 10 oscillations is t s the period T of one oscillation is calculated from $T = t/10$ s. Calculate the value of g from $g = 4\pi^2 \, l/T^2$ and calculate the average value of g from your results. Alternatively, plot a graph of l against T^2 and find g from $g = 4\pi^2 \times \text{gradient}$.

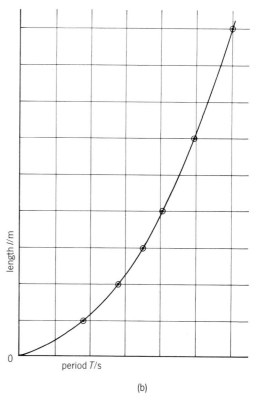

(b)

Note   The graph of l against T is a curve; a straight-line graph is obtained only if l is plotted against T^2.

Questions

Q1   The periodic time of oscillation of a simple pendulum can be significantly reduced by
    A   increasing the mass of the pendulum bob.
    B   increasing the volume of the pendulum bob.
    C   decreasing the amplitude of swing of the pendulum.
    D   decreasing the length of the pendulum.
    E   decreasing the atmospheric pressure acting on the bob.

Q2   Force per unit mass is equivalent to
    A thrust
    B density
    C pressure
    D velocity
    E acceleration

Q3   A stone is dropped from rest from the top of a tall building. The fraction

$$\frac{\text{(distance fallen in the first 4 seconds)}}{\text{(distance fallen in the first 2 seconds)}}$$

is approximately
    A $\frac{1}{4}$
    B $\frac{1}{2}$
    C $\frac{2}{1}$
    D $\frac{4}{1}$
    E $\frac{16}{1}$

(L)

Questions 4–8 The graph below represents a ball thrown vertically upwards and returning to its original position. Use it to answer the questions.

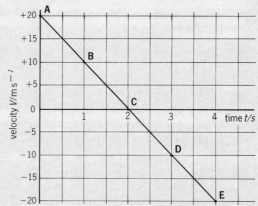

At which of the points labelled **A**, **B**, **C**, **D** and **E** has the ball
Q4   reached it maximum height?
Q5   reached its minimum velocity?
Q6   stopped moving?
Q7   The total *displacement* of the ball is
    A 0 m **B** +10 m **C** +20 m **D** −10 m **E** −20 m
Q8   The *distance* travelled by the ball is
    A 0 m **B** 20 m **C** 30 m **D** 40 m **E** 80 m

Q9 A train travelling at $10\ \mathrm{m\ s^{-1}}$ increases its speed uniformly to $25\ \mathrm{m\ s^{-1}}$ in 3 s. Find its acceleration.

Q10 A diving bell is lowered into the sea at a speed of $6\ \mathrm{m\ s^{-1}}$ and comes to rest with uniform retardation at a distance of 20 m below the surface. Calculate its retardation and the time it takes to come to rest.

Q11 A rocket accelerates from rest to $9600\ \mathrm{m\ s^{-1}}$ in 2 minutes. Calculate the average acceleration and how far the rocket travels in 2 minutes.

Q12 A moon probe has its velocity reduced from $9000\ \mathrm{km\ h^{-1}}$ to $360\ \mathrm{km\ h^{-1}}$ in 40 s. Find the average retardation.

Q13 A car travelling at $5\ \mathrm{m\ s^{-1}}$ is being accelerated uniformly and travels a distance of 300 m in 20 s. Calculate (a) the acceleration of the car and (b) the speed of the car at the end of the 20 s.

Q14 A motor car of mass 1100 kg starts from rest and accelerates steadily until it is travelling at $36\ \mathrm{km\ h^{-1}}$.
(a) If it takes 11 s to attain this speed, what is its acceleration?
(b) Calculate the force exerted between the tyres and the road to produce this acceleration.
(c) How far does the car travel during these 11 s? (*O*)

Q15 Plot the appropriate displacement–time or velocity–time graph of the results given.

(a)

displacement x/m	-20	-10	0	10	20	20	20
time t/s		0	1	2	3	4	5	6

From the graph calculate the velocity of the particle when it is moving. State where the particle is at when the time is (i) 2 s and (ii) 5 s.

(b)

displacement x/m	4	4	4	5	6	7	8	8	8
time t/s	0	1	2	3	4	5	6	7	8

From the graph calculate the velocity of the object when it is moving. Calculate the average velocity over the 8 s period.

(c)

velocity v/m s^{-1}	4	2	0	0	1	2
time t/s	0	1	2	3	4	5

From the graph calculate (i) the acceleration, (ii) the retardation and (iii) the total displacement.

(d)

velocity v/m s^{-1}	15	10	10	10	12.5	15
time t/s	0	2	4	6	8	10

From the graph calculate (i) the total displacement and (ii) the average velocity.

(e)

velocity v/m s^{-1}	0	8	8	4	4	0
time t/s	0	10	20	25	35	40

From the graph calculate (i) the acceleration, (ii) the retardation, (iii) the total displacement and (iv) the average velocity.

Q16 A trolley is pulled from rest along a horizontal track by a constant force. Assume that friction may be neglected.
(a) What type of motion is produced?
(b) At 10 s the force is doubled. How does the motion change?
(c) After a further 10 s the force is suddenly removed. How does the motion change?
(d) Sketch a velocity–time graph to represent the motion of the trolley during the first 30 s of its motion. (*AEB*)

Q17 (a) Sketch a velocity–time graph for a car moving with uniform acceleration from $5\ \mathrm{m\ s^{-1}}$ to $25\ \mathrm{m\ s^{-1}}$ in 15 seconds.
(b) Use the sketch graph to find the values for (i) the acceleration, (ii) the total distance travelled during acceleration. Show clearly at each stage how you used the graph. (*JMB*)

Q18 A car, initially at rest, moves with uniform acceleration for 20 s until it attains a velocity of $15\ \mathrm{m\ s^{-1}}$. It then proceeds at this velocity for 60 s and finally comes to rest after retarding uniformly for a further 10 s. Draw a velocity–time graph of the motion and calculate (a) the retardation, (b) the total distance moved. (*S*)

Q19 (a) In an experiment to determine g, the acceleration of free fall, it is necessary to make careful measurements both of *length* and *time*. Values for these two quantities are then substituted in an appropriate formula to enable g to be calculated.
(i) Draw a diagram of the arrangement of the apparatus you would use to determine g. Indicate on the diagram the exact length that must be measured for the calculations.
(ii) Describe fully how the time interval needed in the calculation is measured.
(iii) Write a relationship of the form '$g = \quad$' which would enable the acceleration of free fall to be calculated using the measurements of length and time you have described in your answers to (i) and (ii). How could you improve the reliability of your determination of g?
(b) When the manned space station *Skylab* was in operation it orbited the Earth above the Earth's atmosphere.
(i) One of Newton's laws of motion states: 'An object will continue with constant speed in a straight line unless an external unbalanced force acts on the object'. Explain why *Skylab* circled the Earth rather than continuing with constant speed in a straight line.
(ii) Experiments conducted by an astronaut in *Skylab* standing on a weighing machine would have shown that he was weightless, i.e. the machine would have read '0'. Explain why the astronaut would have appeared weightless in this situation.
(iii) If *Skylab* had been suddenly halted in its orbit, describe and explain its motion in the next few seconds after it had been stopped, assuming that it was now free to move again. (*L*)

6 Linear momentum and kinetic energy

6.1 Linear momentum

If a table-tennis player misses the ball and it hits him, it does not hurt him even if it is hit very hard. On the other hand, spectators will get well out of the way of a cricket ball hit for six. A small mass such as a bullet can kill when fired from a gun. A motor car can also kill a person standing in its path, even when it is rolling quite slowly. From these examples there appears to be some property derived from an object and its motion which can produce a lesser or greater damaging effect. One such property is called **linear momentum**. The linear momentum p of the object is defined as **the product of its mass m with its velocity v.** (Angular momentum will not be discussed in this book, therefore 'linear momentum p' will be referred to as 'momentum p' $= mv$.) Since mass is a scalar and velocity is a vector, the quantity p given by mv is a vector whose direction is the same as that of the velocity v. The units of momentum from $p = mv$ are kg m s^{-1} which will be shown to be equivalent to N s since N $\equiv$ kg m s^{-2}.

Consider a small particle of mass m kg moving towards a wall with a velocity v m s^{-1}; it strikes the wall normally and rebounds at the same speed (Fig. 6.1). When moving towards the wall the particle's velocity is $+v$ m s^{-1}. After the rebound it will travel in the opposite direction, so to show the velocity of the particle after the rebound we write $-v$ m s^{-1}. Hence the momentum p_B before it strikes the wall is $+mv$ while the momentum p_A after it strikes the wall is $-mv$. Therefore, the sense of the momentum has changed from $+mv$ to $-mv$, although the numerical value is the same both before and after collision.

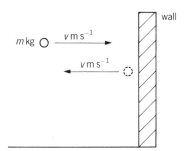

6.1 *Change of momentum of a particle rebounding from a wall*

change in momentum Δp = momentum after collision − momentum before collision
$$= p_A - p_B$$
$$= -mv - (+mv)$$
$$= -2mv$$

i.e. in the direction away from the wall.

6.2 Newton's Second Law of Motion

Newton's Second Law of Motion can be stated as '**the rate of change of momentum of an object is equal to the unbalanced force applied to it causing the change in momentum to take place in the direction of the force.**'

Consider a mass m moving with an initial velocity u. It is accelerated to a velocity v in a time t by the application of a constant unbalanced force F throughout the t seconds (Fig. 6.2).

6.2 *A mass being uniformly accelerated*

change in momentum $\Delta p = (+mv) - (+mu)$
$$\Delta p = mv - mu$$

rate of change of momentum $\dfrac{\Delta p}{t} = \dfrac{mv - mu}{t}$

unbalanced force $F = \dfrac{m(v - u)}{t}$

$$F = ma$$

where a = acceleration which by definition is the rate of change of velocity. The force F has units of kg m s^{-2} which are known as **newton** (N): a tribute to the man whose law we are discussing. It follows from $Ft = mv - mu$ that momentum has units of N s. This equation also shows that the change in momentum Δp is equal to the product of the unbalanced force F and the time t for which it acts. It is important to remember that a given change in momentum could be the result of a large force acting for a short time or a small force acting for a long time.

   Note Newton's First Law of Motion (see p.32) is a special case of the Second Law expressed in the form $Ft = mv - mu$. That is, when $F = 0$ the change in momentum Δp will be zero. Therefore v must equal u for whatever time t is considered. If u is zero then v will also be zero, i.e. the object will remain at rest. If u has a non-zero value then v will have the same value for the duration of t; i.e. the object will continue with uniform velocity throughout the time t.

Example

A pile driver of mass 150 kg falls from a height of 5 m above the pile and is brought to rest in 0.5 s. Ignoring the motion of the pile, calculate the average force exerted on the pile.

$m = 150\,\text{kg} \quad h = 5\,\text{m} \quad v = ? \quad t = 0.5\,\text{s}$
$v_1 = 0\,\text{m s}^{-1} \quad u = 0\,\text{m s}^{-1}$

$$v^2 = u^2 + 2gh$$
$$v^2 = 2 \times 10 \times 5$$
$$v^2 = 100$$
$$v = 10\,\text{m s}^{-1}$$
$$Ft = mv_1 - mv$$
$$F \times 0.5 = 0 - 150 \times 10$$
$$F = -1500/0.5$$
$$= -3000\,\text{N}$$

F is the force exerted by the pile on the driver. Thus the force the driver exerts on the pile is $+3000$ N.

6.3 Dynamics trolleys

From Newton's Second Law expressed in the form $F = ma$ it can be seen that, for a fixed mass m, the acceleration a is directly proportional to the applied unbalanced force F. We can test the relationship $a \propto F$ for a given mass using the dynamics trolley and elastic cords (see investigation 6.1).

   It is interesting to look first at the free-body force diagram (Fig. 6.3a) for a moving trolley. W is the vertical downward pull of the Earth on the trolley, F_1

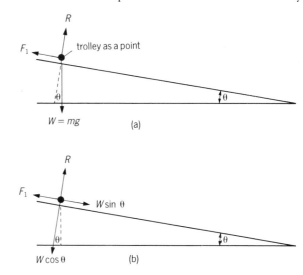

6.3   *The friction-compensated runway*

Investigation 6.1   To test the relationship $a \propto F$

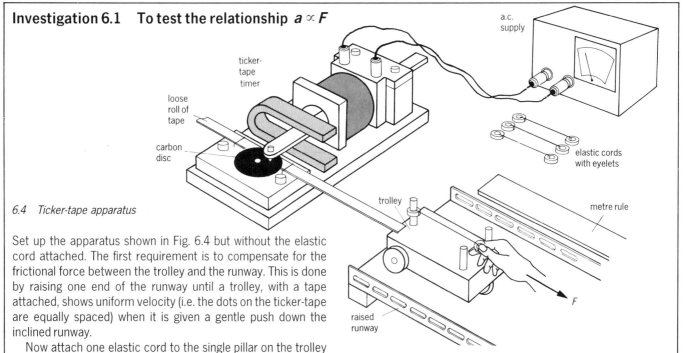

6.4   *Ticker-tape apparatus*

Set up the apparatus shown in Fig. 6.4 but without the elastic cord attached. The first requirement is to compensate for the frictional force between the trolley and the runway. This is done by raising one end of the runway until a trolley, with a tape attached, shows uniform velocity (i.e. the dots on the ticker-tape are equally spaced) when it is given a gentle push down the inclined runway.

   Now attach one elastic cord to the single pillar on the trolley and stretch it until it is level with the double pillars. A force F is required to stretch the cord, and this force F will remain constant provided the length of the stretched cord is kept constant while you pull the trolley down the runway. Thread part

of a 3 m length of ticker-tape under the carbon disc and then stick it on one end of the trolley. Start the timer and stretch the cord while still holding the trolley. After you release the trolley you must move alongside the runway holding the stretched cord

continued

is the frictional force of the runway on the trolley and R is the normal reaction of the runway on the trolley. If the trolley is moving with constant velocity down the slope then, from Newton's First Law, there must be zero unbalanced force acting on it. This is not clear from the three forces shown in Fig. 6.3(a), but if W is replaced by its two resolved components $W\sin\theta$ parallel to the inclined plane and $W\cos\theta$ perpendicular to the inclined plane, as in Fig. 6.3(b), it is easier to understand. If $W\sin\theta$ is equal and opposite to F_1 there is no resultant force acting parallel to the

plane and so uniform velocity is possible along the runway. Also $R = W\cos\theta$ giving zero unbalanced force at right-angles to the plane.

(**Note** An unbalanced force perpendicular to the plane would not affect the motion of the trolley parallel to the plane.

Investigation 6.1 demonstrates that a is directly proportional to F. The equation $F = ma$ also states that for a given unbalanced force F, the acceleration a is inversely proportional to the mass m, i.e. $F \times 1/m = a$.

---

so that its length remains constant. You may have to practise this because the cord will try to shorten when the trolley is first released and you must apply just the right force to prevent this happening.

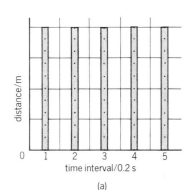

(a)

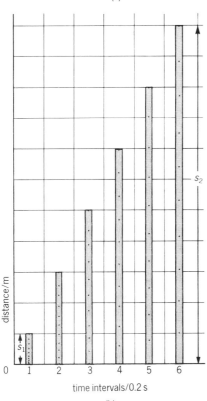

(b)

6.5 Tape charts for (a) uniform motion on the friction-compensated runway and (b) accelerated motion

After a successful run, detach the tape and, disregarding the first series of dots, cut it up into strips which each represent 10 vibrations or 0.2 s (10 × 0.02 s). These strips can be stuck on a sheet of graph paper to give a chart like that in Fig. 6.5(b).

Figure 6.5(a) shows the chart obtained when the trolley runs down the runway at uniform velocity, i.e. covering equal distances in equal time intervals on a **friction-compensated** runway. Using the chart in Fig. 6.5(b) the average acceleration a can be calculated from $a = (v - u)/t$. The average final velocity v for the sixth length of tape is calculated from $v = s_2/0.2$. Likewise, the original velocity is calculated as $u = s_1/0.2$ from the first length of tape. The time interval t between the first and sixth tapes is 5×0.2 s $= 1.0$ s. Hence

$$a = \frac{s_2}{0.2} - \frac{s_1}{0.2} \quad /1$$

$$= (s_2 - s_1)/0.2 \text{ m s}^{-2}$$

When two elastic cords of the same original lengths and made of the same elastic are both stretched by the same amount as the one in the first part of the experiment, the new force will be twice the original force. Repeat the experiment using two, three and four stretched cords to apply forces of $2F$, $3F$ and $4F$ respectively to the same trolley. In each case calculate the acceleration a as shown above. A graph of a against F should be a straight line passing through the origin as shown in Fig. 6.6.

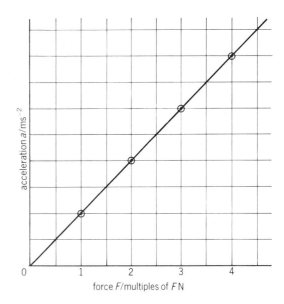

6.6 A graph of acceleration against the force applied to the trolley

Investigation 6.2 To test the relationship $a \propto 1/m$

Again set up the apparatus shown in Fig. 6.4, but this time keep the accelerating force F constant by using two or three elastic cords and instead vary the mass the force acts upon. First run a single trolley, then two, three and four trolleys stacked together. All the trolleys should be of equal mass m so that the total mass is increased by the same amount each time. Alternatively, you could add metal blocks or standard masses equal in mass to the trolley, to a single trolley. Once again one end of the runway must be raised to compensate for friction so that the trolley with ticker-tape attached will move with uniform velocity when given a gentle push.

What will the spacing of the dots on the tape look like when uniform velocity is achieved? Why do you test that frictional forces are compensated for with the tape attached to the trolley? What is the numerical value, if any, of the unbalanced force on the trolley as it moves down the runway with uniform velocity?

When the preliminary adjustments are complete, attach a 3 m length of tape to the trolley and apply a steady force using two or three stretched elastic cords. Using the technique shown in Fig. 6.5(b), calculate the acceleration a and hence find $1/a$ for the single trolley.

Next double the mass to be accelerated by stacking a second identical trolley on top of the first one or by adding standard masses equal in value to the mass of the trolley. Since the mass is now double the weight is also double and therefore the frictional force will increase. Thus the runway must be raised a little higher so that it is friction-compensated for the double mass. Now accelerate the double mass using the same two or three cords and determine a and $1/a$ from the tapes. Repeat the experiment with the mass trebled and quadrupled. A graph of mass m against reciprocal of acceleration $1/a$ should be a straight line through the origin similar to Fig. 6.7.

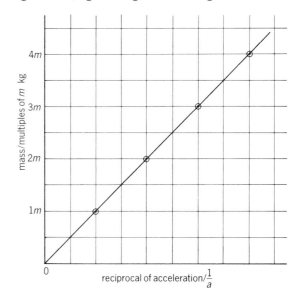

6.7 A graph of the mass of the trolley against the reciprocal of its acceleration

6.4 Newton's Third Law of Motion

Newton's Third Law of Motion states that '**if a body A exerts a force $+F$ on a body B, then body B exerts a force $-F$ on A, that is a force of the same size and along the same line of interaction but in the opposite direction**'. This law says that forces always occur in pairs as the result of the interaction between two objects. Note that *two* objects are involved and the two forces each act on a different object, never on the same object. The two opposing forces are sometimes called the **action** and **reaction** forces.

A mass m above the Earth's surface experiences a pull on it due to the mass of the Earth. The unbalanced force $F = mg$ causes the mass to accelerate towards the Earth's surface at g m s^{-2}. At the same time, the mass m exerts an equal and opposite pull on the Earth, but because the mass of the Earth is enormous, the 'upward' acceleration of the Earth is insignificant. When you walk the Earth pushes on you in response to your push on the Earth. Therefore a frictional force between your shoe and the ground is essential for forward motion. Motor cars are able to move along a road because the reaction of the road pushes the car along in response to the action of the wheels pushing on the road.

6.5 Impulses

An important principle arising out of the Third Law of Motion is that, '**when two objects interact on each other the time for which the two equal and opposite forces act must be the same for both objects**'. Therefore the product of the force F and the time t for which the force acts must be the same for *both* objects. The product Ft, known as the **impulse** of the force, is a vector quantity and has units of N s. From Newton's Second Law $F = (mv - mu)/t$ it follows that $Ft = mv - mu$, i.e. **the impulse of the force p is equal to the change in momentum**. Even when the force F varies throughout the time t, the change in momentum still gives the quantity known as the impulse of the force. This is very important in that both the force F, which may be constant or variable, and the time t are often difficult to measure, e.g. where a sharp blow is involved. The impulse of the force can instead be measured by determining the mass and the change in velocity of the objects.

The idea of the impulse of a force is important when considering a hammer driving a nail into a block of wood, a boy kicking a football and a girl striking a hockey ball. There are many other examples and you should list some of them as an exercise.

skateboard

(a)

javelin

(b)

6.8   *Impulse of a force*

Example

A girl standing at rest with her right foot on a skateboard thrusts backwards on the ground with her left foot as in Fig. 6.8(a). The push of the ground on her left foot will increase the forward momentum of the girl and skateboard. From $Ft = mv - 0$ the velocity v acquired by the girl will depend on the force F which can be applied and the time t for which it acts.

Exercise 6.1

A boy throwing a javelin is shown in Fig. 6.8(b). Show that, for a javelin of a given mass, the distance it will travel depends upon the force exerted by the boy's arm and the time for which it is exerted. Why does the boy hold his arm as far behind his body as he can before he starts to launch the javelin?

Note   An impulse can be a steady force acting for some time as well as a large force acting for a short time.

6.6   Conservation of momentum

Suppose two objects are travelling in the same direction at different speeds and there are no other external forces acting on them, as shown in Fig. 6.9(a). (By convention left to right is taken as positive and thus right to left is negative.) On impact (Fig. 6.9b) the mass A experiences an impulse from B; $F_{BA}t = m_A v_A - m_A u_A$. During the same time t the mass B experiences an impulse from A of $F_{AB}t = m_B v_B - m_B u_B$. Since the two forces F_{AB} and F_{BA} are equal and opposite, $-F_{BA}t = F_{AB}t$. Hence

$$-(m_A v_A - m_A u_A) = m_B v_B - m_B u_B$$
$$-m_A v_A + m_A u_A = m_B v_B - m_B u_B$$
$$m_A u_A + m_B u_B = m_A v_A + m_B v_B$$

i.e. the total momentum before impact equals the total momentum after impact and the momentum has been conserved.

The Principle of Conservation of Momentum states that '**if there is a direction in which there is zero unbalanced force acting on a system then the total momentum of that system in that direction is constant even if the bodies act on each other**'. Note that other forces, e.g. the pull of the Earth, do act on the bodies, but the result can still be used if there is a direction in which the external forces are balanced.

The Principle of Conservation of Momentum is applied in the following problems.

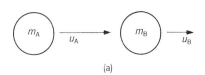

(a)

(b)

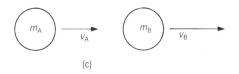

(c)

6.9   *Conservation of momentum*

77

Example

A bullet of mass m is fired from a gun of mass M with a horizontal velocity of v. What is the recoil velocity of the gun?

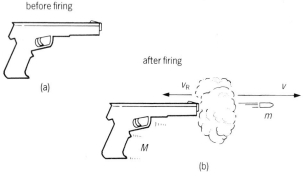

before firing

after firing

v_R v

(a)

(b)

m

M

6.10   Recoil velocity

Choose a suitable direction (the horizontal direction) in which the effect of the external forces is zero. Choose a sign convention for the direction of the velocities: here left to right is positive $(+)$. Let v_R be the recoil velocity of the gun.

$$\text{momentum before gun is fired} = m \times 0 + M \times 0$$
$$= 0 \text{ (gun at rest)}$$
$$\text{momentum after gun is fired} = m \times (+v) + M \times (-v_R)$$
$$\text{momentum before firing} = \text{momentum after firing}$$
$$0 = mv - Mv_R$$
$$Mv_R = mv$$
$$v_R = \frac{mv}{M}$$

In hand-held guns the recoil can be absorbed by the person holding the gun. In very large guns which fire massive shells at high velocity the recoil could rip the gun from its mountings unless special provision is made to absorb the force.

Example

What would happen if an astronaut on a space walk outside an orbiting spacecraft fired a gun? Assuming the mass of the astronaut, his spacesuit and the gun is 120 kg and that he fires a 50 g bullet from the gun at a velocity of 400 m s^{-1}, calculate the velocity of recoil.

$m_1 = 120 \text{ kg}$ $u_1 = 0 \text{ m s}^{-1}$ $m_2 = 0.05 \text{ kg}$ $v = 400 \text{ m s}^{-1}$
$v_R = ?$

$$\text{momentum before firing} = m_1 \times 0 + m_2 \times 0$$
$$= 0$$
$$\text{momentum after firing} = 0.05 \times (+400) + 120 \times (v_R)$$
$$0 = 20 + 120 v_R$$
$$-120 v_R = 20$$
$$v_R = \frac{-20}{120}$$
$$v_R = -\tfrac{1}{6} \text{ m s}^{-1}$$

The astronaut would drift off into outer space unless he were tethered to the spacecraft.

Example

A boy of mass 58 kg jumps with a horizontal velocity of 3 m s^{-1} onto a stationary skateboard of mass 2 kg. What is his velocity as he moves off on the skateboard?

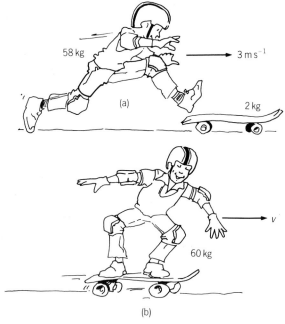

58 kg   3 m s^{-1}

(a)

2 kg

60 kg v

(b)

6.11   Jumping onto a skateboard

Assume there is zero unbalanced horizontal force in the horizontal direction and that left to right is the positive $(+)$ direction.

$$\text{momentum before interaction} = 58 \times 3 + 2 \times 0$$
$$\text{momentum after interaction} = 58 \times v + 2 \times v$$
$$= 60v$$
$$\text{equating momenta } 60v = 58 \times 3$$
$$v = \frac{58 \times 3}{60}$$
$$v = +2.9 \text{ m s}^{-1}$$

Collisions

Did you notice that in the last example the momentum before and after interaction is conserved but the kinetic energy is not? The original kinetic energy of $\frac{1}{2} \times 58 \times 3 \times 3 = 261$ J is reduced to 252.3 J because some energy has been transformed into heat energy and sound energy. This interaction or **collision** of the boy and skateboard is known as an **inelastic collision**. Collisions in which there is no loss of kinetic energy, i.e. kinetic energy is conserved, are called **perfectly elastic collisions**. An example of perfectly elastic collisions is provided by molecules colliding in a gas (see p.139). A few examples, such as the interaction of very hard objects, approximate to elastic collisions but in real life kinetic energy is usually transformed into heat energy, sound energy and work done in deforming the colliding objects.

Example

Two ice hockey players suitably padded collide directly with each other and immediately become entangled. One has a mass of 110 kg and is travelling at 4 m s^{-1} while the other has a mass of 90 kg and is travelling at 6 m s^{-1} towards the first player. In which direction and at what speed do they travel after they become entangled?

Let left to right be the positive (+) direction and assume that any other horizontal forces such as frictional forces can be neglected in this problem.

$$\text{momentum before collision} = 110 \times (+4) + 90 \times (-6)$$
$$\text{momentum after collision} = (110 + 90)(+v)$$

where v is the common velocity of the pair.

Equating momenta before and after collision:

$$200\,v = 440 - 540$$
$$200\,v = -100$$
$$v = -0.5 \text{ m s}^{-1}$$

Note that the players do not move together in the direction of the arrow in Fig. 6.12(b), as can be seen from the negative sign (−) in the final answer. The two players move from right to left at 0.5 m s^{-1}.

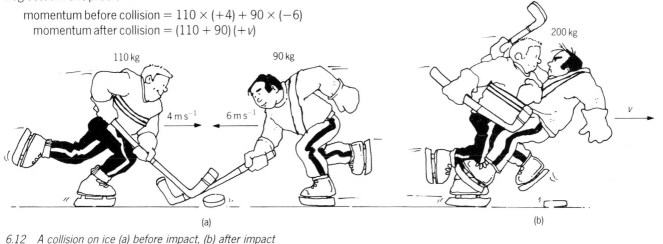

6.12   A collision on ice (a) before impact, (b) after impact

6.7   Illustrating the Principle of Conservation of Momentum

Investigation 6.3   To test the Principle of Conservation of Momentum

6.13   Apparatus to verify the Principle of Conservation of Momentum

Set up the two trolleys and a friction-compensated runway as shown in Fig. 6.13. Fit a strong pin or needle to the front of the first trolley and determine its total mass m_1 using a balance. Fit a stout cork to the second trolley and determine its total mass m_2 using a balance. Position the second trolley at rest about halfway down the runway. Attach a length of tape to the first trolley. After switching on the timer, give the first trolley a push so that it travels along the runway until it meets the second trolley, the pin then enters the cork and the two trolleys continue as one. The tape produced will look like that in Fig. 6.14. Measurements from the tape enable the initial velocity u of the first trolley and the combined velocity v of the two trolleys to be calculated.

$$\text{momentum before collision} = m_1 u + m_2 \times 0$$
$$\text{momentum after collision} = (m_1 + m_2)v$$

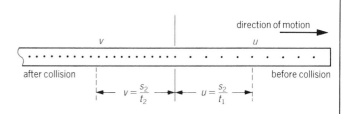

6.14   Tape showing velocity before and after collision

When you substitute the measured values into the above equations you should find that $m_1 u = (m_1 + m_2)v$ within the limits of experimental error. The experiment can be repeated for different values of m_1 and m_2 by placing additional masses on the trolleys.

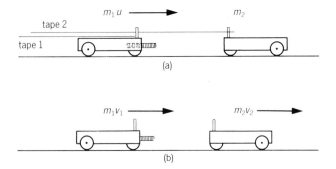

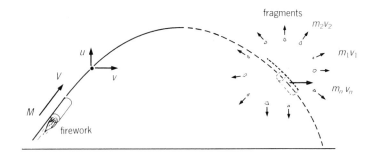

6.15 *Momentum (a) before impact and (b) after impact*

6.17 *Momentum is conserved in an exploding firework*

A similar experiment can be performed using a loaded trolley of mass m_1 fitted with a spring plunger which collides with a second trolley of mass m_2 ($m_2 < m_1$) at rest halfway along the runway. On collision, the more massive trolley will slow down and set the stationary trolley moving. Two ticker-tape timers are needed in this experiment, one connected to each trolley.

$$\text{momentum before impact} = m_1 u + m_2 \times 0$$
$$\text{momentum after impact} = m_1 v_1 + m_2 v_2$$

Within the limits of experimental error it should be found that $m_1 u = m_1 v_1 + m_2 v_2$. This is an example of a partially elastic collision and shows that the Principle of Conservation of Momentum applies to both elastic and inelastic collisions.

Investigation 6.4   To demonstrate that momentum is conserved in an 'explosion'

Place two trolleys fitted with compressed springs in contact and at rest in the centre of the runway as in Fig. 6.16(a). Fit each trolley with a tape passing through its own timer. Then tap the spring plungers smartly with a ruler. The two trolleys will move apart in an 'explosive' collision (Fig. 6.16b) and their velocities can be determined from their respective tapes.

$$\text{momentum before 'explosion'} = m_1 \times 0 + m_2 \times 0$$
$$= 0$$
$$\text{momentum after 'explosion'} = m_1 \times (-v_1) + m_2 (+v_2)$$
$$-m_1 v_1 + m_2 v_2 = 0$$
$$m_2 v_2 = m_1 v_1$$

6.16 *An 'explosive' collision*

Notice that in this investigation there is a gain in kinetic energy. When objects collide there is usually a decrease in kinetic energy. However, in the case of 'exploding' objects there is an increase in the kinetic energy which is released from the potential (stored) energy in the compressed springs. The Principle of Conservation of Momentum can be applied to a spectacular firework exploding in mid-air. When the firework bursts the release of chemical energy increases the kinetic energy of the burning fragments. If there are n fragments then clearly the mass of the firework $M = m_1 + m_2 + m_3 + \ldots m_n$, i.e. the sum of the masses of all the fragments. Assume that the firework is projected with a velocity V at an angle to the horizontal, then the velocity has a vertical component u and a horizontal component v. Ignoring air resistance, the horizontal velocity v of the system remains unchanged after the firework is let off. Therefore there are no external forces acting on the system (firework or fragments) in a horizontal direction and so momentum is conserved in this direction. Hence the total horizontal momentum of the fragments after the explosion must equal the momentum before the explosion. Although some velocities are positive and some are negative, the speed of the fragments and hence the kinetic energy $\frac{1}{2}mv^2$ of the firework can be greatly increased by the chemical energy released.

6.8   Propulsion

Change of momentum can be used as a means of propulsion. Consider a toy balloon which has been inflated and then released. The pressure of the air molecules inside the balloon is greater than the external atmospheric pressure and so air molecules rush out of the open neck of the balloon. The backward movement of the escaping air is responsible for the forward motion of the balloon. Hence it darts around the room as the air rushes out of the balloon. The action force of the air molecules rushing out of the balloon causes a reaction force on the balloon fabric to move it in the opposite direction. A rocket in a

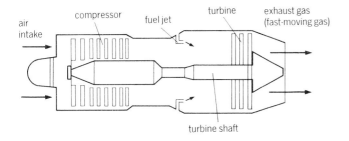

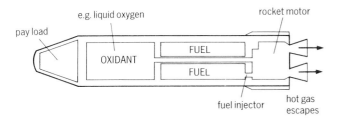

6.18   (a) Jet engine and (b) rocket engine

fireworks display also uses this principle. After the touch paper has been lit the chemicals inside the rocket ignite and force out a fast stream of molecules which thrusts the rocket up into the sky. The explosion which gives the aerial display is timed to occur when the rocket is high in the sky. In both the jet engine (Fig. 6.18a) and the rocket motor (Fig. 6.18b) a chemical reaction forces out a fast stream of molecules which propels the vehicle. However, there is one very important difference in their operation: the jet engine needs air to supply the oxygen required for combustion of the fuel and so cannot operate outside the Earth's atmosphere, while space rockets carry their own supply of oxygen and can thus be used in outer space. Because of the very high velocity and large number of molecules escaping on combustion the momentum is very large even though the mass of the molecules is quite small. An equal and opposite momentum is given to the jet or the rocket.

6.9   Summary of the chapter

Force is equal to the **rate of change of momentum**. An unbalanced force F causes a mass m to accelerate with acceleration a given by $F = ma$. The impulse p of a force F acting for a time t is Ft and is equal to the change in momentum. The change in momentum is calculated from the difference between the final momentum and the initial momentum. Momentum is always conserved in collisions but kinetic energy is not necessarily conserved.

The following worked examples will illustrate some of these points.

Example

A car of mass 1200 kg is brought to rest from a speed of 20 m s^{-1} by a constant braking force 3000 N. Calculate the retardation and the time the car takes to come to rest.

$F = -3000 \text{ N} \quad m = 1200 \text{ kg} \quad a = ?$

$$F = ma$$
$$-3000 = 1200a$$
$$a = \frac{-3000}{1200}$$
$$a = -2.5 \text{ m s}^{-2}$$

The retardation is -2.5 m s^{-2}.

$v = 0 \quad u = 20 \text{ m s}^{-1} \quad a = -2.5 \text{ m s}^{-2} \quad t = ?$

$$v = u + at$$
$$0 = 20 - 2.5\,t$$
$$2.5\,t = 20$$
$$t = \frac{20}{2.5}$$
$$t = 8 \text{ s}$$

The car comes to rest in 8 s.

Example

An ice hockey puck of mass 0.1 kg travelling at 20 m s^{-1} is struck by a stick so as to return it along its original path at 10 m s^{-1}. Calculate the impulse of the force applied by the hockey stick.

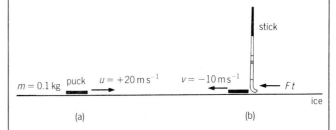

6.19   Impulse of an ice hockey stick on a puck

Let p be the impulse produced by the Force F applied by the stick for the time t.

$m = 0.1 \text{ kg} \quad u = +20 \text{ m s}^{-1} \quad v = -10 \text{ m s}^{-1} \quad F = ?$
$t = ?$

$$\begin{aligned} p &= Ft \\ &= mv - mu \\ &= 0.1 \times (-10) - 0.1 \times (+20) \\ &= -1 - 2 \\ &= -3 \text{ N s} \end{aligned}$$

The impulse applied by the stick is -3 N s. The minus sign indicates that the direction of the impulse is in the opposite direction to the original direction of motion of the puck.

Example

A rifle pellet of mass 5 g is fired horizontally into a block of wood fixed to a model truck which runs freely on a straight track. The mass of the truck and the block is 495 g and these move with a velocity of 0.8 m s^{-1} when the pellet embeds itself into the wood. Calculate the initial velocity of the pellet.

$$m = 0.005 \text{ kg} \quad u = ? \quad M = 0.495 \text{ kg} \quad v = 0.8 \text{ m s}^{-1}$$
$$mu = (m + M)v$$
$$0.005 \times u = (0.005 + 0.495) \times 0.8$$
$$u = \frac{0.5 \times 0.8}{0.005}$$
$$u = 80 \text{ m s}^{-1}$$

The initial velocity of the pellet is 80 m s^{-1}.

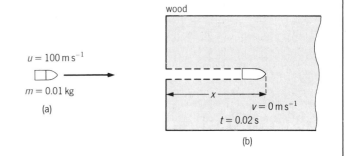

$m = 5\,\text{g} \qquad u$

$M = 495\,\text{g}$

$v = 0.8\,\text{m s}^{-1}$

track

6.20   The velocity of a rifle pellet

Example

A bullet of mass 0.01 kg travelling horizontally at 100 m s^{-1} penetrates a fixed block of wood and comes to rest in 0.02 s. Calculate (a) the distance of penetration x of the bullet into the wood and (b) the average retarding force exerted by the wood on the bullet.

(a) $u = 100 \text{ m s}^{-1} \quad v = 0 \text{ m s}^{-1} \quad a = ? \quad t = 0.02 \text{ s}$

$$v = u + at$$
$$0 = 100 + a \times 0.02$$
$$0.02a = -100$$
$$a = -100/0.02$$
$$a = -5000 \text{ m s}^{-2}$$

$$v^2 = u^2 + 2ax$$
$$0 = 100^2 - 2 \times 5000 \, x$$
$$10\,000\, x = 10\,000$$
$$x = 1 \text{ m}$$

The bullet penetrates 1 m into the block (note the deep penetration).

wood

$u = 100 \text{ m s}^{-1}$

$m = 0.01 \text{ kg}$

(a)

$v = 0 \text{ m s}^{-1}$

$t = 0.02 \text{ s}$

(b)

6.21   A bullet penetrating a wooden block

(b) $F = ? \quad m = 0.01 \text{ kg} \quad a = -5000 \text{ m s}^{-2}$

$$F = ma$$
$$F = 0.01 \times (-5000)$$
$$F = -50 \text{ N}$$

The average retarding force exerted by the wood is -50 N.

Questions

Q1 Which of the following is *not* a vector quantity?
A momentum **B** velocity **C** acceleration
D kinetic energy **E** impulse

Q2 What is the momentum of a body of mass m moving with a velocity v?
A mv^2 **B** $(mv)^2$ **C** mv **D** $\frac{1}{2}mv$ **E** $\frac{1}{2}mv^2$

Q3 Which of the following is a unit of momentum?
A N **B** N s^{-1} **C** kg m s^{-2}
D kg m s^{-1} **E** kg m^{-1}

Q4 A constant horizontal force is applied to a body initially at rest on a smooth horizontal table. Which of the following quantities will **not** change during the application of the force?
A The position of the body.
B The acceleration of the body.
C The velocity of the body.
D The momentum of the body.
E The kinetic energy of the body.   *(L)*

Q5 A horizontal force of 20 N is applied to a mass of 5 kg at rest on a smooth horizontal surface. Calculate the acceleration of the mass. If the same force is applied to the same mass when resting on a rough surface, a constant frictional force of 5 N acts throughout the motion of the mass. What is the acceleration of the mass on the rough surface?

Q6 A balloon of total mass 2200 kg hovers stationary at a height of several metres above the ground. A mass of 200 kg is released from rest from the balloon. Calculate the acceleration of the balloon as it starts to rise.

Q7 A hot air balloonist tries to estimate the motion of his balloon by suspending a 50 N weight from a spring balance in his balloon. Describe the motion of the balloon when the spring balance reads
(a) 60 N and   (b) 30 N.

Q8 A man whose mass is 70 kg stands on a spring balance inside a lift. What reading will the balance register when the lift is (a) at rest, (b) accelerating upwards at 1.5 m s^{-2}, (c) descending at uniform velocity, (d) falling freely after the cable snaps?

Q9 State the equation relating the mass m of a body and the force F which will give it an acceleration a. State the SI unit of each of the three quantities. What force is needed to give a body of mass 0.5 kg, initially at rest on a smooth horizontal surface, an acceleration of $0.1\,\text{m s}^{-2}$? If the force acts on the body for 2 s and is then removed, describe the subsequent motion of the body.

Q10 A car of mass 1000 kg travelling at $20\,\text{m s}^{-1}$ crashes into a brick wall and comes to rest in 0.5 s. Calculate the average force exerted by the wall on the car.

Q11 State and explain the principle of conservation of momentum. Describe an experiment you would perform to test this principle.

A trolley of mass 1.0 kg moves horizontally with a velocity of $0.3\,\text{m s}^{-1}$. A 0.5 kg mass of putty is dropped vertically onto the trolley where it sticks to the trolley. Calculate the final velocity of the trolley.

Q12 Two identical snooker balls are placed on a smooth horizontal surface. One ball is at rest while the other is pushed at the first with a constant velocity of $0.2\,\text{m s}^{-1}$. Assuming a perfectly elastic collision takes place calculate the velocity of each ball immediately after impact. Explain your answer stating any physical principles involved.

Q13 An object of mass 2 kg travelling in a straight line with a velocity of $20\,\text{m s}^{-1}$ collides with, and sticks to, a stationary object of mass 3 kg. They both move off together in the same straight line with a velocity of $v\,\text{m s}^{-1}$. If no external forces are acting, calculate (i) the total momentum just before impact, (ii) the total momentum just after impact, (iii) the velocity v.

(AEB part question)

Q14 A steadily increasing force applied to a moving motor car could result in a change in each of the following *except* the car's

A acceleration.

B direction of motion.

C mass.

D momentum.

E speed. *(L)*

Q15 Write down Newton's three laws of motion. A body of mass 5 kg falls freely from rest through a height of 80 m. Calculate (i) the time taken to reach the ground, (ii) the velocity of the body just before impact, (iii) its maximum kinetic energy.

If the body does not rebound on impact, suggest what has happened to the kinetic energy. *(W)*

Q16 Define *velocity* and *acceleration*.

Explain how Newton's Second Law of Motion relates force and momentum and use this relationship to derive the unit of force.

A 0.5 kg mass is placed on a smooth slope inclined at an angle of 30° to the horizontal. Calculate

(a) the component of the weight acting down the slope,

(b) the acceleration of the mass as it slides down, and

(c) the distance it would move from rest in 0.5 seconds. *(W)*

Q17 State Newton's Second Law of Motion and explain how a formula relating force, mass and acceleration is derived from it.

A body of mass 100 kg is accelerated uniformly from a velocity of $2\,\text{m s}^{-1}$ to $5\,\text{m s}^{-1}$ in 6 seconds. Calculate (i) its initial momentum, (ii) its final momentum, (iii) the resultant force acting on the body.

Describe carefully what happens when a space-rocket is launched and explain why it accelerates at an increasing rate as it burns its fuel. *(W)*

Q18 A small steel ball of mass 80 g is released from rest at a height of 1.25 m above a rigid horizontal metal plate. After the rebound the ball rises vertically to a height of 1.00 m above the plate. Calculate

(a) the velocity of the ball just before impact,

(b) the momentum of the ball just before impact,

(c) the kinetic energy of the ball just before impact,

(d) the loss of energy on impact. Give reasons for this loss of energy.

Suggest some practical arrangements in carrying out such an experiment in order (i) to release the ball carefully at the desired height, (ii) to estimate the height of rise accurately. *(S)*

Q19 State the principle of conservation of momentum.

Describe how you would demonstrate the truth of the principle by means of experiments.

A firework is placed at rest in the middle of a sheet of ice, and then explodes. The firework breaks into three fragments. One fragment, of mass 0.100 kg, moves off with a velocity of $10\,\text{m s}^{-1}$ due North. The second, of mass 0.200 kg, moves off with a velocity of $10\,\text{m s}^{-1}$ due East.

(a) What is the total momentum of the firework (i) just before it explodes, (ii) just after it explodes?

(b) What is the momentum of the third fragment just after the explosion?

(c) The third fragment has a mass of 0.100 kg. What is its velocity just after the explosion? *(O & C)*

Q20 A trolley runs freely down a small-angle slope at constant speed. It pulls a length of ticker-tape through a timer which marks a dot every $\frac{1}{50}$ second. On a second run, the trolley is given a steady pull down the slope.

(a) Draw a diagram of all the forces acting on the trolley on the first run, and explain why the speed is constant.

(b) Explain how a steady pull could be provided for the second run, and describe a way of providing a steady pull of twice the size.

(c) Describe how to use the apparatus to measure the acceleration of the trolley for a given force, and hence to show that acceleration is proportional to force.

(d) Describe how to use the apparatus to investigate the variation between acceleration and mass of the trolley for a constant force. Sketch a suitable graph which could be used to display the results and explain what you would expect to find. *(O)*

7 Addition, subtraction and resolution of vectors

7.1 Simple addition and subtraction of vectors

In earlier chapters various physical quantities have been classified as either a **vector** or a **scalar** quantity. Most notable are displacement, velocity, momentum, acceleration, force and impulse, all of which are vector quantities. **A vector quantity has both magnitude and direction.** Scalar quantities include distance, speed, time, mass, work and energy. **A scalar quantity has magnitude only.** Adding scalar quantities is quite simple: you just add the quantities algebraically, e.g. a mass of 50 g added to a mass of 100 g gives a mass of 150 g. However, adding (or subtracting) two vector quantities is more complicated. We will illustrate what happens when we add vector quantities by taking forces as our example.

When two forces act on an object a single force can be found which will replace these two forces and produces the same effect on the object as the two forces does. This single force is called the **resultant** force. When the two given forces act in the same straight line, the resultant force is relatively easy to find. In Fig. 7.1 one boy alone, exerting a force F_1, is unable to pull the large container P along the ground. However, when a second boy helps by pulling at his waist with force F_2, the two of them can manage to move the container steadily across the ground. A woman is also just able to exert sufficient force R to move the container steadily across the ground. Clearly

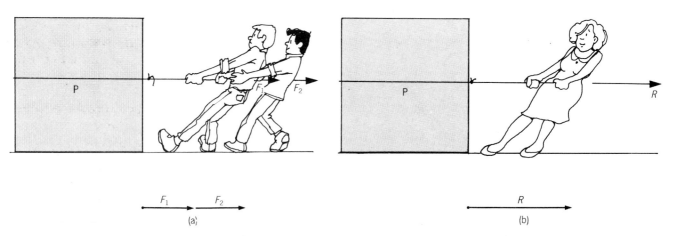

7.1 *Resultant force*

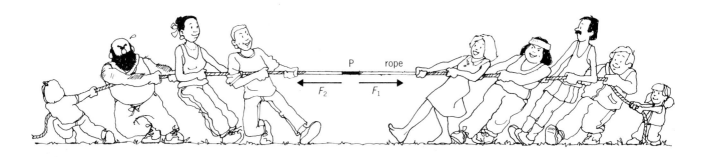

7.2 *Tug-of-war*

$R = F_1 + F_2$, and the resultant force R can be obtained by adding together the forces F_1 and F_2. As both boys are pulling from left to right these forces are, by convention, given a (+) sign to indicate their direction (see p.59). Hence $+ R = (+ F_1) + (+ F_2)$, written more simply as $R = F_1 + F_2$.

Now consider two teams in a tug-of-war. The team on the right pull on the rope from left to right while the other team exerts its pull from right to left. If the team on the right is pulling with a force F_1 this can be shown as $+ F_1$ to indicate that the force acts from left to right. However, the force exerted by the other team should be written as $- F_2$ to indicate that its direction is exactly opposite to F_1.

In this example the resultant force R is given by $R = (+ F_1) + (- F_2) = F_1 - F_2$. If the value of the forces F_1 and F_2 are equal then $R = 0$, zero unbalanced force. In this case **equilibrium** exists, i.e. the piece of rope marked P does not move in either direction. If F_1 is numerically greater than F_2 then the resultant $R = F_1 - F_2$ is positive and hence acts from left to right, P will therefore move to the right, i.e. in the direction of the unbalanced force R, and the team on the right will win. However, if F_2 is numerically greater than F_1 the resultant force $R = F_1 - F_2$ will have a negative sign and the team on the left will win.

Note   Here the resultant force is obtained by *adding* the two forces together, taking account of their direction of application by using either a (+) or (−) sign.

Example

A loaded test tube of weight 0.6 N floats in equilibrium in a tank of water. Calculate the upthrust U of the water on the test tube.

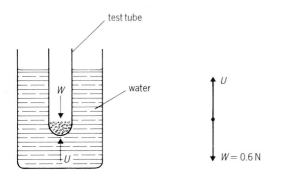

7.3   Forces on a test tube floating in water

For equilibrium $(+ U) + (- W) = R$
$$= 0 \text{ taking up as positive } (+)$$
$$U + (- 0.6 \text{ N}) = 0$$
$$U = + 0.6 \text{ N}$$

The (+) sign in the answer confirms that the upthrust is indeed upward.

7.2   Relative velocity

When a passenger sitting in a fast-moving train looks out of the window, the countryside appears to flash past the window. Although he knows the countryside is not moving, it appears to be moving relative to the observer in the train. A rambler standing in the field alongside the train would see the train hurtle past.

If a car, travelling with velocity v_A, overtakes another car B, travelling with velocity v_B (see Fig. 7.4a), the driver of car A sees car B apparently moving towards her. However, a passenger in the back of car B sees car A gradually catching up with him. The **velocity of A relative to B is the velocity which A appears to have to an observer who is moving with B.** Thus the velocity of A relative to B is effectively the resultant velocity of A when B is made stationary and the same retarding force is applied to A. One method of making B stationary would be to apply the reverse velocity $v_{B \text{ rev}}$ to B. Thus the resultant velocity of A is $v_A + v_{B \text{ rev}}$, and this is the velocity of A relative to B. However, $v_{B \text{ rev}} = - v_B$ (the reversed direction is shown by the negative sign). Hence the relative velocity $(v_A - v_B)$, is obtained by subtracting the two vector quantities.

To find the relative velocity of two cars, both moving from left to right as shown in Fig. 7.4(a), you must calculate the difference in their velocities. However, there are two relative velocities that you could find: the velocity of car A relative to car B and the velocity of car B relative to car A.

velocity of A relative to B
$$= \text{velocity of A} - \text{velocity of B}$$
$$= v_A - v_B$$
$$= v_A + (v_{B \text{ rev}})$$
Adding v_B reversed is equivalent to subtracting v_B.
$$= v_A + (- v_B)$$
$$= + 30 + (- 20)$$
$$= + 10 \text{ m s}^{-1}$$

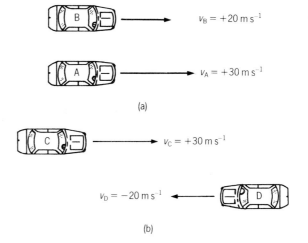

7.4   Relative velocities

velocity of B relative to A
$$\begin{aligned} &= \text{velocity of B} - \text{velocity of A} \\ &= v_B - v_A \\ &= v_B + (v_{A\,rev}) \end{aligned}$$

Adding v_A reversed is equivalent to subtracting v_A.
$$\begin{aligned} &= v_B + (-v_A) \\ &= +20 + (-30) \\ &= -10\,\mathrm{m\,s^{-1}} \end{aligned}$$

The driver in car B sees car A moving away from him (from left to right, + sign) at 10 m s^{-1}, while the driver of car A sees car B falling behind her (from right to left, − sign) at 10 m s^{-1}.

Now look at Fig. 7.4(b) which shows two cars C and D approaching each other at velocities of 30 m s^{-1} and 20 m s^{-1} respectively, the relative velocities are calculated as follows:

velocity of C relative to D
$$\begin{aligned} &= \text{velocity of C} - \text{velocity of D} \\ &= v_C - v_D \\ &= v_C + (v_{D\,rev}) \\ &= v_C + (-v_D) \\ &= +30 + (20) \\ &= 30 + 20 \\ &= +50\,\mathrm{m\,s^{-1}} \end{aligned}$$

velocity of D relative to C
$$\begin{aligned} &= \text{velocity of D} - \text{velocity of C} \\ &= v_D - v_C \\ &= v_D + (v_{C\,rev}) \\ &= v_D + (-v_C) \\ &= -20 + (-30) \\ &= -20 - 30 \\ &= -50\,\mathrm{m\,s^{-1}} \end{aligned}$$

The calculation shows that, seen from car D, the car C approaches from left to right (+) at 50 m s^{-1}. When viewed from car C the car D is observed to approach from right to left (−) at 50 m s^{-1}.

7.3 Parallel forces

Until now we have only considered forces or vectors acting in the same straight line. What happens when, for example, two parallel forces are not acting through the same point? Consider two equal and parallel forces of 5N acting in the same direction at either end of a light (theoretically weightless) rod of length l (Fig. 7.5a). It is not difficult to believe that a 10 N force acting at the centre of the rod will produce the same effect as the two 5 N forces. Fig. 7.5(b) shows the general case of two parallel forces F_1 and F_2 acting at either end of the rod. The two forces F_1 and F_2 cause the rod to accelerate downward *without* rotating. Therefore there must be a point P about which the two forces exert no resultant moment of a force (see p.96). Let P be a distance x from F_1 and a distance y

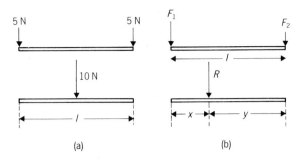

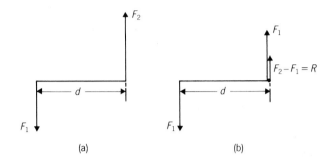

7.5   *Parallel forces not acting in the same straight line*

7.6   *Couples*

from F_2 ($x + y = l$). Hence $+ F_1 x - F_2 y = 0$, i.e. $F_1 x = F_2 y$. This point P is the point where a single force $R = |F_1 + F_2|$ can be exerted, which causes no resultant moment of force about P and so makes the rod accelerate downwards without rotating.

Couples

If two unequal and opposite parallel forces are not acting in the same straight line a resultant force must exist and therefore the object on which they act cannot be in equilibrium. In Fig. 7.6 the two forces F_1 and F_2 act in opposite directions at a distance d apart.

If $F_1 = F_2$ numerically, then R, the resultant force, is given by
$$\begin{aligned} R &= +F_2 + (-F_1) \\ &= F_2 - F_1 \\ &= 0 \end{aligned}$$

(where + means upward). These two equal parallel forces constitute a **couple** which provides a torque of $F_1 \times d$ or $F_2 \times d$ so that the object rotates (spins) at the position shown. The object does not translate (move sideways) because there is no resultant force: the spin is due to the resultant couple.

If F_2 is numerically greater than F_1 (Fig. 7.6b), then
$$\begin{aligned} R &= +F_2 + (-F_1) \\ &= +F_2 - F_1 \end{aligned}$$

so the object moves upwards (+). At the same time it rotates with a torque of $F_1 \times d$. Thus we can think of F_2 as $+ (+ F_1) + (+ R)$, i.e. the two forces F_1 and F_2 can be divided into two equal and opposite forces F_1 which combine to give a couple whose torque is $F_1 d$, and a resultant force R which accelerates the spinning object upwards.

7.4 The parallelogram of forces

When two given forces are not acting in the same straight line, nor are parallel to each other, they must be acting at some angle to each other. If the object they act on does not break apart it cannot move in two different directions at once! Therefore the object will move in some direction between the two lines of the forces. To find the resultant force R and the direction in which it acts we use the **parallelogram of forces** rule. This rule states that 'if two forces F_1 and F_2, acting at a point, are represented to scale in both magnitude and direction by the two adjacent sides of a parallelogram, then the diagonal from their point of intersection to the opposite corner of the parallelogram represents the resultant force R in both magnitude and direction'.

In Fig. 7.9(a) the length of the line OA represents the magnitude of the force F_1, acting at a point O in the direction OA, i.e. at an angle θ to the direction of the force F_2. Likewise OB represents the magnitude and direction of the force F_2 also acting at O. By drawing AC parallel to OB and BC parallel to OA the parallelogram OACB can be constructed with F_1 and F_2 as adjacent sides. The diagonal from O to the

---

Investigation 7.1 To verify the parallelogram of forces rule

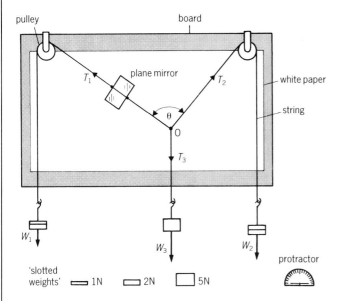

pulley, board, plane mirror, white paper, string

7.7 To verify the Parallelogram of Forces Rule

Set up the board with white paper, pulleys and weights as shown in Fig. 7.7. Slotted iron masses and the hanger have been adjusted so that the pull of the earth on them is 1 N, 2 N, 5 N, 10 N or 20 N. These act as the standard weights W_1, W_2 and W_3 which exert tensions of T_1, T_2 and T_3 in each of the parts of the string shown in the figure. Note that the resultant force R of T_1 and T_2 would cause the piece of string at O to accelerate upwards and an equilibrant force T_3 is applied at O to prevent this. The resultant R and T_3 are therefore equal in size and act in opposite directions through the point O. Hang suitable weights W_1, W_2 and W_3 from the string and allow them to settle in their equilibrium position. Measure the angle θ between the two forces T_1 and T_2 using a protractor.

An accurate method of marking the lines of the string on the paper attached to the board is as follows:

1 Place a plane mirror on the paper behind the string. View the string and its image in the mirror with one eye, positioning the eye so that the string covers its own image as seen in the mirror.

2 Mark two pencil dots on the paper, one on each side of the mirror, so that these dots also appear to be hidden by the string.
3 Repeat the procedure for the other inclined string.
4 Join up the two pairs of dots with straight lines.

The angle θ can easily be measured with the protractor.

Vary the values of W_1, W_2 and W_3 and obtain the appropriate value of θ in each case. Record the results in a table similar to Table 7.1. For each set of results in the table draw a scale diagram similar to Fig. 7.8 to determine the resultant force R. The scale drawing could be drawn on graph paper to increase its accuracy.

Table 7.1 Table of results for investigation 7.1

Force T_1/N	Force T_2/N	Angle θ/°	Resultant R/N	Angle α/°	Equilibrant T_3/N
3	4	90			5

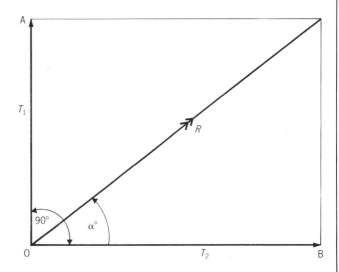

7.8 Finding the resultant force by scale drawing

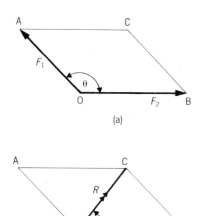

7.9   Parallelogram of forces

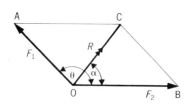

7.10   Either R acting at α or forces F₁ and F₂ acting at θ

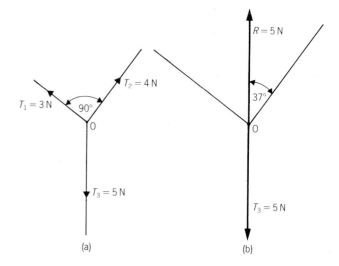

7.11   Three forces in equilibrium

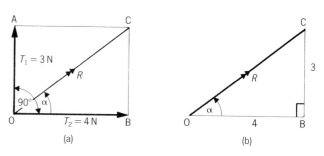

7.12   Finding the resultant force using trigonometry

opposite corner C of the parallelogram represents the resultant force R in magnitude and direction. Figure 7.9(b) shows an identical parallelogram with the resultant $R = OC$ marked in. Since the resultant force R is the single force which replaces the two given forces F_1 and F_2 it should strictly not be shown on the *same* diagram as F_1 and F_2. However, to save space and time F_1, F_2 and R are often shown on the same diagram (as in Fig. 7.10). If you use this shorthand method you must clearly understand that the diagram represents either R or F_1 plus F_2 but *not both*. Never read this diagram as showing three forces — unfortunately, a common mistake.

Using the set of example results shown in Table 7.1, the resultant R in Fig. 7.8 is calculated as follows:

1 Choose a suitable scale (as large as possible), e.g. 1 N ≡ 2 cm.
2 Draw two lines at an angle $θ$ to each other (here $θ ≡ 90°$.
3 Mark off on OA a length of 6 cm ≡ 3 N and on OB a length of 8 cm ≡ 4 N.
4 Complete the parallelogram (here a rectangle) with OA and OB as adjacent sides.
5 Join O to C and measure the length of OC = 10 cm ≡ 5 N; therefore $R = 5$ N.

6 Use a protractor to measure the angle $α$ that R makes with T_2, $α = 37°$.

The resultant force R is a force of 5 N acting at an angle of 37° to the force T_2. Figure 7.11 shows the forces acting when point O is at rest, i.e. the forces T_1, T_2 and T_3 are in equilibrium.

The two forces 3 N and 4 N in Fig. 7.11(a) can be replaced by a single force of 5 N at 37° to the 4 N force, i.e. vertically upwards as in Fig. 7.11(b). The resultant force R and T_3 are in equilibrium, therefore they are exactly equal in magnitude and opposite in direction and both pass through point O. The value of R from calculated T_1 and T_2 should be equal in magnitude to T_3.

This special case of two forces acting at right angles to each other has been chosen because at this level it is the most likely example to occur in calculations and problems. It is also possible to apply simple trigonometry to the solution using a sketch diagram instead of a scale drawing. (Of course, the sine and cosine rules can be applied to the general parallelogram case but this will not be covered in this book.) In Fig. 7.12 CB = AO = 3 N. Applying Pythagoras' Theorem to triangle OBC (Fig. 7.12b) gives $R^2 = 3^2 + 4^2$, $R^2 = 25$, hence $R ≡ 5$ N. The angle $α$ can be calculated from $\tan α = \frac{3}{4} = 0.75$, i.e. $α = 36°52'$.

7.5 Resolution of vectors

Clearly if two forces can be replaced by a single resultant force, then a single force can be 'split' into two forces acting at some appropriate angle between them. If, as is often convenient, the angle between these two **component forces** is 90°, the procedure is known as **resolving a force into two components at right angles**.

Example

A 10 N force acting at an angle $\alpha = 60°$ to the horizontal can be resolved into two components at right angles, e.g. a horizontal component and a vertical component.

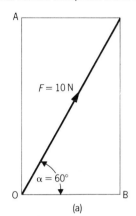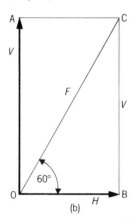

7.13 Resolution of a force into two components at right angles

Figure 7.13(a) shows a sketch diagram of the force $F = 10$ N at 60° to the horizontal and Fig. 7.13(b) the two components V and H, resolved in the vertical and horizontal directions respectively. The triangle OBC enables the values of V and H to be calculated using trigonometry.

$$\sin \alpha = V/F$$
$$F \sin \alpha = V$$
$$V = 10 \sin 60$$
$$V = 10 \times 0.8660$$
$$V = 8.66 \text{ N}$$
$$\cos \alpha = H/F$$
$$F \cos \alpha = H$$
$$H = 10 \cos 60$$
$$H = 10 \times 0.50$$
$$H = 5.0 \text{ N}$$

A useful aid to calculating components is to remember that the component which makes the angle α with the force F to be resolved is always $F \cos \alpha$, i.e. the value of the force to be resolved times the cosine of the angle between the force and the component. Then the 'other' component will be $F \sin \alpha$.

A force can be resolved into two components by using a scale drawing. Begin by drawing the given single force and then construct the four-sided figure which has this line as a diagonal.

Exercise 7.1

Draw a scale diagram of a 10 N force at 60° to the horizontal and show that its vertical and horizontal components are 8.7 N and 5.0 N respectively.

Example

A boy pulls a friend sitting in a home-made trolley by means of a rope inclined at 30° to the horizontal (Fig. 7.14). If the tension T in the rope is 200 N, find (a) the effective force pulling the trolley along; (b) the force tending to lift the trolley off the ground.

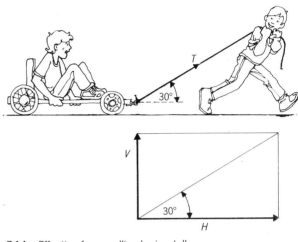

7.14 Effective force pulling horizontally

Resolving the force $T = 200$ N into its horizontal component H and its vertical component V:

$$H = T \cos 30$$
$$H = 200 \cos 30$$
$$H = 173 \text{ N}$$
$$V = T \sin 30$$
$$V = 200 \sin 30$$
$$V = 100 \text{ N}$$

7.6 Projectiles

If a body is projected with velocity v at an angle α to the horizontal, then the velocity can, like the force F in Fig. 7.13, be resolved into two components at right angles, i.e. a vertical component $V = v \sin \alpha$ and a horizontal component $H = v \cos \alpha$. The horizontal component is at right angles to the direction of the acceleration of free fall and so will be unaffected by the acceleration of free fall. If the effect of air resistance is neglected, the horizontal component remains constant throughout the flight of the body. The vertical component is subject to the acceleration of free fall. When solving problems involving **projectiles**, you should deal with each component separately, as illustrated in the worked example below.

Example

A golf ball is struck from a tee with a velocity of 40 m s^{-1} at an angle of 30° to the horizontal (Fig. 7.15). Find (a) its time of flight; (b) the horizontal distance it travels.

Resolve the velocity of projection into its vertical and horizontal components:

$$\text{vertical component} = v\sin 30$$
$$= 40 \times 0.5$$
$$= 20\,\text{m s}^{-1}$$
$$\text{horizontal component} = v\cos 30$$
$$= 40 \times 0.8660$$
$$= 34.64\,\text{m s}^{-1}$$

Treating each component separately:

(a) The vertical motion consists of an initial upward velocity of 20 m s^{-1}; and the flight is complete when the displacement of the ball is zero.

$$u = +20\,\text{m s}^{-1} \quad s = 0\,\text{m} \quad a = -10\,\text{m s}^{-2} \quad t = ?\,\text{s}$$
$$s = ut + \tfrac{1}{2}at^2$$
$$0 = 20t + \tfrac{1}{2}(-10)t^2$$
$$0 = 20t - 5t^2$$
$$0 = 5t(4 - t)$$
$$t = 0\,\text{s (at the start) or } t = 4\,\text{s}$$

Therefore the time of flight is 4 s.

(b) Horizontal motion is constant (neglecting air resistance). The ball moves horizontally at 34.64 m s^{-1} for 4 s.

$$\text{horizontal distance travelled}$$
$$= \text{velocity} \times \text{time}$$
$$= 34.64\,\text{m s}^{-1} \times 4\,\text{s}$$
$$= 138.56\,\text{m}$$

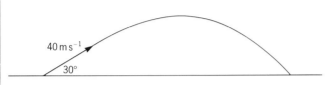

40 m s^{-1}

30°

7.15   *Parabolic path of a projectile (golf ball)*

Note   It can be shown that the vertical and horizontal velocities of the ball at the end of its flight are −20 m s^{-1} and +34.64 m s^{-1} respectively. This gives the resultant velocity of the ball as it strikes the ground as 40 m s^{-1} at 30° to the ground. The path of the ball is a curve (a parabola) symmetrical about a vertical line through the mid-point of its horizontal range. It is also of interest to note that the time the ball takes to reach its highest point is half the time of flight.

Example

The muzzle velocity of a rifle bullet is 400 m s^{-1}. If the rifle is held horizontally at a height of 1.25 m above the ground, find the horizontal distance travelled by the bullet before it hits the ground.

The bullet has two independent components of velocity:
(a) a constant horizontal velocity of 400 m s^{-1}; (b) a variable (increasing) vertical velocity starting at $u = 0$. The initial vertical height (1.25 m) and the acceleration of free fall (10 m s^{-2}) determine the time the bullet takes to reach the ground.

$$u = 0\,\text{m s}^{-1} \quad s = 1.25\,\text{m} \quad t = ?\,\text{s} \quad a = 10\,\text{m s}^{-2}$$
$$s = ut + \tfrac{1}{2}at^2$$
$$1.25 = 0 + \tfrac{1}{2} \times 10t^2$$
$$1.25 = 5t^2$$
$$0.25 = t^2$$
$$t = 0.5\,\text{s}$$

$$\text{horizontal distance travelled}$$
$$= \text{horizontal velocity} \times \text{time}$$
$$= 400\,\text{m s}^{-1} \times 0.5\,\text{s}$$
$$= 200\,\text{m}$$

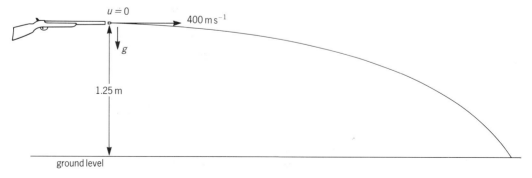

$u = 0$

400 m s^{-1}

g

1.25 m

ground level

7.16   *Parabolic path of a projectile with no initial vertical velocity*

Example

Two tugs tow a boat into harbour. Each tug exerts a force of 5000 N at an angle of 30° to the direction in which the boat moves (Fig. 7.17). Calculate, by scale diagram or otherwise, the resultant force pulling the boat forward.

Choose a suitable scale, e.g. 1000 N ≡ 1 cm, hence 5000 N ≡ 5 cm; draw lines OA and OB at 30° on either side of a horizontal 'line' and mark off lengths of 5 cm on each line. Complete the parallelogram 'around' OA and OB (see Fig. 7.18) and measure the length of the diagonal OC.

OC = 8.7 cm, therefore R = 8700 N at 30° to OB.

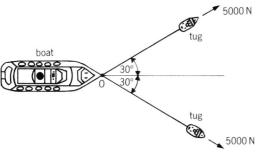

7.17   Resultant force of two tugs on a boat

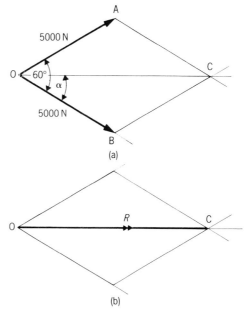

7.18   Resultant force on the boat found by scale drawing

Exercise 7.2

Resolve the two forces OA and OB into two components along and at right angles to the line OC.

Example

A magnetic compass needle is subjected to a force of 0.02 N acting north and a force of 0.04 N acting east (Fig. 7.19).

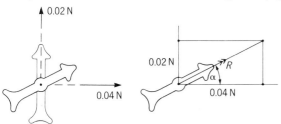

7.19   Deflection of a magnetic compass needle

Calculate the resultant force on the needle and the direction in which it sets.

$$R^2 = 0.02^2 + 0.04^2$$
$$R^2 = 0.0004 + 0.0016$$
$$R^2 = 0.0020$$
$$R = 0.0447 \text{ N}$$

$$\tan \alpha = BC/OC$$
$$= 0.02 \cancel{N}/0.04 \cancel{N}$$
$$\tan \alpha = 0.5$$
$$\alpha = 26° 34' \text{ north of east}$$

The resultant force of 0.0447 N sets the needle in the direction N 63° 26′ E.

Example

(a) A block of metal of weight 80 N rests on a rough plane which is inclined at 30° to the horizontal (Fig. 7.20a). Explain how the block is able to remain at rest.

Resolve the vertical force W into two components at right angles to each other; for ease of working make one perpendicular to the slope and the other parallel to the slope (Fig. 7.20b).

$$\cos 30 = F_1/W$$
$$W \cos 30 = F_1$$
$$80 \times 0.8660 = F_1$$
$$69.28 \text{ N} = F_1$$
$$\sin 30 = F_2/W$$
$$W \sin 30 = F_2$$
$$80 \times 0.50 = F_2$$
$$40 \text{ N} = F_2$$

continued ⌐

Example *Continued*

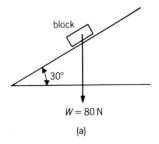

(a)

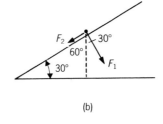

(b)

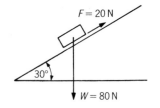

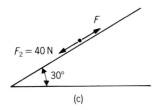

(c)

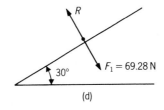

(d)

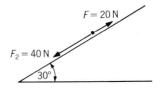

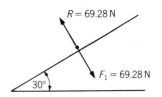

7.20 Forces on a block at rest on an inclined plane

Since the block does not slide down the plane there must be zero unbalanced force acting *along* the plane. Therefore a frictional force F must act up the plane (fig. 7.20c). As the two forces F_2 and F act in the same straight line, $F - F_2 = 0$, i.e. $F - 40 \text{ N} = 0$. Hence the frictional force F must have a value of 40 N acting parallel to and up the plane. Because the block does not fall through the plane, there must be zero unbalanced force acting perpendicular to the plane. Figure 7.20(d) shows the normal reaction R which is the push of the plane on the block caused by the action of force F_1 pushing on the plane (see Newton's Third Law of Motion, p.76). Thus $R - F_1 = 0$, i.e. $R - 69.28 \text{ N} = 0$ and so $R = 69.28 \text{ N}$.

Note The reaction R is always normal (perpendicular) to the plane and is directed away from the plane.

(b) The 80 N block (mass 8 kg) in part (a) above is transferred to a less rough inclined plane which is also inclined at 30° to the horizontal. Describe what happens to the block when it is placed at the top of the slope if the frictional force is now 20 N (Fig. 7.21).

As before the resolved components of W give a force $F_2 = 40 \text{ N}$ acting down the slope and $F_1 = 69.28 \text{ N}$ acting perpendicular to and into the slope. F_1 is balanced by the normal reaction $R = 69.28 \text{ N}$ acting perpendicular to and away from the slope. Since the block does not lift off or fall through the plane, $R - F_1 = 0$. However, the forces parallel to the plane have a resultant force $P \equiv F - F_2 = (20 - 40) \text{ N} = -20 \text{ N}$ that acts down the plane. This unbalanced resultant force causes the block to accelerate down the slope.

$$P = -20 \text{ N} \quad m = 8 \text{ kg} \quad a = ?$$
$$P = ma$$
$$-20 \text{ N} = 8 \text{ kg} \times a$$
$$-20 \text{ N}/8 \text{ kg} = a$$
$$a = -2.5 \text{ m s}^{-2}$$

7.21 Motion of a block down an inclined plane

(c) What force is required to keep the block at rest on a *smooth* plane inclined at 30° to the horizontal (Fig. 7.22).

Note If the term **smooth** is used you should assume that the frictional force F is zero.

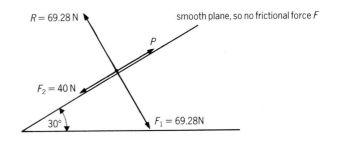

7.22 Motion of a block down a smooth inclined plane

As before, F_1 and R are both 69.28 N, and act in opposite directions, so there is no resultant force perpendicular to the plane. If P is the force required to keep the block from sliding down the plane

$$P - F_2 = 0$$
$$P - 40 \text{ N} = 0$$
$$P = +40 \text{ N}$$

A force of 40 N acting parallel to and up the plane keeps the block from sliding down a smooth plane.

Example

A straight river 240 m wide flows at a rate of 1.5 m s^{-1}. A man who can row at 2.5 m s^{-1} in still water wants to cross the river in the shortest possible time. In which direction must he row and how long does he take to cross?

For the shortest crossing the resultant velocity of the boat should be in a direction straight across the river. However, if the man rows in this direction the current will carry him downstream making the journey longer. He must instead 'head' the boat upstream in such a way that the resultant velocity of the boat and the stream acts perpendicular to the bank (see Fig. 7.23b).

In triangle OAC, AC $= 2.5$ m s^{-1} OA $= 1.5$ m s^{-1} OC = ?

$$AC^2 = OA^2 + OC^2$$
$$2.5^2 = 1.5^2 + OC^2$$
$$2.5^2 - 1.5^2 = OC^2$$
$$4.0 = OC^2$$
$$2 \text{ m s}^{-1} = OC$$
$$\tan \alpha = 2/1.5$$
$$\tan \alpha = 0.75$$
$$\alpha = 53°$$

Hence the man must row upstream at an angle of 53° to the bank so that his effective velocity is 2 m s^{-1} in a direction perpendicular to the bank.

$$s = 240 \text{ m} \quad v = 2 \text{ m s}^{-1} \quad t = ?$$

$$s = vt$$
$$240 \text{ m} = 2 \text{ m s}^{-1} \times t$$
$$240 \text{ m}/2 \text{ m s}^{-1} = t$$
$$120 \text{ s} = t$$

To cross the river, the man must row for 2 minutes.

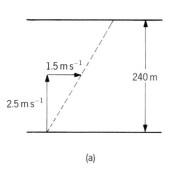

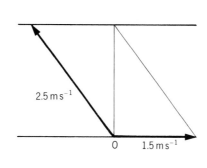

(a)

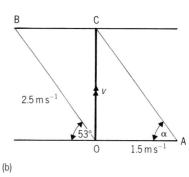

(b)

7.23   Resultant velocity of rower across a river

Questions

Questions 1–3 The following are five quantities which are related to forces:

A   component
B   direction
C   magnitude
D   moment
E   resultant

Which one of these
Q1   implies that more than one force is acting?
Q2   is measured in newton metre?
Q3   for a force of 10 N, might have a value anywhere between 0 N and 10 N?   *(L)*
Q4   A physical quantity which has direction as well as magnitude is known as a
   A force **B** mass **C** scalar **D** vector **E** weight.   *(L)*
Q5   Which of the following is **not** a scalar quantity?
   A mass **B** energy **C** power **D** velocity **E** work
Q6   Which of the following is **not** a vector quantity?
   A displacement **B** density **C** force **D** acceleration
   E momentum

Q7   A couple is defined as any two parallel, coplanar forces which are
   A equal, opposite and acting in the same straight line.
   B equal, opposite and not acting in the same straight line.
   C equal and both acting in the same straight line.
   D unequal and not acting in the same straight line.
   E unequal and acting in the same straight line.
Q8   Two forces act on a block of mass *M*. Which arrangement gives the block the greatest acceleration?

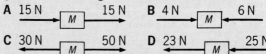

   (SEG)
Q9   Two forces of magnitude 8 N and 6 N act on the same body. The angle between the directions of the forces is 90°. The magnitude of the resultant of the forces will be
   A 7 N **B** 10 N **C** 14 N **D** 24 N **E** 48 N   *(L)*
Q10   A body is in equilibrium under the action of three forces. One force is 6.0 N acting due East and one is 3.0 N in a direction 60° North of East. What is the magnitude and direction of the third force?   *(O & C, part question)*

Q11 Why is *force* referred to as a vector quantity?

Two forces acting at a point have magnitudes 5 N and 8 N. Explain why their resultant may have any magnitude between 3 N and 13 N.

Forces of 7.0 N and 11.0 N act at a point so that the angle between their lines of action is 35°. By means of a scale diagram, determine the magnitude of the resultant of these two forces.

Describe an experiment which demonstrates that the application of a force to a mass produces an acceleration.

A resultant force of 50 N acts on a mass 4.0 kg. Calculate the acceleration produced. *(C)*

Q12

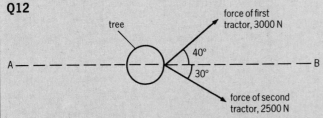

The diagram shows the horizontal forces exerted on a tree by two tractors in an attempt to pull it out of the ground.

(a) Draw a diagram to a stated scale and use it to determine the magnitude and direction of the resultant force exerted on the tree by the two tractors.

(b) Once pulled out of the ground the tree is dragged away at constant speed by a steady force. Explain why a force is necessary to maintain a constant speed.

(c) Finally the tree trunk of mass 4000 kg is dropped into a fast-moving river. Assuming the water exerts a resultant force of 1440 N on the trunk in the direction of the flow of the water, calculate the initial acceleration of the trunk in this direction. *(C)*

Q13 (a) State, with a brief explanation, whether it is possible, given forces of 3 N and 8 N, to produce a resultant force of (i) 5 N, (ii) 15 N, (iii) 8 N.

(b) An elephant is dragging a tree trunk along a horizontal surface by means of an attached rope which makes an angle of 30° with the horizontal. The tension in the rope is 4000 N.

   (i) By scale drawing, or otherwise, determine the horizontal force exerted by the rope on the tree trunk.

   (ii) Determine also the vertical component of the force exerted by the rope on the tree trunk. Explain why it serves a useful purpose.

   (iii) Name the other forces which act on the tree trunk and show clearly the directions in which they act. *(L)*

Q14 A large stone, mass 2.0 kg, is projected horizontally at 40 m s^{-1} from the top of a cliff over the sea and hits the water after 4.0 s.

(a) Taking the acceleration of free fall as 10 m s^{-2}, calculate

   (i) the vertical velocity of the stone just before it hits the water,

(ii) the height of the cliff-top above the sea.

(b) The *rate* at which the stone loses potential energy increases as the stone nears the water. Why is this?

(c) Determine, by means of a scale diagram or otherwise, the direction in which the stone is moving just before it hits the water.

(d) On hitting the water, the stone slows down. State, with a reason, what happens to the kinetic energy it loses. *(C)*

Q15 What do you understand by a *vector quantity*? Which of the following are vectors: mass, momentum, speed, energy, velocity, acceleration?

Explain how a vector can be resolved into two components at right angles to one another.

A trolley of mass 1 kg is placed on a long smooth plane which is inclined at an angle θ to the horizontal where sin θ = $\frac{1}{20}$. It is then released.

(a) What is the component of the weight, acting parallel to the plane?

(b) Find the acceleration of the trolley.

(c) Find the kinetic energy and the momentum of the trolley after it has travelled a distance of 2 metres from rest along the plane. *(O)*

Q16 A man who swims at 2 m s^{-1} relative to the water sets out at right-angles to the bank of a river 12 m wide. The river is flowing at 1.5 m s^{-1} so that it carries him downstream as he swims.

(a) How long would the crossing take in still water?

(b) How long does the crossing take in moving water? Explain.

(c) How far downstream does he land?

(d) What is his speed relative to the bank?

(e) Show on a scale diagram the direction in which he should set out to be able to reach the point on the far bank which is directly opposite his starting point. *(O)*

Q17 (a) Describe an experiment to show that, for a projectile, the horizontal and vertical components of its velocity are independent of each other. Your answer should include

   (i) a labelled diagram of the experimental arrangement,

   (ii) an account of the measurements and/or observations you would make,

   (iii) an explanation of how you would use these measurements and/or observations to show the independence of the two components of velocity.

(b) (i) An object is thrown horizontally with a velocity of 15 m s^{-1} from the top of a cliff. If the acceleration of free fall (due to gravity) is 10 m s^{-1}, calculate the vertical component of its velocity after it has fallen a vertical distance of 20 m. Assume that the effect of friction is negligibly small.

   (ii) Show clearly on a diagram, the size and direction of the horizontal and vertical components of the object's velocity at this point.

(JMB part question)

94

8 Turning forces

8.1 A turning effect

A carpenter has a door waiting to be hung in its frame. The door is firmly fixed on a flat trolley (see Fig. 8.1a). If he pulls with a force F on the door handle, the door and the trolley will move towards him under the action of an unbalanced force. However, if he pulls on the handle after he has hung the door, it will rotate about its hinges (Fig. 8.1b). As the whole door does not move (as it did in Fig. 8.1a) there can no longer be an unbalanced force acting on it. In fact, the two forces r of the door acting at the hinges, and therefore their reaction force $R = 2r$, are equal and opposite to the pulling force F. Thus, two equal, parallel forces acting in opposite directions but not acting at the **same** point will form a couple (see p.86) and so produce rotation, i.e. a turning effect.

Note Two equal and opposite forces acting in the same straight line cancel out: they produce zero unbalanced force and hence no movement.

Two other examples of the turning effect of two equal and opposite forces not acting in the same straight line are the steering wheel of a car and the pedals of a bicycle. In Fig. 8.2(a) the left hand is pulling with force F on the steering wheel while the right hand is pushing. The two forces make the wheel turn in an anticlockwise direction. In Fig. 8.2(b) one pedal is being pushed forward while the other is being pushed back. This rotates the sprocket wheel and the attached chain anticlockwise. Can you think of other everyday examples in which a turning effect or rotation takes place?

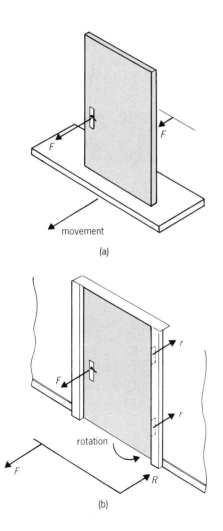

8.1 Movement and rotation

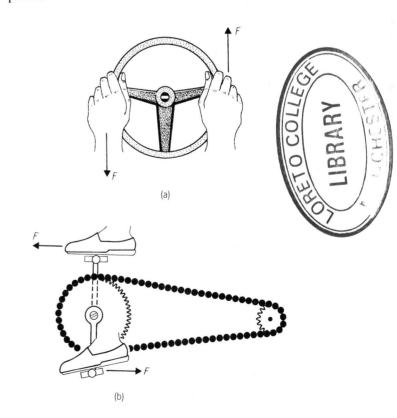

8.2 Rotating forces: couples

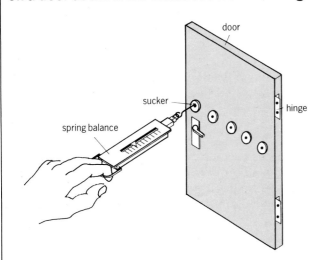
This investigation shows that the force varies with the distance from the hinges for a given rotating effect. In general, **if a force F acts at a point A on a body which is fixed at a point P, there is a turning effect about the point P.**

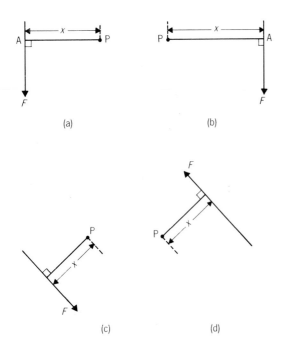

8.4   Moment of force about a point $M = Fx$

8.2   Moment of a force about a point

A **moment of a force** about a point is the product of the force F and the **perpendicular** distance from the point to the line of action of the force. In Fig. 8.4 the moment of a force M about the point P is given by Fx. The moment of the force produces a turning effect (rotation) about the point P. This rotation will be anticlockwise in Figs 8.4(a) and (c) and clockwise in Figs 8.4(b) and (d). The SI unit of moment of a force is the newton metre (N m) as the force is measured in newton (N) and the distance in metre (m). However, in practice it is often convenient to use the non-SI units N cm, i.e. measure the force in N and the distance in cm. Some method of indicating anticlockwise and clockwise rotation should be used. This is usually done by giving a plus sign (+) to anticlockwise moments of force and a negative sign (−) to clockwise moments of a force. In reality, rotation is caused by two equal and opposite parallel forces *not* acting at the same point (in Fig. 8.4 an equal and opposite reaction force should have been shown at P). The pair of equal forces is known as a **couple** and the turning effect produced is called a **torque**. To calculate the torque (moment of a couple) T, take moments of the forces about any point (see Fig. 8.5).

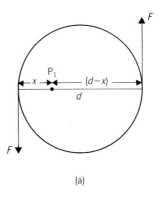

(a)

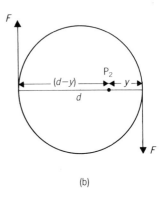

(b)

8.5   Torque or moment of a couple

(a) Taking moments of forces about P_1:
$$\text{total moments} = + Fx + F(d - x)$$
$$= + Fx + Fd - Fx$$
$$= + Fd$$
(+ indicates anticlockwise rotation)
(b) Taking moments of forces about P_2:
$$\text{total moments} = - Fy - F(d - y)$$
$$= - Fy - Fd + Fy$$
$$= - Fd$$
(− indicates clockwise rotation)

In both cases the magnitude of the torque T is found to be the product of *one* of the forces and the perpendicular distance between them, and is independent of the point P. Hence it was possible to use the single force F and the distance x when calculating the turning effects in Fig. 8.4. (All rotation is really due to an unbalanced couple acting on a system but at this level, where mainly parallel forces are being considered, it is simpler to deal with moments of forces about a point.)

Figure 8.6 shows a metre rule of weight 1 N balanced on a knife-edge. The forces acting on the rule must be in equilibrium, i.e. the pull of the Earth on the rule — its weight W — must have an equal and opposite force R – the push of the pivot on the rule — to prevent the rule falling to the ground. Also, since the rule is not rotating about P, the two equal and opposite forces must pass through the same point. Therefore there is no moment of a force about P. Note that a force acting through the point about which its moment is being taken exerts no turning effect, i.e. it has no moment of a force about that point. This is so because

the distance between the point and the line of action of the force is zero, that is, $x = 0$ hence $M = Fx = F \times 0 = 0$. If a 2 N force F is applied at P as in Fig. 8.7, the reaction force R_1 becomes 3 N, equal and opposite to the total downward force of $F + W = 3$ N. As before, no rotation takes place. If, however, the force F is applied, say, 10 cm to the left of P (Fig. 8.8a), the rule immediately tilts downwards at the left, i.e. it rotates anticlockwise. The weight W and the W-force from R_1 cancel leaving F and the F-force from R_1 to form a couple with a torque $T = Fx$. More simply, the moment of the force F about P is Fx.

If the rule is re-balanced and the force F is applied at the left-hand end of the rule 50 cm from P, the rule rotates anticlockwise even more quickly than before. You should verify that R_1 combines with F and W so that the weight W is 'cancelled out' leaving a torque $T = Fy$ or a moment of a force about P of Fy.

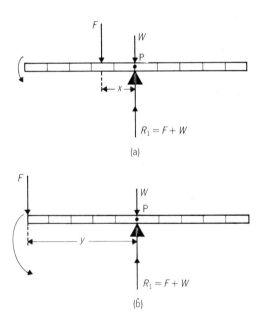

8.8 *Moment of a force varies with the distance of the force from the pivot*

This simple demonstration shows the importance of the distance between the force and the pivot P when dealing with moments of a force about P. Clearly a larger force F_1, say 5 N, applied at 10 cm and then at 50 cm to the left of P would produce a greater turning effect than the 2 N force F applied at the same points.

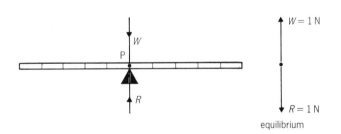

8.6 *A metre rule balanced on a knife-edge*

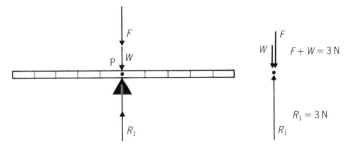

8.7 *Reaction force is equal and opposite to the action force*

Exercise 8.1

Draw diagrams similar to those in Fig. 8.8 to verify the above statement. If a 2 N force F is applied at 10 cm and at 50 cm to the *right* of the pivot P in Fig. 8.7, in what way will the moment of the force about P be similar to that shown and in what way will it be different?

A boy of weight 50 N and a girl of weight 40 N sit at opposite ends of a 2 m plank of wood of weight 20 N which rests on a log to form a see-saw (Fig. 8.9). The plank is of uniform thickness; its weight acts at the centre, and it is balanced on the log before the boy and girl sit on its ends. Clearly, when they are both on the plank the boy will tip down and the girl will rise up.

This example can be used to illustrate a typical calculation of moments of a force about a point. First draw a line to represent the plank. Above this line mark in the value and direction of all the forces acting on the plank, i.e. draw a free-body force diagram. Then mark all the distances below the line, as shown in Fig. 8.9(b). Next choose a suitable point about which to take moments; in this case the point P is used because the forces 20 N and 110 N do not exert any moment of force (turning effect) about P.

moments of the forces about P
$$= + 50 \text{ N} \times 1 \text{ m} + 20 \text{ N} \times 0 \text{ m} - 110 \text{ N} \times 0 \text{ m}$$
$$- 40 \text{ N} \times 1 \text{ m}$$
$$= + (50 - 40) \text{ N m}$$
$$= + 10 \text{ N m}$$

The plank rotates anticlockwise (+ sign) about P. This confirms that the boy goes down while the girl rises up.
Note The sign (+ or −) given to each moment of the forces about P is found by considering each force separately and deciding which type of rotation, anticlockwise (+) or clockwise (−) it would cause about the point P. Note also that since the forces 20 N and 110 N have no turning effect about P they have disappeared from the calculation. If you understand why this is so you could write the first line of the calculation more simply as

moments of forces about P
$$= + 50 \text{ N} \times 1 \text{ m} - 40 \text{ N} \times 1 \text{ m}$$

without affecting the final answer.

It is interesting to note the effect on the calculation if moments of the forces are taken about some other point, e.g. the end X.

moments of the forces about X
$$= + 50 \text{ N} \times 0 - 20 \text{ N} \times 1 \text{ m} + 110 \text{ N} \times 1 \text{ m}$$
$$- 40 \text{ N} \times 2 \text{ m}$$
$$= 0 - 20 + 110 - 80 \text{ N m}$$
$$= + 110 - 100 \text{ N m}$$
$$= + 10 \text{ N m}$$

This time the 20 N and 110 N forces do play a part in the calculation and it is the 50 N force which has no rotating effect about X. However the answer, + 10 N m, remains the same.

Exercise 8.2

Take moments of the forces about a point Y which is 1 m away from the right-hand end of the plank.

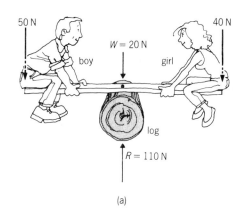

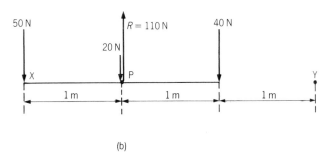

8.9 See-saw

This exercise should convince you that moments of a force can be taken about *any* point inside or outside the body without changing the resultant moment of the forces about that point (+10 N m in this example). There is also a 'best' point about which to take the moments of the forces. This point makes the calculation easiest; in the above example it is the point P. It is usually preferable to take moments of forces about the point through which any 'unknown' force acts (e.g. R in the above example). Remember that any force acting through a given point exerts no moment of a force (turning effect) about that point. Always try to take moments of forces about the point through which most of the forces act. This eliminates as many forces as possible from the calculation.

8.3 The Principle of Moments

To balance the see-saw the boy must move along the plank towards the log. To calculate exactly where he should sit for the plank to balance horizontally, draw a new diagram as in Fig. 8.10, and take moments of the forces about P.

moments of forces about P
$$= + 50 \text{ N} \times x \text{ m} + 20 \text{ N} \times 0 \text{ m} - 110 \text{ N} \times 0 \text{ m}$$
$$- 40 \text{ N} \times 1 \text{ m}$$
$$= 50 x - 40 \text{ N m}$$

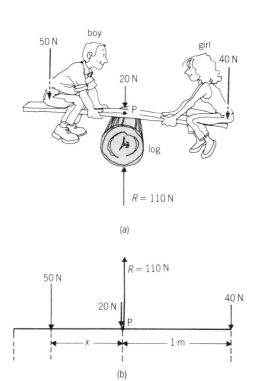

(a)

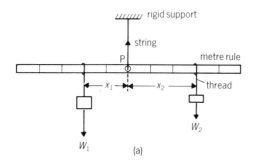

(b)

8.10   Balancing the see-saw

When the see-saw balances the resultant moment of the forces is zero (no rotation), so

$$0 = 50\,x - 40$$
$$40 = 50\,x$$
$$\frac{40}{50} = x$$

Hence x is 0.8 m from P.

This example illustrates the conditions for the equilibrium of a system of forces:

(a) the resultant force is zero ($R \equiv 50 + 20 + 40$ N); and

(b) the resultant moment of the forces about any point is zero.

The second condition is usually expressed as the Principle of Moments which states that **'for a body in equilibrium, the sum of the anticlockwise moments of force must equal the sum of the clockwise moments of force about any point.'**

Investigation 8.2   To verify the Principle of Moments

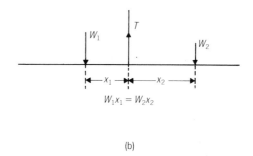

8.11   To verify the principle of moments

Support a metre rule with a hole drilled at its centre on a string tied to a rigid support (Fig. 8.11). If the rule does not balance horizontally add a small piece of plasticene to the 'raised' end to level the rule. Position a weight W_1 tied to a loop of thread on the left of the rule to an accuracy of 1 mm. Hang a second weight W_2 on the right of P and move the loop holding W_2 until the rule is once again balanced horizontally. Read and record the distances x_1 and x_2 from the metre rule itself. Then move the weights W_1 and W_2 to other positions and record the results as before. Calculate $+W_1 x_1$ and $-W_2 x_2$ (in N cm, for convenience)

Table 8.1   Table of results for investigation 8.2

W_1/N	x_1/cm	W_3/N	x_3/cm	$(W_1 x_1 + W_3 x_3)$/N cm

W_2/N	x_2/cm	W_4/N	x_4/cm	$(W_2 x_2 + W_4 x_4)$/N cm

— *continued* —

Investigation 8.2 *Continued*

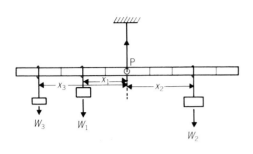

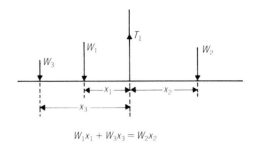

$$W_1 x_1 + W_3 x_3 = W_2 x_2$$

(a)

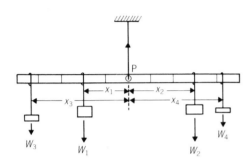

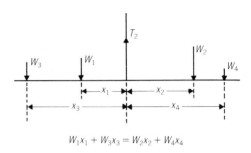

$$W_1 x_1 + W_3 x_3 = W_2 x_2 + W_4 x_4$$

(b)

8.12   Principle of moments using several forces

to show that $W_1 x_1$ is numerically equal to $W_2 x_2$, within the limits of experimental error. Using further weights W_3 and W_4 as shown in Fig. 8.12, you can show that at equilibrium $W_1 x_1 + W_3 x_3 = W_2 x_2$ (Fig. 8.12a) and $W_1 x_1 + W_3 x_3 = W_2 x_2 + W_4 x_4$ (Fig. 8.12b). By adjusting the positions of W_1, W_2, W_3 and W_4 take a series of

readings for the distances x_1, x_2, x_3 and x_4 and record them in a table of results similar to Table 8.1.

This calculation should show that, within the limits of experimental error, $W_1 x_1 + W_3 x_3 = W_2 x_2 + W_4 x_4$ when the rule is in equilibrium, and so it verifies the Principle of Moments.

The equation can also be expressed as
$$W_1 x_1 + W_3 x_3 - W_2 x_2 - W_4 x_4 = 0$$
i.e. the sum of the moments of the forces about a given point is zero when the rule is in equilibrium. In calculations and the solution of problems involving moments of a force about a point it is recommended

that the Principle of Moments is expressed in this alternative form.

Note It is sloppy and imprecise to write about 'moments' or even 'moments of a force'; the correct expression is 'moment of a force about point P' with the point P clearly labelled on the diagram.

Example

A painter of weight 330 N sets up two trestles and a 4 m plank of weight 60 N on which to stand while he paints a wall. Trestles A and B are placed 1 m from each end of the plank as in Fig. 8.13. He sets his can of paint, which weighs 20 N, 0.5 m from the left-hand end of the plank and he gradually works towards the right. How far to the right can he move before the plank just lifts from trestle A?

When the plank *just* lifts from trestle A then $R_1 = 0$ since there is no contact force. For equilibrium, the sum of the moments of

the forces about P must be zero. So, taking moments of the forces about P:

$$0 = + 20 \times 2.5 - R_1 \times 2 + 60 \times 1 - R_2 \times 0$$
$$- 330 \times x \qquad (R_1 = 0)$$
$$0 = + 50 + 60 - 330\,x$$
$$330x = 110$$
$$x = 110/330$$
$$x = \tfrac{1}{3}$$

The plank just lifts from trestle A when the painter stands $\tfrac{1}{3}$ m from P.

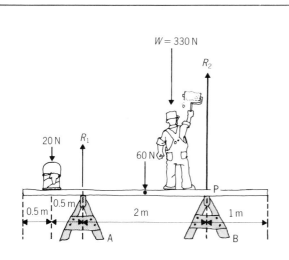

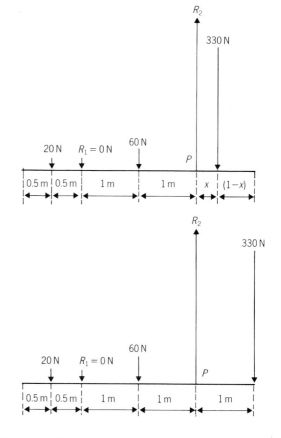

8.13   *A painter on a plank on two trestles*

What would happen if the painter stood on the right-hand end of the plank? The free-force body diagram is shown in Fig. 8.14. Taking moments of forces about P:

$$M = + 20 \times 2.5 - R_1 \times 2 + 60 \times 1 - R_2 \times 0$$
$$\qquad - 330 \times 1 \qquad\qquad\qquad (R_1 = 0)$$
$$M = 50 + 60 - 330$$
$$\quad = + 110 - 330$$
$$\quad = - 220 \text{ N m}$$

The resultant clockwise moment of force (-220 N m) means that the painter would tip the right-hand end of the plank downwards, throwing the can of paint up into the air.

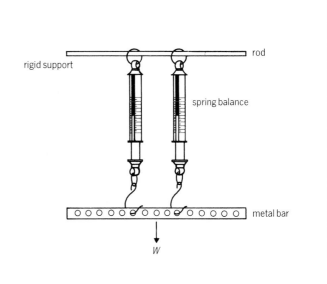

8.14   *Free-body force diagrams for the painter*

8.4   Equilibrium and the centre of gravity

Investigation 8.2   To investigate the equilibrium of parallel forces

Suspend two spring balances from a long metal rod and then attach a metal bar, with holes drilled at equal intervals, to the ends of the spring balances, as in Fig. 8.15. Vary the position of the rod and the distance between the spring balances, recording the readings on the balances for each position. Wherever the rod is placed the sum of the spring balance readings is equal to the weight W of the metal bar.

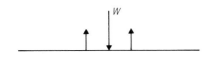

8.15   *Parallel forces*

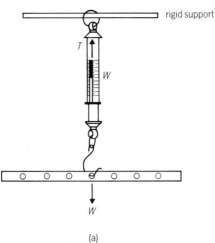

(a)

(b)

8.16   *The weight of a uniform bar acts at the mid-point*

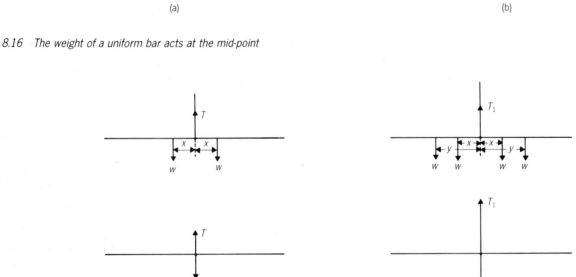

(a)

(b)

8.17   *Adding parallel forces*

For a uniform metal bar of weight W it is possible for

(a) the spring balances to record $W/2$ each;
(b) the spring balances to record unequal fractions of W;
(c) one balance to record W while the other records zero.

Even if extra weights are hung from the metal bar the readings will show that the sum of the upward forces is always equal to the sum of the downward forces and that the sum of the moments of force about any point is zero.

The special case in (c) above where one spring balance supports the bar in equilibrium deserves further investigation. There is only one point on the bar where the spring balance can hold the bar in equilibrium. Clearly only one force, the tension in the

spring of the balance, is being applied in an upward direction at the centre of the bar. For equilibrium, an equal and opposite force must also act at the same point. Thus it would *appear* that the whole weight W of the uniform metal bar acts through the mid-point of the bar. However, the weight is known to be distributed evenly along the length of the uniform bar. If two equal small weights w are hung from the bar so that they are equidistant from the centre (Fig. 8.16b), the bar remains in equilibrium and the spring balance records a total weight of $(W + 2w)$. The same effect is achieved if the two weights w are hung from the centre of the bar. Thus two equal parallel forces acting in the same direction have a resultant force which is equal to the sum of the forces and acts at a point mid-way between the forces. By adding more pairs of equal weights to the bar as in Fig. 8.17(b), the result is confirmed.

It should now be easy to understand why the total weight W of the metal bar in Fig. 8.16(a) is placed at the bar's centre in the diagram. Consider the metal bar to be made up of ten equal pieces each of weight w as shown in Fig. 8.18(a). By pairing up the forces on either side of the centre point P it is clear that the resultant force is $10w$, i.e. the weight W of the bar, acting at P. Each pair of forces will produce no turning effect because the moments of the forces about P will always balance. Figure 8.18(b) shows a free-body force diagram with the tension T in the spring equal and opposite to the weight W. Both T and W act at point P.

In the same way it is possible, for all bodies, to find a point through which the whole weight W of the body appears to act. This one point through which the total weight W of a body *appears* to act is known as the **centre of gravity of the body** and is usually labelled 'G' in diagrams. This is extremely useful when solving problems involving real objects with physical shape and hence distribution of weight throughout that shape. It is now possible to insert a force equal to the total weight W of the body at a point G, the centre of gravity of the body, and to ignore the shape and size of the body. The spring balance holding the metal bar in Fig. 8.18(a) can be reduced to the two vertical lines

representing T and W acting at the point P in Fig. 8.18(b). The horizontal line, which just represents the location of the bar, could be omitted. If, however, other external forces were acting on the bar the horizontal line would be a useful reference line on which to show how and where these forces act.

Now consider a *uniform* metre rule, i.e. one in which the mass is distributed evenly along its length. In Fig. 8.19(a) the rule is shown 'subdivided' into four equal numbered pieces, each of mass m. (**Note** It would be more rigorous to subdivide the rule into a very great number of very small pieces but four are enough to demonstrate the principle involved.) For the purpose of performing calculations in statics or dynamics the total mass M of the rule can be considered to act at a point P (see Fig. 8.19a), and this point is known as the **centre of mass**.

Figure 8.19(b) shows the pull of the Earth acting on each of the pieces m_1, m_2, m_3 and m_4, giving them weights w_1, w_2, w_3 and w_4 respectively. Provided the value of g is the same for each piece, then $w_1 = m_1 g = w_2 = w_3 = w_4$ and the resultant of these parallel forces is the weight W of the rule acting through the centre of gravity G, as before. Thus, provided g does not vary along the length of the rule, the centre of gravity G will coincide with the centre of mass P. This will generally be true for work at this level, but further study will reveal that it is not always the case. If the object is *very* large the value of g varies over its mass, hence the weight distribution is uneven for an equal distribution of mass. Therefore the position of the centre of gravity can differ from the position of the centre of mass. Variation in g is not required at this level, and so the position of the centre of mass and the centre of gravity will be identical.

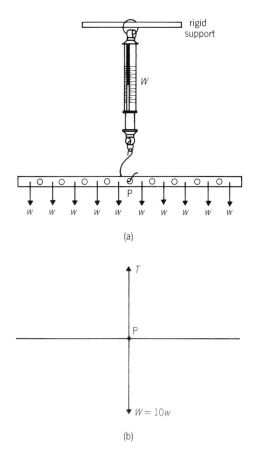

(a)

(b)

8.18   *The point of a body through which its whole weight acts*

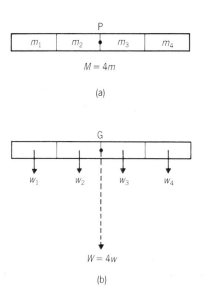

$M = 4m$

(a)

(b)

8.19   *Centre of mass of a uniform metre rule*

103

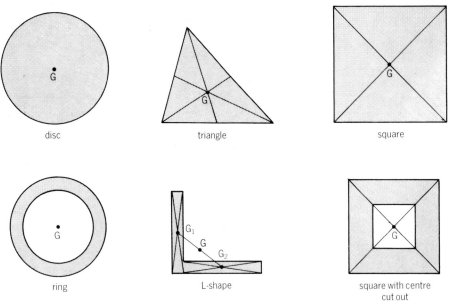

disc | triangle | square

ring | L-shape | square with centre cut out

8.20 *Centre of gravity of some regular shaped laminas*

Investigation 8.3 To find the centre of gravity of an irregular shaped lamina

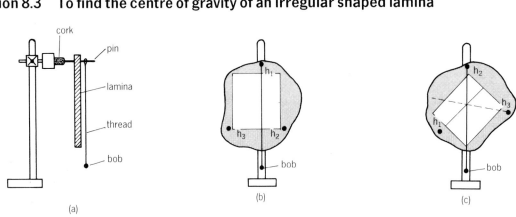

8.21 *To find the centre of gravity of an irregularly shaped lamina*

Cut an irregular shaped lamina from a thin sheet of any material of uniform thickness e.g. cardboard, plywood, plastic etc. Drill three holes (h_1, h_2 and h_3) in it near the edge and at approximately 120° to each other as measured from the 'centre' (see Fig. 8.21b). If the lamina is to be used more than once, cover most of the area between h_1, h_2 and h_3 by sticking on a piece of paper. Set up a pivot (a pin or a needle pushed through a cork held in a clampstand as in Fig. 8.21a) and hang the lamina on the pivot at hole h_1. Next suspend a plumbline (made from a metal bob tied to a length of thread) from the pivot (pin). Slightly displace the lamina and release it. Allow it to oscillate (swing) freely until it comes to rest. After it comes to rest, mark three pencil dots *directly* behind the thread of the vertical plumbline. Remove the plumbline and the lamina from the pivot and join the three pencil dots with a straight line. The centre of gravity G lies somewhere on this straight line.

Re-hang the lamina on the pivot from the hole h_2 and again attach the plumbline. Repeat the procedure as before to obtain a second straight line which will intersect the first line at G, the centre of gravity of the lamina. To ensure accuracy, suspend the lamina from the hole h_3 also. The third line should pass through the point of intersection of the first two lines. A simple test to confirm that G is the centre of gravity can be performed by balancing the lamina horizontally on the point of an upturned drawing pin placed at G as shown in Fig. 8.22.

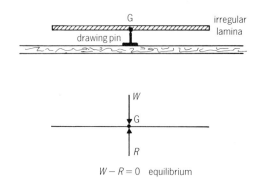

$W - R = 0$ equilibrium

8.22 *Balancing on a pin*

The centres of gravity (or centres of mass) of some regular shaped laminas are shown in Fig. 8.20. Note that G can be either inside the object or near the object. For this reason, it is incorrect to say that the centre of gravity is the point at which the object balances. The triangle, square and disc in Fig. 8.20 can all be balanced on a pin placed at their centre of gravity; however, the other three shapes cannot.

When the lamina is of irregular shape its centre of gravity cannot be found by drawing construction lines to locate G as in the example in Fig. 8.20. Therefore another technique must be used.

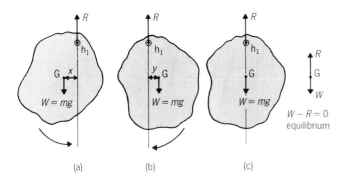

8.23   Equilibrium conditions for the lamina

Why is point G directly below the pivot when the lamina comes to rest after swinging to and fro? When the lamina is displaced to the left, as in Fig. 8.23(a), the weight W acting at G exerts a moment of force $M = +Wx$ about the pivot at h_1. This causes the lamina to swing down in an anticlockwise direction and its (angular) momentum carries it past the vertical position and the point G rises again. When G is to the right of the vertical line the weight W exerts a clockwise moment of force $(-Wy)$ about h_1, i.e. an opposing moment of force, which slows down the swinging lamina until it stops momentarily. Then the clockwise moment of force about h_1 causes the lamina to swing back from right to left (Fig. 8.23b). The lamina will overshoot the vertical line and the whole procedure will be repeated over and over again. As the lamina pushes through the air, the air exerts a drag or retarding force; there is also a frictional force at the pivot. These forces oppose the motion of the lamina; its kinetic energy is gradually reduced so that it slows down and finally stops. When the lamina is stationary it must have zero unbalanced force acting on it. Therefore the weight W must act in the same straight line as the reaction force R and these two forces must be equal in magnitude and opposite in direction. Hence the point G must lie somewhere on the vertical line through h_1.

Note   When the force W acts along a line which passes through G it cannot exert a turning effect about h_1.

8.5   Applications of moments of forces

Simple beam balance

The principle of a simple beam balance used to compare masses can be demonstrated with the apparatus in Investigation 8.4. Once again the rule is balanced horizontally on a pivot placed at its centre of gravity G. It is convenient to have G at the 50-centimetre mark and this can be arranged, if necessary, by 'loading' the rule with a small piece of plasticene. The object whose mass m_0 is required is placed at some point O to the right of G and its distance y from G is recorded in a table of results similar to Table 8.2. A known mass m is placed to the left of G and its distance from G is adjusted until the rule is balanced horizontally. The position X of the mass m is noted and the distance x is recorded. Applying the Principle of Moments gives

$$m_0 = mx/y$$

By varying the distance y and finding the corresponding distance x several values of m_0 can be calculated; from which the average value of m_0 can be found.

Table 8.2   Table of results for the demonstration of a beam balance

$GX = x$/cm	$OG = y$/cm	$m_0 = (mx/y)/g$

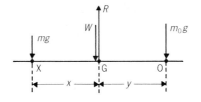

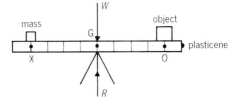

8.24   Principle of the beam balance

Investigation 8.4   Using the Principle of Moments to find the mass of a metre rule

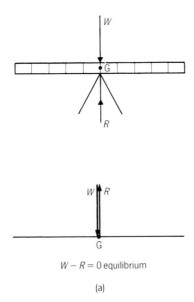

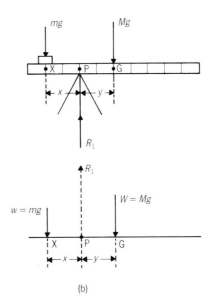

8.25   Finding the mass of a metre rule

Balance the metre rule horizontally on a knife-edge (Fig. 8.25a) and note the position of the centre of gravity G. Then move the pivot to a new position P, as in Fig. 8.25(b), and restore the balance of the rule by adding a known mass m at X. (A 100 g mass would be suitable.) Record the distances x and y.

Taking moments of the forces about P gives

$$mgx - Mgy = 0$$
$$m\!\!\!/gx = M\!\!\!/gy$$
$$M = mx/y$$

Note   The reaction R_1 at P exerts no turning effect about P.

By varying the distance y and finding the corresponding distance x several calculations of M can be made, from which the average value of M can be obtained. Record the results in a table similar to Table 8.3.

Note   Moments of *force* are involved here; the forces involved are the weight of the rule W and the force exerted on the rule by the mass m because of its weight w. Here $W = Mg$ and $w =$

mg and hence the value of g will cancel in the equation for the moments of the forces about P. Be careful to work either with the *mass* or the *weight* of the objects. Thus if the mass m of the metal is used the equation will give the mass M of the rule. However if the weight w in N of the metal is used the equation would be $W = wx/y$ in N, thus giving the weight W of the rule.

Table 8.3   **Table of results for investigation 8.4**

GP = y/cm	PY = x/cm	M = (mx/y)/g

Spinning and rotation

An interesting effect of a couple is the swerve that can be imparted to a ball in such games as football, cricket, tennis, table tennis and golf. To make a ball move in a straight line, the applied force F must act through the centre of gravity G of the ball, as in Fig. 8.26(a). To make a ball swerve the force F can be applied anywhere other than G. In Fig. 8.26(b) the force F is shown applied at the bottom edge of the ball. This has the effect of making the ball rotate anticlockwise and move forward. Hence the ball will 'curve' upwards. This can be explained by adding two imaginary forces of $+F$ and $-F$ acting at G (Fig. 8.26c). Since $+F$ and $-F$ cancel each other out, Fig. 8.26(c) is effectively the same as Fig. 8.26(b). However, $-F$ combined with the applied force F produces a couple whose torque

(moment of force about G) is $F \times r$ where r is the radius of the ball. The remaining imaginary force $+F$ at G is 'responsible' for the forward motion. As the ball spins through the air it receives lift and hence curves upwards.

Exercise 8.3

Draw diagrams and explain how
(a) a footballer can 'bend' the ball around a 'wall' from a free kick;
(b) a bowler can 'swing' the ball in cricket;
(c) a golfer can 'hook' (swing from left to right for a right-hand player) a golf ball if she mishits it;
(d) a tennis player can apply 'top-spin' to a ball.

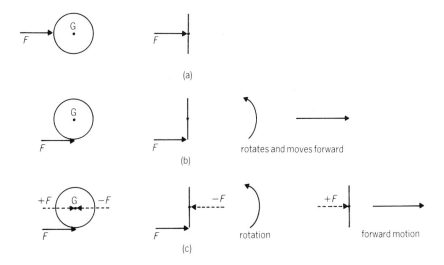

8.26 *Spinning and rotation*

8.6 Machines

Another important practical application of moments of forces about a point is in simple 'machines' such as the **lever**. Here a 'machine' is any device which enables a force applied at one point to overcome another force at some other point. The applied force is called the **effort** E and the force which the 'machine' must overcome is known as the **load** L.

Mechanical advantage

The **ratio of load L to effort E** is known as the **mechanical advantage** (MA) of the 'machine'. Thus MA = (load L N)/(effort E N) and hence has no unit. A load of 100 N is raised by applying an effort of 20 N to a machine. The mechanical advantage = L/E = 100 N/20 N = 5. 'Machines' can have a value for MA of 1, greater than 1 or even less than 1. A single fixed pulley has MA $\approx$ 1 and here the 'advantage' is in applying a downward force rather than an upward force. The structure of the human frame makes it easier to apply downward (pull) forces than upward (push) forces. A bicycle is a typical example of a 'machine' which has MA < 1. Here the 'advantage' is that the rider can control the bicycle more easily than if it has MA > 1, when it might become dangerous. One advantage of using a larger effort than force is to gain an increase of speed. Another 'advantage' is that the rider can 'free-wheel' down slopes or along level ground and thus has periods of rest from pedalling. Most 'machines' do, however, have MA > 1 and hence a real advantage is obtained in using such machines.

Velocity ratio

Another term applied to 'machines' is **velocity ratio** (VR), defined as **the ratio of the velocity of the effort to the velocity of the load**. Hence VR = (velocity of the effort m s^{-1})/(velocity of the load m s^{-1}) which has no unit. It follows from the definition that VR is given by displacement of the effort per second/displacement of the load per second. Since the effort and the load are both moving for the same time the velocity ratio can be quoted as (displacement of the effort d_E)/(displacement of the load d_L) in the same time. Thus in practical determinations of velocity ratio it is sufficient to measure the respective distances moved by the effort and the load as the machine is operated because both effort and load will be moving for the same time. It is also possible to obtain a *theoretical* value for VR from the dimensions of the machine. For example, VR for a pulley system is the number of strings which support the load; for the inclined plane it is the reciprocal of the sine of the angle of inclination of the plane to the horizontal; for a screw jack it is the ratio of the circumference of the 'turning arm' to the pitch of the thread; for the wheel and axle it is the ratio of the diameter of the wheel to the diameter of the axle. The theoretical values for VR can be used when solving numerical problems or when d_L and d_E are not available.

Efficiency

Efficiency is defined as **the ratio of the useful work output to the work input**. The useful work that can be obtained from any machine is always less than the work put in because some of the work is used in overcoming frictional forces and in moving the parts of the machine. Therefore the efficiency is always less than 1. Efficiency = (useful work output J)/(work input J) and hence has no unit. In some cases the percentage efficiency is quoted when dealing with machines; this is the efficiency multiplied by 100%. For a 'machine' in which 40 J of the 200 J of work put into the machine are used in overcoming frictional forces and in moving the mechanical parts, the efficiency will be $(160\,J/200\,J) = 0.8$ (80% if expressed as a percentage).

When calculating efficiency, remember that the useful work obtained from the machine should be divided by the work put into the machine. Since work done = force × displacement of the force, it follows that

$$\text{efficiency} = \frac{\text{load} \times \text{displacement of the load}}{\text{effort} \times \text{displacement of the effort}}$$

$$\text{efficiency} = \frac{\text{load}}{\text{effort}} \times \frac{\text{displacement of the load}}{\text{displacement of the effort}}$$

$$= \text{MA} \times \frac{1}{\text{VR}}$$

So efficiency $\equiv$ MA/VR, or (MA/VR) × 100% if percentage efficiency is required.

In practical experiments you should use the correct definition of efficiency in terms of work done. However, in numerical problems it is often more convenient to use the alternative formula, efficiency $\equiv$ MA/VR, to solve the problem. It is important to remember that the percentage efficiency of a machine is *always less* than 100% because the moving parts of the machine are neither frictionless nor weightless.

8.7 Machines you use

Levers

A number of household gadgets and tools rely on the Principle of Moments for their operation. They all have a pivot (or axis) P about which the forces involved exert turning effects. The velocity ratio is fixed by the design (dimensions) of the machine and the mechanical advantage can never quite reach the value of the VR.

Consider a crowbar used to lever off the nailed-down lid of a packing crate as shown in Fig. 8.27(a). In the force diagram $d_E/d_L = y/x$, hence VR = y/x.

Applying the Principle of Moments, $L \times x = E \times y$ or $L/E = y/x = $ MA. However, this cannot be true because the weight of the crowbar and frictional forces have not been taken into account. In fact, MA will be *greater* than y/x because the weight of the crowbar assists the leverage. The weight W of the crowbar acts downwards at a distance d from the pivot P. The full equation of the moments of force about P gives $Lx = Wd + Ey$. Hence $(L/E) = $ MA $= y/x + Wd/Ex$. Thus MA $> y/x$. In Fig. 8.27(b) a pair of pliers is shown nipping wire into a holder. Once again the velocity ratio is y/x but this time the mechanical advantage is less than y/x. Since x and y can be varied by moving the 'load' nearer to P and applying the 'effort' further from P a larger VR (and also MA) can be obtained. A pair of scissors operates on this principle; can you list other examples of what are known as **first class levers**?

Figures 8.28(a) and (b) show examples of **second and third class levers** respectively. In the case of the wheelbarrow the effort is applied at the 'maximum' distance from P, and so 'large' loads can be lifted (VR $= y/x > 1$). Note that the effort and load are acting in opposite directions. Other examples of second class levers include bottle openers used to lever off metal bottle tops, nut crackers, the oars of a rowing boat and the safety valve on a steam engine.

Figure 8.28(b) shows a pair of tweezers holding a stamp. (If you are a philatelist you will know that stamps should never be picked up with the fingers because they could become creased or pick up dirt or grease and so lose value.) The third class lever also has a special value for VR and MA. From the diagram VR $= y/x$ and, since y is clearly less than x, VR < 1 and hence also MA < 1. This means that the effort is greater than the load and hence the force exerted by the tweezers on the stamp can be delicately controlled. This should ensure that the stamp is not damaged if picked up and held by tweezers. Other examples of third class levers are sugar tongs and the forearm of a person picking up an object (with the elbow acting as a 'pivot').

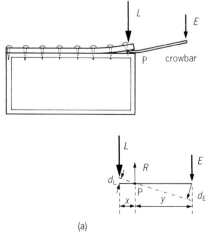

(a)

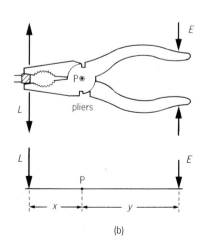

(b)

8.27 First class levers

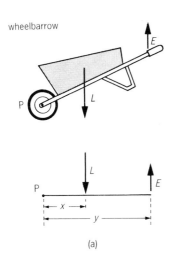

wheelbarrow

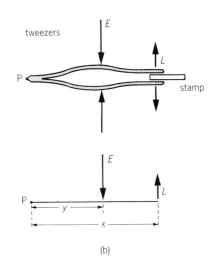

tweezers

stamp

(a)   (b)

8.28   *Second and third class levers*

Exercise 8.4

Sketch some of the second class levers listed above and draw the free-body force diagram associated with each. Can you think of any other examples?

Pulleys

Another form of machine in common use is the pulley. This is a grooved wheel free to rotate on an axle. Figure 8.29 (p.110) shows pulley systems with velocity ratios of 1, 2, 3 and 4. A single fixed pulley with a rope passing over it enables the load L to be lifted by a downward force $E = T_1$, the tension in the rope (Fig. 8.29a). Since forearms behave as third class levers

---

Example

A labourer on a building site has to lift bricks weighing 100 N to the top of a building 10 m high. He can (a) haul them up in a crate weighing 10 N using a single fixed pulley or (b) carry them in the crate up a ladder. If the labourer weighs 600 N calculate the work done in both cases.

(a)   work = force × displacement
   work done raising bricks = 100 N × 10 m
   work done raising crate = 10 N × 10 m
      total work done = 100 N × 10 m + 10 N × 10 m
                = 1000 J + 100 J
                = 1100 J

(b)   work = force × displacement
   work done raising crate = 10 N × 10 m
   work done raising bricks = 100 N × 10 m
   work done raising labourer = 600 N × 10 m
      total work done = (10 + 100 + 600) N × 10 m
                = 710 × 10 J
                = 7100 J

---

when pulling upwards it is much less tiring to pull downwards. Since the distances moved by the effort and the load are equal, VR = 1. Thus a single fixed pulley can be added to any pulley system without changing the velocity ratio of the system but giving the advantage of allowing the final effort force to be applied downward. The effort $E = T_1$ must support the load L and overcome any frictional forces F. Hence $E = T_1 = L + F$; by making F as small as possible E becomes nearly equal to L and the MA nearly equal to 1.

In Fig. 8.29(b) two methods of operating a single movable pulley with VR = 2 are shown. The effort E is equal to T_2 which must support the load L, the weight w of the lower pulley and also overcome frictional forces F. Thus MA $= L/E = 2L/(L + w + F)$ and will always be less than 2. The three-stringed pulley system (Fig. 8.29c) uses a double pulley and a single pulley while in the four-stringed pulley system (Fig. 8.29d) two double pulleys are used. The double pulleys are mounted side by side in a frame (see Fig. 8.29e) but are drawn one above the other for convenience as in Fig. 8.29(c) and (d).

By combining the results obtained in the previous experiment the efficiency of the pulley system can be calculated from

efficiency = work output/work input

$$= \frac{(\text{load} \times \text{displacement of the load})}{(\text{effort} \times \text{displacement of the effort})}.$$

It was shown on p.108 that efficiency is equivalent to MA/VR, but this formula should not be used to find efficiency in an experiment because it has been derived from the correct definition of efficiency. Occasionally, the information given in numerical problems may force you to use the relationship efficiency $\equiv$ MA/VR to calculate the efficiency.

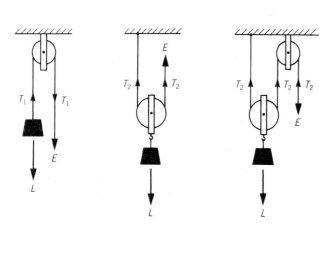

(a) $VR = 1$; $E = T_1$; $T_1 = L + F$

(b) $VR = 2$; $E = T_2$; $2T_2 = L + w + F$

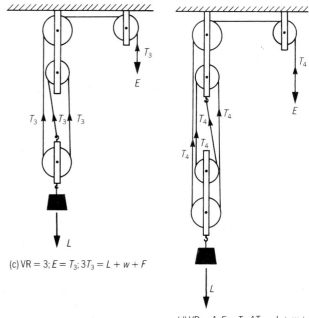

(c) $VR = 3$; $E = T_3$; $3T_3 = L + w + F$

(d) $VR = 4$; $E = T_4$; $4T_4 = L + w + F$

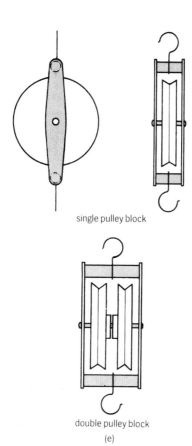

single pulley block

double pulley block

(e)

8.29 *Pulley systems.*
Note *The drawings of strings in pulley system diagrams must be straight lines as the strings are under tension.*

A pulley system in use

Investigation 8.5   To find the mechanical advantage and velocity ratio of a four-stringed pulley system

String together two double-pulley blocks and attach a load L and effort E as shown in Fig. 8.30. For a given load, increase the effort gradually until the load *just* begins to rise steadily, i.e. without acceleration. Record the value for this effort in a table of results similar to Table 8.4. Determine several values of load and effort in this way and record the results. For each pair of values of L and E calculate the mechanical advantage from $MA = (\text{load } L)/(\text{effort } E)$.

You should find that as the load increases the mechanical advantage increases. The effort has to raise the load and the lower pulley block which has weight, and overcome the frictional forces both between the string and the pulley and at the axles of the pulley blocks. When the value of the load is nearly the same as the weight of the lower pulley block about half of the effort does useful work in raising the load while the rest does 'useless' (but necessary) work. When the load is much larger than the weight of the lower pulley block the proportion of the work 'wasted' in raising the pulley block is much less. Therefore the pulley system is more efficient when using loads much greater than the weight of the lower pulley block.

The velocity ratio is calculated from measurements of the distance moved by the effort d_E and the distance moved by the load d_L when the effort moves the load. Place rules alongside the load and the effort, as in Fig. 8.29(b), to measure the distances d_E and d_L. Measure several pairs of values of d_E and d_L and so calculate the average value of the velocity ratio. Within the limits of experimental error, the velocity ratio should be constant and equal to 4. However, as all the strings are not vertical or inextensible, the calculated value may not be exactly 4. In theory, if the load rises by, say, 1 cm then each of the four supporting strings must 'shorten' by 1 cm. Therefore 4 cm of string must unwind so that the effort moves down by 4 cm. That is why the velocity ratio of a stringed pulley system is equal to the number of supporting strings. This method of gauging the velocity ratio is no substitute for measuring d_E and d_L but it can be used in simple numerical calculations.

Table 8.4   Table of results for investigation 8.5

Load L/N	Effort E/N	$MA = (L/E)$/no units

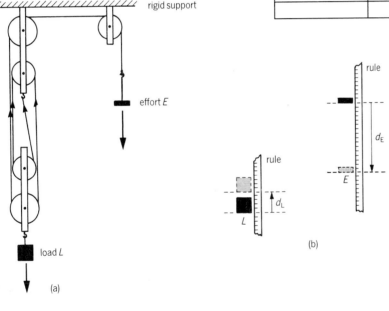

8.30   MA and VR of a four-stringed pulley system

Sketch graphs of mechanical advantage against load and efficiency against load are shown in Fig. 8.31. Reducing the weight of the lower pulley block will improve the efficiency of the system, as will oiling the axle of the pulley wheel. The pulleys used in school laboratories are usually made of aluminium or plastic so that they are fairly light.

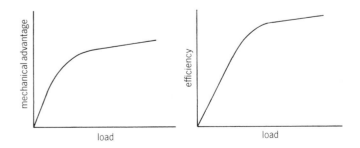

8.31   Graphs of MA and efficiency against load

111

Inclined plane

Another simple 'machine' is the inclined plane. Figure 8.32(a) shows a farmer and his son loading identical bales of hay onto a cart. The farmer lifts the bale vertically up and onto the cart while the son uses a plank of wood as a loading ramp. The farmer must exert a force of at least W the weight of the bale. The son exerts a force $E = W\sin\theta + F$ where F is the frictional force between the bale and the plank. For 'small' angles of θ (up to 30°), $\sin\theta$ is less than 0.5, hence E is less than W. Therefore if the son is physically unable to lift the bale directly onto the cart like his father he will be able to push the bale up the inclined plane and onto the cart.

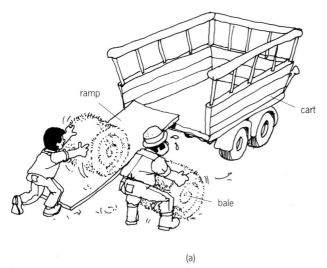

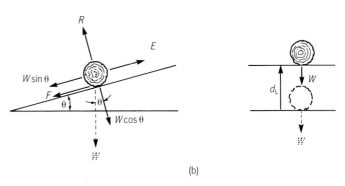

(a)

(b)

8.32   The inclined plane

Investigation 8.6   To find the mechanical advantage and velocity ratio of an inclined plane

First set the angle of inclination θ of the plane at a fixed angle so that the velocity ratio is constant. Then place a load L on the plane, attach a string to it, pass the string over the pulley and then attach the effort as shown in Fig. 8.33. Increase the effort E by small amounts until the load *just* begins to move steadily up the incline. Record the load L and effort E in a table of results similar to Table 8.5. Repeat the procedure for several different values of the load and find the corresponding effort. Calculate MA for each pair of values of load L and effort E from $MA = L/E$ (no units).

The velocity ratio of an inclined plane varies according to the angle of inclination of the plane to the horizontal. Set the angle of inclination θ to some fixed angle (say 30°). Arrange two metre rules as shown in Fig. 8.34 so that you can measure the distance moved by the effort d_E and the vertical distance moved by the load d_L and then record them in a table of results like Table 8.6. The distance moved by the effort can be varied and the corresponding distance moved by the load determined. For

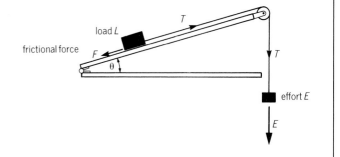

8.33   MA of an inclined plane

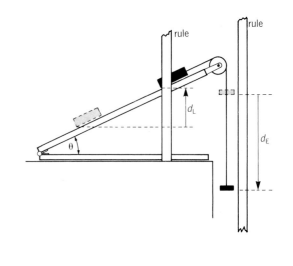

8.34   VR of an inclined plane

Table 8.5   Table of results when finding the MA of an inclined plane

Load L/N	Effort E/N	$MA = L/E$ (no unit)

each pair of values of d_E and d_L the velocity ratio is calculated from VR $= d_E/d_L$ (no unit). The practical value for VR may be compared with the theoretical value of VR $= 1/\sin\theta$, derived as follows. If an effort is applied over the length l of the plane the load 'rises' up through a *vertical* distance h, hence VR $= l/h$. From trigonometry (Fig. 8.35) it follows that VR $= 1/\sin\theta$.

Table 8.6   Table of results when finding the VR of an inclined plane

Distance moved by effort d_E/cm	Distance moved by load d_L/cm	VR $= d_E/d_L$ (no unit)

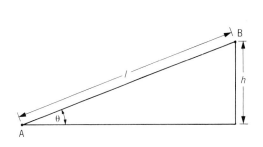

8.35   Theoretical value of VR for an inclined plane

Note   The theoretical methods should *not* be used when a question asks for the practical measurement for VR. However, in numerical problems the reader may have to use any one of the methods listed above in order to solve the problem.

Questions

Q1 A uniform metre rule is balanced at its mid-point P on a pivot. A 10 N weight is hung from the rule at various positions. Which one of the following moments of force about the point P is **not** possible?
A 0 N m   **B** −1 N m   **C** +1 N m   **D** +5 N m
E +10 N m

Q2 Which of the following changes will increase the velocity ratio of an inclined plane?
A Increase the load being drawn up the plane.
B Increase the effort being applied to the load.
C Increase the angle of inclination of the plane.
D Increase the length of the plane.
E Increase the smoothness of the plane.

Q3

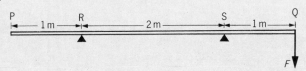

In the diagram PQ is a uniform beam of length 4 m resting on supports at R, 1 m from P, and S, 1 m from Q.
If the beam has a weight equal to 150 N what would be the minimum downward force, F, applied at Q which would lift the beam clear of the support at R?
A 150 N   **B** 100 N   **C** 75 N   **D** 50 N   **E** 37.5 N   *(L)*

Q4 Which of the following does NOT give the value of the velocity ratio of a pulley system?
A The ratio of the distance moved by the effort to the distance moved by the load.
B The ratio of the size of the effort to the size of the load.
C The ratio of the speed of the effort to the speed of the load.
D The ratio of the mechanical advantage to the efficiency.
E The number of strings supporting the load.   *(L)*

Q5 (a) A uniform plank of length 4.4 m and weighing 200 N is placed horizontally and symmetrically on two supports which are 3.2 m apart. A man weighing 800 N stands on the plank over one of the supports.
Draw a diagram of the arrangement, showing clearly the forces acting on the plank. Calculate the force on each support.
How far could the man move towards the nearer end of the plank before it starts to tip?
(b) An object moves in a circular path at uniform speed. Explain why its velocity is not uniform and that a force is necessary to maintain it in this path. What is the direction of this force?   *(S)*

Q6 What is meant by the *centre of gravity* of an object?
Describe how you would find by experiment the centre of gravity of a thin, irregularly shaped sheet of metal.
Explain why a minibus is more likely to topple over when the roof-rack is heavily loaded than when the roof rack is empty.
A metre rule is supported on a knife-edge placed at the 40 cm graduation. It is found that the metre rule balances horizontally when a mass which has a weight of 0.45 N is suspended at the 15 cm graduation, as shown in the diagram.

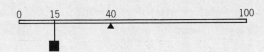

Calculate the *moment*, about the knife-edge in this balanced condition, of the force due to the mass of the rule.
If the weight of the rule is 0.90 N, calculate the position of its centre of gravity.   *(C)*

Q7 Weights of 2 N and 5 N are hung from a light, rigid rod AB of length 80 cm. The 2 N weight hangs freely from the end A and the 5 N weight from a point on the rod 10 cm from end B. Determine how far from end A that a fulcrum must be placed so that the rod and weights will remain in equilibrium when resting across it.

Q8 (a) What is meant by (i) the centre of gravity of a body, (ii) a couple?

A metal sheet of irregular shape is suspended so that it can swing freely about a fixed horizontal needle which passes through a hole P near its edge. Draw a diagram showing the sheet at an instant during the swing when the sheet is not at its rest position. Show on the diagram the direction and point of application of each force acting on the metal sheet.

Draw a second diagram showing the forces on the sheet when it has stopped swinging. Explain why the sheet comes to rest in this position.

(b) In order to 'weigh' a boy in the laboratory, a uniform plank of wood AB 3.0 metres long, having a mass of 8.0 kg, is pivoted about a point 0.5 m from A. The boy stands 0.3 m from A and a mass of 2 kg is placed 0.5 m from B in order to balance the plank horizontally.

Sketch the arrangement, representing each force acting on the plank by an arrow showing the direction of the force. Indicate the value of each force. Calculate the mass of the boy. (Assume that the acceleration due to gravity is 10 m s^{-2}.) *(JMB)*

Q9 Draw a labelled diagram of a block and tackle pulley system which has two pulley wheels in each block.

How would you measure the effort necessary to lift a load of 45 N using this system? Explain how far the effort would move if the load rises vertically by 20 cm. Calculate the efficiency of the system if an effort of 15 N is required.

Why is the efficiency likely to be different for a much smaller load? State *two* methods by which the efficiency could be increased for a given load. *(S)*

Q10 The efficiency of a machine is equal to

A $\dfrac{\text{Mechanical Advantage}}{\text{Velocity Ratio}}$

B Mechanical Advantage × Velocity Ratio

C $\dfrac{\text{Load}}{\text{Effort}}$

D Load × Effort

E $\dfrac{\text{Distance moved by Effort}}{\text{Distance moved by Load}}$ *(L)*

Q11 (a) Describe and explain how you could measure the mass of a banana using only a metre rule, a 100 g mass and some strong, light thread.

(b) (i) A stone and a feather were released at the same time from the same height. Explain why the stone accelerated until it hit the ground, but the feather quickly reached a terminal velocity.

(ii) Describe and explain what would happen if the experiment in (b) (i) were to be repeated on the Moon, where there is no atmosphere. *(C)*

Q12 Draw a labelled diagram of a pulley system which has a velocity ratio of **three**. Briefly describe how the **mechanical advantage** of this system could be found experimentally. Explain why the **efficiency** is less than 100%.

A machine for weighing potatoes is set up as shown below.

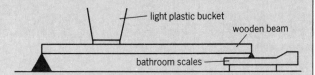

The uniform wooden beam is 2 metres long and has a mass of 10 kg. Calculate the distance of the centre of the light plastic bucket from the left-hand end for the bathroom scales to read 20 kg when 50 kg of potatoes are in the bucket. *(W)*

Q13 Draw a diagram of a simple pulley system which has a velocity ratio of 4. State clearly what you understand by velocity ratio, and explain how your machine satisfies the requirement.

Describe briefly how you would use your machine to find how the efficiency varied with the load applied.

Typical results for a working pulley system are:

load/N	0	50	100	150	200	250
efficiency %	0	15	30	40	45	47

Plot these results on a graph and explain the shape of the curve. *(L)*

Q14 Define the *efficiency* of a simple machine, and derive the relationship between *efficiency, mechanical advantage* and *velocity ratio*.

Draw a diagram of a pulley system having a velocity ratio of 5.

A man uses this pulley system to raise a load of 440 N at a steady speed of 0.1 m s^{-1}. If he applies an effort of 120 N, find the efficiency of the system, and the power developed by the man.

Give **two** reasons for the pulley system being less than 100 per cent efficient. *(W)*

Q15 An inclined plane of length 4 m is used to raise a load of mass 20 kg through a vertical height of 1 m. It is found that an effort of 80 N is necessary to move the mass up the slope at a constant speed.

(i) Describe how you would apply the 80 N force.

(ii) What is the velocity ratio of this inclined plane as a machine?

(iii) Calculate the work done by the effort and the useful work done on the load. (Give your answers in joules.) Account for the difference between these two quantities and explain why they can never be equal in such a situation.

(iv) Calculate the efficiency of this inclined plane as a system for raising loads. *(L)*

9 Energy

9.1 Introducing energy

Importance of studying energy

How often do you see the headline 'Energy Crisis'? Often enough to show that a study of the different sources of energy, and the ways in which they may be utilised to the best advantage, is of the utmost importance. Socially and economically it is essential that energy should not be wasted. This means that production and transfer of energy should be clearly understood. You will see that energy considerations run through the whole of Physics.

Thunderstorms

The thunderstorm is a natural phenomenon which can tell us a great deal about energy. On a hot clear morning in summer, heat from the Sun strikes the ground. Some of this heat is absorbed, raising the temperature of the ground. The remainder of the heat is reflected. Air in contact with the ground is heated, and so it expands, becomes less dense than the air above it and rises. This creates an upcurrent of air. Water vapour in the air current condenses and forms a cloud. Surrounding air flows in to replace the air which has risen, thus setting up local winds. Because of the rotation of the Earth the winds do not flow directly towards the centre of the warmer area and a small circulation is set up (see Fig. 9.1). As the day progresses the effects become more pronounced: the cloud becomes deeper and darker, the upcurrents stronger and the winds increase in strength. The outcome may be a violent thunderstorm, with vivid flashes of lightning, loud rolls of thunder, and torrential rain or hailstones accompanied by strong gusts of wind. In tropical latitudes the effects are often much more pronounced. What starts as a quiet day may well end with widespread damage due to a gradual build-up of energy followed by its violent release.

It will be instructive to look at the thunderstorm in more detail, to see the different forms of energy which are present and consider how they are interrelated. But before this can be done, some of the terms that will be used must be defined.

Work

Work is said to be done when a force moves its point of application in the direction of the force.

work done = magnitude of force × distance moved by force in the direction of the force

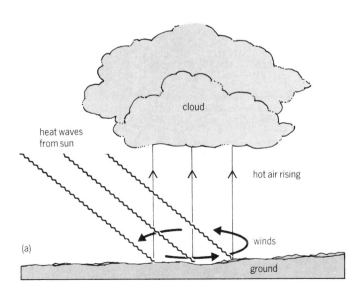
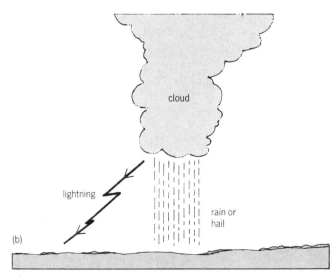

9.1 The thunderstorm: (a) formation, (b) p.e. released as thunder, lightning, rain or hail

If the force is measured in newton and the distance in metre, the work done is in joule. Hence the SI unit of work is the joule: newton × metre = joule.

Note Work done is a *scalar* quantity even though it is the product of two vector quantities.

Energy

Energy is the capacity for doing work and hence is also measured in joule. Since there are many different ways in which a body may be capable of doing work, there are many different forms of energy.

9.2 Mechanical energy

A body may be capable of doing work because it is moving or because of its state or position. These types of energy are called **mechanical energy**.

Kinetic energy

This is the ability to do work which a body possesses by virtue of its motion. It is given by $\frac{1}{2}mv^2$ where m is the mass of the body and v its speed. Thus every moving body possesses kinetic energy and this is obviously one way in which energy may be transmitted. Since before David used a stone from a sling to slay Goliath, through the ages of arrows from bows, and bullets from guns, energy has been transmitted by missiles, often for destructive purposes. It is generally true that the larger the missile and the faster it can move, the more damage it can do.

Example

A stone of mass 0.2 kg is projected by a catapult with a velocity of 20 m s^{-1}. Calculate the kinetic energy of the stone.

$m = 0.2$ kg $\quad v = 20$ m s^{-1} $\quad$ k.e. = ?

$$
\begin{aligned}
\text{k.e.} &= \tfrac{1}{2}mv^2 \\
&= \tfrac{1}{2} \times 0.2 \times 20^2 \\
&= 0.1 \times 400 \\
\text{k.e.} &= 40 \text{ J}
\end{aligned}
$$

Example

A hiker of mass 50 kg climbs to a height of 300 m above the ground level. Calculate the work he does in raising his body to this height and hence his potential energy.

$m = 50$ kg $\quad g = 10$ m s^{-2} $\quad h = 300$ m

$$
\begin{aligned}
\text{force} &= mg \\
\text{work} &= \text{force} \times \text{displacement} \\
&= 50 \text{ kg} \times 10 \text{ m s}^{-2} \times 300 \text{ m} \\
\text{work} &= 150\,000 \text{ J}
\end{aligned}
$$

The potential energy of the hiker is the work done in raising his body to that height, and so is 150 000 J.

Potential energy

This is the ability to do work which a body possesses as a result of its position or state. For example, if a body is raised above the ground work has to be done against the gravitational pull of the Earth, i.e. against the weight of the body. As before,

$$
\begin{aligned}
\text{work done} &= \text{force} \times \text{distance moved by the force} \\
&= mg \times h \\
&= mgh
\end{aligned}
$$

If the body is released it is capable of doing work by its motion as it falls to the ground. The bow and arrow mentioned above are a good example of this form of energy. When the bow is bent it possesses potential energy; when it is released most of this is transferred into kinetic energy of the arrow.

9.3 Nuclear energy

Nuclear fusion

The energy in the thunderstorm was initially heat from the Sun. The Sun is the main source of energy on Earth, and without it life would be impossible. How is the Sun's energy produced? Very little was known about this until Albert Einstein (1879–1955) postulated the theory that matter (mass) could be converted into energy. The temperature in the Sun reaches several million degrees and hydrogen atoms there move with great speeds. They move so fast that they can overcome the strong repulsive forces between each other, and fuse together to form new elements, e.g. helium. The mass of the new element is less than the sum of the masses of the individual particles which fused together to form it. What happened to the lost mass? It was converted into energy (heat). The energy produced is given by $\Delta E = \Delta mc^2$, where Δm is the 'lost mass' and c the speed of light. If Δm is in kilogram and c in m s^{-1} then ΔE will be in joule.

Note Do not confuse this equation with that for kinetic energy. There is no factor of $\frac{1}{2}$ and the speed c is the speed of light and not the speed of the particle.

The production of energy from the fusion of atoms is known as **nuclear** fusion. Obviously the change in mass during the formation of one new atom is extremely small, but since there are extremely large numbers of transformations taking place, large amounts of energy are liberated. Suppose it were possible to change all of one gram of matter into energy. How much energy would be released?

$$
\begin{aligned}
\Delta E &= \Delta mc^2 \\
&= 0.001 \times 10^8 \times 10^8 \\
&= 10^{-3} \times 10^{16} \\
&= 10^{13} \text{ J}
\end{aligned}
$$

This shows the vast quantities of energy which would be available if hydrogen atoms could be made to fuse together. At present the technology needed to produce this type of energy in a controlled manner has not been developed. However, it is nevertheless interesting to compare the value given above with the values obtained from burning common substances:

1 g wood produces approximately 16 000 J
1 g coal produces approximately 32 000 J
1 g petrol produces approximately 45 000 J

Thus converting one gram of matter into energy produces 300 million times more energy than burning one gram of coal. You can work out the ratio for petrol yourself. The implications of these comparisons for the world's energy problems are obvious.

Nuclear fission

There is another type of nuclear reaction known as **fission** (splitting up). In it an unstable (radioactive) nucleus splits when it is bombarded by neutrons. Again there is a difference between the mass of the reactants and that of the product. The sum of the masses of the former is less than the mass of the latter and the 'spare' mass is released as energy (heat). The great advantage of this reaction is that it can be controlled, and so it is used in nuclear power stations to produce electrical energy and in nuclear engines to drive submarines etc.

The first atomic bombs were uncontrolled fission reactions. The extremely high temperatures these reactions produce can be used to cause nuclear fusion. This is the basis of the hydrogen bomb. A conventional atomic bomb produces the high temperatures needed to set off the fusion reactions in the hydrogen bomb.

9.4 Transmission of energy

How is the heat energy produced in the Sun transmitted to Earth? The energy is transmitted by **electromagnetic waves** (see p.216). It is obvious to anyone sitting on a cliff and watching the sea dash against the rocks, that energy can be transmitted by waves. It is not so obvious that energy can be transmitted by waves through the vacuum between the Sun and the Earth. This same process transfers heat from an electric fire. You can feel the heat on your hands if you hold them on the same level as the fire but at some distance from it.

Internal energy

When you look at a solid or liquid at room temperature you would not realise that the molecules are in rapid motion. In Chapter 1 it was shown that the molecules in a liquid move rapidly and haphazardly (randomly) in a process known as Brownian Motion. The molecules in a solid do not move about from place to place but they do vibrate about an equilibrium position. Thus they have kinetic energy. In both solids and liquids each molecule also has potential energy because it is bound to the molecules around it by attractive forces. To increase the distance between two molecules, work has to be done against the attractive forces between the molecules and thus there is an increase in the molecule's potential energy. Thus the energy in solids is a mixture of potential energy and vibrational kinetic energy. The picture is further complicated by the kinetic energy of any electrons which may be moving about in the matter. When energy is transmitted to a solid it may be written as

energy absorbed = increase in internal kinetic energy + increase in internal potential energy

This results in a rise in temperature of the solid.

Note The heat contained by a body is a measure of the internal energy of the body.

The internal energy in a liquid is a mixture of the translational kinetic energy of the moving molecules and the potential energy between the molecules. The internal energy in a gas is mainly kinetic energy since the gas molecules are in rapid motion and are, at normal temperatures and pressures, well separated so the attractive forces between the molecules are negligible.

Energy transfer in a thunderstorm

When part of the incoming energy from the Sun is absorbed by the ground there is an increase in the internal energy of the ground and a consequent rise in its temperature. Some of this energy is transferred to the air which is in contact with the ground. The kinetic energy of the air molecules increases and as a result the number of molecules per unit volume decreases, causing a decrease in density. As a result the air rises, some of the water vapour in it condenses and rising drops of water are formed. As the molecules rise there is a consequent increase in their potential energy.

As the water drops move through the Earth's electrical field they become charged. There is a separation of charge and the top of the cloud acquires a different charge from the bottom. Strong electric fields are set up between different parts of the cloud, and between the bottom of the cloud and the ground. Thus there is a build-up of electrical potential energy.

Eventually the energy is released by the passage of electric charge which produces a flash of lightning. If the lightning flash is between the base of the cloud and the ground, buildings may be damaged or trees torn asunder. The flashes of lightning are accompanied by a roll of thunder produced because some of the energy is dissipated as sound. The potential energy of the water drops is released as kinetic energy when the drops fall as rain or hail. Depending upon the circumstances there may be considerable kinetic energy released and a lot of damage caused. Any farmer who has surveyed his crops after a violent thunderstorm will testify to this.

So far only brief mention has been made of the winds that accompany the storm. Sometimes the circulation becomes very strong, whirlwinds form, and a vast amount of damage is done. These effects are usually more pronounced in tropical than in temperate regions.

The thunderstorm is an example of a naturally occurring phenomenon in which energy from the Sun is converted into other forms of energy. It may be regarded as a natural generator: heat energy from the Sun is converted into mechanical energy as wind, rain etc. Unfortunately the energy output cannot be controlled. One benefit of studying Physics is that you will develop an understanding of energy transfers so that available sources of energy may be used in a controlled and beneficial manner.

9.5   Other forms of energy

Chemical energy

When chemical changes take place, energy is released, often in the form of heat. The food we eat burns slowly in our bodies and produces both the heat necessary to maintain the temperature of the body and the energy necessary for us to move about. It also builds up the body and repairs tissue. Birds need to build up their body mass before migrating because during a long flight their mass will be reduced as they use the stored energy.

In the internal combustion engine a mixture of petrol vapour and air is ignited in the cylinder. The

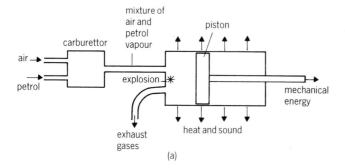

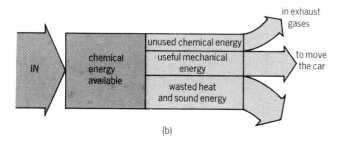

9.2   Energy diagram for the internal combustion engine

chemical change which occurs during this explosion releases heat which causes a rapid expansion of the gas and so the piston is driven downwards (Fig. 9.2a). The kinetic energy of the piston is used to turn the drive shaft and move the car. From Fig. 9.2(b) you can see what happens to the total chemical energy available. Some of the gas does not burn and comes out with the exhaust gases. By far the greater quantity of the heat produced is wasted and only about a quarter of the total energy available is turned into useful mechanical energy.

Fuel is also burnt in a rocket and chemical energy is turned into heat. The hot gases produced are expelled in one direction and the rocket moves off in the opposite direction. You can illustrate the principle by blowing up a balloon and then releasing the neck. Air escapes through the neck and forces the balloon to fly around the room.

In an electric torch, the chemical energy stored in the battery is converted into electrical energy. Electric charge passes through the filament in the bulb and heat and light energy are emitted. The proportions in which these are released depend upon the temperature of the filament. As the temperature rises the proportion of energy emitted as light becomes greater. However there is always more heat produced than light, and the bulb is not a particularly efficient means of producing light. As the energy is produced the chemicals in the battery change and the battery does not have an indefinite life. When all the chemicals have changed their form, the battery will cease to function.

Both heat energy and light energy are produced when the electric charge passes through the filament. What is the difference between them? Both are electromagnetic waves, but they have different wavelengths and frequencies.

Wave energy

The energy E possessed by an electromagnetic wave is proportional to the frequency f of the wave.

$$\text{energy} = \text{constant} \times \text{frequency}$$
$$E = hf$$

h is known as **Planck's Constant**. You can see that the higher the frequency the greater the energy in the wave. Light waves have a higher frequency than heat waves and thus contain more energy. This means that higher energy levels are necessary to produce light than to produce heat.

X-rays are electromagnetic waves whose frequencies are much greater than the frequencies of light waves. They have a much greater penetrating power than light and can be dangerous. Extreme care should be taken about exposure to X-rays.

Gamma radiation has the highest frequency and thus the greatest energy of all electromagnetic radiation. Gamma rays come in from outer space, from naturally occurring radioactive substances and are also emitted by atomic bombs.

Photo-cells

On p.131 you found that electrical energy can release electromagnetic radiation. Can electromagnetic radiation release electrical energy? The answer is yes, and various cells are available for this purpose. A photo-cell converts electromagnetic radiation into electrical energy. One type is the **photo-emissive cell** shown in Fig. 9.3. The cathode is a curved metal plate and the anode is a metal rod which is at a positive potential (i.e. has greater positive charge) with respect to the cathode. When light falls onto the cathode electrons are emitted which are attracted to the anode and so a current is produced. This current can be used to switch on another electrical circuit. The cell has wide uses in industry, e.g. automatic sorting. Figure 9.4(a) shows a beam of light being shone onto a metal cap containing a layer of cork. The light is absorbed and not reflected. In the cap in Fig. 9.4(b) there is no layer of cork, and the light is reflected into the cell. This activates a circuit which makes a robotic arm shoot out and knock the metal cap off the conveyor belt. Thus those caps without a layer of cork are rejected. The cell can also be used for automatic counting. Every time a person (or object) interrupts a beam of light the current in the cell is switched off. Whenever the current is switched off the counter clocks up one unit.

Photo-emissive cells are also used to reproduce the sound on a film. A diagram of the sound track is shown in Fig. 9.5(a). Light is passed through this sound track, and falls onto the photo-cell. The quantity of light passing through depends upon the width of the transparent part of the sound track, and the current produced in the photo-cell varies accordingly. This current produces a voltage across a load-resistor R (see Fig. 9.5b) which is amplified and used to activate a loudspeaker.

The **photo-voltaic cell** is another type of cell converting light energy into electrical energy. Basically it consists of a very thin film of metal which is deposited on a layer of semi-conducting material such as copper oxide. The copper oxide is itself deposited on a sheet of copper. Connections are made to the copper and to the thin sheet of metal on top of the copper oxide (Fig. 9.6). The film of metal is translucent and allows the light to pass. Photo-electrons in the copper oxide are liberated and a current passes through the resistor. It is important to note that this cell generates a voltage without an external battery. The photo-voltaic cell can be used as a light meter because the value of the current produced gives an indication of the intensity of the light. There is no reason why the cell cannot be used to drive a small radio, the source of power being the natural light which is incident upon the cell.

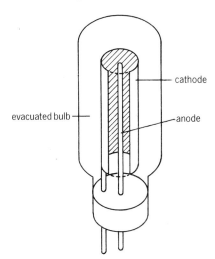

9.3 Photo-emissive cell

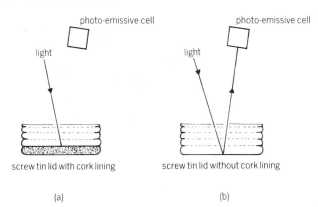

9.4 Automatic sorting of metal caps

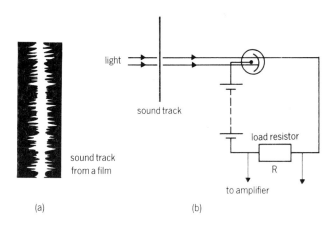

9.5 Reproduction of sound from film

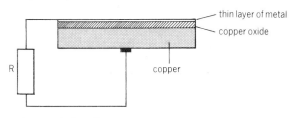

9.6 Photo-voltaic cell

Potential energy

Potential energy, the energy possessed by a body by virtue of its position above the ground, was mentioned on p.14. It will be discussed in more detail now. A compressed spring possesses elastic potential energy by virtue of its state. Work has to be done to compress the spring, and when the spring is released most of this energy can be recovered. A wound-up spring also possesses potential energy, and these were widely used to store the energy needed to drive clocks and watches. Although digital watches and quartz clocks are now coming into fashion, it will be a long time before the old spring type are completely superseded. Young children will be playing with clockwork toys for many years to come and will get fun out of recovering the energy from a wound-up spring.

Energy can also be stored in a length of stretched elastic. Boys and girls have long been familiar with the catapult which can project a missile with greater speed than can be achieved by the hand alone. The potential energy in the elastic is converted into kinetic energy of the missile. This process is reversed in the use of arrester wires to bring a plane landing on an aircraft carrier to a halt. The kinetic energy of the plane is converted to potential energy in the wires.

It should be clear by now that wherever there are forces which may or do cause movement in the direction of the force, then energy is available. You should also now be aware that energy exists in many different forms and may be converted from one form into others.

9.6   Law of Conservation of Energy

This law states that 'energy can neither be created nor destroyed but only transformed from one form into others.' The total energy must remain constant. What happens when a piece of metal is sawn with a hacksaw? Chemical energy from the food we eat is changed into kinetic energy of the hacksaw blade. Some of this energy is used to separate the metal filings from the metal and some is converted into heat energy. The hacksaw blade and metal will get very hot. Some energy will be dissipated as sound.

Consider the energy chain for a coal-fired power station.

heat from Sun → plants (trees) → coal → steam → turbine → generator → electricity

The initial source of energy is the Sun which provides the energy for the trees and plants to grow. These in turn decay and over the years form coal. When this is burnt it releases heat energy and vaporises water to form steam which in turn drives the turbine. The kinetic energy of the turbine is converted into electrical energy in the generator.

Machines and energy

A machine is a device which makes work easier either by changing the line of action of a force, or by enabling the work to be done by using a smaller force. Using a smaller force does not mean that less work can be done, because the smaller force always has to be moved over a larger distance. In fact more work has to be done. So there is no saving in energy. The best that can be hoped for is that the energy used will be the same, i.e. smaller force × larger distance = larger force × smaller distance, but this is not likely to happen. Using a machine results in an increase in the energy used.

Since energy cannot be created, but only transformed from one form to another it is not possible to produce a machine which, once started, will run for ever without any further input of energy. This is because there are always losses of energy due to friction of the moving parts producing heat, sound etc. These energy losses can be minimised but they cannot be eliminated and so a 'perpetual motion machine' is impossible.

Efficiency

The efficiency of a machine is defined as the ratio of the work got out to the work put in, or energy output to energy input (see p.107). It follows that it is all-important to cut down the energy wasted so that the useful work obtained from the machine is as high as possible. It is obvious that the useful energy got out of the machine in Fig. 9.7(a) is equal to the energy put into the machine, so its efficiency is 1 or 100%. The energy given out by the machine in Fig. 9.7(b) is also the same as the energy put in, but two-thirds of it is wasted energy. One third of the output is used, so the efficiency is $\frac{1}{3}$ or $33\frac{1}{3}\%$.

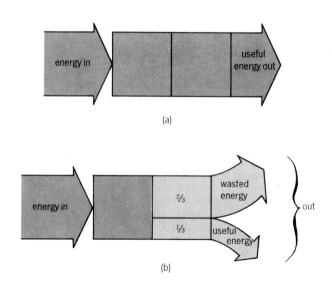

9.7   Energy diagrams showing efficiency

120

Power

This is defined as the rate at which work is done, or the rate at which energy is used and is the ratio of the work done to the time taken. The SI unit of power is the watt (W) and 1 watt = 1 joules per second ($J\,s^{-1}$). Two machines, one producing 500 J in 2 s and the other producing 2500 J in 10 s, both have the same power rating, namely 250 W.

A constant force F is applied to an object of mass m to give it constant acceleration a. The power needed to increase the velocity increases with the velocity:

$$\text{power } P = \frac{\text{work}}{\text{time}}$$
$$= \text{force} \times \frac{\text{displacement}}{\text{time}}$$

hence
$$P = \text{force} \times \frac{\text{displacement}}{\text{time}}$$
$$= F \times v$$

If v increases as F remains constant then P must increase. This is due to the increase in kinetic energy ($\frac{1}{2}mv^2$). So it is also true to write efficiency = (power output)/(power input). Power is a scalar quantity.

Collisions

Collisions were mentioned in Chapter 6 (p.78). The Law of Conservation of Momentum always holds during a collision, and collision problems should be approached from this point of view. What about the Law of Conservation of Energy? This also holds, but remember that it applies to all forms of energy. The *total* energy is constant. Students often make the mistake of assuming that the *kinetic energy* is *conserved*. This is only true if the collision is **elastic**. (**Note**   Elastic collisions only occur at atomic levels.) Consider two identical steel spheres A and B suspended by strings of equal length (Fig. 9.8a). When A is pulled to one side and released (Fig. 9.8b) it will stop after colliding with B and B will rise to approximately the height A was at before it was released (Fig. 9.8c). The process will be reversed when B falls and the spheres will keep moving for a long time. This is a close approach to an elastic collision. Each sphere will take almost all the kinetic energy from the other on colliding although sound energy (as clicks) and some heat energy are lost. If, however, a blob of plasticene is put onto B so that the spheres stick together after colliding, the kinetic energy after collision will only be half the kinetic energy before collision. The momentum before collision is mv_1 where m is the mass of a sphere and v_1 its initial velocity. The momentum after collision is $2mv_2$ where v_2 is the final velocity. So

$$mv_1 = 2mv_2$$
$$v_2 = \tfrac{1}{2}v_1$$
$$\text{k.e. before collision} = \tfrac{1}{2}mv_1{}^2$$
$$\text{k.e. after collision} = \tfrac{1}{2}(2m)v_2{}^2$$
$$= \tfrac{1}{2}(2m)(\tfrac{1}{2}v_1)^2$$
$$= \tfrac{1}{4}mv_1{}^2$$

The lost kinetic energy will partly have been used to change the shape of the plasticene and partly dissipated as heat.

If a lump of lead is dropped from a height to the ground, most of its kinetic energy will be changed to heat when it collides with the ground. As a result the temperature of the lead will rise. Water at the top of a waterfall possesses both kinetic and potential energy. As it falls the potential energy changes to kinetic energy, so the kinetic energy increases. On reaching the bottom of the fall the water collides with the river bed, and some of the kinetic energy changes into heat energy and sound energy. There is a slight rise in the temperature of the water at the bottom of a waterfall.

The Law of Conservation of Energy applies for a freely falling body. Consider a body of mass m at rest at A which is at a height h above the ground (Fig. 9.9). Since it is at rest the body has no kinetic energy and so its energy is the potential energy mgh. The body is released and when it reaches B has acquired a speed v_1. B is a distance h_1 below A. Thus at B the *kinetic energy* is $\frac{1}{2}mv_1{}^2$ and the *potential energy* is $mg(h - h_1)$. So the total energy at B is $\frac{1}{2}mv_1{}^2 + mg(h - h_1)$. From the

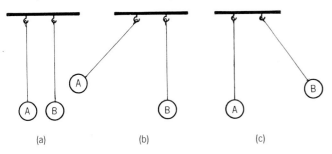

9.8   Collisions of balls on the ends of strings

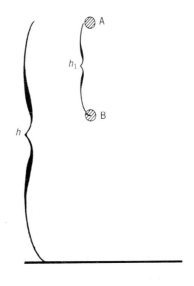

9.9   Conservation of energy in a falling object

equations of motion $v_1^2 = u^2 + 2gh_1$, and since the body started from rest $u = 0$; so $v_1^2 = 2gh_1$. Hence

$$\begin{aligned}\text{total energy at B} &= \tfrac{1}{2}mv_1^2 + mgh - mgh_1\\&= \tfrac{1}{2}m(2gh_1) + mgh - mgh_1\\&= mgh\end{aligned}$$

Thus the energy the body has at B is the same as its initial energy at A.

Problems in Physics can often be solved by using energy considerations.

Example

A car of mass 1200 kg travelling at 72 km h^{-1} is brought to rest in 80 metres. Find the average braking force on the car. What has happened to the original kinetic energy?

The work done in stopping the car, which is given by the retarding force $F \times$ the distance moved by the car after the force is applied, must equal the original kinetic energy. Thus $F \times 80 = \tfrac{1}{2}mv^2$. The speed must be expressed in m s^{-1}.

$$72 \text{ km h}^{-1} = 72 \times \frac{1000}{60 \times 60}$$
$$= 20 \text{ m s}^{-1}$$

$F = ?\text{ N} \quad m = 1200\text{ kg} \quad s = 80\text{ m} \quad v = 20\text{ m s}^{-1}$

$$F \times 80 = \tfrac{1}{2}\,1200 \times 20 \times 20$$
$$F = \frac{600 \times 20 \times 20}{80}$$
$$= 60 \times 5 \times 10$$
$$= 3000 \text{ N}$$

Most of the kinetic energy will be changed into heat energy in the brake drums and these will experience a rise in temperature.

9.7 Future trends in energy production

Natural resources of chemical energy such as coal, oil and gas are being used at a rapid rate. The rate of usage is likely to increase as under-developed countries become more industrialised. No doubt more reserves will be discovered and utilised although the costs of production will increase as they become less easy to tap. Nuclear power plants, which at present rely on fission, are becoming increasingly unpopular because of fears about leakage of radio-activity and the disposal of the waste products. But what are the alternative sources of energy?

Attempts will undoubtedly be made to harness the energy which is stored in the tides. The windmill, which used the kinetic energy of the winds, may return to favour in a more efficient form. Solar cells are already used to produce electricity, and this is one area in which there are likely to be important new developments. A car powered by solar energy has already crossed Australia.

Machines such as the internal combustion engine are not very efficient. Attempts will be made to improve the efficiency of machines and to cut down energy wastage. Heating a normal house is achieved far more efficiently than it was a few years ago, but there is still room for improvement.

9.8 Energy and transport

Oil and its derivatives are the main source of energy for transport. Now many people possess a car, and most of these are driven by petrol engines.

The four-stroke petrol engine

In the carburettor, petrol vaporises and the petrol vapour is mixed with air. This mixture is drawn into the cylinder and exploded by a spark from the sparking plug. There are four strokes.

(i) **Induction stroke**   The piston moves down, and the inlet valve opens allowing petrol vapour and air to enter. The exhaust valve remains closed.

(ii) **Compression stroke**   The piston rises and compresses the mixture of gases. Both valves remain closed.

(iii) **Expansion (power) stroke**   The plug sparks and the gases explode, forcing the piston down. Again, both valves remain closed.

(iv) **Exhaust stroke**   The piston rises and the exhaust valve opens. The exhaust gases are forced out. The inlet valve remains closed, thus it is seen that there is only one working stroke. This drives the car and provides the momentum for the other three strokes. Obviously a large quantity of heat energy is produced and a cooling system is essential. The valves are opened at the correct times by eccentric (specially placed) cams on the shaft.

Other fuels

If **diesel oil** is used instead of petrol, there is no sparking plug. The heat produced during the compression is sufficient to ignite the vapour. This engine is more economical.

Both four-stroke and diesel engines produce carbon and pump polluting waste gases (e.g. carbon monoxide) into the atmosphere. In certain countries cars have to be fitted with devices to cut down pollution of the atmosphere. This tends to increase the cost and cut down the efficiency, and the four-stroke engine is not particularly efficient.

Liquid petroleum gas is another oil derivative which is becoming more widely used. It is cleaner than petrol and diesel and has no carbon problems. Also it does not pump lead into the atmosphere. It is expensive to fit but is more economical on long mileages.

Alcohol can also be used as a fuel. In a petrol engine

the fuel ratio is 1 petrol:15 air, but with alcohol it is 1 alcohol:8 air. Alcohol engines run at lower temperatures than petrol engines. Alcohol has the advantage that it can be produced from organic substances such as sugar. 'Gasohol' is a fuel made from a mixture of alcohol and petrol.

Transport driven by batteries is sometimes seen. These electric vehicles have no pollution problems but the batteries need recharging frequently. Normally they can only move at low speeds.

Where **electricity** is playing an increasing role is on the railways which are becoming more electrified. Diesel replaced coal as a fuel and electricity is now replacing diesel. This method of propulsion is more efficient and much cleaner. The atmosphere is not polluted.

Questions

The following are examples of objects possessing energy or converting energy from one form to another:

A car slowed by its brakes   B hot gas
C melting ice   D red hot steel bar
E steam turbine

Which of these is the best example of

Q1 heat energy converting to mechanical energy?
Q2 mechanical energy converting to heat energy?
Q3 kinetic energy of random movement?
Q4 vibrational energy?   (L)
Q5 At what average rate is electrical energy being converted into potential energy when an electric motor raises a weight of 30 N through a distance of 3 m in 5 s?
  A 0.5 W B 2.0 W C 18 W D 50 W E 450 W (L)
Q6 Potential energy is measured in
  A newton seconds.   B joules.   C newtons.
  D watts.   E kilograms/second.
Q7 A girl whose weight is 600 N runs up a flight of stairs 10 m high in 12 s. The average power she develops is
  A 72 W B 500 W C 720 W D 5000 W
  E 7200 W
Q8 A motor pumps water from a well 10 m deep and projects it at a speed of 15 m s^{-1}. The water issues from the pipe at the rate of 1200 kg min^{-1}. Find the power of the motor.
Q9 A hammer head of mass 0.5 kg strikes the head of a nail at a speed of 10 m s^{-1}. The nail is driven 1 cm into a piece of wood. Find the average retarding force on the nail.
Q10 Solar cells are used to provide the electromotive force to charge the batteries on a car driven by an electric motor. Describe the energy changes which take place. What differences would you expect (i) in bright sunlight, (ii) on a cloudy day, (iii) at night?
Q11 A lift of mass 500 kg containing a load of mass 700 kg rises through 25 metres in 20 seconds. In the absence of friction, calculate the average power output of the motor driving the lift. Explain why, in practice, the power output will not be constant during this time. Assume the acceleration of free fall is 10 m s^{-2}.   (JMB)
Q12 A water wheel is used to operate a dynamo in order to supply electric lighting. Give a brief account of the energy transformations involved.   (S)
Q13 Which of the following are *not* vector quantities: force, energy, momentum, work, velocity?
  A snooker ball **B** makes an impact with an identical stationary ball **C**. Before impact **B** has a velocity of 2 m s^{-1} and it follows along the same path with a velocity of 0.2 m s^{-1}; calculate the velocity of **C** after impact.   (S)

Q14

A crate, of mass 70 kg, is pulled a distance of 12 m up an inclined plane and in the process its centre of gravity is raised 2.0 m. In order to do this a force of 150 N is applied to the crate in a direction parallel to the inclined plane.
(a) What is the increase in the potential energy of the crate?
(b) What is the work done by the force?
(c) Why do your answers to (a) and (b) differ?   (O)

Q15

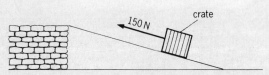

(a) A small trolley is placed as shown at the top, A, of a uniformly rough descending track. (BC is horizontal.) After being released the trolley eventually comes to rest at C. Describe how you could use a ticker-timer to show that the deceleration of the trolley between B and C is constant.
(b) The track is now changed to a *smooth* one with the profile shown below, where WXZ is horizontal. The mass of the trolley is 0.40 kg. What is the potential energy of the trolley when at V, relative to W? After being released, what is the speed of the trolley when it reaches W? (Ignore air resistance acting on the trolley.)

The trolley collides with a second, stationary trolley of mass 0.40 kg at X and the two stick together. It is observed that the combined trolleys have *just* sufficient energy to reach the top of the hump Y. Calculate the energy lost in the collision. What has happened to this energy?   (L)

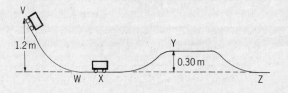

123

10 Heat

10.1 Specific heat capacity

In Chapter 9 it was stated that heat is a form of energy. Students often get confused between the terms *temperature* and *heat*. For example, a red-hot spark from a fire is at a much higher temperature than a pail of boiling water, but contains much less heat energy. The spark will not injure you if it falls on your hand, but the boiling water will certainly do so. Temperature is a measure of the heat energy level, whereas heat is a measure of the total internal energy contained in the body. Internal energy is made up of both potential and kinetic energy, and the kinetic energy may be made up of either vibrational or translational energy or a mixture of both.

When the same quantity of heat energy is given to equal masses of different substances, they do not experience the same rise in temperature. This may be demonstrated by the following experiment.

If an immersion heater of the same power is used in a block of copper of mass 1.0 kg for the same length of time, the temperature rise will be found to be about ten times that of the water. Paraffin, which is less dense than water, has a higher temperature rise when an equal quantity of heat is given to it, and copper, which is much denser than water, has a much higher temperature rise. It would appear that when equal quantities of heat energy are given to equal masses of different substances the relative density has nothing to do with the rise in temperature. The property which is responsible for the different temperature rises is known as the specific heat capacity of the substance.

Specific heat capacity is defined as **the quantity of heat energy which will raise the temperature of unit mass (1 kg) of a substance by 1 K.** It is usually denoted by the letter c and its SI units are $J\,kg^{-1}\,K^{-1}$ to read joule per kilogram kelvin. Temperature scales will be covered in Chapter 13, but you should note that the 'size' of one degree on the Celsius scale is equal to the 'size' of one degree on the Kelvin scale:

10 °C to 15 °C is a rise of 5 °C.
283 K to 288 K is a rise of 5 K.

Both are measures of the same temperature change.

Investigation 10.1   To investigate the rise in temperature produced by a given quantity of heat energy

Find the mass of an empty glass beaker by placing it on a top-pan balance. Then pour a known mass of water, e.g. 1.0 kg, into the beaker. Place an immersion heater, stirrer and thermometer in the water and connect the circuit as shown in Fig. 10.1. A jacket of felt or cotton-wool can be put round the container to cut down loss of heat. Switch on the heater for a fixed time, say 15 minutes (depending upon the power of the heater). During this time stir the water continually and keep the reading on the ammeter constant by adjusting the rheostat if necessary. At the end of the 15 minutes note the rise in temperature.

Pour the water out and repeat the experiment with an *equal mass* of another liquid, e.g. paraffin. After running the immersion heater for the *same time* with the *same* ammeter reading you will note that the rise in temperature of the paraffin is approximately twice that of the water. If the same mass of a third liquid is used a different rise in temperature will be obtained.

Note   Be careful to use the *same mass* and not the *same volume*.

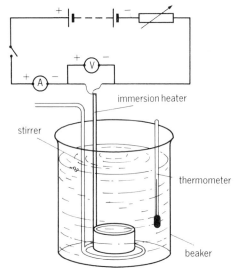

10.1   Apparatus for determining the specific heat capacity of a liquid

Thus if temperatures are measured in °C and their difference is recorded the unit of the difference may be expressed in °C or K, whichever is more suitable.

It follows from the definition of specific heat capacity that c joule of heat energy will raise the temperature of 1 kg of a substance by 1 K. Thus the quantity of heat that raises the temperature of m kg by 1 K is mc J, and the quantity of heat that raises this mass through $\Delta\theta$ K is $mc\Delta\theta$ J. The general equation is given by $\Delta Q = mc\Delta\theta$ where ΔQ is the change in heat energy of the mass m and $\Delta\theta$ is the change in temperature.

Note Heat energy may be absorbed *or* emitted from the substance. If it is absorbed there will be a rise in temperature, and if it is emitted there will be a fall in temperature.

Investigation 10.2 To determine the specific heat capacity of a solid (electrical method)

The solid used in this investigation is in the form of a cylindrical metal block. A metal block is used because it has a high specific heat, and is a good conductor, so the heat from the heater spreads rapidly to the whole of the block. A different method, found in more advanced textbooks, must be used for a poor conductor such as a rubber bung.

Find the mass of the solid using a top-pan balance. Usually the mass is about 1 kg and there is no point in reading the mass more accurately than to 1 g as the temperature is unlikely to be accurate to less than 0.1 K. Then place the solid in a felt jacket which covers it completely and insert the immersion heater and thermometer into the holes drilled in the block. Adding a small amount of oil to the thermometer hole before the thermometer is inserted will ensure good thermal contact between the block and the thermometer. Connect the immersion heater as shown in Fig. 10.2. Switch on the d.c. supply temporarily and adjust the rheostat until you obtain suitable values of the current and voltage. You are now ready to begin the experiment. First note the initial temperature. Then start a stopclock at the same time as you close the switch. When a reasonable rise in temperature has occurred, stop the stopclock at the same time as you switch off the current. Note the time t second and the highest temperature reached by the thermometer. This may occur slightly *after* the current is switched off. You can now calculate the rise in temperature $\Delta\theta$.

During the experiment you must keep the ammeter reading constant by adjusting the rheostat. Note the readings of the voltmeter at fixed intervals and work out the average reading. c is calculated from

$$VIt = mc\,\Delta\theta$$

$V I t$ is the electrical energy given out by the heater during the experiment and $m c \Delta\theta$ is the heat energy received by the block.

If you take readings of the thermometer and voltmeter at 1 minute intervals and note them in a table similar to the example for an aluminium block, you can plot a graph of temperature against time. Draw the best straight line as in Fig. 10.3. The slope of this line gives $\Delta\theta/t$. Note that the time must be in seconds. Then $VI = mc\Delta\theta/t$ or $c = VIt/m\Delta\theta$ and c may be calculated.

Time/s	Temperature/°C	Voltage/V	Current/A

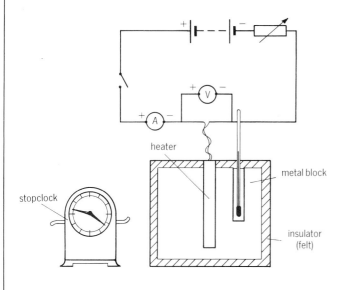

10.2   Apparatus for determining the specific heat capacity of a solid

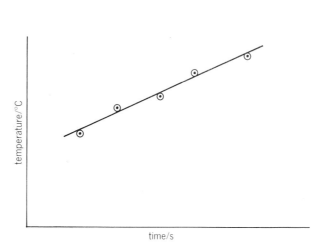

10.3   Graph of temperature against time for investigation 10.2

The felt jacket is used to prevent loss of heat energy by conduction and convection. It is assumed that all the electrical energy is used to raise the temperature of the block. If some escapes $\Delta\theta$ will be lower than it should be and the calculated value of the specific heat capacity will be too high. Felt is a bad conductor so heat cannot escape by conduction. Since the felt prevents air from coming into contact with the block, convection will be almost completely eliminated. The block is usually polished to cut down the heat lost by radiation since shiny surfaces are bad radiators. In this manner the heat losses will be cut to a minimum, but the result will still not be completely accurate because heat energy will be used to raise the temperature of the immersion heater itself and that of the thermometer.

Example of a typical set of results for an aluminium block

$$\text{Mass of block } (m) = 1.0 \text{ kg}$$
$$\text{Initial temperature of block } (\theta_1) = 21.5\,^\circ\text{C}$$
$$\text{Final temperature of block } (\theta_2) = 31.5\,^\circ\text{C}$$
$$\text{Rise in temperature } (\Delta\theta) = 10.0 \text{ K}$$
$$\text{Ammeter reading } (I) = 2.0 \text{ A}$$
$$\text{Voltmeter reading } (V) = 4.5 \text{ V}$$
$$\text{Time} = 1000 \text{ s}$$

$$c = VIt/m \text{ J kg}^{-1}\text{K}^{-1} = \frac{4.5 \times 2 \times 1000}{1 \times 10}$$

$$c = 900 \text{ J kg}^{-1}\text{K}^{-1}$$

Investigation 10.3   To determine the specific heat capacity of a liquid

The specific heat capacity of a liquid may be found in a similar manner. Place a dry empty copper calorimeter and a stirrer on a top-pan balance and determine their mass m^1. Fill it about two-thirds full with liquid and determine the mass m_2. Place the calorimeter in an insulated jacket, insert an immersion heater and fit a cork lid which prevents evaporation and convection from the surface of the liquid. Then follow the procedure of Investigation 10.2. When calculating the result you must remember that heat energy is required to heat the calorimeter, so the equation becomes: electrical energy given out by heater = heat energy gained by liquid + heat energy gained by calorimeter, or

$$VIt = m_1 c_1\Delta\theta + m_s c_s\Delta\theta$$

where the suffix 1 represents the liquid and the suffix s the calorimeter.

One way of cutting down the heat losses is to pre-cool the liquid so that it is several degrees below room temperature at the start of the experiment. Heating then starts and continues until the liquid reaches the same number of degrees above room temperature. The idea is that the quantity of heat gained from the surroundings while the liquid is below room temperature should compensate for the heat lost to the surroundings while it is above room temperature.

Example of a typical set of results for water

$$\text{Mass of calorimeter + stirrer } (m_1) = 0.070 \text{ kg}$$
$$\text{Mass of calorimeter + stirrer + water } (m_2) = 0.170 \text{ kg}$$
$$\text{Mass of water } (m_2 - m_1) = 0.100 \text{ kg}$$
$$\text{Initial temperature of water } (\theta_1) = 18.2\,^\circ\text{C}$$
$$\text{Final temperature of water } (\theta_2) = 35.1\,^\circ\text{C}$$
$$\text{Rise in temperature } (\Delta\theta) = 16.9 \text{ K}$$
$$\text{Ammeter reading } (I) = 2.0 \text{ A}$$
$$\text{Voltmeter reading } (V) = 3.8 \text{ V}$$
$$\text{Time } (t) = 1000 \text{ s}$$

Specific heat capacity of calorimeter and stirrer = $400 \text{ J kg}^{-1}\text{ K}^{-1}$. Assuming no heat losses,

$$VIt = m_1 c_1 \Delta\theta + m_s c_s\Delta\theta$$
$$3.8 \times 2.0 \times 1000 = 0.1 \times c \times 16.9 + 0.7 \times 400 \times 16.9$$
$$7600 = 1.69\,c + 473.2$$
$$7126.8 = 1.69\,c$$
$$c = 7128.8/1.69$$
$$c = 4217 \text{ J kg}^{-1}\text{ K}^{-1}$$

Example

How much heat energy is required to raise 2 kg of water from 20 °C to its boiling point at 100 °C?

$$m = 2 \text{ kg} \quad c = 4200 \text{ J kg}^{-1}\text{ K}^{-1}$$
$$\Delta\theta = 100 - 20 = 80\,^\circ\text{C} = 80 \text{ K}$$

$$\text{heat energy required} = mc\Delta\theta$$
$$= 2 \text{ kg} \times 4200 \text{ J kg}^{-1}\text{ K}^{-1} \times 80 \text{ K}$$
$$= 2 \times 4200 \times 80 \text{ J}$$
$$= 672\,000 \text{ J}$$

However, a liquid must have a container. Suppose the water is in an electric kettle of mass 1 kg and specific heat capacity $400 \text{ J kg}^{-1} \text{ K}^{-1}$.

$$m = 1 \text{ kg} \quad c = 400 \text{ J kg}^{-1} \text{ K}^{-1} \quad \Delta\theta = 80 \text{ K}$$

extra heat energy required to heat kettle
$$= mc\Delta\theta$$
$$= 1 \text{ kg} \times 400 \text{ J kg}^{-1} \text{ K}^{-1} \times 80 \text{ K}$$
$$= 1 \times 400 \times 80 \text{ J}$$
$$= 32\,000 \text{ J}$$

This 32 000 J is wasted energy as it is not used to heat the water. About 4.5% of the energy is wasted.

Table 10.1 Specific heat capacities of various substances in $\text{J kg}^{-1} \text{ K}^{-1}$.

Aluminium	900	Mercury	140
Brass	380	Water	4200
Copper	400	Ice	2100
Iron	450	Paraffin	2270
Lead	130		

However this is a much more efficient method of heating water than using a saucepan on either a gas or an electric cooker because the heating element is *inside* the kettle. On an electric cooker the element may make contact in only a few places and there will be a layer of air between the heat source and the saucepan. On the gas cooker there is probably a layer of unburnt gas below the saucepan. Gases are bad conductors of heat and the time taken to boil the water will increase, thus decreasing the efficiency.

You may have heard that a chest-type freezer is more efficient than an upright type because every time the door of the upright freezer is opened the cold air, which is more dense than the surrounding air, escapes. In the chest-type freezer the dense cold air stays in the freezer, and very little escapes. However, the mass of air involved is very small, so not much electrical energy is required to cool the new air in the freezer to the required temperature. This is an instance where it may be worth losing a little efficiency to gain convenience. It is easier to see where things are in an upright freezer.

10.2 Specific heat capacities of gases

Does a gas have a specific heat capacity? It does because giving a quantity of heat to a gas increases the internal energy. It is a very complex subject, which you can read about in more advanced textbooks.

10.3 Flow of heat energy

Earlier in the chapter it was stated that temperature is a measure of the level of the heat energy. In hydrostatics water always flows from a higher to a lower level irrespective of the quantity of water at each level. The same is true of heat energy. Heat energy always flows from a higher to a lower level, i.e. from a higher temperature to a lower temperature, irrespective of the quantity of heat energy at each level. When a red-hot spark falls into a pail of water heat energy flows from the spark to the water, although the water contains far more heat energy than the spark. The flow of heat energy continues until the two temperatures are equal.

Energy equations

Assuming that heat is not lost to the surroundings, it follows from the Law of Conservation of Energy that the heat energy lost from the body at the higher temperature will equal the heat energy gained by the body at the lower temperature. Hence

$$m_1 c_1 (\theta_1 - \theta_3) = m_2 c_2 (\theta_3 - \theta_2)$$

where m_1 and m_2 are the mass of the hot and the cold body respectively, c_1 and c_2 are the specific heat capacities of the hot and cold bodies, θ_1 the initial temperature of the cold body, θ_3 the final temperature of both bodies.

Example

A blacksmith cools an iron bolt mass 0.5 kg, temperature 400 °C by putting it into a pail containing 9 kg water at 20 °C. Find the final temperature of the water and bolt. Ignore the heat gained by the pail itself and any steam which may be emitted. (Specific heat capacities of water and iron are 4200 J kg^{-1} K^{-1} and 450 J kg^{-1} K^{-1} respectively.)

Using the equation above, $m_1 = 0.5$ kg $m_2 = 9$ kg
$c_1 = 450$ J kg^{-1} K^{-1} $c_2 = 4200$ J kg^{-1} K^{-1}
$\theta_1 = 400$ °C $\theta_2 = 20$ °C $\theta_3 = ?$ °C.

$$m_1 c_1 (\theta_1 - \theta_3) = m_2 c_2 (\theta_3 - \theta_2)$$

0.5 kg × 450 J kg^{-1} K^{-1} × (400 − θ_3) K
$$= 9 \text{ kg} \times 4200 \text{ J kg}^{-1} \text{ K}^{-1} \times$$
$$(\theta_3 - 20) \text{ K}$$
$$0.5 \times 450 (400 - \theta_3) = 9 \times 4200 (\theta_3 - 20)$$
$$0.5 \times 50 (400 - \theta_3) = 4200 (\theta_3 - 20)$$
$$(400 - \theta_3) = 168 (\theta_3 - 20)$$
$$400 - \theta_3 = 168\theta_3 - 3360$$
$$3760 = 169\theta_3$$
$$22.2 \text{ °C} = \theta_3$$

Thus the final temperature is approximately 22.2 °C.

When a body falls to the ground from a height the potential energy it has changes into kinetic energy; if the body does not rebound most of this kinetic energy is changed into heat energy. If we assume that all the kinetic energy is changed into heat energy, then

$$mgh = \tfrac{1}{2}mv^2 = mc\Delta\theta$$
$$mgh = mc\Delta\theta$$
$$gh = c\Delta\theta$$

Notice that the mass cancels, so you can deduce that the rise in temperature does not depend upon the mass of the falling body.

Example

A lead weight is dropped from a helicopter hovering at 100 m above the ground. Assuming that all the energy is converted into heat energy, what will be the rise in temperature of the lead? (Specific heat capacity of lead = 130 J kg^{-1} K^{-1}.)

$$gh = c\,\Delta\theta$$
$$10 \text{ m s}^{-2} \times 100 \text{ m} = 130 \text{ J kg}^{-1} \text{ K}^{-1} \times \Delta\theta$$
$$1000 = 130\,\Delta\theta$$
$$7.7 = \Delta\theta$$

Thus the rise in temperature will be 7.7 °C.

It can be seen from this type of calculation that the temperature of the water at the bottom of a waterfall will be slightly higher than that at the top. You can now work out that if all the increase in kinetic energy due to the fall were converted into heat energy, the temperature of the water at the bottom of a waterfall 100 m high would be ≈ 0.25 °C higher than the temperature of the water at the top.

Transfer of heat energy

There are various ways by which heat energy may be transferred. **Conduction, convection** and **radiation** are the main ways in which heat energy is lost from a hot solid. **Evaporation** also plays a very important part in the transfer of heat from a liquid.

10.4 Conduction

If you pick up a metal bar and a piece of cloth with your bare hands on a cold day, the metal will feel much colder than the cloth. If the objects have been outside for any length of time they will both be at the same temperature. So why does the metal feel colder? The answer is that it conducts heat energy from your hand much more quickly than the cloth. There are many simple experiments which can be performed to show that different materials conduct heat energy at different rates.

Although the wax melts much farther along the copper rod than along the lead rod, showing that copper is a much better conductor of heat energy, the wax melts first on the lead rod. Why is this? Lead has a smaller specific heat capacity than copper so its temperature rises more rapidly. That is why it is necessary to leave the experiment long enough for a **steady state** to be reached. This occurs when the rate of loss of heat is equal to the rate at which heat is supplied. As a result the temperature remains steady.

What is the process by which heat energy is transmitted in conduction? In a solid the particles vibrate but do not change their equilibrium positions. As the temperature rises the speed and amplitude of vibration becomes larger. It is reasonable to assume that some of this increased energy is passed on from particle to particle. However, there are large numbers of free electrons in metals. There is ample space for these to move and in fact they transfer the greater part of the heat energy. You could expect good conductors of heat to be good conductors of electricity.

Investigation 10.4   To compare the thermal conductivity of copper and glass

Hold a solid copper rod in one hand and a solid glass rod in the other. Both rods should be of the same length and diameter. Place the other ends of the rods in a Bunsen flame (see Fig. 10.4). After a short time you will probably have to let go of the copper because it is far too hot to hold, whereas the glass rod still feels quite cool, although the end in the flame may have started to melt.

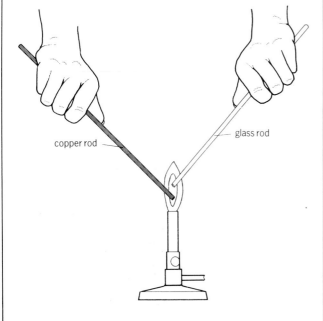

10.4   To show different conducting powers of copper and glass

---

Investigation 10.5   To compare the thermal conductivities of different substances

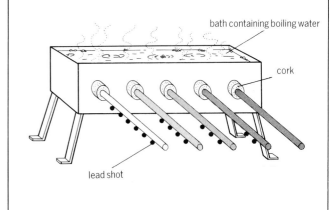

10.5   Ingenhausz apparatus

You will need the Ingenhausz apparatus shown in Fig. 10.5. Push rods of the same dimensions but of different substances through the corks so that their ends stick inside the metal bath. Coat the parts of the rods outside the tank with melted wax and allow it to solidify. Stick ball bearings onto the rods at equal intervals. Then pour boiling water into the bath so that the ends of the rods are submerged. After a time measure how far the wax has melted, or count how many ball bearings have fallen off each rod. The length of wax which has melted is a measure of the conductivity of the rod. You will find that copper is the best conductor and non-metals are the worst.

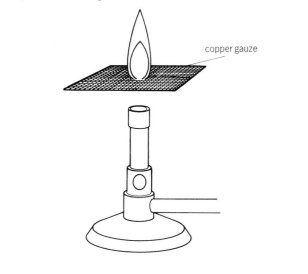
This property of copper gauze is still used in the miner's safety lamp (Fig. 10.7), invented by Sir Humphrey Davy in 1815. If there is any methane in the mine, the gas burns inside the gauze and the colour of the flame in the lamp changes. The gauze prevents the gas outside reaching its ignition temperature, and so an explosion does not occur.

Uses of bad and good conductors

Handles of kettles, saucepans etc. are always made of poor conductors so that the hot vessel can be picked up quite easily and safely. When hot objects such as casseroles have to be carried, oven gloves or some other non-conducting material has to be used to hold them. Table mats are made of non-conducting materials such as cork, so that hot plates and dishes will not damage the polished table. It is well to remember that dishes of toughened glass (a poor conductor) take much longer to cool than metal dishes. They also keep the vegetables in them hot for a long time.

In order to transfer heat as quickly as possible, good physical contact needs to be made between the different substances and good conductors are used. What are the advantages of the toughened glass saucepans that can be obtained today? Another example of a good conductor in the home is the hot

10.7 Flame safety lamp

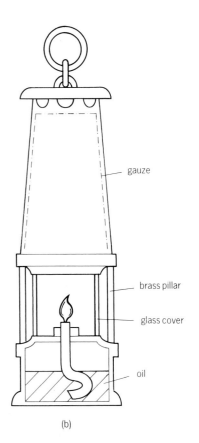

(b)

water 'radiator'. This is made of metal so that heat energy from the hot water inside is conducted quickly to the outside of the radiator. Here it heats air in contact with it by conduction; the hot air then rises and cooler air takes its place.

Exercise 10.1

Write down three examples of the uses of good conductors and three of bad conductors in the home.

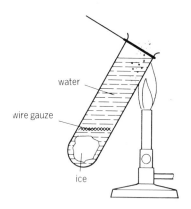

10.8 To show water is a bad conductor of heat

Liquids are poor conductors of heat. In Fig. 10.8 a lump of ice is weighted with some wire to make it stay at the bottom of the water in the test tube. A Bunsen burner heats the water at the top of the tube and the water at the top soon boils. However, it takes a long time for the ice at the bottom to melt. This indicates that both water and glass are poor conductors of heat.

It is interesting to consider the relative thermal conductivities of various substances.

thermal conductivity of copper

$$= 6 \times \text{thermal conductivity of iron}$$
$$= 600 \times \text{thermal conductivity of glass}$$
$$= 7200 \times \text{thermal conductivity of water}$$
$$= 9000 \times \text{thermal conductivity of cork}$$
$$= 18000 \times \text{thermal conductivity of cotton-wool}$$
$$= 18000 \times \text{thermal conductivity of air}$$

The conductivities of air and cotton-wool are approximately the same because cotton-wool contains such large quantities of trapped air.

On frosty mornings in winter you may see birds with their feathers puffed out. This traps a lot more air between the feathers and so the bird is better insulated against the cold.

Conduction is a two-way process. Any insulator which will prevent heat energy from escaping will also prevent heat energy from entering. Bad conductors can be used just as effectively to keep things cool as they can to keep things hot.

A material medium is necessary for conduction. The perfect non-conductor is a vacuum because there are no particles present to transfer the heat.

10.5   Convection

A second way of transferring heat energy is by convection. In this heat energy is transferred by the substance moving *en bloc*. Consequently it does not occur in solids, but only in liquids and gases. It cannot occur in a vacuum. When a certain mass of the substance is heated, the rise in temperature causes the volume to increase. There is thus a decrease in the density of the sample, it becomes less dense than its surroundings and rises. This may lead to the meaningless statement 'heat rises'. What should be said is that the *substance which has been heated* rises. When air is heated, the less dense warm air rises to be replaced by colder more dense air. Hence a **convection current** is set up with the less dense warm air carrying heat energy upwards.

The hot water system in a house (Fig. 10.10) is an example of convection. In its simplest form the water is heated and rises, and cold water falls to replace it. The water in the tank A (boiler) is heated, often by a gas burner. This hot water expands, becomes less dense, rises and flows into the top half of the cylinder B. Cold water from the cistern D falls due to

Investigation 10.7   To show convection currents

Put some water in a large round-bottomed flask. Place an open tube in the water with one end on the bottom of the flask and drop potassium permanganate crystals down it. Then put one finger over the top end and remove the tube and coloured water, leaving the crystals on the bottom of the flask. Place a small Bunsen flame underneath the crystals. You will see purple streamers rise gently up the middle of the liquid and then fall down the outside of the flask. A convection current has been set up, and it will not be long before the water becomes a uniform purple.

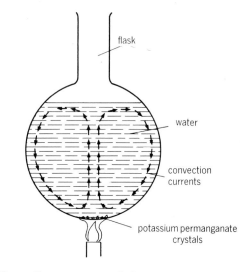

10.9   Convection currents in a flask

hydrostatic pressure into the bottom of the cylinder B and thence to the bottom of the tank A to replace the hot water which has risen. The overflow pipe C is needed in case the water in B reaches too high a temperature. The hot water tap is led from the overflow pipe. Pressure from the water in D forces the hot water out of the tap.

A modern hot water system is rather more complicated. The tank B is double-walled, with one cylinder inside another, one part serving the hot water taps and the other the central heating system. The part serving the taps works by natural convection, but the water is driven round the hot water system by an electric pump. This ensures that all radiators acquire roughly the same temperature.

The element in an electric kettle is placed as near as possible to the bottom of the kettle so that the water can be heated by convection. Putting the element near to the top would be most inefficient since only the water near the top would be heated; that near the bottom would remain cool because water is a bad conductor. Moreover, it would always be necessary to fill the kettle completely in order to cover the element.

Some hot water cylinders which are heated electrically contain two immersion heaters. A low-wattage one near the top of the tank is used when only a small quantity of hot water is needed quickly, e.g. for washing up. When a large amount of hot water is needed, the larger heater near the bottom is switched on.

It is essential to surround the hot water cylinder B in Fig. 10.10 by an insulating jacket so that as little heat as possible is lost to the surroundings. The temperature of the water is controlled by a thermostat which switches off the heater when the water temperature in the cylinder reaches a certain level. Do you think it is more economical to keep the heating on continuously with the thermostat cutting in and out or to switch on only once or twice a day until the water reaches the required temperature?

10.6 Radiation

Radiation is a third method of transferring heat energy. If you stand directly in front of an electric fire, how does the heat reach you? Not by conduction because air is a bad conductor. Not by convection because the hot air rises vertically from the fire. The answer is by radiation in the form of electromagnetic waves. These are partly or wholly absorbed by substances upon which they fall. When they are absorbed they give up their heat energy. As mentioned on p.117, this is the method by which heat reaches us from the Sun. The waves do not need a medium but can travel through a vacuum.

When there is an eclipse of the Sun, the heat and light are cut off at the same time. Thus it is reasonable to assume that they travel at the same speed. The different colours of light have different wavelengths. Heat radiation also has a range of wavelengths. The higher the temperature (energy level) of the body emitting radiation, the shorter the wavelength and the greater the energy.

If a small electric heater behind a slit is used as a source, a metal screen as a mirror and a thermopile and slit as a detector, it can be shown that the laws of reflection also hold for heat. The laws of refraction can be demonstrated by using a prism of rock salt instead of the mirror.

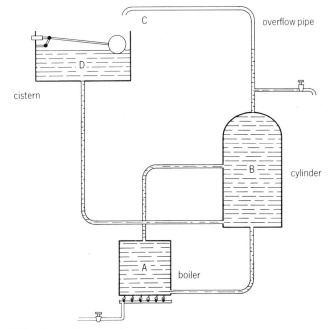

10.10   *Domestic hot water system*

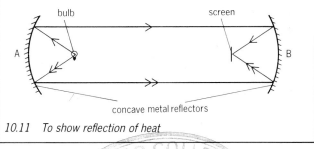

Investigation 10.8   To show the similarity between heat and light

Set up two concave metal reflectors A and B as shown in Fig. 10.11. Place a source of light at the focus of A and a screen in the focal plane of B. The image of A will be received on the screen. If you replace the source of light by a small electric heater and put a match head at the focus of B, the match will ignite. If you then remove reflector B and put a match head in the same position as before, it will not ignite. This shows that heat waves can be focussed in the same manner as light waves.

10.11   *To show reflection of heat*

131

Investigation 10.9 To demonstrate the absorption of heat waves

This can be shown using Leslie's Differential Air Thermometer (Fig. 10.12). A and B are two identical glass bulbs which are connected to each other as shown. Leave A untreated but blacken B with either lampblack or soot. Open the tap T to ensure that the pressure in each bulb is the same. The levels of the coloured liquid in the U-tube will then be the same. Close T and place a small electric heater midway between A and B, and on the same horizontal level. Since they are on the same level as the heater, no heat will be transferred to the bulbs by convection and the same small amount will be transferred to both by conduction. The liquid level falls on the side nearer to B and rises on the side nearer to A. This indicates that the pressure in B is higher than the pressure in A. Since the pressures were the same originally, the conclusion is that the temperature in B is higher than the temperature in A. This is because the black surface has absorbed radiation more quickly than the clear surface.

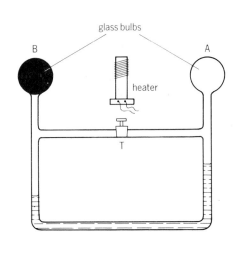

10.12   Leslie's differential air thermometer

Investigation 10.10 A further demonstration of the absorption of heat waves

Figure 10.13 shows two identical sheets of copper A and B supported in wooden bases. A is painted matt white and B matt black. On the back of each plate is a blob of wax which supports a large nail. Place a small electric heater midway between the two plates and at the same level as the wax and turn it on. Very soon the wax at the back of the matt black plate melts and the nail falls. If plate A is highly polished it will take even longer for the wax at the back to melt.

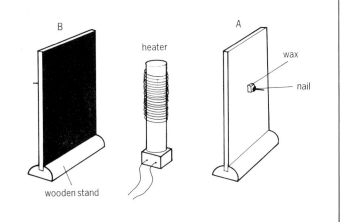

10.13   Demonstration of absorption of radiation

Investigation 10.11 To investigate heat emission using Leslie's Cube

Leslie's Cube (Fig. 10.14) is a hollow copper cube with four different side surfaces. One is lampblackened, another roughened, another white, and the fourth polished. Pour boiling water into the cube, and place a thermopile connected to a sensitive galvanometer equidistant from each of the four faces in turn. The deflection is greatest when the thermopile faces the matt black surface, and least when it faces the polished surface.

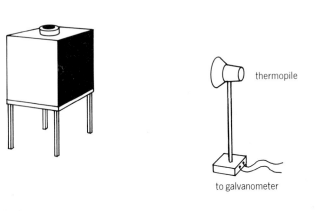

10.14   Leslie's cube

These two experiments lead to the conclusion that black surfaces are good absorbers of radiant heat energy whereas white or polished surfaces are not. This is why the glass in greenhouses in England is often covered with a layer of whitewash in summer. Metal roofs in hot countries are also often painted white. The heat radiation will be reflected rather than absorbed, and the interior of the house remains cool.

Is it also better to have a white car, rather than a black or coloured car, in a hot country? In fact it makes very little difference because the cars are so highly polished that the colour has little effect. It also makes little difference if people in hot countries wear white clothes to keep themselves cool. Cloth is a bad conductor and the long flowing robes often worn trap air which insulates the wearer from the heat.

So far only absorption of radiation has been considered. What about emission?

From this investigation it seems that matt black is the best radiator, followed by roughened, white, and then polished surfaces. Comparing this with absorption, the general rule can be stated that good absorbers are good radiators, and bad absorbers are bad radiators.

A secondary experiment can be performed using Leslie's Cube to compare the ability of various substances to transmit radiation. Sheets of the different substances are placed between the black surface and the thermopile and the readings of the thermopile are noted. The experiment can be repeated using a small electric fire instead of the cube. It must be remembered that, since Leslie's Cube is only at about 100 °C the radiation will have a long wavelength, whereas that from the electric fire will be much shorter. You should find that glass transmits some radiation from the electric fire, but not the longer wavelength from Leslie's Cube. This explains the working of a cold frame or greenhouse (see Fig. 10.15). Short wavelength heat radiation from the Sun (short wavelength because of the Sun's high temperature) is transmitted by the glass and is absorbed by the plants, soil and other objects in the greenhouse. These objects experience a rise in temperature, but since their temperature is not very high they emit radiation of longer wavelength. This cannot pass through the glass, and is reflected and retained in the greenhouse. As a result the temperature inside the greenhouse rises considerably.

It should be stressed that all objects emit and receive radiation all the time. There is a continual transfer. When an object is in a steady state the quantity of radiation absorbed each second is equal to the quantity emitted each second. If the quantity absorbed is greater than the quantity emitted, the temperature of the object will rise. This causes an increase in the quantity of radiation emitted and the temperature will rise until a steady state is reached.

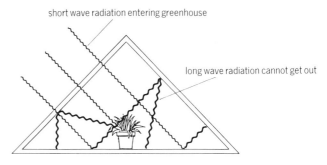

10.15 Greenhouse effect

10.7 Preventing heat transfer

Although it is convenient to consider conduction, convection and radiation separately so that the mechanism of each can be understood, in practice all three operate at once. When designing any apparatus or machine all three must be taken into account so that the apparatus operates as efficiently as possible. The requirements differ according to the situation concerned. In some it is necessary to retain heat. In others, e.g. the motorcycle engine, it is very important to get rid of the heat. The cylinder is encased in a metal block which has fins radiating from it. Metal is a good conductor so the heat is transferred quickly from the inside to the outside. The fins increase the surface area of the metal and so the quantity of air in contact with the metal is increased. Heat energy is passed by conduction from the metal to the air and large convection currents are set up. Also the greater the surface area the greater the quantity of heat energy lost by radiation.

Despite its name, radiation plays little part in the transfer of heat from the household radiator because the temperature is not high enough. In addition the radiators are usually painted white, which cuts down the heat energy radiated. Conduction plays a large part in transferring heat energy from the hot water in the radiator to the air in the room. Convection then plays the major part in distributing the heat energy.

In the motor-car engine the heat from the cylinder is carried away by water. Water is used as the cooling liquid, because in addition to being plentiful it has a high specific heat capacity. The hot water passes into metal tubes in the 'radiator' of the car. Heat energy is conducted to the outside of the tube and carried away by the strong air flow through the radiator produced by a fan.

Much thought has to be given to the transfer of heat energy when designing space ships and space suits. In space the obvious problem is radiation and the design should attempt to cut down radiation to the minimum. The inside of the ship or suit should obviously also be well insulated from the outside to prevent the transfer of heat energy in either direction.

133

The Thermos flask

The Thermos flask is a useful device which almost eliminates conduction, convection, and radiation. It consists of a double-walled glass container with a cork or hollow stopper (Fig. 10.16). The air is pumped out from between the walls of the flask to create a vacuum. The inner surfaces of the walls which enclose the vacuum are silvered to reduce loss of heat energy by radiation. The inner wall is a bad radiator and the outer wall is a bad absorber. Heat energy cannot be transferred across the vacuum by conduction or convection because a medium is necessary for these processes. Glass is a bad conductor, but this is not really significant. A disadvantage of glass is the ease with which it breaks. In flasks built to contain liquid oxygen or liquid hydrogen the flask is made of metal. The walls are very thin so conduction up or down the neck is very small. Elsewhere heat energy conducted through the metal walls does not get any further because of the vacuum.

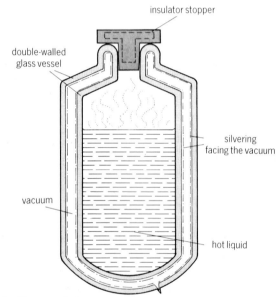

10.16   Thermos flask

The role of the stopper is important. It prevents heat loss by evaporation from hot liquids or from convection currents set up above the surface of the liquid. The transfer of heat energy is a two-way process and the vacuum flask is used as much to keep things cool as it is to keep things hot.

House insulation and heating

In recent years much attention has been focussed on the insulation of houses. This is an economic necessity because of the rising costs of fuel. Cavity walls were introduced as a means of insulation. As air is a better insulator than brick, the introduction of a cavity presumably improves the insulation. However, if the cavity is large, convection currents are set up inside the cavity and heat energy is carried away by convection.

Nowadays the cavity is filled with a substance such as plastic foam which traps small bubbles of air. Convection no longer takes place and the insulation is improved.

Double-glazed windows also increase the insulation by trapping a layer of air between the two sheets of glass. The extra thickness of glass in the two sheets improves the insulation and the layer of air between them is also a very good insulator. The width of the air gap is important. Double glazing has added advantages in that is stops condensation on the inside of windows, and also insulates from sound.

In the roof, layers of an insulating material, or granules, are spread to prevent loss of heat energy by conduction. Once again the insulating properties depend upon the pockets of air trapped between the fibres. A minimum depth of about 10 cm of fibre is recommended.

Central heating is much more efficient that the old-fashioned open fires. Most of the hot air from an open fire goes up the chimney and is lost, and cold air is drawn in under the doors, so creating draughts. Although pleasant to look at, an open fire warms by illusion more than by heat!

The position of heating appliances is very important. A convector heater should be placed on the floor so that hot air can rise and circulate around the room. It is unfortunate that the warmest part of a room will be near the ceiling. The freezing compartment in a refrigerator is placed at the top. Cold air then falls to the bottom and the warmer air at the top is continually cooled.

Electric storage heaters contain dense blocks of material which have a high specific heat capacity. They are heated during the off-peak periods when electricity is cheaper and give off their heat energy slowly throughout the remainder of the day.

U-values

The prevention of energy losses from buildings has become of major importance. To make calculations more precise the U-values of materials have to be known.

The U-value of a material is the rate at which heat flows through it by conduction, per unit area of surface, when unit temperature difference exists between the two sides, i.e.

$$\text{U-value} = \frac{\text{rate of loss of heat energy}}{\text{surface area} \times \text{temperature difference}} \text{ W/m}^2\text{K}$$

It follows that rate of heat loss = U-value × surface area × temperature difference.

Obviously good thermal **conductors** have high U-values, and good thermal **insulators** have low U-values. Note that the thickness of the material is not in the equation, so the U-value depends not only upon the material, but also upon the thickness. A thick layer of insulator has a lower U-value than a thin layer. A layer of double glazing with an air gap in between has a lower U-value than a single sheet of glass. A double brick wall with an air cavity has a lower U-value than a double brick wall with no air cavity. The U-value is further reduced if the air cavity is filled with foam. U-values also depend upon conditions, e.g. moisture. If the outside walls of a house are wet, the U-value is increased.

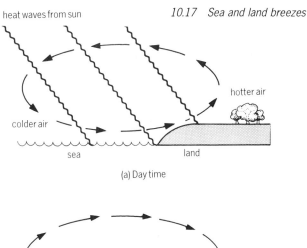

(a) Day time

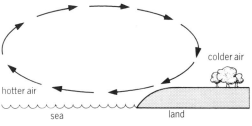

(b) Night time

Example

A room has a wall of 10 m^2 and a double glazing area of 6 m^2 exposed to the outside. The walls are foam filled and the U-value is 0.6 W/m^2 K. The U-value of the double glazing is 2.8 W/m^2 K. The inside temperature is 20 °C and the outside temperature 5 °C. What is the rate of loss of heat?

Temperature difference = 20 °C − 5 °C = 15 °C

Rate of loss through walls
$$= 0.6 \frac{W}{m^2 K} \times 10\,m^2 \times 15\,K = 90\,W$$

Rate of loss through windows
$$= 2.8 \frac{W}{m^2 K} \times 6\,m^2 \times 15\,K = 252\,W$$

Total rate of heat loss to outside = 90 W + 252 W = 342 W
If the walls are not foam filled (U-value 1.7 W/m^2 K) and the window is single glazed (6 mm glass) (U-value 5.6 W/m^2 K) the rate of heat loss become:

wall $1.7 \frac{W}{m^2 K} \times 10\,m^2 \times 15\,K = 255\,W$

window $5.6 \frac{W}{m^2 K} \times 6\,m^2 \times 15\,K = 504\,W$

total   225 W + 504 W = 759 W

thus an extra 417 W are lost.
In a day the energy saved by having the walls foam-filled and the windows double glazed is:

power × time = 417 W × (24 × 60 × 60) s = 36 MJ (approx)

Note   Energy will also be lost through the floor and ceiling and through the walls to adjoining rooms unless these are at the same temperature.

10.8   Natural phenomena

Substances with high specific heat capacities take longer to heat than substances with low specific heat capacities. The reverse is also true: substances with high specific heat capacities take longer to cool than substances with low specific heat capacities under similar conditions. These facts have important natural consequences. The daily variation in temperature over a sandy area when there are clear skies will be much larger than that over water. This accounts for the formation of land and sea breezes (Fig. 10.17). During the day the temperature of the land becomes appreciably higher than that of the sea because of the much lower specific heat capacity of the land. Consequently the air in contact with the ground becomes warmer, expands and becomes less dense. This air rises and colder more dense air from over the sea moves in to replace it. Thus a circulation current is set up. During the night the reverse effect takes place. The land soon cools to below the sea temperature. Thus the air over the sea is warmer than the air over the land and a circulation current is set up in the opposite direction to the daytime current. In daytime the surface wind is from the sea to the land and at night-time from the land to the sea.

Small islands have a much more temperate climate than large land masses in the same latitude. Because of the high specific heat capacity of the surrounding water, temperature variations are small.

On clear nights in winter hoar frost forms quickly on stationary cars. The car radiates heat; the metal, which has a low specific heat capacity, cools quickly and its temperature soon falls below the freezing point.

Questions

Q1 A 700 W heater raises the temperature of some water from 20 °C to 100 °C in 10 min. If the specific heat capacity of water is 4200 J kg^{-1} K^{-1} and if heat losses are neglected, the mass of water heated is

A $\frac{1}{48}$ kg   **B** 1 kg   **C** $1\frac{1}{4}$ kg   **D** 5 kg   **E** 100 kg   *(L)*

Q2 A piece of iron of mass m and specific heat capacity c, and a piece of aluminium of mass $2m$ and specific heat capacity $2c$ each received the same quantity of heat. The temperature of the aluminium rose by 8 K. By how much did the temperature of the iron rise?

A 2 K   **B** 4 K   **C** 8 K   **D** 16 K   **E** 32 K   *(L)*

Q3 In order to keep the contents of a lagged, sealed container cool, a sachet of a gelatinous liquid is pre-cooled and placed in the container. The contents remain cool for some hours. This is possible because

A all other liquids have a larger heat capacity than water.

B heat cannot be lost to the surroundings.

C heat lost by convection does not occur in a lagged container.

D heat lost by radiation still occurs.

E the heat capacity of the sachet is large.   *(L)*

Q4 Hot water at 100 °C is added to 300 g of water of 0 °C until the final temperature is 40 °C. The mass of hot water added must be at least

A 60 g   **B** 75 g   **C** 120 g   **D** 180 g   **E** 200 g   *(L)*

Q5 Which of the following, all initially at a temperature of 20 °C, will have absorbed the greatest quantity of heat energy?

A A steel needle heated to red heat

B A kettle of water heated to boiling point

C A bathtub of water heated to 50 °C

D A mercury thermometer heated to body temperature

E A piece of lead shot heated to its melting point   *(L)*

Q6 Name and describe the *three* main methods by which a hot body may lose heat energy. During the winter, a particular house loses 432 million joules of energy per day to the outside atmosphere. Calculate how many kilowatts of electrical fire heating are needed to maintain the inside temperature.   *(W)*

Q7 A lagged copper calorimeter of mass 75 g contains 125 g of water at 20 °C. When a 200 g mass of copper is transferred from an oven to the calorimeter and water the steady temperature reached is 50 °C. Estimate the temperature of the oven, and give reasons why your calculated value will be different from the true temperature. (Assume specific heat capacities: water = 4000 J kg^{-1} K^{-1}; copper = 400 J kg^{-1} K^{-1}.)

Q8 (a) (i) 'The *double walls* of a *vacuum* flask are *silvered* to reduce heat transfer between the contents of the flask and its surroundings.' Explain the purpose of each of the three features in italics in this statement.

   (ii) List the possible reasons why the contents of a well-sealed vacuum flask eventually reach the same temperature as that of its surroundings.

(b) In coastal regions during periods of hot sunny weather a steady light wind, reversing its direction every twelve hours, is often noticed. Account for the existence of the day-time breeze and with the help of a diagram show the direction of the air currents over the land.

(c) Many householders in Great Britain have built 'sun porches' (rooms with very large windows) on the south side of their houses. Explain, with the aid of a diagram, why the day-time temperature of these rooms is always higher than that of the air outside.   *(L)*

Q9 Describe an experiment you would perform to find the specific heat capacity of a liquid. State the precautions you would take to obtain an accurate result and show how you would calculate the result.

A saucepan of mass 0.7 kg containing 0.50 kg of water is placed on a gas burner. The initial temperature of the water is 20 °C. It takes 5 minutes before the water starts to boil. Find the rate at which heat is supplied to the water by the burner. (Specific heat capacity of water = 4000 J kg^{-1} K^{-1}; specific heat capacity of the material of the saucepan = 600 J kg^{-1} K^{-1}.)

It is found to take less time to boil water and cook vegetables in a saucepan with a lid than in a similar saucepan without a lid. Explain why this is so.   *(L)*

Q10 (a) Describe an experiment which you would carry out to show how the nature of a surface affects the heat radiated from that surface in a given time. State any precautions which you would take and state your finding for two named surfaces.

   How would you then show that the surface which was the better radiator was also the better absorber of radiation?

(b) As the surface of a pond freezes it is found that each equal increase in the thickness of the ice takes longer to form, even when the air above the ice remains at the same low temperature. Explain why this is so.

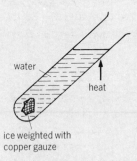

water

heat

ice weighted with copper gauze

(c) In the experiment shown above the ice remains intact for several minutes as heating progresses. Explain how this can be so.   *(L)*

Q11 Two identical metal blocks, one lagged and the other unlagged, have identical immersion heaters inserted and are connected in circuits as in Fig. 10.2 (p.125). Sketch the temperature–time graphs which you would expect for each block, and explain the differences.

The mass of the block is 1 kg and the power of the coil is 48 W. It takes 5 minutes for the temperature of the lagged block to rise from 20 °C to 50 °C. Find the specific heat capacity of the block.

11 The Gas Laws

11.1 The behaviour of ideal gases

When considering the behaviour of ideal gases it is as well to recall the simple assumptions of the kinetic theory. These are

(a) Gases consist of small solid particles which are in constant, rapid and random motion.
(b) The particles move in straight lines and their motion is only affected by collisions with other particles or the walls of the containing vessel. This assumes that attractive forces between the molecules can be neglected.
(c) All collisions are perfectly elastic.
(d) The time that particles are actually in contact with each other is very small and may be neglected.
(e) The actual volume of the molecules is very small compared with the space in which they move.

Since the collisions are perfectly elastic there is no loss of kinetic energy when two particles collide. Students answering examination questions often say that there *is* a loss of energy. If kinetic energy were lost the gas would cool unless heat energy were supplied from outside, because the temperature of a gas is a measure of its total kinetic energy and any loss of internal energy would therefore result in a fall in temperature.

Consider a simple collision between two particles X and Y of the same mass (Fig. 11.1). Before the collision X moves with a speed v and Y is stationary. After the collision X is stationary and Y moves with speed v. This is a necessary consequence of the conservation of momentum and the conservation of kinetic energy. The net effect is the same as if there had not been a collision.

Before collision   After collision

11.1   An elastic collision

11.2 Speed distribution in a gas

The molecules in a gas at the same temperature do not all move at the same speed. There is a speed distribution as shown in Fig. 11.2 where n represents the number of molecules moving with a given speed v. Obviously an increase in temperature increases the average kinetic energy of the molecules. This results in an increase in the speeds of the molecules. The solid curve represents the speed distribution at a higher temperature than the dotted curve for the same gas.

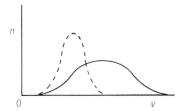

11.2   Speed distribution of molecules in a gas

It is important not to be confused between *speed* and *velocity*. In unit volume of a gas at normal pressure there are billions of molecules, and it is reasonable to assume that at any given instant equal numbers are moving in each different direction. Thus if a certain number are moving with a speed v in one direction, there will be an equal number moving with the same speed in the opposite direction. *Velocity* is a vector quantity and depends upon direction, so the average velocity along this particular line is zero. This applies equally to all other directions and so the average velocity of the molecules of a gas is zero. *Speed* is a scalar quantity and does not depend upon the direction of motion, so it is possible to talk about the average speed of the molecules. You may wonder whether molecules of different gases at the same temperature have the same average speed. The answer is no! They have the same *average kinetic energy*. Assuming that each gas contains the same number of molecules, n

$$\tfrac{1}{2}nm_1\overline{v_1^2} = \tfrac{1}{2}nm_2\overline{v_2^2}$$

or $$\tfrac{1}{2}m_1\overline{v_1^2} = \tfrac{1}{2}m_2\overline{v_2^2}$$

If m_1 is larger than m_2 it follows that $\overline{v_1^2}$ will be less than $\overline{v_2^2}$.

Note $\overline{v^2}$ is the average of the squares of the speeds, and is *not* equal to the square of the average speed. However, the average speed of the lighter gas will be greater than the average speed of the heavier gas at the same temperature.

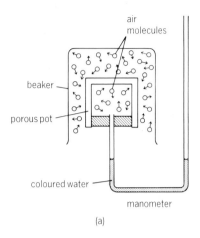

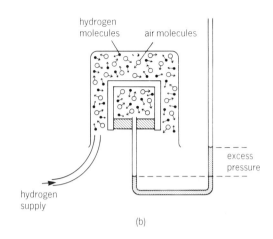

11.3   Demonstration of diffusion of lighter molecules

(a) Cover a porous pot fitted with a U-tube manometer with a beaker as shown in Fig. 11.3(a). With air molecules moving around both inside and outside the pot the pressure of the molecules inside the pot is equal to the atmospheric pressure, and the water levels in the manometer limbs are equal. Now introduce hydrogen into the beaker as shown in Fig. 11.3(b). The level of the water falls in the closed limb and rises in the open limb of the manometer, indicating that the pressure inside the porous pot has increased. This can be explained by noting that hydrogen molecules have a smaller mass than air molecules, and thus have a larger average speed. Hence in a given time the number of hydrogen molecules entering the porous pot is greater than the number of air molecules leaving. The number

of molecules inside the pot increases and therefore the pressure increases also.

(b) The effect of surrounding the porous pot with a gas which is more dense than air is demonstrated using the apparatus in Fig. 11.4. When air molecules are both inside and outside the pot the levels in the manometer arms are the same. When carbon dioxide is put into the beaker the water level in the open limb becomes lower than that in the closed limb. Remembering that carbon dioxide is more dense than air, explain, in terms of molecular movements and speeds, the reason for this difference in levels.

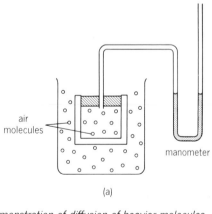

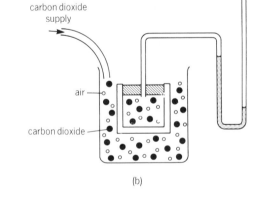

11.4   Demonstration of diffusion of heavier molecules

11.3   Pressure in gases

Why does a gas exert a pressure on the walls of a container? Consider only those molecules which are moving horizontally. Each molecule hits the container wall and bounces back with the same speed, because the collision is elastic. The molecule then travels in the

opposite direction. If the direction left to right is considered to be positive, then the direction right to left is negative.

$$\text{original velocity} = +v$$
$$\text{final velocity} = -v$$
$$\text{change in velocity} = +v - (-v) = +2v$$
$$\text{change in momentum} = +(mv) - (-mv) = +2mv$$

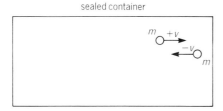

sealed container

11.5   *Change of molecular momentum on rebound*

During one second the molecule crosses the container many times because of its great speed, and makes a very large number of impacts. The change in momentum each second gives the force exerted on the wall by the molecule. There are very large numbers of molecules involved so a large force is exerted on the wall. This force divided by the area of the wall gives the pressure exerted on the wall.

The average person has very little idea of the force exerted by the molecules in the air. This is because the forces usually cancel. Consider a person reading a newspaper. The force acting upon the surface of the newspaper due to its bombardment by the air molecules is 100 000 (10^5) N for each square metre of the paper's surface. How does the paper stand up to this force, and how does the reader manage to hold the paper? The answer is simple. There is an equal and opposite bombardment on the other side of the paper and the two forces cancel. The reader only supports the weight of the newspaper.

Similarly, there is a very large force on the outside of a large patio window due to the pressure of the air outside the house. The window does not break because fortunately an equally large force is exerted in the opposite direction by the molecules of air inside the room. Actually the force on the inside may be slightly larger, because the air temperature inside the room is probably slightly higher than the air temperature outside.

If you are not careful you may easily form an erroneous impression. There are about 10 000 m air above the roof of a house and only about 10 m air beneath it. Why then is the pressure exerted by the air the same on both sides of the roof? Simply because there are the same number of molecules *per unit volume* on each side of the roof. One of the reasons why air pressure decreases with height is because the number of molecules per unit volume decreases. Another is because the temperature also decreases.

The effect of removing air from one side of a sheet of metal has already been shown in the collapsing can experiment on p.47. A popular misconception is that there are no air molecules in a vacuum. There are in fact millions of molecules per unit volume inside the can as opposed to billions of molecules per unit volume outside the can. Thus the pressure exerted on the outside of the can is very much greater than the pressure exerted inside the can and so the walls of the can collapse. You may have experienced this effect yourself. If you replace the cork in an empty flask which you have just washed out with hot water, it may be difficult to remove the cork when the air in the flask has cooled because there will be a fall in pressure inside the flask.

Aneroid barometer

This uses the effect described above to measure the air pressure. The corrugated metal box in Fig. 11.6 has been partially evacuated (contains fewer air molecules) and sealed. It is prevented from collapsing by the strong spring attached to A and B. When the air pressure increases there is a greater *difference* between the pressure outside and inside the box and the distance AB decreases. Conversely, if the air pressure decreases the *difference* in pressure between the outside and inside of the box decreases, and the tension in the spring causes AB to increase. Any change in the distance AB is magnified by levers and pulleys and shown by a pointer which moves round a calibrated dial to show the air pressure. This instrument is often seen hanging in the hall of a house.

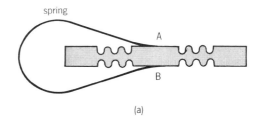

(a)

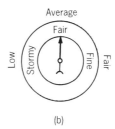

(b)

11.6   *Aneroid barometer*

Unfortunately the makers usually also put weather predictions on the dial, equating bad weather with low pressure and good weather with high pressure. This is at best a very rough guide and should not be taken too literally!

The advantage of the aneroid barometer is that it can be made to record the pressure continuously by attaching a pen to it. In this form it is known as a **barograph** and serves a very useful purpose (see Fig. 11.7). The instrument should be reset to read the same as a Fortin's Barometer every time the paper chart is changed.

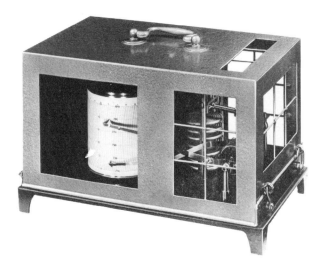

11.7 The barograph

line of constant
altimeter reading

high pressure

low pressure

11.8 Plane flying from area of high pressure to area of low pressure

The partially evacuated box was also used as an altimeter in aircraft. Pressure decreases with altitude and the dial was calibrated to show height. However, the instrument actually recorded the atmospheric pressure, and so if the aircraft flew from an area where the pressure was high to one where the pressure was low, it could lose height although the altimeter reading remained constant (see Fig. 11.8). This was dangerous, especially when flying in cloud over hilly regions. The pilot had to keep obtaining the ground pressure on the radio and resetting the instrument accordingly.

11.4 Boyle's Law

The cylinder in Fig. 11.9(a) has a tightly fitting piston which traps air below it. When the piston is at rest the total upward force on it is equal to the total downward force. When weights are added to the pan, the piston moves downwards, coming to rest when the upward force is again equal to the downward force (Fig. 11.9b). The new upward force is larger than before. The total number of molecules in the cylinder is unchanged and, since there has been no change in temperature, they are moving with the same average speed. So why has the upward force increased? Simply because the vertical height of the cylinder is less so there are more impacts per second of the molecules on the piston and hence a greater upward force. Another

way of looking at it is to say that there are more molecules per unit volume and so the pressure inside the cylinder increases.

Now look at the cylinder in Fig. 11.10(a). When its volume is V the pressure inside the cylinder is p. If the piston is depressed very slowly (so that there is no temperature change) until the volume is $\frac{1}{2}V$ then, considering only those molecules moving horizontally, the same number of molecules strike half the original area. Their average speed remains the same, as does the horizontal distance across the cylinder, and so they will make the same number of impacts in unit time. Hence the total force is the same but the area it acts on is halved; and so the pressure is $2p$. Those molecules moving vertically strike the same

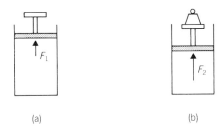

11.9 Force exerted by molecules in a closed cylinder

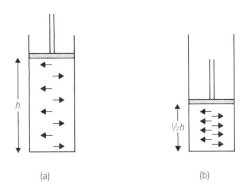

11.10 Simple explanation of Boyle's Law

area, but since the vertical distance they travel is halved, the number of impacts per second is doubled. This means that the force and pressure are doubled.

Halving the volume doubles the pressure, and it can be shown in the same way that decreasing the volume to $\frac{1}{3}V$ will increase the pressure to $3p$. This was first investigated by Robert Boyle in 1660. Boyle's Law states 'at constant temperature the volume of a fixed mass of gas is inversely proportional to the pressure', i.e.

$$V \propto \frac{1}{p}$$
$$V \div \frac{1}{p} = \text{constant}$$
or $\qquad p\,V = \text{constant}$

Investigation 11.2 To verify Boyle's Law

You will need the apparatus shown in Fig. 11.11. Connect a foot pump, via an adaptor and rubber tubing, to the inlet tube of the apparatus and increase the pressure inside the apparatus using the foot pump. Make sure you get 6 to 8 equally spaced readings. After each increase in pressure, allow the apparatus to return to room temperature before taking readings of the volume V and pressure p. Readings can also be taken as the pressure is released, but as the oil level in the tube is lowered, the oil clings to the walls of the tube and takes a little time to drain down to the final level. Tabulate the results as shown in Table 11.1 and plot the corresponding graphs (see Fig. 11.12). If the value of pV in the last column of the table is constant then Boyle's Law is verified. It is also verified if graphs of p against $1/V$ and V against $1/p$ give straight lines passing through the origin, or if the graphs of pV against v or p give straight lines parallel

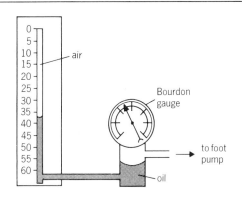

11.11 Verification of Boyle's Law

to the axis. There is no need to plot all three graphs; any one is sufficient.

Table 11.1 Table of results for Investigation 11.2

Volume/m³	Pressure/Pa	Reciprocal of volume/m⁻³	Reciprocal of pressure/Pa⁻¹	Pressure × volume/Pa m³

The graph of p against V gives the smooth curve shown in Fig. 11.12(d). This curve is known as an **isothermal** because the temperature is constant. It is of interest when the behaviour of gases is looked at in greater detail.

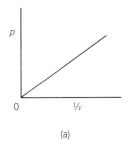

(a)

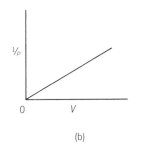

(b)

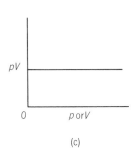

(c)

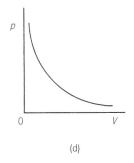

(d)

11.12 Boyle's Law graphs

Example

A bubble of gas released at the bottom of a lake increases to eight times its original volume when it reaches the surface. Assume that atmospheric pressure is equivalent to the pressure exerted by a column of water 10 m high. What is the depth of the lake?

Original volume $= V$; final volume $= 8V$.

Let P be atmospheric pressure and P_1 the pressure at the bottom of the lake. Then using Boyle's Law

$$P \times 8V = P_1 \times V$$
$$8P = P_1$$

$P_1 =$ atmospheric pressure + pressure due to water in lake, so pressure of water in lake $= 7P$. Since $P \equiv$ pressure exerted by 10 m of water, the depth of lake $= 70$ m.

11.5 Pressure Law

So far only the behaviour of a gas at *constant temperature* has been considered. The pressure in a gas depends upon the change of momentum at each impact and upon the number of impacts each second, both of which are proportional to the speed of the molecules, so it is reasonable to assume that the pressure is proportional to (speed)². Since the Kelvin temperature is a measure of the kinetic energy of the

Investigation 11.3   To demonstrate the Pressure Law

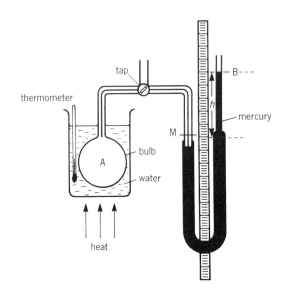

11.13 ·Demonstration of Pressure Law

This experiment uses the apparatus shown in Fig. 11.13. A glass bulb A is connected by capillary tubing and pressure tubing to a tube B which contains mercury. Using the three-way tap in the capillary tube, pump the air out of the bulb A and replace it with dry air which has been passed through a calcium chloride drying tube. Close the capillary tube and connect A to the tube B. There is a mark M on the capillary tube. Immerse A in a beaker of cold

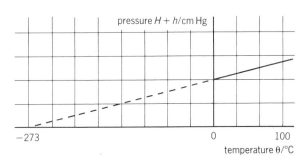

11.14   Pressure Law graph

water and leave it for a few minutes until it reaches the same temperature as the water. Read off this temperature θ on the mercury thermometer. Adjust B until the mercury in the capillary tube is level with the mark M. Note the difference in level h between B and M and read off the atmospheric pressure H on a Fortin's Barometer. The pressure of the air in A is thus ($H + h$) cm mercury. Use a Bunsen burner to heat the water in the beaker by a few degrees, then remove the burner, stir the water, and leave the apparatus for a few minutes until the bulb A reaches the same temperature as the water. Again adjust the mercury to the mark M, note the new difference in level between B and M and also the temperature. Repeat the process, heating the water by about 10 °C each time until the water boils. Plot a graph of pressure ($H + h$) cm Hg against temperature θ °C (see Fig. 11.14). You should obtain a straight line like that in Fig. 11.14. When produced this line will cut the temperature axis at approximately −273 °C.

gas which itself depends upon (speed)^2, we would expect $p \propto T$ as long as the volume of the gas remains constant. If the volume increases work has to be done to push back the surroundings, and some of the energy supplied is not used to raise the temperature of the gas. This leads to the Pressure Law which states that **'the pressure of a fixed mass of gas is directly proportional to the absolute temperature provided the volume remains constant'**, i.e.

$$P \propto T$$
$$\frac{P}{T} = \text{constant}$$
$$\text{or} \quad \frac{P_1}{T_1} = \frac{P_2}{T_2}$$

where P_1 is the pressure at temperature T_1 and P_2 the pressure at T_2.

Capillary tubing is used to ensure that the volume of air which is not at the same temperature as the air in A is as small as possible. Pressure tubing (thick-walled rubber tubing) is used because the pressure exerted by the mercury might split ordinary tubing. Adjusting the mercury level to the mark M every time ensures that the volume is constant.

Constant Volume Air Thermometer

The apparatus in Fig. 11.13 and the graph in Fig. 11.14 may together be used as a thermometer. Place the bulb in a liquid whose temperature is not known, adjust the mercury to the mark M and obtain the new value of h. From this you can determine ($H + h$) and read the value of the temperature from the graph. The temperature to be measured does not need to be between 0 °C and 100 °C.

One obvious disadvantage of using this apparatus is that it is far too cumbersome for a thermometer. Another is that a large amount of the substance whose temperature is to be measured is required. A more sophisticated form of the apparatus contains hydrogen instead of air, and is used as a standard thermometer against which other thermometers are calibrated. Its advantages are that it is extremely accurate and has a very wide range. The lowest temperature it can measure is near to the liquefying point of hydrogen (−200 °C) and the upper limit is determined by the temperature which the material of which the bulb is made will stand (about 1500 °C). An ordinary mercury-in-glass thermometer is not very accurate, and has a very limited range.

11.6 Charles' Law

This law refers to the change in volume of a gas with temperature when the pressure remains constant. It can be stated as follows: '**the volume of a fixed mass of gas is proportional to the absolute temperature provided the pressure remains constant**', i.e.

$$V \propto T$$

$$\frac{V}{T} = \text{constant}$$

$$\text{or} \quad \frac{V_1}{T_1} = \frac{V_2}{T_2}$$

where V_1 is the volume at temperature T_1 and V_2 the volume at T_2.

11.7 General Gas Law

The three gas laws can be combined into a single law known as the General Gas Law:

$$\frac{pV}{T} = \text{constant}$$

$$\text{or} \quad \frac{p_1 V_1}{T_1} = \frac{p_2 V_2}{T_2}$$

At constant temperature $T_1 = T_2$ and $p_1 V_1 = p_2 V_2$
(Boyle's Law)

At constant volume $\quad V_1 = V_2$ and $p_1/T_1 = p_2/T_2$
(Pressure Law)

At constant pressure $\quad p_1 = p_2$ and $V_1/T_1 = V_2/T_2$
(Charles' Law)

Note It is important to remember that *the mass of the gas remains constant* throughout. A change in the mass of the gas will cause a change in the number of molecules per unit volume.

Investigation 11.4 To verify Charles' Law

The apparatus used in this investigation (Fig. 11.15) consists of a narrow tube (quill tube) closed at one end, containing a pellet of concentrated sulphuric acid. Attach the tube and a thermometer to a scale by rubber bands, and place in a tall beaker of water with the open end of the tube upwards. Gently heat the water in the beaker. The sulphuric acid plug removes any water vapour and ensures that the air is dry. Throughout the experiment the pressure of the air trapped in the tube is constant and is equal to the atmospheric pressure plus the pressure exerted by the sulphuric acid. Take readings of the temperature and the length *l* at temperature differences of about 10 °C, with the following precautions:

(a) remove the source of heat before each reading, stir the water well and leave it for a short time to ensure that the air in the tube is at the same temperature as the water;

(b) always keep the pellet of sulphuric acid below the level of the water in the beaker.

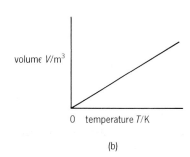

11.15 *Demonstration of Charles' Law*

Since the area of cross-section of the tube is constant the length *l* is proportional to the volume *V* occupied by the air.

Plot a graph of length *l* of the air column against the Celsius temperature θ (see Fig. 11.16a). It will be similar to the pressure–temperature graph in Fig. 11.14, namely a straight line cutting the temperature axis at approximately −273 °C. If the temperature is converted to K the graph of volume *V* (or length *l*) against temperature *T* is a straight line through the origin (Fig. 11.16b) showing that volume *V* is proportional to kelvin temperature *T*.

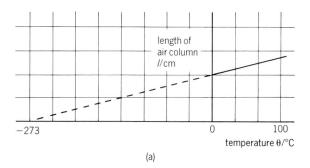

11.16 *Charles' Law graph*

Example

A balloon, volume 0.5 m^3, containing hydrogen at a pressure of $2 \times 10^5 \text{ Pa}$ is released from the ground when the temperature is $17 °C$. What will be the volume when it reaches a height where the pressure inside the balloon is $1.5 \times 10^5 \text{ Pa}$ and the temperature is $6 °C$?

$$\text{original pressure } p_1 = 2 \times 10^5 \text{ Pa}$$
$$\text{original volume } V_1 = 0.5 \text{ m}^3$$
$$\text{original temperature } T_1 = 17 + 273 = 290 \text{ K}$$
$$\text{final pressure } p_2 = 1.5 \times 10^5 \text{ Pa}$$
$$\text{final volume } V_2 = ?$$
$$\text{final temperature } T_2 = 6 + 273 = 279 \text{ K}$$

(Always remember to convert the temperature into K.)

From the General Gas Law,

$$\frac{(2 \times 10^5) \text{ Pa} \times (0.5) \text{ m}^3}{290 \text{ K}} = \frac{(1.5 \times 10^5) \text{ Pa} \times V_2}{279 \text{ K}}$$

$$\frac{279}{290} \times \frac{1}{1.5} \text{ m}^3 = V_2$$

$$0.64 \text{ m}^3 = V_2$$

Example

A cylinder contains 20 litre of gas at a pressure of $25 \times 10^5 \text{ Pa}$. The tap is opened until the pressure drops to $20 \times 10^5 \text{ Pa}$ and then closed. Assuming that the temperature remains constant, what would be the volume of the released gas measured at atmospheric pressure $(1 \times 10^5) \text{ Pa}$?

$$\text{original pressure } p_1 = 25 \times 10^5 \text{ Pa}$$
$$\text{original volume } V_1 = 20 \text{ l}$$
$$\text{final pressure } p_2 = 1 \times 10^5 \text{ Pa}$$
$$\text{final volume } V_2 = ?$$

Assuming that all the original gas expands, then, using Boyle's Law $p_1 V_1 = p_2 V_2$,

$$(25 \times 10^5) \text{ Pa} \times 20 \text{ l} = (1 \times 10^5) \text{ Pa} \times V_2$$

$$\frac{25 \times 10^5}{1 \times 10^5} \times 20 \text{ l} = V_2$$

$$500 \text{ l} = V_2$$

Using the same method for the gas left in the cylinder, the volume it would occupy at atmospheric pressure is 400 l. Thus the volume of the released gas at atmospheric pressure is $500 - 400 = 100 \text{ litre}$.

It can be seen from this example why it is convenient to transport gases at high pressures.

On aerosol cans there is usually a warning saying that the cans must be kept in a cool place and not exposed to direct sunlight, and that empty cans must not be thrown onto a fire. The warning is put there because the can contains a volatile liquid and even when no more can be sprayed out there is always a little liquid left in the can. When the temperature in the can rises there is

(a) rapid evaporation of the liquid which increases the number of gas molecules per unit volume in the can, and

(b) an increase in the speed of the molecules.

These two factors cause a large increase in pressure which may be sufficient to explode the can.

Expansion of gases

The expansion of gases is complicated because both pressure and volume can change. It is usual therefore to keep either the volume or the pressure constant. When the volume is constant the **pressure coefficient of expansion** can be found:

pressure coefficient of expansion

$$= \frac{\text{increase in pressure}}{\text{pressure at } 0 °C \times \text{rise in temperature}}$$

$$= \frac{p_{100} - p_0}{p_0 \times 100}$$

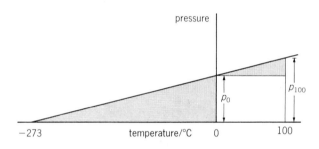

11.17 Finding the pressure coefficient of expansion

The two triangles in the pressure graph (Fig. 11.17) are similar so $p_0/273 = (p_{100} - p_0)/100$ or $1/273 = (p_{100} - p_0)/(p_0 \times 100)$ and the pressure coefficient of expansion is $\frac{1}{273}$ per K. You will have no difficulty in obtaining the same result at constant pressure from the volume–temperature graph. Thus the volume coefficient of expansion is equal to the pressure coefficient of expansion. What is more, if different gases are used the value is the same for all gases. This contrasts with solids and liquids, where the cubical expansivities are all different, and suggests that there is something fundamental about the behaviour of all gases. This will be important for those of you who study Physics at a higher level.

11.8 Other properties of gases

Certain other properties of gases are worth mentioning briefly.

Anyone who has pumped up a bicycle tyre knows that after a few strokes the barrel of the pump becomes quite hot. What is the reason for this? Is it because of friction between the washer and the side of the pump?

This possibility can be eliminated by pumping for the same number of times with the pump disconnected from the tyre. The friction is the same but there is no noticeable increase in temperature. The rise in temperature is due to the compression of the air. Some of the work done in compressing the air increases the kinetic energy (internal energy) of the molecules and so the temperature rises.

This property is made use of in the diesel engine. When the mixture of diesel vapour and air is compressed rapidly its temperature rises above the ignition temperature and the mixture explodes. By contrast the mixture in the cylinder of a petrol engine has to be ignited by a spark from a sparking plug.

When a gas is allowed to expand rapidly the kinetic energy (internal energy) decreases and the gas cools. This is *not* the same effect as the cooling produced by evaporation. The cooling effect produced by the expansion of gases is used in their liquefaction. Until this effect was discovered it was believed that hydrogen and helium could not be liquefied.

Water vapour

The quantity of water vapour in the atmosphere plays a very important part in everyday life because it is a key factor in determining the weather. When a sample of air is cooled sufficiently the water vapour it contains becomes saturated and some condenses into water droplets. The temperature below which air has to be cooled for condensation to take place is known as the **dew point**, and depends upon the quantity of water vapour in the air. The **relative humidity** is the ratio between the quantity of water vapour in the air and the quantity required to saturate the air. When the air is dry, both the dew point and relative humidity are low.

If you wear spectacles you will be conscious of the presence of water vapour in the air. When you enter a warm room after being outside on a frosty evening your spectacles 'steam up' because the temperature of the glass is below the dew point of the air in the room and so water vapour condenses upon it. If a bottle of wine is brought out of a refrigerator, water vapour condenses upon it unless the air is very dry.

The earth radiates heat energy. On a cloudy night a lot of this energy is reflected by the clouds but on a clear night the energy escapes and the ground temperature falls rapidly. The cold ground cools the air in contact with it below the dew point and mist or fog forms when the water vapour in the air condenses. Another method of fog formation is when warm moist air flows over land or sea which is much colder. This accounts for the incidence of sea fog.

On a clear day white (condensation) trails may be seen behind high-flying aircraft. Water vapour from the engines condenses to form cloud. If the surrounding air is moist (high relative humidity) the trails are long and take a long time to disperse. If the relative humidity is low the trails are short or may not form at all.

The situation is different in a cloud chamber (Chapter 34). Here the vapour (ether) is supersaturated. Any disturbance will cause condensation. The disturbance is caused by a particle travelling through it. A keen-eyed observer can sometimes see a similar effect when an aircraft takes off below cloud when the humidity is very high. Short trails appear at the wing tips.

Questions

Q1 100 cm³ of dry air at a pressure of 1 atmosphere and temperature 27 °C are compressed to 5 atmospheres and heated to 77 °C. The new volume is

A $\frac{3000}{7}$ cm³   B $\frac{350}{3}$ cm³   C $\frac{1540}{27}$ cm³   D $\frac{70}{3}$ cm³

E $\frac{120}{7}$ cm³   *(L)*

Q2 2 litre of gas at a temperature of 27 °C and a pressure of 1 atmosphere is compressed to a volume of 1 litre and heated to 127 °C. What is the final pressure of the gas in atmosphere?

A $\frac{3}{8}$ B $\frac{2}{3}$ C $\frac{3}{2}$ D $\frac{8}{3}$ E $\frac{254}{27}$ *(L)*

Q3 What is the relationship between the pressure P and volume V of a fixed mass of gas at constant temperature?

A PV = constant   B PV^2 = constant
C P/V^2 = constant   D P/V = constant
E V/P = constant   *(L)*

Q4 A fixed mass of gas occupies a volume of 1000 cm³ at a pressure P and absolute temperature T. What will its volume be when the pressure is $2P$ and the temperature is $2T$?
A 250 cm³   B 500 cm³   C 1000 cm³
D 2000 cm³   E 4000 cm³   *(L)*

Q5 (a) Describe how you would investigate the variation of volume with temperature of a fixed mass of dry air at constant pressure. Explain (i) how you ensure that the air is dry, and (ii) how the pressure is kept constant in your experiment. Draw a sketch graph showing the results you would expect to obtain.

(b) On aerosol cans there is a warning not to leave them in strong sunlight or to throw them on to a fire when empty. Give the physical reasons for this warning.

(c) Early in the morning the pressure in a car tyre was 2.00 × 10⁵ Pa when the temperature was 7 °C. What would you expect the pressure in the tyre to be when the temperature has risen to 27 °C in the afternoon? (Assume that the volume of the tyre does not change.)

(L)

Q6 Draw a labelled diagram to show any **one** type of apparatus which can be used to check whether Boyle's Law applies to a given sample of gas at room temperature. How, with the apparatus, would you vary the pressure of the sample of gas? What purpose, if any, is achieved by having a thermometer and a barometer near the apparatus? Give your reasoning.

The following observations were obtained for a sample of butane at 16.8 °C (290.0 K).

pressure P (atm)	0.50	0.70	1.00	1.50	2.00	3.00
volume V (cm^3)	30.0	21.5	15.0	9.0	6.0	1.0*

*Including 0.1 cm^3 of liquid.
atm = standard atmospheric pressure.

Explain why Boyle's law can be applied to calculate the value of V (at 16.8 °C) when the pressure is 0.75 atm and also when the pressure is 0.25 atm, but not when the pressure is 1.75 atm nor when the pressure is greater than 3 atm.

Give a reason why the value of V (at 16.8 °C) at a pressure of 4 atm is not likely to be much greater than 0.1 cm^3.

Calculate the value of V when $P = 0.25$ atm and the butane is at 26.8 °C. *(C)*

Q7 (a) (i) Describe how you would investigate the relationship between the volume and temperature of a fixed mass of *dry* air at *constant pressure*.

(ii) Draw a graph showing the results you would expect, labelling your axes.

(iii) Suppose you then used another pure gas (e.g. hydrogen or helium). What feature would the two graphs have in common?

(b) A cylinder of volume 0.4 litre contains a mixture of petrol vapour and air at atmospheric pressure and a temperature of 27 °C. The gas is compressed suddenly by a piston until the volume is 0.05 litre and the pressure 20 times atmospheric pressure. What is the new temperature of the gas? (Assume the mixture obeys the gas equation.) *(L)*

Q8 State the assumptions on which the Kinetic Theory of Gases is based.

State Boyle's Law and explain it in terms of the behaviour of the molecules of a fixed mass of gas.

Describe an experiment which may be performed to estimate the value of the absolute zero of temperature.
(W)

Q9 Give an explanation, in terms of the kinetic theory, of the expansion of a gas heated at constant pressure. *(C)*

Q10 A bicycle pump, with its exit hole closed, contains 80 cm^3 of air at atmospheric pressure of 760 mm of mercury and a temperature of 280 K. When the air has been compressed to 38 cm^3 and the temperature has risen to 301 K, what is the pressure of the enclosed air?

(S part question)

Q11 Apply the kinetic theory to account for the pressure exerted by a gas. Also apply this theory to account for the increased pressure when a gas has

(a) its volume reduced at constant temperature,
(b) its temperature increased at constant volume.

Calculate the ratio of the final pressure to the initial pressure when a fixed mass of gas at 17 °C is heated to 100 °C and compressed to half its initial volume.

Draw a labelled diagram of a simple type of constant-volume gas thermometer. Write *brief* notes on how you would use this thermometer to find the boiling point of a salt solution. *(C)*

Q12 State the basic ideas (assumptions) of the kinetic theory of matter. Give explanations, in terms of molecules, of the following:

(i) the pressure exerted by a gas on the walls of its container;
(ii) the cooling which occurs when a liquid evaporates;
(iii) the diffusion of a gas through a porous pot;
(iv) the definite shape and volume of a solid substance.
(W)

Q13 The results shown in the table below were obtained in an experiment to verify Boyle's Law.

pressure /kN m^{-2}	400	320	160	80
volume /mm^3	2.0	2.5	5.0	10.0
$\dfrac{1}{\text{volume}}$ /mm^{-3}	0.5			

(a) Copy the table and complete it.
(b) Plot a graph of pressure on the *y*-axis against 1/volume on the *x*-axis.
(c) State the relationship which this graph shows between pressure and volume.
(d) **From your graph** calculate the volume when the pressure was 240 kN m^{-2}.
(e) State which **two** physical properties of the gas were kept constant. *(JMB)*

Q14 Kinetic theory suggests that the molecules of a gas or a liquid are in continual random motion.

(a) Explain in terms of kinetic theory why a gas exerts a steady pressure, which increases as the temperature rises, and which increases when the gas is compressed into a smaller space.

(b) A small bottle containing liquid bromine is broken inside a larger glass vessel which has been evacuated. At once a brown coloration is seen throughout the larger vessel and the volume of the liquid is considerably decreased. After a short while the intensity of the coloration and the quantity of liquid remain constant. Explain these observations in terms of the movements of bromine molecules.

(c) Explain in terms of kinetic theory why evaporation produces cooling.

(d) Give a brief account of the manner in which heat is transferred by (i) conduction, and (ii) convection. *(O)*

12 Expansion due to heat

12.1 Expansion and contraction of solids

When a substance is heated, its temperature rises and its volume normally increases, i.e. it expands. There are exceptions to this, and the most notable example is water. Above 4 °C water expands as the temperature rises, but water also expands as the temperature falls between 4 °C and 0 °C. Thus a given mass of water has its smallest volume, and consequently its highest density, at 4 °C.

When heat energy is given to a solid there is an increase in both the kinetic and potential energies of the molecules. This means that they vibrate more rapidly and move farther apart. As the molecules move farther apart the length and width of the solid increase. The expansion is not very large and it has to be magnified in some way to be appreciated.

Later it will be shown that the heating effect, and hence the expansion, is proportional to the square of the current. So if the scale were calibrated this apparatus could be used to measure electric current. An instrument of this type was once used to measure the value of an alternating current, because the heating effect does not depend upon the direction of the current. It is now very rarely used.

This investigation shows that care should be taken when fixing overhead electricity cables or wires. If the work is done in summer, the wires should be allowed to sag so that, when they contract in winter, they will not snap as they tighten. The additional length required to ensure that they do not become taut can be calculated.

The apparatus in Fig. 12.1 could also be used to measure the expansion of the bar. The angle moved by the pointer could be calculated from the distance it

Investigation 12.1 To demonstrate the expansion of a solid

The apparatus used in this investigation is shown in Fig. 12.1. AB is a metal rod which is firmly clamped at A. End B rests upon a roller C to which is attached a long pointer. Heat the bar by several gas jets along its length. As the temperature rises the bar expands and B moves over C, rotating the roller and so moving the pointer over the scale. The longer the pointer the greater the deflection produced.

An alternative apparatus is shown in Fig. 12.2. A resistance wire is firmly clamped at M and N and attached to an external electric circuit. A second wire is attached to the resistance wire midway between M and N. This wire is wrapped once round a pulley and a weight is suspended at the other end. When the current in the external circuit is switched on, the temperature of the resistance wire rises and it expands and sags. The weight falls to take up the slack, turning the pulley and moving the pointer, which is attached to the pulley, over the scale. When the current is switched off again the wire cools and contracts. This raises the weight and the pointer moves back to its original position.

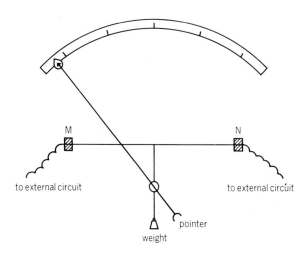

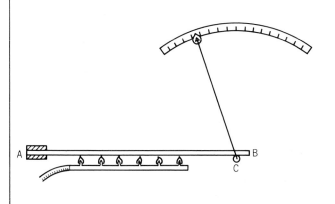

12.1 Demonstration of expansion of a solid

12.2 To show expansion of a wire

moved over the scale; this angle is the same as the angle turned by the roller. The length by which the bar had increased could be calculated from this angle and the radius of the roller. The bar needs to be heated by a Bunsen flame so that its increase in temperature produces a measurable expansion.

Forces on expansion and contraction

If a steel rod of area of cross section 1 cm² is heated to 100 °C and then prevented from contracting while it is cooled to 10 °C, it can be calculated that the force exerted in the rod is about 21 500 N. The same force would be exerted by the rod if an attempt were made to prevent it from expanding when it was being heated. It is obvious that when substances expand and contract considerable forces are exerted.

In everyday appliances allowances have to be made for expansion or contraction, otherwise the large forces produced may cause considerable damage. Railway lines are a good example. They are made of steel and the track used to be laid in 18 m lengths on wooden sleepers. Between the lengths a gap of about 1 cm at 0 °C was left. The rails were connected to each other by 'fishplates' in which the bolt holes are elongated instead of being circular. This allowed the bolts which connected the 'fishplates' to the rails to slide inside the hole, and take up any expansion or contraction. The rails tended to wear at the junctions.

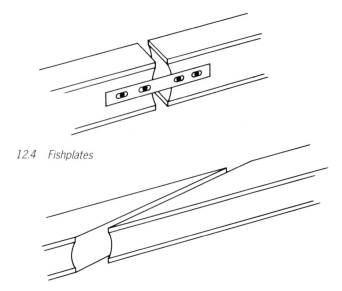

12.4   Fishplates

12.5   Allowing for expansion of railway lines

Nowadays continuously welded rails are used. They are much longer, e.g. several 300 m lengths welded together. The rails are clamped in position much more firmly than the old 18 m rails. Pre-stressed concrete is used instead of wooden sleepers, and the clamps are much stronger. Obviously the rails will expand and contract, and since they cannot move, large stresses will be set up. To make allowance for this the rails are laid so that they are stress-free at a temperature of about 20–25 °C. When the temperature is below this, the rails want to contract but cannot, so they are stressed and under tension. When the temperature is above this, the rails want to expand and cannot, so they are compressed. The central portion of each rail cannot move because it is clamped tightly, but the rails are allowed to move towards the ends by joining them as shown in Fig. 12.5. This gives a much smoother ride than the old-fashioned joint.

Large steel-framed roofs, and other roofs for that matter, contract and expand with fall and rise of temperature, and it is usual to fix only one side of the roof. The other side of the roof may rest on roller bearings (Fig. 12.6) so that the frame can move. When covering roofs with metal panels, it is wise to use small panels instead of very large panels. Although the overall expansion is the same, it is taken up over smaller distances.

Investigation 12.2   The bar-breaker experiment

The apparatus used in this experiment is shown in Fig. 12.3. Heat bar B with a gas burner, and as it expands tighten the screw C. This keeps the cast iron rod A which passes through a hole in B tight against the knife-edges. Switch off the gas when the bar expands no further, and allow the apparatus to cool. Cooling can be speeded up by pouring water over the bar or placing a wet cloth on it. Soon the bar A snaps due to the large force exerted by B when it contracts.

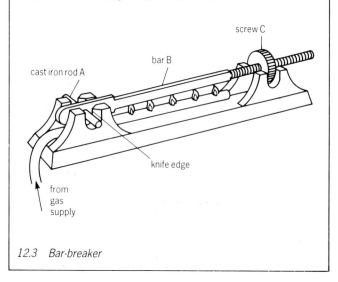

12.3   Bar-breaker

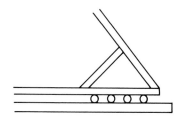

12.6   Rollers under a roof

Allowance also needs to be made for expansion in bridges. In a bridge as long as the Forth Bridge in Scotland, rollers allow for expansion at the ends, but expansion must also be allowed for at various points along the length of the span. When you are driving along a motorway, you may notice the expansion points in the bridges and in the roadway. These are filled with pitch which changes its shape to allow for the expansion.

Pipes which carry steam or hot water also expand and contract. Central heating pipes have to have allowance made for expansion. Industrial steam pipes have a bend in them which alters its shape to take up expansion and contraction.

In accurate work allowance has to be made for the expansion and contraction of measuring instruments. On a hot day a steel measuring tape will give too low a reading. As the tape expands the graduations get slightly farther apart, so that the metre mark on the tape is more than a metre away from the zero. An object one metre long will be measured as less than one metre on the tape. Conversely on a cold day the graduations will get slightly closer together and the tape will give too high a reading.

12.2 Linear expansivity

When allowing for the effects of expansion, it is necessary to be very precise. To do this it is essential to know the **linear expansivity** of the material being used. This is defined as **the increase in length of unit length of the material for a rise in temperature of 1 K**. It is usually denoted by the letter α and

$$\alpha = \frac{\text{increase in length}}{\text{original length} \times \text{rise in temperature}}$$

Strictly the original length should be the length at 0 °C denoted by l_0. l_θ is the length at θ °C and is the final length. $\Delta l = l_\theta - l_0$ is the increase in length. The change in temperature $\Delta\theta$ will be the same whether it is measured on the Celsius scale or on the Kelvin scale: $\Delta\theta \,°\text{C} \equiv \Delta\theta \,\text{K}$. Hence

$$\alpha = \frac{\Delta l}{l_0 \Delta \theta}$$

If the experiment starts at 0 °C

$$\Delta\theta = (\theta - 0) = \theta \,\text{K and } \alpha = \frac{l_\theta - l_0}{l_0 \theta}$$
$$l_0 \alpha \theta = l_\theta - l_0$$
$$l_0 + l_0 \alpha \theta = l_\theta$$
$$l_0(1 + \alpha \theta) = l_\theta$$

It is usual in calculations to take the original length l_0 as the length at room temperature. The error in doing this is very small and is usually ignored at this level.

Investigation 12.3 To find the linear expansivity of a metal

There are several different types of apparatus available for this determination, and only one will be described. The requirements of the apparatus are:
(a) a suitable length of rod (or hollow tube) of metal ≈ 500 mm;
(b) a micrometer or spherometer to measure accurately the expansion which is ≈ 1–2 mm;
(c) a chamber so that the metal experiences a temperature rise which is as large as possible;
(d) a reasonable period of heating so that the apparatus reaches a steady final temperature.

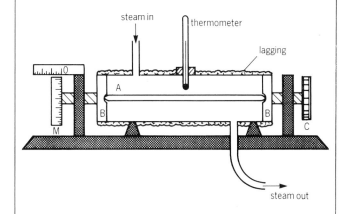

12.7 Apparatus for measuring the expansion of a rod

A is the rod whose linear expansivity is required (Fig. 12.7). Measure its length l_0 to the nearest millimetre using a metre ruler. This length is normally 500 mm. Then place it in the chamber as shown. The two ends B of the chamber are removable and have hollows into which the tapered ends of the rod A fit. Fit the lagged chamber into the solid metal stand, and set the micrometer screw M at the zero reading. Tighten the screw C until it is just finger tight, taking care not to bow the rod by screwing too tightly. Loosen (unscrew) M and take the thermometer reading. Then pass steam through the chamber until the thermometer reading is steady, and note this steady reading. Screw in M until it is just tight and take the micrometer reading. The difference between the two micrometer readings gives Δl and that between the two thermometer readings $\Delta\theta$. Then $\alpha = \Delta l / l_0 \Delta\theta$. The lagging on the chamber helps to produce a steady temperature reading.

By using bars of different materials you can determine their linear expansivities. The units of linear expansivity are K^{-1}.

Table 12.1 Some common values of α where linear expansivity is $\alpha \times 10^{-6} \text{K}^{-1}$

Aluminium	25.0	Iron and steel	11.0
Brass	18.7	Platinum	8.86
Copper	16.7	Invar	0.1
Pyrex	3.0	Soda glass	8.5

Concrete has a linear expansivity of $10-14 \times 10^{-6}$ K^{-1}. It will be noticed that invar, which is an alloy of iron and nickel, has a very low expansivity. Obviously very little correction for expansion is required when invar is used. Platinum and soda glass have approximately equal expansivities. This is useful as it means that platinum wire can be sealed into soda glass. Changes in temperature will not affect the seal as both materials expand and contract at approximately the same rate. If an aluminium wire were used to plug a hole in glass at a high temperature, then when the apparatus cooled the wire would have contracted more than the hole, would have a smaller diameter and would fall out.

Example

The Forth Bridge is constructed of steel and is 2.5 km long. The linear expansivity of steel is 11×10^{-6} K^{-1}. The minimum winter temperature may be as low as $-20\,°C$ and the maximum summer temperature as high as $40\,°C$. (These temperatures may seem rather extreme, but they are the temperatures of the steel and not the surrounding air.) What distance must be allowed for the change in length of the bridge?

change in length = original length $\times$ linear expansivity $\times$ change in temperature

$$\Delta l = l_0 \alpha \Delta$$
$$\Delta l = ? \quad l = 2.5 \times 10^3\,m \quad \Delta\theta = 40\,°C - (-20\,°C) = 60\,°C = 60\,K$$
$$\alpha = 11 \times 10^{-6}\,K^{-1}$$
$$\Delta l = 2.5 \times 10^{-3}\,m \times 11 \times 10^{-6}\,K^{-1} \times 60\,K$$
$$= 2.5 \times 10^{-3} \times 11 \times 10^{-6} \times 60\,m$$
$$= 165 \times 10^{-2}\,m$$
$$= 1.65\,m$$

This is quite a large change in length.

Example

A railway line is laid with 20 m lengths of rail on a day when the temperature is 5 °C. Gaps of 1 cm are left between the rails. At what temperature will the gaps close? (Linear expansivity of steel $11 \times 10^{-6}\,K^{-1}$.)

The rail will have to expand 0.5 cm in each direction for the gaps to close. The total increase in the length of each rail will be 1 cm.

$$\Delta l = 10^{-2}\,m \quad l = 20\,m \quad \alpha = 11 \times 10^{-6}\,K^{-1} \quad \Delta\theta = ?$$
$$\Delta l = l\alpha\,\Delta\theta$$
$$10^{-2}\,m = 20\,m \times 11 \times 10^{-6}\,K^{-1} \times \Delta\theta$$
$$\Delta\theta = \frac{10^{-2}}{20 \times 11 \times 10^{-6}}\,K$$
$$= \frac{10^2}{2.2} = 45.5 \quad K\,or\,°C$$

Thus the gap will close at a temperature of $45.5 + 5 = 50.5\,°C$.

One question which often causes confusion is whether the size of a hole in a metal plate increases or decreases when the temperature of the plate is increased. It is often argued incorrectly that the size of the hole will decrease because the metal expands in all directions.

Investigation 12.4   To determine the direction of expansion

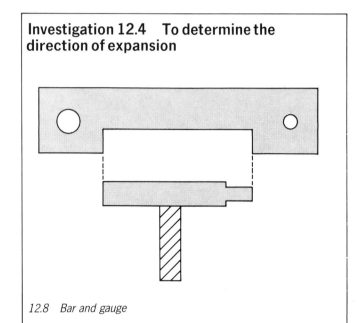

12.8   Bar and gauge

The bar in Fig. 12.8 just fits the hole in the metal gauge when both are at the same temperature. Both are made of the same metal. Strongly heat the gauge alone in a Bunsen flame. The bolt will now slip through it easily. This shows that the size of the hole has increased. On the other hand, if you leave the gauge for a few minutes in a pail containing ice while the bar remains at room temperature, the bar will no longer pass through the hole because the size of the hole has decreased. If both bar and gauge are treated the same, i.e. are kept at equal temperatures, then the bar will always just fit the hole.

12.3   Differential expansion

The principle of differential expansion in this example is used in fitting steel rims on railway carriage wheels. The rims are heated until they slide easily onto the wheel; when they cool they fit very tightly.

Differential expansion has many useful applications. Sometimes the metal screw cap on a glass or plastic bottle is very difficult to remove. If the top of the bottle is held in hot water, for example under a running hot water tap, the metal will expand more than the glass or plastic and will unscrew quite easily.

A glass stopper stuck tightly in the neck of a glass bottle may also be loosened by holding the neck in hot water. Although the expansivity of the neck is the same as that of the stopper, glass is a very bad conductor, and the neck expands before the stopper gets hot, thus loosening the stopper.

Example

A man wishes to fit an aluminium ring onto a steel rod which is 2.5 cm in diameter. The diameter of the aluminium ring is 0.025 mm too small. By how much must the temperature of the ring be raised before it will just slip on to the rod? Subsequently he wishes to remove the ring. Through what temperature must the rod now be heated? (Linear expansivities of aluminium and steel are 25×10^{-6} K^{-1} and 11×10^{-6} K^{-1} respectively.)

Note There is no need to find the circumference of the ring. It is much easier to work with the diameter.

The diameter of the aluminium ring must increase by 0.025 mm.

$\Delta l = 0.025$ mm $= 0.025 \times 10^{-3}$ m $= 25 \times 10^{-6}$ m
$l_0 =$ diameter $= 2.5$ cm $= 2.5 \times 10^{-2}$ m $\quad \Delta \theta = ?$
(Actually l_0 will be $25 - 0.025$ mm, but this can be ignored.)

$$\Delta l = l_0 \, \alpha \, \Delta \theta$$

$$25 \times 10^{-6}\text{m} = 2.5 \times 10^{-2}\,\text{m} \times 25 \times 10^{-6}\text{K}^{-1} \times \Delta \theta$$

$$\Delta \theta = \frac{25 \times 10^{-6}\,\text{K}}{2.5 \times 10^{-2} \times 25 \times 10^{-6}}$$

$$\Delta \theta = \frac{1}{2.5 \times 10^{-2}}\,\text{K}$$

$$= \frac{100}{2.5}\text{K} = 40\,\text{K or }40\,°C$$

When the ring and rod cool to room temperature, the ring will be a very tight fit. Re-heating them through the same temperature range will not cause the ring to become loose because the steel rod is also heated. Since both are heated together it is the *difference* in linear expansivities which must be used, i.e.

25×10^{-6} K^{-1} $- 11 \times 10^{-6}$ K^{-1} $= 14 \times 10^{-6}$ K^{-1}.
As before $\Delta l = 25 \times 10^{-6}$ m $\;\; l_0 = 2.5 \times 10^{-2}$ m $\;\; \Delta \theta = ?$

$$\Delta l = l_0 \times (\text{difference in expansivities}) \times \Delta \theta$$

$$25 \times 10^{-6}\text{m} = 2.5 \times 10^{-2}\,\text{m} \times \frac{14 \times 10^{-6}}{\text{K}} \times \Delta \theta$$

$$\Delta \theta = \frac{25 \times 10^{-6}}{2.5 \times 10^{-2} \times 14 \times 10^{-6}}$$

$$= \frac{1}{14 \times 10^{-3}}\,\text{K}$$

$$= \frac{10^3}{14}\,\text{K}$$

$$= 71.4\,\text{K or }71.4\,°C$$

The expansion of glass is often a nuisance in the home. Pouring hot liquids into thick glass containers often breaks them. The reason is that the part of the glass in contact with the hot liquid acquires the liquid temperature very quickly and expands, whereas the outside remains cold because glass is a bad conductor. As a result a stress is set up inside the glass, and the container breaks. When making jam the prudent cook heats the jam-jars in the oven before pouring in the hot jam. This ensures that glass and jam will be at approximately the same temperature. A valuable cut-glass dish can be saved from disaster by thinking carefully before plunging it into hot water.

Compound bar or bimetallic strip

This is a very important application of differential expansion. It can be demonstrated by a strip of copper and a strip of iron of the same dimensions, riveted or welded together to form a single bar and attached to a wooden handle. (The rivet itself is a useful example of expansion. When hot it is pushed through a hole in the metal strips, and is flattened at the top and bottom. When it cools it contracts, and holds the two plates firmly together.) When the metal bar is heated it bends with the metal with the larger expansivity on the outside of the curve. In Fig. 12.9 copper is on the outside. When the temperature rises the copper becomes longer than the iron and since it cannot slide over the iron the bar curves to form an arc of a circle. If, instead of being heated, the bar is placed in a mixture of ice and salt the bar will be cooled, and will curve in the opposite direction with the copper on the inside.

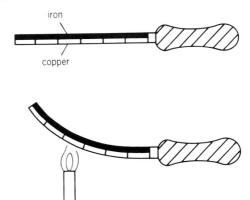

iron
copper

12.9 Compound bar

The bimetallic strip is widely used as a **thermostat**, a device which keeps the temperature approximately constant (Fig. 12.10). It has a variety of applications, e.g. in electric irons, domestic hot water systems, fish tanks and so on. In a thermostat a bimetallic strip is part of an electrical circuit, and curves and breaks contact when the temperature reaches a certain value, thus switching off the current in the heater. When the

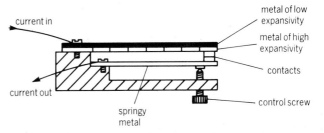

current in
metal of low expansivity
metal of high expansivity
contacts
current out
springy metal
control screw

12.10 Bimetallic thermostat

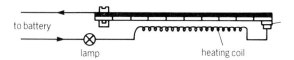

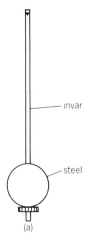

12.11 Car indicator circuit

temperature drops below the required value, the strip bends back and remakes contact, switching on the heater. The temperature at which the thermostat cuts out and in is adjusted by the control screw. If the control screw is turned clockwise, the contacts will be forced closer together, and a higher temperature will have to be reached before contact is broken.

Another use of the bimetallic strip is in the flashing indicators on a car. A small heating coil, in series with the lamp, is placed close to the bimetallic strip (see Fig. 12.11). When the indicator is switched on, the lamp lights and the heating coil gives out heat, raising the temperature of the bimetallic strip. This makes it bend away and break contact, thus switching off the lamp and the coil. It soon cools, straightens, re-makes contact, and the lamp and coil are switched on again. The process is repeated continually.

Watches and clocks run by springs and pendulums may soon become collectors' items as they are replaced by digital timers. They do not keep good time unless the effects of expansion are compensated. When the temperature rises the elasticity of the hair spring in a watch is weakened, and the diameter of the balance wheel increases. Both of these effects tend to slow down the watch. However, a rise in temperature causes the bimetallic strips in a compensated balance wheel to bend inwards, and this compensates for the other effects. In modern watches the spring may be made of an alloy of iron and nickel, and the balance wheel of invar. The effects of temperature are much less pronounced in these alloys.

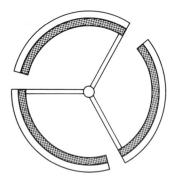

12.12 Compensated balance wheel

Differential expansion in the home

The period of a pendulum depends upon the length of the pendulum. When the temperature rises the length of the pendulum increases and its period is increased.

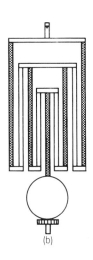

12.13 Compensated pendulum

Thus a pendulum clock goes more slowly. Figure 12.13 shows two types of compensated pendulum. In Fig. 12.13(a) the rod is made of invar and the bob of steel. The expansion of the invar downwards is compensated by the expansion of the bob upwards, and the position of the centre of gravity, and hence the period, remains unchanged. The screw at the bottom raises or lowers the bob so that the correct period can be obtained. Once set in the correct position this pendulum should be self-compensating. Figure 12.13(b) shows a more complicated pendulum. The non-shaded rods have the larger expansivity and will expand enough to compensate for the expansion of the longer shaded rods. Nowadays, when most buildings are fitted with central heating, a more or less uniform temperature is maintained but it is still important to compensate for the effects of heat.

The thermostat in a gas oven (Fig. 12.14) depends upon differential expansion. Gas enters through the inlet tube and passes through the openings D, E and F and into the burners. The cylinder B is made of brass, and the rod A of invar. When the temperature of the oven rises the brass expands much more than the invar, causing the valve C to move to the left and close the holes E and F. Thus the supply of gas to the oven

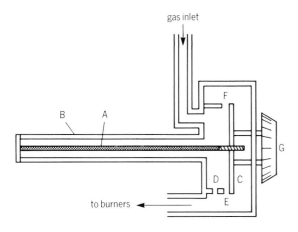

12.14 Gas oven thermometer

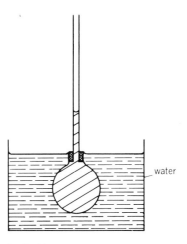

12.15 Expansion of a liquid

is reduced and the jets burn very low. The hole D is essential to admit a supply of gas to keep the burners alight when the valve is closed. As the oven cools B contracts and C moves to the right allowing more gas to the burners. The outside knob G allows C to be screwed in or out, thus decreasing or increasing the flow of gas, and decreasing or increasing the temperature setting of the oven.

12.4 Area and volume expansion

Most substances expand equally in all directions, although some, such as wood, have different expansivities along and across the grain. Obviously a metal rod expands in all directions, but since it is really only the length which is considered it is convenient to consider only the expansion along the length and talk about linear expansivity.

The **area or superficial expansivity** is defined as

$$\frac{\text{increase in area}}{\text{original area} \times \text{rise in temperature}} = \frac{\Delta A}{A_0 \Delta\theta} = \beta \, K^{-1}$$

The **volume or cubical expansivity** is defined as

$$\frac{\text{increase in volume}}{\text{original volume} \times \text{rise in temperature}} = \frac{\Delta V}{V_0 \Delta\theta} = \gamma \, K^{-1}$$

The relationship between these and linear expansivity is $\beta = 2\alpha$ and $\gamma = 3\alpha$. If you are interested in mathematics you will have no difficulty in showing that $\beta = 2\alpha$ and *not* α^2 and that $\gamma = 3\alpha$ and *not* α^3.

12.5 Expansion of liquids

There is no such thing as the linear expansivity of a liquid, because liquid can flow. When considering, for example, a thread of mercury in a tube the volume expansivity is used. Since the thread is narrow the volume expansivity is sometimes divided by 3 to obtain a non-existent 'linear expansivity'.

If a glass flask containing liquid is placed into a bowl of hot water (Fig. 12.15), the level of the liquid first falls and then rises. Why does the level fall? The glass, which is a bad conductor, gets hot and expands before the heat reaches the liquid. Thus the volume of the flask increases and the level of the liquid falls. However when the liquid eventually acquires the temperature of its surroundings it expands more than the glass, and its level then rises. Liquids have larger volume expansivities than solids.

Since a liquid has to have a containing vessel, the cubical expansion of the vessel normally has to be taken into account and it is only the apparent expansion of the liquid which is noted:

apparent expansivity of liquid = real expansivity of liquid − volume expansivity of container

Table 12.2 Some common value of γ where cubical expansivity is $\gamma \times 10^{-5}$ K^{-1}.

Alcohol	122	Mercury	18
Paraffin oil	90	Water (10–20°C)	15
Soda glass	2.5	Water (20–40°C)	40

12.6 Variation of density with temperature

The mass m of any substance is equal to its volume V multiplied by its density ρ: $m = V \times \rho$. When a substance is heated its mass m does not change. So when its volume increases as the temperature rises, its density must decrease. This change in density is not particularly significant in solids but it is very important in liquids and gases (which can flow) because it is the cause of the convection currents that are set up.

The expansion of a U-tube does not have to be taken into account when considering the expansion of a liquid. In the balancing columns of a manometer the pressure at the bottom of the tube ($h\rho g$) depends upon the height of the liquid column and its density and not upon the quantity of liquid in the tube. Thus the area of cross-section of the tube does not matter.

Example

What will be the effect of a rise in temperature upon the reading of a mercury barometer? Consider the three factors which are affected, namely the tube, the metal scale and the mercury.

(a) *The tube*   This will increase both in length and in area of cross-section. Neither will have any effect upon the reading, because it is only the density of mercury which affects the difference in column heights.

(b) *The metal scale*   This will expand, increasing the distance between marks on the scale, and will give a lower reading.

(c) *The mercury*   The density will decrease, so the height of the mercury column will increase to give the same pressure at the base. Since the cubical expansivity of mercury is greater than the linear expansivity of the brass of the scale, there will be a net increase in the barometer reading.

Anomalous expansion of water

Water is such a vital everyday substance that its behaviour is of the utmost importance.

Figure 12.18 shows how the volume of a fixed mass of water varies between $-10\,°C$ and $100\,°C$. The ice expands slowly until it reaches $0\,°C$ and then melts. The volume of water at $0\,°C$ is 10/11 of the volume of ice at $0\,°C$, and the volume continues to decrease until $4\,°C$ is reached. After this the volume increases, but not uniformly, until $100\,°C$ is reached. However the volume of water at $100\,°C$ is still less than the volume of ice at $0\,°C$. At $100\,°C$ the water changes to steam, and its volume increases by a factor of 1650.

It can be seen that water has its minimum volume and maximum density at $4\,°C$. This is fortunate for skaters and pond life. Ice, being less dense than water, forms on top of the water. Since it is a bad conductor it protects the water below. Pond life benefits because the water temperature at the bottom of a deep pond is not likely to fall below $4\,°C$. Once this temperature is reached, convection currents due to cooling cease. **Note**   Convection currents are caused by cooling as well as by heating.

One adverse consequence of the peculiar behaviour of water is the bursting of water pipes in very cold

Investigation 12.5   To discover the changes in density as water freezes

Put a flask containing a thermometer and an expansion tube into a large beaker and pack a freezing mixture of ice and salt around it (Fig. 12.16). At intervals read the temperature of the water and its level. It will be easier to see the meniscus if the water is slightly coloured, and it is as well to give the flask an occasional shake to ensure that mixing of a sort takes place. Plot a graph of scale reading against thermometer reading (see Fig. 12.17). As the temperature decreases the volume of the water decreases until the temperature is around $4\,°C$. The volume then starts to increase, and when the temperature reaches $0\,°C$ there is a large increase in volume (the water probably overflowed from the tube). The conclusion is that a given mass of water has its minimum volume at $4\,°C$.

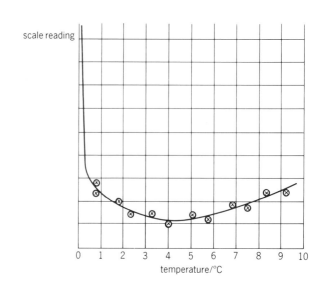

12.16   Expansion of water

12.17   Graph showing expansion of water

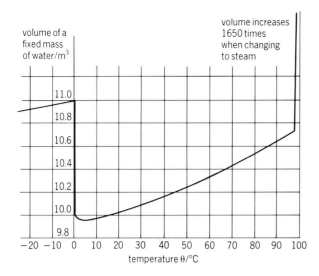

12.18 Anomalous expansion of water

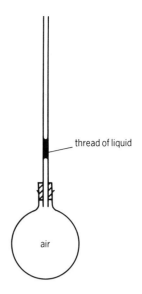

12.19 Expansion of air

conditions. When water at 0 °C changes into ice the volume increases by $\frac{1}{11}$. This is a very big expansion and an enormous force is exerted if there is no room for this expansion to be taken up. As a result the water pipe may split open, or a joint may be blown out. Some people believe that water pipes burst during a thaw. In fact the pipes burst when the water inside them freezes, but the burst does not become evident until the water flows through the hole during the thaw. Sensible precautions to take during a cold spell are

(a) drain the pipes if possible;
(b) lag thoroughly those which cannot be drained;
(c) keep a source of heat near pipes which may freeze. (Using heat may be expensive, but it is better than the expense and inconvenience of a burst pipe.)

If your morning milk is delivered very early you may have noticed, in very cold conditions, a column of frozen cream projecting from the top of the bottle, with the milk bottle top on the top. Obviously if the cap did not come off easily the bottle would break. Similarly, care must be taken when putting foodstuffs which contain a lot of water into a domestic freezer. Enough space must be left in the container for expansion when it freezes, otherwise the liquid may overflow or the container crack.

A natural example of the large force exerted when water freezes is the splitting open of rocks and the weathering of soil. When in winter the ground is saturated with water and the water freezes, there is a large expansion which forces the soil apart so that it crumbles when dry. When a crevice in a rock is filled with water, the water on the surface freezes first. If the temperature falls low enough to freeze the whole of the water, the force of the expansion may cause a large chunk of rock to split off.

12.7 Expansion of gases

The expansion of a gas is much larger than that of a liquid which experiences the same rise in temperature. Air expands just over three times as much as alcohol and about ten times as much as water. If you hold the flask shown in Fig. 12.19, which contains air, in your hands the liquid column will shoot out of the top of the tube, showing that the air has expanded. Gases always occupy all the space available, and when considering the expansion of gases the conditions have to be stated very precisely. This was covered in detail in Chapter 11 (p.137).

Questions

Q1 The length of a metal rod is 100 cm and the linear expansivity of the metal is 0.000 02 K^{-1}. By how many centimetre will it contract when cooled through 50 K?
A 1.001 **B** 0.150 **C** 0.100
D 0.50 **E** 0.001   (AEB)

Q2 If a fixed mass of water is cooled slowly from 10 °C to 0 °C, its volume
A increases steadily.
B decreases steadily.
C first increases and then decreases.
D first decreases and then increases.
E remains unchanged.   (L)

Q3 The fact that the level of the mercury in a mercury-in-glass thermometer rises when the temperature of the thermometer is raised shows that

A mercury is a good radiator of heat.
B glass is a poor conductor of heat.
C glass does not expand when heated.
D glass expands less than mercury when heated.
E mercury expands uniformly with rise in temperature.

(L)

Q4

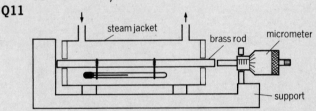

The apparatus shown in the diagram consists of a long hollow metal tube with closed ends resting on wooden supports with the end A firmly held against the fixed block F. (The wooden supports allow the tube to expand and contract freely.) The micrometer M is mounted on the same board so that it is level with the end B of the tube.

The apparatus is to be used to measure the change in length of the tube when its temperature is increased from room temperature to 100 °C. Suggest how this measurement could be carried out, giving full experimental details of the procedure you would adopt. Make clear how you would raise the temperature of the tube and how you would attempt to ensure that all parts of the tube are at 100 °C when your measurement is taken. Also indicate the precautions you would take to reduce errors in the measurement of the expansion. Would you expect to be able to measure the change in the *diameter* of the tube with a micrometer? Give a reason for your answer. Suggest an experiment you could carry out to demonstrate that the volume expansion of liquids is generally greater than that of solids. *(C)*

Q5 (a) Describe simple experiments to demonstrate that for the same temperature change (i) copper and steel expand or contract by different amounts, (ii) equal volumes of air and water expand by considerably different amounts.

(b) Indicate, preferably using a sketch graph, how the volume of a mass of water changes over the temperature range 270 K (when it is ice) to 285 K. Show clearly any special features and refer briefly to a practical consequence of ONE of these. *(S)*

Q6 Draw a labelled sketch of an experimental arrangement for measuring the expansion, accurate to a tenth of a millimetre, of an iron rod (either solid or hollow) when it is heated by steam, the rod being initially at room temperature. (For a length of a metre, the expansion is of the order of a millimetre.) Explain, with the aid of a diagram, the action of any *one* type of thermostat used for temperature control. What adjustment to the thermostat is needed if a higher controlled temperature is required?

Give *one* example of a disadvantage of thermal expansion and show how it is allowed for, or corrected. *(C)*

Q7 When equal volumes of water and mercury are heated, the mercury expands more than the water over the range 0 °C to 10 °C, but the water expands more than the mercury over the range 30 °C to 40 °C.

Describe in detail how you would check this experimentally; draw a diagram of the apparatus you would use.

Given that the volume of the water at 0 °C is equal to its volume at 10 °C, show how you could use your observations to compare the expansion of the mercury with the expansion of the containing vessel. *(C)*

Q8 A galvanised iron wire is hung between two posts 20 m apart, in the middle of summer when the temperature is 30 °C. Assuming that the lowest winter temperature will be −10 °C how long should the wire be so it will just become taut at the lower temperature? (Linear expansivity of wire $11 \times 10^{-6}\,K^{-1}$.)

Q9 The graduation on a steel tape is correct at 0 °C. What will be the true distance between two posts which is read on the scale as 10 m at 20 °C? (Linear expansivity of steel $11 \times 10^{-6}\,K^{-1}$.)

Q10 A steel tyre of diameter 1 m at 15 °C is to be fitted on to a wheel of diameter 1.005 m. To what temperature must the tyre be heated? (Linear expansivity of steel $11 \times 10^{-6}\,K^{-1}$.)

Q11

(a) The apparatus shown in the diagram was used to determine the linear expansivity of a brass rod.

(i) Why is it preferable to choose a long brass rod rather than a short one for this experiment?

(ii) What important physical properties are necessary for the material from which the support is made?

(iii) After passing steam through the jacket, how could you make sure that the rod had stopped expanding?

(iv) Why is it necessary to use a micrometer in this experiment?

(v) The following results were obtained from this experiment:

Initial length of rod = 700 mm
Initial temperature of rod = 20 °C
Initial micrometer reading = 3.58 mm
Final temperature of rod = 100 °C
Final micrometer reading = 4.70 mm

Calculate the linear expansivity of the brass rod.

(b) Draw a labelled diagram of the arrangement of the apparatus needed to test whether the 100 °C graduation mark of the thermometer used in part (a) is correct.

What precautions would you take to ensure the accuracy of this test? *(L)*

13 Temperature

13.1 Measurement of temperature

The difference between heat energy and temperature was mentioned on p.124. An analogue of this difference is a well. The total amount of water in the well is not usually of interest, but the level of water in the well is. If x m^3 of water are added to the well, the increase in level Δh is important, as is the decrease in level if a quanitity of water is drawn out. In the same way the total quantity of heat energy in an object is not usually of interest. However, it is very important to know the change in temperature if Q joule heat energy are absorbed or given out by the object. Some method of measuring the change in the heat energy level of a body is needed, or a way of comparing the level of heat energy in different bodies. The **level** of the heat energy or **temperature** of the body is the important factor, because heat energy will always flow from a higher to a lower temperature (heat energy level), although the body at the lower temperature may contain more heat energy.

Bodily senses are not good estimators of temperature. On p.128 it was stated that a metal rod feels colder than a piece of cloth when both are at the same temperature, which is lower than the body temperature. The reason is that the metal conducts heat energy from the hand far more rapidly than the cloth. What you feel with your hand also depends upon its initial state.

What, then, is required to measure temperature? Any physical property of a body which varies *uniformly* with temperature will serve to measure temperature. Some of these properties are:

(a) the variation in volume of a fixed mass of liquid;
(b) the variation in resistance of a metal, for example a length of platinum wire;
(c) the variation in the electromotive force of a thermocouple when the two junctions are at different temperatures;
(d) the pressure of a fixed mass of gas at constant volume.

There are others which could be used. How do we know that the properties vary uniformly? This is difficult, because if one property is used to check another, and they do not agree, it is not possible to know which is at fault, and if all four thermometers are used to measure the same temperature, say 200 °C, then all will give slightly different readings. Which, if any, is correct?

All gases have the same expansivity, so it is probable that there is something fundamental about the constant volume gas thermometer. Moreover, the gas scale of temperature is the same as the theoretical Kelvin thermodynamic scale of temperature. The constant volume gas thermometer is described on p.142. It is taken as the standard, and other thermometers are calibrated against it. Water cannot

---

Investigation 13.1 To demonstrate that two bodies at the same temperature may feel different

Take four cups or beakers and half fill one (**A**) with hot water, another (**D**) with ice-cold water, and the middle two (**B** and **C**) with luke-warm water, both at the same temperature (Fig. 13.1). Persuade a friend to put a finger from the left hand in **A** and one from the right hand in **D**. Then transfer the finger which was in

A into **B** and that which was in **D** into **C**. Ask your friend which feels hotter, **B** or **C**? Persuade other people to try the experiment. Do they all say that **C** is at a higher temperature than **B**? Thermometers placed in **B** and **C** will show them to be at the same temperature. The reason the people think that **B** and **C** are at different temperatures is because the left hand experiences a fall in temperature, whereas the right hand experiences a rise in temperature.

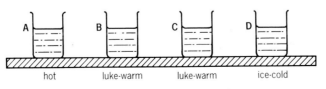

13.1 Apparatus for investigation 13.1

be used as a thermometer liquid because of its unusual expansion. It has other disadvantages, namely a low boiling point and a high freezing point. Its colourlessness is not really a problem as there is no difficulty in adding a little colouring matter so that it can be seen easily.

Liquid-in-glass thermometers

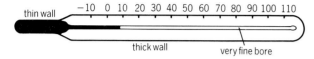

13.2   Liquid-in-glass thermometer

The thermometer in Fig. 13.2 is probably the most familiar type. The two liquids normally used in it are mercury and alcohol. The liquid is contained in a thin-walled bulb at the end of a long thick-walled capillary tube. Glass is a bad conductor of heat energy so the walls of the bulb are thin to enable the heat energy to pass through quickly, and the liquid to attain the temperature of its surroundings. Since the bulb is small, the bore of the capillary tube must be very fine so that a small change in temperature produces a reasonable movement of the liquid column. If you look end-on at a broken thermometer stem, you will need a magnifying glass to see the bore of the tube. It is easy to see the liquid thread in the thermometer, because the thick-walled tube acts as a cylindrical magnifying glass.

Liquid-in-glass thermometers are not particularly accurate. They have a limited range and are easily broken. They can be read more accurately if the size of the interval between the graduations is increased. This is done either by increasing the size of the bulb or by using a finer bore capillary tube or by a combination of both. If the bulb is larger the increase in volume of the liquid will be greater for the same rise in temperature, and the mercury will move a longer distance along the stem. Decreasing the bore produces a greater length of liquid for the same increase in volume and the same rise in temperature.

How long does it take for a thermometer to reach the temperature of its surroundings? This depends upon the quantity of liquid in the bulb. The larger the quantity of liquid the longer it takes. Some clinical thermometers are known as 'half-minute thermometers' and some as 'one-minute thermometers' for obvious reasons!

13.2   Scales of temperature

In order that temperature readings have the same meaning wherever they are taken, it is necessary to have a fixed **scale of temperature**. A scale must be defined by two fixed reference points which are easily obtainable and easily reproducible.

Lower fixed point   This is the temperature of pure melting ice, at a pressure of one standard atmosphere.

Upper fixed point   This is the temperature of dry steam from water boiling at a pressure of one standard atmosphere. It is important to stipulate the pressure, since both the freezing point and the boiling point of water vary with pressure.

Fundamental interval   This is the distance between the fixed points. It is divided into a number of equal divisions. Each division is one **degree**.

Determination of the lower fixed point

This point is fixed by submerging the bulb and the lower part of the stem of the thermometer in a funnel containing pure melting ice. Care is taken to ensure that the bulb is in good contact with the ice, and that the mercury level is just above the surface of the ice. When the liquid level in the thermometer remains steady for some time a mark is made at that point on the stem. Suppose the distance of this mark above the bulb is l_0.

Determination of the upper fixed point

This point is fixed by suspending the thermometer in steam above boiling water. The thermometer is contained in a double-walled jacket so that it is completely surrounded by steam, and the mercury thread protrudes just above the cork. When the liquid level remains steady for some time a mark is made at this point on the stem. Suppose the distance of this mark above the bulb is l_{100}. A manometer is incorporated in the apparatus to check that the pressure inside the apparatus is the same as that outside, and the external pressure is noted.

Celsius scale of temperature

On this scale the lower fixed point is 0 °C and the upper fixed point is 100 °C. The fundamental interval is divided into one hundred equal divisions. If the thermometer is needed to measure temperatures outside the fixed points, then the scale markings are continued below the 0 °C mark and above the 100 °C mark. The distance between consecutive marks on the scale remains the same. This assumes that the liquid expands uniformly.

When dealing with the expansion of a liquid volumes are needed, but if it is assumed that the area of cross-section of the stem remains constant then lengths may be used instead of volumes. Then the length of a degree interval on the Celsius scale is $(l_{100} - l_0)/100$ because $l_{100} - l_0$ is the fundamental interval.

When the thermometer is placed in a liquid whose temperature θ is unknown, the liquid level is at a distance l_θ above the bulb. Then the value of the temperature θ is obtained by simple proportion:

$$\theta = \frac{l_\theta - l_0}{l_{100} - l_0} \times 100$$

Example

In an unmarked mercury thermometer the length l_0 was 4 cm, and l_{100} 24 cm. What are the temperatures when l_θ is (a) 16 cm, (b) 28 cm and (c) 2 cm?

(a) $l_0 = 4$ cm $l_{100} = 24$ cm $l_\theta = 16$ cm $\theta = ?$

$$\theta = \frac{l_\theta - l_0}{l_{100} - l_0} \times 100 = \frac{(16 - 4)\,\text{cm}}{(24 - 4)\,\text{cm}} \times 100$$

$$= \frac{12}{20} \times 100 = 60\,°\text{C}$$

(b) $l_0 = 4$ cm $l_{100} = 24$ cm $l_\theta = 28$ cm $\theta = ?$

$$\theta = \frac{l_\theta - l_0}{l_{100} - l_0} \times 100 = \frac{(28 - 4)\,\text{cm}}{(24 - 4)\,\text{cm}} \times 100$$

$$= \frac{24}{20} \times 100 = 120\,°\text{C}$$

(c) $l_0 = 4$ cm $l_{100} = 24$ cm $l_\theta = 2$ cm $\theta = ?$

$$\theta = \frac{l_\theta - l_0}{l_{100} - l_0} \times 100 = \frac{(2 - 4)\,\text{cm}}{(24 - 4)\,\text{cm}} \times 100$$

$$= \frac{-2}{20} \times 100 = -10\,°\text{C}$$

General equation Earlier it was stated that any physical property of a body which varied uniformly could be used to measure temperature. The general equation for the Celsius temperature θ is

$$\theta = \frac{X_\theta - X_0}{X_{100} - X_0} \times 100$$

where X is the property which varies 'uniformly' with temperature. For example, X could be the resistance of a platinum wire or the electromotive force of a thermocouple.

Kelvin scale of temperature

This is the scale used for all scientific work. The lower fixed point on the Kelvin scale is also the temperature of pure melting ice at a pressure of one standard atmosphere and its value is 273.15 K. The upper fixed point is the temperature of dry steam from water boiling at a pressure of one standard atmosphere and its value is 373.15 K. Both the fundamental interval and the size of the degree are the same on the Celsius and Kelvin scales. It follows that changes in temperature on both scales will be equal: $\Delta\theta\,°\text{C} \equiv \Delta\theta\,\text{K}$.

Figure 13.3 shows a simple comparison table between the Celsius and Kelvin scales. For convenience, temperatures in the laboratory and everyday life are measured in °C. There is no difficulty in converting to K.

13.3 Celsius and Kelvin scales of temperature

13.3 Thermometric liquids

The two liquids used in thermometers are mercury and alcohol. Both have advantages and disadvantages.

Mercury

The advantages of using mercury in a thermometer are:

(a) it does not wet (cling to the sides of) the tube;
(b) it is a good conductor and the whole liquid quickly acquires the temperature of the surroundings;
(c) it expands uniformly;
(d) it has a high boiling point (357 °C);
(e) it has a low specific heat capacity.

The disadvantages of using mercury are:

(a) it has a high freezing point (-39 °C);
(b) its expansivity is fairly low.

The high freezing point means that it cannot be used in winter in countries where the temperature gets very low.

Alcohol

The advantages of using alcohol in a thermometer are:

(a) it expands uniformly;
(b) it has a large expansivity;
(c) it has a low freezing point ($-115\,°C$).

The disadvantages of using alcohol are:

(a) it wets the tube;
(b) it has a low boiling point ($78\,°C$);
(c) it has a high specific heat capacity.

It is sometimes stated that being colourless is a disadvantage, but this is not really a problem as it is quite easy to add a little colouring matter. Alcohol is used in cold countries in winter because of its low freezing point.

13.4 Maximum and minimum thermometers

A maximum thermometer records the highest temperature it has reached during a given period, while a minimum thermometer records the lowest temperature it has reached.

Clinical thermometer

A very important maximum thermometer is the clinical thermometer, which is used to take the temperature of the human body. Mercury is the liquid used in this thermometer, which is shown in Fig. 13.4. The glass wall of the bulb is very thin so that the mercury quickly acquires the temperature of the body.

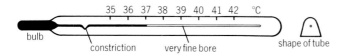

35 36 37 38 39 40 41 42   °C

bulb   constriction   very fine bore   shape of tube

13.4 Clinical thermometer

The bore of the capillary tube is very fine to give a large change in length for a small change in temperature. The feature that transforms it into a maximum thermometer is the constriction in the capillary just above the bulb. When the temperature rises the expansion of the relatively large volume of mercury in the bulb produces a force which pushes the mercury through the constriction and up the tube. When the thermometer is taken out of the patient's mouth or armpit, the mercury cools and contracts. The cohesive forces between the mercury molecules are not strong enough to pull the mercury back through the constriction, and the thread breaks at the constriction. Thus the mercury in the capillary tube cannot get back into the bulb, and the maximum temperature (the patient's temperature) can be read off. The thermometer stem is usually triangular in shape to increase the magnification, and enable the thermometer to be read more easily. The thermometer is given a sharp shake to get the mercury back into the bulb.

Note The scale is restricted to a small range, 35–42 °C. Normal body temperature is 36.9 °C (37 °C to the nearest degree). The short range enables the stem to be reasonably short. Under no circumstances should the thermometer be washed in very hot water after being taken out of the patient's mouth or the thermometer is likely to burst. It should be sterilised using a sterilising solution.

Maximum thermometer

Figure 13.5 shows another maximum thermometer in which a steel index is inserted in the capillary tube above the mercury column. As the temperature rises the index is pushed up by the mercury column because steel floats on mercury. When the temperature falls, the index remains in position helped by the small spring. The bottom of the index gives the maximum reading. A magnet is used to reset the thermometer by bringing the index back to the top of the mercury column.

Minimum thermometer

Alcohol is used in the minimum thermometer in Fig. 13.6 and the index is inside the liquid. When the temperature falls the alcohol contracts and the index is pulled back by the force of surface tension in the

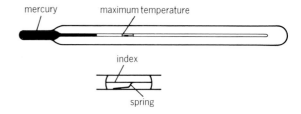

mercury   maximum temperature

index

spring

13.5 Maximum thermometer

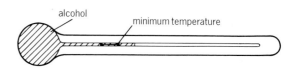

alcohol   minimum temperature

13.6 Minimum thermometer

meniscus. When the temperature rises the alcohol flows past the index which remains in position. The index does not fit as tightly as that in the maximum thermometer, and the thermometer is used in a horizontal position (e.g. to measure the minimum temperature of the ground at night). If the thermometer is tilted gently the index slides down the tube and comes to rest at the meniscus. This resets the thermometer.

Six's combined Maximum and Minimum Thermometer

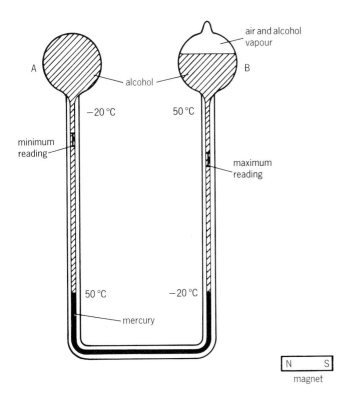

13.7 Combined maximum and minimum thermometer

This thermometer (Fig. 13.7) is used in meteorological stations to measure the maximum and minimum air temperature over twenty-four hours. Alcohol is the thermometric liquid and is contained in the bulb A. Bulb B also contains alcohol and in the space above the alcohol is a mixture of alcohol vapour and air. A thread of mercury separates the two columns of alcohol. This thread of mercury pushes up the indexes, which are made of steel and have a spring so that they remain in position when no force acts upon them. When the temperature increases the alcohol in A expands, flowing past the minimum index and pushing the mercury thread round the tube. This in turn pushes up the maximum index and the air in B is compressed. When the temperature falls the alcohol in A contracts. The air in B is now under less pressure and expands to push the alcohol and mercury thread

round the tube. The maximum index remains in position as the alcohol flows past and the mercury pushes the minimum index towards A. Thus the *bottom* of the index in the right-hand column gives the maximum reading, and the *bottom* of the index in the left-hand column gives the minimum reading. A magnet is used to reset the indexes by drawing them down to their respective mercury levels. (Of course the alcohol in B also contracts and expands, but this affects only the pressure of the gas in bulb B.)

13.5   Other thermometers

Bimetallic thermometer

A bimetallic strip (see p.151), wound into a coil, may be used to make a thermometer (Fig. 13.8a). When the temperature increases the curvature of the coil increases causing the pulley to which the movable end is attached to rotate and thus move the pointer over

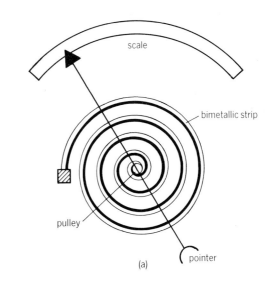

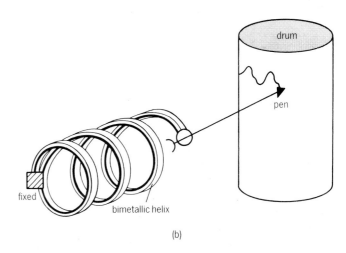

13.8   (a) Bimetallic thermometer, (b) thermograph

the scale. This type of thermometer can be robust and very compact (about as big as a pocket watch) and is used to record the temperature in freezers, ovens etc. The coil can also be made into a helix (Fig. 13.8b) and a pen attached to the end of the pointer. If the pen is positioned to touch a rotating drum it will give a continuous recording of the temperature. This instrument is called a **thermograph**. The tension in the helix can be adjusted by turning a screw and the instrument should be checked at regular intervals against another type of thermometer.

Platinum resistance thermometer

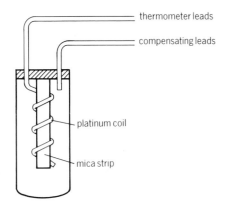

13.9   Platinum resistance thermometer

This thermometer uses the variation with temperature of the resistance of a coil of platinum wire as its standard. It is made from a double coil of platinum wire wound on a strip of notched mica and placed inside a porcelain tube. The coil is doubly wound to counteract the effects of electromagnetic induction. A pair of compensating leads are added to nullify the change in resistance of the leads to the platinum coil. The thermometer is placed where the temperature is required and the resistance of the coil is measured on a Wheatstone Bridge. Usually a scale will be calibrated to read the temperature directly, but if the actual resistance R_θ is measured the temperature can be calculated from

$$\theta = \frac{R_\theta - R_0}{R_{100} - R_0} \times 100$$

where R_0 and R_{100} are the resistances at $0\,°C$ and $100\,°C$ respectively. This temperature will obviously be in $°C$.

The advantages of a resistance thermometer over a liquid-in-glass thermometer are:

(a) it is far more accurate;
(b) it has a very large range;
(c) it can be read at a distance if it has long leads. The observer does not need to be close to where the temperature is being measured, e.g. in a furnace.

162

Example

The resistance of a platinum resistance thermometer at $0\,°C$ is $6.0\,\Omega$, at $100\,°C$ $8.4\,\Omega$ and at $\theta\,°C$ $14.4\,\Omega$. Find the value of θ. The thermometer is then placed in a thermos flask containing liquid nitrogen at $-200\,°C$. What will be the value of its resistance?

$R_0 = 6.0\,\Omega \quad R_{100} = 8.4\,\Omega \quad R_\theta = 14.4\,\Omega \quad \theta = ?$

$$\theta = \frac{R_\theta - R_0}{R_{100} - R_0} \times 100 = \frac{(14.4 - 6.0)\,\Omega}{(8.4 - 6.0)\,\Omega} \times 100$$

$$= \frac{8.4}{2.4} \times 100 = 3.5 \times 100 = 350\,°C$$

$R_\theta = ? \quad R_0 = 6.0\,\Omega \quad R_{100} = 8.4\,\Omega \quad \theta = -200\,°C$

$$\theta = \frac{R_\theta - R_0}{R_{100} - R_0} \times 100$$

$$-200 = \frac{(R_\theta - 6.0)\,\Omega}{(8.4 - 6.0)\,\Omega} \times 100$$

$$-2 = \frac{R_\theta - 6.0\,\Omega}{2.4\,\Omega}$$

$$-4.8\,\Omega = R_\theta - 6.0\,\Omega$$
$$R_\theta = 6.0\,\Omega - 4.8\,\Omega$$
$$R_\theta = 1.2\,\Omega$$

Thermo-electric thermometers

Different metals contain different numbers of free electrons per unit volume. Suppose metal A contains n_1 m^{-3} and metal B has n_2 m^{-3}. When A and B are brought into contact so that the electrons can move freely from one to the other (Fig. 13.10), they will redistribute themselves until the number on each side is the same, say n. Thus if A loses electrons it will have a net positive charge, and if B gains electrons it will be negatively charged, and thus an electromotive force is set up across the junction. Whether or not this electromotive force produces a current depends upon what happens to the other ends of A and B. Obviously these ends have to be joined, either directly or by other wires, and charge will only flow if these ends are at a different temperature from the junction of the metals.

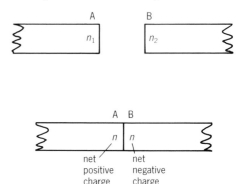

13.10   Electromotive force when different metals are in contact

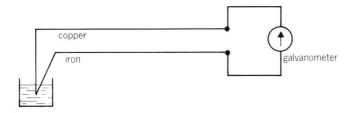

13.11 Thermocouple

The value of the net electromotive force produced, and hence the current, depends upon this temperature difference. The copper connecting wires have no effect on the electromotive force.

Basically the thermometer is made by joining one pair of ends and placing these where the temperature is to be determined (see Fig. 13.11). The other pair of ends are well away from the heat and are connected to a sensitive galvanometer. The galvanometer deflection is proportional to the electromotive force

$$\theta = \frac{E_\theta - E_0}{E_{100} - E_0} \times 100$$

The advantages of a thermo-electric thermometer are

(a) it has a low thermal capacity and can be used to measure fluctuating temperatures;
(b) it has a very large range, from $-200\,°C$ to $1500\,°C$ depending upon the metals used for the thermocouple;
(c) it can measure the temperature at a point.

Note Both the thermocouple and the resistance thermometer can only be used over a certain temperature range. These are the ranges over which the variation of resistance with temperature and variation of electromotive force with temperature are uniform. Above certain temperatures, which differ for different metals, they cease to be uniform.

Thermopile

By using a lot of thermocouples in series a sensitive heat-detecting device called a **thermopile** can be made.

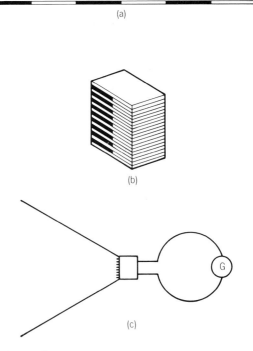

13.12 Thermopile

(This is the instrument used to detect the radiation emitted by the sides of Leslie's Cube, see p.132.) Strips of two metals are joined alternately (Fig. 13.12a) and then wound round a non-conducting frame so that half the junctions are on one side and half on the other (Fig. 13.12b). One side, with junctions, is painted black to absorb radiation and so become hot more easily. The rest of the junctions remain cool. The frame is then placed at the end of a cone (Fig. 13.12c) so that radiation is concentrated onto the black surface. The free ends of the thermocouples are connected to a sensitive galvanometer. Since the thermocouples are in series, the electromotive forces add up and a measurable deflection is obtained on the galvanometer. This instrument is sensitive enough to detect the heat from a lighted match some distance away.

Questions

Q1 There is a constriction in the bore of the tube of a clinical thermometer in order to
  A allow a restricted scale.
  B give a steady reading.
  C reach the final reading more quickly.
  D keep the mercury at its maximum reading.
  E allow each degree interval to be larger.

Q2 A temperature scale X has an ice point of 40° and a steam point of 240°. What is the temperature in °X when the Celsius temperature is 50 °C?
  A 80 **B** 100 **C** 120 **D** 140 **E** 160 *(AEB)*

Q3 Alcohol is sometimes used as a thermometric liquid because of its
  A ability to conduct heat.
  B cohesive properties.
  C high specific heat capacity.
  D low density.
  E low freezing point. *(L)*

Questions 4–5
  A 37 K **B** 273 K **C** 310 K **D** 350 K **E** 373 K
Q4 Which of the above is the temperature at which pure ice melts (at standard pressure)? *(L)*
Q5 Which of the above is the temperature of the normal human body? *(L)*

Q6

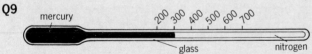

(a) You are provided with an uncalibrated thermometer as shown in the diagram. The mercury level is about one quarter of the way up the stem at room temperature. Describe how you would calibrate the instrument by marking two fixed points and then use it to determine room temperature.

Explain why, in the above instrument,
  (i) the glass surrounding the bulb is thin even though this makes it fragile,
  (ii) the mercury level will not immediately rise to its final steady level when the thermometer is placed in a warm liquid.

(b) Explain why
  (i) an alcohol-filled thermometer might be preferred to a mercury-filled one by an Arctic explorer,
  (ii) in a clinical thermometer the bulb is not quite full of mercury at room temperature. *(L)*

Q7 Draw a labelled diagram of a clinical thermometer, naming the liquid used and suggesting why it is suitable. State the reasons for any special features in the design of the thermometer. Some thermometers have different sized bulbs but give the same readings. Explain why this is possible. *(L)*

Q8 A mercury-in-glass thermometer is graduated from $-5\,°C$ to $105\,°C$. Describe how you would test experimentally that the 0 and 100 marks are correct. Illustrate with diagrams where necessary.

Explain why, if water is used to check the $0\,°C$ reading the water must be pure, but for checking the $100\,°C$ temperature the water need not be pure. Indicate the effect on the water at both these temperatures of the impurities normally considered.

State, giving a reason, a circumstance in which an alcohol thermometer could be used but a mercury one could not. *(L)*

Q9

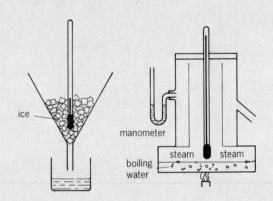

The diagram shows a mercury-in-glass thermometer containing nitrogen, graduated on the Kelvin or absolute scale. (Boiling point of mercury = 633 K, melting point of mercury = 230 K, softening point of glass about 750 K.) Mark on the diagram the position of the steam point.

Give the reason why the scale need not be graduated below the 200 mark.

Give *one* advantage of having nitrogen in the tube, rather than a vacuum.

Give a reason why the scale is not graduated above the 700 mark. *(C)*

Q10 A mercury thermometer with only the $0\,°C$ and $100\,°C$ markings on it was given to a student and the student was asked to estimate the temperature of a block of ice cream. Explain how the student could do this. *(AEB)*

Q11 Describe how you would check the $0\,°C$ mark on a mercury-in-glass thermometer. State the advantages of mercury for use as a thermometric liquid. Why is a mercury-in-glass thermometer not suitable for use in the Antarctic?

Q12 An ungraduated thermometer is attached to a centimetre scale and reads 7.5 cm in melting ice and 23.5 cm in steam at $100\,°C$ and 5.5 cm in a freezing mixture. What is the temperature of the freezing mixture?

Q13 Draw a diagram of and explain the action of a combined maximum and minimum thermometer.

Q14 Describe a thermometer suitable for measuring the temperature of liquid air. Why would a mercury-in-glass or alcohol-in-glass thermometer not be suitable?

The resistance of a coil of platinum wire is $10\,\Omega$ at $0\,°C$ and $14\,\Omega$ at $100\,°C$. What will be the temperature when its resistance is $15.4\,\Omega$?

Q15 What features in design would you expect to find in a thermometer which was required to measure temperatures between $0\,°C$ and $20\,°C$ very accurately to one hundredth of a degree centigrade? Give your reasons for the design features. Give reasons why you would not expect this thermometer to be suitable for measuring rapidly varying temperatures between $0\,°C$ and $20\,°C$.

Q16 The resistance of a platinum resistance thermometer is $10\,\Omega$ at $\theta\,°C$ and $14\,\Omega$ at $100\,°C$. What will be its resistance when it is placed in liquid nitrogen at $-200\,°C$?

Q17 Describe an instrument which can be used to measure the quantity of heat radiation falling upon it.

Q18

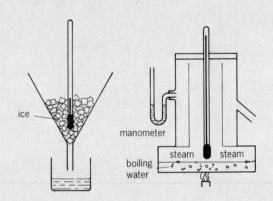

The diagrams illustrate two stages in the calibration of a thermometer.

(a) Briefly outline the procedure you would carry out to calibrate the thermometer.

(b) Give **one** reason in each case for (i) ensuring that the ice is made from pure water, (ii) placing the thermometer bulb in the steam rather than in the boiling water, (iii) the presence of the manometer.

(c) (i) One important property of a liquid for use in a thermometer is its ability to conduct heat. Explain why it is an advantage for the liquid to be a good conductor of heat.
  (ii) State **two** other properties which would make a liquid suitable for use in a thermometer and explain why these properties are advantageous. *(O & C)*

14 Freezing, melting and vaporisation

14.1 Cooling and heating curves

The **melting point** of a substance is **the temperature at which the solid phase and the liquid phase of the substance are in equilibrium under the stated pressure** which is usually taken as standard atmospheric pressure. It will be shown later that the melting point varies with the pressure and is altered when impurities are present.

A standard cooling curve is shown in Fig. 14.3. Consider the various parts of the curve. **AB** represents the substance in the liquid state. Here the molecules are free to move, and they move in random directions,

colliding with each other and with the walls of the containing vessel. The liquid is above the temperature of the surroundings so there is a net loss of heat energy, and the temperature of the liquid falls. As a result the molecules lose both kinetic and potential energy. This means that they move more slowly and become closer together.

BC represents a mixture of liquid and solid states. Near **B** the mixture will be mainly in the liquid state, and near **C** the mixture will be mainly in the solid state. Since the temperature is well above room temperature, heat energy must be given out, but the temperature does not fall. This is because heat energy is being

---

Investigation 14.1 To plot the cooling curve for naphthalene

Clamp a boiling tube containing naphthalene into a stand and then lower the tube into a beaker containing boiling water. When the naphthalene melts insert a thermometer into the tube and clamp it to the stand. When the temperature of the naphthalene reaches about 95 °C, lift the tube out of the boiling water and wipe the outside dry. Start a stopclock and take the temperature

of the naphthalene at half-minute intervals until the readings become more or less constant, then continue to take temperature readings at one-minute intervals. The whole experiment takes about 40 minutes. Whilst the liquid is cooling it should be shielded from stray draughts and stirred as much as possible to prevent irregular solidification. At the end of the experiment reheat the naphthalene before trying to remove the thermometer, otherwise you may leave the thermometer bulb in the naphthalene.

Plot a graph of temperature against time, as shown in Fig. 14.2, and extrapolate the horizontal part of the graph to the temperature axis to determine the melting point of naphthalene.

Paradichlorobenzene may be used in the experiment instead of naphthalene. The curve obtained is of a similar shape, but the melting point is much lower.

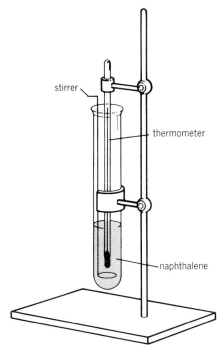

14.1 Apparatus to measure cooling in naphthalene

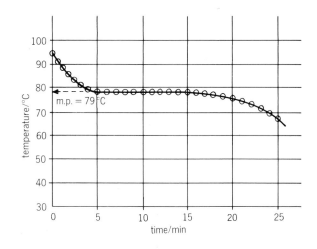

14.2 Cooling curve for naphthalene

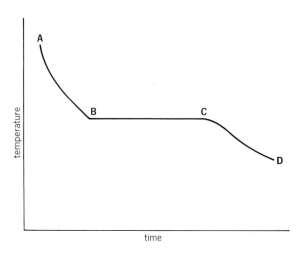

14.3 Standard cooling curve

Consider the various parts of the heating curve. **AB** represents the solid ice. The ice gains both potential and internal kinetic energy as it is heated and the temperature rises. **BC** represents the ice melting. The heat energy absorbed causes a gain in the potential energy of the molecules, which enables them to move with random motion. The kinetic energy and temperature remain constant. **CD** shows the liquid state with the temperature rising. There is a gain in both potential and kinetic energy. The distance between individual molecules increases and they move faster. **DE** represents a mixture of liquid and vapour. The temperature and hence the kinetic energy remain constant until all the liquid has changed into vapour. The heat energy absorbed increases the potential energy of the molecules, i.e. it is used to do the work necessary to pull the molecules apart from their neighbours, and transform the liquid into a vapour.

Further heating in a closed space would enable the dotted curve **EF** to be produced. This mainly represents an increase in kinetic energy and temperature. There will only be a small increase in potential energy since the molecules are so far apart.

released inside the substance as it changes from the liquid state to the solid state. The internal kinetic energy will stay at the same value, but will change from translational to vibrational kinetic energy. This means that the molecules will no longer move about with random motion but will vibrate about a fixed position with the same average kinetic energy. The potential energy will decrease because the molecules are much closer together. It is this release of potential energy which keeps the temperature constant.

CD represents the substance in the solid state. The only motion of the molecules is by vibration, and as the heat energy is released the kinetic energy of vibration decreases.

14.2   Specific latent heat of fusion

The horizontal part of all the cooling and heating curves represents a change in state without a change in temperature. In a solid, heat energy is required to do work to break the molecular bonds to change the substance into a liquid. Conversely, when the change

Investigation 14.2   To plot the heating curve for water

Take some ice from the freezing compartment of a refrigerator and crush it into a beaker. Insert a thermometer so that it is well inside the ice but does not touch the bottom of the beaker. Heat the beaker from beneath and take readings of temperature and time every minute. Plot the graph of your results. You should obtain a curve of the type shown in Fig. 14.4.

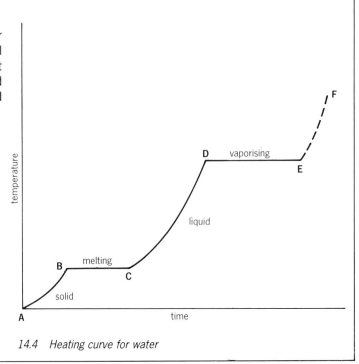

14.4   Heating curve for water

166

is from liquid to solid the molecules get closer together, causing a decrease in potential energy, and heat energy is released. This heat energy is known as **latent heat**. The specific latent heat of fusion is **the quantity of heat required to change unit mass of a solid into a liquid without changing its temperature**. It is also the quantity of heat energy given out when unit mass of a liquid changes into a solid without a change of temperature. In SI units the specific latent heat l has units of J kg^{-1}. If a mass m of a substance changes state from solid to liquid the gain in heat energy ΔQ is given by $\Delta Q = ml$.

Investigation 14.3 To determine the specific latent heat of ice

Put equal quantities of crushed ice into two identical filter funnels **P** and **Q** (see Fig. 14.5). If the ice has been taken out of a freezer, it must be left until it attains a temperature of 0 °C and starts to melt. Place an immersion heater connected to an ammeter, voltmeter and rheostat in **P**, making sure that it is completely covered with ice. At the same time as you switch on the immersion heater, place dry empty beakers of known mass under **P** and **Q**. Note the readings of the ammeter and voltmeter, and if necessary adjust the rheostat to keep them constant throughout the experiment. After several minutes, when a reasonable amount of water is in the beaker under **P**, note the time, remove the beakers and switch off the heater. Find the masses of the beakers and their content.

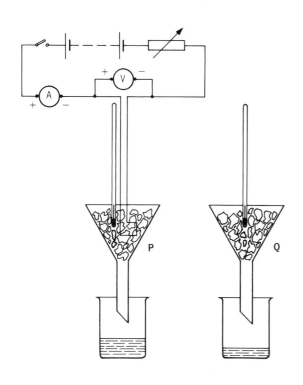

14.5 Apparatus used to determine specific latent heat of water

Suppose the results are as follows:

mass of beaker under **P** before experiment = m_1 kg
mass of beaker under **P** after experiment = m_2 kg
mass of ice melted in **P** during experiment = $(m_2 - m_1)$ kg
mass of beaker under **Q** before experiment = m_3 kg
mass of beaker under **Q** after experiment = m_4 kg
mass of ice melted in **Q** during experiment = $(m_4 - m_3)$ kg
reading of ammeter = I A
reading of voltmeter = V V
time for which heater was switched on = t min
= $60t$ s

The funnel **Q** is a control. It enables the mass of ice melted due to the temperature of the room during the experiment to be obtained. It is reasonable to assume that the same mass will be melted in **P**. Thus the mass of ice melted by the heater is $(m_2 - m_1) - (m_4 - m_3)$ = m. If l is the specific latent heat of fusion of ice the heat energy needed to melt the ice is ml joule. This must be equal to the electrical energy given out by the heater, which is $VI \times 60t$ J. Hence

$$ml = VI \times 60t$$

$$l = \frac{VI \times 60t}{m} \text{J kg}^{-1}$$

The value for the specific latent heat of fusion of ice is 336 000 J kg^{-1} or 336 J g^{-1} and 336 000 J of heat energy are needed to melt 1 kg of ice at 0 °C. Conversely the same quantity of heat energy is released when 1 kg of water freezes.

Note If the initial temperature of the ice is below 0 °C then additional heat will be required to raise the temperature to 0 °C before the ice starts to melt.

Many old houses have cellars underneath them and vegetables were often stored there during the winter. Due to the insulating property of the earth, a cellar remains relatively cool during the summer and relatively warm during the winter. When severe weather was expected a barrel containing water was put in the cellar. When this froze the latent heat energy liberated helped to keep the cellar temperature round about 0 °C and ensure the vegetables were not harmed by the cold.

Example

How much heat energy is liberated when 20 kg of water freezes to form ice at 0 °C?

This is quite straightforward and simply involves multiplying the mass by the specific latent heat.
$m = 20$ kg $l = 336\,000$ J kg^{-1} $\Delta Q = ?$
$$\Delta Q = ml$$
$$= 20 \text{ kg} \times 336\,000 \text{ J kg}^{-1}$$
$$= 6\,720\,000 \text{ J}$$

Example

How much heat energy is required to change 100 g of ice at $-10\,°C$ into water at $20\,°C$? (Specific heat capacity of ice $= 2100\ \mathrm{J\,kg^{-1}\,K^{-1}}$; specific heat capacity of water $= 4200\ \mathrm{J\,kg^{-1}\,K^{-1}}$; specific latent heat of fusion of ice $= 336\,000\ \mathrm{J\,kg^{-1}}$.)

This problem must be tackled in three stages, following the three events that occur.

(a) Find the heat energy required to raise the temperature of the ice from $-10\,°C$ to $0\,°C$.

(b) Find the heat energy required to melt the ice at $0\,°C$.

(c) Find the heat energy required to raise the temperature of the water from $0\,°C$ to $20\,°C$.

Note One mistake often made is to multiply the specific latent heat by the change in temperature. This should *never* be done. During the period when the change of state takes place, there is no change in temperature.

(a) $m = 0.1\ \mathrm{kg}$ $c = 2100\ \mathrm{J\,kg^{-1}\,K^{-1}}$ $\Delta\theta = 0 - (-10) = 10\ \mathrm{K}$

$$\Delta Q_1 = mc\,\Delta\theta$$
$$= 0.1\ \mathrm{kg} \times 2100\ \mathrm{J\,kg^{-1}\,K^{-1}} \times 10\ \mathrm{K}$$
$$= 2100\ \mathrm{J\ or\ 2.1\ kJ}$$

(b) $m = 0.1\ \mathrm{kg}$ $l = 336\,000\ \mathrm{J\,kg^{-1}}$

$$\Delta Q_2 = ml$$
$$= 0.1\ \mathrm{kg} \times 336\,000\ \mathrm{J\,kg^{-1}}$$
$$= 33\,600\ \mathrm{J\ or\ 33.6\ kJ}$$

(c) $m = 0.1\ \mathrm{kg}$ $c = 4200\ \mathrm{J\,kg^{-1}\,K^{-1}}$ $\Delta\theta = 20 - 0 = 20\ \mathrm{K}$

$$\Delta Q_3 = mc\,\Delta\theta$$
$$= 0.1\ \mathrm{kg} \times 4200\ \mathrm{J\,kg^{-1}\,K^{-1}} \times 20\ \mathrm{K}$$
$$\Delta Q_3 = 8400\ \mathrm{J\ or\ 8.4\ kJ}$$

$$\mathrm{Total\ heat\ energy} = \Delta Q_1 + \Delta Q_2 + \Delta Q_3$$
$$= 2100\ \mathrm{J} + 33\,600\ \mathrm{J} + 8400\ \mathrm{J}$$
$$= 44\,100\ \mathrm{J\ or\ 44.1\ kJ}$$

Investigation 14.4 To demonstrate that pressure affects the melting point

Take a length of fine bare copper wire and attach to its ends the largest weights which the wire will support without breaking. Place the wire across a block of ice as shown in Fig. 14.6. The copper wire sinks slowly through the block and the weights fall to the floor. Is the ice in one piece or two?

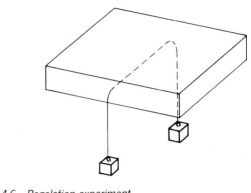

14.6   Regelation experiment

temperature must be round or above the freezing point. It is not advisable to try this investigation out of doors on a cold day, when the temperature is well below the freezing point, because the depression of the freezing point produced by the pressure is not sufficient to melt the ice.

Ice skating

The depression of the freezing point due to pressure is supposed to explain the mechanism of ice skating. The high pressure exerted by the narrow blades of the skates is supposed to melt the ice, forming a thin layer of water which acts as a lubricant. Some argue that the depression of the freezing point (found by using weight of skater/area of skate blade) is not sufficient to melt the ice, and say that melting is caused by friction. Maybe the true explanation is a combination of both effects. The area of the skate in contact with the ice may be only a small fraction of the area of the blade and the pressure may thus be large enough to melt the ice.

Snow

When walking on snow the pressure exerted by the foot is often sufficient to melt the snow. It freezes again when the foot is raised and sticks to the sole of the boot making walking difficult. Snowballs are formed because the pressure of the hands causes the snow to melt sufficiently for the particles to stick together when the pressure is released and refreezing takes place. When the temperature is well below the freezing point it is easy to walk and impossible to make snowballs because the pressure is insufficient to melt the powdery snow.

14.3   Effect of pressure and impurities on the melting point of water

In the previous chapter when considering the lower fixed point on a thermometer (p.158) it was stated that the pressure should be one standard atmosphere when the point was fixed. The inference is that pressure affects the melting point.

This process is known as **regelation**. The explanation is that the large pressure exerted by the wire slightly lowers the freezing point of the ice and so the ice underneath the wire melts. The water flows round the wire and refreezes when it gets above the wire, releasing latent heat energy which is conducted through the bare copper wire. This helps to melt the ice beneath and the process continues until the wire cuts through the block. Conduction through the copper wire plays an important part in the process, which will not work if an insulator is used. In addition, the

Impurities

Another factor which affects the freezing point of water is the presence of impurities. Adding salt to water lowers the freezing point. This is useful in making a freezing mixture of ice and salt if it is necessary to cool something below 0 °C. 0 °C is warmer than the freezing point of the mixture of ice and salt. Salt is spread on roads and pavements to melt ice and snow or to prevent any water from freezing. There is a limit to how far the freezing point can be lowered and it cannot be lowered sufficiently to melt snow and ice in very severe conditions (extremely low temperatures). Fortunately in these conditions the pressure exerted by car tyres is not enough to melt the snow and so allow ice to form.

14.4 Evaporation

The other change of state is between liquid and vapour. Molecules of a liquid escape from the surface and become vapour. This process is known as **evaporation**. Molecules in a liquid are free to move in any direction because the bonds which bound them together in the solid state have been broken. However there are still strong attractive forces between the molecules in a liquid. In Fig. 14.7 molecule **A** in the body of the liquid is attracted equally in all directions, and there is no resultant force upon it. It has kinetic energy but only travels a very small distance before colliding with other molecules. Under normal conditions it is extremely unlikely that it will escape from the liquid. It moves about in random directions. The same is true of the other molecules in the vicinity, but they will not all move with the same speed. Some have more kinetic energy than others; the average kinetic energy of all the molecules is a measure of the temperature of the liquid (see p.137).

Molecule **B** is in the surface layer of the liquid. The attractive forces in the horizontal directions are all equal, as with molecule **A**. There are some molecules just above the surface of the liquid and thus there is a small upward force. This is much less than the large downward force, so there is a resultant force towards the body of the liquid. Whether or not the molecule can overcome this force and escape from the liquid depends upon its kinetic energy.

Only the fastest-moving molecules have a large enough kinetic energy to escape from the liquid. Since some of the fastest-moving molecules leave the liquid it follows that the average kinetic energy of the molecules remaining in the liquid is decreased. Consequently the temperature of the liquid falls. This cooling is not noticed normally because heat energy flows in from the surroundings to keep the temperature constant. You can experience it by placing a drop of volatile liquid such as ether or eau de cologne on the back of your hand. The liquid evaporates rapidly and the area feels cold, because latent heat is drawn rapidly from the hand. A more convincing demonstration is given in the following investigation.

Investigation 14.5 To demonstrate that evaporation produces cooling

Place an empty copper calorimeter on a large drop of water on a wooden block (Fig. 14.8) in a fume cupboard. Fill the calorimeter about one-third full with a volatile liquid such as ether. Using a bellows, rapidly bubble air at room temperature through the ether. This causes a very large increase in the surface area of the ether exposed to the air and produces rapid evaporation. After a very short period of time the outside of the calorimeter will be covered with a coating of hoar frost, and the layer of water under the calorimeter will be frozen solid.

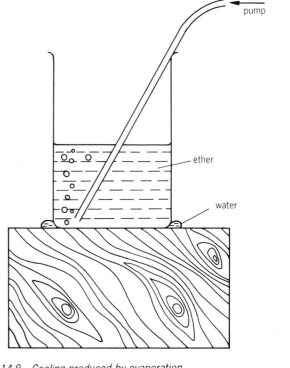

14.8 *Cooling produced by evaporation*

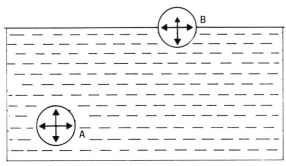

14.7 *Forces between molecules in a liquid*

The loss of large numbers of the more energetic molecules from the ether lowers its temperature to below 0 °C, and heat energy flows in from the surrounding area. The immediate surroundings, i.e. the water, supply most of this heat energy and the water loses so much heat energy that it freezes.

A simple application which uses the cooling produced by evaporation is shown in Fig. 14.9. A milk bottle is placed in the water, and the unglazed earthenware jar is inverted over it. Water rises up the earthenware jar by capillary action, and evaporates. The cooling produced helps to keep the milk fresh. This device is useful when no refrigerator is available, e.g. when camping. If no earthenware jar is available, a wet muslin cloth can be used instead.

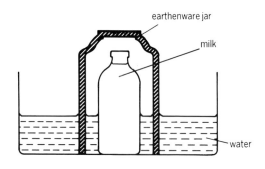

14.9   Keeping milk cool

If you have swum in the open air you will know the difference between a dry and a humid day. If the air is dry evaporation is rapid. Latent heat is taken from the body as the water evaporates and you will feel very cold on leaving the water. On a humid day there is little evaporation and so there is no need to dry off as soon as you leave the water.

More facts about evaporation

1 Evaporation only takes place from the surface of a liquid, so one way of cutting down evaporation is to decrease the surface area. Conversely, increasing the surface area increases evaporation and enables a liquid to cool more quickly.
2 Evaporation takes place at any temperature. However, raising the temperature of the liquid increases the number of molecules in the surface layer with sufficient kinetic energy to escape, and hence increases the rate of evaporation.
3 Decreasing the atmospheric pressure increases the rate of evaporation as there is less likelihood of the escaping molecules rebounding into the liquid.
4 A wind over the surface increases evaporation as it removes the molecules as soon as they escape from the liquid and thus increases the rate of evaporation.

Work done in pushing back atmosphere

Whenever there is a large increase in the volume of a gas work has to be done to push back the surrounding atmosphere. Energy is required for this. When water changes into steam the volume increases about seventeen times. Most of the heat energy supplied is used to break away from the attractive forces of the molecules but about one-twentieth is used to push back the atmosphere. The same occurs with other liquids. When a solid changes to liquid the change in volume is very small and the energy lost effecting this can be neglected. With ice, of course, the volume decreases as it liquefies and so the energy change is in the opposite direction.

14.5   Boiling

Boiling also involves the release of molecules from a liquid, but it differs from evaporation in the following ways:

1 Boiling takes place throughout the whole body of the liquid. When the temperature reaches the boiling point the average kinetic energy of the molecules is such that they can break free from the attractive forces of the molecules surrounding them. Bubbles of vapour are formed throughout the liquid.
2 Boiling takes place at a fixed temperature which is the boiling point of the liquid at that particular pressure.

One definition of the **boiling point** is **the temperature at which the saturated vapour pressure of the liquid is equal to the pressure of the surroundings.** It follows that the boiling point is raised if the pressure of the surroundings is increased.

The effect of pressure

The pressure cooker works on the above principle. By preventing the steam from escaping, the vapour pressure above the water is increased and thus the boiling point is raised. Consequently the cooker's contents are at a higher temperature and so take less time to cook. When the pressure inside reaches a certain value the weights on the lid are pushed up, and

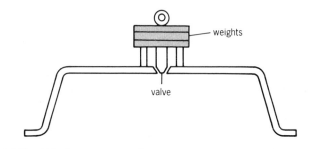

14.10   Lid of a pressure cooker

Investigation 14.6 To demonstrate boiling under reduced pressure

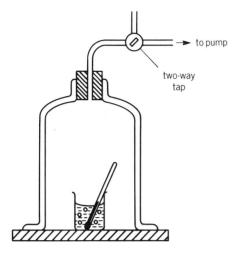

14.11 Boiling under reduced pressure

Place a beaker, half-full of water at room temperature, under an inverted bell jar to which a pump is attached (Fig. 14.11). Pump out the air from inside the bell jar. Soon the water will start to boil, although the thermometer shows that the water is still at room temperature.

a valve is opened to allow some steam to escape and so prevent the cooker exploding. The boiling point can be adjusted by changing the value of the weights on the lid.

Cooking at camps which are high on mountains is not likely to be successful unless a pressure cooker is used. The temperature of the boiling water will be too low to cook satisfactorily. Car radiators used to boil over when crossing high mountain passes, but cars now have sealed radiator systems which make them less likely to boil.

The effect of impurities

The addition of impurities will also affect the boiling point of water. Adding salt or sugar to water raises the boiling point. Salt or sugar molecules are more massive than water molecules and as a result the attractive forces are increased. More kinetic energy is required to overcome them, and the boiling point is raised.

14.6 Specific latent heat of vaporisation

The specific latent heat of vaporisation is **the quantity of heat energy required to change unit mass of liquid into vapour without changing the temperature.** Conversely it is the quantity of heat energy given out when unit mass of a vapour condenses into a liquid without the temperature changing.

Investigation 14.7 To determine the latent heat of vaporisation

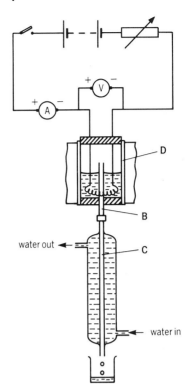

14.12 Apparatus used to find specific latent heat of vaporisation

The apparatus used in this investigation is shown in Fig. 14.12. **D** is a wide glass tube with a tight-fitting cork at the bottom. A glass tube **B** runs through the cork and is connected to the condenser **C**. Half-fill **D** with the liquid under consideration, then place a heating coil inside the liquid. Pass the leads through a cork that fits tightly into the top of **D** and switch on the current. Eventually the liquid boils and vapour issues freely from the bottom end of **C**. Run cold water through the condenser so that drops of liquid come out of the bottom of **C**. Place a clean dry beaker whose mass has been determined under the condenser to catch the drops, and at the same time start a stopclock. Note the readings of the ammeter and voltmeter when the heater is switched on and check them at various times during the experiment. After several minutes stop the clock, remove the beaker and determine its mass.

Suppose the results are as follows

$$\text{mass of clean dry beaker} = m_1 \text{ kg}$$
$$\text{mass of beaker and condensed liquid} = m_2 \text{ kg}$$
$$\text{mass of liquid condensed } (m_2 - m_1) = m \text{ kg}$$
$$\text{time taken} = t \text{ min}$$
$$= 60t \text{ s}$$
$$\text{average ammeter reading} = I \text{ A}$$
$$\text{average voltmeter reading} = V \text{ V}$$

The mass of liquid condensed will be the same as the mass of liquid boiled off, and the electrical energy released by the coil must be equal to the heat energy

171

taken in by the liquid. Hence, if l is the latent heat of vaporisation,

$$VI \times 60t = (m_2 - m_1)l$$

$$l = \frac{VI \times 60t}{(m_2 - m_1)}$$

$$= \frac{VI \times 60t}{m} \text{ J kg}^{-1}$$

This is not strictly true. Although the tube is well lagged, some heat energy is still lost to the surroundings. This heat loss is eliminated by running the experiment for the *same time* with a different current I_1 and voltage V_1 and noting the new mass M of liquid condensed. Then

$$(V_1 I_1 - VI)60t = (M - m)l$$

This eliminates the heat loss to the surroundings and the value of l calculated is quite accurate. The specific latent heat of vaporisation of water is $2\,260\,000$ J kg^{-1} (2260 kJ kg^{-1}).

Example

A kettle which does not switch itself off contains 1 kg of water. If the user forgets to switch it off after the water starts to boil, how long will it take for the kettle to boil dry? Why is the calculated time likely to be an underestimate? (The kettle has a 1.5 kW heater. Specific latent heat of vaporisation of water is $2\,250\,000$ J kg^{-1}.)

$m = 1$ kg $\quad l = 2\,250\,000$ J kg^{-1}
Heat energy required to vaporise all the water $= \Delta Q$

$$\Delta Q = ml$$
$$= 1 \text{ kg} \times 2\,250\,000 \text{ J kg}^{-1}$$
$$= 2\,250\,000 \text{ J}$$

$P = IV = 1500$ W $\quad t = ?$
Electrical energy required $= VIt = 1500$ J s^{-1} t s $= 1500\,t$ J

$$1500\,t = 2\,250\,000$$
$$t = \frac{2\,250\,000}{1500} \text{ s}$$
$$= 1500 \text{ s}$$
$$= 25 \text{ min}$$

This time is likely to be an underestimate because the temperature of the kettle is well above that of the surroundings and quite a lot of heat energy is lost. This lowers the quantity of energy available to vaporise the water, so the time taken to boil dry will increase. On the other hand the element is likely to burn out before all the water is vaporised because it will not be completely covered with water.

Example

Compare the quantities of heat energy released when 200 g steam cool from 100 °C to 40 °C and 200 g water cool from 100 °C to 40 °C. (Specific latent heat of vaporisation $2\,260\,000$ J kg^{-1}. Specific heat capacity of water 4200 J kg^{-1} K^{-1}.)

Heat energy lost when 200 g steam condense at 100 °C $= \Delta Q_1 = ml$.
$m = 0.2$ kg $\quad l = 2\,260\,000$ J kg^{-1} $\quad \Delta Q_1 = ?$

$$\Delta Q_1 = ml$$
$$= 0.2 \text{ kg} \times 2\,260\,000 \text{ J kg}^{-1}$$
$$= 452\,000 \text{ J or } 452 \text{ kJ}$$

Heat energy lost when 200 g of water cool from 100 °C to 40 °C $= \Delta Q_2 = mc\Delta\theta$.
$m = 0.2$ kg $\quad c = 4200$ J kg^{-1} K^{-1} $\quad \Delta\theta = 100 - 40 = 60$ K

$$\Delta Q_2 = mc\Delta\theta$$
$$= 0.2 \text{ kg} \times 4200 \text{ J kg}^{-1}\text{K}^{-1} \times 60 \text{ K}$$
$$= 50\,400 \text{ J or } 50.4 \text{ kJ}$$

Total heat energy released by steam
$$= \Delta Q_1 + \Delta Q_2$$
$$= 452 \text{ kJ} + 50.4 \text{ kJ}$$
$$= 502.4 \text{ kJ}$$

Total heat energy released by water $= 50.4$ kJ.

Thus approximately ten times as much heat energy is released by the steam as by the same mass of boiling water. It follows that scalding by steam is much more severe than scalding by the same mass of boiling water.

14.7 Transfer of heat energy on melting and condensation

Domestic refrigerator

One very important application of the transfer of heat energy on evaporation and condensation is the domestic refrigerator (see Fig. 14.13). When the pump **P** is started the pressure is rapidly reduced in the pipes **F** in the freezing compartment. This causes Freon, the volatile liquid in the pipes, to evaporate rapidly (or boil under reduced pressure). The latent heat energy required is taken from the Freon itself and from the surroundings and cooling occurs. The gas is compressed as it passes through the pump **P** and condenses into a liquid. Latent heat energy is released in this compression and must be removed before the Freon again enters the refrigerator, otherwise the heat removed would be taken straight back again. Copper vanes are attached to the pipes which conduct heat energy from the Freon and dissipate it to the surroundings, mainly by convection. The cooled Freon then passes into the freezing compartment, and

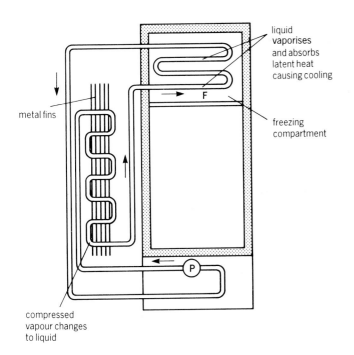

metal fins

liquid vaporises and absorbs latent heat causing cooling

freezing compartment

compressed vapour changes to liquid

14.13 Domestic refrigerator

the cycle is repeated. The walls and door of the refrigerator are hollow and are filled with a poor conductor such as expanded polystyrene. A thermostat inside the refrigerator controls the temperature by switching the pump on and off.

A room cannot be cooled by leaving open the door of a refrigerator since the heat energy taken from inside the refrigerator is released into the room. If the system were 100% efficient the quantity of heat energy released would equal the quantity taken from the refrigerator and the temperature of the room would remain the same. In fact the system is not likely to be 100% efficient and the temperature of the room is likely to rise.

It is important that a refrigerator or freezer should be sited where there is a good air flow around it. This is necessary to dissipate the heat from the copper vanes. It would be foolish to put a small freezer into a confined space such as a cupboard just because this happened to be convenient. There is a strong probability that the motor driving the pump would overheat and burn out.

Heating or cooling by mixing

Water can be heated by passing steam through it or cooled by adding ice to it. It is useful to know how to do calculations involving the above processes.

Example

A refrigerator converts 500 g of water at 20 °C into ice at −10 °C in 2 hours. What is the rate at which heat energy is extracted from the water? (Specific latent heat of fusion of water = 336 000 J kg^{-1}; specific heat capacity of water = 4200 J kg^{-1} K^{-1}; specific heat capacity of ice = 2100 J kg^{-1} K^{-1}.)

Heat energy extracted in cooling the water from 20 °C to 0 °C = ΔQ_1
$m = 0.5$ kg $c = 4200$ J kg^{-1} K^{-1} $\Delta\theta = 20 - 0 = 20$ K
$\Delta Q_1 = ?$

$$\Delta Q_1 = mc\Delta\theta = 0.5 \text{ kg} \times 4200 \text{ J kg}^{-1}\text{K}^{-1} \times 20 \text{ K}$$
$$= 42\,000 \text{ J or } 42 \text{ kJ}$$

Heat energy extracted when the water changes to ice = ΔQ_2
$m = 0.5$ kg $l = 336\,000$ J kg^{-1} $\Delta Q_2 = ?$

$$\Delta Q_2 = ml = 0.5 \text{ kg} \times 336\,000 \text{ J kg}^{-1}$$
$$= 118\,000 \text{ J or } 118 \text{ kJ}$$

Heat energy extracted when the ice cools from 0 °C to −10 °C = ΔQ_3
$m = 0.5$ kg $c = 2100$ J kg^{-1} K^{-1} $\Delta\theta = (0 - (-10)) = 10$ K
$\Delta Q_3 = ?$

$$\Delta Q_3 = mc\Delta\theta = 0.5 \text{ kg} \times 2100 \text{ J kg}^{-1}\text{K}^{-1} \times 10 \text{ K}$$
$$= 10\,500 \text{ J or } 10.5 \text{ kJ}$$

total heat energy
extracted $= \Delta Q_1 + \Delta Q_2 + \Delta Q_3$
$= 42\,000 + 118\,000 + 10\,500$ J
$= 170\,500$ J

This heat is extracted in 2 hours so the heat energy extracted each second is 170 500 (2 × 60 × 60) J s^{-1} = 24 J s^{-1}. The rate of extraction is 24 J s^{-1} or 24 W.

Example

What is the mass of steam at 100 °C which is needed to raise the temperature of 2 kg water from 15 °C to 60 °C? Ignore the heat required to raise the temperature of the containing vessel. Specific latent heat of vaporisation of water = 2 260 000 J kg^{-1} and specific heat capacity of water = 4200 J kg^{-1} K^{-1}.

The heat energy ΔQ_1 gained by the cold water must equal the heat energy ΔQ_2 lost by the steam.
Heat energy gained by cold water:
$M_1 = 2$ kg $\Delta\theta = 60$ °C − 15 °C = 45 K
$c = 4200$ J kg^{-1} K^{-1}.

$$\Delta Q_1 = m_1\,c\,\Delta\theta$$
$$= 2 \text{ kg} \times 4200 \text{ J kg}^{-1}\text{K}^{-1} \times 45 \text{ K}$$
$$= 90 \times 4200 \text{ J}$$

Heat lost by steam:
$m_2 = ?$ $l = 2\,260\,000$ J kg^{-1} $c = 4200$ J kg^{-1} K^{-1}
$\Delta\theta_2 = 100$ °C − 60 °C = 40 K

$$\Delta Q_2 = m_2\,l + m_2\,c\Delta\theta_2 = m_2\,(l + c\Delta\theta_2)$$
$$= m_2\,(2\,260\,000 \text{ J kg}^{-1} +$$
$$4200 \text{ J kg}^{-1}\text{kg}^{-1} \times 40 \text{ K})$$
$$= m_2\,(2\,260\,000 + 40 \times 4200) \text{ J kg}^{-1}$$
$$= m_2\,2\,428\,000 \text{ J kg}^{-1}$$

$$\Delta Q_2 = \Delta Q_1$$
$$m_2\,2\,428\,000$$
$$\text{J kg}^{-1} = 378\,000 \text{ J}$$
$$m_2 \approx 0.156 \text{ kg}$$

Example

A glass containing 500 g of squash at 20 °C has 100 g of ice at 0 °C put into it. What will be the temperature of the squash when the ice has all melted? Specific latent heat of fusion of ice = 336 000 J kg^{-1}; specific heat capacity of water = 4200 J kg^{-1} K^{-1}. Assume squash has the same specific heat capacity as water.)

Let θ °C be final temperature of the squash. Ignore the heat lost by the container. Heat lost by squash ΔQ_1 = heat gained by ice ΔQ_2.

Heat lost by squash:
$m_1 = 0.5$ kg $\quad c = 4200$ J kg^{-1} K^{-1} $\quad \Delta\theta_1 = (20 - \theta)$ K

$$\Delta Q_1 = m_1 c \Delta\theta$$
$$= 0.5 \text{ kg} \times 4200 \text{ J kg}^{-1} \text{ K}^{-1} \times (20 - \theta) \text{ K}$$
$$= 0.5 \times 4200 \times (20 - \theta) \text{ J}$$

Heat gained by ice:
$m_2 = 0.1$ kg $\quad l = 336\,000$ J kg^{-1}
$c = 4200$ J kg^{-1} K^{-1} $\quad \Delta\theta_2 = (\theta - 0)$ K

$$\Delta Q_2 = m_2 l + m_2 c \Delta\theta = m_2 (l + c\Delta\theta)$$
$$= 0.1 \text{ kg} \times 336\,000 \text{ J kg}^{-1} + 0.1 \text{ kg} \times 4200 \text{ J kg}^{-1} \text{ K}^{-1} \times \theta \text{ K}$$
$$= (0.1 \times 336\,000 + 0.1 \times 4200 \times \theta) \text{ J}$$
$$= (33\,600 + 420\theta) \text{ J}$$

$$\Delta Q_1 = \Delta Q_2$$
$$0.5 \times 4200 \times (20 - \theta) \text{ J} = (33\,600 + 420\theta) \text{ J}$$
$$42\,000 - 2100\,\theta = 33\,600 + 420\,\theta$$
$$8400 = 2520\,\theta$$
$$3\tfrac{1}{3} = \theta$$

The final temperature of the squash is $3\tfrac{1}{3}$ °C.

Questions

Q1 The temperature of water boiling in a vessel can be raised by
  A adding pieces of porous solid to the water.
  B adding salt to the water.
  C decreasing the pressure in the vessel.
  D heating the vessel more strongly.
  E stirring the water vigorously. *(L)*

Q2 If air is pumped with a bicycle pump into ether at room temperature contained in a test tube, cooling results. This is because
  A ether has a lower boiling point than water.
  B heat is conducted from the ether to the glass and to the air.
  C latent heat has to be supplied to the ether in order to evaporate it.
  D the air is cooled when it is compressed in the pump.
  E the specific heat capacity of ether is low. *(L)*

Q3 How much heat is evolved when a mass m of water initially at a Celsius temperature θ is frozen into ice at 0 °C? (Let the specific heat capacity of water be c and the specific latent heat of fusion of ice be l.)
  A $mc\theta$ B ml/θ C $mc + ml/\theta$ D $mc\theta + ml$
  E $mc\theta + ml/\theta$ *(L)*

Q4 (a) The results in the table were obtained when a hot liquid in a test tube was allowed to cool in a laboratory.

temperature (°C)	85	61	56	56	56	50	40
time (minutes)		0	1	2	3	4	5	6

  (i) Draw a graph of temperature on the y-axis against time on the x-axis. On the graph show clearly the freezing point of the liquid.
  (ii) Describe what could be seen happening inside the test tube during the cooling process.
  (iii) Explain the shape of the graph, by stating what is happening in the test tube at each stage of the cooling process.
  (b) Calculate the total quantity of heat required to change

0.01 kg of ice at −10 °C completely into steam at 100 °C. (Specific heat capacity of ice = 2100 J kg^{-1} K^{-1}; specific heat capacity of water = 4200 J kg^{-1} K^{-1}; specific latent heat of fusion of ice = 336 000 J kg^{-1}; specific latent heat of vaporisation of water = 2 260 000 J kg^{-1}.)
  (c) Explain how a hot-water radiator heats a small room.
  (JMB)

Q5 Define *specific heat capacity* and show how you would determine its value for water by an electrical method.
  Calculate the minimum mass of ice at 0 °C that would have to be added to 160 g of water at 15 °C to bring its temperature down to 0 °C. (Latent heat of fusion of ice = 336 000 J kg^{-1}; specific heat capacity of water = 4200 J kg^{-1} K^{-1}.) *(W)*

Q6 An 8 W heating coil is embedded in a 0.2 kg block of ice standing in an insulated container without a lid. A thermometer in the block reads −20 °C at the start. The heater extends throughout the block so that it is in contact with all the ice. (Take the specific heat capacity of ice to be 2000 J kg^{-1} K^{-1}, the specific heat capacity of water to be 4000 J kg^{-1} K^{-1} and the specific latent heat of fusion of ice to be 300 000 J kg^{-1}.)
  (a) Explain what is meant by the terms (i) *specific heat capacity* and (ii) *specific latent heat of fusion*.
  (b) Without calculation, draw a sketch graph to show how the temperature changes with time from the moment the heater is switched on until the temperature rises to 20 °C. Explain the shape of the sketch graph.
  (c) Once all the ice melts, how long does it take to raise the temperature of the water from 0 °C to 20 °C?
  (d) With the heater still on, the temperature of the water continues to rise but more and more slowly and eventually settles at 82 °C for a long time. How is this accounted for? *(O)*

Q7 What do you understand by *specific latent heat*?
  By considering the molecular nature of matter, explain what happens to the latent heat of fusion of ice and to the latent heat of evaporation of water, when each is supplied

to cause the corresponding change of state.

A jet of dry steam (at 100 °C) flowing at the rate of 0.30 g per second is directed onto crushed ice at 0 °C in a copper can which has a hole in its base. 2.80 g of water at 0 °C flows out through the hole per second. If the specific latent heat of condensation of steam is 2 260 000 J kg^{-1} and the specific heat capacity of water is 4200 J kg^{-1} K^{-1}, calculate the heat per second given out by the steam in condensing and cooling to 0 °C. Use this result to estimate a value for the specific latent heat of fusion of ice, and explain whether you would expect this value to be larger or smaller than the correct value. *(C)*

Q8 A small electric heater is immersed in crushed ice contained in a funnel. Before the heater is switched on, water drips from the funnel at a constant rate of 0.5 g min^{-1} and this is increased to 4 g min^{-1} when the heater is working. Determine (i) the rate at which heat is being absorbed from the surroundings and (ii) the power of the immersion heater in watts. (Specific latent heat of fusion of ice 336 000 J kg^{-1}.)

Q9 A jet of dry steam at 100 °C is played onto the surface of 100 g of dried ice at 0 °C contained in a well-lagged calorimeter of negligible heat capacity, until all the ice has melted and the temperature begins to rise. The mass of water in the calorimeter when the temperature reaches 40 °C is found to be 120 g. Assuming that the specific latent heat of fusion of ice is 336 000 J kg^{-1} and that the specific heat capacity of water is 4000 J kg^{-1} K^{-1}, determine a value for the specific latent heat of vaporisation of water.

Explain carefully why the escape of steam to the atmosphere during this operation has no effect on the result.

Q10 (a) Why must energy be supplied to change the state of a substance without change in temperature?

(b) Define *specific latent heat of vaporisation* of a liquid. Describe an experiment you would perform to determine the specific latent heat of vaporisation of a liquid. Point out two sources of experimental error and explain, briefly, the steps you would take to minimise their effect.

(c) The diagrams show two identical filter funnels with crushed ice surrounding similar immersion heaters. In apparatus A the heater is unconnected and, when the ice is melting steadily, 0.015 kg of water is collected in 300 s. In apparatus B the heater is connected to a power supply of 50 W. When water drips at a steady rate, 0.058 kg of water is collected in 300 s. Calculate a value for the specific latent heat of fusion of ice.

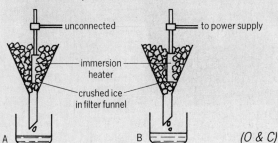

A   B   *(O & C)*

Q11 Define specific latent heat of fusion and state the unit in which it is measured.

Describe an experiment which may be performed to determine the specific latent heat of fusion of ice.

Explain why water at the bottom of a pond rarely freezes, even in a very severe winter. *(W)*

Q12 A 180 watt heater and a thermometer were immersed in 0.5 kg of water in a copper calorimeter. The following readings were obtained:

temperature/°C	30	36	40	45	49	54	57
time/minutes	3	4	5	6	7	8	9

On the graph paper provided plot a graph of temperature against time. Start the axes from the origin and draw the best straight line through your points.

Using your graph, or otherwise, find
(a) room temperature (the temperature at which heating started), and
(b) the specific heat capacity of water.
Give two reasons why the value obtained for the specific heat capacity is more than the accepted value.

State two precautions you would take in carrying out this experiment to ensure a more accurate value for the specific heat capacity. *(L)*

Q13 (a) Describe fully a method for the determination of the specific latent heat of fusion of ice indicating any precautions taken to achieve an accurate result. Show how the result is obtained from your observations.

(b) Explain the following:
(i) Low temperatures can be effectively maintained in the cold display cabinet of a supermarket with the lid kept open continuously. (Details of the refrigerator are not required.)
(ii) Frost is less likely to occur on a winter evening if the sky is cloudy than if it is clear.
(iii) On unpacking a metal instrument from a close-fitting packing case made of expanded polystyrene on a cold day, the instrument feels much cooler than the case. *(L)*

Q14 The *specific heat capacity* of water is 4200 J kg^{-1} K^{-1} and the *specific latent heat of vaporisation* of water is 2 260 000 J kg^{-1}. Define the terms in italics.

What is the least time in which a 1200 W heater could boil away 2.40 kg of water, initially at 100 °C?

A saucepan containing 1.50 kg of water at 10 °C is placed on a gas stove. With the burner full on, the temperature of the water is observed to rise to 30 °C in 2.0 minutes.
(a) Using these figures, estimate (i) the power of the burner, (ii) the time it would take for the temperature to rise from 30 °C to 100 °C.
(b) (i) Will your estimate of power in (a) be greater than or less than the actual value?
(ii) What quantitative information about the saucepan would enable you to make a better estimate of power?
(iii) Will your estimate of time taken in (a) be greater than or less than the actual value? *(O & C)*

15 Light and mirrors

15.1 How the eye sees

Light is that form of energy which enables people to 'see' things. For a person to see any object, light energy must enter the eye. This energy is converted into a 'picture' in a very complex process, but a simplified version is as follows:

(a) light enters the eye (Fig. 15.1) through a 'hole' in the iris, called the pupil;
(b) the crystalline lens focusses the light to form a real, inverted image on the retina;
(c) energy is collected by the rods and cones making up the retina;
(d) this energy is transmitted as electrical impulses via the optic nerve to the brain;
(e) the brain re-inverts the image and produces a 'picture'.

The brain has the ability to interpret or assemble a 'picture' even from very slight information, and it can easily be deceived into producing a 'picture' that it *expects* to see.

Investigation 15.1 To show that our eyes deceive us!

Look at Fig. 15.2(a). Which line do you think is the longer? Measure the two lines to prove that they are, in fact, equal in length. Why do you think the lower line 'looks' longer than the upper line?

Now look at Fig. 15.2(b). What do you see — a pretty young girl or an old hag with a hook nose? By concentrating on the drawing and, if necessary, blinking you will be able to see both 'views' of this picture as it changes from one to the other. The brain wants to produce a 'picture' from the drawing and the view you see depends on which prominent feature of the drawing you select. Concentrating on the wavy line at the left of the drawing produces the young girl, while focussing your attention on the thick black line towards the bottom of the drawing gives the old hag image.

Stare hard, if possible without blinking, at Fig. 15.2(c) for about two minutes. Hold the page quite close to your eye and focus on the spot in the middle. Now look away from the figure and stare at a sheet of white paper or the wall. What do you 'see' when you blink while looking at the white paper? You should see a picture which resembles the Mona Lisa.

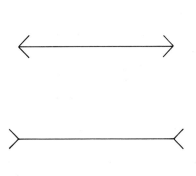

(a)

(b)

(c)

15.2 Optical illusions

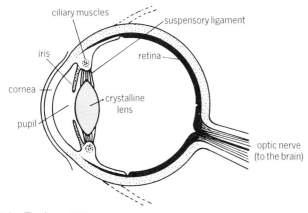

15.1 The human eye

Note A number of books (e.g. *Optical Illusion Puzzles* by Paraquin (Sterling, 1984)) are available which deal with many more examples of optical and visual illusions.

Accommodation

Light that enters the eye can reach it in several ways:

(a) directly from a luminous source such as the Sun, an electric lamp, a neon tube, a candle etc.;

(b) from an object reflecting light directly to the eye;

(c) as direct or reflected light which has been (i) further reflected to the eye, e.g. by a plane mirror, (ii) refracted (bent) to the eye, e.g. by a lens, (iii) diffracted to the eye, e.g. by a diffraction grating or a very narrow slit.

The normal human eye can accommodate itself to cope with light which is in a parallel beam or a diverging cone but *not* with a converging cone (see Fig. 15.3).

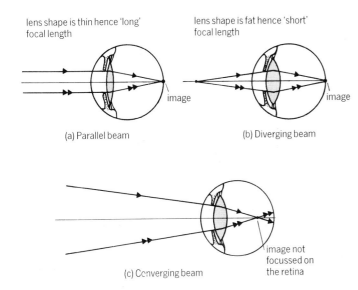

15.3 The eye can 'see' parallel and divergent beams but not a convergent beam

The crystalline lens in the eye is held in position by the suspensory ligament which is controlled by the ciliary muscles. This enables the focal length of the lens to be varied so that parallel light and divergent light can be focussed sharply onto the retina of the eye. When the eye is at rest, as it is when viewing a distant object, the ciliary muscles are relaxed and the lens is pulled out thin by the suspensory ligament. This gives the lens a long focal length and thus parallel rays are focussed onto the retina of the eye. When a near object is being viewed the ciliary muscles contract, releasing the tension in the suspensory ligament so that the lens becomes fatter. It thus has a shorter focal length and is able to focus a sharp image of the near object onto the retina of the eye.

The ability to focus on both distant and near objects is known as **accommodation**. The eye is said to be 'fully accommodated' when viewing an object at the shortest distance of distinct vision, usually taken as 25 cm from the eye. However, converging light is always brought to a focus in front of the retina and therefore a patch of light rather than a clear image is seen. In Fig. 15.4(a) sunlight (represented by a parallel beam of light) illuminates an object which reflects the light to the eye as a parallel beam (see p.178). In Fig. 15.4(b) light travelling directly from the lamp reaches the eye as a diverging cone of light. In Fig. 15.4(c) divergent light from a neon tube is reflected by a plane mirror into the eye as an even wider diverging cone of light. In all these cases the eye can adjust (accommodate) to see the object or light source clearly. In Fig. 15.4(d) light from the lamp is refracted by the lens. When the eye is at position 1 no image can be seen because it receives a converging cone of light. However, when the eye is at position 2 a real image can be seen because it now receives a diverging cone of light.

Binocular vision

Another important aspect of normal vision is that the two eyes give slightly different pictures. The brain merges them into a single picture which simulates depth and three dimensions. Look at an object with your right eye while keeping the left eye closed. Now close your right eye and open the left eye: the object appears to 'jump' slightly sideways. This gives an indication of the different images received by the eyes.

Photographs and drawings are two-dimensional images and thus cannot show a 3-D effect. However it is possible to simulate 3-D effects by several well known processes. One such process is to produce red and green pictures of the object which are slightly offset. To observe the 3-D effect the photograph must be viewed with a red filter over one eye and a green filter over the other eye. The red filter allows the 'red image' through to the eye but 'blacks out' the green

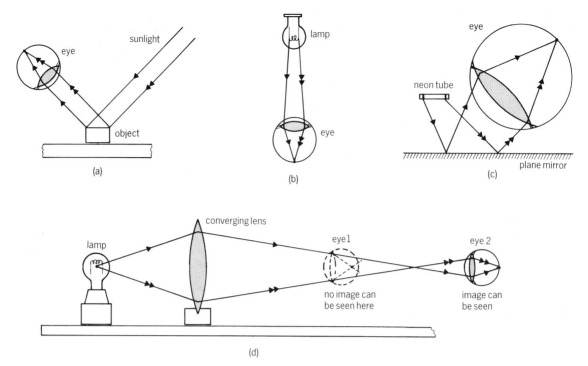

15.4 *Various ways in which light can reach the eye*

image, while the green filter allows the 'green image' to be seen by the other eye but cuts out the red image. Hence the brain receives two separate images coming from slightly different positions and can then produce the 3-D effect. (This effect was used spectacularly before the War to produce 3-D movies. All viewers were supplied with special red and green spectacles as they entered the cinema.) A similar process uses polarised images and Polaroid filters, and a third uses stereo camera pictures and a plane mirror. For this two cameras placed 65 mm apart take simultaneous photographs of the same scene. One of the

15.5 *3-D effect*

photographs is printed normally while the other is printed in reverse. They are then laid side by side and a 20 cm square plane mirror is stood midway between the two pictures. When the left picture is looked at directly with the left eye, and the right picture seen 'through' the plane mirror, as shown in Fig. 15.5, a 3-D effect is produced.

15.2 Light travels in straight lines

Light energy travels as a short-wavelength electromagnetic wave. If an object absorbs all the light incident upon it, and reflects none to the eye, it appears black. Similarly, none of the objects in a completely blacked-out room can be seen because no light energy comes from the objects to the eye. Everything therefore appears black. Black is thus 'seen' when there is no light energy coming from an object.

The three rays in Fig. 15.6 are spreading outwards from a point on the lamp and form a **divergent beam**. Strictly speaking, each 'ray' of light is a divergent cone of light but at this level simple straight rays of light in two-dimensional drawings will suffice. Although light energy travels as a wave, for simple explanations of most optical phenomena it is said to travel in straight lines.

Note It is important to remember that, in Physics, rays of light are represented by straight lines with an arrowhead to indicate the direction in which the light is travelling (usually taken as from left to right). Many examination candidates omit the arrowhead and are penalised.

Investigation 15.2 To show that 'light travels in straight lines'

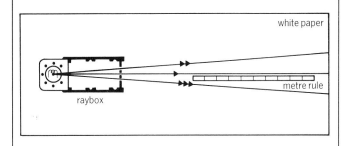

15.6 Light travels in straight lines

Place a raybox, fitted with a triple slit, on a sheet of white paper resting on a bench. The raybox should have the cylindrical lens removed so that it emits a divergent beam. Three straight tracks of light, called **rays of light**, can be seen forming a divergent beam on the paper. Place a metre rule close to the central ray as shown in Fig. 15.6. This ray of light can be seen to travel in a line which is as straight as the edge of the metre rule. Placing the rule alongside each of the other two rays, in turn, will confirm that these rays are also straight but travelling at different angles.

Shadows and eclipses

(a) The shadow produced by a point source of light
You must always remember that rays of light from a source travel outwards in *all* directions. In Fig. 15.7 only *two* of the many rays from the bulb have been used to complete the diagram. Rays of light within the triangle bounded by the two rays, the disc and the point P will be stopped by the disc. Hence no light reaches the screen in the area bounded by the rays (see Fig. 15.7), and this area appears black. The area of shadow has the same outline as the obstacle (disc) which blocks off the light. Its sharply defined shape is called the **umbra** or area of total shadow. Rays of light which lie outside the limits of the two rays shown in Fig. 15.7 will, of course, reach the screen and illuminate it.

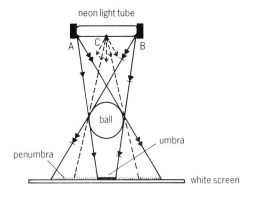

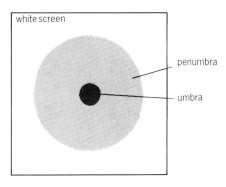

15.8 Umbra and penumbra

(b) The shadow produced by an extended source of light Every point on the extended source of light sends out its own set of rays in *all* directions. By choosing the two extreme points A and B at the ends of the neon tube in Fig. 15.8 and drawing a ray from both points to enclose the obstacle (ball) and continue to the screen, the shadow image formed can be explained. The region where the two triangles overlap is the area where no light reaches the screen (the umbra). Verify for yourself that no ray of light coming from *any* point *between* A and B, e.g. point C, can get past the ball and into the umbra. A shadow is also cast in the two outer regions where the triangles meet the screen, but here the shadow is not *completely* black. In these areas only some of the rays coming from the

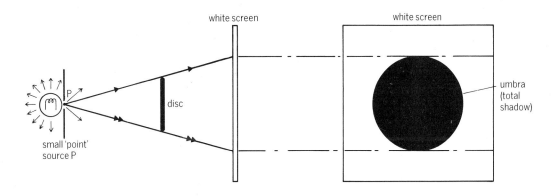

15.7 Umbra

Exercise 15.1

neon tube 1   neon tube 2

A   B   C   D

square plate

white
screen

15.9   Shadow image of a plate

Copy Fig. 15.9 accurately into your book and complete the ray diagram to show how the umbra and penumbra are formed. Assume the obstacle to be a square-shaped plate. Draw a front (plan) view of the shape of the shadow images. Two small neon tubes are used as the extended source and eight rays of light can be drawn from points A, B, C and D; only *four* of these rays are really necessary for the overall pattern. State which two points are required and why only four rays are necessary to complete the ray diagram.

neon tube are blocked off by the ball; others are able to reach them. This produces a partial shadow called the **penumbra** which is rather fuzzy and not a clearly defined shape. Figure 15.8 also shows five rays from a point C. One of these rays is absorbed by the ball, two of the rays pass close to the edge of the ball and reach the penumbra region, while the two remaining rays illuminate the screen.

Eclipses

Other phenomena which can be explained by assuming that light travels in straight lines include eclipses of the Sun or the Moon. For the Sun to be eclipsed it is necessary that 'something' (the Moon) blots out some light from the Sun which is travelling towards the Earth. Therefore Sun, Moon and Earth must be in a straight line as in Fig. 15.10. Here the four rays drawn from the extremities of the Sun show a region of total shadow, where an observer will see a **total eclipse** of the Sun, and an outer region of partial shadow where an observer will see a **partial eclipse** of the Sun. Beyond this outer region the Sun will be visible as normal.

Since the Moon is visible from Earth by the light it reflects from the Sun it will be eclipsed when it is in a position where it cannot receive sunlight. This occurs when it is in the shadow cast by the Earth as in Fig. 15.11. When the Moon, which is orbiting the Earth, passes into the region of shadow, the Earth blocks out the Sun's rays and a partial or total eclipse of the Moon can be seen from the Earth as the Moon moves through its orbit.

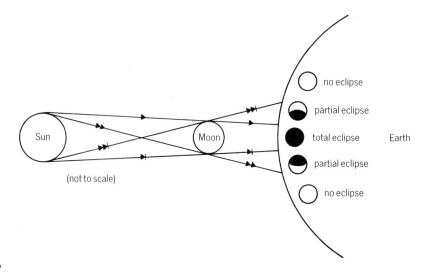

(not to scale)

no eclipse

partial eclipse

total eclipse   Earth

partial eclipse

no eclipse

15.10   Eclipse of the Sun

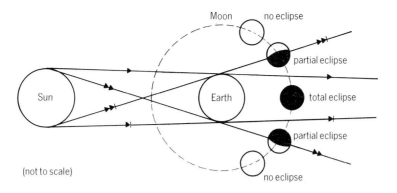

(not to scale)

15.11   Eclipse of the Moon

Pinhole camera

The pinhole camera relies on the fact that the extremely narrow cones of light entering the tiny aperture, a small pinhole, approximate to rays of light travelling in straight lines. Figure 15.12 shows the construction of a pinhole camera and the rays show how an inverted image is produced on the light-sensitive film. Note that the incident rays intersect at the pinhole. Because the rays cross over at this point, the top of the object will appear at the bottom of the image, and the bottom of the object will appear at the top. Figure 15.12 represents a side elevation showing a vertical object but it can just as easily serve as a plan view with the object lying horizontally, showing that an object would also be 'inverted' in the horizontal plane. That the inversion occurs in all planes is illustrated in Fig. 15.13.

Note If a translucent screen is used in place of the film, the image viewed from behind the camera is as

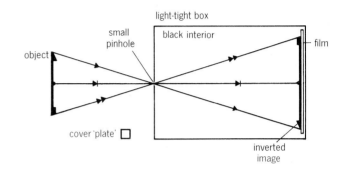

15.12   Pinhole camera

shown in Fig. 15.13(c). Since the observer has moved through 180° the image is different from that in Fig. 15.13(b).

The pinhole camera has several minor disadvantages: only one picture can be taken at a time:

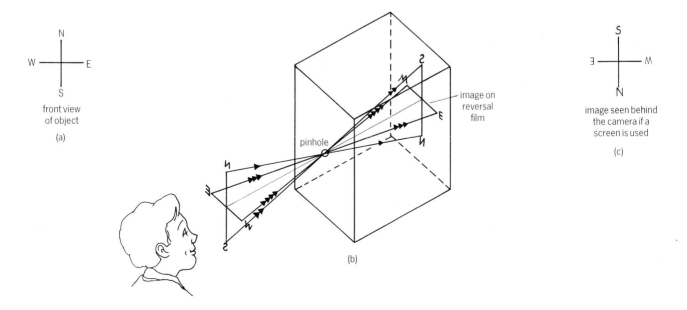

15.13   The image in a pinhole camera is inverted

Investigation 15.3 To make a pinhole camera

It is interesting to make a pinhole camera with a translucent screen in place of the film so that images of brightly lit objects can be viewed directly. Make two hollow boxes from stiff card such that one slides easily into the other. Cover one end of the larger box with stiff card from which a large circular hole has been cut. Cover this hole with a piece of black paper. Cover one end of the other box with a sheet of tracing paper. Fit the two boxes together with the closed ends outwards to produce a pinhole camera with an adjustable screen position. Prick a small pinhole in the centre of the black end plate and point the camera towards a bright source of light. You should then see a sharp, inverted image of the light source on the tracing paper.

Now prick a second pinhole in the front of the camera. Two images should be formed as in Fig. 15.14. Copy Fig. 15.14 and include a third pinhole midway between the two already in the diagram. Complete the ray diagram to show the formation of three images.

As you add more and more pinholes to your camera, more and more images appear on the screen and these images

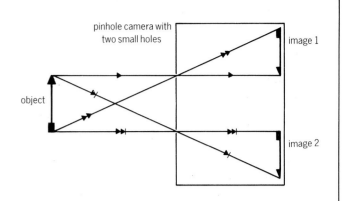

15.14 The image in a pinhole camera with two pinholes

overlap and cause blurring. Punch out all the pinholes to form one 'large' hole. A blurred image should be seen on the screen. This image is much brighter than the image obtained with just one pinhole because much more light energy enters through the enlarged hole.

---

a 'long' time exposure is needed so that pictures of moving objects cannot be taken. (A pinhole camera *is* used in astronomy to show the rotation of the Earth on its axis by taking a long time exposure of a star which does not remain at the same point in the sky due to the Earth's rotation.) However it does have one big advantage over lens cameras in that it produces distortion-free images on the film. Surveyors use the pinhole camera to examine a building or structure for true vertical and horizontal lines.

The blurring of the image can be explained by treating the 'large' hole as a series of small pinholes each giving its own image in a slightly different place. An alternative way of explaining the blurring is illustrated in Fig. 15.15, in which cones of light from three small points on the object form patches of light in the image. If any more cones of light from points on the object are shown in this diagram, the image 'points' (patches of light) will overlap, showing how the blurring is caused.

15.3 Laws of reflection of light

When rays of light strike any surface the rays are reflected, unless the surface is black, when they are absorbed.

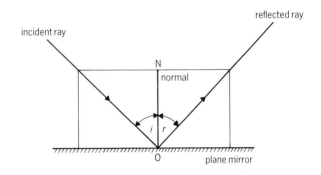

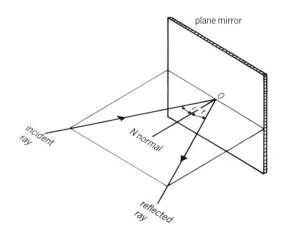

15.16 Laws of reflection of light

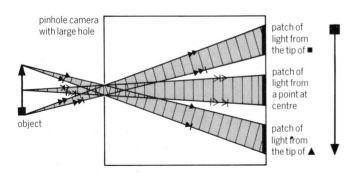

15.15 The image in a pinhole camera with a large hole

Investigation 15.4   To verify that the angle of incidence *i* is equal to the angle of reflection *r* for a plane mirror

On a large sheet of white paper construct, using a protractor or otherwise, two lines at right angles to each other. One of these lines (M_1M_2) represents the position in which the plane mirror is placed while the other line (ON) represents the normal at the point O. Using a protractor, mark off angles of 45°, 50°, 60°, 70° and 80° to the normal line. These large angles will serve as angles of incidence *i* which can be measured to a reasonable degree of accuracy with a protractor.

Place the plane mirror on the line M_1M_2 with its silvered surface standing vertically on the line. Position a raybox so that a thin ray of light tracks along the 45°-line. This ray is reflected at O and the path of the reflected ray can be marked with three pencil dots, P_1, P_2 and P_3. Remove the mirror and join P_1, P_2 and P_3 with a straight line which should also pass through O. With a protractor measure the angle of reflection *r* between the normal and the reflected ray. Record the value of *r* in a table of results similar to Table 15.1.

Reposition the mirror and repeat the experiment for *i* = 50°, 60°, 70° and 80°. Plot a graph of angle of incidence *i* against angle of reflection *r*. This should be a straight line passing through the origin (0,0), confirming that angle *i* = angle *r*.

Table 15.1   Table of results for Investigation 15.4

angle of incidence *i*/°	45	50	60	70	80
angle of reflection *r*/°					

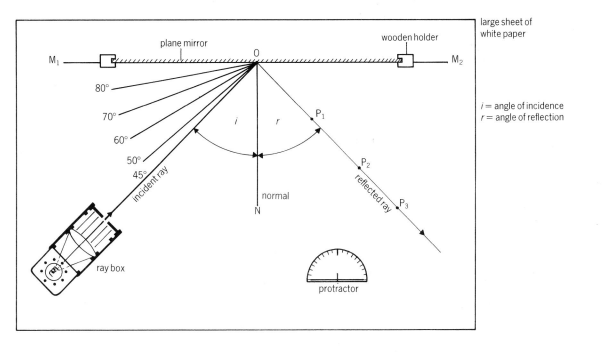

15.17   *Showing that the angle of incidence equals the angle of reflection*

The incident and reflected light obeys two simple laws:

1. The incident ray, the reflected ray and the normal to the mirror at the point of incidence all lie in the same plane.

2. The angle of incidence is equal to the angle of reflection.

The **angle of incidence** *i* is the angle between the normal and the incident ray; the **angle of reflection** *r* is the angle between the normal and the reflected ray (Fig. 15.16); a **normal** ON is a line drawn at right angles to the mirror.

15.4   Plane mirrors

Regular and diffuse reflection

When light is reflected from a surface it must obey the laws of reflection. How the light is reflected depends on the nature of the surface. If a parallel beam of light is incident on a *smooth* surface such as a plane mirror or highly polished metal surface it is reflected as a parallel beam (Fig. 15.18a). This is known as **regular** reflection. The angle of incidence is the same for every ray because the surface is so smooth (flat) and hence the angle of reflection is the same for every ray.

Most surfaces which appear to the naked eye to be smooth are in fact quite rough, as can be seen when they are viewed under a microscope. In Fig. 15.18(b) a parallel beam of light is incident on a 'rough' surface.

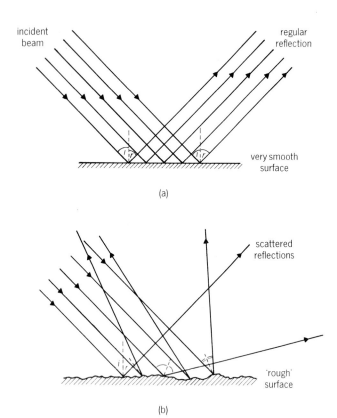

15.18 (a) Regular and (b) diffuse reflection

Since the rays strike the surface at many different angles of incidence, they are reflected at many different angles. This irregular reflection is known as **diffuse** reflection. Most objects are rough and so the reflected light that reaches the eye is diffuse. They therefore appear dull rather than shiny.

Images in plane mirrors

Figure 15.19 shows two diverging rays of light from an object which are each reflected by the mirror at an angle of reflection equal to the angle of incidence. This produces a more widely diverging beam which enters the eye. The lens of the eye focusses this light onto the retina and the brain interprets the picture as if the light, travelling in straight lines, had come from a point I behind the mirror. Simple geometry will show

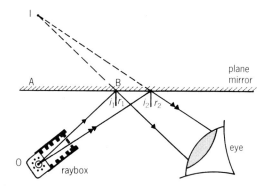

15.19 Virtual image in a plane mirror

Investigation 15.5 To find the position of an image in a plane mirror

On a large sheet of white paper construct, using a protractor or otherwise, two lines at right angles to each other. One of the lines (M_1M_2) represents the position in which the plane mirror is placed while the other line represents a normal line. Mark points O_1, O_2, O_3 and O_4 on the normal line at 10 cm, 15 cm, 20 cm and 25 cm respectively from M_1M_2. Place the plane mirror on the line M_1M_2 with its silvered surface standing vertically on the line. Place the raybox such that the three diverging rays radiate from the point O_1, giving an object distance d_O of 10 cm, as marked on the normal line. The central ray strikes the mirror normally and is reflected back along its original path. The other two reflected rays are marked with points P_1, P_2 and P_3 as shown in Fig. 15.20. Remove the mirror and join each set of points with a straight line produced behind the mirror. The two reflected rays appear to come from the point I. Measure, with a rule, the image distance d_i from I to the mirror line M_1M_2. Record the value of d_i in a table of results similar to Table 15.2.

Reposition the mirror on the line M_1M_2 and move the raybox to give object distances of 15 cm, 20 cm and 25 cm and locate the corresponding image distances. Plot a graph of object distance d_o against image distance d_i. This should be a straight line passing through the origin, confirming $d_o = d_i$.

It is important to note also that the image lies on the perpendicular from the object to the mirror.

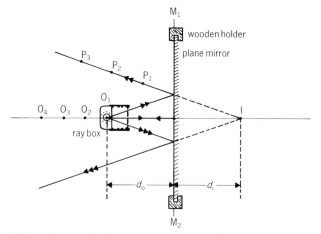

15.20 Showing that the image lies as far behind the mirror as the object is in front

Table 15.2 Table of results for investigation 15.5

object distance d_o/cm	10	15	20	25
image distance d_i/cm				

triangles ABI and ABO are congruent and AI = AO. The image is known as a **virtual** image, that is **an image through which the rays of light do not pass.**

Note Real rays are shown as solid lines with arrowheads, while imaginary (virtual) rays are shown as dashed lines behind the mirror.

Virtual images are normally upright images which can be seen by the eye but which, since they are formed by a divergent beam, cannot form a picture on a screen. The image in a plane mirror lies as far behind the mirror as the object is in front of the mirror.

Investigation 15.6 To show that the image in a plane mirror is laterally inverted

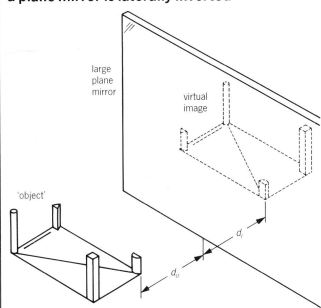

15.21 *Lateral inversion of an asymmetric object*

Place a rectangular piece of card with a diagonal drawn on it in front of a large plane mirror. Insert four different-shaped pieces of wooden dowel at the corners of the card to produce an asymmetrical object (Fig. 15.21). The image seen in the mirror is very similar to the object but, however the object is lifted or twisted, it is impossible to produce an exact replica of the virtual image. The two pieces of dowel, here square and semicircular, which are at the right-hand side of the object are also at the right hand side of the image as seen by the observer. Likewise, the left-hand side of the object appears on the left-hand side in the image. However, the 'faces' of the dowels on the object which are visible to the observer are not visible in the image. The 'faces' of the dowels seen in the mirror image are those which are facing the mirror and are not visible to the observer. The two dowels which are closer to the observer are furthest from the mirror and hence their image lies further behind the mirror than the image of the other two dowels.

Using a duplicate set of pieces, try to construct an *exact* replica of the image seen in the mirror. Versions which look *almost* the same as the mirror image can be produced but can easily be shown *not* to be exact replicas of the image.

The image of an object seen in a plane mirror is upright and virtual, lies as far behind the mirror as the object is in front and is also the same size as the object. In addition the image is laterally inverted (see Fig. 15.21).

In fact it is not possible to reconstruct the image. The image has *not* been reversed, turned inside out or turned upside-down. What has happened to the image can only be described as **lateral inversion.**

Figure 15.22 shows a piece of clear acetate with a letter E written on it and held in a right hand in front of a plane mirror. An observer looking through the acetate sheet will see the letter E and the back of a right hand. The image seen in the plane mirror will be a letter E apparently held in what looks to be like the front (palm) of a left hand. Of course, the face of the acetate sheet nearest the mirror is responsible for the formation of the image. The shape of the letter on this face is Ǝ.

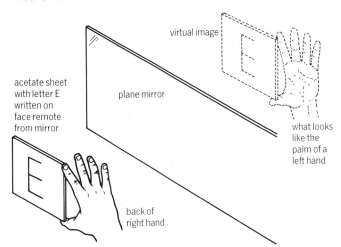

15.22 *Lateral inversion of a 'see-through' object*

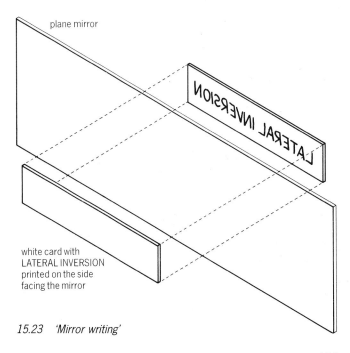

15.23 *'Mirror writing'*

If the words 'LATERAL INVERSION' are written on a piece of white card which is presented to a plane mirror the image seen in the mirror is as shown in Fig. 15.23.

Uses of plane mirrors

Plane mirrors can be used to view 'inaccessible' objects, e.g. a dentist uses a plane mirror to look at a patient's teeth; people use plane mirrors to see how they appear to others, and plane mirrors are fitted on corners so that drivers can 'see' out of concealed driveways or round 'blind' turns. Optical instruments such as periscopes, telescopes and overhead projectors use plane mirrors to bring the final image to a more convenient place. A large plane mirror hung at an angle of 45° to the vertical above a horizontal table enables people or television cameras facing the mirror to 'see' what is on the table (see Fig. 15.24). This principle is used in art and cookery demonstration programmes.

Opticians require letters of a standard height to be placed at a specific distance from the eye of a patient who is taking an eye-test. Often the room in which the test is conducted is not long enough to meet this distance requirement. However, this problem can be overcome (see Fig. 15.25) by using a plane mirror and an illuminated test card positioned above the patient's head! The test is conducted in a completely darkened room with the letters painted on a translucent screen and illuminated from within. The letters on the screen must be laterally inverted so that the patient sees the correct letter shapes when viewed in the plane mirror.

15.25 Sight testing in a small room

Multiple images in plane mirrors

Two square pieces of plane mirror placed face to face can be 'joined' with a strip of sticky tape fixed to one edge. When the mirrors are stood on a bench the tape acts as a 'hinge' enabling the mirrors to be 'opened' to any angle required. A few pieces of coloured paper placed between the two mirrors will form various image patterns as the angle between the mirrors is varied. Symmetrical image patterns will be formed

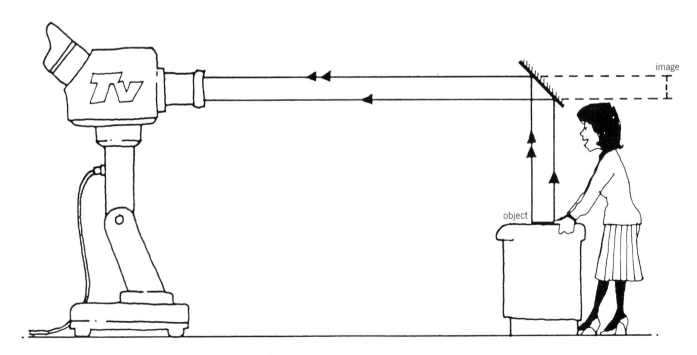

15.24 Looking 'vertically' down

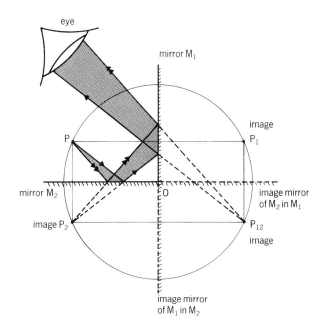

15.26 Images in mirrors inclined at 90°

whenever the angle is a factor of 360°. Figure 15.26 represents a ray diagram showing how three images P_1, P_2 and P_{12} of an object P are formed when the angle between the mirrors is 90°. The images all lie on a circle, centred on O, passing through the object P. Mirror M_1 acts as an object in mirror M_2 and vice versa, producing the virtual image mirrors shown. Image P_1 is the image of P in the mirror M_1 and P and P_1 are equidistant from M_1. Image P_2 is the image of P in mirror M_2 and P and P_2 are equidistant from M_2. Image P_{12} is actually two images superimposed, the images produced by P_1 and P_2 reflected in their appropriate image mirror.

Mirrors at an angle to one another are used on dressing tables and in hairdressers to enable you to view the sides and back of your head. A special case of the use of two plane mirrors is when they are placed parallel to and facing each other (Fig. 15.27). In theory, an infinite number of mirror images and images of an object are formed.

Exercise 15.2

Draw the ray diagram which shows that five images of an object are formed when the angle between the mirrors is 60°. A children's toy called a kaleidoscope is based on the principle of two mirrors set at 60° with coloured pieces between them as the object.

You might also like to try to produce the drawing for two mirrors at 30°, which gives eleven images.

15.5 Concave mirrors

A concave mirror has a hollow or 'cave' when viewed from the front. It could have been formed by coating the outside of a glass sphere with silver and cutting out a circular portion. The central point of the mirror is called the **pole** P, and the line which passes through this point perpendicular to the surface is known as the **principal axis** (Fig. 15.28). All rays close to and parallel to the principal axis pass through a common point F on the axis after reflection by the mirror. This point is called the **focal point**. The distance from the pole P of the mirror to the focal point F is known as the **focal length** f of the concave mirror.

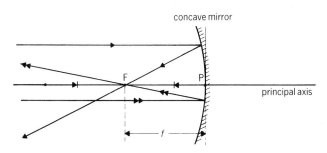

15.28 Focal length, pole and principal axis of a concave mirror

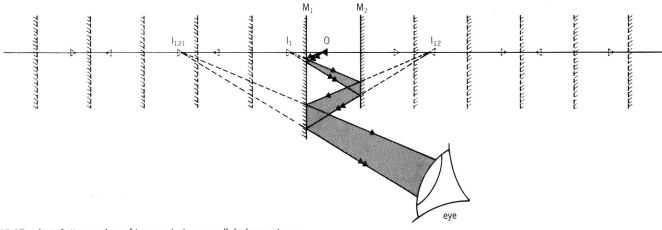

15.27 An infinite number of images in two parallel plane mirrors

Investigation 15.6 To show parallel rays are brought to the focal point F and a point source of light placed at F produces a parallel beam for a concave mirror

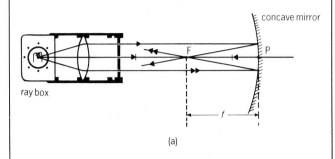

(a)

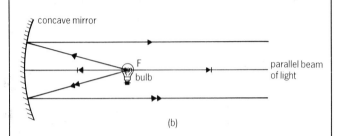

(b)

15.29   Parallel beams and a concave mirror

Using a raybox fitted with a triple slit, direct three parallel rays on to a cylindrical strip of mirror (Fig. 15.29a). Measure the distance FP with a rule to obtain the focal length *f*.

As an illustration of the principle of reversibility of light, place a 'point' source of light at F, the focal point of the strip of mirror (see Fig. 15.29b). A parallel beam of light is formed.

If parallel rays which are *not* parallel to the principal axis are incident on the mirror these rays will also focus at one point F_1 which lies directly below F (Fig. 15.30).

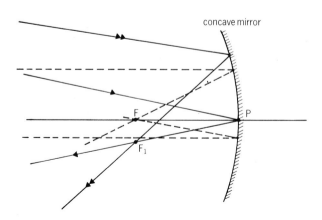

15.30   Focal plane of a concave mirror

Investigation 15.7 To measure the focal length *f* of a concave mirror

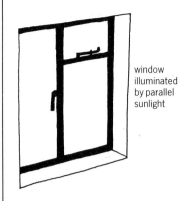

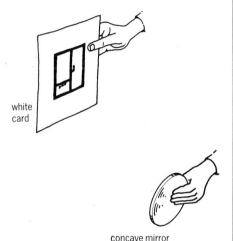

15.31   Rough method of finding the focal length of a concave mirror

Point a concave mirror towards a brightly lit window on a sunny day. Hold a piece of white card between the mirror and the window, as in Fig. 15.31. Move the card (or the mirror) until a sharp inverted image is formed on the card. When this image is formed on the card, the card is at the focal plane. Measure the distance from the mirror to the card with a rule. Repeat the focussing of the image of the windows several times to obtain several values of *f*. Calculate the average value of the focal length *f* of the concave mirror.

There is a point C on the principal axis such that all rays of light from it strike the mirror normally (perpendicularly) and are reflected back through the same point C (Fig. 15.32a). This point is called the **centre of curvature** C of the mirror and is the centre of the sphere of which the mirror forms a part. The distance from the pole P of the mirror to the centre of curvature C is known as the **radius of curvature** *r* of the

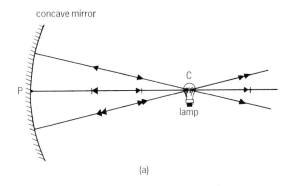 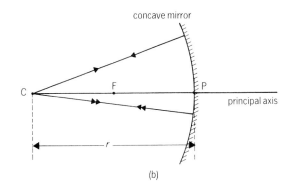

| (a) | (b) |

15.32   Radius of curvature of a concave mirror

concave mirror (Fig. 15.32b). A small light source placed at C will improve the intensity of the light shining to the right of the source, since light from the left-hand side of the lamp will be reflected back through C after striking the mirror.

It can be shown theoretically and experimentally that $r = 2f$, which means that the focal length f of the concave mirror can also be calculated from $f = r/2$.

15.6   Ray construction diagrams

Schematic diagrams called **ray construction diagrams** can be used to illustrate the formation of an image when light rays are reflected by a concave mirror and received by the eye or, in the case of real images, on a screen. Two main construction rays are used in these diagrams.

Investigation 15.8   To measure the radius of curvature *r* of a concave mirror

A small luminous object placed at the centre of curvature C of a concave mirror sends rays of light to the mirror which then reflects them back to the point C to form a real inverted image alongside the object. Set up the apparatus as shown in Fig. 15.33(a) with the mirror facing the light source. If necessary slightly tilt the mirror in its holder so that a patch of light is thrown on to the 'screen' alongside the object. Move the light source towards (or away from) the mirror until a sharp inverted image is formed alongside the object. With a metre rule, measure the distance from the pole P of the mirror to the object which is now at C. Record the value of *r* in a table of results like

Table 15.3. Repeat the experiment but this time leave the light source fixed and move the mirror in its holder until the image is once more correctly focussed. Measure and record the second value for *r*. Calculate the average value of the radius of curvature *r*.

Table 15.3   Table of results for investigation 15.8

	1	2
radius of curvature *r*/cm		
average *r*=	cm	

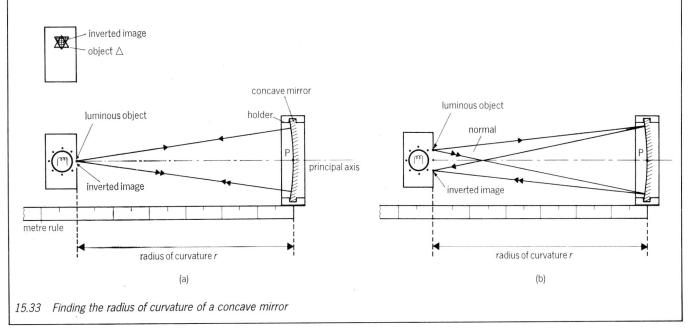

15.33   Finding the radius of curvature of a concave mirror

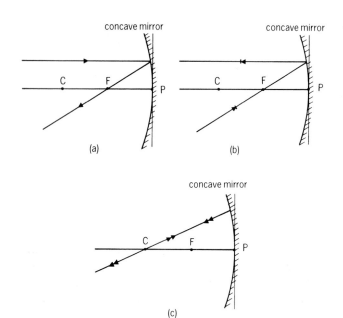

(a)

(b)

(c)

15.34 *Construction rays*

In Fig. 15.34(a) the ray parallel to the principal axis is reflected through the focal point F. In Fig. 15.34(b) a ray passing through F is reflected so that it emerges parallel to the principal axis; this ray is the same as that in Fig. 15.34(a) because of the Principle of Reversibility of Light. In Fig. 15.34(c) the ray from the centre of curvature C strikes the mirror normally and is therefore reflected along its same path through C.

The position of the 'top' of the image can be located using two construction rays from a point on the top of an object standing perpendicular to the principal axis. It is situated at the point of intersection of these two rays after reflection. Since the object is perpendicular to the principal axis the image will also lie perpendicular to the axis. In Fig. 15.35 the images are constructed by dropping a perpendicular onto the principal axis from the point of intersection of the two

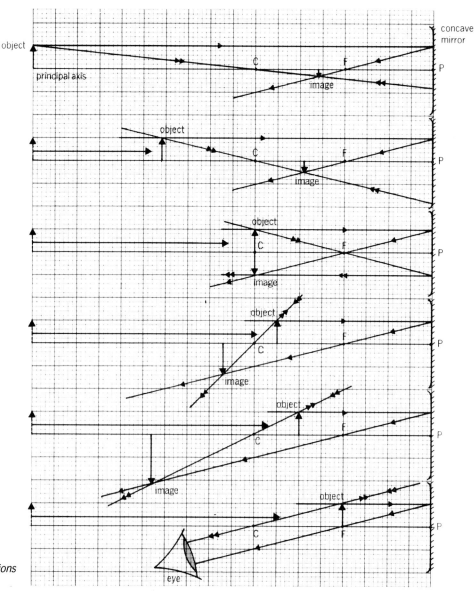

15.35 *Image sizes for different object positions for a concave mirror*

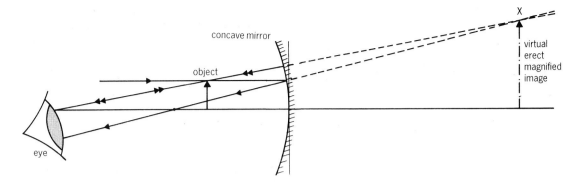

15.36 *Virtual, erect and magnified image in a concave mirror*

reflected rays. When a scale diagram is drawn the image represents the size and position of the image in relation to the object.

Note As the object moves towards the concave mirror from a great distance, the image formed near the focal point F will move away from the mirror. The size of the image increases from a diminished image near F to magnified images beyond C. When the object reaches the focal point F the emergent rays are parallel but the eye is still able to cope with this light and form an image. If the object is moved closer to the mirror than the point F the two rays which emerge are *diverging* (Fig. 15.36). While these diverging rays do not form a real image on a screen the human eye can still produce an image using this light. The two rays appear to be diverging from a point X, located by producing the rays backwards until they intersect at X.

The virtual, erect image is represented by a dotted line to emphasise its non-real nature. A concave mirror used in this way is acting as a magnifying mirror and is sometimes known as a shaving mirror or a make-up mirror.

Note This image is laterally inverted, as in a plane mirror.

15.7 Convex mirrors

A convex mirror could be formed by coating the inside of a glass sphere with silver and cutting out a circular portion. The line which passes through both the central point of the mirror (the pole P) and the focal point F is called the principal axis (Fig. 15.37). All rays

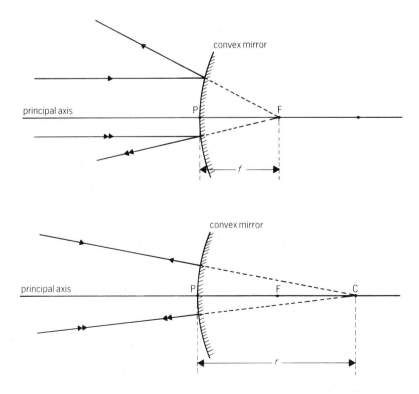

15.37 *Focal length and radius of curvature of a convex mirror*

close to and parallel to the principal axis are reflected by the mirror so that they appear to come from the focal point F of the mirror. The distance from the pole of the mirror to the focal point F is known as the focal length *f* of the convex mirror. There is a point C on the principal axis towards which incident rays strike the mirror normally (perpendicularly) and will be reflected back along the same path apparently coming from C. The point C is called the centre of curvature, and is the centre of the sphere of which the mirror forms part. The distance from the pole P of the mirror to the centre of curvature C is known as the radius of curvature *r* of the convex mirror. All images formed by a convex mirror are diminished, erect and virtual, and laterally inverted.

Convex mirrors are used in supermarkets to show a wide field of view so that the assistants can see large areas of the store, they allow bus drivers to see the passengers on the top deck of a double-decker bus and are used in wing mirrors on motor cars.

Schematic diagrams (ray construction diagrams) are used to illustrate the formation of an image when light rays are reflected by a convex mirror and received by the eye. Two main construction rays are used in these diagrams, one from the top of the object parallel to the principal axis, and the other from the top of the object passing through the focal point.

Figure 15.38 shows an object at a large, medium and small distance from the convex mirror. In all cases the image is diminished and virtual. The reflected rays always form a diverging beam. However, the human eye can form an image from a diverging beam. The two rays appear to be diverging from a point X, located by producing the rays backwards until they intersect at X.

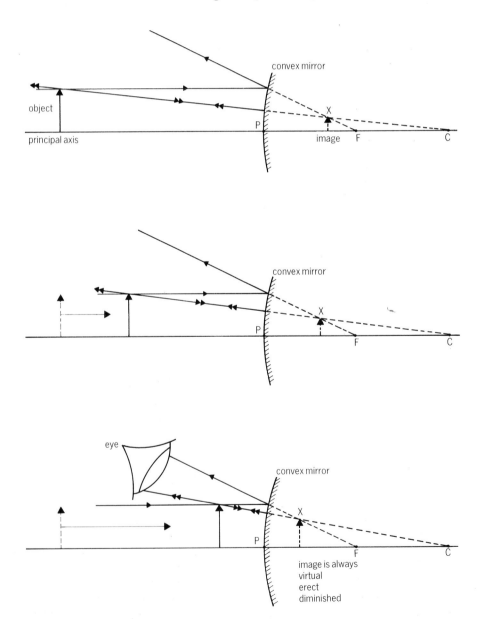

15.38   The image in a convex mirror is always virtual, erect and diminished

Comparing the fields of view of a plane mirror and a convex mirror

For a fair comparison to be made the two mirrors must be the same size and the eye must be placed at the same distance from each of them. The maximum angle of view is obtained when the angle of reflection at the mirror is a maximum, i.e. when the normals to the mirror are drawn at the extreme edges of the mirror.

Note The normals to the convex mirror are lines which are continuations of the radii at the edges of the mirror. Once the angles of reflection have been drawn, equal angles must be drawn on the other side of the normals to give the position of the incident rays. The angle of incidence for the convex mirror is much greater than the angle of incidence for the plane mirror, hence the convex mirror has a greater field of view than the plane mirror.

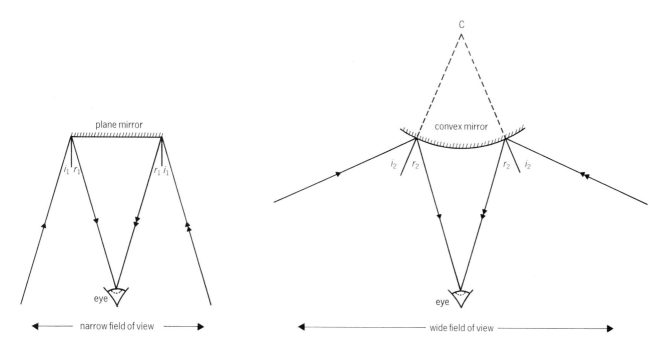

15.39 Wide field of view of a convex mirror

Questions

Q1 Which of the following controls the amount of light entering the eye?
 A Ciliary muscle **B** Cornea **C** Iris **D** Lens
 E Retina (L)

Q2 A concave mirror may be used for all but **one** of the following. This is
 A a magnifying mirror.
 B a torch reflector.
 C a reflecting telescope.
 D a dentist's mirror.
 E a car wing mirror. (WY & LREB)

Q3 An object is placed 20 cm in front of a plane mirror. The mirror is moved 2 cm towards the object. The distance between the positions of the original and final images seen in the mirror is
 A 2 cm **B** 4 cm **C** 10 cm **D** 18 cm
 E 22 cm

Q4 Two plane mirrors are supported with their surfaces at right angles and a small object is placed between them. How many reflected images of this object can be seen in the mirrors?
 A 1 **B** 2 **C** 3
 D 4 **E** 5 (L)

Q5 The sharpness of an image formed in a pinhole camera may be increased by
 A illuminating the object more strongly.
 B increasing the distance between the pinhole and the film.
 C making the pinhole smaller.
 D placing the camera nearer to the object.
 E using a smaller object. (L)

Q6 The term 'accommodation', as applied to the eye, refers to its ability to
 A control the light intensity falling on the retina.
 B distinguish between different colours.
 C erect the inverted image formed on the retina.
 D vary the distance between the lens and the retina.
 E vary the focal length of the lens. (L)

Q7 Describe the essential features of a pinhole camera, and state one property of light that it demonstrates. What would happen to the image if (i) the camera were made longer, (ii) the pinhole were triangular but still very small, (iii) the pinhole were increased in size? *(L part question)*

Q8 Describe how you would establish by experiment the relationship between the angles of incidence and reflection for a plane mirror.

With the aid of a diagram explain why three images can be seen when an object is placed between two plane mirrors set at right angles. Give a ray diagram to show how an eye suitably placed sees the image most distant from a point on the object between the mirrors.

Why does a plane mirror produce an image whereas a piece of white paper reflecting the same amount of light does not? *(L)*

Q9 State the laws of reflection of light, and describe how you would verify them experimentally.

Explain, with the help of a ray diagram, how the eye sees the image of a bright point formed by a plane mirror.

A man sits in an optician's chair, looking into a plane mirror which is 2 m away from him, and views the image of a chart which faces the mirror and is 50 cm behind his head. How far away from his eyes does the chart appear to be? *(O)*

Q10 Explain, with appropriate diagrams in each case, **two** of the following:
(a) how an eclipse of the Sun occurs, distinguishing clearly between total and partial eclipses;
(b) why three images are formed when an upright pin is placed between the reflecting surfaces of two vertical plane mirrors meeting at right angles;
(c) the use of plane mirrors to make a simple periscope — why are lenses usually fitted to periscopes? *(W)*

Q11 A real object is 100 mm in front of a concave mirror, which produces an upright image. What is the radius of curvature of the mirror?
A Less than 100 mm
B Exactly 100 mm
C Between 100 mm and 200 mm
D Exactly 200 mm
E More than 200 mm *(L)*

Q12 A man 1.75 m tall stands at a distance of 7.0 m from the pinhole of a pinhole camera. The distance of the film from the pinhole is 0.20 m. Find the length of the image of the man which is formed on the film.

State **two** ways in which the appearance of the image will change if the size of the pinhole is increased. *(C)*

Q13 Draw a ray diagram showing how a concave mirror can be used to produce a *real, inverted, diminished* image of a suitable object. *(W)*

Q14 Draw a labelled diagram to show how a converging (concave) mirror may be used to produce a wide parallel beam of light. State *one* different use of a converging mirror. *(S)*

Q15 Draw **two** ray diagrams, **one** for each case, showing how an image of a real object is formed by (i) a plane mirror; (ii) a concave (converging) mirror. Describe the image formed in each case. *(JMB)*

Q16 State where an object must be placed so that the image formed by a concave mirror is (i) erect and virtual, (ii) at infinity, (iii) the same size as the object. *(W)*

Q17 (a) State the laws of reflection for light meeting a mirror and use them to predict the reflected path of one ray meeting a concave spherical mirror.
(b) An observer close to a large concave mirror sees an enlarged upright image of himself. Draw a ray diagram to show how one point (not on the axis) of this image is produced.
(c) Describe an experiment in which, by making the image coincide with the object, the focal length of a concave mirror may be found. What is measured and how is the result calculated?
(d) A bright object 50 mm high stands on the axis of a concave mirror of focal length 100 mm and at a distance of 300 mm from the concave mirror. How big will the image be? *(O)*

Q18 (a) Draw diagrams to show how
(i) a *convex* mirror can be used to give a large field of view,
(ii) a *concave* mirror can be used to give an enlarged upright image,
(iii) a *concave* mirror and a small source of light can be used to produce an approximately parallel beam of light.
(b) An illuminated object and a concave mirror are used to produce a sharp image of the object on a screen. The corresponding magnifications (linear) and image distance are as given below.

magnification m	0.25	1.5	2.5	3.5
image distance v/cm	20	40	56	72

Draw a graph plotting m along the vertical axis and v along the horizontal axis. Use the graph to find the image distance when $m = 1.0$.
What is the object distance when $m = 1.0$?
What is the focal length of the mirror? *(L)*

Q19 Describe how you would construct a pinhole camera. Draw a labelled ray diagram to show how this camera forms an image of an object several metres distant from the camera and describe the image formed.

What conclusion concerning the properties of light can be drawn from the action of this camera?

(C part question)

16 Refraction

16.1   The refractive index

Refraction is the **bending of light (or the change in direction of the wavefront) as it crosses the boundary between two media at a glancing angle**. This deviation of the ray (or the wavefront) occurs because light travels at different speeds in the different media. However, when the ray of light (or wavefront) is incident normally (at 90°) to the interface (boundary) between two media, no such deviation of the light is observed. In fact the ray of light continues in a straight line (see Fig. 16.1a). Although the wavefronts do not change direction, a change does take place: the wavefronts are closer together in the water and even closer together in the glass. That is, the light travels slower in the water than in the air and even slower in glass.

Figures 16.1(b) and 16.1(c) show ray and wavefront diagrams for light crossing the boundary between air and water, and between air and glass. The ray of light

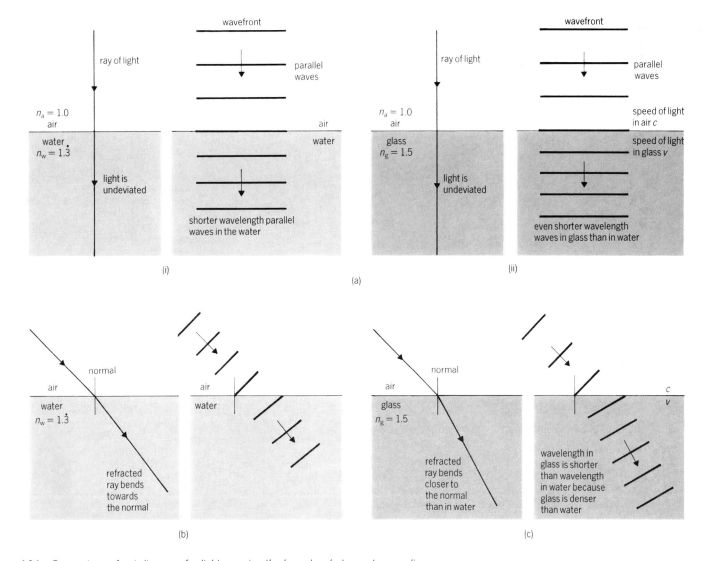

16.1   Ray and wavefront diagrams for light crossing the boundary between two media

is refracted *towards* the normal in water because water is an 'optically' denser medium than air (i.e. water has a greater refractive index than air). The ray is refracted even more towards the normal in the glass because the glass is even more 'optically' dense than water (i.e. glass has a greater refractive index than water). 'Optically' denser also means that the light travels more slowly in the medium.

The refractive index n is a constant for a given pair of media and is defined as $n = c/v$ where c = speed of light in air and v = speed of light in the medium. It is also determined from the ratio $n = \sin i/\sin r$ where i = the angle of incidence or the angle that the ray makes with the normal in the air and r = the angle of refraction or the angle that the ray makes with the normal in the second medium (see Fig. 16.2a).

Snell's Law Snell's Law states that the ratio of $\sin i$ to $\sin r$ is a constant n, the refractive index.

In Figure 16.2(b) a ray of light is shown leaving the medium and being refracted away from the normal in the air (that is, the less dense medium).

At this level only two media will be encountered, one of which will be air. Therefore two important points must be noted:

1 The angle to be measured must be the angle between the ray and the normal constructed at the point where the ray meets the interface;
2 One angle will be measured in the air medium while the other angle will be in the denser medium.

Reversibility of light

Figure 16.2 also illustrates the principle of **reversibility of light**. This principle states that '**light travelling from A to B through any "system" can reverse its path by travelling from B to A through the same "system"**', i.e. it follows the same path in either direction. The angles which the ray makes with the normal in Fig. 16.2(b) are the same as those in Fig. 16.2(a); the only difference is the *direction* of the rays. Thus angle x = angle i and angle y = angle r. To avoid having to define two refractive indices for each pair of media (depending on the direction of the light ray), the refractive index n will be shown as

$$n = \frac{\sin (\text{angle ray makes with normal in air})}{\sin (\text{angle ray makes with normal in medium})}$$

rather than referring to angles of incidence and refraction. Thus the refractive index n of the medium is given by either $n = \sin i/\sin r$ (Fig. 16.2a) or $n = \sin x/\sin y$ (Fig. 16.2b).

What happens when a ray of light passes through a parallel-sided medium such as a glass block is shown in Fig. 16.3. By geometry, $\angle y = \angle r$ (alternate angles in parallel lines). Since $n = \sin i/\sin r = \sin x/\sin y$ it follows that $\sin x = \sin i$, and thus $\angle x = \angle i$. So the angle of emergence equals the angle of incidence.

Thus when a ray of light passes through a parallel-sided block the emergent ray is parallel to the incident ray. The ray is displaced sideways but not deviated. The sideways (lateral) displacement d is shown in Fig. 16.3.

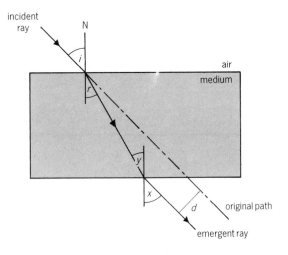

16.3   Refraction through a glass block

The critical angle

The angle the ray makes with the normal in air is always larger than the angle it makes with the normal in the medium, i.e. the angle x is always greater than the angle y (Fig. 16.5a). It is obvious that the maximum value of x is 90° (Fig. 16.5b). The angle of

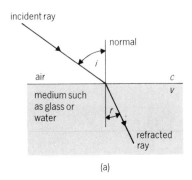

(a)

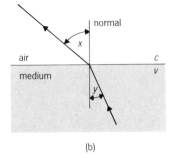

(b)

16.2   Principle of reversibility of light

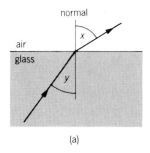
(a)

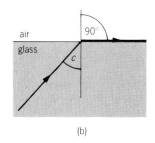
(b)

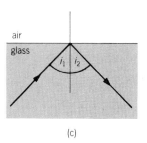
(c)

16.5   Critical angle

Example

Using the information given in Fig. 16.4, calculate the value of the refractive index of glass, n_g and hence find the value of the angle x.

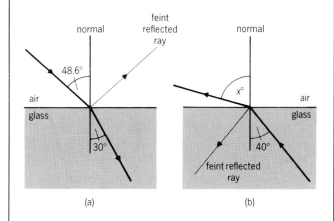

16.4   Refractive index and angle of emergence

From Fig. 16.4(a)
$\angle i = 48.6°$ $\angle r = 30$ $n_g = ?$

$$n_g = \frac{\sin i}{\sin r}$$

$$n_g = \frac{\sin 48.6}{\sin 30}$$

$$n_g = \frac{0.7501}{0.5000}$$

$$n_g = 1.5$$

From Fig. 16.4(b)
$\angle i = x$ $\angle r = 40°$ $n_g = 1.5$

$$n = \frac{\sin i}{\sin r}$$

$$1.5 = \frac{\sin x}{\sin 40}$$

$$1.5 \times \sin 40 = \sin x$$
$$\sin x = 1.5 \times 0.6428$$
$$\sin x = 0.9642$$
$$x = 74.6°$$

incidence in the denser medium for which the angle of refraction in the air is 90° is called the **critical angle c**. Calculating the refractive index in this situation gives $n = \sin 90°/\sin c$, i.e. $n = 1/\sin c$, a useful alternative formula for n which will be used later.

What happens if the angle of the incident ray inside the glass is greater than the critical angle c? In this case no light can escape from the glass (denser medium) and the ray is said to be **totally internally reflected** such that angle i_1 = angle i_2 (Fig. 16.5c). Total internal reflection is dealt with more fully on p.203.

Note   When drawing a ray diagram it is essential to construct the normal at the point where the ray meets the interface (boundary) between the air and the other medium. This allows correct illustration of the ray being refracted towards or away from the normal, depending on the media being used.

Change in wavelength

In Fig. 16.6 a wavefront XX′ is shown travelling in air towards the boundary between air and a medium. In time t the point X has reached A and X′ has reached B. Clearly the wavefront XX′ has advanced to the

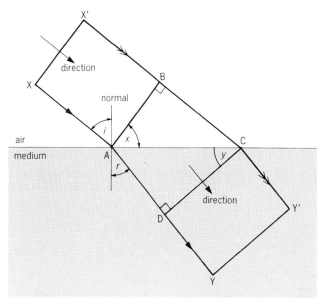

16.6   Refraction of wavefronts

197

position AB in time t. In the same amount of time, t, the point B will have reached the point C ($X'B = BC$), while the point A will have advanced to the point D, where $AD < BC$ because the wave travels more slowly in the medium. The new wavefront CD will *not* be parallel to the original wavefront XX', or to AB; there is a change in the direction of the wave. (Rays of light XADY and X'BCY' are shown in Fig. 16.6.)

The angle that the incident ray makes with the normal in the air is $\angle i$ (the angle of incidence) and the angle that the ray makes with the normal in the medium is $\angle r$ (the angle of refraction). Using the fact that the wavefront is perpendicular (90°) to the ray, and also that the normal is perpendicular (90°) to the boundary between the two media, it is easy to show $\angle i = \angle x$ and $\angle r = \angle y$.

$$n = \frac{\sin i}{\sin r} \text{ from Snell's law}$$

$$n = \frac{\sin x}{\sin y} \text{ since } x = i \text{ and } y = r$$

$$\sin x = \frac{BC}{AC} \text{ from the right-angled triangle ABC}$$

$$\sin y = \frac{AD}{AC} \text{ from the right-angled triangle ACD}$$

$$n = \frac{BC}{AC} \div \frac{AD}{AC}$$

$$n = \frac{BC}{AC} \times \frac{AC}{AD}$$

$$n = \frac{B\cancel{C}}{\cancel{A}D} = \frac{\text{speed of light in air} \times \text{time}\,\cancel{t}}{\text{speed of light in medium} \times \text{time}\,\cancel{t}}$$

$$n = \frac{\text{speed of light in air}}{\text{speed of light in medium}} = \frac{c}{v}$$

Now wave speed = frequency (f) × wavelength (λ); the frequency of the light remains the same regardless of the medium in which the light is travelling. It follows that different speeds of light must be due to different wavelengths. So

$$n = \frac{c}{v} = \frac{\cancel{f}\lambda_{\text{air}}}{\cancel{f}\lambda_{\text{medium}}}$$

$$n = \frac{\lambda_{\text{air}}}{\lambda_{\text{medium}}}$$

The wavelength of the wave in the medium will be shorter than the wavelength in the air.

Example

The speed of light in air is $3.0 \times 10^8 \, \text{m s}^{-1}$. Calculate the speed of light in glass of refractive index 1.5. Calculate the wavelength of the light (a) in air, (b) in glass, if the frequency of the light is 6.0×10^{14} Hz.

$n = 1.5 \quad c = 3.0 \times 10^8 \, \text{m s}^{-1} \quad v = ?$

$$n = \frac{c}{v}$$

$$1.5 = \frac{3.0 \times 10^8}{v} \, \text{m s}^{-1}$$

$$v = \frac{3.0 \times 10^8}{1.5} \, \text{m s}^{-1}$$

$$v = 2.0 \times 10^8 \, \text{m s}^{-1}$$

The speed of light in glass is $2.0 \times 10^8 \, \text{m s}^{-1}$.

(a) $c = 3.0 \times 10^8 \, \text{m s}^{-1} \quad f = 6.0 \times 10^{14} \, \text{Hz} \quad \lambda_{\text{a}} = ?$

$$c = f\lambda_{\text{a}}$$

$$3.0 \times 10^8 \, \text{m s}^{-1} = 6.0 \times 10^{14} \, \text{s}^{-1} \times \lambda_{\text{a}}$$

$$\frac{3.0 \times 10^8}{6.0 \times 10^{14}} \, \text{m} = \lambda_{\text{a}}$$

$$\lambda_{\text{a}} = 5.0 \times 10^{-7} \, \text{m}$$

The wavelength of the light in air is 5.0×10^{-7} m.

(b) There are two methods of finding the wavelength of the light in glass:

(i) $n = 1.5 \quad \lambda_{\text{a}} = 5.0 \times 10^{-7} \, \text{m} \quad \lambda_{\text{m}} = ?$

$$n = \frac{\lambda_{\text{a}}}{\lambda_{\text{m}}}$$

$$1.5 = \frac{5.0 \times 10^{-7}}{\lambda_{\text{m}}} \, \text{m}$$

$$= \frac{5.0 \times 10^{-7}}{1.5} \, \text{m}$$

$$= 3.3 \times 10^{-7} \, \text{m}$$

(ii) $v = 2.0 \times 10^8 \, \text{m s}^{-1} \quad \lambda_{\text{m}} = ? \quad f = 6.0 \times 10^{14} \, \text{Hz}$

$$v = f\lambda_{\text{m}}$$

$$2.0 \times 10^8 \, \text{m s}^{-1} = 6.0 \times 10^{14} \, \text{s}^{-1} \times \lambda_{\text{m}}$$

$$\frac{2.0 \times 10^8}{6.0 \times 10^{14}} \, \text{m} = \lambda_{\text{m}}$$

$$\lambda_{\text{m}} = 3.3 \times 10^{-7} \, \text{m}$$

The wavelength of the light in glass is 3.3×10^{-7} m.

Investigation 16.1   To determine the refractive index *n* of a rectangular block of glass using Snell's Law

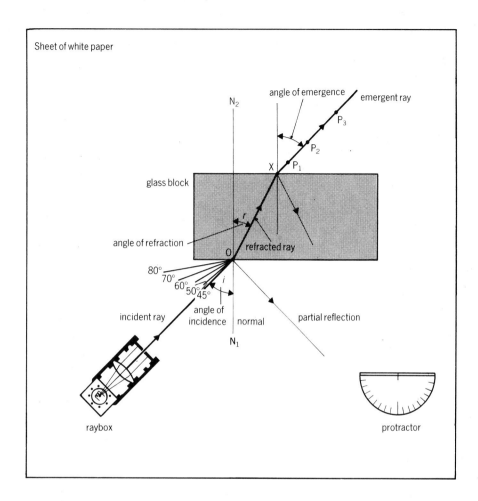

16.7   Finding the refractive index of a glass block

Place the glass block on a large sheet of white paper and very carefully trace around its outline. Remove the block. Construct a normal N_1N_2 to one of the longer sides of the block outline. With the aid of a protractor, construct angles of incidence *i* of 45°, 50°, 60°, 70° and 80° to the normal in the air (see Fig. 16.7).

Replace the block accurately in its outline. Direct a ray of light from the raybox along the line drawn such that *i* = 45°. (If the lower face of the block is 'frosted' or painted white, the refracted ray can be seen.) Mark the emergent ray accurately with three points P_1, P_2 and P_3. This enables the emergent ray for the angle of incidence *i* = 45° to be drawn in when the block is removed. Keeping the block in place, repeat the procedure for rays of light with angles of incidence of 50°, 60°, 70° and 80°, marking three points on each emergent ray.

Remove the block and join the three points P_1, P_2 and P_3 with a straight line to meet the outline of the block at X. Join X to O with a straight line to represent the refracted ray for *i* = 45°.

Using a protractor, carefully measure the angle of refraction *r* between the normal and the refracted ray in the glass. Measure

the angle of refraction *r* for each of the other rays and record each value in a table of results like Table 16.1. Great care must be taken to join up the correct points and to measure the appropriate angle in each case.

Using sine tables, record the values of sin *i* and sin *r*. For each pair of values *i* and *r* calculate the refractive index *n* from $n = \sin i/\sin r$. Hence calculate the average value for the refractive index *n* for glass. Alternatively, plot a graph of sin *i* against sin *r*. This should give a straight line passing through the origin. The gradient (slope) of the line is the refractive index *n* of the glass.

Table 16.1   Table of results for investigation 16.1

Angle of incidence *i*/degree	Angle of refraction *r*/degree	sin *i*	sin *r*	$n = \dfrac{\sin i}{\sin r}$
45		0.7071		
50		0.7771		
60		0.8660		
70		0.9397		
80		0.9848		

16.2 Real and apparent depth

Image of a pencil in water

Figure 16.8(a) shows a pencil standing in a tank of water. The light rays from the point O of the pencil which is resting on the bottom of the tank are refracted away from the normals N_1 and N_2 as shown. To the eye they appear to come from point I. When the pencil is viewed from above through the surface of the water it looks bent (as shown by the dotted outline).

Image of a coin in water

The ray construction diagram for the eye viewing a coin at the bottom of a tank of water is given in Fig. 16.8(b). It shows a direct ray from the coin passing straight out of the water into the air without deviation; one other ray showing refraction away from the normal N is used to complete the diagram. Again the image seen by the eye appears nearer the surface of the water than the real object.

Note The image I of the pencil point O in Fig. 16.8(a) is not on the vertical line through O. When the eye is viewing normally or nearly normally as in Fig. 16.8(b) the image does lie above the object O. Both diagrams in Fig. 16.8 have been exaggerated for clarity. Because both rays in Fig. 16.8(a) are deviated, this diagram is more accurate than Fig. 16.8(b).

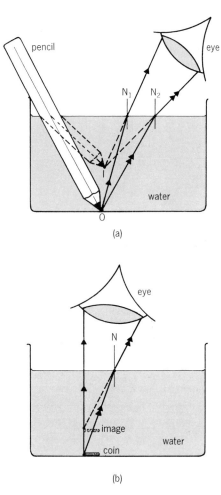

16.8 Bent pencil and raised coin seen in water

Exercise 16.1

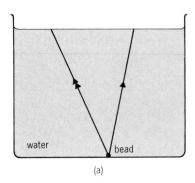

(a)

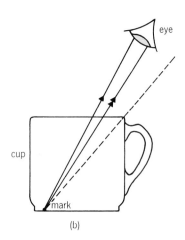

(b)

16.9 Raised bead and re-appearing mark seen in water

Figure 16.9(a) shows two rays of light reflected from a small bead resting on the bottom of a tank of water. Copy the figure and complete the ray diagram to show where an eye sees the image of the bead.

Figure 16.9(b) shows how an eye is able to see a mark on the bottom of an empty cup. If the eye is to the right of the boundary line the mark is not visible because the side of the cup prevents light going directly into the eye. However, if the eye is placed a little below the boundary line (from where the mark cannot be seen) the mark will become visible if water is poured into the cup.

Copy Fig. 16.9(b) and, by constructing two rays from the mark, show how the mark can be seen by an eye below the boundary line when the cup is full of water.

A measure of the refractive index using real and apparent depth

A mark O is drawn on the side of a rectangular glass block with a water-based felt-tipped pen (easily removed with a damp cloth). This mark serves as an 'object'. Figure 16.10 shows the image I of O when the mark is viewed normally through the other side of the glass block. OX is a normal ray. The ray OY bends away from the normal when it emerges into the air.

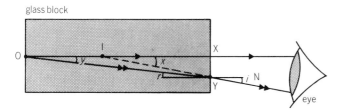

16.10   Real and apparent depth

The angles that the ray makes with the normal in the glass and the air are labelled r and i respectively. The refractive index n of the glass is given by $n = \sin i/\sin r$. From the geometry of the figure

$$\angle x = \angle i \text{ (corresponding angles)}$$
$$\angle y = \angle r \text{ (alternate angles)}$$
$$n = \frac{\sin i}{\sin r} = \frac{\sin x}{\sin y}$$

In $\triangle IXY$ $\qquad \sin x = \dfrac{XY}{IY}$

In $\triangle OXY$ $\qquad \sin y = \dfrac{XY}{OY}$

$$n = \frac{XY}{IY} \div \frac{XY}{OY}$$
$$n = \frac{\cancel{XY}}{IY} \times \frac{OY}{\cancel{XY}}$$
$$n = \frac{OY}{IY}$$

Suppose point Y moves closer and closer to X. The OY and IY will get shorter and nearly equal to the distances OX and IX respectively. Therefore the refractive index n, which is equal to OY/IY, is also nearly equal to OX/IX.

The distance OX is known as the **real depth** and the distance IX is known as the **apparent depth**. For rays of light very close to the normal, the refractive index n = real depth/apparent depth.

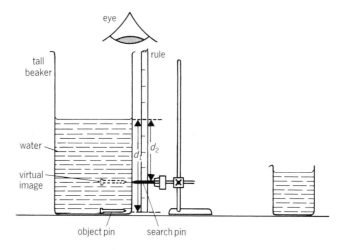

16.12   Finding the refractive index of water

Clearly, a rectangular block of any transparent material can be used in this experiment.

The method of investigation 16.2 can be adapted to find the refractive index of water (see Fig. 16.12). A steel optical pin on the bottom of a tall beaker serves as the object. A search pin held in a clamp is moved (just outside the beaker) to locate the image position by no parallax. Vary the real depth d_1 of the water (say 10 cm, 12 cm, 16 cm, 20 cm and 24 cm) by adding water carefully. Find the corresponding apparent depths d_2. Process the results as above or plot a graph of d_1 against d_2. A graph of real depth d_1 against

---

Investigation 16.2   To determine the refractive index of Perspex by the real and apparent depth method

This method requires the accurate measurement of the real and apparent depth which, in turn, requires the location of the virtual image by the method of no parallax.

Place a Perspex block on a sheet of white paper and carefully trace around its outline. Draw a vertical line at the centre of one of the shorter sides of the block. This line will act as the object. When the object line is viewed normally through the Perspex from the opposite side of the block its image appears inside the block. A search pin in a cork 'holder' can be used to locate the position of the virtual image. Place the search pin on top of the Perspex block and move it into position so that, when looking

directly at the object line through the block, the pin appears to form a continuous, vertical line with the image (Fig. 16.11a). Viewing must be done using one eye only (close the other eye as shown in Fig. 16.11b). Test the alignment of the pin by moving your head slightly from side to side. If the pin and the image remain together the pin is then directly (vertically) above the virtual image. However, if they 'break' apart they are not correctly aligned. Note whether the pin or the image moves to the left when your eye is moved to the right. Whichever one moves to the left is the one which is nearest to you. Move the search pin backwards or forwards according to your observation.

Move the search pin until it exhibits **no parallax** with the image (no separation from the image when the eye is moved). Leaving the pin in position, measure the apparent depth from

— continued —

the front (viewing) edge of the block to the search pin which marks the position of the image. Measure the real depth from the front (viewing) edge of the block to the object line either before locating the image or after measuring the apparent depth. Repeat the experiment to obtain the second reading for the real and apparent depths and record your results in a table like Table 16.2.

Calculate real depth/apparent depth for both pairs of values and average the results to give the refractive index *n* of Perspex.

Table 16.2   Table of results for investigation 16.2

real depth/cm		
apparent depth/cm		
$n = \dfrac{\text{real depth}}{\text{apparent depth}}$		

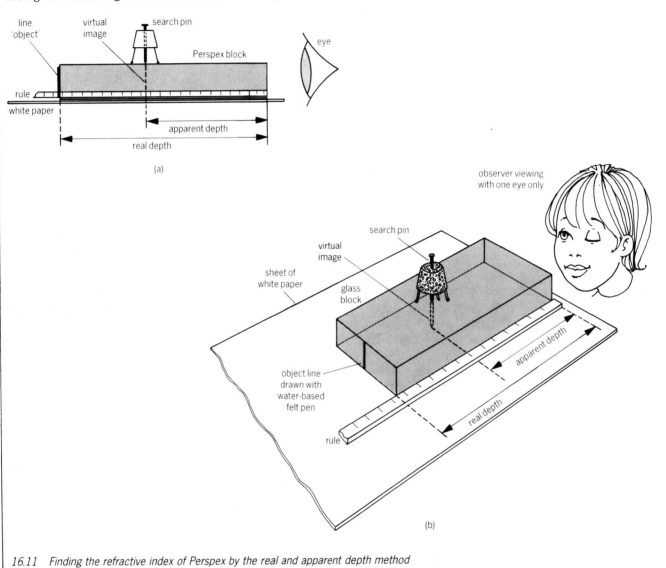

16.11   Finding the refractive index of Perspex by the real and apparent depth method

apparent depth d_2 should be a straight line passing through the origin. The refractive index *n* is given by the gradient (slope) of this straight line.

A much more accurate method of determining the refractive index for either a solid or a liquid by the real and apparent depth method uses a travelling microscope. This microscope measures to an accuracy of 0.01 mm, and can be focussed onto the image itself which avoids the errors of the no parallax method.

When using this method to determine the refractive index of a solid, such as glass, the microscope should be focussed on a mark on a sheet of white paper. Then it is focussed on the mark seen through a glass block placed on top of the mark. Finally the microscope is focussed onto lycopodium powder which has been lightly dusted onto the top surface of the glass block. The three readings are processed as in the previous experiment.

Investigation 16.3   To determine the refractive index of a liquid by the travelling microscope method

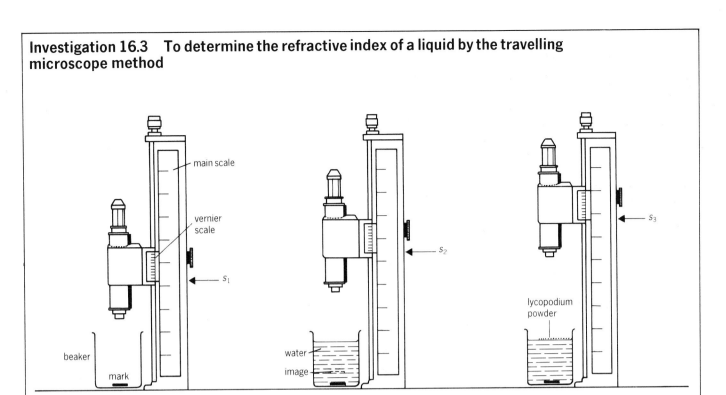

16.13   Finding the refractive index of water by the travelling microscope method

Adjust the eyepiece of the microscope so that the cross-wires are in focus. Make a mark on the base inside the beaker and adjust the microscope, up or down, until this mark is sharply in focus (Fig. 16.13a). Note the reading s_1 on the main scale opposite the vernier zero and record it in a suitable table of results.

Now carefully pour water into the beaker until a suitable depth of water is obtained. Re-adjust the microscope so that the mark is in focus when seen through the water (Fig. 16.13b). Record the second reading s_2 on the main scale, including the vernier scale reading. Lightly sprinkle lycopodium powder on the surface of the water. Adjust the microscope further to bring the lycopodium powder into focus (Fig. 16.13c). Note and record the third reading s_3.

Calculate the real depth from $(s_3 - s_1)$ and the apparent depth from $(s_3 - s_2)$. Hence calculate the refractive index n of the water using $n = (s_3 - s_1)/(s_3 - s_2)$.

16.3   Critical angle c and total internal reflection

A ray of light incident *normally* on the boundary between two media will not be deviated or bent but will pass straight across the boundary. A semicircular-shaped block of Perspex (or glass) is very useful in this context as light rays are able to enter the curved face along *any* radius line without being deviated. Figure 16.14(a) shows the normal ray which goes into and out of the Perspex block without suffering any deviation at either of the two air–Perspex boundaries. Figure 16.14(b) shows a ray of light entering the block normally without deviation but making an angle y with the normal at O inside the Perspex. When the ray leaves the denser medium (Perspex) it travels with greater speed in the less dense medium (air). Therefore it is refracted *away* from the normal making an angle x to the normal in the air which is greater than y. Using

$$n = \frac{\sin (\text{angle ray makes with the normal in air})}{\sin (\text{angle ray makes with the normal in medium})}$$

the refractive index of Perspex $n_p = \sin x/\sin y$. If several measurements of x and y are taken then the refractive index of Perspex can be calculated by averaging the results for each pair of values.

The angle y can be increased by moving the raybox on an arc of a circle centred on O. This results in an increase in angle x until the stage shown in Fig. 16.14(c) is reached, i.e. x is 90°. Angle x clearly cannot be made greater. The angle that the ray now makes with the normal inside the Perspex is called the **critical angle** c (the angle in the denser medium produced when the angle of refraction in the less dense medium

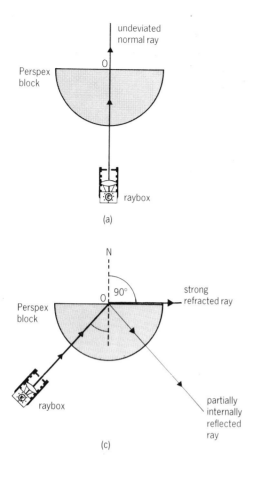

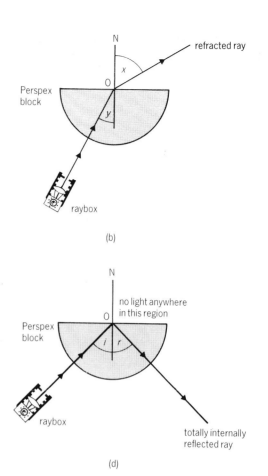

(a)

(b)

(c)

(d)

16.14   Critical angle and total internal reflection

is 90°). A faint reflected ray is usually observed as well as the bright ray which is refracted along the straight edge of the block. This is due to **partial internal reflection**. Note also that when white light is used the light emerging along the straight edge is split up into the colours of the spectrum.

If the raybox is moved further round the arc, as in Fig. 16.14(d), so that the angle of incidence i inside the Perspex is greater than the critical angle c, no refraction occurs at the straight-edge boundary. Instead the ray is **totally internally reflected** at an angle r to the normal where $r = i$. For total internal reflection to occur the angle of incidence i must be measured inside the *denser* medium (Perspex) and must be *greater* than the critical angle c. Note that for all angles of incidence greater than the critical angle, the law of reflection holds true.

Example

Diamond has a refractive index n_d of 2.4, calculate the critical angle c for diamond.

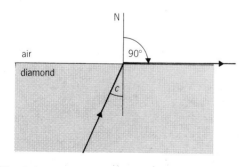

16.15   Critical angle for diamond

In Fig. 16.15
$n_d = 2.4 \quad x = 90° \quad y = c$

$$n = \frac{\sin 90°}{\sin c}$$

$$2.4 = \frac{1}{\sin c}$$

$$\sin c = \frac{1}{2.4}$$

$\sin c = 0.4167$ (from reciprocal tables)
$c = 24° \, 38'$

The critical angle for diamond is only 24° 38′. Its 'sparkle' is thus due to the ease with which multiple total internal reflections occur when light shines on it, especially when it has been expertly cut and polished to enhance this effect.

On page 197, it was shown that $n = 1/\sin c$. An accurate measurement of the critical angle c will therefore enable n to be calculated.

Exercise 16.2

(a) Show that the critical angle for glass of refractive index $n_g = 1.5$ is 41° 49′, i.e. approximately 42°.
(b) Determine the critical angle for water of refractive index $n_w = 1.\dot{3}$.

Investigation 16.4   To determine n for Perspex by the critical angle method

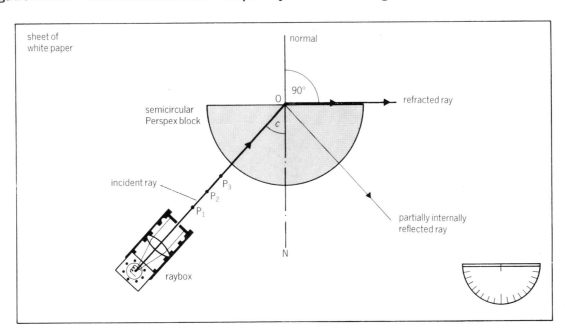

16.16   Finding the refractive index for Perspex by the critical angle method

Place the semicircular Perspex block at the centre of a large sheet of white paper and carefully trace its outline. Find the mid-point O of the straight edge of the block. Construct, using a protractor, a normal NO perpendicular to this straight edge at O. Replace the block in its outline. Move the raybox in an arc to the left of NO, always directing the incident ray at the point O. When the refracted ray emerges along the straight edge, as shown in Fig. 16.16, mark the path of the incident ray with three points P_1, P_2 and P_3. Remove the block temporarily and join the three points with a straight line which should pass through O. Using a protractor, measure the critical angle c between the incident ray drawn and the normal.

Replace the block carefully in its outline and repeat the procedure, but this time move the raybox in an arc to the right of NO, always directing the ray at the point O. Record the two measured values of c in a table of results like Table 16.3 and calculate the average value of the critical angle c. Then calculate the refractive index n_p for Perspex from $n_p = 1/\sin c$.

Table 16.3   Table of results for investigation 16.4

	1st reading	2nd reading	average
critical angle c/degree			

The apparatus of investigation 16.4 can also be used to show that the angle of incidence i is equal to the angle of reflection r for light incident in a denser medium (Perspex) for angles greater than the critical angle c.

Right-angled isosceles prism

A glass (or Perspex) prism with angles of 90°, 45° and 45° is a very useful device for reflecting light. Its main advantage is that it *totally* reflects light whereas mirrors absorb some of the incident energy. In addition, the silvering on mirrors can become tarnished or flake off but a glass (or Perspex) prism can remain undamaged for a long time. This type of prism is used in binoculars, periscopes and certain types of telescopes and microscopes.

Figure 16.18(a) shows a ray of light incident normally on the face AB of a 90°, 45°, 45° glass prism. It travels straight on into the glass without deviation to

Investigation 16.5 To verify the Law of reflection of light for angles greater than the critical angle

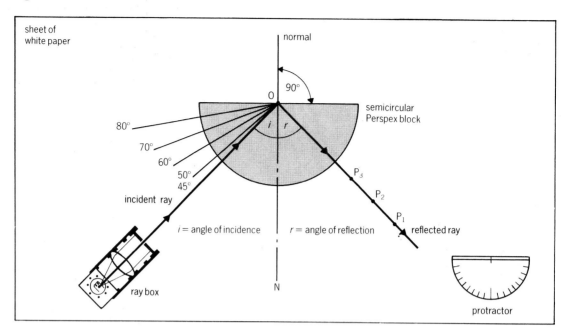

16.17 Law of reflection for angles greater than the critical angle

Place the semicircular Perspex block on a large sheet of white paper and carefully trace its outline. As before find the mid-point O and construct the normal NO, (see Fig. 16.17). For Perspex the critical angle $c = 42°$, thus angles of incidence $i > 42°$ are greater than the critical angle. Using a protractor, construct angles of 45°, 50°, 60°, 70° and 80° to the normal NO.

Replace the block carefully in its outline and direct a ray of light from the raybox along the 45°-line. The ray will be heading towards O and will be reflected to emerge from the curved face on the other side of the normal. Mark three points P_1, P_2 and P_3 on the reflected ray. Remove the block temporarily and join the three points with a straight line which should pass through O.

Using a protractor, measure the angle of reflection r between

the normal and the reflected ray and record the result in a table like Table 16.4. Replace the block carefully in its outline and repeat the procedure for angles of 50°, 60°, 70° and 80° to the normal. Record the values of r in the appropriate places in the table of results. Plot a graph of angle of incidence i against angle of reflection r. A straight line graph covering the range 45° – 80° is sufficient to show that angle i is equal to angle r.

Table 16.4   Table of results for investigation 16.5

angle of incidence i/degree	45	50	60	70	80
angle of reflection r/degree					

strike the face AC at the point D. A normal N must be constructed at D and the angle which the ray inside the glass makes with this normal determined in order to decide what happens (refraction or total internal reflection) to this ray. From geometry, the angle the ray makes with the normal is 45°, which is greater than the critical angle $c = 42°$ for glass of refractive index 1.5. Therefore the ray will be totally internally reflected at 45° to the normal. Hence the ray is deviated through an angle of 90°. The ray then travels in the glass towards the face BC to strike the face BC normally and hence emerge without deviation.

The face AC acts like a reflecting mirror, except that all the light incident on it is totally reflected and none

absorbed. Hence it is a better reflector than a plane mirror.

When a ray of light is incident normally on the hypotenuse face AC of the prism (see Fig. 16.19a), the light is deviated through 180°. The first reflection on AB deviates the ray through 90° and the second

Exercise 16.3

Copy Figs. 16.18(b) and (c) and complete the path of the ray incident normally on the faces shown. Draw any normals required, mark important angles and show clearly where the ray emerges from the prism. (Assume the critical angle $c = 42°$ for the material of the prism.)

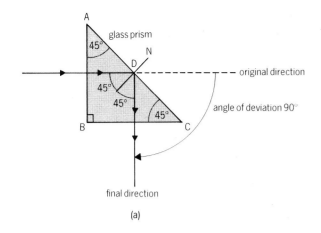

(a)

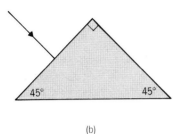

(b)

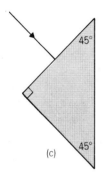

(c)

16.18   Totally internally reflecting prisms

reflection on BC deviates the ray through a further 90°, making a total deviation of 180°. As before, the light enters the prism without deviation and suffers total internal reflection because the angles inside the glass are 45° (greater than the critical angle of 42°).

When the ray of light is incident normally on the hypotenuse face, the prism has an inverting effect as well as undergoing a deviation of 180° (see Fig. 16.20a). When the prism is used as shown in Fig. 16.20(b) there is again an inverting effect, but this time there is no deviation (the image is observed in the same direction as the object).

Exercise 16.4

Copy Fig. 16.19(b) and complete the path of the ray into and out of the prism. Mark clearly any angles required to complete the diagram.

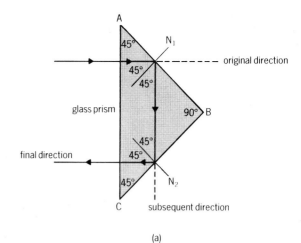

(a)

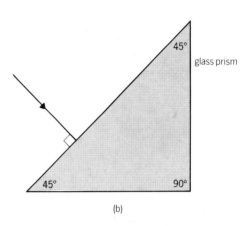

(b)

16.19   Deviation of ray through 180°

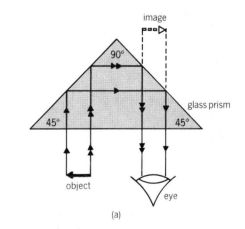

(a)

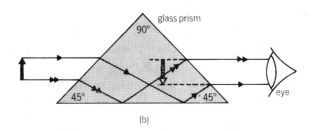

(b)

16.20   Inversion with or without deviation

16.4 Some applications of refraction and total internal reflection

Mirage effect

The density, and hence the refractive index, of air changes gradually with height. There is no abrupt change from one medium to another. Thus a ray of light in air is bent gradually without any abrupt change of direction. This is known as continuous refraction. Usually this does not produce any noticeable effect; the most striking is probably the apparent increase in the size of the Sun as it dips below the horizon. However, the effect is much more dramatic on a hot sunny day in summer. Since the air close to the ground is warmer and hence less dense than that above, the ray of light is bent away from the normal. (Usually the air near the ground is denser and the ray will be bent towards the normal.) Thus a ray of light from the sky is bent as shown in Fig. 16.21. The eye does not realise this and interprets the light as if it were reflected from the ground, as if by a mirror. It looks like a pool of water, and if the driver is in the correct position, images of trees and houses can also be seen. The 'pool' always appears to be at the same distance from the driver. This distance depends upon the height of the driver's eye above the ground. This effect is known as a **mirage**.

Continuous refraction occurs all the time, but mirages are not always seen. They are seen more easily when the driver is going up a slope. When driving downhill, or in a dip, they will not be seen because it is not possible for the light to be 'bent' into the eye.

Note Mirages are *not* due to total internal reflection, otherwise they would be seen in all circumstances. A little thought will show that a surface such as a dry road cannot produce regular reflection, thus the effect must be due to continuous refraction in the air.

The mirage effect is also seen in very cold regions. Here, however, because of the opposite variation in density of the air, a ray of light from near ground level will curve in the opposite direction. Thus 'objects' (such as a polar bear or land feature) appear to be upside down in the sky.

Fibre optics

One application of total internal reflection is found in fibre optics. Good quality glass of high refractive index is coated with a thin layer of glass of lower refractive index. A ray of light entering the end of a thin fibre that strikes the interface between the two glass surfaces at an angle greater than the critical angle will be totally internally reflected along the whole length of the fibre (Fig. 16.22). Light can thus travel the length of the fibre and emerge from the other end without loss of intensity.

Surgeons use a special device which looks like a flexible tube to view a patient's internal organs without surgery. The device consists of two bundles of fibres mounted co-axially in a tube. Light is sent down one bundle of the fibres and is reflected from the internal organs to return up the other bundle of fibres. Because the bundles are flexible they can be separated at the viewing end of the tube. One bundle is fitted with a light source and the other bundle is fitted with an eyepiece for the surgeon to view through.

A similar use of total internal reflection is in creative gardening. Spectacular fountains are created by placing a coloured light bulb in a position so that the light will be totally internally reflected in a jet of water. Jets of different colours can be combined for an effective display.

Vanishing coin

Place a coin on the bench and stand a glass block on top of the coin (Fig. 16.23a). The coin is only visible when you look down through the top horizontal surface. Cover the top of the block with black tape so that you can concentrate on viewing through the vertical faces only. You cannot see the coin through any of the four vertical faces no matter what angle you view from. Light reflected from the coin cannot emerge from any vertical face because of total internal reflection.

A mirage, Algeria

warm air

hot air

very hot air

light from sky

'pool' on road

16.21 Mirage effect

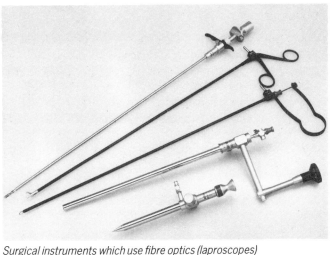

Surgical instruments which use fibre optics (laproscopes)

View of internal organs through a laproscope

low refractive index

high refractive index

16.22   Fibre optics

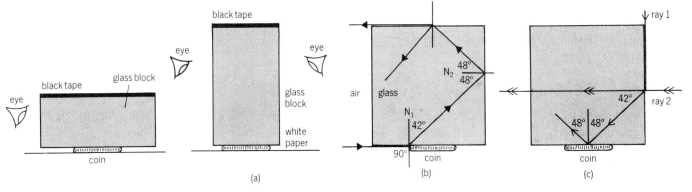

16.23   Vanishing coin

The geometry of this demonstration is shown in Figs 16.23(b) and (c). For the coin to be seen, light must be reflected off it, then travel through the glass and finally emerge into the air. First consider a ray of light which grazes the bottom edge of the block and the top of the coin (Fig. 16.23b). This ray will refract at an angle of $42°$ to the normal N_1, inside the glass. Hence it makes an angle of $48°$ with the normal N, that is, an angle greater than the critical angle $c = 42°$. Any ray entering the base at an angle between $0°$ and $90°$ will make an angle of *less* than $42°$ with the normal N_1. The ray will then either pass through the glass and be refracted out at the top surface or it will make an angle with the normal N_2 at the vertical face of $48°$ or greater. In this case it will be totally internally reflected again. Therefore, no light can emerge from the vertical faces (sides) of the block.

Another possibility is for light to enter through a vertical face of the block, be refracted down towards the coin and emerge again. However, Fig. 16.23(c) shows that light entering a vertical face can never reach the coin because it must suffer total internal reflection at the bottom face. It can be shown by simple geometry that when a ray of light passes through the side, the angle of refraction must be $42°$ or less. Thus the angle of incidence on the bottom face is $48°$ or greater and it is totally internally reflected (see ray 1). Thus a person looking in the other side cannot see the coin. Obviously some rays pass through the block without touching the bottom face (see ray 2).

Exercise 16.5

Explain why the coin will be visible through the vertical faces if water is placed on top of the coin before the glass is put in position.

Questions

Q1 A glass block of length 18 cm and refractive index 1.5 contains a small air bubble. Viewed from one side the bubble *appears* to be 8 cm from this side. How far in the block will it *appear* to be when viewed from the opposite side?

A 12 cm
B 10 cm
C 9 cm
D 6 cm
E 4 cm

Q2 (a) What is meant by the refractive index of a material? Describe how you would measure the refractive index of glass by tracing rays through a glass block.

(b) For a glass 45 ° prism of refractive index 1.53, rays of light which normally fall on a face can be deviated either through 90 ° or through 180 °, the light in each case being totally reflected.

(i) Explain why total internal reflection occurs.

(ii) Calculate the least value of the refractive index of a material which produces total internal reflection with an angle of incidence of 45 °.

Q3 A ray of light is incident on the plane surface of a transparent material at such an angle that the reflected and refracted rays are at right angles to each other. Draw a diagram to illustrate this and calculate the refractive index if the angle of refraction = 30°. *(S)*

Q4 State clearly what is meant by the refractive index of a substance. Describe in detail how you would determine this quantity for a transparent solid, showing how you would use the readings which you obtain.

What are the conditions necessary for total internal reflection to take place?

Often when you are travelling in summer a pool of water appears to lie on the road in front of you. Explain why this effect occurs, and say why you can never approach close to it. *(L)*

Q5 Define the term *refractive index*. Describe, with full experimental details, how you would find the refractive index of a given rectangular block of glass.

A swimmer is standing on the edge of a pool looking vertically downwards at the tiles on the bottom. Explain why the swimming pool looks shallower than it really is. *(C)*

Q6 State the laws of refraction and explain what is meant by the refractive index of a substance.

Describe how you would determine the refractive index of glass by measurements of the real and apparent depth of a glass block.

A travelling microscope is focused on to some lycopodium powder which rests on the bench. When a rectangular glass block is placed over the powder, the microscope must be raised by 1.6 cm to refocus on the powder. It is raised by a further 3.2 cm when focused onto powder on the top of the block. Calculate the refractive index of the glass of the block. *(JMB)*

Q7

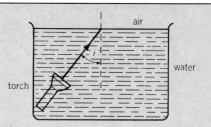

(a) The diagram above shows a torch being held under water in such a way that a ray of light is produced which can strike the surface of the water at different angles *i*. Calculate a value for the critical angle; the refractive index of water is 4/3.

Draw sketches to show what will happen to the ray of light after it has struck the water–air boundary when *i* is about 20° and when *i* is about 60°. Account for the different behaviour of the ray in the two cases.

Why in one case has the resulting ray coloured edges whereas in the other case it has not?

(b) In an experiment to determine the refractive index of water a black line is painted on the bottom of a tall glass container which is then partially filled with water. On looking vertically down into the water the black line appears to be closer than it really is. Explain, with the help of a ray diagram, why this is so.

The following results were obtained in such an experiment.

real depth/cm	8.1	12.0	16.0	20.0
apparent depth/cm	5.9	9.1	12.0	15.1

Plot a graph of real depth (*y*-axis) against apparent depth (*x*-axis) and hence determine a value for the refractive index of water. *(L)*

Q8 The diagram shows a side view of a water-filled aquarium PQRS. An electric lamp, surrounded by a shield with a narrow slit, is immersed in one corner of the aquarium at S. The light ray from the slit shines on the water surface PQ at an angle of 40° as shown.

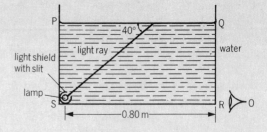

(i) If the refractive index of water is 1.33, calculate the critical angle for a ray travelling from water to air.

(ii) Draw a diagram of the light ray shown above meeting the water surface PQ, and show its path after meeting the surface. Calculate the angle that this new path makes with PQ and label the angle.

(iii) The shield surrounding the lamp is turned slightly so that when an observer O looks perpendicularly at the side QR the lamp is directly visible. Calculate how far the image of the lamp appears to be from QR. *(L)*

17 Light dispersion, colour and the electromagnetic spectrum

17.1 Dispersing and combining white light

Deviation

A ray of light of a single colour incident on an equilateral glass prism is refracted *towards* the normal N_1 and travels through the glass at reduced speed. When it emerges into the air it is refracted *away* from the normal N_2 and speeds up again. The ray has been **deviated** from its original direction; the **angle of deviation** D is the angle between the original and final directions, as shown in Fig. 17.1. The three prisms in Fig. 17.2(a) have been placed so that they 'deviate'

three parallel rays to a single point F. A converging (convex) lens can be thought to consist of a set of differently shaped prisms. In Fig. 17.2(b) rays of light from a point O are deviated by the different sections of the lens to form a real image at I. This is covered in greater detail in Chapter 18, p.221.

Dispersion

A ray of white light entering a glass prism is **dispersed** (split up) into its component colours of red, orange, yellow, green, blue, indigo and violet. These colours are collectively called the **spectrum of white light** (see Fig. 17.3).

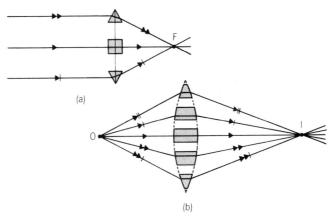

17.1 *Angle of deviation*

17.2 *A convex lens as a series of prisms*

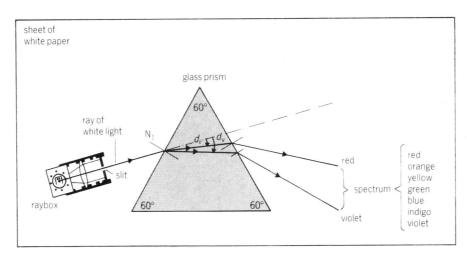

17.3 *Dispersion of white light*

Investigation 17.1   To produce a pure spectrum

Set up the apparatus shown in Fig. 17.4. The narrow slit, positioned at the focal point of the first achromatic lens, is strongly illuminated with white light, so that a parallel beam of white light emerges from the lens. (An achromatic lens does not disperse the white light into its colours in the way an ordinary single lens does. It is usually made of a combination of two lenses of different refractive indices.) The parallel beam of white light is dispersed on entering the prism. As is usual, two of the seven colours, red and blue, will be used to illustrate what happens to the beam. A parallel beam of red light is formed inside the prism. This emerges from the prism as a parallel beam and is focussed by the second achromatic lens onto a white screen placed at the focal plane of the second lens. A parallel beam of blue light is also formed inside the prism, at a slight angle to the parallel red beam. The parallel beam of blue light emerges from the prism at an angle to the red beam and so it will be focussed at a different place on the focal plane (white screen). Similarly, each different coloured parallel beam will be focussed on a different point on the white screen, giving a range of sharply defined colours.

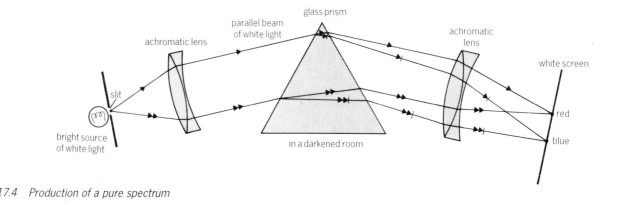

17.4   Production of a pure spectrum

The spectrum of white light is generally said to consist of seven colours although indigo and violet are very difficult to distinguish. It must be stressed that the dispersion takes place immediately the light enters the prism, and further dispersion occurs as the light leaves the prism. The colours in white light are separated by the prism because the glass has slightly different values of refractive index for each of the different colours (wavelengths) in the white light. Red rays, which have the longest wavelength, are deviated least while the violet rays, with the shortest wavelength, are deviated most. The spectrum formed is not very pure because the colours overlap and only the edges of red and violet, the outer colours, are sharply defined. All 'colour' experiments are best performed in a darkened room to exclude light which may confuse the result.

A less pure spectrum can be obtained using one lens only. This spectrum is better than the one produced with no lens (Fig. 17.3), but is clearly not so good as that formed in the investigation. White light from a slit is focussed by the converging lens to a point such as X (see Fig. 17.5). The prism is then placed in the path of the light and the white screen adjusted until the colours are 'in focus' on the screen. Again the effect is best observed if the demonstration is carried out in a darkened room.

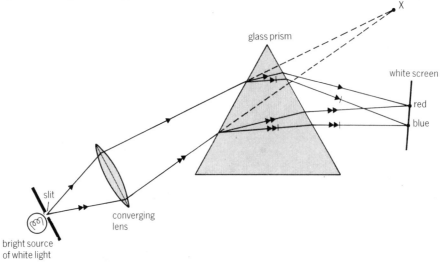

17.5   An impure spectrum

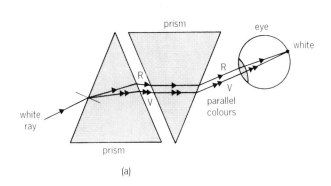

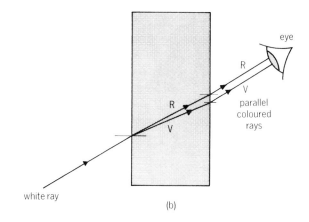

(a)

(b)

17.6   Re-combining colours to form white light

The colours of the spectrum can be recombined to form white light by using a second prism as shown in Fig. 17.6(a). All the colours emerge from the second prism in rays parallel to each other and, since all wavelengths are present, white is seen by the eye. This also explains why a parallel-sided glass block does not appear to disperse white light (Fig. 17.6b). The white light incident on the rectangular glass block does suffer dispersion inside the block but each coloured ray emerges parallel to the others and to the original ray. The lens in the eye focusses all the parallel coloured light onto one spot on the retina of the eye, hence white is seen.

Newton's Disc

Another way of showing that red, orange, yellow, green, blue, indigo and violet combine to give white light involves spinning Newton's Disc. A disc with coloured sectors painted on it (see Fig. 17.7) is rotated. As the speed of rotation increases the disc looks white or, more correctly, greyish white because paints are not pure colours.

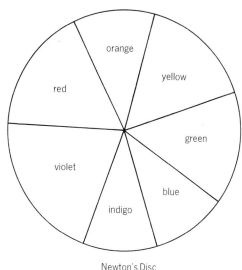

17.7   Newton's Disc

17.2   Colour

Primary and secondary colours

When white light is dispersed by a prism seven colours (red, orange, yellow, green, blue, indigo and violet) are seen on a white screen. However, only **three** coloured lights need to be combined to give white light; these are red, green and blue mixed in the correct intensities. Using three rayboxes fitted with a red, a green or a blue filter, the coloured rays can be made to overlap as shown in Figure 17.8.

Where all three colours overlap, at W, white light is seen. When just red and green light overlap, as at Y, yellow light is seen. When green and blue light overlap, as at C, cyan is seen. When blue and red light overlap, as at M, magenta is the colour seen. Red, green and blue are called **primary colours** because they cannot be made by the combination of other colours, they can be combined to form all the other colours and all three combined together give white light. Yellow, cyan and magenta, the three colours formed by the combination of various pairs of primary colours are known as

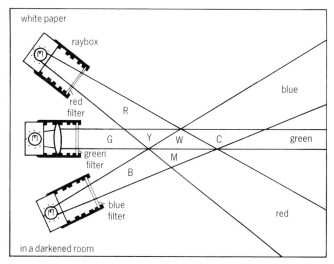

17.8   Primary and secondary colours

secondary colours. When a secondary colour is combined with the remaining primary colour white light is seen.

$$\text{yellow (red + green) + blue = white}$$
$$\text{cyan (green + blue) + red = white}$$
$$\text{magenta (red + blue) + green = white}$$

Colours which add together to give white light are called **complementary** colours.

A microcomputer program, *Colour* by G. and P. Rowell (BBC cassette) is available from Cambridge University Press. It demonstrates primary, secondary and complementary colours and what happens when coloured filters are placed in front of a light source. It also shows the appearance of a coloured object in different coloured lights.

All colours can be produced by the addition of red, green and blue light in the correct proportions and intensities. The cones in the retina of the human eye are stimulated by either red, green or blue light, and so send a message to the brain which 'sees' the colour composed in this way. The rods in the retina of the eye receive black and white images and are able to respond to very low levels of light. Cones are not able to operate effectively in low levels of light so at night coloured objects appear black or grey.

Colour addition

Colours in stage lighting and in colour television are produced by the addition of the primary colours red, green and blue. In stage lighting just three projectors, with red, green and blue filters can be used. The intensity of the coloured light from each projector is varied by varying the brightness of the lamp in the projector. By shining these three colours onto a white background and combining the colours in pairs it is possible to produce yellow, cyan or magenta. When red and green light are added and reflected by the white screen this has the same effect on the eye as yellow light. Likewise, green and blue added together appear as cyan and red and blue as magenta. Other colours are produced by varying the proportions and intensities of the overlapping primary colours. The colours on a colour television are produced by the combination of the primary colours in differing intensities. Spots of phosphors are stimulated by electrons to emit either red, green or blue light. The screen is covered in a myriad of groups of three spots of phosphors. Each individual group can be stimulated by three split beams of electrons to give either red, green or blue. Also by stimulating pairs of the three spots in a group yellow, cyan and magenta can be produced. To obtain white light, all three colours are stimulated in equal proportions. Black is obtained when no light is emitted, i.e. when the electron beams are suppressed and do not stimulate the phosphors on the screen. All other colours are produced by stimulating red, green and blue in varying proportions.

Colour subtraction

If the surface of a material absorbs all the colours (wavelengths) incident upon it it will appear black. If the surface absorbs all colours in equal proportions but reflects some of the light it will appear grey in white light. However, if a surface absorbs the colours in different proportions the surface appears coloured. Any surface which reflects all colours completely will appear white.

Printers make use of absorption of colour to produce coloured pictures in magazines and books. They print three versions of the same picture in inks of different colours: yellow, cyan and magenta. Yellow reflects red and green while absorbing blue, cyan reflects green and blue while absorbing red and magenta reflects red and blue while absorbing green. To increase the contrast another picture in black ink is usually added. When all the pictures are printed on top of each other on the same sheet of white paper a full colour picture is obtained. Clearly, to obtain white no ink is used; the white paper reflects all the colours. Red is obtained from yellow and magenta inks which together absorb green and blue but reflect red. Green is obtained from yellow and cyan inks which together absorb red and blue while reflecting only green. Blue is reflected from cyan and magenta inks which together absorb red and green. Black is obtained where all three inks overlap because yellow, cyan and magenta will absorb red, green and blue. Therefore no light is reflected and that part will appear black. Other colours such as pink, orange, brown, purple etc. can be obtained by varying the proportions of the three inks to provide all the various shades and hues. This is an example of producing colour pictures by **subtraction**, in direct contrast to the **addition** of coloured lights.

Why does a red book appear red while a green filter appears green when used in white light? Will the book and filter still appear red and green respectively if illuminated by blue light? The colour of an object depends on

(a) the colour of the light falling on the object;
(b) the colour(s) which the object reflects or transmits.

In Fig. 17.9 the book appears red because red light is reflected by the book cover while all the other colours contained in white light are absorbed. The green filter appears green because it absorbs all colours except green, which is reflected and transmitted by the filter. When blue light is used instead of white light the book and the filter appear black because they both absorb blue light. Since no colour besides blue is present in the blue light, no light is reflected from the book or

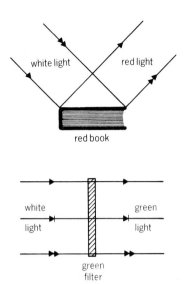

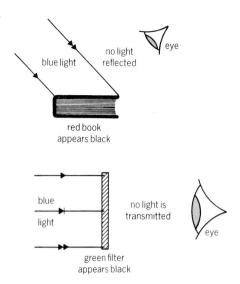

17.9   Coloured objects and filters

reflected or transmitted by the filter. The book will appear red when illuminated by white, red, yellow and magenta light because all of these colours contain red light.

Just as a prism can be used to show that white light consists of seven colours, it can also be used to show that yellow light consists of red, yellow and green wavelengths.

Combinations of a primary colour filter and a secondary colour filter can also be tested by the method of investigation 17.2. Try to predict the colour transmitted before you make the test.

Mixing coloured paints

Paints are *not* pure colours, e.g. blue paint reflects green and indigo as well as the predominant blue colour. Yellow paint reflects yellow light but also reflects some orange and green light. Therefore, when yellow and blue paints are mixed together the only colour reflected is green. Hence the mixture appears green. Figure 17.11 (overleaf) illustrates how each paint absorbs certain colours while reflecting others.

Exercise 17.1

Which colours can be used to illuminate the green filter so that it appears green?

Exercise 17.2

If the yellow and cyan filters are placed together in front of the slit which colour(s) is (are) seen on the screen? Which colours are seen when (i) the cyan and the magenta filters are placed together, (ii) the yellow and magenta filters are combined in front of the slit?

Explain why no light will be transmitted when all three filters are placed together.

Investigation 17.2   To find the colours in yellow light

Set up a raybox, prism and white screen as shown in Fig. 17.10. Place a yellow filter over the slit so that the colours in yellow light are shown on the screen. The yellow filter can be replaced by a cyan and by a magenta filter to display the colours contained in these secondary colours.

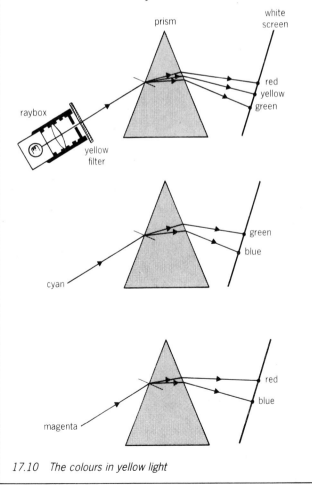

17.10   The colours in yellow light

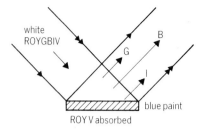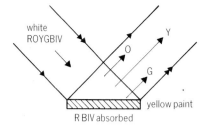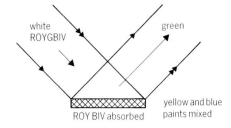

17.11 *Mixing coloured paints*

17.3   The electromagnetic spectrum

The electromagnetic spectrum includes wavelengths other than those visible to the human eye.

Infrared radiation, visible light and ultraviolet radiation are all members of the same **electromagnetic spectrum**. All are transverse waves travelling at the speed of light $c = 3 \times 10^8 \text{ m s}^{-1}$ and can travel through a vacuum. Unlike longitudinal sound waves, which must have a material medium for their transmission, electromagnetic waves can travel through a medium or a vacuum. They are characterised by their different frequencies (or wavelengths); ultraviolet radiation has a greater

---

Investigation 17.3   To detect infrared and ultraviolet radiation

This demonstration can be performed using a very powerful (intense) source of light such as a carbon-arc or quartz-iodine lamp and a rock salt prism. A glass prism is useless here because glass absorbs infrared and ultraviolet radiations.

Note   It is very dangerous to look directly at a carbon-arc or quartz-iodine lamp. During this investigation it is important to look *only* at the spectrum cast on the screen.

It is important that this investigation is performed in a completely darkened room. Set up the light source, prism and white screen so that a visible spectrum is cast onto the screen. Place a suitable detector in the visible spectrum and note the 'reading' of the detector. Move the detector slowly towards the red end of the spectrum and then into the dark region beyond the red end, taking a reading at each stage.

For infrared radiation suitable detectors are (i) a thermopile connected to a sensitive galvanometer (microammeter) which registers tiny currents when the invisible radiation falls on the thermopile; (ii) a phototransistor with a battery and galvanometer; (iii) the blackened bulb of a thermometer which shows a rise in temperature when infrared radiation strikes it. An increase in the detector's reading when it is placed just beyond the red end of the spectrum shows the presence of the invisible radiation known as infrared radiation.

Change the detector to one which responds to ultraviolet light, i.e. either (i) a piece of photographic film which becomes blackened when exposed to ultraviolet light or (ii) a piece of card coated with a phosphor or fluorescent paint which glows when ultraviolet is absorbed. Take readings as you move the detector from the visible spectrum to just beyond the violet end.

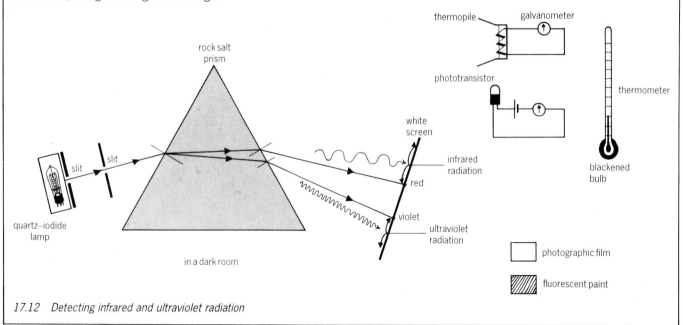

17.12   *Detecting infrared and ultraviolet radiation*

frequency than visible light and infrared a lower frequency. Since $c = f\lambda$, i.e. speed = frequency × wavelength, it follows that ultraviolet radiation has a shorter wavelength than visible light while the infrared wavelength is longer than that of visible light.

Visible light

A very narrow band of radiation of wavelength from about 7×10^{-7} m to 4×10^{-7} m, i.e. from red to violet, is known as the **visible spectrum**. It is produced by a flame or any incandescent object and can be detected by the human eye, photographic film, a light-dependent resistor or a photo-electric cell.

Infrared radiation

A band of radiation of wavelength from about 10^{-6} to 5×10^{-3} m characterised by warmth is known as the infrared region of the spectrum. This heat radiation is produced from hot bodies such as the Sun, electric fires and furnaces and can be detected by a thermopile, phototransistor, the blackened bulb of a sensitive thermometer or thermochromic (special heat-sensitive) paper.

Radio waves

Beyond the infrared region is a wide range of wavelengths from about 10^{-4} m to 5×10^{4} m known as **radio waves**. This region can be subdivided into particular types of wave, e.g. microwaves, radar and television waves. Radio waves are produced by electrical oscillations in circuits containing inductance and capacitance and can be detected by diodes fitted to similar tuned circuits in the receiver. Just as light waves can be totally internally reflected so also can radio (wireless) waves, e.g. by the Kennelly–Heaviside layer in the Earth's upper atmosphere. Radio waves can be reflected from this layer to reach places which, because of the Earth's curvature, would be out of reach for waves travelling directly from the transmitter. However, the shorter wavelength television waves are not totally internally reflected by the Kennelly–Heaviside layer and hence can only be relayed around the world by satellites. In fact all electromagnetic waves can experience total internal reflection in suitable circumstances.

Electric waves of very long wavelength, 5×10^{4} m to 10^{8} m or beyond, exist beyond the radio region of the electromagnetic spectrum, but these are beyond the scope of this book.

Ultraviolet radiation

At its name suggests, ultraviolet radiation is just beyond the violet end of the visible spectrum and has wavelengths in the range 5×10^{-7} m to 5×10^{-9} m. Notice that this overlaps the violet end of the visible spectrum. This is a common feature of the 'boundary'

between any pair of radiations, i.e. there is no sharp distinction between the radiations, as illustrated in the electromagnetic spectrum chart on p.218.

Ultraviolet radiation is produced by such objects as a carbon-arc lamp, electric spark, discharge tube, mercury vapour lamp, hot bodies and the Sun. The radiation can be detected by photographic film and by the fluorescence it causes in certain mineral salts. Ultraviolet radiation from the Sun causes sun-tanning of the skin (infrared radiation from the Sun causes the heating effect). Ultraviolet radiation is used in burglar alarms, automatic door openers and counters, for detecting real pearls and forged banknotes, for photofinishes in races and discriminating between the values of postage stamps which have been phosphor-coated.

Note Excessive ultraviolet radiation can be harmful to the eyes and the skin, so **take care** when using this radiation in the laboratory. This warning also applies to the two radiations, X-rays and gamma-rays, which are described below.

X-rays

X-rays have a wide range of wavelengths from about 5×10^{-8} m to 5×10^{-15} m and hence overlap into the ultraviolet region at one end and into the gamma-ray region at the other. They are produced when very fast-moving electrons are stopped by a heavy metal target. They can be detected by photographic plates and film, producing photo-electric effects on metals and ionisation of gases. X-rays are used in radiology, the science of applying X-rays to medicine to produce 'pictures' of internal organs in the body. They are also used to kill dangerous cells and tumours in the body but it should be noted that healthy cells are also killed when the dangerous radiation is used. X-rays can be used for detecting flaws or cracks in metal castings; the method relies on total internal reflection.

Figure 17.13 represents an X-ray tube in which electrons produced by thermionic emission at the

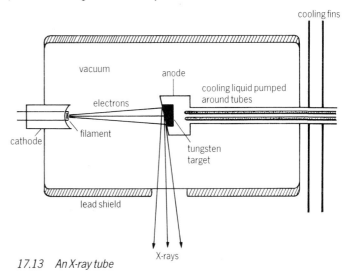

17.13   An X-ray tube

217

filament are accelerated to very high speed by a large potential difference between the anode and the cathode (several kilovolts to several hundred kilovolts). These high-energy electrons smash into the target metal (e.g. tungsten) releasing energy in the form of heat (internal energy), light and X-rays. The amount of heat energy produced is quite considerable and thus a cooling liquid (oil) has to be pumped through the anode to prevent it from melting. In addition, cooling fins of large surface area are fitted to help dissipate the heat to the surroundings. The temperature of the filament controls the number of electrons produced per second and hence the quantity of X-rays generated. The potential difference across the tube controls the frequency of the X-rays emitted and so is responsible for the penetrating power of the X-rays (the higher the potential difference the greater is the frequency of the X-rays produced and hence the greater their penetrating power). All but the most penetrating X-rays can be absorbed by a sheet of lead a few millimetres thick, hence the tube is surrounded by a lead shield for safety. X-rays emerge from a small 'window' in the lead shield.

Gamma rays

Gamma rays have a range of wavelengths from about 5×10^{-11} m to 10^{-15} m or below, and in terms of wavelengths overlap the X-ray region. These rays are emitted from *within* the nucleus of a radioactive nuclide, such as cobalt-60. They can be detected by a Geiger–Müller tube (p.387) and photographic plates or film. Gamma rays can be used to kill cancerous cells in humans but care is needed in their use because they also attack and kill healthy cells.

17.4 Properties of electromagnetic radiation

All forms of electromagnetic radiation have the following properties:

(a) they are all transverse waves travelling in free space at $c = 3 \times 10^8$ m s^{-1} and obey the inverse square law for intensity;

(b) the wave equation $c = f\lambda$ can be applied to any known wavelength (or frequency f) to determine its frequency f (or wavelength λ);

(c) they all, under suitable conditions, can be reflected, refracted and diffracted and exhibit the phenomenon of interference;

(d) they do not necessarily need a medium through which to travel and thus can travel in a vacuum;

(e) they can be plane polarised (this distinguishes them from longitudinal waves such as sound waves which cannot be polarised).

Investigation 17.4 To demonstrate polarisation

This simple demonstration of polarisation can be performed using two sheets of Polaroid or the 'lenses' from an old pair of Polaroid sunglasses. Observe light through one sheet of Polaroid; the light will not appear as bright (Fig. 17.14a). Place the second sheet of Polaroid between your eye and the first sheet so that the light is still visible. Slowly rotate the second sheet until it cuts off the light completely as shown in Fig. 17.14(b). Polaroid is a material which allows only vibrations in one plane to pass through it. When the Polaroids are 'crossed' as in Fig. 17.14(b) no vibration can pass through to the eye; hence the pair appear black.

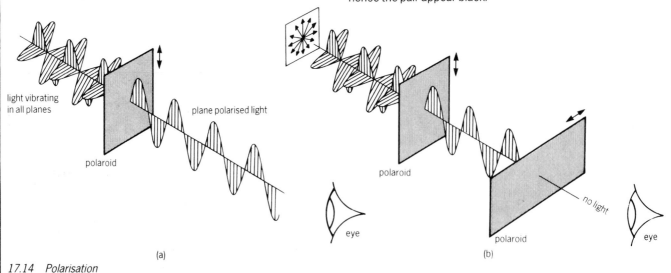

light vibrating in all planes

polaroid

plane polarised light

(a)

polaroid

polaroid

no light

eye

eye

(b)

17.14 Polarisation

Table 17.1 shows the complete electromagnetic spectrum with approximate values for the wavelengths and frequencies of the different radiations. Examples of ultimate source, production, detection and applications are given for each of the main classifications of the radiations.

wavelength λ/m	10^{-15} 10^{-14} 10^{-13} 10^{-12} 10^{-11} 10^{-10} 10^{-9} 10^{-8} 10^{-7} 10^{-6} 10^{-5} 10^{-4} 10^{-3} 10^{-2} 10^{-1} 10^{0} 10^{1} 10^{2} 10^{3} 10^{4} 10^{5} 10^{6} 10^{7} 10^{8}

γ-rays from cosmic rays	γ-rays from radioactive sources	ultra-violet	VIOLET visible RED	infra-red	radar and microwaves	radio	TV waves	radio waves	very long electronic waves	radiation

X-rays

frequency f/Hz	10^{23} 10^{22} 10^{21} 10^{20} 10^{19} 10^{18} 10^{17} 10^{16} 10^{15} 10^{14} 10^{13} 10^{12} 10^{11} 10^{10} 10^{9} 10^{8} 10^{7} 10^{6} 10^{5} 10^{4} 10^{3} 10^{2} 10^{1}

	γ-rays	X-rays	Ultra-violet	Visible	Infra-red	Radar and microwave	Radio
Ultimate source	Nuclear changes	Bombardment of heavy metals by very fast electrons	Movement of electrons in M, N, and O shells	Vibrations of electrons in outer orbit	Vibration and bending of molecules	Inversion and rotation of molecular arrangement	Motion of electrons and nuclei in magnetic and electric fields at right angles
Production	Cyclotron; Cobalt–60	X-ray tube; X-rays	Discharge tube; Carbon arc	Filament lamp; Discharge tubes; Lightning, flames	Electric fire; Heater	Klystron	Transistor circuits
Detection	Geiger tube	Photographic plate; Photo-electric effect	Fluorescence; Photo action; ZnS; Photo-voltaic cell	Eye, photo-cells, camera; Light-sensitive diode	Thermopile; Photo transistor	Wave guide tubes	Aerial and diodes; Earphone
Applications	Detecting flaws in metal castings; Sterilisation; Medicine, e.g. cancer treatment	Radiography; Radiology; Detecting flaws in metals; Diffraction to find crystal structure; Detection of art forgeries	Treatment of skin complaints; Killing bacteria; Fluorescent lighting; Burglar alarms; Automatic counting in industry	Observation of visible world, mainly by reflection; Photography; Splits into various colours	Cooking, heating, drying, e.g. paint; Infra-red photography; Photocopiers (thermal)	Radar communication; Microwave cooking	Communication and navigation

Table 17.1   The electromagnetic spectrum

Questions

Q1 A ray of white light is shone onto a glass prism. The light **cannot** be
A deviated. B dispersed. C focused.
D reflected. E refracted. *(L)*

Q2 In a dark room, light of a pure primary colour shines on to a surface painted with the colour complementary to that of the light. What will be seen by an observer looking at the surface?
A The primary colour
B The complementary colour
C A white surface
D A black surface
E A spectrum of colours *(L)*

Q3 A leaf which contains only a green pigment is illuminated with monochromatic red light. The leaf will appear to be
A black. B brown. C green.
D red. E yellow. *(L)*

Q4 Which one of the following examples of electromagnetic radiation has the shortest wavelength?
A Radio waves B Infrared C Ultraviolet
D Visible light E X-rays *(L & EAG)*

Q5 Draw a series of labelled diagrams to show what happens to a ray of white light when the following occur:
(i) refraction; (ii) critical angle; (iii) total internal reflection; (iv) deviation by a prism (v) dispersion; (vi) lateral displacement.
Light travels through air at 300 million $m\,s^{-1}$. On entering water it slows down to 225 million $m\,s^{-1}$. Calculate the refractive index of water. *(W)*

Q6 Describe how you would use a rectangular block of glass to determine the refractive index of the glass.
Given that the refractive index of the glass is 1.65, calculate the angle of refraction in the glass when a ray of light strikes one surface of the block at an angle of incidence of 60°.

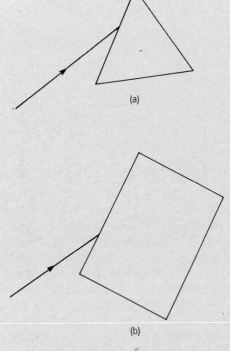

(a)

(b)

When a ray of white light is incident, as shown in diagram (a), on one face of a triangular glass prism, a spectrum is observed on a screen on the other side of the prism. Draw a labelled diagram to show the paths of the differently coloured rays which produce the spectrum observed on the screen; the position of the screen should be indicated. The triangular prism is replaced by a rectangular block of the same glass as shown in diagram (b). Suggest whether or not a spectrum will be observed in this case, giving reasons for your answer. *(C)*

Q7 (a) (i) Draw a ray diagram to show how a pure spectrum of white light can be projected onto a screen using a prism and any other necessary apparatus.

   (ii) Describe and explain the appearance of a red-coloured pen as it is moved through the white-light spectrum.

(b) If the screen of a working colour television set is closely observed it may be seen that it is made up of a lattice of regularly arranged minute spots of light. Each spot of light emits one of the three primary colours and the lattice of these coloured spots A, B and C is regularly arranged as in the diagram. Any colour can therefore be formed on the screen by various combinations of one, two or three spots emitting their individual colours.

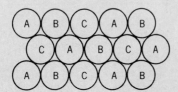

   (i) Name the three primary colours used in the screen lattice.

   (ii) Explain how the television screen can appear magenta using this lattice.

   (iii) Describe and account for the appearance of a yellow coloured screen when it is viewed through a red filter. *(L part question)*

Q8 (a) An optical system which transmits well into the ultraviolet and infrared regions of the spectrum is used to form the spectrum of a white-hot arc source on a screen. Draw a labelled diagram showing only this spectrum and indicate on it the approximate wavelength of each part that you name.

(b) What would you expect to observe if a thermopile with a blackened surface, connected to a suitable meter, were moved along the whole of the spectrum? Explain.

(c) What would you expect to observe if a strip of fluorescent material, which fluoresces green, were moved along the whole of this spectrum? Explain.

(d) Mention **one** property or effect shown by all these types of radiation which suggests that they are propagated as wave-motions and **one** property or effect which suggests that they carry energy in small packets (photons). *(O)*

Q9 List the principal regions of the complete electromagnetic spectrum, arranged in order of increasing wavelength. For each region, state a typical value of wavelength in metres. Describe (i) how a beam of ultraviolet radiation can be produced in the laboratory, (ii) how you would demonstrate that ultraviolet radiation can ionise air. Explain the ionisation process.

Calculate the wavelength of radio waves of frequency 1.2 MHz, taking the velocity of electromagnetic radiation to be $3 \times 10^8\,\mathrm{m\,s^{-1}}$.

Q10 Consider the following types of wave: infrared, ultraviolet, sound, X-rays, radio

   (i) Which of these is **not** part of the electromagnetic spectrum?

Of those that are electromagnetic,

   (ii) which has the shortest wavelengths,

   (iii) which has the lowest frequencies,

   (iv) which is unlikely to be detected by a photographic method,

   (v) what is significant about their speed? *(S part question)*

Q11 Radio transmission is possible with a certain spectrum of waves that travel through space at $3 \times 10^8\,\mathrm{m\,s^{-1}}$.

(a) Draw a diagram of the complete electromagnetic spectrum, labelling the various types of radiation.

(b) State two differences between radio waves and the other types of radiation in the electromagnetic spectrum.

(c) What is the importance of the ionosphere in radio-wave propagation?

(d) What is the frequency of the radio transmission on wavelength 1500 m? *(O)*

18 Lenses

18.1 Converging lenses

Lenses are usually made of glass or clear plastic. A **converging lens** is one which is thicker in the middle than at its edge. Figure 18.1 shows three shapes which act as converging lenses, i.e. they will converge (bring together) parallel rays of light passing through them.

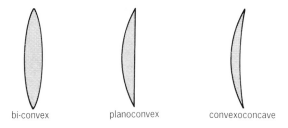

bi-convex   planoconvex   convexoconcave

18.1   Converging (convex) lenses

Focal length and focal plane

The line which passes symmetrically through the optical centre O of the lens is called the **principal axis** of the lens. All rays close to and parallel to the principal axis pass through a common point F on the axis called the **focal point**. The distance from the optical centre O of the lens to the focal point F is known as the **focal length** f of the lens. If parallel rays which are *not* parallel to the principal axis are incident on the lens these rays will also focus at one point F_1 which lies directly below F. A plane passing through F and F_1 is called the **focal plane** of the lens. Any parallel beam of rays incident on the lens will be refracted so as to form a point which lies on the focal plane. Lenses are used in many different kinds of instruments — cameras, telescopes, microscopes, binoculars etc. — and the focal length f of the lens is an important constant to know when deciding which lens to use in which instrument.

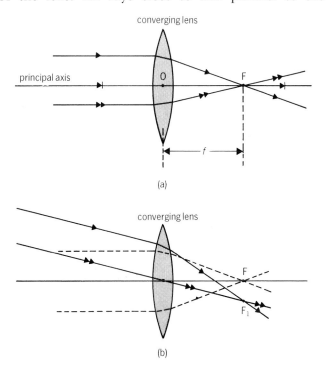

(a)

(b)

18.2   (a) Focal length and (b) focal plane of a converging lens

---

Investigation 18.1   To measure the focal length f of a converging lens

Sunlight coming from the Sun, 150 million kilometres away, arrives in parallel beams. Using the windows of the laboratory as an object, you can form a sharp, inverted image on a sheet of white card (acting as a screen) by adjusting the converging lens between the window and the screen (see Fig. 18.3).

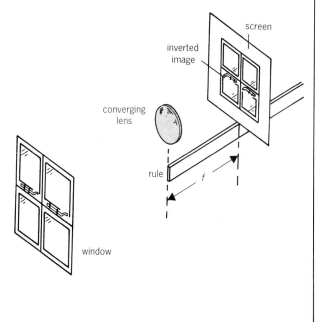

18.3   A rough determination of the focal length of a converging lens

---

Notice that the image formed on the screen is inverted in both the vertical and horizontal planes, and is real. If a 'distant' object is used in this experiment the light rays are almost parallel and, if a sharp image is formed on the screen, the distance from the lens to the screen is very nearly equal to the focal length of the lens. For example, if the object distance (the distance from the lens to the object) is ten times the image distance (the distance from the lens to the real image) then the image distance will be about 11% greater than the focal length. However, if the object distance is one hundred times the image distance then the image distance is only 1% greater than the focal length. Therefore a converging lens of focal length 10 cm will focus the image of an object 10 metre away at a distance of 10.1 cm from the lens. The greater the distance between the object and the lens, the more nearly the image forms on the focal plane of the lens, hence the distance between the lens and the real inverted image on the screen is closer in value to the focal length of the lens.

Investigation 18.2   To determine the focal length *f* of a converging lens by the plane mirror method

From the principle of reversibility of light, a point source of light placed at the focal point F of a converging lens will give a parallel beam of light emerging from the lens. If a plane mirror is placed perpendicular to the parallel beam it will reflect the beam through the lens and hence form an image at F coincident with the object (Fig. 18.4).

Set up an illuminated object, a converging lens in a holder and a plane mirror as shown in Fig. 18.5(a). Move the object so that a sharp, real, inverted image is formed alongside the object. Figure 18.5(b) shows the formation of an image I_1 of an object O_1 *not* on the principal axis. When the image is sharply focussed measure, with a metre rule, the distance from the centre of the lens to the image. Repeat the focussing procedure three more times to obtain four values for the focal length, and use them to calculate the average value of *f*. It may be necessary to adjust the lens in its holder or the alignment of the plane mirror, or both, to achieve the correct positioning of the image.

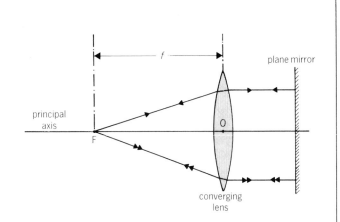

18.4   *Finding the focal length of a converging lens using a plane mirror*

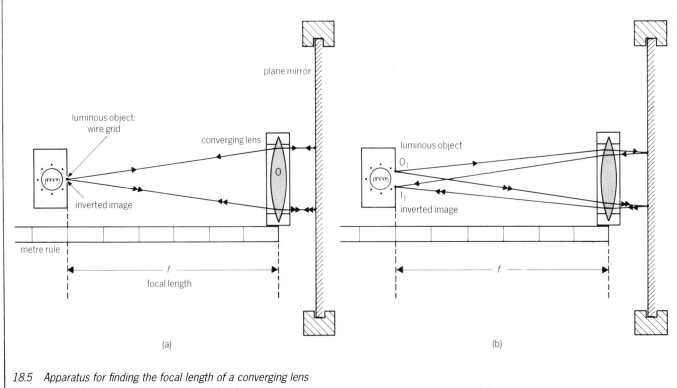

18.5   *Apparatus for finding the focal length of a converging lens*

222

Investigation 18.3 To determine the focal length f of a converging lens by the object and image distance method

When a real, inverted image is focussed onto a screen using a converging lens the relationship between the object distance u, the image distance v and the focal length f is

$$\frac{1}{u} + \frac{1}{v} = \frac{1}{f}$$

Set up an illuminated object, a converging lens in a holder and a white screen as shown in Fig. 18.6(a). A real image can be produced only if the object distance u is greater than the focal length distance f. Therefore, set the object distance u at some suitable (large) value such as 80 cm to be reasonably sure of focussing a real image. It may be necessary to adjust the lens in its holder until a circular patch of light is seen on the screen. Then move the screen until a sharp, inverted image is focussed on the screen. An illuminated wire grid is a suitable object which can be focussed to give a sharp image. Figure 18.6(b) shows the formation of an image I_1 of an object O_1 not on the principal axis.

Using a metre rule, measure the object distance u from the centre of the lens to the object and the image distance v from the centre of the lens to the sharp image formed on the screen. Record the values of u and v in a table of results like Table 18.1. Repeat the experiment for other values of u (say 70 cm, 60 cm, 50 cm and 40 cm) and determine the corresponding values of v. Taking each pair of values of u and v, calculate the focal length f using $1/u + 1/v = 1/f$. Hence calculate the average value of the focal length f.

Table 18.1   Table of results for investigation 18.3

Object distance u/cm	Image distance v/cm	Focal length f/cm
80		
70		
60		
50		
40		

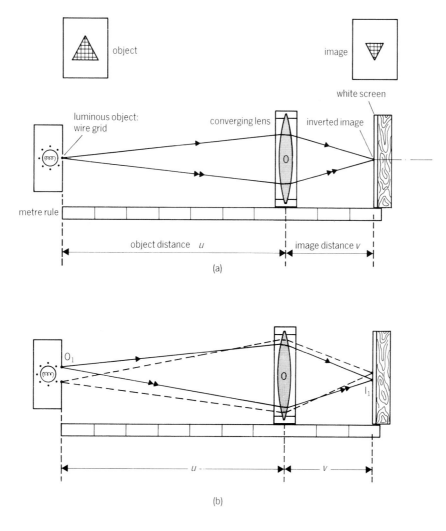

18.6   *Finding the focal length of a converging lens by object and image distance method*

Example

A typical calculation of f using the **Real is Positive** sign convention.

$u = +80$ cm $v = +26\frac{2}{3}$ cm $f = ?$

$$\frac{1}{u} + \frac{1}{v} = \frac{1}{f}$$

$$\frac{1}{80} + \frac{3}{80} = \frac{1}{f}$$

$$\frac{4}{80} = \frac{1}{f}$$

$$4f = 80$$

$$f = +20 \text{ cm}$$

Example

An alternative method of calculating f from the results is to use reciprocal tables.

$u = 40$ cm $v = +40$ cm $f = ?$ 'real is positive'

$$\frac{1}{u} + \frac{1}{v} = \frac{1}{f}$$

$$\frac{1}{40} + \frac{1}{40} = \frac{1}{f}$$

$$0.0250 + 0.0250 = \frac{1}{f}$$

$$0.05 = \frac{1}{f}$$

$$f = \frac{1}{0.05}$$

$$f = +20 \text{ cm}$$

Note Whenever the formula $1/u + 1/v = 1/f$ is used the sign convention should be stated as different conventions appear in other textbooks.

18.2   Linear magnification

Linear magnification m is defined as **the ratio of the size (height) of the image to the size (height) of the object**:

$$m = \frac{\text{size of image}}{\text{size of object}}$$

Linear magnification m can have a value less than 1 when the image is diminished, equal to 1 when the object and image are the same size or greater than 1 when the image is magnified. Using the apparatus shown in Fig. 18.6(a), the size of the image and the object can be measured along with the image distance v and the object distance u. The measurement of the

size of the image can be simplified by using graph paper with 1 mm squares as the screen on which to focus the image. It is helpful to choose object distances which lie in the range f–$2f$ so that real enlarged images are formed on the screen.

Investigation 18.4   To verify that the ratio of object to image equals the ratio of object distance to image distance

Set up the apparatus as in Fig. 18.6(a) and adjust the object distance u to $2f$. Move the screen until a sharp inverted image is focussed on it. With vernier callipers measure the height h_1 of the image and the height h_2 of the object. Alternatively use the mm graph paper to measure h_1. Also measure the image distance v and the object distance u using a metre rule. The measurements should be repeated several times for different distances of u and the results entered in a table like Table 18.2. Within the limits of experimental error, it should be found that $m = h_1/h_2 = v/u$.

Note It is important to use a luminous object such as a brightly illuminated wire grid so that the image can be sharply focussed, thus the sizes of the object and image can be measured accurately.

Table 18.2   Table of results for investigation 18.4

Size of image h_1/cm	Size of object h_2/cm	$m = h_1/h_2$	Image distance v/cm	Object distance u/cm	v/u

---

It is interesting to repeat this experiment with half of the lens covered with masking tape. If the same object and image distances are used, the sizes of the images are also unchanged. The only difference is that the images are less bright because only half of the lens is collecting and focussing the light from the object grid. The focal length f of the lens has not been altered even though its aperture has been reduced by half.

Ray construction diagrams

Any ray of light parallel to the principal axis passes through the focal point F after refraction by the lens. Another important set of rays passes through the optical centre O; these pass, undeviated, straight through the lens. If a ray from each of these sets is drawn from a point on an 'object' standing perpendicular to the principal axis then the intersection of the two emerging rays gives the position of the corresponding point on the image. The image will also be perpendicular to the principal axis.

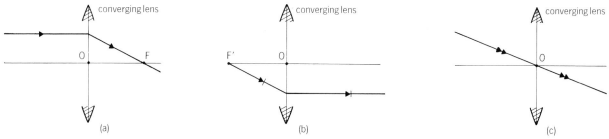

18.7   Construction rays

Schematic diagrams, called **ray construction diagrams**, can be used to illustrate the formation of an image when light rays pass through a converging lens and are received by the eye or, in the case of real images, on a screen. Two main construction rays are used in these diagrams. In Fig. 18.7(a) a ray parallel to the principal axis is refracted through the focal point F. In Fig. 18.7(b) a ray passing through F' (OF = OF') is refracted so as to emerge parallel to the principal axis; this ray is the same as in Fig. 18.7(a) because of

the Principle of Reversibility of Light. In Fig. 18.7(c) the ray passing through the optical centre O of the lens emerges undeviated.

If you draw two construction rays from a point on the top of an object standing perpendicular to the principal axis, the point of intersection of these two rays after refraction locates the position of the 'top' of the image. Since the object is perpendicular to the principal axis the image will also lie perpendicular to the axis. In Fig. 18.8 the images are constructed by

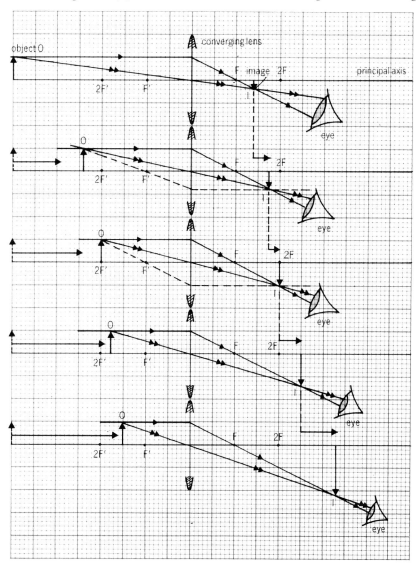

18.8   Images seen in a converging lens for different object positions

dropping a perpendicular from the point of intersection of the two refracted rays onto the principal axis. When a scale diagram is drawn the image represents the size and position of the image in relation to the object. As the object moves closer to the lens the image moves away from the lens and increases in size from a diminished image near the focal point to magnified images beyond 2F.

When the object reaches the focal point F' the emergent rays are parallel and two images are formed: one at minus infinity which is upright and virtual and can be seen by the eye and the other which is real and at plus infinity but cannot be seen. Figure 18.9(a) shows the parallel emergent rays, apparently coming from minus infinity; the lens in the eye is still able to form an image on the retina.

If the object is moved closer to the lens than the point F' the two rays which emerge are diverging (see Fig. 18.9b). While these diverging rays do not form a real image on a screen the human eye can form an image using this light. The two rays appear to be diverging from a point X, located by producing the rays backwards, as dotted lines, until they intersect at X. The virtual, erect image is represented by a dotted line to emphasise its non-real nature. A converging lens used in this way is acting as a magnifying lens and is sometimes known as a **simple microscope.**

If an object is placed between F' and 2F' (OF' = OF) a real, inverted, magnified image can be shown to be formed at I on a ray construction diagram (Fig. 18.10). The two shaded triangles in this diagram are similar ($\angle ACO = \angle OIB = 90°$, $\angle AOC = \angle IOB$ opposite angles). By proportion $h_2/v = h_1/u$ or $h_2/h_1 = v/u$. However $m = h_2/h_1$, hence m is equivalent to v/u. When performing calculations involving magnification it is important that you recall

$$m = \frac{h_2}{h_1} \equiv \frac{v}{u}$$

However, you must remember that the definition of linear magnification m is size of image divided by size of object.

Example

An image formed on a screen is three times the size of the object. The object and screen are 80 cm apart when the image is sharply focussed. State (a) which type of lens is used and (b) calculate its focal length.

(a) A converging lens is used; it is the only lens which will give a real, magnified image. The image must be real because the rays of light intersect at the image and so it can be formed on the screen.
Note At this level all 'objects' are assumed to be real.

(b) $m = +3 \quad u + v = 80$

$$m \equiv \frac{v}{u}$$

Hence
$$+3 = \frac{v}{u}$$

$$+3u = v$$
$$u + 3u = 80 \qquad \text{(substitute for } v\text{)}$$
$$4u = 80$$
$$u = +20 \text{ cm and } v = 3 \times u$$
$$= 3 \times 20$$
$$= +60 \text{ cm}$$

$u = +20 \text{ cm} \quad v = +60 \text{ cm} \quad f = ? \text{ cm}$

$$\frac{1}{u} + \frac{1}{v} = \frac{1}{f}$$
$$\frac{1}{20} + \frac{1}{60} = \frac{1}{f}$$
$$\frac{3+1}{60} = \frac{1}{f}$$
$$\frac{4}{60} = \frac{1}{f}$$
$$4f = 60$$
$$f = \frac{60}{4} = +15 \text{ cm}$$

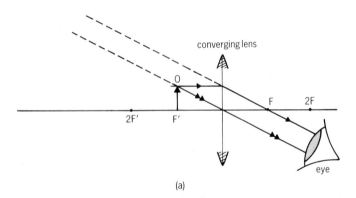

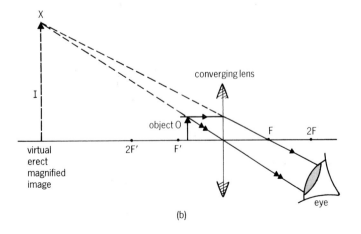

18.9 *Simple microscope: virtual, erect and magnified image*

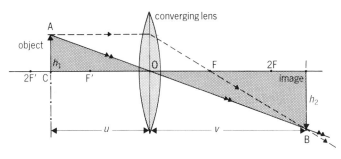

18.10   Linear magnification

Long sight

A practical use of a converging lens is in the correction of the defect of vision known as long sight. A person who is long-sighted is one who can see distant objects clearly but for whom objects at a short distance are not clear. Figure 18.11 shows how the lens in a long-sighted eye can focus light from a 'distant' object onto the retina of the eye but that light from a 'near' object

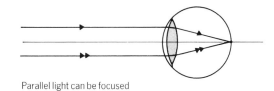

Parallel light can be focused

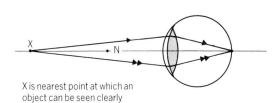

X is nearest point at which an object can be seen clearly

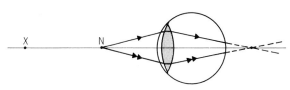

Objects between X and the normal near point N cannot be focused

18.11   Long sight

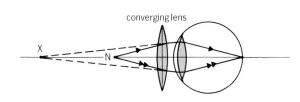

18.12   The correction of long sight: light from N is refracted by the lens so that it appears to come from X

would be focussed at a point behind the retina. This means the 'defective' eye can cope with diverging light of a certain angular width, but not if the divergence is too great.

By selecting a converging lens of suitable focal length and placing this close to the eye the widely diverging cone can be refracted so that it appears to come from a point where the eye can just cope with the divergent beam (see Fig. 18.12). The eye can now see clearly objects from N, the near point for normal vision 25 cm from the eye, to infinity when using the converging lens. An optician measures the power (strength) of lenses in **dioptres**. Dioptre d is determined from $d = 100/f$ where f = focal length of the lens in centimetres or from $d = 1/f$ (f is in metres). A lens of $+2$ dioptres is a converging (positive) lens of 50 cm (0.5 m) focal length. (**Note**   The dioptre is *not* an SI unit.)

18.3   Diverging lenses

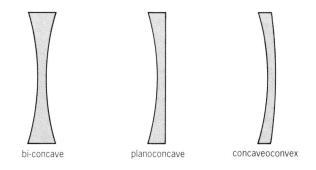

18.13   Diverging (concave) lenses

A **diverging lens** is one which is thinner in the middle than it is at its edge. Figure 18.13 shows three shapes which all act as diverging lenses, i.e. they diverge (spread out) parallel rays of light that pass through the lens (see Fig. 18.14). All images of real objects seen through a diverging lens will appear upright, virtual and diminished.

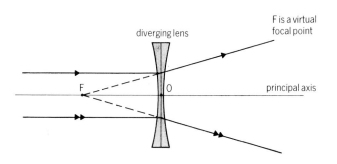

18.14   Virtual focal point of a diverging lens

227

Short sight

One of the main practical uses of a diverging lens is in the correction of the defect of vision known as short sight. A short-sighted person is one who can only focus clearly on objects very close to the eye (usually 1 metre or less). Figure 18.15 shows how the lens in an eye can focus light from a 'near' object onto the retina of the eye but cannot focus parallel light from a distant object onto the retina. This parallel light is brought to a focus in front of the retina, so the retina receives a blurred image. This means that the 'defective' eye can only cope with a rather widely divergent beam of light. By selecting a diverging lens of suitable focal length and placing this close to the eye the parallel light can be refracted so as to appear to come from a point where the eye can cope with the divergent beam (see Fig. 18.15).

The concavoconvex diverging lens (see Fig. 18.13) is used in the correction of short sight because this shape has a better appearance and gives better transmission of light than the other two. The short-sighted eye can see clearly objects from N, the normal near point at 25 cm, to infinity when using the diverging lens. An optician measures the strength of these lenses in dioptres and these would be quoted as negative values. For example, a lens power −1 dioptre is a diverging lens of focal length 1 m.

Note Using the real is positive sign convention, the focal length of a diverging lens is negative.

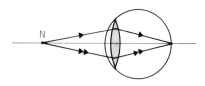

'Near' object seen clearly

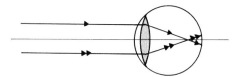

Object between the near point and
infinity cannot be focussed

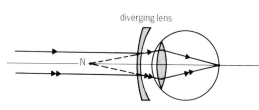

Parallel light is refracted by the lens so that
it appears to come from N

18.15   Short sight and its correction

Questions

Questions 1–4   The following are descriptions of five kinds of optical image:

    A diminished and virtual
    B enlarged and real
    C enlarged and upright
    D real and inverted
    E virtual and the same size

Which one of these describes the image formed

Q1 on the retina of the eye?
Q2 by a magnifying glass when used to read a newspaper?
Q3 by a convex driving mirror on a car?
Q4 when a camera is used to photograph a distant object?   *(L)*

Q5 If an object is placed 21 cm from a converging lens the image formed is slightly smaller than the object. If the object is placed 19 cm from the lens the image formed is slightly larger than the object. The approximate focal length of the lens is

    A 5 cm   **B** 10 cm   **C** 18 cm
    D 20 cm   **E** 22 cm   *(L)*

Q6 (a) Draw a ray diagram to show what is meant by the *principal focal point (focus)* of a convex (converging) lens. On your diagram indicate the *focal length* of the lens.

(b) Describe an experiment to measure as accurately as possible the focal length of a convex (converging) lens. Your account should include
    (i)   a ray diagram;
    (ii) a statement about the measurements you would make;
    (iii) an explanation of how the final result would be obtained from your measurements.

(c) Draw **two** ray diagrams, **one** for each case, showing how a single convex (converging) lens could be used with a real object to produce
    (i)   a real diminished image;
    (ii) a virtual magnified image.
In each case, the position of the principal focus should be clearly marked. Name **two** practical devices, **one** for each case, in which a convex (converging) lens is used in these two ways.   *(JMB)*

Q7 What is meant by the term *focal length* as applied to a converging lens? How would you find this quantity for a given converging lens by experiment?

A camera fitted with a lens of focal length 50 mm is being used to photograph a flower that is 5 cm across. The flower is placed 20 cm in front of the camera lens. At what distance from the film should the lens be adjusted to obtain a sharp image of the flower?

What would be the diameter of the image of the flower on the film? *(C)*

Q8 (a) Draw a labelled ray diagram to show how a converging lens produces a real image of a *distant* object.

(b) Describe and explain, with the aid of diagrams, how adjustment is made to bring near and distant objects into focus in a camera and by the human eye (details of the anatomical structure are **not** required).

(c) Describe and explain **two ways** in which camera setting can be adjusted to take account of an increase in the brightness of the scene to be photographed.

How does the eye adjust to take account of an increase in brightness?

(d) The lens of a camera is replaced by a piece of metal with a pinhole in it. Is it now necessary to make any adjustment to obtain a clear picture on the film to take account of the distance of the object from the camera? *(O & C)*

Q9 (a) Explain, or show by a diagram, what is meant by the *principal focus* and the *focal length* of a converging lens.

Determine, graphically or otherwise, how far an object must be placed in front of a converging lens of focal length 10 cm in order to produce an erect (upright) image of linear magnification 4.

(b) Describe how you could demonstrate that white light is composed of a number of colours. *(L part question)*

Q10 (a) A small source of light (e.g. illuminated cross wires) is set up on the axis of a converging lens. A plane mirror is placed behind the lens at right angles to the lens axis so that light is reflected back through the lens. For one position of the lens, relative to the object, a clear image appears at the side of the object. Draw a ray diagram to explain this. What is significant about the distance between lens and object in this position? Does the distance between lens and mirror matter? Give a reason.

(b) Describe the essential differences between the focusing action of the lens in the eye and that in a simple camera. *(S part question)*

Q11 (a) With the aid of a diagram, give an account of the eye as an optical instrument. What determines the apparent size of an object that is seen?

(b) Draw a diagram to show how a converging lens held close to the eye acts as a simple magnifying glass. Why

is it usual to choose a lens of short focal length for this purpose rather than one of long focal length?

(c) A thin converging lens of focal length 30 cm is used to form a real image on a screen 90 cm from the lens. **Either**, find, by graphical construction, the object distance from the lens and the magnification, and explain your construction. **Or**, calculate the value of the object distance from the lens and the magnification using the appropriate formulae, and draw a diagram (not necessarily to scale) showing how the image is formed. *(O)*

Q12 An object 2 cm tall is placed on the axis of a converging lens of focal length 5 cm at a distance of 3 cm from the optical centre of the lens. Draw a ray diagram to show how the image is formed and observed. Find also the position and height of the image.

Without drawing further ray diagrams, state the nature and position of the image, saying also whether it is large or small, when the object is at a distance from the lens of (a) 5.5 cm, (b) 10 m. (N.B. Exact numerical answers are not required.)

State a practical application of the use of such a lens with the object in each of positions (a) and (b). *(S)*

Q13 An object 3 cm high is placed 15 cm in front of a converging lens of focal length 6 cm. It is perpendicular to the principal axis of the lens. Determine the position, height and character of the image.

Q14 (a) Describe fully, showing the arrangement used, an accurate method of finding the focal length of a converging (convex) lens.

(b) Explain what is meant by a virtual image. Show by means of a ray diagram how a lens can produce such an image. State a use for the arrangement you describe.

(c) Explain what is meant by a long-sighted eye and show how a suitable lens can correct this defect. *(L)*

Q15 (a) Give a ray diagram to show the action of a simple magnifying glass. Name the type of lens used and state fully the nature of the image.

(b) Explain, with diagrams, how the human eye can produce clear images for object at different distances.

With the aid of a diagram explain the use of a diverging lens in correcting a named eye defect.

(L part question)

Q16 Explain what is meant by the *principal focus and focal length* of a converging lens. If you were given such a lens, describe how you would make a reliable experimental determination of its focal length.

Name the defect of vision which can be corrected by this type of lens, and show clearly by a ray diagram how the lens corrects the defect.

Explain clearly why a person who has lost the sight of one eye is at a disadvantage compared with the normal person who has two good eyes. *(L)*

19 Optical instruments

19.1 The periscope

The periscope is used to raise the line of sight of the observer. It is useful for 'seeing' over the crowds at race meetings and golf tournaments! This instrument consists of two plane mirrors or, preferably, two right-angled isosceles prisms arranged in some form of tube or holder (see Fig. 19.1). The reflecting surfaces of the mirrors and the prisms are arranged so that they are parallel to each other and at 45 ° to the vertical. Light received at the top plane mirror (or prism) is incident at 45 ° and therefore also reflected at 45 °, hence is deviated by 90 ° in a clockwise direction. The light is then deviated by 90 ° in an anticlockwise direction at the lower plane mirror (or prism). Thus the image is upright, virtual and appears at a lower level than the object. The first reflection produces lateral inversion but the second reflection compensates for this.

The disadvantages of using mirrors in periscopes are that they easily become tarnished or the silvering peels off. Therefore prisms are used in precision instruments, such as the periscope of a submarine (Fig. 19.1b). Glass prisms are not affected by the weather and are less likely to be damaged. Moreover, the light

is *totally* internally reflected by the prism, whereas there is about a 9% loss of light on each reflection by a mirror.

19.2 Angular magnification

Microscopes and telescopes are optical instruments used to magnify the image seen by the eye. The type of magnification they produce is called **angular magnification** and is different from linear magnification. To understand angular magnification you must first understand how the size of the image formed on the retina of the eye varies with the distance of the object from the eye. Figure 19.2 shows the same object at different distances from the eye. Bringing the object closer to the eye makes the image appear larger because the angle α it subtends at the eye has been increased. However, there is a limit to how close the object may be to the eye and the image still be clearly seen. The limiting distance is known as the **least distance of distinct vision** D, and is taken as 25 cm for the normal eye (see Fig. 19.3a). With the object at the near point N, a distance D from the eyeball, the size of

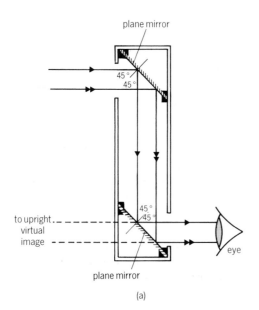

(a)

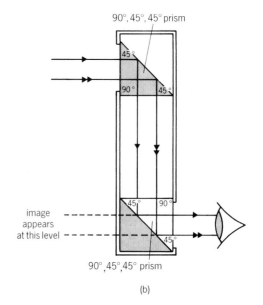

(b)

19.1   (a) Mirror and (b) prism periscopes

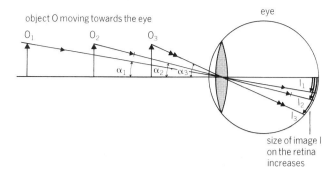

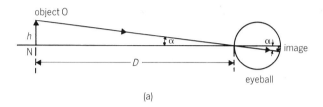

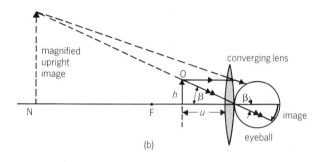

19.2 Angular magnification

19.3 Angular magnification of a simple microscope

For a lens of focal length $f = 5$ cm, $v = 25$ cm, so $1/u + \frac{1}{25} = \frac{1}{5}$, i.e. $1/u = \frac{1}{5} + \frac{1}{25} = \frac{6}{25}$; therefore $M = 25 \times \frac{6}{25} = 6$. If the object O is moved back to the focal point F of the lens the angle β will reduce slightly but the light emerging from the lens gives an image at infinity. This produces least strain on the eye. For the image at infinity, $u = f$ the focal length of the lens and hence $M = D/f$. For the 5 cm lens, $M = 25$ cm/5 cm = 5. The difference in magnification is hardly noticeable but the effects of the eye strain over long periods of viewing could be considerable. Therefore a person will often view the final image at infinity because it is more comfortable.

19.3 Compound microscope

A converging lens can produce magnified images in two ways:

(a) with the object inside (or at) the focal length of the lens resulting in an upright, virtual image as in the simple microscope,

(b) when the object is between the focal length f and 2f from the lens, when the image is inverted, real and magnified.

By combining these two effects an even greater magnification of the final image can be achieved.

Figure 19.4 shows a microscope made from two converging lenses. The object is placed between F_o and $2F_o$ for the short-focus **objective lens**. A real, inverted magnified image is formed at I_1 and this image is viewed through a very short-focal-length **eyepiece lens**. Note the lenses are arranged so that the image at I_1 is inside the focal point F_e of the eyepiece lens. Hence the magnified image at I_1 is further magnified by the eyepiece lens acting as a simple microscope. The object, or slide, is normally inserted upside down into the microscope so that the final image appears the right way up.

If a microscope is too long the specimen is not within handling distance while it is being viewed. Since the minimum distance between an object and a real image is four times the focal length f_o of the lens, the focal length of the objective lens is usually about 5 cm or less. This can give a linear magnification m_o of the objective lens of about $10\times$. The eyepiece lens has a short focal length with a magnification m_e of about $25\times$. Clearly the total magnification $M = m_o \times m_e$, the product of the individual linear magnifications. Therefore it is not unusual to have a magnification $M = 10 \times 25 = 250\times$ for a microscope.

the focussed image on the retina will be largest for the unaided eye. If the object is moved any closer to the unaided eye the image becomes blurred. If, however, a converging lens is placed close to the eye (Fig. 19.3b) then the object can be moved nearer to the eye than N and the light coming from the lens will still be focussed into a clear image on the retina of the eye. This image on the retina is larger than the largest image that could be seen with the unaided eye. The converging lens is acting as a simple microscope or magnifying glass.

Note When viewing an object at the near point N, the eye is fully accommodated and is under most strain.

Angular magnification $M = \beta/\alpha$ is defined as **the ratio of the angles subtended at the eye by the image at D and the object at D**. From Fig. 19.3(b), $\alpha = h/D$ and $\beta = h/u$ hence

$$M = \beta/\alpha$$
$$= \frac{h}{u} \div \frac{h}{D} = \frac{h}{u} \times \frac{D}{h}$$
$$= \frac{D}{u}$$

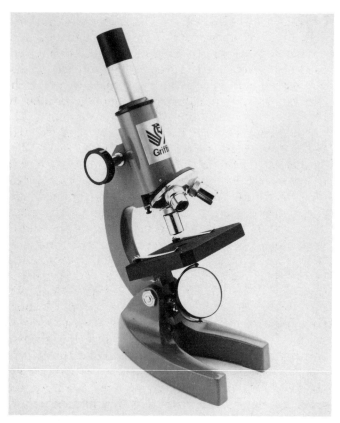

19.4 *Compound microscope*

19.4 Telescopes

Telescopes are used to magnify the images of distant objects. Very distant objects appear to be very small because of the very small angle they subtend at the unaided eye. There are two main types of telescope: refracting telescopes employing lenses and reflecting telescopes employing mirrors.

Refracting telescopes

In the refracting telescope two or more lenses are used. A simple astronomical telescope can be made from two converging lenses of different focal lengths. The objective lens is of long focal length f_o while the eyepiece lens is of short focal length f_e. The angular magnification M produced by this telescope in normal adjustment is $M = f_o/f_e$ and hence is greatest when f_o is largest and f_e is smallest. However, there are practical limitations on how short the focal length f_e can be made without major distortion of the image. The objective lens should have as large an aperture (diameter) as possible in order to collect the maximum amount of light. This makes the objective lens very heavy, very expensive and difficult to grind with precision and accuracy.

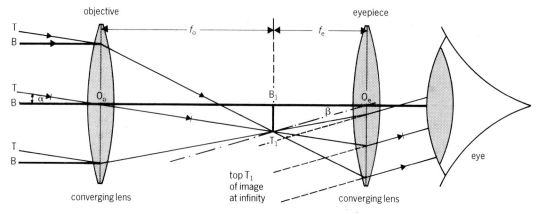

19.5 *Astronomical telescope*

Note Angular magnification is the comparison of the size of the image seen with the optical instrument to the size of the object seen with the naked eye. Angular magnification is the ratio of the angles β/α (Fig. 19.5), i.e. the angle subtended at the eye with the instrument compared to the angle subtended at the objective lens (strictly at the unaided eye, but the length of the telescope is insignificant compared with the object distance).

Figure 19.5 shows a ray diagram illustrating the formation of an image in an astronomical telescope. Two sets of parallel rays from the top T and bottom B of a star or planet are included. These rays will form an inverted, real image B_1T_1 at the focal plane of the objective lens. This real image is viewed through the short focal length eyepiece lens acting as a magnifying glass. When the image is at the focal plane of the eyepiece lens all the rays emerging from the eyepiece are parallel to the chain-dotted line T_1O_e, i.e. the final image is at infinity, causing minimum eye strain. This final image is inverted but this does not matter when the object is the Moon etc. An extra converging lens could be used to re-invert the first image so that the final image is upright, but it would increase the length of the telescope by four times the focal length of the inverting lens. The distance between the two lenses is normally equal to the sum of the focal lengths of the objective and eyepiece lenses $(f_o + f_e)$. You could make a model telescope with an objective lens of focal length $f_o = 30$ cm and an eyepiece lens of focal length $f_e = 2.5$ cm set 32.5 cm apart. The refractor with the largest objective aperture (100 cm) is in Wisconsin, USA.

Galilean telescope and prismatic binoculars

A final erect image can be formed using a Galilean telescope (sometimes known as opera glasses). In this type of telescope the eyepiece is a diverging lens (see Fig. 19.6). As before, a converging lens of long focal length is used as the objective lens. This would form a real, inverted image at I if the light had not been intercepted by the short-focal-length diverging lens used as the eyepiece. The eyepiece lens is placed so that the distance O_eI is equal to the focal length f_e of the eyepiece lens. Hence the rays all emerge parallel to O_eX, giving a final upright image at infinity. The distance between the two lenses is numerically equal to the difference in their focal lengths $(f_o - f_e)$. The angular magnification $M = \beta/\alpha$ is also equivalent to f_o/f_e as before. By using a diverging eyepiece an upright image with no loss in magnification is obtained from a telescope that is shorter in length. The main disadvantage of this arrangement is that the field of view is very small, like looking down a hollow tube.

One method of converting an astronomical telescope (inverted image) into a terrestrial one (upright image) by using an additional lens was mentioned opposite. An alternative and much more practical solution is to use two isosceles right-angled prisms to re-invert the image that is formed by the two converging lenses. In prismatic binoculars the prisms are placed at right angles to each other with the longer faces towards each other (see Fig. 19.7 overleaf). The image formed by the converging objective lens is both inverted and laterally inverted. One prism re-inverts the image to make it the right way up for viewing through the eyepiece used as a simple microscope. The other prism corrects the lateral inversion.

Some of the advantages of binoculars over other telescopes include:

(a) the final image is upright;
(b) the image is the right way round;
(c) the short compact length (introducing prisms reduces the overall length by two-thirds);
(d) two telescopes placed side by side (one for each eye) enable both depth and perspective to be seen;
(e) they have a wide field of view.

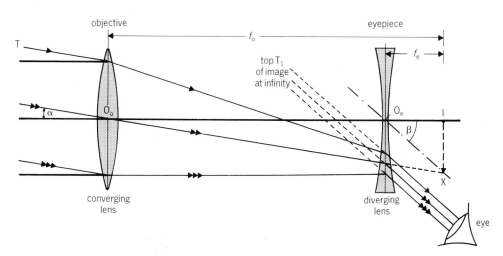

19.6   Galilean telescope (opera glasses)

Reflecting telescopes

The second type of telescope is the reflecting telescope. An astronomical reflecting telescope consists of a large concave (converging) mirror set in a frame with a small plane mirror positioned slightly nearer to the concave mirror than the focal point F. A convex (converging) lens is positioned to view the image seen in the plane mirror. The action of an astronomical reflector is shown in Fig. 19.8. The concave mirror used in an astronomical telescope is large so that it collects as much light as possible. It is usually 'silvered' on the *front* surface of the glass base (unlike laboratory mirrors which are normally silvered on the back surface) to cut out the internal reflection and refraction which occurs when the back of the mirror is silvered. It is also easier to 'work' the shape of the mirror and then to apply an even layer of aluminium. Why is a mirror used instead of a lens? Mirrors are easier and cheaper to produce than lenses and are less liable to flaws or imperfections. The mirror is lighter than an equivalent lens and is therefore easier to suspend. In fact, the largest astronomical telescopes are of the reflector type. One of the best known of these instruments is the 500 cm reflecting telescope at Mount Palomar, USA, shown in Fig. 19.9.

Radio telescope Another kind of telescope which collects energy and then reflects this energy to a focal point is the radio telescope (Fig. 19.10). It is *not* an optical instrument. Instead of visible light, weak radio signals are reflected by a parabolic-shaped 'dish' to a sensitive antenna at the principal focus of the 'dish'. Radio telescopes are used for detecting radiation from outer space as well as for sending and receiving signals from spacecraft. Radio astronomy plays an important part in helping scientists to unravel the mysteries of the universe.

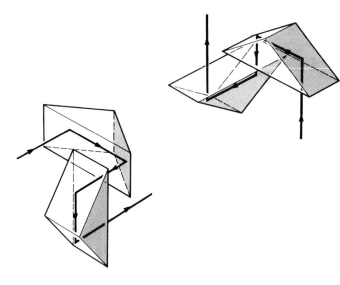

19.7   Prism binoculars

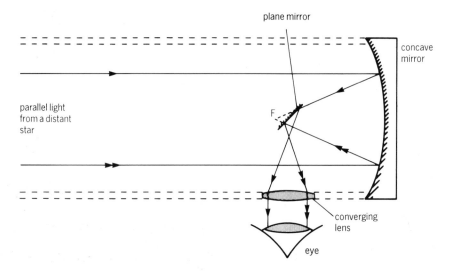

19.8   Reflecting astronomical telescope

234

19.9   Mount Palomar reflecting telescope

19.10   Radio telescope

19.5 The camera

The camera is made from a converging lens mounted in a rotatable ring which can be moved towards or away from a light-sensitive film (see Fig. 19.11a). The lens is positioned so that a sharp image is produced on the film, depending on the distance of the object from the lens. A variable-speed shutter behind the lens allows the light to enter the camera for the amount of time needed to expose the film correctly. If a fast-moving object is to be photographed then the fastest shutter speed should be used to prevent the photograph from being blurred. Behind the shutter there is a variable-diameter aperture or stop which controls the amount of light which can pass through the lens and on to the film. The aperture also controls the depth of field which can be focussed by the camera. A narrow aperture gives a large depth of field, while a wide aperture gives a small depth of field around a given object. Objects outside this narrow range are out

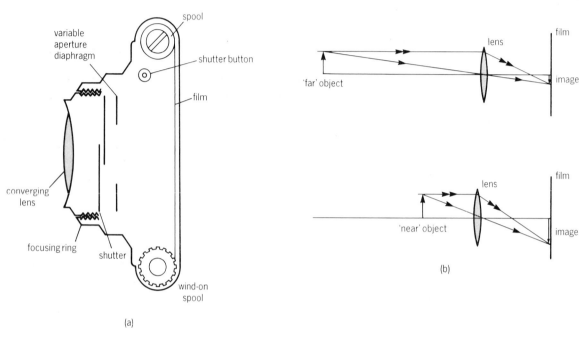

(a)

(b)

19.11   Lens camera

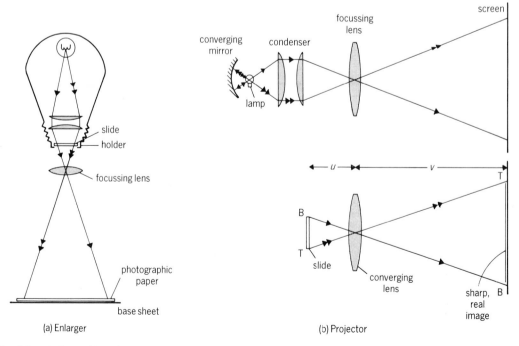

(a) Enlarger

(b) Projector

19.12   Principle of the photographic enlarger and slide projector of focus. The converging lens is positioned so that a real, inverted image is formed on the film; to take distant objects the lens is moved closer to the film and for near objects the lens is moved away from the film (Fig. 19.11b).

When the film is developed it can be printed on paper using an enlarger or on a transparent material to produce a slide.

19.6 Projectors and enlargers

The principles of the enlarger and the projector are shown in Fig. 19.12. To print a photograph, the negative film is placed 'upside down and back to front' in the slide holder in the enlarger (see Fig. 19.12a). A powerful lamp and two lenses are arranged to give even illumination of the frame of the film. First the image of the frame is pre-focussed clearly onto the base sheet using the focussing (converging) lens. The lamp is then switched off while a sheet of photographic (light-sensitive) paper is placed in position on the base sheet. The lamp is switched on again for a set time to **expose** the paper which is then developed, fixed and glazed.

Note Photographs must be printed in a darkroom to protect the photographic paper.

Figure 19.12(b) illustrates the principle of a slide projector. A quartz-halide lamp is placed with its line filament at the centre of curvature of a concave

(converging) mirror. The concave mirror prevents about half of the light produced from being lost because it reflects the light travelling in the 'wrong' direction. The filament is placed at the centre of curvature C of the mirror because any ray of light from C will strike the mirror normally and return through C. A pair of converging lenses called the condenser controls the beam of light so that it evenly illuminates the region where the slide is to be placed. The condenser concentrates as much light as possible onto the slide.

The lower diagram in Fig. 19.12(b) shows the inverted slide at an object distance u from the converging, focussing lens producing an 'inverted' real image on the screen at an image distance v. The slide is positioned so that $2f > u > f$ which ensures that a real, magnified inverted image is produced. Since magnification m is equivalent to v/u and v is very much greater than u, the magnification m is very large. The final image will appear 'upright' on the screen because the slide was inverted in the holder. The slide should also be reversed in the holder so that the lateral inversion produced by the focussing lens will be compensated for.

Overhead projector

Another type of projector in fairly common use in education is the overhead projector (o.h.p.). This consists of a quartz–halogen line-filament lamp sited at the centre of curvature of a converging mirror such

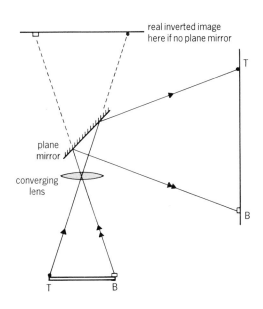

19.13 Principle of the overhead projector

that light goes directly from the lamp and by reflection from the mirror to a special type of lens called a Fresnel lens. A Fresnel lens is made from a flat sheet of clear plastic on which concentric grooves are cut at special angles so that light is converged by it. This provides strong, even illumination over the 'square' glass plate mounted above the lens. A roll of clear acetate can be moved across the glass plate. The teacher or lecturer can write or draw on the acetate sheet without turning away from the audience and the image is projected onto a white screen which is also facing the audience.

Figure 19.13 (p.237) shows the main components of an o.h.p. in use and a ray diagram of the formation of the image on the screen. The projector has a focussing lens and a plane mirror mounted on an adjustable arm so that the image can be focussed sharply onto the screen. If the plane mirror is removed a real, inverted image forms on the ceiling. This image is inverted and laterally inverted. When the mirror is replaced it reflects the light onto a vertical screen and reflection by the mirror corrects for both lateral inversion and the 'vertical' inversion.

In common with most other projectors, this projector has an electric fan which operates before, during and after the lamp is switched on. A large amount of heat energy is produced by projector lamps, therefore some method of forced cooling is required to prevent the filament from melting. The fan blows 'cold' air over the lamp and helps to stabilise the temperature. The fan runs after the lamp is switched off because the hot filament is very easily broken. Therefore the projector should not be moved until the fan stops, indicating that the filament is cool enough to withstand mechanical vibrations.

Questions

Q1 The human eyes possess the power of accommodation. This is the power to
- **A** alter the diameters of the pupils as the intensity of illumination changes.
- **B** distinguish between lights of different colours.
- **C** focus on objects at different distances.
- **D** see a series of still pictures as a moving picture.
- **E** decide which of two objects is the closer. *(L)*

Q2 How does the eye change in order to focus on near or distant objects?
- **A** The lens moves in or out.
- **B** The retina moves in or out.
- **C** The iris changes colour.
- **D** The pupil gets larger or smaller.
- **E** The lens bulges or relaxes. *(NWREB)*

Q3 In which one of these ways is a simple camera very different from the normal eye?
- **A** The amount of light entering it is adjusted by means of a diaphragm.
- **B** A small inverted image is formed.
- **C** An image is formed on a light-sensitive surface.
- **D** It can be adjusted for far and near objects by altering the position of the lens.
- **E** A real image is formed. *(L)*

Q4 A single diverging lens is used in
- **A** a magnifying glass.
- **B** a simple camera.
- **C** the focusing lens for a projector.
- **D** spectacles for the correction of short sight.
- **E** the objective lens in a telescope. *(C)*

Q5 Describe with the aid of a diagram how you would measure the focal length of a converging lens.

Draw a further diagram to show how such a lens is used as the eyepiece in a telescope or microscope.

An illuminated object is set up 2 m from a white screen. Where should a converging lens be placed in order to give a clear image, four times the height of the object, on the screen? What focal length lens is necessary? *(S)*

Q6 Describe an experiment you would perform to determine the refractive index of glass.

Explain what is meant by *critical angle* and *total internal reflection* and calculate the refractive index of a transparent substance which has a critical angle of 43° 39′.

With suitable diagrams, explain **Either**, (a) how an optical fibre works, **Or**, (b) how a prism periscope is constructed.
(W)

Q7 (a) Describe how you would
- (i) show experimentally that the angle of incidence is equal to the angle of reflection when light is *totally internally reflected*;
- (ii) make a measurement of the *critical angle* for light passing from glass to air. What is the relationship between the critical angle and the refractive index of the glass in this case?

(b) Explain why, in periscopes and binoculars, glass prisms are preferred to plane mirrors to deviate a beam of light. Draw diagrams to show how light can be deviated by a prism through (i) 95°, (ii) 180°. *(L)*

Q8 (a) What is the difference between a real and a virtual image?

Draw a ray diagram to show how an image of a suitably-placed object is formed by (i) a plane mirror, and (ii) the lens in a camera. Point out three ways in which the images differ.

(b) The diagram shows a lens, of focal length 10 cm, being used as a simple magnifier. By a ray diagram drawn to

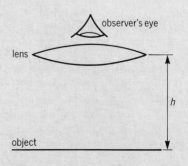

scale, or otherwise, find the value of the height, *h*, of the lens above the object if the virtual image is to be formed 25 cm from the lens.

If the object is 7.0 mm wide, what is the width of the image? *(O & C)*

Q9 A **convex lens** of focal length 6 cm is held 4 cm from a newspaper which has print 0.5 cm high. By calculation or scale drawing, determine the size and nature of the image produced.

Draw a diagram showing how **two** suitable lenses can be used to produce a compound microscope. Indicate on your diagram (i) the focal points of the lenses; (ii) the position of the object; (iii) the position and nature of the final image. *(W)*

Q10 Describe with the help of a diagram, how you would set up two suitable lenses to form a compound microscope.

Draw a diagram showing the passage through such a microscope of a pencil of rays starting from a point object which does not lie on the axis of the instrument. *(O)*

Q11 (a) Explain the meaning of the term 'focal length' as applied to a convex (converging) lens and a concave (diverging) lens.

Describe briefly an experiment you would use to measure accurately the focal length of a convex (converging) lens.

(b) Draw a ray diagram to show how two lenses may be used to construct a compound microscope. State the type of each lens and its approximate focal length. Show on the diagram the positions of the principal foci of the lenses in relation to the object and image positions. Specify the nature of each image. *(JMB)*

Q12 State and explain **one** practical use for each of the following: (i) convex mirror; (ii) concave mirror; (iii) convex lens; (iv) concave lens. *(W)*

Q13 (a) A converging lens is suitably set up to show the image on a screen of an illuminated object. Describe how you would measure the linear magnification produced by the lens for various object and image distances from the lens. Indicate the result you would expect. Draw a ray diagram to illustrate the image formation.

(b) Describe, with a ray diagram, the action of a converging lens as the eyepiece of either a compound microscope, or an astronomical telescope. *(S)*

Q14 Explain, with the aid of clearly labelled diagrams, the following:

(a) the refraction of light from air into water;

(b) critical angle and total internal reflection at an air–water boundary;

(c) the use of two convex lenses as an astronomical refracting telescope.

A **concave** lens produces an image, 7 cm from the lens, of an object placed 21 cm from the lens. Find the focal length of the lens. *(W)*

Q15 (a) A converging (convex) lens has a focal length of 5 cm.

(i) What is the power of the lens?

(ii) If this lens were used in an astronomical refracting telescope for which part of the telescope would it

be most suitable? Describe the other lens which would be used in the telescope, stating a suitable value for its focal length.

(iii) What would be the distance between the two lenses if the telescope were in normal adjustment (i.e. with the final image at infinity)?

(b) Explain the purpose of the reflector in a radio-telescope. *(JMB)*

Q16 (a) Define *refractive index*.

Describe how you would determine the refractive index of a liquid. Indicate the readings which you would take and explain how you would work out the result.

(b) Sketch **two** diagrams indicating the type of lenses used and the positions and nature of the images in (i) a Galilean telescope, (ii) an astronomical telescope. *(JMB)*

Q17 Explain with the aid of ray diagrams, how a lens, of focal length 100 mm, can be used

(a) in a simple camera to photograph a distant object,

(b) in a slide projector to project the image of a transparency ('slide') onto a screen,

(c) as a magnifying glass to examine the transparency.

In each case show clearly where the photographic film or transparency should be placed in relation to the focal plane of the lens, and state the type of image being formed by the lens. The details of the other parts of the instruments are not required.

When the lens is used as a magnifying glass, the final image produced has a linear magnification of 2.5. Determine, by using a ray diagram drawn to scale, or otherwise, the distance from the lens to the object. *(O & C)*

Q18 (a) Contrast the method of focusing in a camera and in the eye, showing clearly how in each the lens system can focus images of objects at different distances.

(b) Draw a ray diagram showing clearly how you would use a lens to correct the defect of vision known as long sight.

(c) Although a pinhole camera can produce a good photograph, lens cameras are much more widely used. State and explain two reasons for this.

(d) A lens of focal length 20 cm is used to produce a ten-times magnified image of a film slide on a screen. How far must the slide be placed from the lens? *(L)*

Q19 A simple lens camera consists of a lens of focal length 100 mm (which is fixed at a distance 100 mm in front of the film) and a shutter.

(a) What are the main similarities and differences between this simple camera and the eye?

(b) When an object 2 m high stands 5 m in front of this simple-camera lens, how big an image will result on the negative?

(c) (i) Explain why this camera would be unsuitable for photographing an object which is 500 mm from the lens,

(ii) Explain how the camera might be modified and used to photograph this object. *(O)*

20 **Waves**

20.1 Oscillations

Waves are one of the ways of transferring energy. When a stone is thrown into a pond, ripples (waves) spread out in concentric circles from the point where the stone enters the water. Any object which is floating on the water, e.g. a toy boat, just bobs up and down. Although the wave moves outwards the boat does not, as you may have discovered when your toy boat was becalmed in the middle of the pond. Throwing stones into the water creates waves but does not bring the boat to the side.

The apparatus in Fig. 20.1 demonstrates the production of waves by making particles vibrate about a fixed point. Consider a mass at rest at the end of a spiral spring (position 1 in Fig. 20.1a). If the mass is depressed slightly to position 2 and released, it oscillates up and down about the mean position. One **complete oscillation** has occurred when the mass has moved through positions 2 – 1 – 3 – 1 – 2, i.e. when it has returned to its starting position *and* is moving in the *same* direction (Fig. 20.1b). If, for example, the particle starts at 1, then 1 – 2 – 1 is *not* a complete oscillation. The particle has returned to its starting position, but it is moving in the *opposite* direction. The oscillation is complete after 1 – 2 – 1 – 3 – 1, when the particle is in the starting position and is moving in the original direction.

There are various important definitions concerning an oscillating body.

The **period** *T* of the oscillation is the time taken in completing one oscillation.

The **frequency** *f* of oscillation is the number of complete oscillations made in one second. $f = 1/T$ where *T* is the period in seconds. The unit of frequency is the hertz (Hz).

The **amplitude** *a* of an oscillation is the distance between the **mean position** and the **extreme position**. It can also be defined as the maximum displacement on either side of the mean position. In Fig. 20.1 the amplitude is the distance between positions 1 and 2 or between positions 1 and 3.

Note A common error is to assume that the amplitude is the distance between the extreme positions. This distance is 2*a*.

The phase is a rather difficult concept which can be explained by considering two vibrating particles. A and B are two identical springs which support identical masses. The masses are depressed the same distance *a* and released at the same time (Fig. 20.2a). Both pass the mean position at the same time while moving in the same direction (Fig. 20.2b). Both reach the top of the oscillation at the same time (Fig. 20.2c). The masses are said to be oscillating in **phase**, i.e. they are always at the same point in the oscillation at the same time, and are moving in the same direction.

Particles A and B have the same amplitude, but two particles which do not have the same amplitude can also be in phase. Provided they both pass their mean position at the same time travelling in the same direction, and are at the maximum displacements at the same time, they are in *phase*. These two particles have the same period and hence the same frequency.

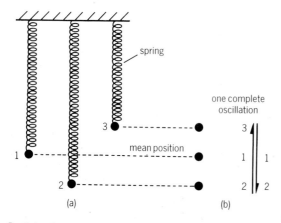

20.1 Particle vibrating on a spring

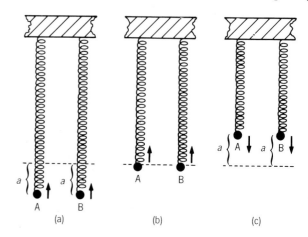

20.2 Particles vibrating in phase

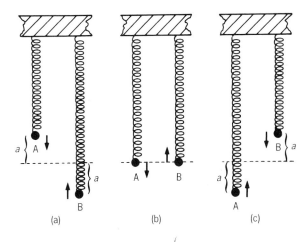

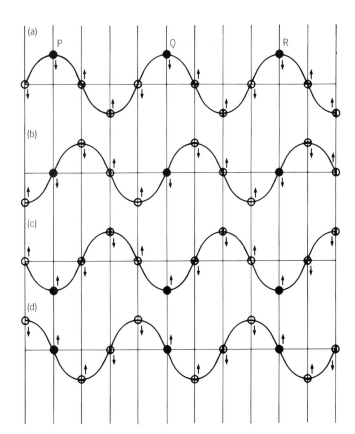

20.3 Particles not in phase

Figure 20.3 represents a different situation. Particle A is released first, particle B is released when A is at the top of its oscillation (Fig. 20.3a). Thus B starts when A has completed half an oscillation and so is half a period $\frac{1}{2}T$ behind A. Both particles are at the mean position at the same time but are moving in *opposite* directions (Fig. 20.3b). Particle B is still half a period $\frac{1}{2}T$ behind A and is moving vertically upwards while A is moving vertically downwards. The directions differ by 180° or π radians. The particles are said to be **out of phase**, and their **phase difference** is 180° or π. In Fig. 21.3(c) A is at the bottom of an oscillation and starting to go up, while B is at the top of an oscillation and starting to come down. They remain 180° or π out of phase and separated by half a period.

It follows that if A is released first and B is released as A passes the mean position, then B will always be one-quarter of a period $\frac{1}{4}T$ behind A. Half a period out of phase is equivalent to 180° or π out of phase, so $\frac{1}{4}T$ is equivalent to the particles being 90° or $\frac{1}{2}\pi$ out of phase.

20.2 Wave motion

Figure 20.4 shows a number of equally spaced particles, all vibrating with the same amplitude and frequency. However, each particle is 90° ($\frac{1}{2}\pi$) out of phase with the particles next to it and $\frac{1}{4}T$ or 90° ahead of the particle to its right. A wave form can be drawn through the particles. Figure 20.4(b) represents the positions of the particles one-quarter of a period $\frac{1}{4}T$ later, Fig. 20.4(c) shows the particles half a period $\frac{1}{2}T$ later, and Fig. 20.4(d) shows the particles three quarters of a period $\frac{3}{4}T$ later. You can see that as the particles vibrate up and down about the mean position, the crest of the wave moves forward.

This wave model may be linked to what happens when a stone is thrown into water. Most of the stone's energy is given to the water molecules at the point of impact. These vibrate up and down like the mass at the

20.4 Transverse waves formed by vibrating particles

end of the spring. However, each particle is bound to the particles around it by attractive forces and so these particles start to vibrate a little later. They in turn affect the particles next to them. Thus a wave spreads outwards from the point of impact, and obviously this will be a circular wave.

Wavelength

Some important observations can be made from a study of Fig. 20.4. Particles P, Q and R are in phase, because they are all at the top of the oscillation (on the crests of the wave), moving in the same direction. The distance between two consecutive crests is known as the **wavelength** λ. This is also the **distance between two consecutive particles in phase**. You should have no difficulty in identifying particles which are in phase (not only those at the top of crests or the bottom of troughs) and will notice that the distance between any two consecutive particles in phase is always the same and equal to one wavelength λ.

Speed of wave

From Fig. 20.4 you can also see that during the time P completes one oscillation, the wave crest travels from P to Q. Thus in a time T s the wave crest travels a distance λ and the speed of the wave c is given by $c = \lambda/T$. However, $T = 1/f$, hence $c = f\lambda$.

This may also be deduced from the fact that the distance travelled by the wave for one oscillation is the wavelength λ. There are *f* oscillations in 1 second so in 1 second the wave travels $f \times \lambda$. Hence speed $c = f\lambda$. For any wave motion

$$\text{speed} = \text{frequency} \times \text{wavelength}$$

This is a very important formula.

Note Speed is used and not velocity. Velocity is a vector and is specified by both speed *and* direction. When a sound is made the waves travel in all directions; consequently the velocity varies, but the speed is constant. When a wave is reflected from a stationary object the velocity changes but the speed does not. Thus velocity is not relevant here.

Transverse progressive waves

The wave in Fig. 20.4 is a **transverse progressive** wave. It is called 'transverse' because the direction of motion of the particles is perpendicular to the direction of motion of the wave, and 'progressive' because the wave crest moves forward.

You should now understand why throwing a stone into the middle of a pool to create a wave does not bring the toy boat to the side. The motion of the boat is similar to the motion of the water particles below: it just bobs up and down.

There is a tendency to think that the direction of motion of the particles in a transverse wave *must* be vertical. This is not so. Imagine a wave to be emerging from the paper (see Fig. 20.5). All the directions of motion shown by the arrows are in the plane of the paper, and therefore perpendicular to the direction of motion of the wave. As you can see, there are many possible modes of vibration in a transverse wave.

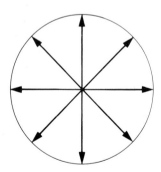

20.5   *Directions of vibration of a transverse wave*

Pressure in a transverse wave When a transverse wave is propagated (i.e. energy is transmitted as a wave) the particles just vibrate in a direction perpendicular to the direction of motion of the wave. The average distance between the particles does not change, so the number of particles per unit volume remains constant, and the pressure does not change.

Types of transverse waves Water waves are transverse waves. So are all types of electromagnetic waves, e.g. radio, TV, laser, infrared, visible light, X-rays, and gamma rays. When a piano wire is struck or a violin string bowed a transverse wave travels along the wire or string.

Note The *sound* wave this produces is *not* a transverse wave.

Longitudinal waves Longitudinal waves are formed when the particle vibrates along the direction of motion of the wave (Fig. 20.6). This process is usually more difficult to understand than the transverse wave. Figure 20.6(a) shows the particles in the rest positions before wave motion starts. The particles then vibrate so that each particle is 90 ° or $\frac{1}{2}\pi$ out of phase with the particle next to it. Figure 20.6(b) shows the positions of the particles one-quarter of a period $\frac{1}{4}T$ later. In order to make the diagram easier to follow, each particle has been drawn differently from its neighbour. You can see that as the particles vibrate, the spacing between them varies. Where the particles are close together the pressure increases slightly and these areas are called **compressions**. Where the particles are further apart the pressure decreases; these areas are called **rarefactions**. The compressions and rarefactions are equally spaced. Figures 20.6(b)–(e) show that as each particle vibrates about its mean position, the compressions and rarefactions move forward. Wave forms have been drawn in to show that as the compressions and rarefactions move forward

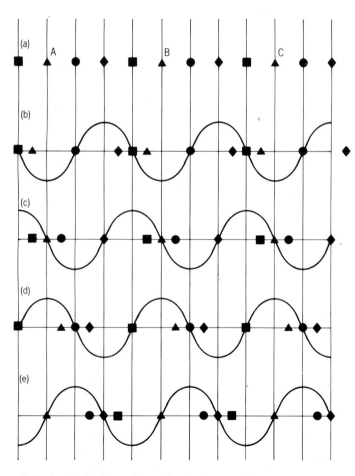

20.6   *Longitudinal wave formed by vibrating particles*

the wave also moves forward. This type of wave is known as a **longitudinal progressive** wave. It is called 'longitudinal' because the direction of vibration of the particles is the same as the direction of motion of the wave, and 'progressive' because, although the particles vibrate about their mean positions, the compressions and rarefactions, and hence also the wave, move forward.

The particles A, B and C in Fig. 20.6 are always in phase. In Fig. 20.6(c) each is at the centre of a compression, in Fig. 20.6(e) each is in the centre of a rarefaction. Thus the distance between A and B is one wavelength λ. The distance between B and C is also λ. The distance between two consecutive compressions is one wavelength, as is the distance between two consecutive rarefactions. In the diagram each particle completes one oscillation.

Longitudinal waves are difficult to represent, but the ordinary wave form is used. Notice that the compressions and rarefactions are not the crests and troughs. They occur at the mean positions. As with transverse waves, $c = f \lambda$, i.e. speed = frequency × wavelength.

20.3   Sound waves

Sound waves are longitudinal waves. The following are necessary for the transmission of sound:

(a) a **source**, the vibrating object which produces the sound;
(b) a **medium** to transmit the sound;
(c) a **receiver** such as the ear or a microphone to receive the sound.

Source   As the source vibrates mechanically about a fixed point the medium in the vicinity is alternately compressed and rarefied. The vibrating object may be the prongs of a tuning fork, skin of a drum, wire in a piano etc.
Note Although the object may be vibrating *transversely* (at right angles to its length), the wave sent through the air will be *longitudinal*.

Medium   Air is the most common medium for the transmission of sound, but solids, liquids and gases all transmit sound. The compressions and rarefactions travel through the medium by the vibration of the molecules. It is obvious that when sound travels along a metal rod, the particles vibrate but do not move along the rod. In the same way air that carries sound does not move along. The air next to the vibrating source stays there.

Receiver   The compressions and rarefactions in the medium reach the receiver, which may be an eardrum or the diaphragm of a microphone, etc. and cause it to vibrate with the same frequency as the source. The louder the sound (the larger the amplitude of vibration of the source), the greater the pressure difference between the compressions and rarefactions, and the larger the amplitude of vibration of the eardrum. Hence the louder the sound appears to the listener.

Audibility

The range of frequencies which the listener can distinguish is known as the **range of audibility**. The top and bottom of this range are known as the **limits of audibility**. The lower limit is supposed to be 20 Hz and the upper limit 20 000 Hz. If a long strip of metal is set into vibration, it can be seen vibrating but no sound can be heard. This is because the sound is below the lower limit of audibility. Musical notes vary in frequency from about 30 Hz to 5000 Hz. The ability of the eardrum to respond to sounds decreases with age, and the range of audibility becomes considerably reduced as the lower limit rises and the upper limit decreases. This tendency will perhaps become more pronounced in future years as background noise levels increase and our eardrums move continually. This cannot be good for them and may even cause premature deafness.

Sounds with frequencies above 20 000 Hz are known as **ultrasonic**. They cannot be heard but they still affect the eardrums and can cause acute pain. With their higher frequency they have a greater penetrating power and can be used to detect mines in the sea and babies in the womb.

Location of underground disturbances

If a disturbance occurs underground, e.g. an earthquake or an atomic explosion, both transverse and longitudinal waves are emitted. The waves travel at different speeds and the time that each arrives at a receiving station is recorded. If the speed of each wave and its time of arrival are known, the distance of the

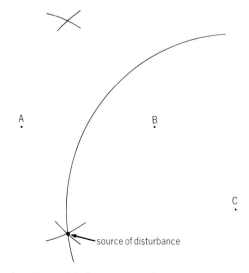

20.7   Locating a disturbance

243

disturbance from the receiving station can be calculated from the difference in speeds multiplied by the difference between the times of arrival. By drawing a circle with the receiving station as centre and the calculated distance as radius, the source of the disturbance can be found on the circumference. Such circles drawn round three receiving stations (A, B and C in Fig. 20.7) will meet more or less at one point. This point is where the disturbance took place. If only two stations are used the circles will meet at two points, and the source of the disturbance may be at either.

20.4 Producing wave pulses and waves

The production of wave pulses and waves can be demonstrated with a long length of rubber tubing or a slinky spring. Figures 20.8(a) and (c) show a transverse pulse travelling along a length of rubber tubing and a slinky spring. These are produced by jerking the end sharply in a direction perpendicular to the length of the tubing or spring and then returning it to the original position. Figures 20.8(b) and (d) show transverse waves produced by moving the end continually from side to side. Figure 20.8(e) shows a

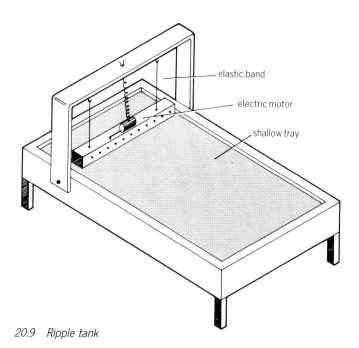

20.9 Ripple tank

longitudinal pulse in a slinky spring produced by moving the end quickly forward and back to its original position, while Fig. 20.8(f) shows a longitudinal wave produced by moving the end continually back and forth. A continuous wave can only be seen for a short time because the wave is reflected when it reaches the end of the rubber or spring. This occurs whether the end is free or fixed. The reflected wave affects the incident wave (see p.254).

In the ripple tank

The ripple tank (Fig. 20.9) is a convenient piece of apparatus for demonstrating the properties of wave pulses and waves. It consists of a sheet of glass in a frame about 5 cm deep. Sheets of sponge line the frame to absorb the ripples and prevent reflection by the sides. The tank stands on legs above a large sheet of white paper or painted hardboard. A lamp above the tank throws the shadows of the waves or ripples onto the white screen. These shadows are seen most clearly if they are *not* viewed through the water. Before use the tank is levelled and water is poured in to a depth of 5–10 mm.

Plane wave pulses are produced by dipping a rule into the water, circular wave pulses are produced by any pointed object. When continuous waves are required a wooden beam is hung above the water by elastic bands. A small electric motor with an eccentric shaft is fitted to the beam which, when switched on, makes both motor and beam vibrate. A wooden strip fitted to the bottom of the beam produces a plane wave, circular waves are formed by a small wooden sphere.

Continuous waves are viewed using a stroboscope.

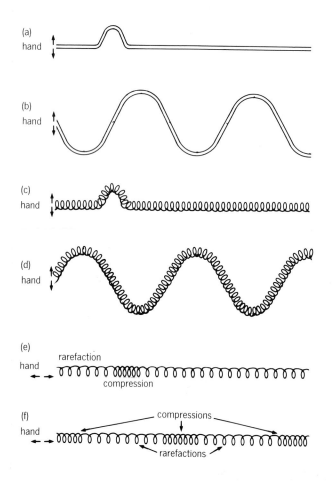

20.8 Wave pulses and waves

One type of stroboscope is simply a flashing light. When this flashes with the same frequency as the frequency of the waves, the waves appear to be stationary. Another type is a hand stroboscope, a disc with a number of radial slits equally spaced around its edge. The disc is attached to an axle passing through its centre and fixed to the handle A. It is rotated by a finger placed in the hole B. The waves are viewed through the slits, and when the frequency with which the slits pass the eye is the same as the frequency of the waves, the waves appear to be stationary.

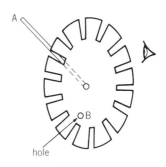

20.10   Hand stroboscope

20.5   Reflection and refraction of waves

Investigation 20.1   To investigate the reflection of plane waves

Set up the ripple tank with the plane wave dipper and stroboscope. Place a block of metal in the tank to reflect the waves. You should see a wave pattern like that in Fig. 20.11, showing that the waves are reflected as plane waves. Put a sheet of white paper on the screen and draw in the wave patterns; mark the angles of incidence and reflection. In this way you can verify that the angle of reflection is equal to the angle of incidence.

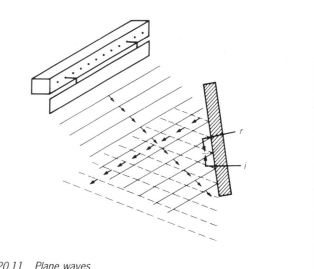

20.11   Plane waves

Investigation 20.2   To investigate the reflection of circular waves

Replace the plane dipper by a sphere to produce spherical waves. After reflection by a plane reflector, the waves are spherical. The centre of these spherical waves appears to be a point as far behind the reflector as the dipper is in front (see Fig. 20.12). This indicates that the distance of the image behind the reflector is equal to the distance of the object in front of the reflector.

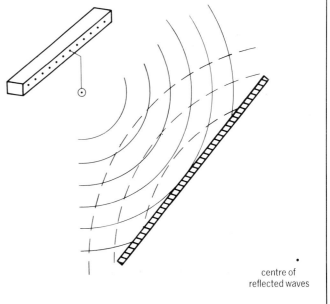

centre of
reflected waves

20.12   Reflection of circular waves

Investigation 20.3 To demonstrate refraction of waves

Set up the ripple tank with the plane wave dipper. Place a plane sheet of glass in the water so that the depth of water over the glass is less than the depth elsewhere in the tank.
(**Note** If you place washers under the glass it is easier to move and adjust.) You should notice the following effects:

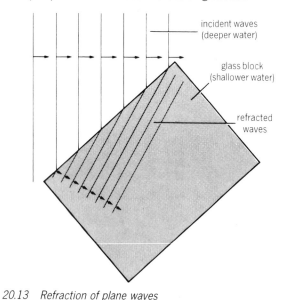

20.13 *Refraction of plane waves*

(a) The direction of the waves changes when the waves strike the shallower water at an angle (Fig. 20.13).
(b) The wavelength decreases in the shallower water.
(c) The wave speed is reduced in the shallower water.

You can check the reduction in speed by allowing a plane wave pulse to approach the shallow water with the wave parallel to the boundary (see Fig. 20.14). It is obvious that there is a decrease in speed in the shallow water, and if you time a wave over a given distance you can calculate it. The shallower the water, the more pronounced the effect.

Circular waves can also be used. Not only is there a change of speed and wavelength in the shallow water, but also a change in curvature.

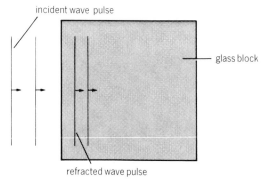

20.14 *Refraction of a wave pulse*

The equation $c = f\lambda$ applies to all types of waves, and so the effects seen in a ripple tank occur elsewhere. In the tank both the speed and wavelength of the water waves were reduced. What happened to the frequency? The frequency of the waves is the same as the frequency of the dipper, which did not change. The waves only change in frequency if their source alters. In general, when waves pass from one medium into another (in a ripple tank a change in depth is equivalent to a change in medium) there is a change in speed, but no change in frequency. However, since $c = f\lambda$ the wavelength must change when there is a change in speed.

Refraction of waves is associated with a change in speed. It follows that factors which cause a change in wave speed also cause refraction. Temperature, wind speed and humidity can cause changes in the speed of sound waves, and hence cause refraction. Ionised layers can cause a change in the speed of electromagnetic waves, and hence cause refraction. This accounts for total internal reflection (continuous refraction) in the Kennelly–Heaviside layers (see p.217).

In Chapter 16 (p.198) you read that

$$\text{refractive index} = \frac{\text{speed of light in vacuum}}{\text{speed of light in medium}}$$

Thus the refractive index of glass n = speed of light in vacuum/speed of light in glass.

Example

The wavelength of red light in vacuum is 7.7×10^{-7} m and its speed in vacuum 3.0×10^8 m s^{-1}. What is its wavelength in glass whose refractive index for red light is 1.5?

$$\text{speed of red light in glass} = \frac{\text{speed of light in vacuum}}{\text{refractive index}}$$

$$= \frac{3.0 \times 10^8}{1.5} \text{ m s}^{-1}$$

$$\text{frequency of red light } f = \frac{c}{\lambda}$$

$$= \frac{3.0 \times 10^8}{7.7 \times 10^{-7}} \text{Hz}$$

The frequency remains constant.

$$\text{wavelength} = \frac{\text{speed}}{\text{frequency}}$$

So

$$\text{wavelength in glass} = \frac{3 \times 10^8}{1.5} \text{ m s}^{-1} \div \frac{3 \times 10^8}{7.7 \times 10^{-7}} \text{s}^{-1}$$

$$= \frac{7.7 \times 10^{-7}}{1.5} \text{m}$$

$$= 5.13 \times 10^{-7} \text{m}$$

Note The refractive index of glass is not always the same: it varies according to the colour of the light. The refractive index given is usually that for yellow light.

20.6 Comparison of transverse and longitudinal waves

Both transverse and longitudinal waves may be represented by sine wave forms. Both types of waves can

(a) be reflected,
(b) be refracted,
(c) interfere,
(d) be diffracted.

In general, what applies to one set of waves applies equally well to the other. Transverse waves can be polarised whereas longitudinal waves cannot, but this is outside the scope of this book.

Differences between sound waves and electromagnetic waves

(a) Sound waves are longitudinal and electromagnetic waves are transverse.
(b) Sound waves travel at a speed of 340 m s^{-1} whereas electromagnetic waves travel at a speed of $3 \times 10^8 \text{ m s}^{-1}$.
(c) Sound waves do not pass through a vacuum but electromagnetic waves (light) do.

This experiment shows that sound waves will not travel through a vacuum and need a material medium for their propagation. Heat and light from the Sun reach Earth through the vacuum of Space, but sound does not. This is fortunate in view of the enormous explosions which occur in the Sun!

On p.242 the propagation of transverse waves was explained in terms of the direction of motion of the particles being perpendicular to the direction of motion of the waves. There are no particles in a vacuum, so how are the transverse waves propagated? A precise explanation is beyond the scope of this book. However, the propagation may be regarded as an energy transfer between electric and magnetic fields. These are carried along without loss of energy and do not require a medium.

Example

An observer notes that there is a 6 second interval between seeing a flash of lightning and hearing the clap of thunder. How far away is the storm?

The light travels at $3.0 \times 10^8 \text{ m s}^{-1}$ and thus may be regarded as reaching the observer instantaneously. The sound takes 6 seconds and the distance it travels is given by speed × time. Sound travels at 340 m s^{-1} so distance $= 340 \text{ m s}^{-1} \times 6 \text{ s} = 2040 \text{ m}$.

Thus the storm is 2040 m from the observer.

Investigation 20.4 To demonstrate that sound waves do not pass through a vacuum

Suspend an electric bell by its leads inside a bell jar (see Fig. 20.15). Pass a tube through the cork and connect it to a vacuum pump. Before starting the pump, close the switch to the electric bell. You can hear the electric bell and see the movement of the striker. When the pump starts the sound gradually becomes fainter and fainter but the striker can still be seen to be moving. The fact that the bell is still seen indicates that the light (electromagnetic) waves travel through the vacuum. If you let air back into the bell jar you can hear the sound again.

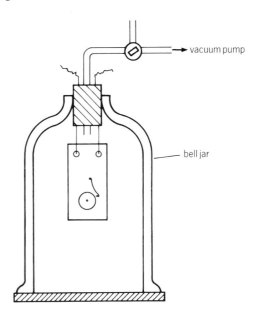

20.15   Demonstration that sound waves do not travel through a vacuum

20.7 Sound

Wave forms

The wave forms in Fig. 20.16 may be regarded as longitudinal sound waves. The wave forms in parts (a), (b) and (e) have the same frequency, as do those in parts (c) and (d).

Pitch The pitch of a note (how 'high' it is) is determined by its frequency, so the notes produced by the waves in (a), (b) and (e) in Fig. 20.16 all have the same pitch. The wavelength of the waves in parts (c) and (d) is half of the wavelength in the others so the frequency and hence the pitch are doubled. These notes are said to be **one octave** higher than the others.

Loudness The loudness of a note depends upon the amplitude of the wave that produces it. The greater the

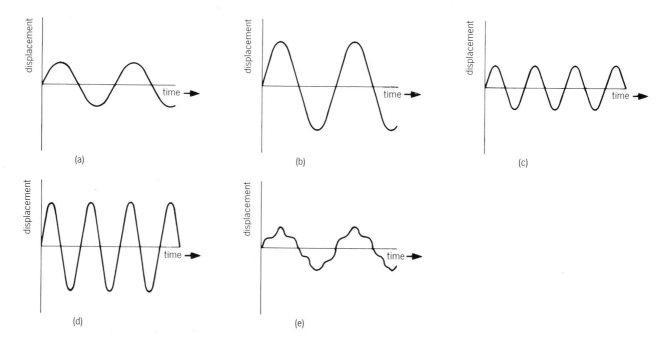

(a)　(b)　(c)

(d)　(e)

20.16　Different wave forms with the same frequency

amplitude the louder the note, because more energy is used to produce a larger amplitude.

Note　The energy transmitted by a wave depends upon the frequency as well as the amplitude. If the frequency of a note is doubled, twice as many compressions and rarefactions strike the ear each second and more energy is received. In fact the energy in a wave is proportional to both $(frequency)^2$ and $(amplitude)^2$.

Quality or timbre　The note in Fig. 20.16(e) has the same frequency and hence the same pitch as the notes in (a) and (b). It has the same amplitude as (a) and will therefore be just as loud. However, (e) sounds different from (a) because it has a different wave form. It is said to differ in quality or timbre. It sounds richer than the other notes because it is not a simple note, but contains **overtones**. Notes of the same pitch played upon different musical instruments are distinguished from each other by their quality.

Sources of sound

Any object which vibrates mechanically produces a sound. Whether or not it is audible depends on the frequency and amplitude of the vibration. What is certain is that the vibrating body sets up pressure waves which impinge on the ear drum.

Tuning fork　When the prongs are set into vibration pressure waves are sent through the air (Fig. 20.17). If the stem of the fork is placed on a bench top, the bench top is set into forced vibration at the same frequency as the tuning fork. The note produced is much louder but lasts for a shorter time, because more energy is used to set a larger volume of air into vibration. Different-sized tuning forks produce notes of different frequencies.

Toothed wheel　A toothed wheel is rotated on its axle with a stiff card or metal plate held against the teeth (Fig. 20.18). As the wheel rotates the teeth impinge

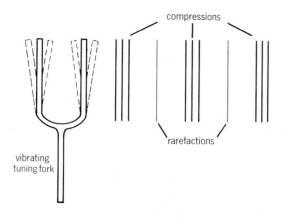

20.17　Vibration of a tuning fork

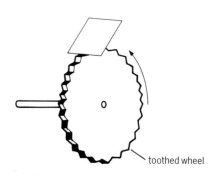

20.18　Toothed wheel

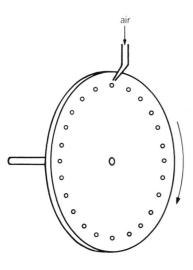

20.19 *Siren*

upon the card and make it vibrate. The frequency of vibration is given by the number of teeth × the number of revolutions per second. The frequency can be varied by varying the number of revolutions per second, or by using a wheel with a different number of teeth.

Siren This is a disc with a ring of equally spaced holes equidistant from the centre. A narrow jet of air is directed onto the holes. When the disc is rotated the air stream is continually interrupted and puffs of air pass through the holes at regular intervals. The frequency of the note is given by the number of holes in the disc × the number of revolutions per second. Usually there are several rings of holes in a disc, allowing the frequency to be varied by using a different ring, or by varying the speed of the disc.

20.8 Measuring of the speed of sound

A direct determination of the speed of sound requires only two measurements: the distance of the source from the observer and the time taken for the sound to travel that distance. Then the speed can be calculated from speed = distance/time.

Early methods of measuring the speed of sound used a cannon on one side of a valley and an observer on the other side. The distance between the cannon and the observer was measured. Using a stopwatch the observer noted the time between seeing the flash and hearing the sound. The time taken for the light to travel the distance was neglected. In order to eliminate as far as possible the effects of wind, each station had

a cannon and an observer and both cannon were fired at approximately the same time. The mean of the two times was taken and the speed calculated. This was found to be about 340 m s^{-1}. The big disadvantage of this method is that cannon are not readily available!

Many examinees describe a similar method. One pupil stands at one end of the playing field with a starting pistol and another at the other end with a stopwatch. The distance between them is measured accurately with a tape measure. The pupil starts the stopwatch on seeing the puff of smoke from the pistol, and stops it on hearing the sound. The performance is repeated in the reverse direction to compensate for any wind effects, and the average time is taken. Since sound travels at 340 m s^{-1} a stopwatch is not likely to be accurate enough, and a centisecond or millisecond timer is preferable.

Echo method

When a short sharp sound, e.g. a clap, is made, the wave pulse may be reflected by a large obstacle, e.g. a wall, and heard by the observer. This reflected pulse is known as an **echo**. Suppose a person stands 50 m in front of a wall and gives a single clap. When the echo is heard the sound has travelled 100 m. Timing this interval with a stopwatch is not very accurate. However, if a second person holds the stopwatch and the first person claps every time an echo is heard, then the time for a large number of echoes can be obtained with reasonable accuracy.

Suppose the distance of the clapper from the wall is 50 m and the time interval between the first and the one-hundred-and-first clap is 30 seconds, then

$$\text{speed of sound} = \frac{\text{distance travelled}}{\text{time taken by one clap}}$$

$$= 100 \text{ m} \div \frac{30}{100} \text{ s}$$

$$= 333 \text{ m s}^{-1}$$

Example

A man standing in a gorge between two large cliffs gives a short sharp shout. He hears two echoes, the first after 1 second and the next after $1\frac{1}{2}$ seconds. The speed of sound is 340 m s^{-1}. What is the distance between the cliffs?

Let x be the distance of the man from one cliff and y his distance from the other (see Fig. 20.20). Then the sound travels a distance of $2x$ in 1 second and a distance of $2y$ in 1.5 s.

Distance travelled in 2.5 s = $2x + 2y = 2(x + y)$. But in 2.5 s sound travels 2.5×340 m = 850 m.

Hence

$$2(x + y) = 850 \text{ m}$$
$$x + y = 425 \text{ m}$$

The distance between the cliffs is 425 m.

Oscilloscope method

A more sophisticated method of measuring the speed of sound directly uses an oscilloscope (p.355). A loudspeaker emits a pulse at regular intervals, and this registers on a cathode ray oscilloscope. When the pulse is received by the microphone it will also register on the oscilloscope. If the characteristic of the timebase is known, the time interval between the two pulses can be found. The distance between the loudspeaker and microphone is measured. Then speed of sound can be found from speed = distance/time.

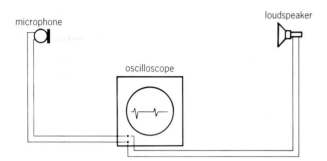

20.20   Oscilloscope method for measuring the speed of sound

Variation in the speed of sound

The speed of sound is greater in solids than in liquids, and greater in liquids than in gases. Early experiments in Lake Geneva showed that the speed of sound in water is much greater than in air. In fresh water the speed of sound is 1410 m s^{-1}, in sea water it is 1540 m s^{-1}. In iron the speed of sound is about 5000 m s^{-1}.

By sending out signals and noting the time interval before the reflected signal (echo) arrives, sound pulses are used to determine the depth of the sea, and to locate the position of shoals of fish. During the war echo sounding with high-frequency sound waves was used to detect the position of mines.

Bats in flight use a form of echo sounding to detect the presence of obstacles. The bat emits a high-frequency sound which is reflected by an object in its path. The echo is heard by the bat which can then pinpoint the object's position and so avoid it.

Atmospheric conditions affect the speed of sound in air. The speed of sound is proportional to the square root of (pressure/density). Changes in pressure do not affect the speed of sound in air. This is because an increase in pressure causes a corresponding increase in density and the ratio pressure/density remains constant.

Changes in temperature do affect the speed of sound in air (or indeed in any gas). The Gas Laws indicate that pressure/density is proportional to the kelvin temperature T. Thus the speed of sound is proportional to $\sqrt{T}$.

Example

A plane takes off when the temperature is 16 °C and the speed of sound 340 m s^{-1}. What will be the speed of sound when it reaches a height where the temperature is -17 °C?

$$\text{initial temperature} = 273 + 16 = 289 \text{ K}$$
$$\text{final temperature} = 273 - 17 = 256 \text{ K}$$

The speed of sound c is proportional to $\sqrt{T}$ so $c_1/c_2 = \sqrt{(T_1/T_2)}$.

$$\frac{c_2}{340} = \sqrt{\frac{256}{289}} = \frac{16}{17}$$
$$c_2 = \frac{16}{17} \times 340 \text{ m s}^{-1}$$
$$= 320 \text{ m s}^{-1}$$

It is easier to break the sound barrier at high altitudes because the temperature is lower.

Changes in humidity affect the speed of sound. The density of water vapour is less than the density of dry air at the same pressure. At night, when the humidity tends to rise, sounds travel faster. Sounds can be heard more clearly on a quiet misty night. This is partly because of the increased humidity, and partly because under such conditions there is usually a temperature inversion which tends to refract the sounds so that they do not escape.

Questions

Questions 1–4
The following are associated with musical notes:
A amplitude
B intensity
C pitch
D timbre (quality)
E speed.
   Which of the above
Q1 is determined by the fundamental frequency of the note?
Q2 is determined by the presence of overtones?
Q3 is constant for all sounds produced by an orchestra?
Q4 can be used to distinguish between different musical instruments?   (L)

Questions 5–8
The diagrams which follow show the waveforms of five musical notes displayed successively on a cathode ray oscilloscope without adjusting its controls.

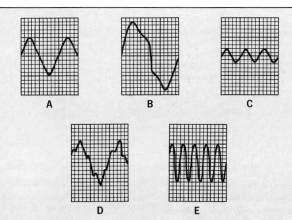

A   B   C

D   E

Which waveform shows

Q5 the note with the greatest number of overtones?
Q6 the note of largest amplitude?
Q7 the note with the highest pitch?
Q8 the note with the lowest frequency? *(L)*

Q9 (a) Define the terms *wavelength, frequency* and *velocity* as applied to a wave. State a relationship between them.

(b) Describe, in detail, an experiment you would carry out to measure the speed of sound in air. Explain how the result would be calculated from your measurements.

(c) State **two** differences between an electromagnetic wave and a sound wave, both of wavelength 1 metre.

(d) Name **two** types of electromagnetic wave with wavelengths **less** than 1 metre. *(C)*

Q10 Which one of the following is *not* an example of a transverse wave?

A a sound wave
B a light wave
C a wave on the surface of the bathwater
D a wave on a skipping rope which is shaken
E a ripple in a flag on a windy day *(NEA)*

Q11 A man sees 'steam' start to come from a factory whistle and 3 seconds later he hears the sound. The velocity of sound in air is 360 m s^{-1}. The distance from the man to the whistle (in metre) is

A 120. **B** 780. **C** 960. **D** 1080. **E** 2160.

Q12 A sonar signal (a high frequency sound wave) sent vertically downwards from a ship is reflected from the ocean floor and detected by a microphone on the keel 0.4 s after transmission. If speed of sound in water is 1500 m s^{-1}, what is the depth, in m, of the ocean?

A 150 **B** 300 **C** 600 **D** 3000 **E** 6000 *(AEB)*

Q13 (a) Explain the meaning of the terms *amplitude* and *frequency* of a vibration.

Describe the effect of changing these two quantities with respect to
(i) the light emitted by a lamp,
(ii) the sound emitted by a source of sound.

(b)

A   B

The diagram shows a vibrating tuning fork. The time taken for a prong to go from A to B is $\frac{1}{500}$ s.

What is the frequency of the vibration? If the velocity of sound in air is 330 m s^{-1} what is the wavelength of the note emitted by the fork? *(AEB)*

Q14 Explain the difference between **longitudinal** and **transverse** waves. Give **one** example of each kind of wave.

Explain how waves transfer energy from one place to another.

Ripples are sent across a pond and a small floating object goes up and down six times in 15 seconds. If the wave crests are 40 cm apart, calculate the speed of the waves across the pond. *(W)*

Q15 State **three** similarities and **three** differences between the water waves on a ripple tank and sound waves in air.

A set of plane waves on a ripple tank reaches a portion of the tank where the water is shallower. The boundary of the shallow water is at an angle of approximately 45° to the wave fronts. Explain, with the aid of a diagram, what happens to the waves as they enter the area of shallow water.

Name **two** types of electromagnetic waves and explain **three** ways in which they differ from each other. *(JMB)*

Q16 Describe how you would find the speed with which sound travels in air, by experiment.

A radio station broadcasts on a frequency of 200 000 Hz and the wavelength of its signal is 1500 m. Calculate
(a) the speed of radio waves in m s^{-1},
(b) the wavelength of the signal of another station that broadcasts on a frequency of 1 250 000 Hz.

State, and explain, two differences between sound waves and light waves. *(C)*

Q17 (a) A flexible metal strip presses lightly against the teeth of a cog wheel as it rotates uniformly at 600 revolutions per minute. If the wheel has 50 teeth find (i) the frequency, and (ii) the wavelength of the note which it emits in air, given that the speed of sound in air is 340 m s^{-1}.

If the wheel is now rotated at 300 revolutions per minute, explain whether the time taken for the sound to reach a distant observer will be charged.

What will be the effect, if any, on the pitch of the note emitted if the temperature of the surrounding air now increases by several degrees, all other factors remaining unchanged? Explain your answer.

(b) Explain the meaning of (i) *echo*, and (ii) *resonance*. Describe in detail how *one* of these two phenomena can be used to determine the speed of sound in air. *(L)*

Q18 A wheel has 50 spokes and rotates at 10 revolutions per second. Calculate the frequency of the note obtained by holding a card lightly against the spokes as they rotate. What would you expect to observe if a source of sound of frequency 502 Hz was placed near the card?

Describe briefly how you would use a stroboscope to check the rate of rotation of the wheel. *(S)*

21   Vibrations and stationary waves

21.1 Vibrations and resonance

Free and forced vibrations

When a body is given an initial impulse, and then left alone, it continues to vibrate. The frequency with which it vibrates is its **natural frequency**. Among numerous examples are a child on a swing who has been pushed once only, a punch-ball which has received just one punch (Fig. 21.1), a simple pendulum and a tuning fork which has been struck. These vibrations are **free vibrations**.

When the child on the swing is pushed as the swing comes forward (Fig. 21.2), the swing does not continue to vibrate with its natural frequency. The swing is not allowed to reach the extreme position, and its **frequency** (number of vibrations per second) is determined by the person who is pushing it. Similarly when the boxer punches the punch-ball continually, the frequency with which the punch-ball oscillates is determined by the frequency with which the boxer punches. These vibrations are known as **forced vibrations**.

Resonance

If you give the bench top a sharp tap you will hear a sound. This is the **natural frequency** of the bench top. When the stem of a vibrating tuning fork is placed on the bench top, the bench top is forced to vibrate at the same frequency as the tuning fork.

Every body has its own natural frequency of vibration and it will vibrate with that frequency when it has the opportunity.

Figure 21.3 shows a stretched wire or string to which are attached five pendulums of different lengths, a, b, c, d and e. A sixth pendulum f of the same length as c is attached as shown. Since the five pendulums a to e are of different lengths they have different natural frequencies; however f has the same natural frequency as c because it is the same length. If f is pulled to one side and released it oscillates freely. After a short time c also starts to oscillate. As the amplitude of c increases, the amplitude of f decreases, and eventually f comes to rest and c oscillates with almost the same amplitude as f had originally. The process is then reversed: the amplitude of f increases as c comes to rest, and so on. During this time the pendulums a, b, d and e show no significant movement, although d and e are between c and f, and you might expect the energy to be transferred along the wire. This effect is known as **resonance**. When a body vibrates in the vicinity of another body which has the same natural frequency, the second body vibrates 'in sympathy'.

Why does the amplitude of f decrease as the amplitude of c increases? Since there is no source of energy in the system, the total amount of energy cannot increase. So as the energy of c increases the energy of f must decrease. Energy is transferred from

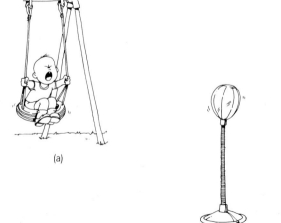

(a)

(b)

21.1 Free vibrations

(a)

(b)

21.2 Forced vibrations

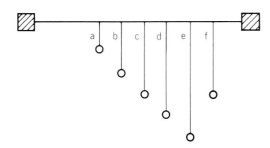

21.3   Resonance

f to c. The *total* vibrational energy will decrease due to work being done against the resistance of the air, and eventually both pendulums will come to rest. Until this happens energy is continually transferred from one pendulum to the other.

Resonance can be a nuisance and is sometimes very dangerous. In the days when columns of soldiers marched they were always made to march out of step when crossing bridges, lest the frequency of their marching should be the same as the natural frequency of the bridge. If the two had been the same, the bridge would have vibrated violently. Trains cross long bridges such as the Forth Bridge very slowly for the same reason.

When turbo-jet engines were first made there were initial teething troubles. At a certain number of revolutions per second, the frequency with which the rotating blades passed the fixed blades was the same as the natural frequency of the blades, and some of them shattered. Sometimes some parts of a car vibrate quite strongly at certain speeds. This is often due to resonance and can be overcome by increasing or decreasing the speed (engine revolutions per minute).

The shattering of a wine glass by a high note which has the same frequency as the natural frequency of the glass is often given as an example of resonance. This is not easy to achieve in practice! However, if you sing a note in a room containing a piano, the piano string with the same natural frequency will vibrate in sympathy.

One example of useful resonance is the tuning circuit on a radio set. Radio waves of all frequencies strike the aerial and only the one which is required must be picked out. This is done by having a capacitance–inductance combination (see p.373) which resonates to the frequency of the required wave. The capacitance is variable; by altering its value other frequencies can be obtained.

A diver wanting to perform a very high dive from a diving board jumps up and down at the board's natural frequency. This resonance increases the amplitude of the springboard and the diver has no difficulty in reaching the required height.

21.2   Producing a stationary wave

Reflected pulses

In Chapter 20 you saw that a pulse will travel along a length of stretched rubber tubing or a spring. When the pulse reaches the end it is reflected, whether the end of the tubing is fixed or free. In Fig. 21.4 one end of the rubber tubing is fixed firmly to a wall and the other end held in the hand. The held end is flicked sharply upwards and brought back to its original position. A pulse travels along the tubing to the wall, where it is

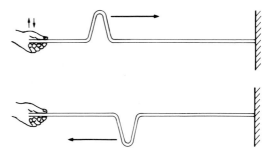

21.4   Reflection of a pulse

reflected. The reflected pulse is below the mean level of the tubing, whereas the initial pulse was above the mean level. Why is there this difference? Consider the end of the rubber tubing fixed to the wall. Since it is fixed it cannot move. The upward force of the original pulse tries to move it upwards (Fig. 21.5). However, since it cannot move there must be an equal and opposite downward force applied by the support to the end of the rubber tubing, and hence the reflected pulse is below the mean level of the tubing. The reflected pulse is 180° out of phase with the original pulse.

upward force due to original pulse

downward force due to reflected pulse

21.5   Forces on the fixed end of a piece of rubber tubing

Stationary waves

When the hand holding the rubber tubing moves up and down and the frequency of the movement is gradually increased, a point is reached when a single loop is obtained (see Fig. 21.6a overleaf). Further increasing the frequency of oscillation of the hand produces a double loop (Fig. 21.6b). If you time the frequency of the hand movements you will see that their frequency has doubled. Since it is difficult to move your hand more rapidly, it is better to use a mechanical vibrator (Fig. 21.7). The metal rod inside the electromagnetic coil vibrates at a frequency controlled by the oscillator.

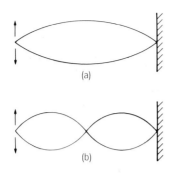

(a)

(b)

21.6   Stationary waves

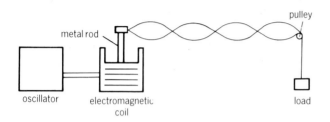

21.7   Production of stationary waves

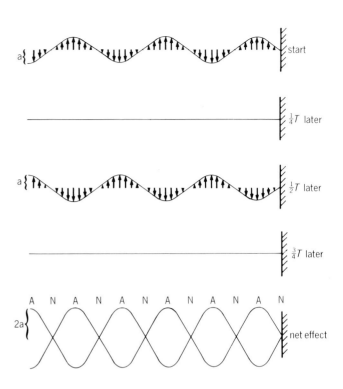

21.8   Nodes and antinodes

Investigation 21.1   To produce stationary waves

Connect one end of a string to the rod in a vibrator. Pass the string over a pulley and attach a load to the other end. Vary the frequency of the oscillator to produce 1, 2, 3, 4 etc. stationary loops between the metal rod and the pulley.

These loops are called **standing** or **stationary waves**. They are formed because the reflected wave is superimposed upon the incident wave. This is known as **interference** and will be dealt with in general in the next chapter (p.262).

In this investigation there are two waves, the **incident** and the **reflected waves**. They have the same frequency, amplitude, and wavelength but are travelling in opposite directions. These waves are **progressive**, but they interfere with each other and so set up stationary waves. The consequences of this are:

(a) all particles in one half wavelength are in phase, i.e. they all move in the same direction at the same time;

(b) each particle has an amplitude different from the particle next to it;

(c) the particles in one half wavelength are 180 ° out of phase with those in the next half wavelength. This simply means that they are either at opposite ends of the oscillation at the same time, or, if they happen to be in the mean position, they are moving in opposite directions.

This is shown in Fig. 21.8, demonstrating that some particles (marked N) never move (they have zero amplitude) since the forces acting upon them are always equal and opposite. These points are called **nodes**, and the distance between two consecutive nodes is half a wavelength, i.e. $\frac{1}{2}\lambda$.

Maximum movement occurs at the points marked A, and the amplitude of these points is *twice* the amplitude of the incident wave. These points are called **antinodes**, and the distance between two consecutive antinodes is half a wavelength. The distance between a node and the next antinode is one-quarter of a wavelength, i.e. $\frac{1}{4}\lambda$.

Note   A stationary wave is different from a progressive wave. In a progressive wave

(a) all particles have the same amplitude;

(b) each particle is out of phase with the particle next to it.

21.3   The sonometer

A sonometer consists of a hollow chamber on which there are two fixed bridges A and B (see Fig. 21.9). A wire fixed at one end passes over A, B and a pulley at the end of the chamber, and weights are attached to the other end. The tension in the wire is altered by adding or removing weights. The third bridge C is movable.

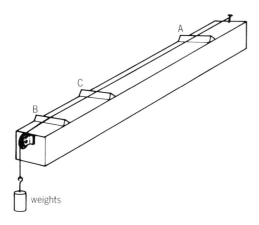

21.9 Sonometer

21.10 Fundamental note

Remove bridge C and add weights until the wire is reasonably taut. If you pluck the wire in the middle it vibrates as a single loop (Fig. 21.10). Since the wire is at rest at A and B these points are nodes; the mid-point of AB is an antinode. This is the simplest manner in which the wire can vibrate, and is known as the **fundamental** mode of vibration. The frequency of the note emitted is the **fundamental frequency**. It is important to stress that the vibrating wire has a

transverse wave motion. However its vibration sets up a *longitudinal* wave in the air. The two waves have the same *frequency* but *not* the same *wavelength* because the speeds of the transverse and longitudinal waves are different. It is possible to make the sonometer wire vibrate longitudinally, by stroking it along its length with resin-covered fingers. This produces a very high-pitched note.

There is another experiment in which the length of wire is constant while the tension in the wire is changed and the fundamental frequency of the length AB is found. It is a very fiddling business to adjust the tension so that the frequency of the note emitted is the same as that of the fork. A better method is to insert the bridge C and move it until the frequency of the length AC is the same as that of the fork. If f is the frequency of the fork, then the frequency of the length AB is given by $f \times$ AC/AB. By using different forks it is found that frequency $f \propto \sqrt{T}$ where T is the tension in the wire.

By using different wires of the same length and keeping the tension constant, it can be shown that $f \propto 1/\sqrt{m}$ where m is the mass per unit length of the wire. The material of the wire does not matter; two different wires of the same mass per unit length will give the same note if the tension and length are the same.

All the above relationships can be combined to give

$$f \propto \frac{1}{l} \sqrt{\frac{T}{m}}$$

In fact

$$f = \frac{1}{2l} \sqrt{\frac{T}{m}}$$

Since the note produced is the fundamental, the length AC of the wire is the distance between two nodes, i.e. half a wavelength. Thus $l = \lambda/2$, or $2l = \lambda$. Since $c = f\lambda = f \times 2l$, the speed $c = \sqrt{(T/m)}$. This is not the

---

Investigation 21.2 To show that the frequency of the fundamental note emitted by a wire is inversely proportional to the length

Set up the sonometer as described above and adjust the tension until the frequency is approximately 256 Hz (by comparison with a 256 Hz tuning fork). Place bridge C under the wire and move it until the frequency of the note emitted by the length AC is exactly 256 Hz. This can be checked by placing a paper rider on the stationary wire midway between A and C and putting the stem of the vibrating 256 Hz tuning fork on the sonometer box. If the length AC is correct the wire will start to vibrate in sympathy with the tuning fork and the paper rider will be thrown off. (**Note** This is an example of resonance.) Measure the length AC.

By using forks of different frequencies, and keeping the tension unaltered, obtain the different values of AC that correspond to the tuning forks. From your results plot a graph of frequency f against $1/l$ (see Fig. 21.11). This is a straight line

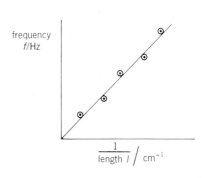

21.11 Graph of frequency against 1/length

through the origin. It shows that the fundamental frequency of the wire AC is inversely proportional to its length.

speed of sound, but the speed with which the transverse wave travels along the wire.

Note This transverse wave produces a longitudinal sound wave of the same frequency.

Example

A sonometer wire vibrates in unison with a tuning fork of frequency 384 Hz. Give two ways in which the sonometer can be adjusted to vibrate in unison with a tuning fork of frequency 512 Hz.

The first method is to alter the length of wire which is vibrating by placing a bridge underneath the wire. $f \propto 1/l$ so $f_1/f_2 = l_2/l_1$ since the tension and mass per unit length of the wire do not change.

$$\frac{f_1}{f_2} = \frac{384}{512}$$

$$= \frac{3}{4} = \frac{l_2}{l_1}$$

Thus the bridge must be placed so that the new length is $\frac{3}{4}$ of the original length. Shortening the length of a vibrating wire gives a note of higher frequency.

The second method is to keep the length of the wire constant and to increase the tension. This time l and m are unchanged so

$$\frac{f_1}{f_2} = \sqrt{\frac{T_1}{T_2}} \quad \text{or} \quad \frac{f_1^2}{f_2^2} = \frac{T_1}{T_2}.$$

$$\frac{T_1}{T_2} = \frac{384^2}{512^2}$$

$$= \frac{9}{16}$$

$$T_2 = \frac{16}{9} T_1$$

The original tension should be increased by a factor of $\frac{16}{9}$. Tightening the wire raises the pitch of the note.

Overtones

Figure 21.12(a) shows the simplest mode of vibration of the wire. There is a node at each end and an antinode in the middle. If the mid-point of the wire is fixed so that it also becomes a node then the wire will vibrate in two loops (Fig. 21.12b). This is the **first overtone**, and its frequency is twice the fundamental frequency. Since it has a higher frequency, the overtone has a higher pitch than the fundamental. The wire is made to vibrate in three loops by placing a bridge one-third of the way from one end and plucking at the mid-point w of the shorter section (Fig. 21.12c). This is the second overtone and its frequency is three times the fundamental frequency. The loops in the wire cannot be seen, but they can be determined. Place paper riders at x, y and z and then pluck w. The riders

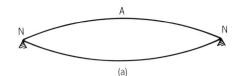

(a)

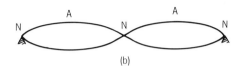

(b)

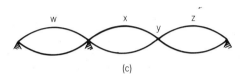

(c)

21.12   Overtones in a wire

at x and z will fly off but that at y will stay on, indicating that there is a node at y. When a violin string is bowed it is possible to produce overtones as well as the fundamental. The overtones combine to produce a richer note or a note of higher quality. Each instrument has its characteristic overtones which enable the instrument producing the note to be identified.

Stationary waves can also be produced when neither end of the string is fixed. In Chapter 20 (p.244) you found that continuous vibration of a length of rubber tubing produced standing waves. If the free end is always an antinode instead of a node, a stationary wave will be produced.

Stationary longitudinal waves can also be produced. A point or particle which does not move is a node and a point which has a maximum displacement is an antinode. One difference between transverse and longitudinal waves is that in a longitudinal wave there is no reversal of phase on reflection at a closed end. A compression is reflected as a compression and a rarefaction as a rarefaction. A change of phase does take place on reflection at an open end, where a compression is reflected as a rarefaction.

21.4   Pressure variation in stationary waves

First consider a progressive *longitudinal* wave. Compressions and rarefactions follow each other along the wave, so at each point the pressure varies between a maximum and a minimum. Thus the pressure variation is the same at every point in the

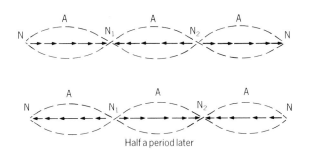

21.13 *Pressure variation in stationary waves*

medium, or the pressure variation is constant throughout the medium. This is not the case for a stationary wave. As with transverse waves, all the particles along a half wavelength are in phase with each other and 180° out of phase with the particles in the next half wavelength. Moreover, each particle has a different amplitude from that next to it. In the wave in Fig. 21.13, air flows towards N_1 from both directions thus increasing the pressure at N_1, and away from N_2 thus decreasing the pressure at N_2. At A there is a change in the direction of flow after half a period but no change in pressure. Half a period later the flow is reversed again. As a result there is quite a large variation in pressure at the nodes, whereas there is no variation of pressure at the antinodes. So in a stationary longitudinal wave the *maximum pressure variation is at the nodes and the minimum pressure variation is at the antinodes*.

When you draw diagrams to represent stationary waves in sound it is easier to use the transverse wave form, *always remembering that the waves are longitudinal*.

21.5   The resonance tube

A resonance tube is a long narrow tube in which the column of air is made to vibrate. Various methods are used to alter the length of the air column, e.g. changing the level of water in the tube. The closed end of a tube is a node because the air in contact with it is stationary. The open end of the tube is always an antinode because the amplitude of vibration there is a maximum. Figure 21.15 shows the fundamental mode of vibration of the air in a tube closed at one end (a closed tube). There is one node and one antinode, and this is the simplest way in which it can vibrate. The length of the tube is approximately one-quarter of a wavelength.

21.15 *Fundamental vibration in a closed tube*

Investigation 21.3   To demonstrate stationary waves with sound

Place a speaker emitting a reasonably high-frequency note at some distance in front of a large metal reflector. Use a microphone as a detector and move it slowly from the reflector towards the speaker. You should hear maximum sounds at a, b, c, d and e (see Fig. 21.14). These are the nodes of the stationary waves where the pressure variation is greatest. Minimum sounds are detected at p, q, r, s and t. These are the antinodes where there is no pressure variation. (The position of these points depends upon the wavelength of the sound.)

The speed of sound in air may be calculated from these positions. Measure the distance from p to t. It is equal to two wavelengths (2λ), so $\lambda = \frac{1}{2}$pt. Let the frequency of the note be f, then speed $c = f\lambda = f \times \frac{1}{2}$pt.

Note   A more accurate determination is obtained if the speaker is farther away from the reflector and the distance between a larger number of antinodes (or nodes) is measured.

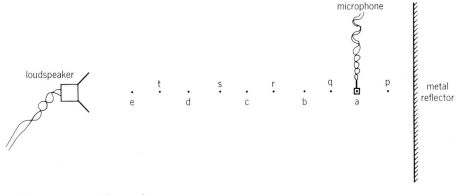

21.14 *Demonstrating stationary waves with sound*

Investigation 21.4 To determine the speed of sound using the resonance tube method

The apparatus used in this investigation is shown in Fig. 21.16(a). The resonance tube is a long narrow tube which is connected to the reservoir B by rubber tubing. Both tubes contain water. When B is raised the length of the air column in A is decreased, and when B is lowered the length of the air column in A is increased. Place a vibrating tuning fork over the top of A when the length of the air column in A is practically zero. You should hear no sound. As you increase the length of the air column in A you will hear the sound increase, reach a maximum and then start to die away again. Repeat the procedure, adjusting B until the length of the air column in A gives maximum sound. Then measure the length l_1 of the air column (Fig. 21.16b).

The loud sound is heard because the natural frequency of the air column of length l_1 is the same as the natural frequency of the fork and so the air column vibrates in sympathy. You have found the **first position of resonance**. In fact the length of air vibrating is slightly longer than the length of the air column in A. Thus

$$\tfrac{1}{4}\lambda = l_1 + e$$

The length e is the extra length which must be added to the air column l_1 to give the length of air vibrating and is known as the **end correction**.

When you lower B still further so that the length of the air column is increased, you will find another position at which the sound is a maximum. Determine this position accurately and measure the length l_2 of the air column. This is the **second position of resonance**. As before, there is an antinode at the open end of the tube, and a node at the water surface. The only way this can be accommodated is shown in Fig. 21.16(c), and the length of the air column in the tube is approximately three-quarters of a wavelength ($\tfrac{3}{4}\lambda$). The end correction is the same as before, so $\tfrac{3}{4}\lambda = l_2 + e$. Subtracting the two measurements gives

$$\tfrac{3}{4}\lambda - \tfrac{1}{4}\lambda = l_2 + e - (l_1 + e)$$
$$\tfrac{1}{2}\lambda = l_2 - l_1$$

and the end correction is eliminated. Thus

$$c = f\lambda$$
$$= f \times 2(l_2 - l_1)$$

where f is the frequency of the tuning fork. This is a quick and quite accurate method of finding the speed of sound in air.

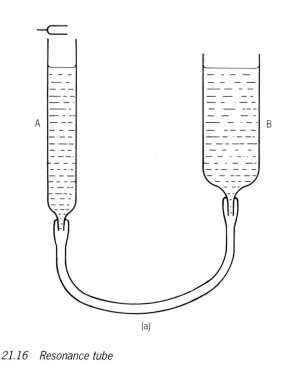

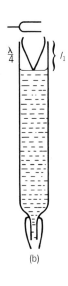

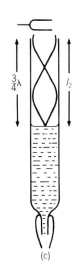

21.16 Resonance tube

A series of forks could be used to show that the length of the air column is proportional to the frequency of the wave. A better method uses a small loudspeaker connected to a calibrated audio-frequency oscillator instead of fixed-frequency tuning forks (see Fig. 21.17). A long tube containing a piston is used instead of tubes of water because it makes adjustment of the column length easier. The steady source of sound is applied a short distance from the end of the tube and the resonant lengths of the air column for frequencies of 300 Hz, 350 Hz, 400 Hz,

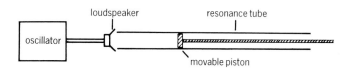

21.17 To show that length of air column is proportional to frequency

258

450 Hz, 500 Hz, 550 Hz and 600 Hz obtained. A graph of 1/frequency against length is plotted as in Fig. 21.18. The negative intercept on the length axis gives the value of the end correction e (about $0.6r$ where r is the radius of the resonance tube).

When water is poured into a bottle, a note is emitted as the air in the bottle is set into vibration. The pitch of the note is raised as the volume of the air in the bottle is decreased. Every bottle has its own natural frequency and a note may be produced by blowing across the open neck of the bottle.

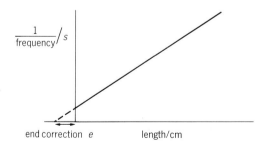

21.18 Graph of 1/frequency against length

During the early part of the 1939–45 war, searchlights controlled by sound-ranging equipment were focussed on to the aircraft. To counteract this some aircrew threw out empty bottles when searchlights picked up the plane. The loud notes made by the falling bottles were picked up by the sound-ranging equipment and the searchlights put out of focus.

21.6 Wind instruments

The sounds produced by wind instruments depend upon the setting up of stationary waves in tubes or pipes. The note depends upon the length of the tube and the mode of vibration of the air in the tube.

Figure 21.19 represents an open organ pipe. Air is blown into the pipe at 0 and strikes the sharp edge E. This causes the air in the pipe to vibrate. Since both ends of the pipe are open, there is always an antinode at each end. The simplest mode of vibration has an antinode at each end and a node in the middle. This is the fundamental (see Fig. 22.19a) and the length of the tube is approximately equal to half a wavelength. The frequency f_0 of the fundamental note $\approx c/2l$ where c is the speed of sound and l is the length of the tube.

Figure 21.19(b) represents the next possible mode of vibration: the first overtone. Here the length l is approximately equal to one wavelength and the frequency is $2f_0$, twice that of the fundamental. The second overtone with a frequency of $3f_0$ is also shown (Fig. 21.19c). It is not difficult to work out other modes of vibration, and you will find that all overtones are possible.

A closed organ pipe has a stop at the end of the pipe, i.e. the end of the pipe is closed. This means that there

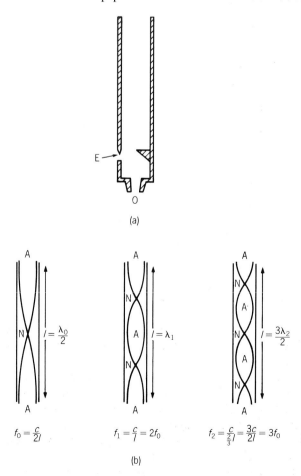

21.19 Modes of vibration of an open pipe

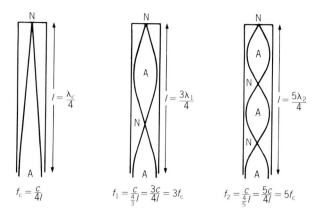

$$f_c = \frac{c}{4l}$$

$$f_1 = \frac{c}{\frac{4}{3}l} = \frac{3c}{4l} = 3f_c$$

$$f_2 = \frac{c}{\frac{4}{5}l} = \frac{5c}{4l} = 5f_c$$

21.20   Modes of vibration of a closed pipe

is always a node at the top; possible modes of vibration are shown in Fig. 21.20. Points which are immediately obvious are:

(a) the fundamental frequency f_c of a closed pipe is half the fundamental frequency of an open pipe of the same length, i.e. $f_o = 2f_c$;
(b) only the odd overtones can be obtained with a closed pipe. Thus the range of notes is greater with an open pipe than with a closed one.

Physical conditions alter the tuning of musical instruments. An increase in temperature causes an increase in the speed of sound in air, and thus an increase in the fundamental frequency. The length of the pipe also increases slightly, causing a slight decrease in frequency. When tuning an organ, for example in a church, the tuners ask for the heating to be turned on so that the organ is tuned at the temperature at which it is normally used. Stringed instruments have the tensions in the strings adjusted by screws or pegs. An increase in temperature causes the wire to expand slightly and reduces the tension.

21.7   Beats

When two notes are sounded, one set of waves is imposed upon the other. This normally has little effect because the frequencies and amplitudes are different. However when two notes of nearly the same frequency are sounded together there is a periodic rise and fall in the intensity of the sound. The sound never dies away completely but the intensity varies. Figure 21.21 shows the combination of two waves of nearly equal frequencies. These periodic variations in intensity are known as **beats**, and are helpful in tuning a wire to a tuning fork. If three beats are heard each second, then the difference in the frequencies of the two notes is 3 Hz. The tension of the wire is adjusted until no beat is heard, and it then has the same frequency as the tuning fork. Beats can be demonstrated using two tuning forks of the *same* frequency. A small piece of plasticene is then attached to a prong of one of the forks to change its frequency slightly. When the forks are sounded together beats will be heard.

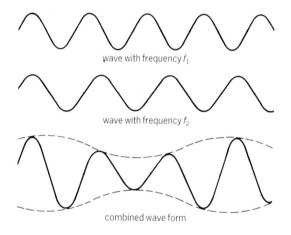

wave with frequency f_1

wave with frequency f_2

combined wave form

21.21   Combining two waves to form beats

Questions

Q1 The following are five physical properties:
A reflection **B** refraction **C** interference
D resonance **E** diffraction
Which is most closely associated with the following observation?
A small paper rider, placed in the centre of a horizontal stretched wire jumps off when a vibrating tuning fork is placed in contact with the end of the wire. *(L, part question)*

Q2 A thin wire under tension is rigidly clamped at its ends. State exactly how the frequency of vibration of the wire depends on its length. What other factors affect this frequency at a given temperature?
Describe *two* methods by which you could measure the fundamental frequency of vibration of the wire, assuming you have a source of sound of known and variable frequency.

By reference to this vibrating wire, explain the terms *amplitude*, *stationary wave*, *antinode* and *wavelength*. *(S)*

Q3 (a) A source of sound, S, is placed in front of a large plane reflector, R.

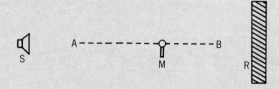

(i)   A microphone, M, which is connected to a cathode ray oscilloscope, is moved along the line AB perpendicular to the reflector. The oscilloscope shows maxima and minima of sound intensity. Explain this and name the maxima and minima.

(ii)   The distance between 11 successive minima is

2.5 m. Assuming the speed of sound to be 340 m s^{-1} find the frequency of the source.

Why is it better to use eleven successive minima instead of two to determine the frequency of the source?

(iii) State, giving your reason, what you would expect to happen to the distance between the minima as the frequency of the source is increased.

 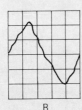 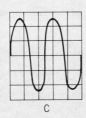

A   B   C

(b) The diagrams A, B and C represent the traces on an oscilloscope of sound waves produced by three different instruments. Compare the pitch, quality and intensity of the three sounds. (Give your reasons.) *(L)*

Q4 (a) Describe an experiment in which a stationary sound wave is produced. Explain how it may be used to determine a value for the wavelength of the sound and hence to determine the speed of sound in air.

(b) A siren consists of a disc with 25 equally spaced holes drilled through it near its edge. A jet of air is directed at the holes as the disc rotates at a rate of 16 rev s^{-1}.
(i) Explain why a note is heard.
(ii) Calculate the frequency of the note.
(iii) Assuming that the speed of sound in air is 340 m s^{-1}, calculate the wavelength of the note in air.
(iv) What effect, if any, will an increase in the rate of rotation have on the pitch of the note and on the time the sound takes to reach a distant observer? Give reasons for your answer. *(L)*

Q5 The table below shows the results of an experiment in which the length of a stretched wire (a sonometer) was varied until it vibrated in unison with each of several tuning forks taken in turn. The tension of the wire was kept constant throughout the experiment.

Frequency of tuning fork/Hz	256	288	341	384	512
Length of wire/mm	942	837	707	628	471

(i) What do you understand by the frequency of a tuning fork?
(ii) Plot a graph of the frequency of the tuning fork against the length of the wire.

(iii) Use the graph to determine the frequency of the tuning fork which will vibrate in unison with a wire of length 754 mm at the same tension as in the experiment. *(L)*

Q6 Describe how you would attempt to show that a material medium is essential for the transmission of sound.

A source of sound S produces vibrations of constant frequency in the air. Describe for some point in the air, e.g. A in the following diagram, (i) the *motion* of the air at the point, (ii) the *pressure changes* occurring at the point. How would the pressure changes at that point alter if the source of sound were (a) louder, (b) of higher pitch?

In the diagram, B is the point nearest to A at which the motion and pressure changes area at all instants identical with those at A when the frequency of the source is 1360 Hz. Given that $AB = 25.0$ cm, calculate the speed of sound in the air. *(C)*

Q7 By blowing across the open end of a bicycle pump the air column inside the cylinder of the pump can be made to resonate and a musical note is obtained. The pitch of this note can be varied by sliding the pump handle in or out.
(i) Sketch a cross-section of the pump when it is emitting its lowest note and mark carefully where the node and the antinode occur in the vibrating air column in the cylinder.
(ii) When the length of the vibrating air column is 0.35 m the frequency of the note emitted is found to be 250 Hz. Calculate the speed of sound in air.
(iii) If the length of the air column inside the bicycle pump is reduced to 0.175 m, find the frequency of the note which is now emitted. Compare the pitch of this note with that in (ii). *(L)*

Q8 Sound waves are *longitudinal* waves; when they travel through air they are associated with *compressions* and *rarefactions* in the air. Explain the meanings of the terms in italics.

The waves from a sound source of frequency 510 Hz travel through air at 340 m s^{-1}. Calculate the wavelength of the waves and deduce the distance from a compression to the nearest rarefaction.

A different source of sound has a frequency of 1020 Hz. How is its pitch related to that of the source of frequency 510 Hz?

Describe in detail an experiment by which the speed of sound waves in air could be determined. State your precautions you would take to reduce the errors in your experiment. *(C)*

22 Interference, diffraction and the photoelectric effect

22.1 Theories of light

The earliest theory of light was the **corpuscular theory**. This stated that light consisted of small particles or corpuscles and these travelled from the object to the eye. Reflection was explained by considering the corpuscles as small elastic spheres bouncing from a perfectly elastic surface. Refraction was explained by assuming that the corpuscles were attracted by the particles of the denser medium, and were thus accelerated. Thus the speed of light was increased in the denser medium and this resulted in a change in direction. On leaving the denser medium the corpuscles were supposed to be retarded to their former speed. Consequently they suffered an opposite change in direction and emerged parallel to the incident rays. This theory is based on the fact that the speed of light must be *higher* in the denser medium.

The next theory was the **wave theory**. This assumed that light energy was transmitted by waves. The explanation of refraction by this theory depended upon the speed of light being *lower* in a dense medium than in a rare medium. When experimental technique improved sufficiently to measure the speed of light in the laboratory, it was found that the speed of light is less in water than in air. This was a very strong point in favour of the wave theory.

If the wave theory is correct it should be possible to make the crest of one wave of light cancel the trough of another, i.e. to get two light waves to combine to produce darkness. When this was achieved in the laboratory it was further evidence in favour of the wave theory.

Two other factors in favour of the wave theory were diffraction and polarisation. Diffraction is the ability of waves to spread around obstacles, and can now be demonstrated with light. Polarisation is the ability to confine the wave motion to one plane only.

Thus it appears that all the evidence is in favour of the wave theory of light. However, it is not possible to explain everything with the simple wave theory. An example is the photo-electric effect, where light shining upon certain metals causes electrons to be emitted. The explanation of this involves waves acting as particles (**photons**). In modern physics both wave and particle properties of light are assumed.

22.2 Interference

In the previous chapter stationary waves are described as a reflected wave superimposed upon an incident wave, and beats are described as the interaction of two waves of nearly equal frequency which produces a periodic rise and fall in intensity. Both of these are examples of **interference**, a topic which will now be studied in more detail.

Figure 22.1 shows two waves travelling in different directions and crossing at O. Suppose the frequencies of the waves are equal and they have equal amplitudes. If the crest of one wave arrives at O at the same time as the trough of the other, they will combine so that the particle at O suffers no displacement. This is true along the length of the wave. As you read on p.241, a crest is 180° out of phase with a trough. Since the waves have the same frequency, they are always 180° out of phase at O, whatever part of the wave is passing. Thus the forces on the particle are always equal and opposite and thus cancel. The same is true for a longitudinal wave; in this case a compression coincides with a rarefaction instead of a crest coinciding with a trough. Obviously the waves only cancel completely if they have the same amplitude. This is known as **destructive interference**.

If two crests or two troughs arrive at O at the same instant they combine so that the amplitude of the wave

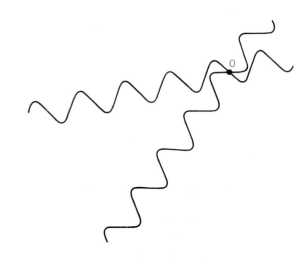

22.1 *Waves crossing*

Investigation 22.1   To demonstrate interference in a ripple tank

It is possible to demonstrate the interference of water waves in a ripple tank. Attach two identical dippers to the horizontal wooden bar about 10 cm apart (Fig. 22.2). When you start the motor the bar vibrates and the dippers vibrate with the bar. Thus they have the same frequency and the same amplitude, and send out circular waves of the same frequency and amplitude. These waves interfere. If you view the waves using a stroboscope of the same frequency the waves appear stationary and the interference pattern is clear. Either two crests or two troughs coincide along the full lines in the diagram and there is constructive interference. (These lines are sometimes known as **antinodal lines** because the displacement is a maximum.) Along the dotted lines crests coincide with troughs and there is destructive interference. (These lines are sometimes known as **nodal lines** because the displacement is a minimum.) The lines fan out from the region between the two dippers as shown.

Look at what happens along a line AB parallel to the line joining the two dippers (sources) and some distance from them. Points of maximum disturbance alternate with points of minimum disturbance and these points are equally spaced. The distance between them depends upon the distance of AB from the dippers.

If you speed up the motor the frequency of the waves increases, and there is a corresponding decrease in wavelength. The nodal and antinodal lines become closer together. They are still equally spaced *along AB* but the distance between them is decreased.

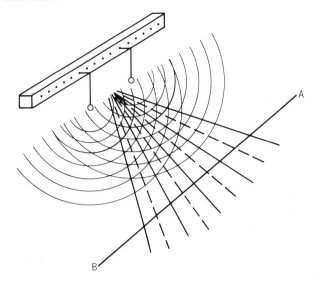

22.2   *Interference in a ripple tank*

is doubled. The waves are in phase at O and the forces on the particle are equal and act in the same direction. This means that the forces on the particle at O always reinforce each other. This also happens to longitudinal waves when two compressions or two rarefactions arrive at the same time. Since the waves are in phase, the amplitude is doubled, whatever part of the two waves arrives at O. This effect is known as **reinforcement** or **constructive interference**.

Obviously whenever two waves pass through the same point they react with each other. Whether or not anything is observed at the point of intersection depends upon the frequency and amplitude of the waves. If the waves have the same frequency and the same amplitude it is possible for them to cancel completely. Because it is difficult to get two different sources to produce waves with the same frequency and amplitude it is usual in laboratory experiments to use a single source and make the waves travel along different paths.

The observations made in this experiment can be summarised as follows:

(a) The points of maximum displacement along AB are equally spaced.
(b) These points become closer together as the frequency increases, i.e. the distance between them decreases.
(c) The distance between the points depends upon the distance of AB from the sources.

Note   The dippers enter the water together and leave the water together, i.e. they are vibrating in phase.

Figure 22.3 shows two sources S_1 and S_2 which are vibrating in phase. Consider the point M on the perpendicular bisector of S_1S_2. M is equidistant from S_1 and S_2 i.e. $S_1M = S_2M$. If two crests leave S_1 and S_2 at the same instant they will arrive at M together because they have travelled equal distances. This is also true for two troughs. Hence the waves are always in phase when they arrive at M and always reinforce each other. Thus M is always a point of constructive interference or maximum displacement. The same reasoning applies to any point along OM.

Now look at N, on LR perpendicular to OM. For N to be a point of destructive interference or zero (minimum) displacement, the waves must be 180 ° out of phase when they arrive at N. The forces at N are then always equal and opposite and so cancel. Thus

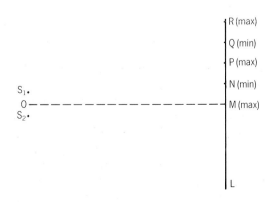

22.3   *Maxima and minima produced by two sources*

the length of the paths taken by the two waves must differ by half a wavelength, i.e. by the distance between a crest and a trough, the two nearest points which are 180 ° out of phase. A phase difference of 180 ° is equivalent to a path difference of $\frac{1}{2}\lambda$ and so $NS_2 - NS_1 = \frac{1}{2}\lambda$.

P is the next point of maximum displacement on LR and the waves are again in phase. The shortest distance between two consecutive particles in phase is one wavelength and thus $S_2P - S_1P = \lambda$. At Q there is destructive interference and no displacement. The waves are again 180 ° out of phase, which means that this time the path lengths differ by one and a half wavelengths, i.e. $QS_2 - QS_1 = \frac{3}{2}\lambda$. R is the next position of constructive interference. The waves are again in phase so $RS_2 - RS_1 = 2\lambda$.

If you continue to work out the positions you will find that for maximum displacement the difference in path length is always a whole number of wavelengths. The general condition for constructive interference is

$$\text{path length difference} = n\lambda$$

where $n = 0, 1, 2, 3$ etc. It follows that for destructive interference the general condition is path length difference $= (n + \frac{1}{2})\lambda$, where $n = 0, 1, 2, 3$ etc. There are also regions of constructive and destructive

interference on ML and beyond. The pattern is symmetrical on both sides of OM.

22.3 Interference of electromagnetic waves

Interference fringes with monochromatic light

Although the ripple tank gives a good demonstration of interference, a more convincing effect is produced when two sources of light are made to interfere. You will then see bright bands formed by constructive interference and dark bands formed by destructive interference. This cannot be shown if two extended light sources, such as two flash lamp bulbs, are used because they emit large numbers of waves of different frequencies, amplitudes and phases. Instead, the technique is to use a single source which is very narrow (e.g. a fine slit) to produce two separate sources close together.

A single source is used in the investigation so that the two sources A and B emit waves which have the same frequency and amplitude and which are in phase. These are known as **coherent sources**. It would be impossible to achieve this similarity with two separate individual sources.

Investigation 22.2 To demonstrate interference with light

Figure 22.4 shows an arrangement of slits similar to that used by Thomas Young, the first person to produce interference fringes. A sodium lamp is used as a light source because it emits monochromatic light, i.e. light of one wavelength. The experiment should be performed in a dark room. Place a screen with a single slit S in front of the lamp. This slit is regarded as the source. Place a second screen with two narrow parallel slits A and B about 1 mm apart as shown so that A and B are

symmetrical with respect to S, i.e. equidistant from S. The distance between the screens should be a few centimetres. View the fringes on a ground glass screen placed about 50 or 60 cm from A and B. After adjusting the screen a little, you should see parallel yellow and black fringes on the screen. These may be viewed more clearly through a microscope (see Fig. 22.4).

If you cover slit B so that A alone illuminates the screen, you should see a patch of yellow light. This is also the case if A is covered and B alone illuminates the screen. This indicates that fringes are produced only when both slits illuminate the screen.

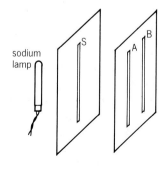

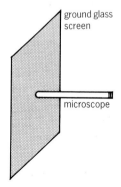

22.4 Production of interference fringes

Distance between consecutive bright (or dark) fringes

In Fig. 22.5 y is the distance between the central bright band (fringe) and the next bright band, d the distance between the sources and X the distance between the sources and the screen. AP is equal to PC and BC is the difference in path length for waves meeting at the first bright band, i.e. BC must be one wavelength long. By considering the geometry, it may be shown to a very close approximation that

$$\frac{\lambda}{d} = \frac{y}{X} \ \text{ or } \ \lambda = \frac{yd}{X} \ \text{ or } \ y = \frac{\lambda X}{d}$$

The bands are equally spaced, and so y is also the distance between any two bright bands. This can also be shown geometrically.

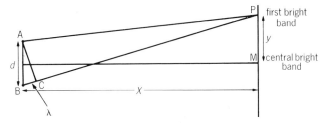

22.5 *Distance between consecutive bright bands of an interference fringe*

By considering $y = \lambda X/d$ several deductions can be made.

(a) The smaller the distance d between the sources, the larger the distance y between the fringes. This is why it is important to have the sources close together.

(b) The greater the distance X, the greater the distance between the fringes.

(c) The longer the wavelength of the light, the greater the distance between the fringes. So blue fringes will be much closer together than red fringes.

To obtain a measurement of y, you must measure the distance between a large number of fringes using a microscope and then divide this distance by the number of fringes. You should also use the microscope to measure d, but it is accurate enough to measure X with a metre rule. The wavelength can be calculated from these measurements.

Interference fringes with white light

If the sodium lamp is replaced by a source of white light the results may be summarised as follows:

(a) There is a white band in the centre. Although white light is made up of a lot of colours of different wavelengths, each wavelength from the two sources is in phase at the centre and so there is a band where each separate colour combines. This gives white light.

(b) There are no dark bands. Consider the position where there is destructive interference of yellow light. There is no dark band here because, although yellow light still cancels here, the other colours do not. So white light minus yellow light is seen.

Note The situation may not be quite so simple as this, because some other colour may reinforce here.

The overall effect is of white light in the centre with parallel bands of different colours on either side.

You can clearly see the effect of wavelength on the interference pattern if you place different coloured filters in front of the white light. If a filter made of two narrow strips of red and blue is used the appearance is similar to Fig. 22.6.

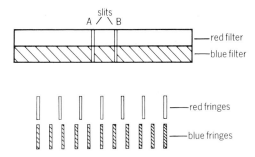

22.6 *Interference fringes with different colours*

Practical use of fringes

Fringes are also produced by reflected light. When a spot of oil or petrol is spilled onto water, coloured fringes are produced. These are formed by the interference of light reflected from the top and bottom surfaces of the very thin film of oil. Thin wedge-shaped air films (e.g. formed by trapping air between two microscope slides slightly inclined to each other) also produce interference fringes when light is reflected from the top and bottom surface. A thin wedge produces fringes parallel to the edge of the wedge when illuminated with monochromatic light. When the bottom plate of the wedge is moved the fringes move across the eyepiece of a microscope and the very small distance moved by the bottom plate can be calculated by counting how many fringes have moved across the microscope cross wires.

The standard of length is now determined by the number of interference fringes of red cadmium light in 1 metre. This has the advantage that it does not depend upon the temperature; the platinum–iridium bar which was used formerly had to be at a fixed temperature. Another example of interference of light is given by the colours seen on soap films. Thin films show interference colours either by reflected or by transmitted light. The thinner the film the brighter the colour.

Investigation 22.3 To demonstrate interference with 3-centimetre electromagnetic waves

An experiment similar to Young's slits can be performed using 3-cm electromagnetic waves. Place a transmitter sending out 3-cm waves symmetrically behind the parallel slits A and B, which are each about 2 cm wide, and separated by a distance of about 6 cm (see Fig. 22.7). As the detector use a probe which modulates the 3-cm waves to produce a 'sound' output from the loudspeaker. As you move this probe along the line XY you will record alternate maxima and minima. Mark the positions of the constructive and destructive interference on a large sheet of paper and so measure the path differences for different maxima and minima. This should verify the conditions for producing interference.

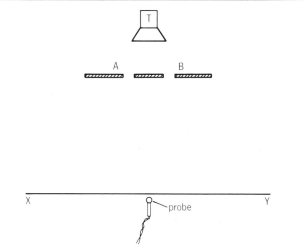

22.7   Interference with 3-cm electromagnetic waves

22.4   Interference of longitudinal waves

Investigation 22.4 To demonstrate interference with sound waves

Set up apparatus similar to that shown in Fig. 22.8(a). The wave source is a loudspeaker attached to an oscillator and the receiver is a microphone to which head phones are attached. Make the sound waves travel from the loudspeaker to the microphone along two different paths, ACB and ADB. The length of ACB is fixed but you can alter ADB by pulling out or pushing in the trombone-like tube D. Turn on the loudspeaker and slowly pull out tube D to increase the length ADB travelled by the sound. You will hear a series of maximum and minimum sounds in the headphones. Maximum sounds are heard when the distance ADB − ACB is a whole number of wavelengths; minimum sounds are heard when ADB − ACB is equal to an odd number of half wavelengths.

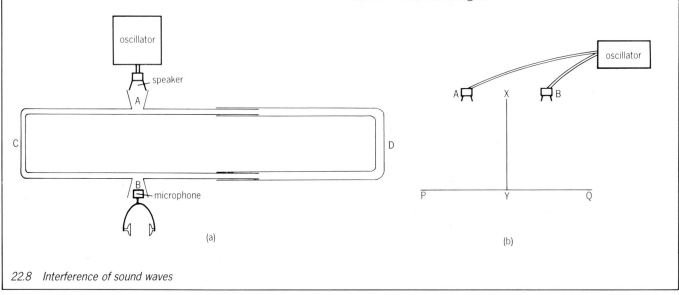

22.8   Interference of sound waves

Example

When the loudspeaker sends out a note of 500 Hz the microphone at B registers a minimum intensity (Fig. 22.8a). As D is pulled out $\frac{1}{3}$ m the intensity in the microphone at B increases to a maximum and returns to a minimum again. Determine the speed of sound in air.

In going from one minimum to the next minimum the length of the path increases by one wavelength. This means that D has been pulled out half a wavelength (the path increases by half a wavelength at both joins). Thus $\lambda/2 = \frac{1}{3}$ m and $\lambda = \frac{2}{3}$ m.

$$c = f\lambda$$
$$= 500\,\text{s}^{-1} \times \tfrac{2}{3}\,\text{m}$$
$$= 333.3\,\text{m s}^{-1}$$

Example

In Fig. 22.8(b) A and B are two loudspeakers which are connected to the same oscillator. The note emitted is of constant frequency. What would you expect an observer to hear when (a) walking along XY and (b) walking along PYQ? XY is on the perpendicular bisector of AB and PQ is perpendicular to XY. Assume that reflection from the ground can be neglected.

(a) The observer walking from X to Y will always hear a loud note, but the intensity will diminish as the distance from AB

increases. When walking along XY the observer is always equidistant from A and B, so the waves are always in phase and there is constructive interference. The intensity decreases as the distance increases because intensity varies as $1/d^2$ where d is the distance from AB.

(b) When walking along PQ the observer will hear alternate maximum sound and no sound at regular intervals. Y is a position of maximum intensity because it is equidistant from A and B. The maximum sounds will be equally spaced around Y.

22.5 Diffraction

If you have watched waves at the seaside or on an inland stretch of water you may have noticed that the waves spread round obstacles, and that they spread out when they pass through an opening. This spreading is called **diffraction**. As with interference, diffraction occurs with both transverse and longitudinal waves. The shorter the wavelength the more difficult it is to demonstrate diffraction. The

wavelength of light is very small and the diffraction (spreading) round obstacles is very little.

Note You must be careful not to confuse *diffraction* with *refraction*. Diffraction is the deviation of waves in a single medium by a narrow aperture or obstacle, and there is no change in wavelength or speed. Refraction is the deviation of waves when they cross the boundary between two different media, and there is a change in both wavelength and speed.

Investigation 22.5 To demonstrate diffraction round a straight edge in a ripple tank

Use a flat dipper to produce parallel wave fronts. Put a block of metal in the tank to act as the straight edge. When the parallel waves pass the straight edge you will see them bend as shown in Fig. 22.9. Decrease the speed of the motor so that waves of longer wavelength are produced. The bending should become more pronounced.

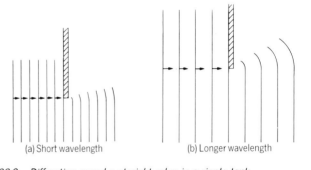

(a) Short wavelength   (b) Longer wavelength

22.9   *Diffraction round a straight edge in a ripple tank*

Investigation 22.6 To demonstrate diffraction through a slit in a ripple tank

Make a slit by placing two blocks of metal close to each other in the tank (see Fig. 22.10). Produce the plane waves using a flat dipper as before. First keep the slit width constant and vary the frequency and hence the wavelength. You should make two observations:

(a) the waves spread out more, i.e. they are diffracted more, when the wavelength is longer;

(b) the wavelength does not change when the waves pass through the slit.

Now keep the frequency, and hence the wavelength, constant (Fig. 22.11). Gradually decrease the width of the slit. As the width decreases you should see the diffraction (spreading) increase; when the width of the slit is less than the wavelength the emerging waves are circular. At this width the slit may be considered to act as a separate point source of waves.

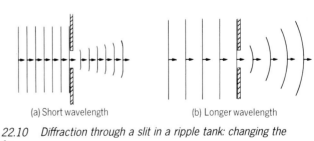

(a) Short wavelength   (b) Longer wavelength

22.10   *Diffraction through a slit in a ripple tank: changing the frequency*

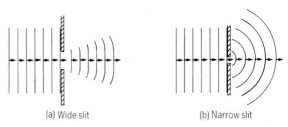

(a) Wide slit   (b) Narrow slit

22.11   *Diffraction through a slit in a ripple tank: reducing the slit*

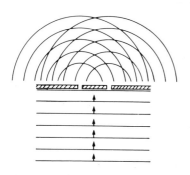

22.12 Diffraction through two slits in a ripple tank

Two narrow slits (Fig. 22.12) can be used instead of the two dippers as in Fig. 22.2, to act as separate wave sources. The interference patterns produced are just as clear. This indicates that diffraction may set up the conditions for interference to occur.

Diffraction of 3-centimetre electromagnetic waves

Similar diffraction experiments can be performed using 3-cm electromagnetic waves. Figure 22.13(a) shows the transmitter behind a slit and the probe in front of the slit detecting the spreading out of the waves. Figure 22.13(b) shows the transmitter behind a straight edge and the probe picking up energy in the geometrical shadow. When the probe is moved parallel to the metal plate and just outside the shadow,

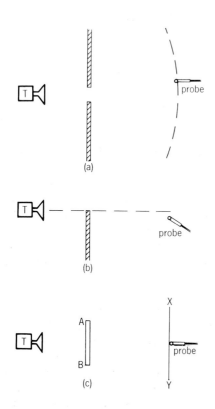

22.13 Diffraction with 3-cm electromagnetic waves

variations in intensity are detected, but they differ from interference in that the intensity remains high in the minima, although not so high as in the maxima. Figure 22.13(c) shows a metal plate symmetrically placed in front of the transmitter. A probe moved along XY records maxima and minima as in interference. In this case the edges A and B of the metal plate act as separate sources.

Diffraction of sound waves

The diffraction of sound waves can be observed in everyday life. If you stand in an open field and shout you can be heard by someone standing behind you. The sound waves emerging from your mouth are diffracted. If you use a megaphone it is much easier for someone in front of you to hear, but not so easy for those behind. This is because the opening from which the waves emerge is so much larger that they are not diffracted so much. Someone shouting from around a corner can be heard but not seen. The long wavelength sound waves are diffracted and bend round the corner, but the very short wavelength light waves are not.

It is not always easy to recognise diffraction with sound waves, because usually reflection and sometimes refraction also take place at the same time.

Diffraction of light waves

It is very difficult to show diffraction with light waves because the wavelength of light is so very short. However, it can be demonstrated if a monochromatic light source is used with a photographic plate acting as a receiver.

22.6 The diffraction grating

So far diffraction has been observed as the waves pass through a single slit and a double slit. It is interesting to see the effect of a large number of parallel slits very close together, in what is known as a **diffraction grating**. The waves spread out in a circular shape from each slit (as the width of the slit is less than the wavelength of the light), as shown in Fig. 22.14.

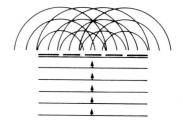

22.14 Diffraction grating

Monochromatic light

If the waves in the diagram are replaced by monochromatic rays, as in Fig. 22.15, and only some diffracted rays are shown, a clearer picture can be obtained. Figure 22.15(a) shows those rays leaving perpendicular to the grating. When a converging lens is placed in their path they are brought to focus at O. All are in phase, so they reinforce each other when they meet and produce a bright band of light.

Figure 22.15(b) shows those rays leaving at an angle θ_1 to the grating. The width of each opening in the grating is a and the width of each opaque part is b. From the enlargement you can see that $\lambda/(a + b) = \sin \theta_1$. Rays are shown leaving from the top of each opening and each ray has to travel one wavelength (λ) further than the one above it. The bottom ray travels three wavelengths further than the top ray, so they are still in phase. When they reach the lens they are all in phase because the difference in path length between successive rays is λ. Thus when brought to a focus by the lens, they will all reinforce and produce a second bright band.

Figure 22.15(c) shows rays leaving at an angle of θ_2 ($\sin \theta_2 = 2\lambda/(a + b)$); the difference in path length between successive rays is 2λ. Again all rays reinforce when brought to a focus by a lens. Similarly if the difference in path lengths is three wavelengths then $3\lambda = (a + b) \sin \theta_3$. In general terms the equation for difference in path lengths may be written $n\lambda = (a + b) \sin \theta_n$ where $n = 0, 1, 2, 3$ etc. The spaces (of width a) have to be very close together (a distance b apart); 600 spaces (lines) per millimetre is quite common. In this case $(a + b) = 1/600$ mm or $10^{-3}/600$ m. The distance $a + b = d$ is known as the grating spacing, and the equation is $d \sin \theta = n\lambda$.

Figure 22.16 combines these results. When monochromatic light falls normally on to a grating and the emerging light passes through a lens, bright bands are formed as shown. The middle band represents $n = 0$ and the second band on either side represents $n = 2$.

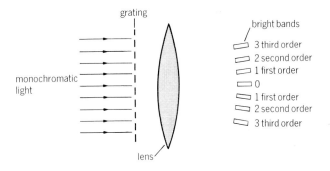

22.16   Spectra formed with a diffraction grating

White light

If white light is diffracted by the diffraction grating the centre bright band remains white. However, since the angles of emergence are slightly different for each different colour, spectra are formed instead of the bright bands of one colour produced by monochromatic light. The spectrum in the position $n = 1$ is known as the **first order spectrum** and that in the $n = 3$ position as the **third order spectrum**.

The spectra formed by a diffraction grating differ from those produced by a prism in that the colours are in the reverse order. Red light, with the longest wavelength, is deviated most by the grating whereas it is deviated least in the prism. Gratings are often used to produce spectra because a wider spread can be obtained than with a prism. The width of the spectrum increases with increasing order.

It is possible to show the diffraction grating effect with 3-cm electromagnetic waves. The grating consists of a series of aluminium sheets about 8 cm wide separated by gaps of about 2 cm. The transmitter is placed behind the grating and the probe moved about in front. The positions of maximum sound show the different order spectra.

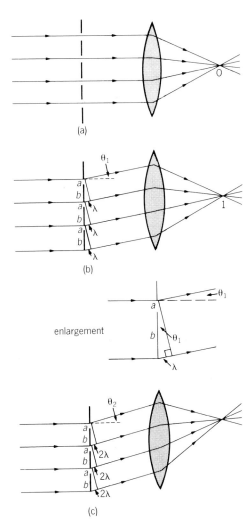

22.15   Theory of the diffraction grating effect

22.7 Photo-electric effect

The photo-electric effect, i.e. the emission of electrons when light falls upon certain metals, was mentioned in Chapter 9.

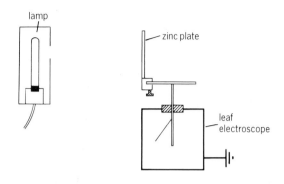

22.17 Photo-electric effect

The electrons emitted are known as **photo-electrons**. The number of photo-electrons emitted depends upon the intensity of the incident light, *as long as the wavelength of the light is below a certain value*. If it is above this value no photo-electron is emitted no matter how great the intensity of the light. This can be tested by using different metals and light of different wavelengths.

Knowledge of the photo-electric effect suggests that the energy of a light wave is in little packets or quanta called **photons**. The energy of a photon = *hf* where *h* is a constant known as Planck's constant and *f* is the frequency of the wave. When a photon releases an electron the energy equation is

energy of photon	=	energy required to release electron from metal	+	kinetic energy of released electron

Investigation 22.8 To demonstrate the photo-electric effect

Attach a clean zinc plate to the cap of a leaf electroscope and illuminate it with a strong source of white light. Note what happens when:

(a) the zinc plate and electroscope are uncharged;
(b) the zinc plate and electroscope are negatively charged;
(c) the zinc plate and electroscope are positively charged.

There should be no response from the electroscope. Replace the white light source by an ultraviolet lamp and repeat the experiment. This time you should observe the following results.

(a) When there is no initial charge the leaf of the electroscope rises initially, indicating that it is acquiring charge.
(b) When the zinc plate and electroscope are negatively charged the leaf of the electroscope falls, indicating that it is losing negative charge.
(c) When the zinc plate and electroscope are positively charged the leaf of the electroscope does not move.

All of these observations can be explained if it is assumed that the ultraviolet light releases electrons from the zinc. In (c) the positive charge immediately attracts the electrons back to the plate, and so there is no loss of charge.

The longer the wavelength, the smaller the frequency and the smaller the energy of the photon. In this respect the photon may be regarded as akin to a small individual particle. The length of time for which the light is incident is not relevant. The energy of the photon is determined simply by the frequency of the wave.

The value of the frequency f_o which will just release a photo-electron from a particular metal is known as the **threshold value**. Light of higher frequency releases the photo-electron and gives it kinetic energy. The equation may be written as $hf = hf_o + \frac{1}{2}mv^2$, where v is the speed of the photo-electron.

Questions

Q1 How do the frequency and wavelength change when waves in a ripple tank pass through a narrow gap in a barrier?

	Frequency	*Wavelength*
A	increase	increase
B	increase	decrease
C	decrease	increase
D	decrease	unchanged
E	unchanged	unchanged

Q2 (a) Explain what is meant by the *thermionic emission* of electrons, and by the *photoelectric emission* of electrons.

(b) Describe an experiment to show that a narrow beam of electrons projected at right angles to a uniform magnetic field describes a circular path.

(c) Describe an experiment which demonstrates photoelectric emission and explain why this gives evidence for the existence of photons. *(O)*

Q3 The following are types of electromagnetic radiation:

A gamma rays **B** infrared rays **C** radio waves
D ultraviolet rays **E** yellow light

Which of these suffers least diffraction on passing though a narrow aperture? *(L)*

Q4 A metal is known to emit photo-electrons under certain conditions, but does not emit any when a parallel beam of light falls upon it. It may be made to emit photo-electrons by

A focusing the light on to a point on the metal.
B increasing the intensity of the light.
C polarising the light.
D using light of a much shorter wavelength.
E using light of a much longer wavelength.

Q5 (a) In an experiment to measure the wavelength (L) of a source of light using Young's slits to form an interference pattern on a screen, the band separation (y) is given by the formula: $y = LD/s$; where s is the distance between slits and D is the distance from the slits to the screen. Calculate y for yellow light ($L = 5.9 \times 10^{-7}$ m) if s = 0.25 mm and D = 50 cm.

Name a possible source of yellow light and indicate how it is situated for this experiment. What changes would you expect in the observed pattern if (i) red, (ii) white light had been used? Give reasons.

(b) Consider the following types of wave: infrared, ultraviolet, sound, X-rays, radio.
(i) Which of these is *not* part of the electromagnetic spectrum?
Of those that are electromagnetic,
(ii) which has the shortest wavelengths,
(iii) which has the lowest frequencies,
(iv) which is unlikely to be detected by a photographic method,
(v) what is significant about their speed? *(S)*

Q6 Describe with the aid of a labelled diagram how you would set up and use a finely ruled grating to produce a spectrum on a screen. Make clear what is meant by the *dispersion* of light by the grating.

When white light is shone on a finely ruled grating a *continuous* spectrum is formed. What is the meaning of *continuous* in this case?

In the continuous spectrum of the sun, there is radiation just beyond the red end of the visible region. Name this radiation. State two properties which this radiation has in common with light, and two which are different from those of light.

Describe with a labelled diagram one experiment for detecting this type of radiation. *(C)*

Q7

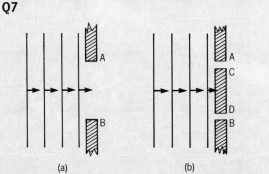

(a) (i) Plane waves strike the aperture AB in diagram (a). Sketch the wave pattern emerging from AB. On the same diagram show by *dotted lines* what would be the effect of doubling the wavelength.
(ii) CD is now placed in the aperture, so that in effect AC and DB are two parallel slits as in diagram (b). The wavelength is returned to its original value. Draw the new wave pattern in the region of the slits.

(iii) If a detector were moved along the line MN what would you expect to find? (Pay particular attention to the point P which is equidistant from C and D.) What differences would you expect along MN if the wavelength were shortened?

(b) Describe a demonstration to illustrate the difference between transverse and longitudinal waves. Give an example of each, other than those you have used in your demonstration. *(L)*

Q8 In certain ways light acts as a wave motion and in others as a stream of particles called photons.
(a) Describe how you would demonstrate interference of light in the laboratory and explain how you could deduce the wavelength of the light from measurements that you could take.
(b) Explain how interference effects support the wave theory rather than the particle theory.
(c) What is meant by photoelectric emission and how might it be demonstrated?
(d) Explain why the photoelectric effect supports the particle theory rather than the wave theory. *(O)*

Q9 (a) The diagram represents the fringe pattern obtained in a double-slit experiment when monochromatic red light was used.

shaded area is red, unshaded area is black

(i) Explain clearly, using the wave theory of light, why dark and red fringes occur.
(ii) State clearly how the pattern would change if monochromatic blue light were used, the rest of the apparatus remaining unchanged.
(iii) What deduction could be made about the difference between red and blue light from the two fringe patterns?

(b) In the experiment referred to in (a) the two slits were 0.0002 m apart and the distance from the double-slit to the screen on which the fringes were formed was 4 m.
(i) Sketch and label the arrangement of the apparatus, showing the positions of the source, slits and screen.
(ii) On the screen, the distance between the first red (bright) fringe and the eleventh red fringe was 0.13 m. Calculate the fringe separation.
(iii) Calculate a value for the wavelength of the red light used in the experiment.

(c) What is meant by dispersion? Sketch a diagram to show the path taken by a narrow beam of white light when it passes through a glass prism. *(JMB)*

23   Introduction to static electricity

23.1   Static charge

Most substances when rubbed against another substance release **static electricity**. This is most noticeable when the rubbed substance is a very good insulating material. If you rub a plastic comb or the barrel of a pen on your coat sleeve it will attract small bits of paper. If you rub an inflated balloon on a nylon jersey it can be stuck to the wall or ceiling. Records, household mirrors and windows all attract dust and other small particles when polished with a dry duster. You may hear a crackling sound when you take nylon clothes off over your head; you may even see sparks in a darkened room. Perhaps you have felt or seen a spark between your hand and the metal door handle when you get out of the family car.

All of these are examples of the formation of **electric charge** caused by the friction between surfaces. In every case *equal* amounts of *opposite* charge are formed. Only two types of electric charges are known to exist and these are called **positive charge** (+) and **negative charge** (−). In early work on electrostatics an ebonite rod rubbed with animal fur gained a negative charge; a glass rod rubbed with silk acquired a positive charge. Modern plastics now enable us to obtain a negative charge by rubbing a polythene rod or strip with a duster and a positive charge by rubbing a cellulose acetate rod or strip with the same duster.

In this book only the polythene and acetate strips will be discussed. When the polythene strip is rubbed with a duster, electrons (e^-) are removed from the duster and go onto the polythene strip where they remain because the polythene is a very good insulator. The duster, which has lost negative charge, acquires a positive charge (Fig. 23.1a). However, the duster is *not* a good insulator and electrons from earth quickly pass through the hand that holds it and neutralise the positive charge. Thus when the duster is tested for charge it is found to be uncharged or neutral.

> ### Exercise 23.1
> Using Fig. 23.1(b) explain how the acetate strip acquires a positive charge by giving up electrons to the duster. Explain how and why the duster remains uncharged (neutral).

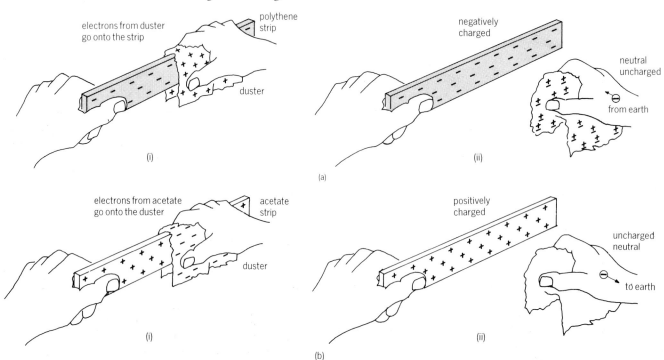

23.1   Charging by friction: (a) negative and (b) positive charge

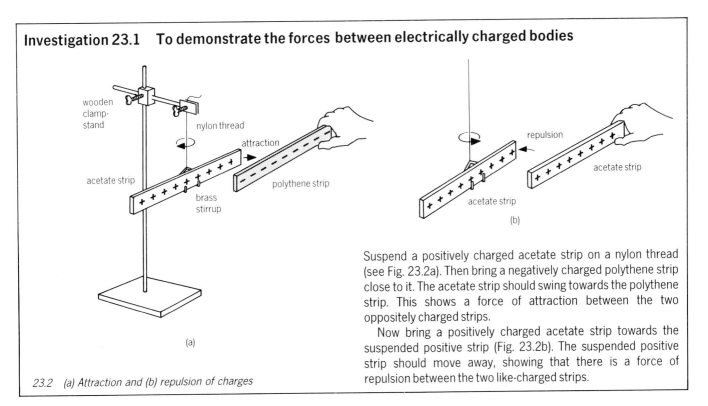

Investigation 23.1 To demonstrate the forces between electrically charged bodies

23.2 (a) Attraction and (b) repulsion of charges

Suspend a positively charged acetate strip on a nylon thread (see Fig. 23.2a). Then bring a negatively charged polythene strip close to it. The acetate strip should swing towards the polythene strip. This shows a force of attraction between the two oppositely charged strips.

Now bring a positively charged acetate strip towards the suspended positive strip (Fig. 23.2b). The suspended positive strip should move away, showing that there is a force of repulsion between the two like-charged strips.

The conclusions which can be drawn from these tests are

1 **Like charges repel** (positive *repels* positive; negative *repels* negative).
2 **Unlike charges attract** (positive *attracts* negative; negative *attracts* positive).

Induction

Figure 23.3(a) shows a light polystyrene sphere which has been coated with a metal (conducting) paint suspended near a positively charged strip. The sphere is standing in the **electric field** (a region where electric forces act on electric charges) set up by the charge on the acetate strip. This field causes the separation of equal amounts of charge on the sphere by **induction** (influence). Negative charges (−) from within the neutral metal move towards the positive strip leaving positive charges (+) at the side of the sphere furthest from the strip (Fig. 23.3b).

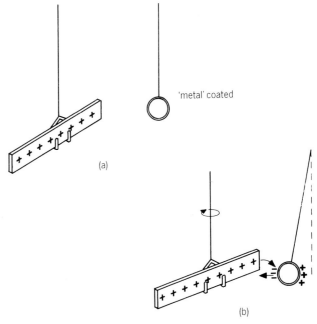

23.3 Electrostatic induction

Exercise 23.2

Redraw Figs. 23.2 and 23.3 with a negatively charged polythene strip in place of the positively charged acetate strip; the other charged strips and metal-coated sphere remain unchanged. Describe and explain what happens in each case. Give reasons why (i) the stirrup should be made of brass, (ii) the thread should be nylon and (iii) the clampstand should be wooden rather than metal.

23.2 Electric potential

An electric charge exerts a force on other electric charges. The region in which the force is exerted is called an **electric field**, and it extends, in theory, an infinite distance away. An uncharged metal sphere (Fig. 23.4) on an insulating stand has no external electric effect. It does contain many electric charges but, since these are present in equal and opposite

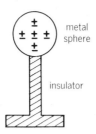

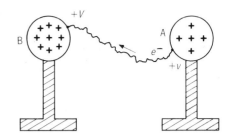

23.4 *Equal and opposite charges produce no external electrical effect*

23.6 *Charge flows when a wire joins two spheres at different potentials*

amounts, the overall effect is **electric neutrality**.

If a metal sphere A (Fig. 23.5a) acquires a small positive charge (by the removal of negative charges from the sphere), the charge acquired can exert a force of attraction on negative charges and a force of repulsion on positive charges. The acquisition of the positive charge is said to raise the **electric potential** of the sphere so that it is greater than that of the Earth (taken as zero potential, see p.275). A small positive charge raises the sphere to a 'small' positive potential $+v$. If an identical sphere B (Fig. 23.5b) were to acquire more positive charge it would be raised to an even higher positive potential $+V$. Hence sphere B is at a higher positive potential than sphere A.

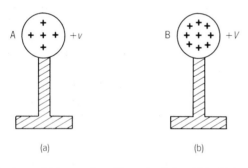

23.5 *A sphere at (a) a small positive potential and (b) a higher positive potential*

If the spheres B and A are connected by an insulated wire (Fig. 23.6), charge will flow because of the potential difference $(V - v)$ between the two spheres. Positive charge, if it were free to move, would flow from high positive potential $+V$ to lower positive potential $+v$. Negative charges (electrons e^-) flow from A to B, i.e. towards the higher positive potential, until the potentials of A and B become equal. The removal of negative charge from A will result in an effective gain of positive charge, hence the potential of A becomes greater than $+v$. The gain of negative charge by sphere B results in an effective loss (neutralisation) of some positive charge, hence the potential of B is lowered to less than $+V$. Electrons (e^-) stop flowing when the potential of B equals the potential of A, i.e. when the potential difference is zero.

Exercise 23.3

Copy the diagrams in Figs. 23.5 and 23.6, but change the positive charges to negative charges. Describe and explain what happens when the spheres A and B are connected with an insulated wire.

The potential near and on the surface of a positively charged sphere

Since charges in a metal conductor will flow until the potential is equal throughout, all points on the surface of the metal sphere are at the same potential. If the surface of the sphere is positively charged (Fig. 23.7) the value of the potential varies from $+V$ on the sphere's surface to zero at an infinite distance away from the sphere. The potential V_E at E is less than the potential V_D at D, which in turn is less than the potential V_C at C which is less than $+V$ at the surface of the sphere. Since infinite distances are not a practical proposition, a sensible arbitrary level of potential must be chosen as **zero potential**.

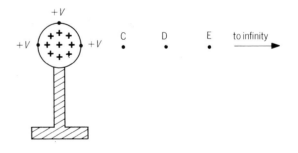

23.7 *Potential decreases with increasing distance from a charged sphere*

In Fig. 23.6, the potential of spheres A and B would be increased if they acquired more positive charges. However the *increase* in potential produced by the same increase in charge would be less noticeable if the spheres were much larger. Hence a very large object will not alter its potential by any significant amount even if large quantities of charge are given to it or taken from it. The potential of this large object can thus be used as the zero level of potential. The most convenient large 'body' to use is our Earth. The Earth contains a vast store of negative charge; however, its potential is approximately constant even when charges are given to it or taken from it. This is similar to the level of a lake remaining unchanged if a bucket of water is poured into it or a cupful of water is scooped out of it. Just as 0 °C on the Celsius scale of temperature is an arbitrary zero and there are temperatures above and below this zero, so also there are electric potentials above and below the arbitrary zero set by the Earth's potential (Fig. 23.8).

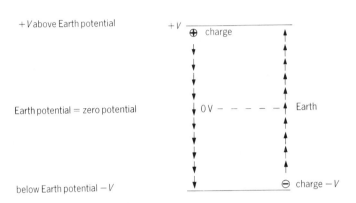

23.8   Earth potential as zero potential

The **potential V of a charged body** is defined as **the work done W in carrying unit charge from zero potential to the charged body**. If a charge of Q coulomb is carried between two points at a potential difference of V volt the work done W is given by $W = QV$ joule.

Potential associated with a charged body

The region around a charged object, a positively charged acetate rod or a negatively charged polythene rod, has different potentials at different distances from the charges as shown in Fig. 23.9. The potential decreases with increasing distance from the rod. An

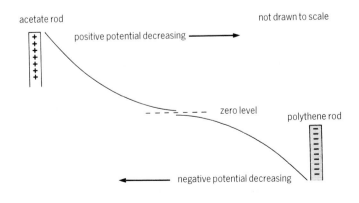

23.9   The potential at a distance from a charged body

uncharged metal conductor (Fig. 23.10) contains equal amounts of positive and negative charge and is therefore neutral. If you place an uncharged metal conductor near a positively charged rod (or a negatively charged rod) the potential difference between the ends A and B of the conductor (produced by the electric field of the charged rod) separates the charges in the conductor until the potential of the conductor is constant (see Fig. 23.11). This produces equal and opposite charges at ends A and B of the conductor. These charges in turn modify the potential due to the charged insulators.

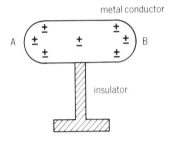

23.10   An uncharged metal conductor

In Fig. 23.11(a) the positive rod attracts electrons to the end A of the conductor, thereby reducing the positive potential at A. The movement of electrons of the conductor to A leaves a net positive charge at the end B, raising the positive potential at B. The potential is now uniform from A to B (no potential difference between A and B) and the charges stop moving. Similarly, the negative rod in Fig. 23.11(b) repels electrons to the end A of the conductor, thereby increasing the negative potential at A. The movement of electrons to A leaves a net positive charge at the end B resulting in a lowering of the negative potential at B. The potential is now uniform from A to B (no potential difference between A and B) and the charges stop moving.

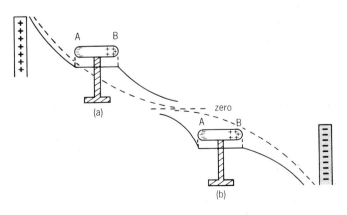

23.11   The effect on potential of introducing an insulated metal conductor: dotted lines show the potential due to the charged rods alone; solid lines show the potential when the conductor is placed near the charged rods

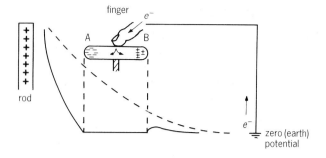

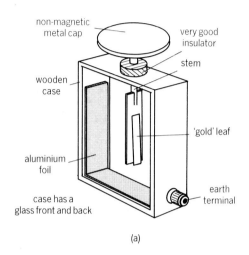

23.12 *Earthing the metal conductor lowers its potential to zero*

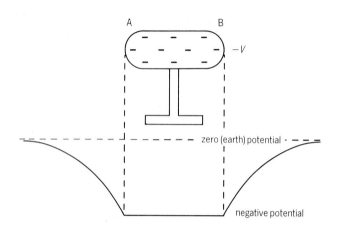

23.13 *Charging by induction*

If *any* point of the conductor AB is momentarily earthed by being touched with a finger (Fig. 23.12), the potential of the conductor becomes zero (earth) potential. Electrons flow from the earth to neutralise the positive charges at B and also provide sufficient negative charge at A to reduce the potential set up by the positively charged rod to zero.

When the finger is removed the negative charge at A remains at A due to the force of attraction between the positive charge on the rod and the negative charge at A. The negative potential set up by the negative charge at A balances or neutralises the positive potentials set up by the positive charge on the rod. Finally when the rod is removed the negative charges at A repel each other and spread out across the conductor to give a uniform negative potential (Fig. 23.13).

Exercise 23.4

Describe and explain what will happen if the conductor AB shown in Fig. 23.11(b) is momentarily earthed with a finger and the negative rod is then removed. Draw diagrams similar to Figs. 23.12 and 23.13, and explain what happens in terms of electron flow to the earth driven by the negatively charged rod.

23.3 Leaf electroscope

The leaf electroscope is a useful instrument in the study of electrostatics. The leaf of the electroscope is deflected whenever a **potential difference** exists between the cap/stem and the case. Since the case is usually earthed (is at zero potential), the deflection of the leaf indicates electric potential.

Note Since electric charge is needed to raise a conductor to a potential, the leaf electroscope does also indicate the presence of electric charge.

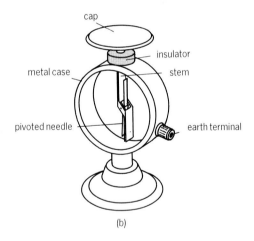

(a)

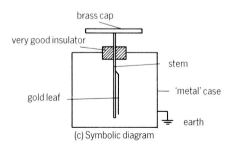

(b)

(c) Symbolic diagram

23.14 *The structure of a leaf electroscope*

Investigation 23.2 To show that a leaf electroscope measures potential difference

Connect a 0–5 kV variable power pack to the cap and the earth terminal of a leaf electroscope (Fig. 23.15). Gradually increase the potential from 0 to 5000 V. As you do so you will see the angle of deflection of the leaf increase from 0 to some maximum value.

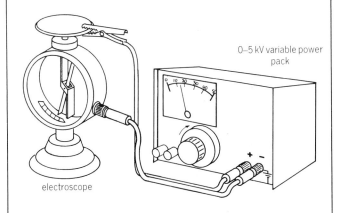

23.15 The deflection of the leaf is a measure of the potential difference between the cap and the earth

Investigation 23.3 To emphasise that the electroscope operates by *potential difference* rather than charge

Charge an acetate strip positively by rubbing it with a dry duster. When you bring the charged acetate strip near to the cap of an electroscope (Fig. 23.16a) the leaf is deflected away from the stem. When you remove the charged strip the leaf falls. If you now bring a negatively charged polythene strip near the cap of the electroscope (Fig. 23.16b) you will again see the leaf deflected away from the stem. Hence the leaf is deflected by both a positive charge and a negative charge. Thus the deflection must be produced by the *potential difference* set up by the charge rather than the sign of the charge.

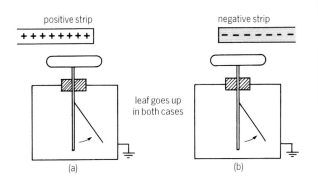

23.16 The potential rather than the sign of the charge causes deflection of the leaf

How the electroscope works

The cap, stem and leaf of an electroscope can be treated as an isolated 'conductor' because the case insulates it from outside influences. The potential of the case remains at zero (earth) potential throughout. When a positively charged rod (Fig. 23.17a) is brought close to the cap of the electroscope (Fig. 23.17b), one end of the 'conductor' is in an electric field which has a potential gradient $+V > v_1 > v_2 > v_3 > v_4 > v_5$. A potential difference is set up across the ends of the 'conductor' which causes a separation of equal amounts of charge of opposite sign. In practice this is achieved by electrons flowing to the cap of the electroscope. This separation of the charges alters the potential gradient set up by the charged rod. The charge will stop flowing when the 'conductor' is at a uniform potential $+v$, i.e. there is no potential difference across its ends.

If the charged rod, and therefore its electric field, are removed the equal and opposite charges on the 'conductor' give rise to a potential difference across the ends of the 'conductor'. The charges recombine as electrons flow to neutralise the positive charges. The leaf and the stem lose their charge and hence the leaf falls.

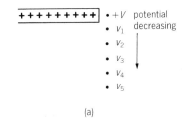

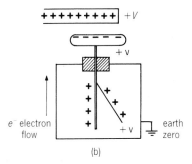

23.17 How the electroscope works

Exercise 23.5

Redraw Figs. 23.17(a) and (b) with a negatively charged rod and explain the movement of the negative charges.

Note The explanations on p.275 concerning potentials of conductors near charged rods apply equally well here even though the 'shape' of the conductor is different.

Investigation 23.4 To charge an electroscope by induction with a known sign of charge

Earth the cap of an electroscope by touching it momentarily with a finger, making it zero potential (Fig. 23.18a). Place a positively charged rod near the cap of the electroscope (Fig. 23.18b); equal and opposite amounts of charge in the cap/stem system separate out leaving the system at a positive potential ($+V$).

Keeping the positively charged rod in place, again earth the cap of the electroscope with a finger and note that the leaf falls.

The potential of the cap/stem V is now zero (Fig. 23.18c), even though the cap of the electroscope carries a negative charge and the stem a positive charge.

(**Note**   On p.276 it was stated that a conductor may be earthed by touching it at any point.) When the earthing finger is removed the leaf remains down because the potential is still zero (Fig. 23.18d). Finally, when the positively charged rod is removed the negative charges on the cap repel each other and are conducted throughout the cap/stem system until the system acquires a uniform negative potential $-V$. This deflects the leaf away from the stem (Fig. 23.18e).

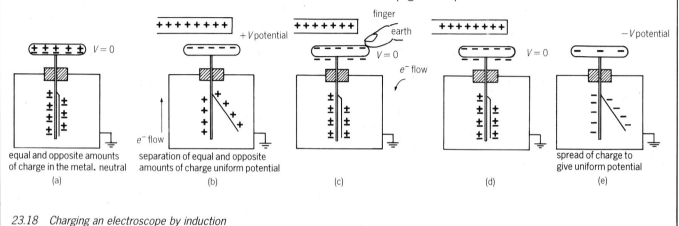

equal and opposite amounts of charge in the metal. neutral	separation of equal and opposite amounts of charge uniform potential			spread of charge to give uniform potential
(a)	(b)	(c)	(d)	(e)

23.18   Charging an electroscope by induction

Investigation 23.5 To show that the charges separated by a potential gradient are equal in size and opposite in sign

Place two identical conducting spheres A and B on insulating stands so that they are in contact. Earth the spheres by touching them with your finger to ensure they are at zero potential at the start of the experiment. Now place a negatively charged rod near to sphere A as shown in Fig. 23.19(a). The potential gradient due to the charge on the rod causes a separation of equal quantities of opposite charge and so electrons flow from A to B until A and B reach a uniform potential. Now move sphere B away from sphere A, keeping the charged rod in position (Fig. 23.19b). Then remove the charged rod (Fig. 23.19c). The charges on A and B distribute themselves evenly over the regularly shaped spheres.

Place a hollow metal can on the cap of an electroscope and charge the whole system positively by induction. Since the electroscope is positively charged the leaf will be deflected. Now carefully lower the sphere A into the hollow metal can. You should see the deflection of the leaf increase (Fig. 23.19d). The increase in deflection of the positively charged leaf proves that A is also positively charged.

Having proved that A is positive and B is negative, all that remains is to prove that the quantities of charge are equal in size. To do this simply bring the two spheres back into contact; the two charges should recombine to make A and B neutral. If the amounts of charge are *not* equal before the spheres touch then the surplus charge (positive *or* negative) would appear on both spheres. Therefore each sphere must be tested for charge. First touch sphere A on to the cap of an uncharged electroscope

and observe the leaf, then do the same with sphere B. You should see no deflection for either sphere. Since A and B have no charge after they have touched but had positive and negative charge respectively before they touched they must have had equal and opposite amounts of charge.

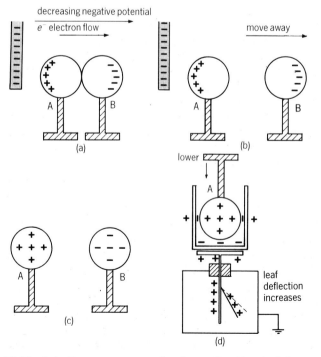

23.19   Induction causes an equal and opposite amount of charge to separate

Exercise 23.6

Redraw Fig. 23.18(a) – (e) with a negatively charged rod in place of the positively charged rod. Describe, with explanation, what happens to the electroscope.

Exercise 23.7

Using the apparatus in Fig. 23.19(d), describe how you can prove that sphere B is negatively charged.

If the two spheres are identical in size and they gain equal amounts of opposite charge then they should each be 'raised' to equal levels of opposite potentials. This may be demonstrated by repeating the part of Investigation 23.5 shown in Fig. 23.19(a), (b) and (c) and then testing the charged spheres A and B by placing each of them into a hollow metal can placed on the top of an uncharged leaf electroscope (Fig. 23.20). You should find that the deflection θ_1 of the leaf produced by sphere A (Fig. 23.20a) is equal to the deflection θ_2 of the leaf produced by sphere B (Fig. 23.20b). Since the deflection of the leaf is a measure of the potential difference between the charged bodies A and B and the case of the electroscope, the potential difference must be the same for each body.

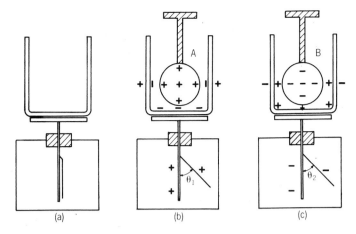

23.20   Testing the potential of the charged spheres

Note   A has a positive potential $+V$ while B has a negative potential $-V$. The case of the electroscope, being earthed, has zero potential.

23.4   Electrophorus

An electrophorus is a simple machine for generating charge. It consists of a brass disc fitted with an insulating handle, together with a piece of good insulating material such as a square of polythene.

Investigation 23.6   To charge an electrophorus

Rub the polythene square or give it a few flicks with a duster. It becomes negatively charged as electrons are removed from the duster and remain on the surface of the polythene square. Since the polythene has gained negative charges (electrons) it acquires a negative potential. Place the metal disc onto the charged insulator square (Fig. 23.21a). The negative potential on the square causes a separation of equal and opposite charges across the thickness of the metal disc with the negative charges (electrons) repelled to the upper surface of the disc. This is another example of the separation of charge by induction.
Note   Although the metal disc is 'touching' the charged insulator the charges do *not* flow off the insulator into the metal. In fact, the metal disc is making contact with very few points on the insulator (see inset in Fig. 23.21a).
   Momentarily earth the metal disc by touching it with a finger. The negative potential on the insulator repels the negative charges (electrons) to earth through the finger (Fig. 23.21b). The metal disc and the insulator are at zero potential; positive charge on the metal disc is needed to bring the negative potential on the insulator square to zero potential. The potential remains zero when the finger is removed (Fig. 23.21c). When the disc is lifted from the charged square, the disc becomes positively charged by a redistribution of electrons (Fig. 23.21d). As the positively charged disc is moved away from a negative potential, work must be done against the force of attraction. Work done is QV (in joule) and this gain in energy is responsible for the metal disc becoming charged.

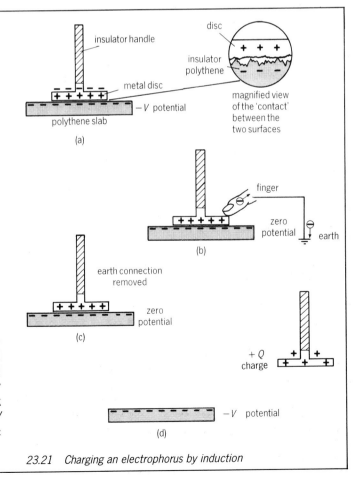

23.21   Charging an electrophorus by induction

The charging of the metal disc by this method is identical to investigation 23.4 in which you held a negatively charged rod near to the cap of an electroscope to charge it by induction. If you turn Fig. 23.2(d) upside down you can see its similarity to Fig. 23.18, the only difference being that the brass disc does not have a metal stem with a gold leaf fitted to it. However, the principle of charging by induction is the same. This means that the electroscope could have been charged by resting the charged rod on the cap of the electroscope, instead of holding it near, and then continuing the procedure for charging by induction.

Exercise 23.8

Redraw Fig. 23.21 but this time use a *positively* charged square of insulating material. Show that the brass disc acquires a negative charge when it is placed on the positively charged square.

Note It must be stressed that charges in solids are caused by the movement of negative electrons.

In all induction processes the charged insulator does not lose *any* of its charge and hence can be used over and over again. A charged insulator can be completely discharged by passing it through the warm air above a Bunsen flame. The heat energy from the flame causes the surrounding air to become ionized, i.e. it contains 'free' negative ions (electrons) and positively charged air molecules (due to the separation of one or more electrons from some of the neutral air molecules). In a gas both positively and negatively charged ions are able to move, and the charged insulator will attract the oppositely charged ions to it while repelling the ions of like charge. The insulator will attract the oppositely charged ions until it becomes neutralised, i.e. it 'loses' all its charge.

Questions

Q1 To remove completely the positive charge from an acetate rod it should be
- A placed inside a 'closed' hollow metal can.
- B placed back into contact with the charging duster.
- C placed in contact with a negatively charged polythene rod.
- D passed to and fro over a bunsen flame.
- E rubbed with one's hand to earth it.

Q2 A positively charged rod is brought close to (but not touching) an uncharged sphere. If the sphere is earthed it
- A becomes positively charged.
- B becomes positively charged on one side and negatively charged on the other.
- C remains uncharged.
- D is attracted by the rod.
- E is repelled by the rod. (L)

Q3 Two metal spheres A and B each stand on an insulating base and are in contact. A negatively charged rod is brought near to the sphere A, as shown below.

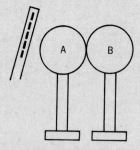

(a) Explain, in terms of electrons, the difference between conductors and insulators.
(b) What effect does the charged rod have on the electrons in A and B? Why?
(c) In what way will A and B differ if separated while the rod is near?

(d) How could the apparatus be used to leave A and B equally positively charged?
(e) How much, if any, of the charge on the rod is lost when the spheres are charged by induction? So how often could it be used to charge similar pairs of spheres without itself being recharged? (O)

Q4 (a) Diagram (a) represents a positively charged conducting sphere of radius *r*, which is insulated and also so far away from other conductors that it can be considered isolated. Draw a diagram representing the pattern of the lines of force of the electric field surrounding the sphere. How would it have differed if the charge had been negative?

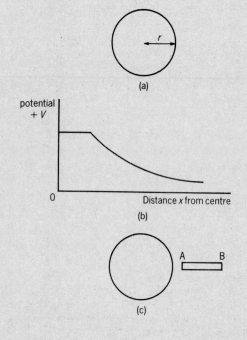

(b) Diagram (b) is a graph showing the way in which the potential *V* varies with the distance *x* from the centre of the sphere. Explain the general form of this graph. In what way would the graph have differed if the charge had been negative?

(c) A copper rod AB is laid along the direction of the field as shown in diagram (c). How does this modify the potential variation in its neighbourhood, and how is it that its own potential is the same all over it?

(d) Describe and explain how you would proceed if asked to remove the rod from the field bearing a free charge. State the sign of this charge, and explain where it has come from. *(O)*

Q5 (a) Draw a diagram of a leaf electroscope, clearly labelling the parts. What does the leaf electroscope measure?

(b) (i) A copper calorimeter containing a piece of dry flannel is placed on top of an electroscope and a dry polythene rod is pushed in. There is no deflection of the electroscope, but when the rod is pulled out the leaves diverge. Explain these observations.

(ii) Why do the rod and the flannel have to be dry?

(iii) If, after the rod is pulled out, it is quickly placed in a similar empty calorimeter on a similar electroscope, what will happen? Explain.

(iv) If instead, the rod is brought near to a metal-coated pith ball suspended by a nylon thread, the pith ball is first attracted to the rod, touches it and is then repelled. Explain.

(v) If instead, the rod is placed over a small light piece of paper the paper sticks to the rod. Explain why the paper is not immediately repelled. *(L)*

Q6 (a) Draw a labelled diagram showing the essential structural features of a leaf electroscope. Describe in detail how the electroscope could be charged by the method of induction.

Explain how it could then be used (i) to determine if another charged body had a charge of the same sign, (ii) to show that a damp cotton thread is a much poorer insulator than one which is perfectly dry.

(b) Explain why a dressing table mirror may become more dusty if wiped with a dry cloth on a warm dry day. *(L)*

Q7 (a) With the help of a diagram, describe the leaf electroscope.

(b) When a polythene rod has been rubbed it carries a negative charge. Describe and explain how such a rod could be used to charge the cap of an electroscope (i) negatively, (ii) positively.

(c) How could a polythene rod and an electroscope be used to test whether a strand of wool or a length of cotton was the better insulator?

(d) When a hand is placed near to the cap of a positively charged electroscope without touching it, the leaf drops. Explain why, in terms of potential and movement of charge. *(O)*

Q8 Describe how you would charge a leaf electroscope positively by the process of electrostatic induction. Explain what happens to (i) the charge, (ii) the potential of the electroscope during the process.

Without touching the can a charged insulated metal sphere is slowly lowered completely into a large metal can standing on the cap of the electroscope and the effect on the deflection of the leaf is noted. The sphere is removed. It is then brought up slowly towards the outside of the can until it makes contact. Compare and explain the effect on the deflection of the leaf in both parts of the experiment.

(JMB)

Q9 Suppose you are supplied with a negatively charged rod and two identical and uncharged metal spheres, A and B, on insulating stands.

(i) How, using the negatively charged rod, would you charge the two spheres equally so that A is negatively charged and B is positively charged?

(ii) How would you show experimentally, using any additional apparatus you may require, that this had, in fact, occurred?

(iii) Account for the production of the two equal charges in terms of the movement of charged particles.

(L part question)

Q10 A polythene rod may be charged negatively by rubbing it with a cloth, but a brass rod held in the hand cannot be charged in this way.

(i) State clearly what happens when the polythene is being charged.

(ii) Explain why the brass cannot be charged by rubbing.

(JMB part question)

Q11 A large metal can standing on an insulating block is to be given a large charge using the electrophorus shown in the diagram. The polythene slab of the electrophorus is initially given a negative charge by vigorously rubbing it with a dry cloth.

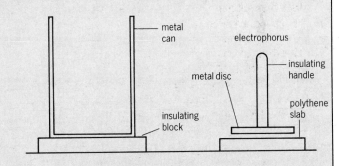

(i) Describe how the metal disc is subsequently charged. Illustrate your answer with diagrams to show each step of the charging process and draw carefully the distribution of charges on the disc at each stage of the procedure.

(ii) Describe how the electrophorus is now used to charge the metal can so that it finally obtains a much larger charge than that on the polythene slab.

(iii) The can's large charge has a much greater amount of energy than that of the electrophorus. How did the can gain this large amount of energy?

(L part question)

24 Further investigations on charge, potential and applications of static electricity

24.1 Faraday's ice pail experiments

Investigation 24.1 To show no charge can exist inside a closed hollow conductor

Give a small positive charge (10+) to a small metal sphere at the end of a long insulator by placing the metal on a negatively charged piece of insulator, momentarily earthing the metal with your finger and then lifting the sphere clear of the charged insulator. Then carefully lower the charged sphere into a hollow metal can standing on the cap of an electroscope. You should see the leaf of the electroscope deflect *slightly* as the charge is *just* introduced into the can. As you lower the charge deeper into the can the deflection of the leaf increases until, when the charge is well inside the can, the deflection remains constant. Even when you move the charge around or even touch the inside of the can with it, the deflection remains unaltered provided you hold the charge 'deep' down in the can.

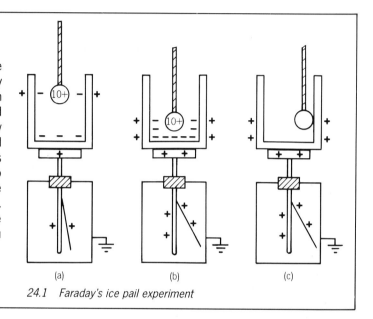

24.1 Faraday's ice pail experiment

The positive potential on the sphere causes a separation of equal and opposite amounts of charge across the thickness of the metal can. When the charge is just inside the can, only some of the charges separate out (see Fig. 24.1a). However, all the charges separate out when the charged sphere is well down inside the can (Fig. 24.1b). In Fig. 24.1(b) ten negative (−) charges are shown on the *inside* surface of the can and ten positive (+) charges are shown distributed on the outside surface of the can and the cap, stem and leaf of the electroscope. However, the total charge inside the can is zero (10+ and 10−) because the twenty charges effectively cancel each other out. Thus lowering a charged sphere with ten positive charges on it 'deep' into a hollow metal can has the effect of placing ten positive charges on the outside of the can and parts of the electroscope.

It is easy to see that if the charged sphere is removed from the can without having touched the inside of the can, the equal and opposite amounts of charge on the inside and outside of the 'can' will recombine to give zero charge. The ten negative charges move to recombine with the ten positive charges and hence the leaf will collapse. If, however, the charged metal sphere is allowed to touch the inside of the can when

it is well down inside the can, the charge induced on the inside of the can exactly neutralises the charge on the sphere (Fig. 24.1c). The deflection of the leaf in Fig. 24.1(c) is the same as that in Fig. 24.1(b), but this time, when the sphere is removed from the can, the deflection of the leaf is permanent.

The angle of deflection of the leaf is a measure of the potential to which the can, cap, stem and leaf system has been raised by acquiring a charge equal in magnitude and sign to the original charge lowered into the can. Clearly, a larger original charge on the sphere produces a greater deflection of the leaf; a smaller charge produces a smaller deflection. Thus the size of the charges on two charged conductors can be compared by measuring the angle of deflection of a leaf electroscope when each of the charges is lowered, in turn, into a hollow metal can resting on the electroscope. (This is true only when the capacitance of the system remains constant.)

Note Charged insulators as well as conductors may be lowered into the metal can to produce the effect shown in Fig. 24.1(b). However, the total charge can only be transferred from a **conductor** onto the inside of the can. A charged insulator will not transfer its charge (or accept charge) from the inside of the can.

Investigation 24.2 Charging by induction

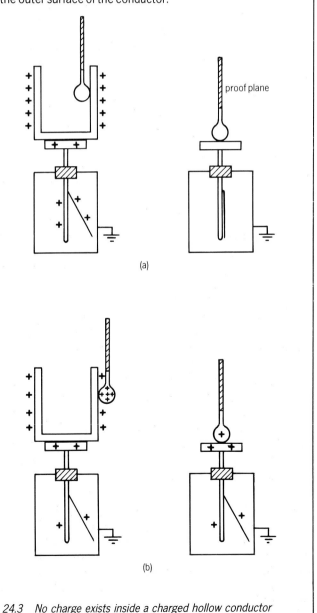

(a)

(b)

(c)

24.2 Charging by induction

The electroscope may be charged by lowering a charged insulator into a hollow can (see Fig. 24.2). As you lower the charged insulator into the can the negative potential set up by the negative charges on the insulator causes a separation of equal and opposite charge on the can (see Fig. 24.2a). Momentarily earth the metal can by touching it with a finger (*anywhere* on the can will do). The leaf collapses immediately. This shows that the negative charges have been driven to earth through your finger by the negative potential on the charged insulator (Fig. 24.2b). Positive charge on the inside of the can 'reduces' the potential of the negatively charged insulator to zero (earth) potential. When you remove the negatively charged insulator from the can, the positive charge remaining raises the can and the electroscope to a positive potential. Electrons (negative charges) from neutral molecules in the can, or from the parts of the electroscope connected to the can, move so that the positive charge is distributed on the outside of the can and the electroscope as shown in Fig. 24.2(c).

Note The positive charges do not actually move but the positive charge distribution is achieved by the removal or re-distribution of negative charges.

Clearly the above procedure will also work if the charged insulator is replaced by a charged conductor. The previous investigations show that no charge can exist inside a 'closed' hollow conductor; either there is no actual charge or, if a charged body is introduced, an equal and opposite charge will appear on the inside of the conductor to neutralise it.

24.2 Distribution of charge

Investigation 24.3 To demonstrate no charge exists inside a charged hollow conductor

Stand a metal can on the cap of an electroscope and give it a positive charge as shown in Fig. 24.3(a). Lower a previously earthed proof plane (a small metal disc on an insulating handle) into the can so that it touches the inside. Withdraw the proof plane and test it for charge by placing it in contact with the cap of a second, uncharged electroscope. The absence of deflection of the leaf proves that no charge has been collected by the proof plane. Now repeat the procedure, but this time touch the outside of the charged can with the proof plane. The second electroscope will show a deflection when the proof plane is placed in contact with the cap of the electroscope. Hence the charge on a hollow (or solid) conductor resides on the outer surface of the conductor.

proof plane

(a)

(b)

24.3 No charge exists inside a charged hollow conductor

A practical application of the knowledge that no charge exists inside a 'closed' hollow conductor could arise if, for example, a crane driver accidentally touched an overhead power line. He would be quite safe inside his metal cab provided he did not try to leave the cab until the outside were discharged or the power switched off. Passengers in an aircraft are safe when lightning strikes it because the discharge is conducted around the outer shell of the fuselage to the atmosphere beyond. Demonstrations have been carried out in which a one million volt potential was applied to the roof of a car being driven past a high-voltage generator. Despite the enormous discharge between the generator and the car the driver was able to repeat the demonstration without any ill effects either to him or the car. These experiments show that charge resides on the outer surface of a conductor.

Note This applies equally to hollow and solid conductors and, of course, to insulators.

If some negative charge is placed on a metal sphere supported on an insulating stand, as in Fig. 24.4(a), the negative charges repel each other and are conducted through the metal. The electrons distribute themselves until every point on the sphere is raised to exactly the same negative potential; the charge flow will then stop. All points on the charged sphere must be at the *same potential* because if this were not so a **potential difference** between different points on the conductor would exist. This would cause the movement of charges until the potentials were equalised. A charged conductor, whatever its shape, must therefore have the same potential at all points both on and inside its surface. The cylindrical-shaped conductor in Fig. 24.4(b) has a constant positive potential at all points on its surface. Likewise, the negatively charged pear-shaped conductor in Fig.

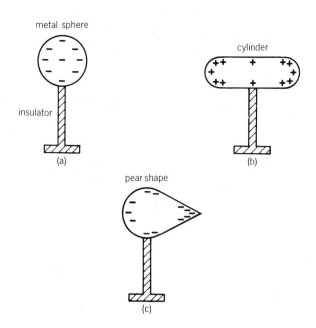

24.4 *Distribution of charge on different-shaped conductors*

24.4(c) has a constant negative potential all over its surface. Thus charge distributes itself so that the *potential* is uniform throughout any given conductor. On a uniform shape, such as a sphere, the distribution of the charge will be equal or uniform. However, non-uniform shapes such as those in Fig. 24.4(b) and (c) do *not* have an equal distribution of charge over their surface. The amount of charge which accumulates at any given point on a surface depends upon the curvature at that point. The greater the curvature, i.e. the smaller the radius, the greater the charge. There is thus a greater concentration of charge at the 'pointed' end of the pear-shaped conductor in order to maintain all points of the shape at the same potential.

Investigation 24.4   To show that any charged conductor is at a uniform potential

Connect a wire to the cap of an electroscope and coil it around a good insulator as shown in Fig. 24.5. The insulator acts as a handle while you trail the 'free' end of the wire over the surface of the charged conductor.

Note The normal plastic insulation on the wire is not good enough for the high voltages involved in electrostatics experiments. Hence the wire must be wrapped round a good insulator such as a polythene rod which you can hold in your hand without any charge leaking through you to earth.

As soon as the 'free' end of the wire makes contact with the charged conductor the leaf is deflected. The angle of deflection θ is a measure of the potential of the conductor. As you trail the 'free' end of the wire over the charged conductor, the angle of deflection θ remains constant. This shows that the potential is constant at all points on the surface of the conductor.

The test can be repeated using different-shaped conductors and with different amounts or signs of charge being given to the

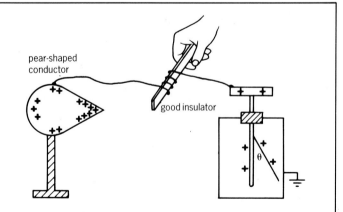

24.5 *The potential on any surface is uniform*

conductor. In each case a constant angle of deflection θ will be obtained for each individual charged conductor; the value of θ will, of course, depend upon the size of the charge given to the conductor and the size of the conductor.

Investigation 24.5 To investigate charge distribution on a pear-shaped conductor

Using a proof plane, collect charge from a small area around points A, B and C on the conductor and then test the amount of charge collected by lowering the proof plane into a hollow can standing on the cap of an electroscope (Fig. 24.6). On p.279 it was shown that the deflection of the leaf of an electroscope can be related to the quantity of charge lowered into the hollow can standing on the cap of the electroscope (see p.279) because the capacitance of the system is constant. When the proof plane touches a point on the conductor it collects an amount of charge which depends on the concentration of charge at A and the size of the metal disc on the proof plane. Note the deflection, θ, produced when you lower the charged proof plane well down into the hollow can and touch it against the inside Fig. 25.6(a). It is often necessary to transfer the charge from the same point several times in order to obtain a reasonable deflection. Do not forget to earth the electroscope each time to remove the charge, and take care that the proof plane touches the surface the same number of times at points A, B and C. You should find that $\theta_A > \theta_B > \theta_C$ indicating a greater charge concentration at A than at B which, in turn, has a greater charge concentration than C.

Note   What do you know about the potential at A, B and C?

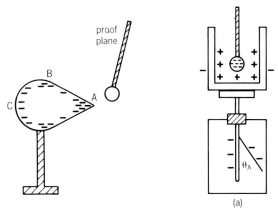

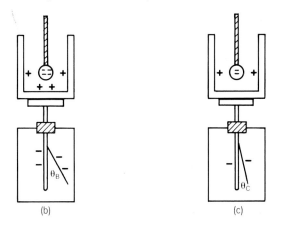

24.6   Investigating the charge distribution on a pear-shaped conductor

Similar experiments can be carried out to test the distribution of charge over the surfaces of conductors of different shapes. You should find that a charged sphere has a uniform distribution of charge over its surface. Can you think of a reason why this should be so for this one particular shape?

If you connect a sharply pointed conductor to a high voltage supply, e.g. by plugging it into the dome of a Van de Graaff generator, you can feel an 'electric wind' if you hold your hand a few centimetres away from the pointed end of the conductor, as in Fig. 24.7(a). A high concentration of positive charge at the point of the conductor will attract negative charges (electrons) until the positive charge is neutralised. At the same time positive ions in the air are being repelled by the positive charge at the point. Among the air molecules in the room there are always some positive ions (molecules of the gases which make up air with one or two electrons removed) and some negative ions (the 'removed' electrons). Figure 24.7(b) shows the charge movement in the air, i.e. the positively charged ions being repelled away from the positively charged point conductor and the negatively charged ions being attracted towards it. The attraction of the negative charges (electrons) to the positvely charged point neutralises the positive charges on the point and hence lowers its positive potential. Thus the charged conductor discharges in a way known as **point**

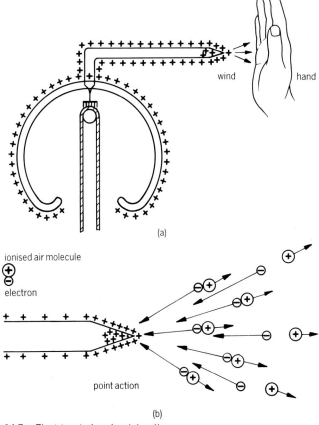

24.7   Electric wind and point action

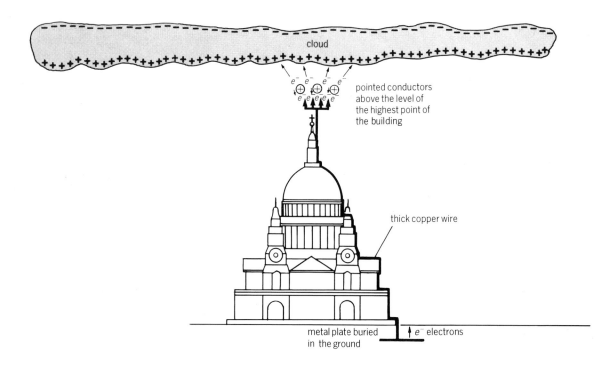

labels in figure:
cloud

e⁻ ... pointed conductors above the level of the highest point of the building

thick copper wire

metal plate buried in the ground

e⁻ electrons

24.8   How a lightning conductor works

discharge. The positive charges which rush away from the pointed conductor are positive ions (almost air molecules) and it is these that cause the air disturbance or 'wind'.

Note   The process is continuous because charge is continually being added to the Van de Graaff dome by the generator. This explanation shows that the pointed conductor is very good at collecting charge as well as holding a large concentration of charge.

Lightning conductor

An important application of point action is used in the design of lightning conductors. The movement of clouds in our atmosphere can produce vast quantities of static charge on a cloud. This build-up of charge can be so great that the potential of the cloud gives a potential difference between the cloud and the earth (zero) potential large enough to break down the insulating properties of the air. When this happens the air becomes conducting and the charge flows to earth, as a lightning flash, striking the nearest or highest building or object which is present, i.e. it takes the shortest route to earth. Never shelter under trees during a thunderstorm; the lightning could strike the tree and could kill or injure you as it runs down the tree to earth. It is best to kneel down in the open with your head as low as possible and your hands resting on your knees with fingers pointing towards the ground. If the lightning does strike you it should hit your shoulders, run down your arms and out of your fingers into the earth. This position thus protects your head and vital organs such as your heart.

If a flash of lightning were to strike a building

serious damage could result. However, a lightning conductor could save the building from damage. A lightning conductor consists of a number of pointed conductors fixed to a high point on the building and connected to a thick copper wire which runs down the side of the building and ends on a metal plate buried in the ground. As a positively charged cloud passes over the building there is a separation of equal and opposite amounts of charge in the copper wire with a high concentration of negative charges on the points of the conductors and positive charge trying to accumulate at the metal plate. However, the earth is a vast store of negative charge and so as soon as the positive charge is formed at the metal plate it is immediately neutralised by negative charges (electrons) drawn from the earth. Electrons are also attracted out of the earth and up to the pointed ends of the conductor by the positive potential on the cloud. A very high concentration of negative charge can build up on the points and this reduces the positive potential of the cloud, thereby making it less able to break down the insulating properties of the air. The charged ions of air are also moving in an electric 'wind'; negative charges (electrons) are repelled by the points and attracted by the cloud, also helping to lower the positive potential of the cloud, i.e. to discharge the cloud. The positive ions of air are attracted by the negatively charged pointed conductors but the vast store of negative charge in the earth can supply unlimited negative charge to the points to neutralise them. If the lightning does strike the conductor it sends its electrical charge through the lightning conductor and 'safely' into the earth.

286

24.3 Van de Graaff generator

The Van de Graaff generator (see Fig. 24.9) is an interesting application of several of the principles stated above. The lower metal roller charges the rubber belt by friction and the lower pointed conductors (comb) 'spray' a negative charge on to the outer surface of the rubber. This negative charge is mechanically carried up inside the metal dome (hollow 'closed' conductor) where a separation of equal and opposite charge is induced: negative charge goes to the outer surface of the dome with positive charge on the inside of the dome. The positive charge on the inside of the dome is immediately neutralised by the negative charge 'collected' by the upper comb of pointed conductors. You discovered on p.283 that 'no charge' can exist inside a 'closed' hollow conductor. This makes it appear that the negative charges carried up into the dome are actually transferred to the outside of the dome, which is not so.

As more and more negative charge is added to the dome its negative potential increases. The upper roller, made of polyethylene, charges the rubber positively and therefore positive charge is carried down by the revolving rubber belt. When these positive charges arrive at the lower comb, which is earthed, negative charge is attracted out of the earth to neutralise the positive charges. As the belt rises again it carries negative charge into the dome and increases the build-up of negative charge on the outside of the dome. The lower roller is usually driven by a small electric motor so that charge is continually fed into the dome. In theory, the dome should go on accepting charge indefinitely and reach an infinite potential. However, in practice, the dome does lose some of its charge to the surrounding air due to ionisation and imperfections in the smoothness of its surface. When the rate at which the dome is receiving charge from the moving belt is equal to the rate at which it is losing charge to the atmosphere it will have gained the maximum charge that it can hold and hence have reached its maximum potential. Using a school laboratory generator it is quite common to be able to achieve potentials of about 250 000 V. Fortunately these generators can only supply very tiny currents; this means that you can point your finger at the dome, receive a 'shock' and not be harmed.

There are many interesting demonstrations which can be performed using a Van de Graaff generator. A selection is described below and illustrated in Fig. 24.10 overleaf.

Hold a metal sphere with metal handle near to the charged dome. An electrical spark will 'jump' the gap (Fig. 24.10a). An estimate of the potential can be made from the fact that a potential difference of 30 000 V is required to produce a spark across a gap of about 1 cm. Thus a spark 'jumping' across a gap of 8 cm

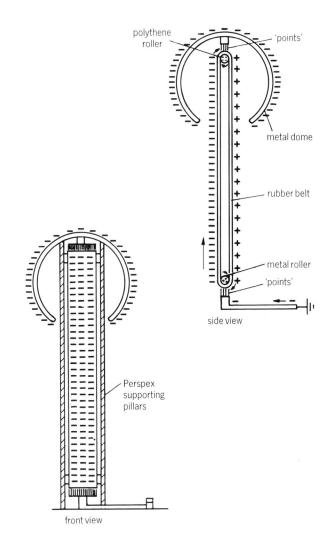

24.9 Van de Graaff generator

indicates a potential of almost 250 000 V on the dome. If you replace the metal sphere by a pointed conductor and bring it close to the charged dome, no spark is produced. The presence of the pointed conductor reduces the potential on the dome by moving the ions in the air to give a 'silent' discharge (Fig. 24.10b). If you stand on a very good insulator (an upturned plastic bucket or dish supported on polythene squares) and place one hand on the dome of the generator before it charges up you can effectively become 'part' of the dome. Hence you too can be charged up to a very high potential when the generator is switched on. Your hair may 'stand on end' and 'sparks' may be received from any part of you or your clothing. Figure 24.10(c) shows a girl receiving a 'shock' as she tries to touch a 'charged' boy's heel. A 'windmill' balanced on a needle inserted in the dome of the generator (Fig. 24.10d) will rotate as shown due to the reaction of the thrust of ions away from the pointed ends of the 'windmill'. If you hold a neon lamp with a pointed wire fitted to its base 'terminal' between your finger and thumb it will light up when held near the charged dome (Fig. 24.10e).

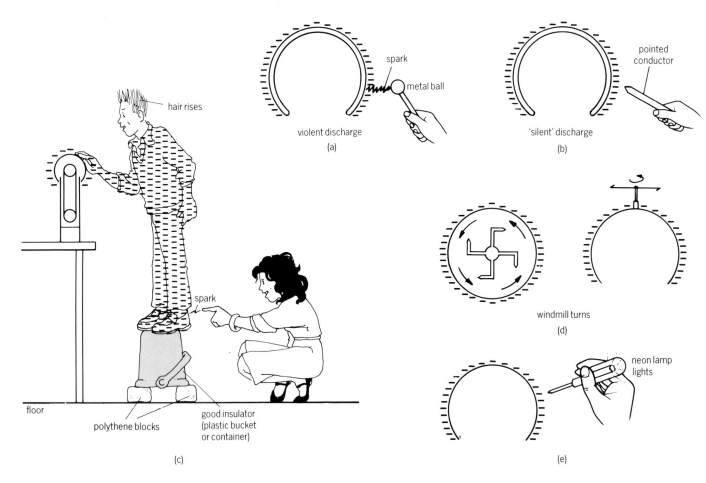

24.10 A selection of experiments using a Van de Graaff generator

24.4 Capacitors and capacitance

The dome of a Van de Graaff generator stores charge and as such is a **capacitor**. A capacitor usually consists of two metal plates, one of which is charged while the other is earthed. (In the case of the charged dome the other 'plate' is the earth itself.) The **capacitance C** of a capacitor is defined as **the ratio of the charge Q that it stores to the potential V to which it is raised.** Thus

$$\text{capacitance } C = \frac{\text{charge } Q}{\text{potential } V} \quad \frac{\text{coulomb}}{\text{volt}}$$

and the unit of capacitance is the farad(F). The farad is an extremely large unit and it is more appropriate to state capacitance in microfarad (10^{-6} F) or even picofarad (10^{-12} F).

If a charge of 1×10^{-3} C is added to a capacitor which raises its potential to 200 V, then the capacitance C of the capacitor is

$$C = 1 \times 10^{-3} \text{ C}/200 \text{ V}$$
$$= 5 \times 10^{-6} \text{ F } (5 \text{ μF}).$$

Parallel-plate capacitor

A simple form of capacitor is the parallel-plate

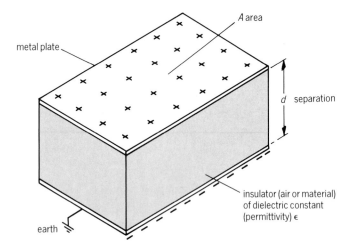

24.11 Parallel-plate capacitor

capacitor, made of two parallel sheets of metal separated by an insulator (called a dielectric) with one of the plates earthed (Fig. 24.11). Its properties can be investigated using a leaf electroscope as a voltmeter, i.e. to measure potential. The capacitance C of the capacitor can be shown to be $C = \epsilon A/d$ where ϵ = the **dielectric constant** of the insulating material between

Investigation 24.6 To investigate the capacitance of a parallel-plate capacitor

Place the metal plate P_1 of a capacitor on the cap of an electroscope as in Fig. 24.12. Support the other plate P_2, which is earthed, at a short distance above P_1. Give a charge of $+Q$ to P_1 using an electrophorus or an extra high tension supply.
(Note An equal and opposite charge of $-Q$ appears on P_2 even though it is at earth (zero) potential.) The capacitance C is given by the charge Q on either plate divided by the potential difference V between the plates (V is the potential of P_1). The deflection θ_1 of the electroscope shows the potential V_1 on the capacitor.

Keeping the separation d of the plates constant, slide an insulator (a sheet of glass or Perspex) into the space between the plates. You will notice a decrease in deflection to θ_2 showing a decrease in potential to V_2. Since the charge Q on the plates has remained constant the capacitance C of the capacitor must have changed. From $V = Q/C$ it follows that the capacitance C must have *increased* if the potential V has decreased from V_1 to V_2.

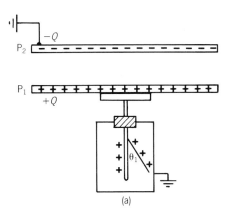
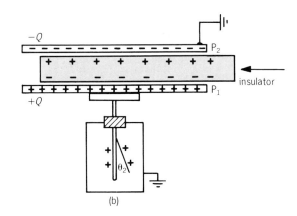

24.12   Capacitance varies with the insulator (dielectric) between the plates

Investigation 24.7 To show how capacitance varies with surface area of the plates

Use the same arrangement as in Fig. 24.12, but this time let the air act as the insulator. As before give the plate P_1 a charge of $+Q$ and hold the plate P_2 in the hand (earthed) at a constant distance d above P_1 (Fig. 24.13). You can vary the effective area A of the plates by moving the upper plate parallel to the lower plate. When the area of overlap A_1 of the plates is small the deflection of the leaf θ_1 indicates a high potential V_1. When you increase the area of overlap to A_2 the deflection of the leaf decreases to θ_2, indicating a lower potential V_2. This demonstrates that the capacitance C increases as the area A of the plates increases. More simply, the capacitor will be able to store more charge for the same potential if it has larger plates. In Fig. 24.13(a) the negative charge is only partly 'covering' the positively charged plate P_1 and hence its influence is not as great as when P_2 totally 'covers' the positively charged plate (Fig. 24.13b). In the latter position the effect of the charge on P_2 is to reduce the potential on P_1, hence the deflection θ_2 is less than θ_1.

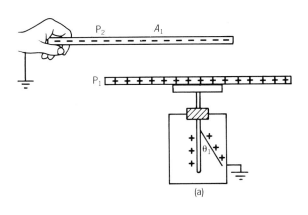
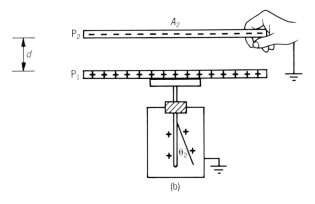

24.13   Capacitance varies with the area of overlap of the plates

Investigation 24.8 To show how capacitance varies with separation _d_ of the plates

Using the same equipment as before, place a charge of $+Q$ on plate P_1 and position the upper plate P_2, which is earthed, at a distance d_1 above P_1. A deflection θ_1 of the leaf of the electroscope indicates the size of the potential V_1. Move the earthed plate closer to the plate P_1. The deflection θ_2 of the leaf decreases, indicating a lower positive potential V_2 on the plate P_1 (Fig. 24.14). As the separation is reduced from d_1 to d_2 the potential on P_1 is also reduced, and so the capacitance must have increased. Thus the plate P_2 can store more positive charge to reach the same potential because the negatively charged earth plate is nearer.

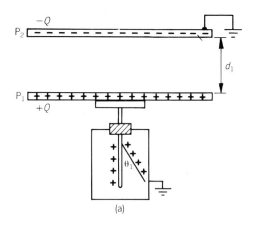

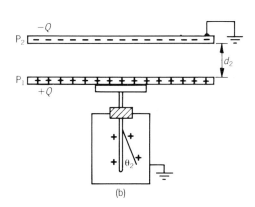

24.14 *Capacitance varies with the separation of the plates*

the plates, A = the surface area of the plates, and d = the separation of the plates.

Figure 24.12(a) shows how the presence of the negative charges on P_2 lowers the positive potential on P_1. When the insulating material is inserted between the plates the material becomes polarised, i.e. its atoms or molecules become slightly distorted to give some positive charge at the 'upper' edge and an equal and opposite negative charge at the 'lower' edge near the positively charged plate. Hence there is a significant lowering of the positive potential on P_1. An alternative explanation is that the two plates with the insulator present can store more charge than Q to raise it to the original potential V_1, when the capacitor is said to have a greater capacitance. Thus capacitance C increases further if a material of greater dielectric constant ϵ is inserted between the plates.

Practical uses of capacitors

Practical applications of capacitors include a tuning capacitor for radios, a smoothing capacitor in rectifier circuits, as a time delay and for coupling or decoupling. The gold leaf electroscope is really a capacitor with the leaf fitted to the charged plate and the casing acting as the earthed plate.

Capacitors 'block' direct current but 'transmit' alternating current. If a capacitor is connected to a d.c. supply it cannot charge up instantaneously; charge flows for a short time until the capacitor reaches the potential difference of the supply. Since the potential of the plates is in opposition to the supply the flow of charge will stop. Current cannot flow between the two plates unless, of course, the voltage is so high that the insulating properties of the material between the plates breaks down. Alternating current is current which 'flows' first in one direction and then in the reverse direction round a circuit. Alternating current can continue its to-and-fro movement even if there is a gap in the circuit. Therefore a capacitor in an a.c. circuit does not prevent the a.c. from 'flowing'. Thus a capacitor has the useful property of being able to 'separate' a.c. from d.c.

Some practical capacitors are shown in Fig. 24.15. Shown alongside each is the electrical symbol used to represent it. There are two main types of capacitor: electrolytic and non-electrolytic. Electrolytic capacitors are usually made from two sheets of aluminium foil separated by paper soaked in a conducting electrolyte. A very thin film of oxide is formed by electrolysis and this oxide layer acts as the insulator. Non-electrolytic capacitors contain flexible strips of material such as waxed paper, polyester, polyethylene or polycarbonate. These flexible strips are the insulator, the plates are formed by depositing a thin metal film on each side of the strip by vacuum coating.

Note Capacitors are discussed further in Chapter 32 (p.371).

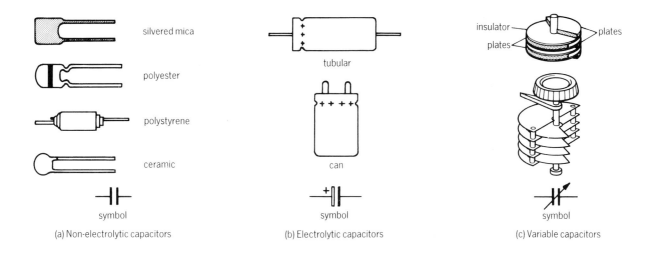

(a) Non-electrolytic capacitors

(b) Electrolytic capacitors

(c) Variable capacitors

24.15   Practical capacitors

24.5   Electric fields

Strength of an electric field

Electric field strength E at a point is defined as **the force per unit charge acting on a charged object placed at that point in the field.** Hence $E = F/Q$ where F is the force in newton and Q is the charge in coulomb. The units of E are thus newton per coulomb ($N\,C^{-1}$).

The electric field strength E between two parallel charged plates is approximately uniform and is given by $E = -V/d$ where V is the potential difference between the plates in volt and d is the separation of the plates in metre. From this equation E has units of volt per metre ($V\,m^{-1}$) which can be shown to be equivalent to the newton per coulomb stated earlier. The minus sign in the equation is to show that a positive charge would be repelled away from a positive potential. If a potential difference of 250 V is applied to two parallel plates which are 10 cm apart the electric field strength $E = 250\ V/0.1\ m = 2500\ V\,m^{-1}$.

Combining the two equations for E gives $F/Q = -V/d$, thus $F = -VQ/d$.

Illustrating electric fields

An electric field can be illustrated by drawing **lines of electric force**. These lines represent the direction of motion of a small 'free' positive charge placed in the field. The density of the lines is used to indicate the strength of the field. Thus the lines of electric force are directed away from the positively charged spheres in Figs. 24.16(a) and (b) but towards the negatively charged sphere in Fig. 24.16(c). More lines are shown in Fig. 24.16(b) to indicate a stronger electric field. Figure 24.17 illustrates a uniform electric field between two parallel oppositely charged plates. The electric lines of force are parallel to each other and equally spaced. The greater number of lines in Fig. 24.17(b) indicates a stronger uniform electric field.

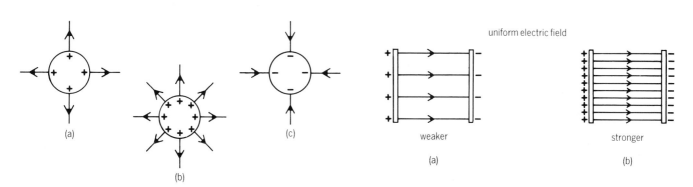

24.16   Electric field around a charged sphere

24.17   Uniform electric field

Questions

Questions 1–2

A A positively charged insulated body whose charge is distributed unevenly over its surface.

B A negatively charged conductor at zero potential.

C A positively charged body whose charge is distributed uniformly over the whole of its surface.

D A body which will lose electrons if it is connected to Earth by a wire.

E A body possessing a positive charge but at zero potential.

Which of the statements above best describes

Q1 a positively charged pear-shaped conductor resting on a block of paraffin wax?

Q2 a metal can, standing on a metal topped bench, when placed close to an insulated negatively charged body? *(L)*

Q3 An electrically charged object may be discharged by being held just above a flame. This is because

A the object becomes conducting when heated.

B the object is oppositely charged to the flame.

C the object is ionised when heated.

D the hot gases in the flame are ionised.

E the hot gases bombard the object and remove its charge. *(L)*

Q4 Many high buildings are protected from lighting by lightning conductors. Which of the following statements about a lightning conductor is **not** true?

A It has a point at its top end.

B It is made from a thick strip of copper.

C It must be insulated from the building.

D Its lower end is buried in the earth.

E Its top must be higher than the highest part of the building. *(L)*

Q5 Draw a labelled diagram of an electroscope and explain how it may be charged by *induction*.

Describe how the distribution of charge on a conductor may be investigated. Draw diagrams showing the results you would expect from (i) a spherical conductor, (ii) a pear-shaped conductor.

Explain the function of the lightning conductor attached to tall buildings. *(W)*

Q6 The diagram shows two metal plates, A and B separated by Perspex. Plate A is connected to the cap of a charged electroscope. The case of the electroscope and plate B are earthed. The leaf of the electroscope shows a small deflection. The electroscope, used in this way, registers variations of potential difference between cap and case.

(a) What is the purpose of earthing the electroscope case?

(b) How in practice, is the earthing carried out?

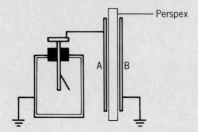

Perspex

(c) When the Perspex is removed, it is observed that the deflection of the leaf increases. What can be deduced about the capacitance of the arrangement from this observation? Explain your answer.

(d) Describe the structure of some practical form of capacitor. *(L)*

Q7 Which of the following changes will *not* increase the charge that can be stored on a capacitor?

A Increase the area of the plates.

B Increase the potential difference between the plates.

C Increase the permittivity of the dielectric between the plates.

D Increase the thickness of the plates.

E Decrease the distance between the plates.

Q8 (a) A pear-shaped conductor is mounted on an insulating stand and given an electrostatic charge. How would you expect the charge per unit area to vary over the surface of the conductor? Describe how you would demonstrate this by experiment. How would you expect the electrostatic potential to vary over the surface? Give a reason.

(b) Describe with a clear diagram the action of a lightning conductor. *(S)*

Q9 (a) A capacitor is a device for storing electric charge.

   (i)   What are the essential features in the construction of a capacitor?

   (ii) Explain how the charge is distributed when a capacitor is charged.

   (iii) Describe and explain what happens when the terminals of a charged capacitor are connected by a piece of copper wire.

(b) In an experiment with a capacitor, the charge which was stored was measured for different values of charging potential difference. The results are tabulated below.

Charge stored/μC	7.5	30	60	75	90
Potential difference/V	1.0	4.0	8.0	10.0	12.0

   (i) Plot a graph of charge stored on the *y*-axis against potential difference on the *x*-axis. (ii) **Use the graph** to calculate the capacitance of the capacitor used in the experiment. *(JMB part question)*

Q10 What do you understand by an *electric field?* Define *capacitance*.

Draw diagrams to represent (i) the electric field due to an isolated positively charged conducting sphere, (ii) the electric field due to an insulated negatively charged conducting sphere which is held above a large horizontal earthed conducting plate.

Two large metal plates *A* and *B* are mounted parallel to one another and at a distance 5 cm apart. *A* is maintained at a constant voltage of $+3$ kV and *B* is earthed. What is the electric field strength between the plates?

An uncharged metal sphere held on an insulating rod is placed in the electric field between the plates. With the help of a diagram, describe and explain the nature of the charge distribution induced on the sphere. *(O)*

25 Electric current and resistance

25.1 Electric symbols

Whenever you are considering any experiment or problem in current electricity it is essential to draw a circuit diagram. Your circuit diagram should be neat and precise, so that the reader can see at once what it shows. A standard set of symbols is in common use so that there should be no confusion over the interpretation of a diagram. These symbols are shown in Fig. 25.1.

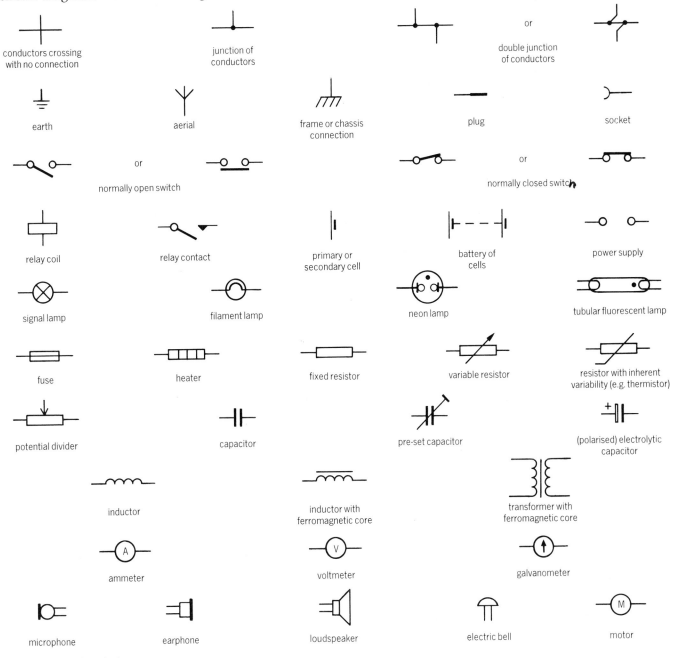

25.1   Electrical symbols

25.2   Current electricity

Both static and current electricity deal with charges and voltages, however they are treated separately. The main difference between them is in the values of the quantities involved. Static electricity mainly involves high or very high voltages and small currents. Current electricity mainly involves low voltages and reasonably large currents. Both mainly study the movement of negative charge.

Fundamental facts

The structure of the atom is considered in greater detail in Chapter 33 (p.383). However, it is useful to know the basic particles which make up the atom and to have some idea of its structure.

Electron   This carries a negative charge of 1.6×10^{-19} coulomb and has a mass of 9.12×10^{-31} kilogram.

Proton   This carries a positive charge of 1.6×10^{-19} coulomb and has a mass of 1.673×10^{-27} kilogram. Thus the proton has a charge equal and opposite to that of the electron and a mass about 1850 times as big as the mass of the electron.

Neutron   This carries no charge and has a mass of 1.675×10^{-27} kilogram. It is very slightly more massive than the proton.

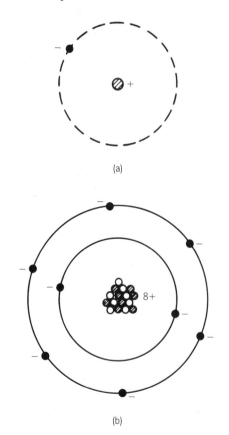

(a)

(b)

25.2   (a) Hydrogen atom, (b) oxygen atom

Atomic structure   Figure 25.2(a) shows a diagram of the simplest atom, the atom of hydrogen, it has a central **nucleus** consisting of a single proton; around this a single electron rotates in a manner which may be assumed to be much the same as the way that the Moon rotates round the Earth. Figure 25.2(b) shows a model of a more complex atom, namely oxygen. The nucleus contains eight protons and eight neutrons. There are eight electrons arranged in two outer **shells**. More complicated atoms contain more protons and neutrons in the nucleus, and a larger number of outer shells of electrons.

Facts about atoms may be summarised as follows.

1   Atoms are electrically neutral and the number of electrons in the outer shells is equal to the number of protons in the nucleus.
2   Nearly all the mass of an atom is concentrated in the nucleus in an extremely small space.
3   The diameter of the atom is the diameter of the outermost electron shell. Since the mass of the atom is concentrated in the nucleus, which only occupies a very small part of the volume of the atom, an atom consists largely of empty space.

It follows from this last point that even solids contain much more space than matter, so any unattached electrons can move about quite freely within them.

Ions   When one or more outer electrons are detached from an atom, the atom is no longer electrically neutral. There are more protons in the nucleus than there are outer electrons, and so the atom has a net positive charge and is known as a **positive ion**. Conversely, if extra electrons become attached, there are more electrons in the outer shells than there are protons in the nucleus, the atom has a net negative charge and is known as a **negative ion**. Molecules which lose or gain electrons are also referred to as ions.

25.3   Electric current

Movement of charge

In Chapter 3 you found that a body moves if it is placed in a gravitational field so that it is acted upon by a force. Similarly, an electric charge will move if it is placed in an electric field so that it is acted upon by a force. Consider the simplest case of a hydrogen atom which loses its electron to become a hydrogen ion. Both the electron and the hydrogen ion have the same magnitude of charge so in an electric field they will be subjected to equal forces, but in opposite directions. The equation $F = ma$ applies to both particles and, since the mass of the electron is approximately 1/2000 the mass of the proton, the acceleration of the electron is approximately 2000 times the acceleration of the proton.

The atoms in solids are bound in a crystal structure by strong electrical forces, and can only vibrate about a fixed mean position. If the solid is a conductor it will contain a vast number of electrons which are not tightly bound and are free to move. These are known as **free electrons**. Since the solid is mainly empty space, the free electrons move within it at random rather like the molecules in a gas. When an electric field is applied there is a net drift of electrons towards the positive end of the electric field. This movement of charge is known as the **electric current**. More specifically, the quantity of charge Q passing a given point in one second is the electric current. Electric current is usually denoted by the letter I. Hence $I = Q/t$ where t is the time in second. The unit of current is the ampere: 1 ampere = 1 coulomb per second.

Example

A charge of 3 coulomb flows past a point in a wire in 4 second. Calculate the current flowing in the wire and the number of electrons passing the point each second.

$Q = 3\,C \quad I = ? \quad t = 4\,s$

$$I = \frac{Q}{t}$$

$$= \frac{3\,C}{4\,s}$$

$$= 0.75\,A$$

Each electron has a charge of $1.6 \times 10^{-19}\,C$, so the number of electrons passing the point is $0.75\,C\,s^{-1}/1.6 \times 10^{-19}\,C = 4.69 \times 10^{18}\,s^{-1}$.

It is interesting that the vast quantity of electrons which drift past the point each second give a small current of 0.75 A.

The flow of charge

When an electric light switch is closed the light comes on immediately. An electric signal in a conductor travels at a speed of about $3 \times 10^8\,m\,s^{-1}$. You should not confuse this speed with the speed of electrons in an electric current. The average drift speed of electrons when a current passes is about $10^{-4}\,m\,s^{-1}$. This speed varies with the strength of the current.

The negatively charged electron was not discovered until the 1890s. Before that the direction of the current was regarded as the direction in which a *positive* charge would flow. This convention is still maintained, although it is now known that in a wire the actual movement is of the electrons (negative charge) flowing in the opposite direction.

The charge carriers in liquids are positive and negative ions. These normally drift at random, forming and recombining. When the liquid is placed in an electric field there is a drift of positive ions in one direction and negative ions in the other. The drift speed is low.

Gases always contain a few ions and electrons. When an electric field is applied the lighter electrons obviously move at much greater speeds than the positive ions. If the gas pressure is reduced the electrons travel much farther before colliding, and may acquire sufficient energy to ionise other gas molecules. When the pressure is very low the speed of the electrons becomes very large and the positive ions also attain a reasonable speed.

Conductors, semiconductors and insulators

Investigation 25.1 To test materials for conductivity

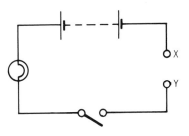

25.3 Circuit to test conductors and insulators

Set up the circuit shown in Fig. 25.3. X and Y are metal clips. Strips or rods of different metals, e.g. glass, wood, plastic etc., are the materials used. Join X and Y with one of the materials to be tested and close the switch. The lamp lights for some materials but not for others, showing that these materials allow charge to flow through them. Liquids can also be tested using this circuit. Attach copper strips to X and Y and dip them into beakers containing the liquids to be tested. The lamp lights for some but not for others.

This investigation shows that solids can be divided into **conductors** (those which allow the charge to pass easily) and **insulators** (those which do not allow the charge to pass easily).

Metals are good conductors because they contain large numbers of free electrons per unit volume, and so the charge flows easily.

Insulators contain practically no free electrons. The electrons are tightly bound and normally charge does not flow. However, strong electrical forces can break the bonds which bind the electrons and so allow conduction. Thus a good insulator at low voltages may be quite a poor insulator at high voltages. Many electrostatics experiments fail because the insulation is not good enough to withstand the high voltages used.

If a sensitive current detector is used instead of the lamp in investigation 25.1, other substances can be identified which allow only small currents to pass. These are called **semiconductors**. Semiconductors contain few free electrons and so the currents are small. However, if their temperature rises more electrons are released and so they are better conductors at higher temperatures.

25.4 Electric potential

In Chapter 3 you found that gravitational potential increases with height above the Earth's surface. When a mass m is moved a distance h from a lower to a higher level work is done against the gravitational field. A force mg is moved a distance h, and the work done is mgh. This is the increase in the potential energy of the mass.

Similar ideas are used in the study of electricity. Here the moving quantity is charge. Work is done against the electric field when charge is moved from a lower potential level to a higher potential level. The difference between the two levels is known as the **potential difference** (p.d.) and it is measured in **volt** (V). If *one joule* of work is done in moving *one coulomb* of charge between two points, the *potential difference* between the two points is *one volt*.

Note This is a definition of the volt.

It follows that if 2 C charge is moved between the same two points, 2 J work is done; if 3 C charge are moved through a potential difference of 2 V, 6 J work are done. The work done or energy expended is thus the product of the charge and voltage:

$$\text{joule} = \text{coulomb} \times \text{volt}$$
$$W = Q \times V$$

This can be rearranged into $V = W/Q$, and thus the potential difference may be defined as the energy per unit charge. Since also $Q = It$, substituting for Q gives $V = W/It$ or

$$V = \frac{W}{t} \times \frac{1}{I}$$

W/t is the rate of dissipation of energy and thus potential difference may also be defined as the rate of dissipation of energy per unit current.

Returning to the gravitational analogy, any mass which is free to move under gravity will move from a higher level to a lower level, e.g. a ball released at the top of a slope rolls down to the bottom. Similarly, charge which is free to move under an electric field moves from a higher potential to a lower potential. (**Note** This refers to the movement of *positive* charge.) Thus if a potential difference is applied between two points on a conductor, charge flows.

Ohm's Law

The German physicist George Ohm stated 'the current I in a conductor is proportional to the potential difference V between its ends, provided that the physical conditions such as temperature remain constant', i.e.

$$I \propto V \text{ or } \frac{V}{I} = \text{constant} = R$$
$$V = IR$$

R is the constant of proportionality and is known as the **resistance** of the conductor. This relationship is known as Ohm's Law. When V is in volt and I in ampere, the units for R are ohm (Ω).

In a good conductor, a small potential difference V produces a large current I, hence V/I is small and R is small. A good conductor has a small resistance. On the other hand some alloys such as nichrome and constantan have quite a high resistance, and resistors are made from them. If the element of an electric iron or an electric fire were made from a good conductor such as copper, it would not work.

Example

Calculate the potential difference V across a 5 Ω resistor carrying a current of 1.2 A.

$V = ?$ $I = 1.2$ A $R = 5\,\Omega$
$$V = I \times R = 1.2\,\text{A} \times 5\,\Omega$$
$$= 6.0\,\text{V}$$

The formula $V = I \times R$ may have to be rearranged to $I = V/R$ or $R = V/I$ to determine I or R when the other two variables are known. One way to remember the variations of the formula is to use the triangle in Fig. 25.4. To obtain the formula for a given quantity cover up the letter required (say V). This leaves two adjacent letters, I and R, and so the formula for V is $I \times R$. If you cover I you are left with V above R, so the formula for I is V/R, similarly $R = V/I$. This method may be applied to any formula containing three variables, e.g. $Q = It$ and $W = QV$. Make sure you arrange them in the correct corners of the triangle!

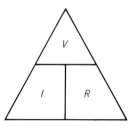

25.4   Formula triangle

Example

Calculate the current flowing through a 4 Ω resistor when a potential difference of 6 V is applied across it.

$V = 6\,V \quad I = ? \quad R = 4\,\Omega$

$$I = V/R$$
$$= \frac{6\,V}{4\,\Omega}$$
$$= 1.5\,A$$

Sometimes it is inconvenient to use the units volt, ampere and ohm, so their multiples or submultiples are used. Some in common use are given in Table 25.1.

Table 25.1 Multiples and submultiples of the ampere, ohm and volt

Name	Symbol	Quantity	
milliampere	mA	$\frac{1}{1000}$ A	$= 10^{-3}$ A
microampere	μA	$\frac{1}{1\,000\,000}$ A	$= 10^{-6}$ A
millivolt	mV	$\frac{1}{1000}$ V	$= 10^{-3}$ V
kilovolt	kV	1000 V	$= 10^{3}$ V
kilohm	kΩ	1000 Ω	$= 10^{3}$ Ω
megohm	MΩ	1 000 000 Ω	$= 10^{6}$ Ω

Electric circuits

Figure 25.5 shows a circuit in which all the components are connected in **series**. This means that there is only one path which the charge can take, so the current is the same throughout the circuit. An instrument which measures the current in a circuit is called an **ammeter**. It is always connected in **series** in the circuit. An instrument which measures potential difference is called a **voltmeter**. It is always connected in **parallel** in the circuit. An electric circuit is the closed path through which charge flows from one terminal of a voltage supply to the other. Figure 25.6 shows a circuit in which some of the components, i.e. the two resistors and the voltmeter, are connected in parallel. At the point M there are three paths which the charge can take, and the charge recombines at the point N. The voltmeter measures the difference in potential between points N and M.

Ammeters and voltmeters have terminals marked either + or −. You must always connect the + terminal to the positive terminal of the battery. If the current enters the wrong terminal of the instrument the sensitive coil inside will probably be damaged and the instrument broken.

A third instrument used is the **centre zero galvanometer** which indicates current direction. This is basically a milliammeter (very sensitive ammeter) with the zero position of the pointer in the centre of the scale.

Kirchhoff's First Law

This law states that 'the quantity of charge entering any junction in a circuit must be equal to the quantity of charge leaving that junction'. It follows that at junction M in Fig. 25.6 the charge entering per second is equal to the charge leaving per second, i.e.

at M $\qquad\qquad I_M = I_1 + I_2 + I_V$

and at N $\qquad I_1 + I_2 + I_V = I_N,$

and so $I_M = I_N$. If more charge entered a junction than left it there would be a build-up of charge at the junction. Conversely, if more charge left than entered there would be a charge deficiency. Obviously neither of these is possible.

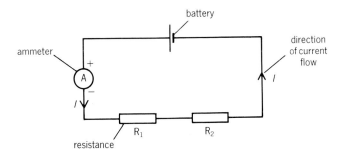

25.5 Series circuit

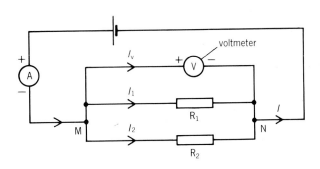

25.6 Parallel circuit

25.5   Resistance and resistors

Resistors in series and in parallel

Investigation 25.1   To check Ohm's Law and measure resistance using an ammeter and voltmeter

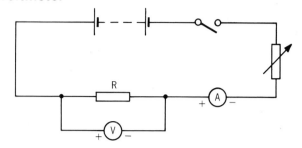

25.7   Circuit to check Ohm's Law

Arrange the apparatus as shown in Fig. 25.7. The fixed resistor R could be a metre length of nichrome wire. Before switching on check that the positive terminals of the instruments are connected to the positive terminal of the battery. After you have closed the switch adjust the rheostat (variable resistor) until a suitable current I is recorded on the ammeter. Record both this reading and the reading V on the voltmeter. Adjust the rheostat to obtain further readings of I and V. Suitable values for I are 0.2, 0.4, 0.6, 0.8 and 1.0 A.

Tabulate the results in a table like Table 25.2 and calculate the value of V/I. Then plot a graph of V against I (Fig. 25.8). You should find that the graph is a straight line passing through the origin, thus verifying Ohm's Law. The slope of this graph gives the value of the resistance R of the nichrome wire. The value of V/I in the last column is constant, which also verifies Ohm's Law, and this constant value is the same as the value of the resistance R obtained from the graph.

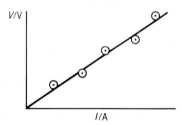

25.8   Graph of voltage against current

Table 25.2   Table of results for investigation 25.1

Voltage V/V	Current I/A	$V/I = R/\Omega$

The method of investigation 25.1 for verifying Ohm's Law has a serious drawback: the voltmeter depends upon Ohm's Law for its working. Thus you have assumed the law to prove the law! Other more valid methods of verifying the law can be found in more advanced textbooks.

Investigation 25.2   To find the resistance of three lengths of nichrome wire

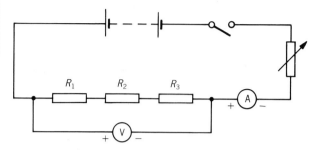

25.9   Resistors in series: experimental method

Set up the apparatus shown in Fig. 25.9 using three separate lengths of nichrome wire (or any three separate resistors) as resistors R_1, R_2 and R_3. Calculate the combined resistance R of the resistors using the formula $R = V/I$. Then replace the three resistors by first R_1, then R_2 and finally R_3 and calculate the resistance of each. You should find that when the resistors are connected in series, the total resistance is equal to the sum of the resistances R_1, R_2 and R_3 of the separate resistors, i.e.

$$R = R_1 + R_2 + R_3$$

Now connect the same resistors in parallel as in Fig. 25.10 and calculate their combined resistance R. This time you should find that the reciprocal of the total resistance is equal to the sum of the reciprocals of the separate resistances, i.e.

$$\frac{1}{R} = \frac{1}{R_1} + \frac{1}{R_2} + \frac{1}{R_3}$$

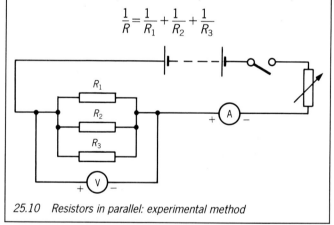

25.10   Resistors in parallel: experimental method

These relationships can also be found theoretically. Consider three resistors in series (fig. 25.11). Since they are in series the current I in each resistor is the

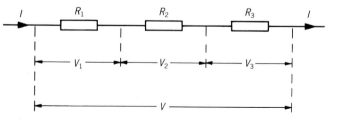

25.11   Resistors in series: theoretical method

298

same. The potential difference between the ends of R_1 is V_1 and, from Ohm's Law, $V_1 = IR_1$. Similarly $V_2 = IR_2$ and $V_3 = IR_3$.

Let R be the combined resistance of the three resistors and V the potential difference between the extreme ends. However, the potential difference across the combination of resistors must be equal to the sum of the potential differences across each separate resistor. Hence $V = V_1 + V_2 + V_3$. Substituting values for V_1, V_2 and V_3 gives $V = IR_1 + IR_2 + IR_3$. But $V = IR$ so $IR = IR_1 + IR_2 + IR_3$. Cancelling throughout by I,

$$R = R_1 + R_2 + R_3$$

When resistors are in series the combined resistance is the sum of the individual resistances and is thus *greater* than any individual resistance.

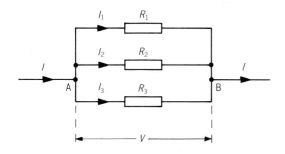

25.12   *Resistors in parallel: theoretical method*

Now consider resistors R_1, R_2 and R_3 connected in parallel as in Fig. 25.12. Here the constant factor is the potential difference between junctions A and B. Whichever path is taken by the charge, the potential difference must be the same. However, the current in each path is different. Using Ohm's Law the potential difference V between A and B is given by $V = I_1R_1 = I_2R_2 = I_3R_3 = IR$ where I is the combined current and R the combined resistance. At A $I = I_1 + I_2 + I_3$, and substituting values for the current gives $V/R = V/R_1 + V/R_2 + V/R_3$. Cancelling throughout by V gives

$$\frac{1}{R} = \frac{1}{R_1} + \frac{1}{R_2} + \frac{1}{R_3}$$

When all the resistors have the same value, i.e. $R_1 = R_2 = R_3$,

$$\frac{1}{R} = \frac{1}{R_1} + \frac{1}{R_1} + \frac{1}{R_1} = \frac{3}{R_1}$$
$$\therefore R = \tfrac{1}{3}R_1.$$

so the effective resistance is equal to $\frac{1}{3}$ of the resistance of each individual resistor. Connecting resistors in parallel ensures that the combined resistance is *less* than the resistance of the smallest individual resistor. For example, if the only resistors available are two 1 Ω resistors a value of $\frac{1}{2}$ Ω is obtained by connecting them in parallel.

Example

6 Ω and 3 Ω resistors are connected in parallel and an 8 Ω resistor is connected in series with them. A current of 2 A passes through the 8 Ω resistor. Find

(a) the combined resistance;
(b) the potential difference across the combined resistor;
(c) the current through the 3 Ω resistor.

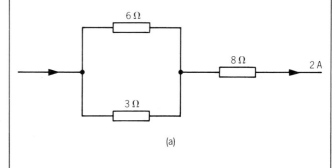

25.13   *Finding combined resistance*

It is *always* a help to draw a diagram (see Fig. 25.13a).

First find the combined resistance R of the resistors in parallel.

$R = ?$ $R_1 = 6\,\Omega$ $R_2 = 3\,\Omega$

$$\frac{1}{R} = \frac{1}{R_1} + \frac{1}{R_2} = \frac{1}{6} + \frac{1}{3}$$
$$= \frac{3}{6} = \frac{1}{2}$$
$$R = 2\,\Omega$$

The equivalent circuit is shown in Fig. 25.13(b).

(a) Let the combined resistance of all three resistors be R.
$R = ?$ $R_1 = 8\,\Omega$ $R_2 = 2\,\Omega$

$$R = R_1 + R_2$$
$$= 8\,\Omega + 2\,\Omega$$
$$= 10\,\Omega$$

(b) Let the potential difference across the combined resistors be V.
$V = ?$ $I = 2\,A$ $R = 10\,\Omega$

$$V = I \times R = 2\,A \times 10\,\Omega$$
$$= 20\,V$$

(c) The combined resistance of the parallel network is 2 Ω. Hence potential difference V across the parallel resistors is

$$V = I \times R = 2\,A \times 2\,\Omega$$
$$= 4\,V$$

For the 3 Ω resistor $V = 4\,V$ $I = ?$ $R = 3\,\Omega$

$$I = V/R = \frac{4\,V}{3\,\Omega}$$
$$= 1\tfrac{1}{3}A$$

In a series circuit the current is constant throughout the circuit. Thus it is obviously impracticable to connect an electric light bulb and an electric fire in series, because they operate with currents of widely differing values. A major disadvantage of a series circuit is that when one component fails the circuit is broken and none of the components works. If you have used 'fairy lights' on a Christmas tree you may have spent a lot of time and trouble locating and replacing the 'dud' bulb – each has to be tested to find which has gone.

Exercise 25.1

Four single $1\ \Omega$ resistors are available. Show that the following resistances may be obtained by using one or more of the resistors: $4\ \Omega,\ 3\ \Omega,\ 2\tfrac{1}{2}\ \Omega,\ 2\ \Omega,\ 1\tfrac{1}{2}\ \Omega,\ 1\tfrac{1}{3}\ \Omega,\ 1\ \Omega,\ \tfrac{1}{2}\ \Omega,\ \tfrac{1}{3}\ \Omega$ and $\tfrac{1}{4}\ \Omega$.

Investigation 25.3   To measure resistance by the substitution method

Connect the circuit as shown in Fig. 25.14. The two-way switch allows either the unknown resistor X or the box of standard resistors to be connected in series with the milliammeter, rheostat and steady voltage supply (accumulator). First insert the plug key into the two-way switch so that the current flows only through the unknown resistor. Then adjust the rheostat until the current is at a suitable value, say 20 mA. Move the plug key so that the current only flows through the box of standard resistors and adjust the plugs in the box until the milliammeter again reads 20 mA. The resistance of the unknown resistor is equal in value to the sum of the values on the plugs which have been removed from the resistance box. Repeat the procedure for several values of the current by adjusting the variable resistor, and find the average resistance of the unknown resistor.

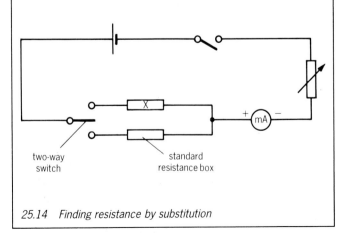

two-way switch   standard resistance box

25.14   Finding resistance by substitution

This method is suitable for fairly large resistances, but is not accurate enough for small resistances.

Variation of resistance

Ohm's Law states that the relationship $V = IR$ holds 'provided the temperature remains constant'. This suggests that resistance varies with temperature. It is possible to investigate this for metals by replacing the unknown resistor in the circuit Fig. 25.7 by the bulb from a pocket torch. As you increase the current, the filament of the bulb first glows a dull red, and then becomes white. Take readings of V and I during this time and calculate the value of $R = V/I$. You will find that as the current increases, and hence the temperature of the filament increases, the value of R also increases.

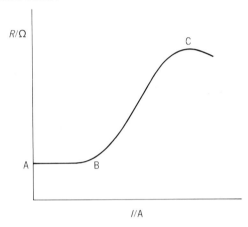

25.15   Graph of resistance against current for changing temperature

Draw a graph of R against I, as shown in Fig. 25.15. Over the horizontal part AB the temperature remains reasonably constant and Ohm's Law is obeyed. Then from BC the resistance increases, and finally the resistance starts to decrease again. It is not possible to measure the temperature of the bulb during the experiment, but it does show the effect on the resistance of increasing the temperature.

Instead of the bulb you could use a coil of insulated copper wire wound on a mica strip and placed in a boiling tube containing paraffin. When this tube is placed in a beaker of water containing a thermometer and the water is heated, the resistance of the coil at different temperatures can be measured. Figure 25.16 shows the graph of R against the temperature θ. This is a straight line, showing that the resistance has increased uniformly with temperature.

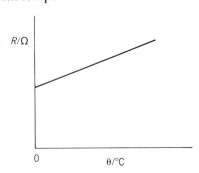

25.16   Graph of resistance against temperature

Thus the resistance of metals increases uniformly with temperature until a certain temperature, which depends upon the metal, is reached. Over this range of temperature the metal may be used as a **resistance thermometer**.

To investigate the variation of the resistance of non-metals with temperature, replace the unknown resistor in Fig. 25.7 by a non-metal conductor such as carbon or a thermistor. Thermistors are made from semiconducting oxides of iron, cobalt and nickel. You should notice that, as the current and hence the temperature increases, the value of $R = V/I$ decreases. So the resistance of these substances decreases with increasing temperature. This occurs because more electrons are freed at higher temperatures, producing a larger current for the same potential difference and a consequent decrease in resistance.

Other factors affecting resistance

You have already met an experiment which shows that the resistance of a wire increases with length. Connecting three identical wires in series causes a threefold increase in resistance. Thus it is reasonable to assume that $R \propto l$ where l is the length of the wire. Putting three identical wires in parallel means in effect that the area of cross-section of the resistor is trebled while the length remains the same. However, the resistance is reduced to one-third of the original value. Thus it is reasonable to assume that $R \propto l/A$ where A is the area of cross-section of the wire.

Investigation 25.4 To confirm that $r \propto l$ and $r \propto 1/A$

The following experiment checks these theories. Connect a length of wire in place of the fixed resistor in the circuit shown in Fig. 25.7, and attach a clip so that the length of the wire can be varied as shown in Fig. 25.17(a). In this way find the resistance of different lengths of wire. Plot a graph of resistance against length (see Fig. 25.17b).

Next use pieces of wire of the same length and material, but with different areas of cross-section, and draw a graph of resistance against 1/area of cross-section (see Fig. 25.17c).

Both graphs should be a straight line passing through the origin, showing that $R \propto l$ and $R \propto 1/A$. Combining both relationships gives $R \propto l/A$, i.e. $R = \rho l/A$.

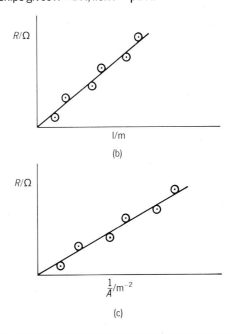

(b)

(c)

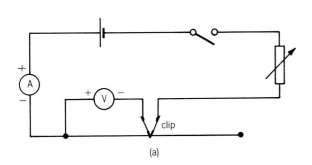

(a)

25.17 *Variation of resistance with length and area of cross-section*

Investigation 25.5 To measure resistivity

Find the slope R/l of the graph of resistance against length (Fig. 25.17b). Measure the diameter d of the wire using a micrometer screw gauge. Take at least six readings at different places on the wire and in different directions and find their average value d. This is done in case the wire is not accurately cylindrical. The area of cross-section of the wire $A = \frac{1}{4}\pi d^2$, giving

$$\rho = \frac{R}{l} \times \frac{1}{4}\pi \, d^2.$$

The constant of proportionality ρ is known as the **resistivity** of the wire. It is possible to re-arrange the equation to give $\rho = R \, A/l$. Thus the units of ρ are $\Omega \, m^2/m$, i.e. Ohm metre. It is seen that the resistivity is numerically equal to the resistance between opposite faces of a metre cube.

Resistivities are very small. A good conductor such as copper has a resistivity of $1.8 \times 10^{-8} \, \Omega$ m, whereas nichrome, an alloy used for making heating elements, has a resistivity of about $110 \times 10^{-8} \, \Omega$ m.

Example

What length of resistance wire of resistivity $100 \times 10^{-8}\,\Omega\,\text{m}$, area of cross-section $2.5 \times 10^{-7}\,\text{m}^2$, would be needed to make a resistor of $57.6\,\Omega$ (an element for a 1 kW electric fire)?

$l = ?$ $R = 57.6\,\Omega$ $A = 2.5 \times 10^{-7}\,\text{m}^2$
$\rho = 100 \times 10^{-8}\,\Omega\,\text{m}$ $R = \rho\, l/A$ so $l = RA/\rho$.

$$l = \frac{57.6 \times 2.5 \times 10^{-7}}{100 \times 10^{-8}}\ \frac{\text{m}^2}{\text{m}}$$
$$= 14.4\,\text{m}$$

This is quite a long length of wire and so it is coiled round a cylindrical insulator to make a compact element.

Example

A wire is stretched until its length is doubled. What effect will this have on its resistance?

Assuming that the volume remains constant, doubling the length halves the area of cross-section. Since the resistivity depends only upon the nature of the material, this does not change as the wire is stretched.

Let the initial resistance be R and the final resistance R_1. If the original length is l the final length is $2l$; if the original area is A the final area is $A/2$.

$$R = \frac{\rho\, l}{A}$$

$$R_1 = \frac{\rho \times 2l}{\frac{1}{2}A} = \frac{4\rho l}{A} = 4R$$

The effect is to multiply the resistance by 4.

Potentiometer or potential divider

The fact that the resistance of a uniform wire is proportional to its length is used to make a potentiometer or a potential divider. Figure 25.18(a) shows a 2 V accumulator connected across the ends AB of a uniform resistance wire of length 1 m. The current is constant throughout the circuit, and the resistance of the wire varies uniformly with its length.

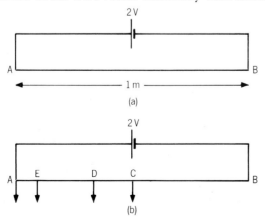

25.18

Each centimetre of the wire has the same resistance r, so the voltage drop across each centimetre of the wire is Ir, and is $\frac{1}{50}$ V. When a potential difference of 1 V is needed connections are made to A and C where C is the mid-point of the wire, i.e. AC = 50 cm (Fig. 25.18b). The potential difference between A and C is $50 \times \frac{1}{50}$ V = 1 V. A potential difference of 0.5 V is obtained by making connections to A and D where AD = 25 cm. A potential difference of 0.1 V is made by making connections to A and E where AE = 5 cm.

25.6   Colour code for resistors

It is useful to know the value of a resistor; this is indicated by the four coloured bands on the resistor, as shown in Fig. 25.19. The first three colours give the 1st digit, the 2nd digit and the number of zeros (noughts), the fourth band, if there is one, gives the tolerance as follows: none $= \pm 20\%$, silver $= \pm 10\%$, gold $= \pm 5\%$, red $= \pm 2\%$ and brown $= \pm 1\%$. The colours black, brown, red, orange, yellow, green, blue, violet, grey and white represent the digits from 0 to 9, respectively.

Example

(a) brown   green   black   (no fourth band)
    1   5   0 $\pm 20\%$
    The resistor has a value of $150\,\Omega \pm 20\%$.

(b) red   violet   orange   gold
    2   7   000 $\pm 5\%$
    The resistor has a value of $27\,000\,\Omega \pm 5\%$.

(c) What is the colour code for a 20 MΩ resistor?

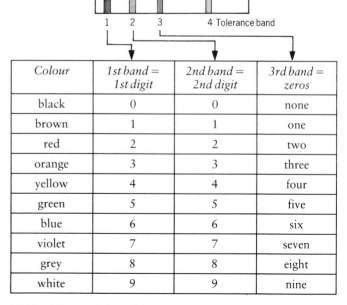

Colour	1st band = 1st digit	2nd band = 2nd digit	3rd band = zeros
black	0	0	none
brown	1	1	one
red	2	2	two
orange	3	3	three
yellow	4	4	four
green	5	5	five
blue	6	6	six
violet	7	7	seven
grey	8	8	eight
white	9	9	nine

25.19   Colour code for resistors

Questions

Q1

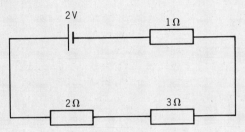

The potential difference, in V, across the 3 Ω resistor, is

A $\frac{1}{9}$ **B** $\frac{1}{2}$ **C** 1 **D** $\frac{6}{5}$ **E** 2   *(AEB)*

Q2

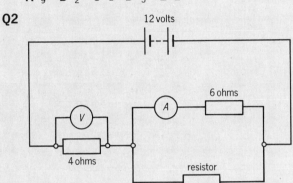

Calculate the readings of the voltmeter V and ammeter A in the above circuit. Also find the power taken from the battery. (Assume that the resistance of V is very high and the resistance of A is zero.)

Explain, without detailed calculation, whether the reading of the voltmeter will increase or decrease if the 3-ohm resistor is now altered to 6 ohms.

Why should voltmeters have as high a resistance as possible but ammeters as low a resistance as possible? *(L)*

Q3 Values of the current I passing through a coil for corresponding values V of the potential difference across the coil as measured on a voltmeter are shown below.

The voltmeter has a zero error which has not been allowed for in the readings given:

I/amperes	0.05	0.20	0.35	0.50	0.65
V/volts	0.85	2.80	4.74	6.70	8.65

Plot a graph to show the relation between V as ordinate (y-axis) and I as abscissa (x-axis). Use the graph to determine (i) the resistance of the coil, (ii) the correction which must be applied to the voltmeter readings, and give the correct value of the first p.d. Explain how each is determined from the graph. *(JMB part question)*

Q4 (a) Describe, with the help of a circuit diagram, how you would measure the resistance of a resistor using an ammeter, a voltmeter, and any other equipment you require. Suggest one error which could affect the accuracy of your result and state the way in which it would affect the result.

(b) Two electric light bulbs, both marked 0.3 A, 4.5 V are connected (A) in parallel, (B) in series, across a 4.5 V battery of negligible internal resistance. Assume that the resistance of the filament does not change. In each case A and B (i) state what might be seen, (ii) calculate the currents through each bulb, and (iii) calculate the current supplied by the battery. *(JMB)*

Q5 (a) Write down the formula for the effective resistance of two resistors in parallel. Calculate the effective resistance of a 12-Ω resistor and a 6-Ω resistor connected in parallel.

(b) Suppose you are supplied with the following equipment:
a steady low voltage d.c. source of low internal resistance,
a 12-Ω resistor and a 6-Ω resistor,
a variable resistor of a maximum value of 10 Ω in 1 Ω stages,
connecting wire,
a suitable ammeter.
Describe how, using only the above apparatus, you can check that the measured value of the resistance of the 6-Ω resistor and the 12-Ω resistor in parallel agrees with the calculated value. Draw a circuit diagram and state clearly the readings which you would take.

If the supply were replaced by one of high internal resistance, explain what effect this would have on the experiment.

(c) Two resistance wires X and Y of the same material and length but of different cross-sectional areas are joined in parallel to a d.c. source of low internal resistance. The cross-sectional area of X is twice that of Y. What is the ratio of

(i) the resistance of X to the resistance of Y,
(ii) the current in X to the current in Y, and
(iii) the power dissipated in X to the power dissipated in Y? *(L)*

Q6 A six volt battery is used, together with a potential divider, to provide a variable voltage first across a 3 ohm resistor alone, then across a torch bulb alone.

(a) Sketch one circuit which shows (i) the arrangement of the potential divider and (ii) how the current through either the resistor or the bulb and the potential difference across it could be measured.

(b) Sketch two graphs, one for each component, showing how the current varies with the potential difference. *(JMB)*

Q7 (a) Show how you would connect three resistors, each of resistance 6 Ω, so that the combination has resistance (i) 9 Ω, (ii) 4 Ω.

In case (i) the combination is connected across the terminals of a battery of e.m.f. 12 V and negligible internal resistance. Calculate (iii) the current through each resistor, (iv) the p.d. across each resistor, (v) the total power consumed.

(b) Describe how you would measure the resistance of a coil or wire by the method of substitution. *(S)*

26 Electromotive force and potential difference

26.1   Flow of charge

Investigation 26.1   To produce an electric current

It is not difficult to produce a flow of electric charge. First twist together the ends of two bare wires made of different metals, e.g. copper and iron, and connect the other ends to the terminals of a sensitive centre zero galvanometer; a mirror type is very suitable (Fig. 26.1). When you hold the junction of the wires in your hand there is a deflection on the galvanometer indicating a flow of charge. If you hold a lighted match under the junction a much larger deflection is produced (you must be careful that it is not too great or the galvanometer may be damaged). All that you have used are two different metals in contact with a temperature difference between the opposite ends of the metals.

Here is another way of producing a flow of electrons. Connect two lengths of copper wire to the terminals of the galvanometer. Clip the other ends of the wire onto two coins of different metals, e.g. a two pence piece and a ten pence piece. Dip a piece of blotting paper into brine and then press the coins together with the blotting paper sandwiched between them (Fig. 26.2). You will see a deflection on the galvanometer. A layer of saliva can be used instead of the blotting paper between the two coins. All that you have used are two different metals separated by a solution.

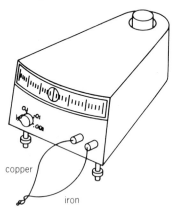

26.1   E.m.f. produced by joining two dissimilar metals

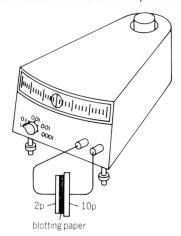

26.2   E.m.f. produced by a very simple cell

In both the examples in investigation 26.1, an **electromotive force** (e.m.f.) is set up. This causes charge to flow and will be dealt with in more detail later.

Simple cell

The apparatus used in investigation 26.2 (copper, zinc and dilute sulphuric acid) is called a **simple cell**. The covering of the copper plate with a layer of hydrogen is known as **polarisation**. You can see that by using different metals and an electrolyte (solution) an e.m.f. is produced which causes charge to flow. This flow of charge is hindered and finally prevented by the layer of hydrogen which forms on the copper plate. If some means is found of preventing the formation of hydrogen or of continually removing it as it forms, the cell will continue to function for a long time.

In the simple cell copper is the positive terminal and zinc the negative terminal. Charge flows from the copper to the zinc in the external circuit. It follows that charge must flow from zinc to copper inside the cell, in order to complete the circuit.

Where does the energy of the electrons come from? It comes from energy released when the zinc reacts with the sulphuric acid. If the zinc rod alone is placed in the sulphuric acid, bubbles of hydrogen will be released unless the zinc is very pure. This is because a particle of zinc and a particle of impurity, together with the sulphuric acid, form a minute cell and so hydrogen is released. This is known as **local action**. It is important because it constitutes a loss of energy: the zinc is being used up even when the cell is not in use. This loss can be prevented by coating the zinc with a layer of mercury in a process known as **amalgamating**

Investigation 26.2   To make a simple cell

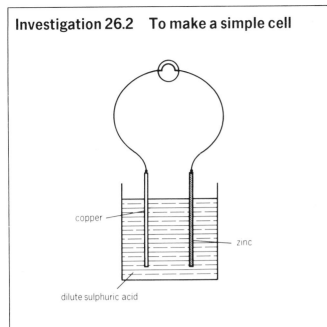

26.3   Simple cell

Set up the circuit shown in Fig. 26.3. Screw a torch bulb into a holder, connect one terminal of the holder to a copper plate and the other terminal to a zinc plate. Immerse the two plates in a beaker containing dilute sulphuric acid. The bulb should glow brightly. It does not glow for long but soon starts to get dimmer and then goes out. The copper plate is covered with a layer of bubbles of hydrogen gas. If you take out the plates, wipe them clean and re-immerse them in the solution the bulb will light again, but will only remain lit for a very short time.

the zinc. The mercury dissolves the zinc and provides a barrier between the impurities and the solution, so preventing local action. The zinc is only used up when the cell is in use.

Leclanché cell

The Leclanché cell (Fig. 26.4) is a type of **primary** cell. It has the advantage that it can be produced in dry form. (Liquid primary cells are not now used.) In this cell the positive terminal is made of carbon and the negative terminal of zinc. The **electrolyte** (liquid or jelly which conducts the charge through the cell) is a jelly of ammonium chloride, and the **depolariser** (the chemical which removes hydrogen and prevents it settling on the positive plate) is manganese (IV) oxide. The manganese (IV) oxide is mixed with powdered carbon, effectively increasing the area of the positive plate and the efficiency of the depolarising process. Since charge has to be driven through the electrolyte the electrolyte offers a resistance to the movement of the charge. This resistance is known as the **internal resistance** of the cell. The internal resistance depends upon the size of the cell.

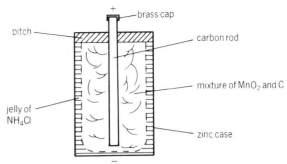

26.4   Leclanché cell

The following points about the Leclanché cell should be noted.

1 It is called a primary cell because it cannot be recharged.
2 During the working of the cell, zinc changes to zinc chloride, hydrogen is released and the zinc and ammonium chloride are used up.
3 The cell has an electromotive force of 1.5 V. (**Note**   The electromotive force in a cell does not depend upon the size of the cell but *only* upon the nature of the chemicals used.)

The Leclanché cell owed its importance to the fact that it was the first cell to be produced in 'dry' form. Latterly, new types of dry cell have been developed which are supposed to have a longer life.

Secondary cells

Secondary cells can be recharged when they run down. The most common type in use is the lead–acid accumulator (battery) which is used in cars (Fig. 26.5). In its working form the positive plate is made of lead(IV) oxide (PbO_2), the negative plate of lead (Pb) and the electrolyte is sulphuric acid. The plates are very close together and are prevented from touching by separators made of an insulator. When the cell discharges two things happen:

1 Both positive and negative plates change to lead(II) sulphate ($PbSO_4$).
2 Water is formed which dilutes the acid.

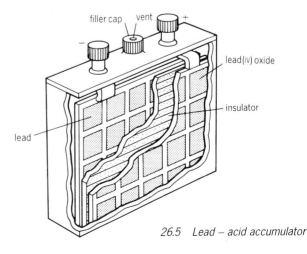

26.5   Lead – acid accumulator

305

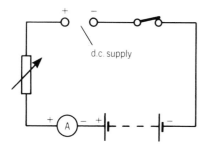

26.6   *Charging circuit for an accumulator*

Figure 26.6 shows the circuit for recharging accumulators. The following points should be noted.

1 A direct current (d.c.) supply must be used which must be of a voltage greater than the combined electromotive forces in the battery of accumulators being recharged.

2 The positive terminal of the battery must be connected to the positive terminal of the supply so that, in the accumulator, the charge flows in the opposite direction to the normal flow.

3 It is more effective to charge for a long time with a small current than for a short time with a large current. The rheostat is used to adjust the value of the current.

4 During recharging the concentration of the acid increases and the liquid level may fall. The accumulator should be topped up with distilled water and *not* with dilute acid.

5 During recharging the positive plate changes from lead(II) sulphate to lead(IV) oxide, and the negative plate from lead(II) sulphate to lead.

6 A single-cell accumulator has an electromotive force of 2 V and the internal resistance is negligible. The very small internal resistance is an advantage in that it allows large currents to be drawn from the cell.

7 The capacity of an accumulator is measured in ampere-hour. A capacity of 40 ampere-hour means that it can be run for 40 hour at 1 A or 20 hour at 2 A etc., before it needs recharging.

26.2   Electromotive force (e.m.f.) and potential difference (p.d.)

In a cell or battery, chemical changes take place which produce the energy needed to drive charge round the circuit. The **electromotive force** is defined as **the total energy expended (work done) per coulomb of electricity when charge is driven round the circuit.** This is similar to the definition of potential difference (p.296), and e.m.f. is also measured in volt.

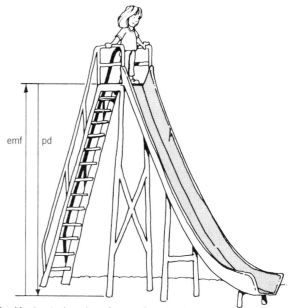

26.7   *Mechanical analogy for e.m.f. and p.d.*

A mechanical analogy of e.m.f. is that of a child playing on a slide (Fig. 26.7). As the child climbs the slide she gains potential energy. This potential energy is released when she slides down. Now imagine that the cell is the steps of the slide and the chute is the external circuit. There is a step-up of energy from the negative to the positive terminal which is obtained from the chemical reaction inside the cell. This step-up of energy puts the positive terminal at a higher potential than the negative terminal and provides the potential difference to drive the charge round the external circuit. (The extra potential energy at the top

---

Investigation 26.3   To differentiate between e.m.f. and p.d.

Set up the circuit shown in Fig. 26.8. Note the reading *E* on the voltmeter when the key K is open. This reading is the e.m.f. of the cell. The e.m.f. of a cell is measured on an **open circuit**, in which there is no charge flowing, and shows the maximum energy per coulomb which is available. Close the key K and again note the voltmeter reading *V*. This second reading is taken on a **closed circuit**, in which charge flows, and denotes the p.d. *V* between the terminals when the cell is in use. This is the energy that can be used per coulomb of electricity.

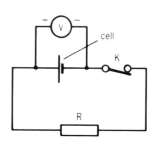

26.8   *Difference between e.m.f. and p.d.*

of the slide drives the child down the chute.) The energy per coulomb to drive the charge from the *negative* to the *positive* terminal *inside the cell* is the e.m.f. The energy per coulomb to drive the charge from the *positive* to the *negative* terminal in the *external circuit* is the p.d.

E is always greater than V unless no charge flows in the circuit, when $E = V$. The difference between E and V is the voltage needed to drive charge through the cell and overcome the internal resistance r of the electrolyte in the cell. Hence $E - V = Ir$ where I is the current. However, $V = IR$ where R is the resistance of the external circuit. So

$$E - IR = Ir$$
$$E = Ir + IR$$
$$= I(r + R)$$

Thus e.m.f. = current × total resistance in circuit, whereas p.d. = current × external resistance. When $r = 0 \ \Omega$, $E = V$ and all the energy is available for use in the external circuit, none being lost in the cell itself. Thus it is an advantage to have the internal resistance as small as possible. Primary cells have reasonably large internal resistances but secondary cells such as the lead–acid accumulator have very small internal resistances.

What happens in a simple circuit containing a cell? In the electrolyte there are positive and negative ions which behave like any other molecules, i.e. they move in random directions with numerous collisions. When the electrodes (terminals) are put in the electrolyte, an e.m.f. is set up *from negative to positive inside the cell*. When the circuit is completed by closing the external circuit, *positive ions* drift to the *positive terminal* and are neutralised by free electrons. At the *negative terminal* a chemical reaction takes place with the negative ions and *electrons* are released. The same number of electrons are neutralised per second at the positive plate as are released per second at the negative plate. The net result is that there is a drift of electrons from the negative terminal to the positive terminal in the external circuit. The conventional current is from positive (+) to negative (−) in the external circuit.

26.3   E.m.f. and p.d. of connected cells

Like resistors, cells can be connected either in series or in parallel or in a combination of both. When connected in series, the negative terminal of one cell is connected to the positive terminal of the next, as shown in Fig. 26.9(a). The electromotive forces add together, and so do the internal resistances. Thus the total e.m.f. of the battery = $3E$ and the total internal resistance = $3r$.

When the cells are connected in parallel, all the positive terminals are connected together and all the

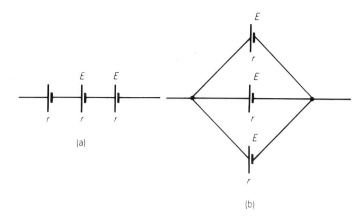

26.9   *Cells in series and in parallel*

negative terminals are connected together (Fig. 26.9.b). This method of connection effectively gives a larger surface area to both the positive and negative plates. Thus the e.m.f. of the battery is E, the same as the e.m.f. of a single cell, and nothing has been gained here. However the internal resistances are in parallel and hence the total internal resistance is $\frac{1}{3}r$. This is usually a considerable advantage.

The internal resistance r of a cell always has to be taken into account when doing circuit calculations unless the question specifically states that the internal resistance is zero or can be ignored. Banks of cells are best treated as a single cell. Thus the cells in Fig. 26.9(a) should be regarded as a single cell of e.m.f. $3E$ and internal resistance $3r$, and those in Fig. 26.9(b) should be regarded as a single cell of e.m.f. E and internal resistance $\frac{1}{3}r$. The internal resistance of a cell or battery is *always* in *series* with the circuit. A common mistake made when dealing with the circuit shown in Fig. 26.10(a) is to assume that resistances R_1, R_2 and r are in parallel. This is *not* the case. You should first find R, the combination of resistances R_1 and R_2. Then draw the equivalent circuit (Fig. 26.10b) with R replacing R_1 and R_2. It is now obvious that R and r are in series.

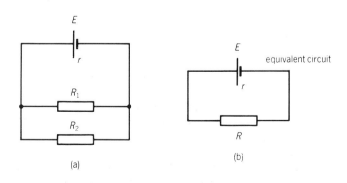

26.10   *Place of internal resistance of a cell in a circuit*

Example

4 Ω and 2 Ω resistors are connected in parallel across the terminals of a cell of e.m.f. 1.5 V and internal resistance 2 Ω. Find the total current in the circuit and the potential difference between the terminals of the cell.

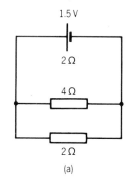 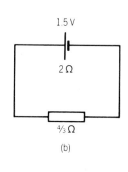

(a)   (b)

26.11   How to calculate internal resistance

First draw the circuit (Fig. 26.11a). Then find the combined resistance R of the 4 Ω and 2 Ω resistors.

$R = ?$ $R_1 = 4\ \Omega$ $R_2 = 2\ \Omega$

$$\frac{1}{R} = \frac{1}{R_1} + \frac{1}{R_2}$$

$$\frac{1}{R} = \frac{1}{4\ \Omega} + \frac{1}{2\ \Omega}$$

$$= \frac{1+2}{4\ \Omega}$$

$$= \frac{3}{4\ \Omega}$$

$$R = \tfrac{4}{3}\ \Omega$$

The equivalent circuit is shown in Fig. 26.11(b).

Total resistance $R_3 = ?$ $r = 2\ \Omega$ $R = \tfrac{4}{3}\ \Omega$

$$R_3 = r + R$$
$$= 2\ \Omega + \tfrac{4}{3}\ \Omega$$
$$= 3\tfrac{1}{3}\ \Omega$$

Now find the total current I.

$I = ?$ e.m.f. $= 1.5$ V   total resistance $= 3\tfrac{1}{3}\ \Omega$

$$I = \frac{\text{e.m.f}}{\text{total resistance}}$$

$$= \frac{1.5\ \text{V}}{3\tfrac{1}{3}\ \Omega}$$

$$= \frac{3/2}{10/3}\ \text{A}$$

$$= \frac{9}{20}\ \text{A}$$

$$I = 0.45\ \text{A}$$

Terminal p.d. $V =$ current × external resistance

$$= \frac{9}{20}\ \text{A} \times \frac{4}{3}\ \Omega$$

$$= \frac{3}{5}\ \text{V}$$

Hence $V = 0.6$ V

This example shows the importance of the internal resistance. Although 1.5 V are available only 0.6 V are used usefully, and more energy is needed to drive the charge through the cell than through the external circuit.

Investigation 26.4   To compare the e.m.f.s of two cells

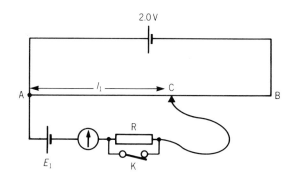

26.12   Potentiometer

The e.m.f.s of two cells may be compared by using a potentiometer (see p.302). Connect the 2.0 V accumulator (Fig. 26.12) across the ends of the uniform 1 m resistance wire AB. The resistor R is included in the circuit to protect the galvanometer and has a value of about 2 kΩ. When you have found the approximate balance point, short-circuit R by closing the key K. You can then determine the exact balance point. There is a uniform fall in potential along AB. Connect the positive terminal of the cell of e.m.f. E_1 to A. It is essential that the two positive terminals are connected to the *same* point. Move the jockey C (by lightly tapping the wire) along AB until no deflection is observed on the galvanometer. Since there is no deflection there is no current flowing and the cell is on open circuit. Thus the e.m.f. E_1 is equal to the potential difference between A and C, which is itself proportional to l_1. Thus $E \propto l_1$.

Replace the cell by another cell of e.m.f. E_2 and obtain a new balance length l_2 where $E_2 \propto l_2$. The e.m.f.s E_1 and E_2 can be compared by

$$\frac{E_1}{E_2} = \frac{l_1}{l_2}$$

If E_1 is known, E_2 may be calculated.

A very close approximation to the e.m.f. E of a single cell may be obtained. Suppose the balance length is l cm. Then, since the internal resistance of the accumulator is negligible, the potential difference along l is $2 \times l/100$ V. Hence $E = l/50$ V.

A voltmeter may be used to find the e.m.f. of a cell simply by connecting it to the terminals of the cell. The e.m.f.s of two cells may be compared in this way, but the method is not as accurate as the potentiometer method because the voltmeter takes a small current, even though it has a very high resistance.

26.4 Electrolysis

Chemical effect of an electric current

On p. 162 you read that an e.m.f. is produced when different substances come into contact. It is reasonable to assume that when an electric charge passes through a solution chemical changes occur. This can be confirmed using a Hoffmann Voltameter (Fig. 26.13).

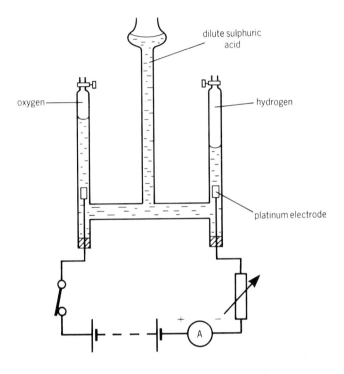

26.13 Hoffmann voltameter

The **electrodes** in the voltameter are made of platinum and the **electrolyte** is water to which a few drops of sulphuric acid have been added. The electrode which is connected to the positive terminal of the battery is called the **anode**; the electrode connected to the negative terminal of the battery is called the **cathode**. When the key is closed current enters the electrolyte at the anode and leaves from the cathode and gases are given off at both electrodes. The gas that escapes when the tap over the anode is opened will rekindle a glowing splint, showing it to be oxygen. If a lighted flame is held over the tap above the cathode and the tap is then opened, the issuing gas ignites with a 'pop' and burns with a blue flame. This gas is hydrogen. The volume of hydrogen liberated is twice the volume of oxygen.

In the electrolyte there are positive hydrogen ions (H^+), negative sulphate ions (SO_4^{2-}) and negative hydroxyl ions (OH^-). The hydrogen ions drift to the cathode where their positive charge is neutralised by electrons and hydrogen is liberated. At the anode, hydroxyl ions give up their electrons and combine to form water and oxygen. The oxygen is liberated. The sulphate ions remain in solution.

What would happen if an alternating current supply were used? Each electrode would be alternately the cathode and the anode. Gases would still be liberated at both electrodes, but it would be a mixture of both gases. In electrolysis experiments a *direct current* supply is essential.

In the simple cell hydrogen is deposited on the positive terminal, whereas in the voltameter it is liberated at the negative terminal. This difference occurs because the charge flows *inside* the simple cell and the current direction is towards the positive plate, whereas in the voltameter the current direction is towards the negative plate in the external circuit. Thus hydrogen is always deposited or released at the plate towards which the positive charge flows.

Electrolysis of copper sulphate solution

Figure 26.14 shows a copper voltameter. The anode and cathode are copper plates and the electrolyte is copper(II) sulphate solution. When the current is switched on copper is deposited on the cathode and the anode loses mass. The strength of the copper sulphate solution remains unchanged because the negative sulphate ions reaching the anode give up their electrons and combine with copper from the anode to form copper(II) sulphate.

When platinum electrodes are used copper is still deposited on the cathode. The reaction at the anode is different in that oxygen is liberated and water is formed, but no copper(II) sulphate is produced to replace that lost at the cathode. Thus the strength of the solution is decreased.

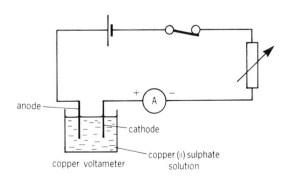

26.14 Copper voltameter

Investigation 26.5 To calibrate an ammeter with a copper voltameter

If you know the mass of copper z deposited by one coulomb of charge, you can check the accuracy of the ammeter used in the circuit in Fig. 26.14. Take the cathode out of the electrolyte, clean it, dry it and determine its mass m_1. Then replace it and pass a *small steady current* through the voltameter for a reasonable time t s, say twenty minutes. (If a large current is passed the copper tends not to adhere to the cathode.) Note down the steady reading on the ammeter. Then take out the cathode, dry it and find its mass m_2 using a balance. Then the mass deposited is $(m_2 - m_1)$ and $(m_2 - m_1) = zIt$ where t is the time in second. Compare the calculated value of I with the steady ammeter reading.

Fundamental facts about electrolysis

The following are a few fundamental facts about electrolysis.

1 Hydrogen and metals are always liberated at the cathode.
2 The mass liberated or deposited at the cathode is proportional to the quantity of charge which flows, i.e. $m \propto Q$ (It). This mass does not depend upon the area of the plates, but only upon the current and the time for which it flows.
3 The mass liberated or deposited depends upon the relative atomic mass and the valency of the substance.
4 A d.c. supply is essential.

Questions

Q1 A high resistance voltmeter is placed in the circuit as shown. Its reading, in V, will be
A 0 **B** 2.0 **C** 2.4 **D** 10.0 **E** 12.0

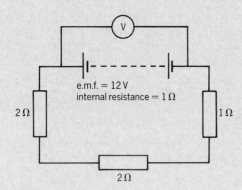

e.m.f. = 12 V
internal resistance = 1 Ω
$2\,\Omega$ $1\,\Omega$
$2\,\Omega$

(AEB)

Q2 The e.m.f. of a cell is quoted as 1.5 V. This means that the cell can supply 1.5
A amperes of current.
B coulombs of charge.
C joules of energy.
D joules of energy per ampere of current it delivers.
E joules of energy per coulomb of charge it delivers. *(AEB)*

Q3 The depolarizer used in a dry cell is
A ammonium chloride
B carbon
C manganese(IV) oxide
D zinc chloride
E zinc sulphate *(L)*

Q4 A cell of e.m.f. 1.5 V and internal resistance $3\,\Omega$ is connected in series with a cell of e.m.f. 2.0 V and internal resistance r so that the cells assist each other. When this arrangement is joined across the ends of a resistor of constant resistance $10\,\Omega$, a current of 0.25 A is produced. Determine (i) the value of r, and (ii) the heat which would be produced in the $10\text{-}\Omega$ resistor if the current were maintained for a continuous period of 4 min.
(L part question)

Q5 Four identical cells, each of e.m.f. 1.5 volts and possessing internal resistance, are connected so as to form a battery of e.m.f. 6.0 volts. The battery is then joined in series with an ammeter of negligible resistance and a coil of fixed resistance 12 ohms. The ammeter then reads 0.3 amperes. Draw a diagram of the circuit and show clearly how the cells must be connected. Determine (i) the internal resistance of the battery and (ii) the value of the resistor which must be connected in parallel with the 12-ohm coil in order to increase the ammeter reading to 0.5 amperes.
  What would a high resistance voltmeter read when connected to the terminals of the 6-volt battery in this latter case? *(L)*

Q6 Three cells, each of e.m.f. 1.5 V and negligible internal resistance, are connected in series with a switch and two coils, P and Q, each of resistance $5\,\Omega$. A coil S is connected in parallel with P, so that the combined resistance of P and S is $4\,\Omega$. Calculate (i) the resistance of S; (ii) the total resistance in the circuit; (iii) the current in Q; (iv) the current in S. Draw a circuit diagram and include an ammeter which could be used to measure the current in S.
  In reality, the cells would have internal resistance. Indicate how this would affect the reading of a voltmeter connected across the cells, when the switch is on. Would the resistance of the voltmeter matter? *(S)*

Q7 A battery consisting of 6 cells each of e.m.f. 1.5 V and internal resistance $0.5\,\Omega$ is joined to two resistors, of $5\,\Omega$ and $20\,\Omega$, which are connected in parallel. An ammeter of resistance $0.5\,\Omega$ is included in the circuit to measure the current through the battery. Draw a diagram of the circuit. Calculate
(i) the reading of the ammeter;
(ii) the reading of a high resistance voltmeter connected across the battery;
(iii) the power wasted in the battery. *(C part question)*

Q8 What do you understand by *potential difference*?

A battery of internal resistance $0.2\,\Omega$ maintains a current of $1.2\,A$ through a resistor of $3.0\,\Omega$ in the circuit shown in the diagram.

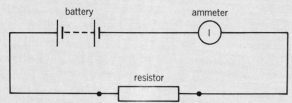

Calculate
(a) the potential difference across the resistor;
(b) the charge flowing through the ammeter in 20 s;
(c) the electromotive force of the battery, if the resistance of the ammeter is $0.3\,\Omega$;
(d) the heat produced in the battery in 250 s.

The potential difference across a resistor through which a current is flowing may be measured by connecting a moving-coil voltmeter which has a high resistance to the terminals of the resistor. Why, to obtain an accurate reading, must the resistance of the voltmeter be large? Explain why, when the current through the resistor is changed, such a voltmeter will record the new potential difference between the ends of the resistor. *(C)*

Q9

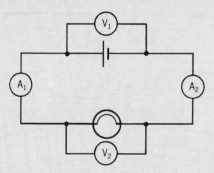

A cell of internal resistance $0.8\,\Omega$ is connected in series with ammeters A_1 and A_2, and a lamp, as shown in the diagram. A voltmeter V_1 is connected across the cell and a voltmeter V_2 is connected across the lamp. The reading of A_1 is $0.3\,A$ and that of V_2 is $1.2\,V$. (Assume that the ammeters have negligible resistances and that the voltmeters draw negligible currents.)
(a) Find the resistance of the lamp.
(b) Find the reading of V_1.
(c) What is the reading of A_2?
(d) Find the electromotive force (e.m.f.) of the cell.
(e) What current would the cell deliver if short-circuited by connecting a copper wire across its terminals? *(O)*

Q10 (a) State Kirchhoff's first law concerning electric currents entering and leaving a junction in a circuit. Describe an experiment you would perform to establish the validity of the law. Draw a circuit diagram showing how you would connect up your apparatus.
(b) The diagram represents part of a car electrical system, comprising a lead–acid battery with an e.m.f. of $12.0\,V$ and internal resistance $0.1\,\Omega$, R_1 representing lamp

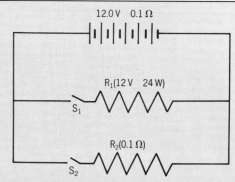

bulbs which dissipate a total power of 24 watts when connected to a 12 V supply, R_2 $(0.1\,\Omega)$ representing the windings of the starter motor and two switches S_1 and S_2.
(i) Calculate the current the battery supplies if S_1 is closed and S_2 remains open. What is the resistance of R_1 assuming the lamps are at their normal working temperatures?
(ii) If both S_2 are closed, calculate the effective resistance of the whole circuit (to the nearest $0.1\,\Omega$).
(iii) What current will now be drawn from the battery? Indicate the principle involved at each stage of your calculation. *(JMB)*

Q11

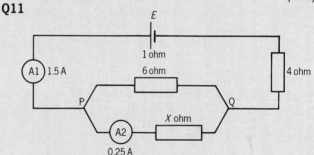

The diagram shows a battery of e.m.f. E volts and internal resistance 1 ohm connected in a circuit containing resistors and ammeters. The ammeters are of negligible resistance and have the readings shown. Calculate the values of the e.m.f. E and the resistance X. What would be the reading of ammeter $A1$ if P and Q were connected by a short length of thick copper wire? *(W)*

Q12 Describe, giving a circuit diagram, an experiment which would show whether a particular cell has an appreciable internal resistance. Indicate briefly what readings would be needed in order to estimate its value. (You are not required to derive the equation for this.)

Explain why a check against a short circuit should be made when using secondary cells such as lead plate accumulators, whereas this is not so important when dry cells are used.

Resistances of 2 ohms and 3 ohms are connected in series with a cell. A high resistance voltmeter connected across the 3-ohm resistor reads 1.0 volt, but this increases to 1.2 volt when an extra 2-ohm resistor is connected in parallel with the first 2-ohm resistor. Calculate the *electromotive force* and *internal resistance* of the cell. *(L)*

27 Using electricity

27.1 Heating effect of an electric current

There are numerous applications of the heating effect of an electric current. Can you imagine life without electric cookers, electric kettles, electric fires, hair dryers, soldering irons etc.? All of these work as they do because when electric charge passes along a wire, the wire gets hot.

In mechanics you learned that when a body falls from a height, the potential energy decreases and the energy lost is changed into some other form of energy. The same applies in electricity. When charge flows from a higher to a lower potential level, energy is released. On p.296 you read that if one joule of work is done in moving one coloumb of charge between two points against the electric field, the potential difference between the two points is one volt. It follows that if one coloumb of charge moves through a potential difference of one volt in the direction of the electric field then one joule of energy is released. Hence, when charge flows, energy W in joule = potential difference $\times$ charge.

$$W = V \times Q$$
$$= VIt$$

The energy is released as heat energy and $W = VIt$. However, since $V = IR$,

$$W = I^2Rt$$

Moreover, $I = V/R$, so

$$W = \frac{V^2}{R} t$$

Thus the formula for the heat produced by an electric current may be written in three different ways. The one that is chosen depends upon the information which is given.

27.2 Power

Power is **the rate of doing work**, or the rate at which energy is produced. Hence

$$P = \frac{\text{energy released}}{\text{time}}$$
$$= \frac{VIt}{t}$$
$$= VI$$

The power equation may be written in three different forms:

$$P = VI$$
$$P = I^2 R$$
$$P = \frac{V^2}{R}$$

Power is measured in joule/second and the unit of power is the **watt**: 1 watt = 1 joule/second or $1 \text{ W} = 1 \text{ J s}^{-1}$.

The watt is a small unit. Larger units are

1 kilowatt (kW) = 1000 W = 10^3 W
1 megawatt (MW) = 1 000 000 W = 10^6 W

The power of normal electrical appliances is usually stated in watt or kilowatt. The potential difference which should be applied to it is also stated, because it is meaningless to state the wattage without also stating the voltage. For example, an electric light bulb for use in the house is marked 100 W 240 V; a car headlamp bulb is marked 48 W 12 V. The resistance of the bulbs may be obtained from the equation $P = V^2/R$ or $R = V^2/P$.

Example

Find the resistance of 100 W 240 V bulb.

$R = ?$ $V = 240$ V $P = 100$ W

$$R = \frac{240 \times 240}{100} \frac{V^2}{VA}$$

$$= 24 \times 24 \text{ V/A}$$

$$= 576 \ \Omega$$

This is the **working resistance** of the light bulb, i.e. the resistance when the bulb is hot. When the bulb is cold the resistance is much less, but putting a potential difference of 12 V across it will not make it light and the power produced will be very low.

Investigation 27.1   To demonstrate the heating effect of a current

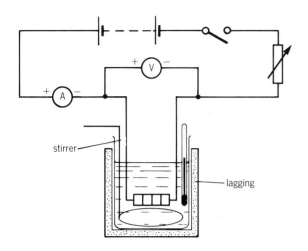

27.1   Heating effect of an electric current

You can demonstrate the heating effect of a current with the apparatus shown in Fig. 27.1. This is essentially the same as the apparatus used to determine the specific heat capacity of a liquid (see p.124). Put a liquid of low specific heat capacity, e.g. paraffin, into a glass beaker or polythene cup. This container should be well lagged to reduce the heat losses to the surrounding air by conduction and convection. Place a low-power immersion heater inside the liquid so that it is completely covered, and connect the circuit as shown. The rheostat allows the values of the voltage and current to be adjusted.

Perform the following experiments.

1   Read the thermometer, then close the switch and keep the readings of the voltmeter and ammeter constant to ensure that the electrical energy is supplied at a constant rate. Stir the liquid well and read the thermometer at regular intervals. Plot a graph of rise of temperature against time (see Fig. 27.2a). This should be a straight line through the origin, showing that the temperature increases uniformly with time.

Since the thermal capacity of the paraffin and container remains constant throughout the experiment, it may be assumed that the heat energy W given out by the heater is proportional to the time t. Hence $W \propto t$ when V, I and R are constant.

2   Find the rise in temperature over a fixed time interval when the values of the voltage and current are kept constant. After the paraffin has cooled to room temperature repeat the experiment for the same time interval, but with different values of the voltage and current. The resistance of the heater remains constant. Plot graphs of rise in temperature against I^2 (Fig. 27.2b) and of rise in temperature against V^2 (Fig. 27.2c). These should both be straight lines through the origin. Again the thermal capacity of the apparatus is constant, hence heat energy released $W \propto I^2$ when R and t are constant and also $W \propto V^2$ when R and t are constant.

3   In this experiment use different heating coils. These may be produced by winding different lengths of resistance wire round a pencil. Repeat the experiment for each different heating coil, starting from room temperature each time and heating for the same length of time with the same current value. Plot a graph of rise in temperature against the resistance R of the heating coil (Fig. 27.2d). A straight line through the origin should be obtained.

Since different lengths of resistance wire are used the thermal capacity of the apparatus will vary very slightly but within the limits of experimental error it is true to say that $W \propto R$ when I and t are constant.

The experiment may be repeated, but this time keeping V and t constant. A graph of rise in temperature against $1/R$ (Fig. 27.2e) is a straight line through the origin, showing that $W \propto 1/R$ when V and t are constant.

These results agree with the equations.

$$W = VIt = I^2 Rt = \frac{V^2}{R} t$$

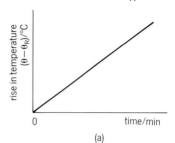

(a)

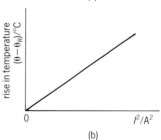

(c)

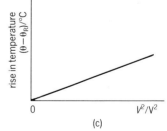

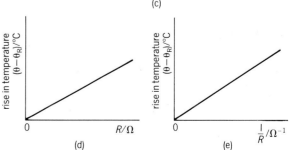

27.2   Graphs of the heating effect of current

Example

Find the resistance of 48 W 12 V car headlamp bulb.

$R = ?$ $V = 12\,V$ $P = 48\,W$

$$R = \frac{V^2}{P}$$

$$= \frac{12 \times 12}{48} \frac{V^2}{VA}$$

$$= 3 \frac{V}{A}$$

$$= 3\,\Omega$$

This is the resistance of the car headlamp bulb when it is hot. The current through the bulb is found from $P = VI$, i.e.

$$I = \frac{P}{V}$$

$$= \frac{48}{12} \frac{VA}{V}$$

$$= 4\,A$$

Example

A man wishes to use a 120 V 100 W appliance which he has bought abroad on the 240 V mains in this country. What should he do?

$R = ?$ $V = 120\,V$ $P = 100\,W$

$$R = \frac{V^2}{P}$$

$$= \frac{120 \times 120}{100} \frac{V^2}{VA}$$

$$= 12 \times 12 \frac{V}{A}$$

$$= 144\,\Omega$$

Thus he should put a 144 Ω resistor in series with the appliance (see Fig. 27.3) to give two equal resistors in series across the 240 V supply with a voltage drop of 120 V across each.

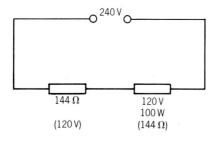

27.3   An example of cutting down voltage

This solution is not really satisfactory. The current through the resistor will be slightly less than 1 A, but the resistor will heat up and energy will be wasted. He should instead use a step-down transformer to change the voltage from 240 V to 120 V.

It is obvious that if a potential difference of 240 V is put across this bulb the current, given by $V/R = 240\,V/3\,\Omega$. is 80 A. This current causes the filament temperature to rise so high that the filament melts and the bulb 'blows'. So you can see that if voltages much lower than the stipulated voltage are applied to electrical appliances the wattage is much less than that required, and if a voltage greater than the stipulated voltage is applied it is likely that the element or filament will burn out. Electrical appliances should not be used with voltages higher than those marked upon them, unless some precaution, such as including a series resistor, is used to reduce the potential difference across the appliance to the required value.

Cost of electricity

Electrical energy that is used has to be paid for. Electricity is sold in units of kilowatt hour (kWh). As the name suggests, if one kilowatt of electricity is used for one hour, 1 kWh of electrical energy is used.

$$1\,kWh = 1000\,J\,s^{-1} \times (60 \times 60)\,s$$
$$= 1000 \times 60 \times 60\,J$$
$$= 3\,600\,000\,J$$

For the price of one unit of electricity a 1 kW electric fire can be used for 1 hour, a 3 kW immersion heater can be used for 20 minutes or a 100 W electric lamp can be used for 10 hours. The power of a 26-inch colour television set is about 150 W, so the TV set can run for about 7 hours on one unit of electricity.

27.3   Uses of the heating effect of current

Fuses

A fuse is a safety device. It is usually made of tinned copper wire. Its diameter (gauge) is such that it melts when the current exceeds a certain value. The fuse protects the appliances in a circuit by limiting the current that passes through it. It is much cheaper to replace a fuse than to replace, for example, the element of an electric iron which has 'burned out'.

Fuses also reduce the danger of fire. Electrical wiring nowadays is placed in a metal conduit, but there are places where it is not, for example, on the leads to appliances. If the current in the circuit becomes too large, the wire may melt and set fire to the insulation. This may spread to the rest of the house if it occurs outside the metal conduit. A fuse wire has a smaller diameter than the remainder of the wiring in the circuit, so it is the weakest point in the circuit.

There are various reasons why fuses melt (blow). Sometimes it is simply because the fuse wire is old and has become oxidised, reducing its diameter. When a fuse wire blows *it should be replaced by fuse wire of the same gauge. On no account* should it be replaced by fuse wire of a heavier gauge. If the fuse blows again immediately after it is replaced, then there is probably a fault in the circuit. This should be located and put right by a qualified electrician. A fuse could also blow when more appliances are being used than the circuit was designed to accommodate, e.g. using extra electric fires when the weather is particularly cold. This is a dangerous practice and is not recommended. A fuse is incorporated in the plug of most appliances. The size of the fuse should be such that it will take a current slightly larger than the maximum current taken by the appliance. For example, a 1 kW heater takes a current of $I = P/V = 1000/240$ VA/A = 4.1 A, so a 5 A fuse would be large enough. There is no point in inserting a 13 A fuse which would not limit the current enough to protect the fire.

Example

What current is taken by a 3 kW electric fire on the 240 V mains? What size fuse should be used in the plug?

$I = ?$ $P = 3000$ W $V = 240$ V

$P = VI$ so $I = \dfrac{P}{V} = \dfrac{3000}{240} \dfrac{VA}{V}$

$= 12.5$ A

The current is 12.5 A and a 13 A fuse is adequate.

Example

What current is taken by a 60 W 240 V electric light bulb and what is its resistance?

$I = ?$ $P = 60$ W $V = 240$ V $R = ?$

$$I = \frac{P}{V} = \frac{60}{240} \frac{VA}{V}$$

$$= \frac{1}{4} A$$

$$= 0.25 A$$

$$R = \frac{V^2}{P} = \frac{240 \times 240}{60} \frac{V^2}{VA}$$

$$= 960 \ \Omega$$

Hence $I = 0.25$ A and $R = 960 \ \Omega$.

The resistance of the electric fire in the first example can also be found.

$R = ?$ $P = 3$ kW $V = 240$ V

$$R = \frac{V^2}{P} = \frac{240 \times 240}{3000} \frac{V^2}{VA}$$

$$= \frac{24 \times 24}{30} \frac{V}{A}$$

$$= \frac{192}{10} \ \Omega$$

$$= 19.2 \ \Omega$$

This fire is probably made of three 1 kW bars in parallel. Each of these has a resistance of 57.6 Ω.

It is noticeable that, for appliances used on the 240 V mains, the resistance decreases as the wattage increases. The resistance of the 3 kW fire is small whereas the resistance of the 60 W light bulb is considerable.

Filament lamps

The filament of an electric lamp gives out a bright light from a very small space. This is produced by using a long length of fine tungsten wire. The finer the wire the greater is the resistance per unit length. Tungsten is used because it has a high melting point (3650 K). The wire is first coiled into a narrow coil, and this coil is itself coiled in turn (Fig. 27.4a). In this way the filament can be made to fit inside the glass bulb (Fig. 27.4b). The bulb also contains a small amount of an inert gas such as nitrogen or argon to prevent oxidation and evaporation of the metal.

Filament lamps are inefficient. They emit both heat energy and light energy, but the greater part of the energy is emitted as heat and not as light.

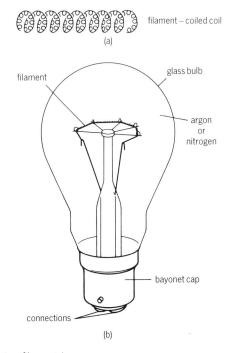

27.4   Tungsten filament lamp

Fluorescent lamps

Fluorescent lamps are about three times as efficient as filament lamps. A fluorescent lamp consists essentially of a mercury vapour discharge tube. The inside of the tube is coated with a chemical which fluoresces under the ultraviolet light released in the discharge. Although initially more expensive than tungsten filament lamps, the running costs are far less because the current is less, and they also last longer.

27.4 Wiring in the home

Wiring circuits

The current taken by a 3 kW electric fire is 12.5 A whereas that taken by a 60 W lamp is 0.25 A. Thus they cannot possibly be connected in *series*, because the current is constant throughout a series circuit. A second disadvantage of a series circuit is that the potential differences across the individual parts are added together, so a large voltage is necessary if many appliances are used. Finally, if one part fails there is no current in any other part of the circuit. That is why house wiring circuits are *parallel* circuits.

Although it is possible to connect a 60 W lamp and a 3 kW fire in parallel (because the potential difference across each is the same), separate circuits are used for lighting and heating. The lighting circuit has finer gauge cable and so lower value fuses are used. Also the heating circuit contains an earthing wire. Figure 27.5 shows a circuit with three different wattage lamps connected in parallel. The current in each lamp must be different, and they would not function properly if connected in series. The total current in the circuit is the sum of the individual currents and so a 1 A fuse is adequate. Although it is unlikely that all the lamps in a house are switched on at one time, the fuse must allow for this possibility.

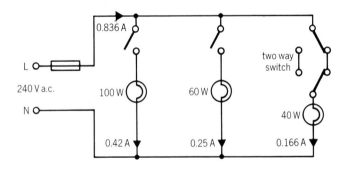

27.5   Lighting wiring circuit

The 40 W lamp is operated by a two-way switch. This is the usual wiring for a lamp on a stairway, and means that it can be switched on or off from both the top and bottom of the stair.

There are two very important points worth noting about the circuit in Fig. 27.5.

1   The switches are all on the *live* side of the lamps. Hence when switched off the light socket is not live. Were the switch to be on the neutral side, the socket would be live when the switch was open,

Exercise 27.1

How many 60 W lamps can be switched on at the same time if there is a 5 A fuse in the lighting circuit?

and anyone touching it, e.g. when changing the bulb, would get a shock and could be electrocuted. If in any doubt it is always advisable to get a qualified electrician to check that the switch does break the live wire.

2   The fuse is also on the live side of the circuit. Thus when the fuse blows the appliance is dead, i.e. is made safe. The fuse would blow just as easily if it were on the neutral side, but the appliance would remain live.

The electricity supply

Electricity is fed into the house by a heavy cable which contains two wires which are well insulated from each other. One of these wires is the **live wire** (L) and the other is the **neutral wire** (N). The potential of the neutral wire is earth potential since it is earthed at the power station. The potential of the live wire varies between about $+340$ V and -340 V. This means that the root mean square (r.m.s.) value of the potential of the live wire is 240 V. This will be explained when the production of alternating voltages is considered (p.357). Whenever an appliance such as an electric fire or lamp is connected to the live and neutral wires charge flows through the appliance. When the live wire is positive, charge flows from live to neutral, and when the live wire is negative charge flows from neutral to live.

The electricity is fed into the house through the mains fuse, the meter and the main switch to the distribution box (Fig. 27.6). Switches are of two types, **single pole** which cuts just one wire, and **double pole** which cuts both wires. The main switch is a double pole switch. From the distribution box there are normally three circuits, namely the lighting circuit, power circuit, and a circuit to the cooker which is separate from the power circuit.

The lighting circuit has already been discussed. It differs from the other two in that there are only two wires, live and neutral. There is no earth wire.

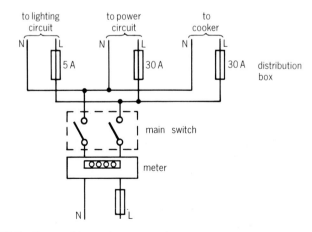

27.6   House wiring system

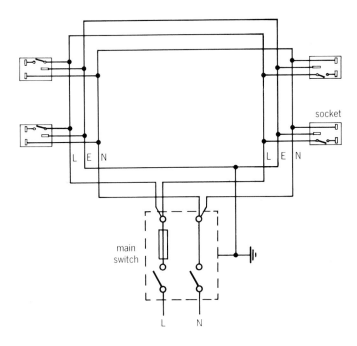

27.7   Power circuit

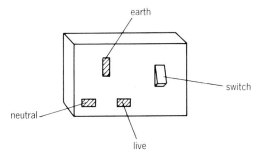

27.8   Three-pin socket

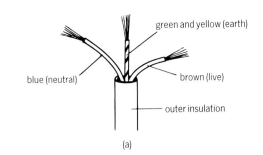

(a)

(b)

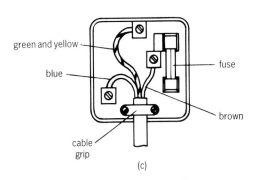

(c)

27.9   Wiring a plug

Power circuit

Nowadays power circuits are usually on **ring mains** (Fig. 27.7). The advantage of ring mains is that there are two paths which the current can take in the live wire and also in the neutral wire. This means that it is possible to use at one time twice as much current as could be taken with a single wire. A much more expensive and clumsy way of wiring the house would be to wire a separate circuit from the distribution box to each different room.

Figure 27.8 shows a three-pin socket. These are connected to the ring mains at different points (see Fig. 27.7). The live terminal of each socket is connected to the live wire, the neutral terminal to the neutral wire, and the earth terminal to the earth wire. There are two important safety precautions in the socket.

1 The switch in the socket breaks the live wire.
2 The sockets have shutters which only open when a plug is inserted. The earth pin of the plug, which is longer than the other two pins, opens the shutters as it is inserted in its hole.

Figure 27.9(a) shows the three-core cable which should always be used to connect appliances such as electric fires to the ring mains. The live wire is covered with brown insulation, the neutral wire with blue insulation and the earth wire with green and yellow striped insulation. All three are enclosed in a tube of moulded insulation. When connecting the cable to an appliance, first strip the insulation from about 5 cm of the cable. Then strip 2 cm insulation from the inner wires. Tightly twist the strands of bare wire together, as it is very important not to have loose strands. Wrap each wire clockwise round the pillar of the correct

terminal so that the screw tightens in the same direction (Fig. 27.9b).

Figure 27.9(c) shows the three-pin plug with the wires attached correctly. The blue wire is connected to the neutral (**N**) terminal, the green and yellow wire to the earth (**E**) terminal and the brown wire to the live (**L**) terminal. The **N** and **E** terminals are connected directly to the plug pins, but the **L** terminal is connected to one end of a fuse, the other end of which is connected to the live pin. There are three further safety precautions in the plug.

1 Each plug contains a separate fuse, so that if a fault occurs in the appliance this fuse will blow

instead of the main fuse. This also has the advantage of pinpointing the faulty appliance. If the main fuse blew each appliance would have to be tested separately to find out which was faulty.

2 The fuse breaks the live wire so that the appliance is not live when the fuse blows.

3 The cable grip prevents the wires from being pulled out of the terminals and shorting the circuit.

Special circuits

As shown in Fig. 27.6 the electric cooker is not run from the ring circuit, but has its own separate circuit. This is because it takes a large current. Other devices which take large currents, e.g. instant showers, may also be connected separately to the distribution box.

Earthing

Earthing the circuit is a most important safety precaution. In any electrical appliance the earthing wire is always connected to the metal case. Figure 27.10 shows the earth lead connected to the case of an electric iron. Many electric irons have a water reservoir and these can be lethal if not properly earthed. Should the insulation inside the iron break down, or the live wire become loose, then the case of the iron would become live and the user may get a severe shock if the case were not earthed. The wire which earths the case has a much smaller resistance than a human being and so the bulk of the charge passes down the wire to earth.

Amateur electricians sometimes earth to the nearest large quantity of metal. This is a mistake because if the metal is not itself connected to earth there is a chance

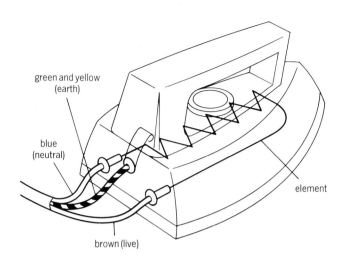

27.10 Connections in an electric iron

that it may become live. It is best to earth to a metal rod which is driven directly into the ground.

Since water conducts electricity, it is dangerous to have appliances such as electric fires in a bathroom unless they are placed high on the wall out of reach of people and water. There are usually no sockets in the bathroom for this reason. On a very cold day it may be tempting to use an extension lead to carry an electric fire into the bathroom when taking a bath. This is a very foolish procedure and could lead to your electrocution. You should also take great care in the kitchen. It is always advisable to dry your hands before switching on electrical appliances. Water dripping from your hand into the socket could carry current to you from the live wire and give you a serious electric shock.

Questions

Q1 A householder installs two room lights operating in parallel from the house mains and he wishes to include a protective fuse. At which of the locations marked **A, B, C, D** and **E** in the circuit diagram below would the fuse be best placed?

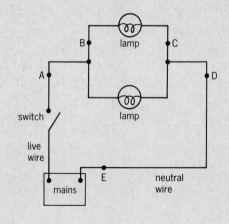

(L)

Q2 Electrical appliances have voltage and power ratings as listed below. Which has the larger working resistance?

	Appliance	Voltage/V	Power/W
A	Washing machine	250	3000
B	Television	240	160
C	Kettle	240	1500
D	Hair curler	250	20
E	Car headlamp	12	36

(L)

Q3 If the potential difference between two parts of a thundercloud is 10^8 V, what is the amount of energy given up during the passage of 20 coulombs?
A 2×10^{-7} J **B** 200 J **C** 5×10^6 J
D 2×10^9 J **E** 2×10^{10} J (L)

Q4 A 3-pin mains plug is fitted to the lead for a 1-kW electric kettle to be used on a 250-V a.c. supply, which of the following statements is NOT correct?
A A 13-A fuse is the most appropriate value to use.
B The brown wire should be connected to the live side of the mains.

C The fuse should be fitted in the live lead.
D The neutral wire is coloured blue.
E The yellow and green wire should be connected to the earth pin. *(L)*

Q5 A 3-kilowatt electric fire is designed to operate from a 240-volt supply. Calculate the resistance of the fire. The fire is connected to the supply by long leads of resistance 0.8 ohm. Assuming their resistance to remain unaltered, determine (i) the current in the leads, and (ii) the power dissipated in the leads.

Explain why a single pole switch (cutting only one wire) should be placed so that it cuts the live wire.
(L part question)

Q6 Two heating coils dissipate heat at the rate of 40 W and 60 W respectively when connected in parallel to a 12-V d.c. supply of negligible internal resistance. Calculate the resistances of the coils.

Assuming that these resistances remain constant, what would be their rates of dissipation of heat when connected together in series with the same supply as before?
(L part question)

Q7

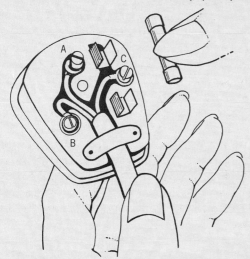

(a) The diagram shows the type of 3-pin electrical plug with the cover removed used in the United Kingdom. The electric cable connected to the plug contains three wires with colour-coded insulation, namely brown, blue and green/yellow stripe. Identify each of the colour-coded wires by stating to which of the terminals A, B or C in the diagram they should be connected.

Identify the terminal through which no current passes in normal circumstances. What is the purpose of the wire connecting this terminal to an electrical appliance such as an electric fire? Describe how it works.

What is the purpose of the device, held above C in the diagram, that is about to be inserted into the plug? Describe how it works.

(b) An electric cooker has the following specification:

Item	No. of items	Power of item/W
Ceramic hob, *small* heating area	2	1250
Ceramic hob, *large* heating area	2	1500
Grill	1	2000
Oven	1	2500

Calculate how much energy (in kW h) the cooker will use in 30 minutes when all the items are used simultaneously.

How much will it cost to run the cooker during this time if electrical energy costs 6p for 1 kW h?

Calculate the maximum current that will be carried by the cable connecting this cooker to a 250-V mains supply. *(L)*

Q8 Describe an experiment to investigate the relationship between the heat produced in a wire and the electric current flowing through it. Your answer should include
(i) a circuit diagram.
(ii) an account of the observations you would make.
(iii) an account of how you would use these observations to deduce the relationship.
(iv) a statement of the result you would expect to obtain.
(JMB)

Q9

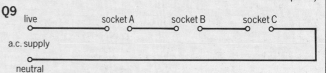

The diagram shows an **incorrect** attempt to wire three sockets A, B and C to the mains supply. When a mains electric heater is plugged into any one of the three sockets, no current flows in the circuit. When similar mains heaters are plugged into *each* of the sockets simultaneously, a current flows in the circuit but the heaters give out much less heat than they were designed to do.

Explain these observations.

Draw a circuit diagram to show the three sockets correctly wired to the mains supply so that the three heaters can operate normally. Include (a) a fuse, (b) an earth wire, in your circuit diagram.

Explain clearly why a fuse and an earth wire are used in a mains wiring circuit.

Draw a labelled diagram of the structure of one type of fuse.

A 3kW heater is fitted with a 35 W indicator lamp and a 15 W fan. These three components of the appliance are connected directly to the 250 V mains and switch on and off together. When the appliance is operating, calculate (i) the total power, (ii) the total current, (iii) the energy used in 4 hours. *(C)*

28 Magnets and magnetism

28.1 Magnets

It has been known for several thousand years that a certain stone, found naturally, always pointed in a certain direction when it was freely suspended. For this reason it was called 'lodestone' or leading stone. It is magnetite, an oxide of iron.

Lodestones were used to make the first compasses. Nowadays a compass is made from a small magnet which is pivoted at its centre of gravity so that it rotates in a horizontal plane. When the compass is disturbed it will oscillate and always come to rest with the same end pointing in a northerly direction (Fig. 28.1a). Any magnet which is freely pivoted will always come to rest with the same pole of the magnet pointing in a northerly direction (Fig. 28.1b).
(**Note** This only happens if there is no iron in the vicinity.) The end which points to the north is known as the **north-seeking pole**, which is usually abbreviated to **N-pole**. The end of the magnet which points to the

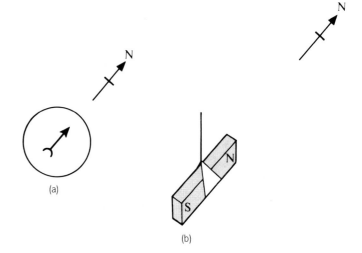

28.1 A magnet that is free to move always sets in the same direction

north pole is marked **N** and the opposite end is marked **S**. A common mistake is to assume that the south pole of a compass or magnet points to the north. If you remember the full name of the south pole, i.e. south-seeking pole, you will avoid this error.

Investigation 28.1 To demonstrate the laws of magnetism

Remove the magnet from its holder, and bring the **N**-pole slowly up to the compass needle. The N-pole of the compass is repelled and the S-pole attracted (Fig. 28.2a). Then bring the south pole of the magnet slowly up to the compass needle. The reverse occurs: the N-pole of the compass is attracted and the S-pole repelled (Fig. 28.2b).

Replace the magnet in its holder and bring up another magnet (Fig. 28.2c). Again the N poles repel each other but N- and S-poles attract. Now bring a piece of soft iron up to the magnet. You will find that both ends of the soft iron attract both ends of the magnet (Fig. 28.2d). If you freely suspend the soft iron it will not point in any fixed direction, and so it is *not* a magnet. This shows that attraction is not a true test of magnetism.

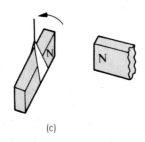

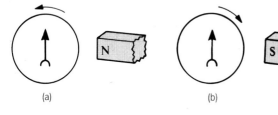

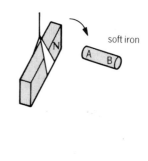

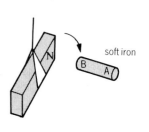

28.2 Attraction and repulsion of magnets

This investigation demonstrates the Laws of Magnetism: **unlike poles attract** and **like poles repel**. A specimen is a magnet if it will repel another magnet, and repulsion is the only true test.

Poles of a magnet

A rough idea of the exact position of the poles may be obtained by suspending a bar magnet, as shown in Fig. 28.3, and allowing it to attract small soft iron nails. Most nails are attracted at two specific points. These points are the **poles** of the magnet and are the regions where the magnetic force is most concentrated. The strength of the magnetic force varies along the magnet.

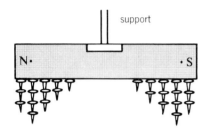

28.3   Location of poles of a magnet

The poles are not quite at the ends of the magnet, but are placed symmetrically a short distance from the ends. The distance between the poles is about five-sixths of the length of the magnet. Thus the poles of a magnet which is 12 cm long are 1 cm from each end. A better way of finding the position of poles is to plot the **magnetic lines of force**, as shown in investigation 28.2.

Magnetic substances

Only certain substances are magnetic. Soft iron is attracted to a magnet, but copper is not. You can check this with copper wire. Try other substances also. You will find that iron, nickel and cobalt, and certain alloys are strongly magnetic. These are known as **ferromagnetic substances**.

28.2   The effect of a magnet

Magnetic induction

If you touch both ends of a soft iron nail with a similar soft iron nail, nothing happens (Fig. 28.4a). However, if you bring one pole of a magnet to touch one end of the first nail, the second nail can be picked up by the first. Thus when the first nail is in contact with the magnet it becomes a magnet itself. This phenomenon is known as **induced magnetism**. Figure 28.4(b) shows the polarity of the induced magnet. The end of the nail in contact with the N-pole of the magnet becomes a S-pole.

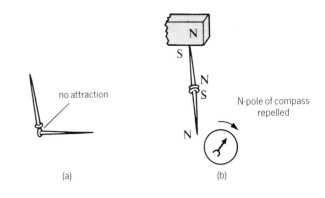

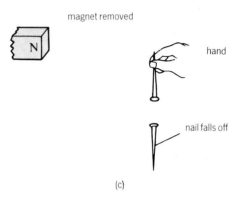

28.4   Magnetic induction

When the magnet is removed the second nail falls off (Fig. 28.4c), i.e. it has lost its induced magnetism. Thus when the inducing force is removed the induced magnetism disappears. This does not always happen. Had a steel nail been used instead of a soft iron one, some of the induced magnetism would have been retained.

A magnet is not the only source of induced magnetism. Whenever a magnetic substance is placed in a strong **magnetic field**, it becomes an induced magnet. It is true to say that induction precedes attraction. This may be shown by a simple demonstration. Bring the N-pole of a strong bar magnet slowly to the N-pole of a much weaker bar magnet. The pole is repelled. However, if you bring it up very quickly attraction takes place. This is because induction has occurred, and the polarity of the weak magnet is reversed.

Theory of magnetism

The mechanism of magnetism is still not perfectly understood. However, the theory regards each individual atom or molecule of a magnetic material as a small magnet with a north and south pole, i.e. as a **dipole**. A close group of atoms (a domain) may have the magnetic axis on each atom or molecule pointing in the same direction (Fig. 28.5a). Assuming that the

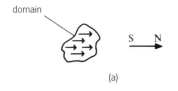
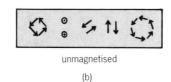
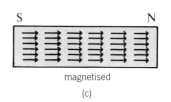

domain

S — N

unmagnetised
(a)
(b)

S   N

magnetised
(c)

28.5   Theory of magnetism

heads of the arrows represent the north poles, the net effect of the domain is represented by a single arrow. In an unmagnetised specimen the axes in the domains lie in closed chains, or pointing in random directions. The total magnetic effect is very small or zero (Fig. 28.5b). When all the domains are aligned in one direction the specimen is magnetised with the poles near the end (Fig. 28.5c). Elsewhere the poles nullify each other.

This effect may be demonstrated by hanging soft iron keepers from each end of two similar magnets (Fig. 28.6a). When you bring the N-pole of one into contact with the S-pole of the other the keepers on these ends fall off, but those at the other ends stay on (Fig. 28.6b). Thus in a magnet or line of magnets the poles are near to the ends, and a magnet only attracts in these regions. The poles are not exactly at the ends, because the unbalanced poles at the very ends repel each other, and tend to splay out.

Magnetic lines of force

The definition of a magnetic line of force is that **it is the path in which an imaginary 'free' N-pole will travel if it is free to do so.** However, free north poles do not exist. The following demonstration gives a reasonable approximation.

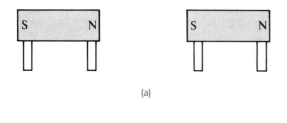

(a)

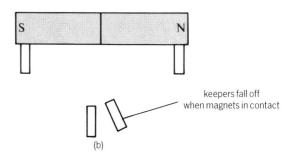

keepers fall off when magnets in contact

(b)

28.6   Magnets only attract at their poles

Investigation 28.2   To show lines of force

Place a strong bar magnet on a cork floating in a dish of water. The cork rotates or oscillates until the magnet comes to rest pointing in a north–south direction. Magnetise a long steel needle so that the eye is a N-pole and the point a S-pole, and push it through a small cork so that the eye is just above the cork. Float the magnetised needle in the water. The S-pole is far enough away from the surface of the water for the N-pole at the eye to act like a free N-pole. Place the floating needle near the N-pole of the magnet and release it. It should follow the path indicated in Fig. 28.7. The path traced by the moving needle eye is a line of force. A different path will be traced if you place the needle in a different starting position.

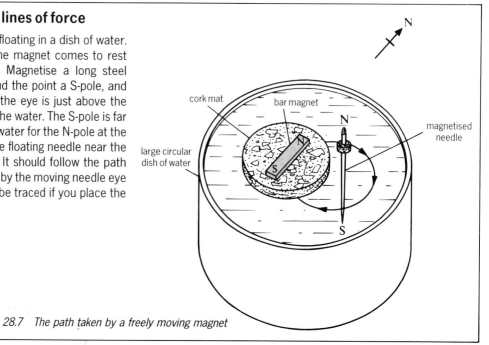

28.7   The path taken by a freely moving magnet

28.3 Magnetic fields

Around every magnet is a field of force known as a **magnetic field**. Any magnetic material placed in this region is affected and modifies the shape of the field.

Investigation 28.3 To plot a magnetic field with iron filings

Place a piece of paper on the top of a bar magnet and sprinkle iron filings lightly over the paper. Then tap the paper gently. The filings fall into the pattern in Fig. 28.8, showing the lines of force. This is not a good representation of a magnetic field as the directions of the lines of force are not shown.

Note Lines of force are vectors and thus have direction and magnitude. The spacing between the lines of force is a measure of the field strength.

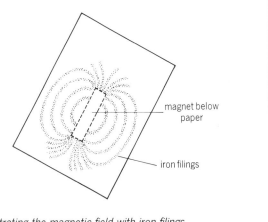

magnet below paper

iron filings

28.8　*Illustrating the magnetic field with iron filings*

Investigation 28.4 To plot a magnetic field with small compasses

Put a bar magnet onto a sheet of paper and place a small compass near to the magnet (position (i) in Fig. 28.9). When the compass has settled mark the ends of the needle with pencil dots. Then move the compass to position (ii) so that the S-pole rests on the dot which previously marked the N-pole, and put a third dot against the N-pole. Move the compass on to position (iii) and repeat the procedure. Continue this until the compass reaches the S-pole of the magnet, then join the dots. The line produced represents a line of force. Repeat the whole operation for other lines of force. The advantage of this method is that the direction in which the N-pole of the plotting compass points indicates the direction of the magnetic field.

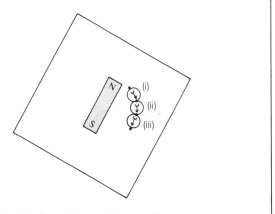

28.9　*Plotting the lines of force with a small compass*

Earth's magnetic field

The horizontal component of the earth's magnetic field may be found by the method of investigation 28.4. Place a sheet of paper on the bench and use the plotting compass alone. You will obtain a number of parallel lines running from south to north.

Combined magnetic fields

Magnetic fields react with each other. The force at any point in a combined field is the resultant of the two fields of force. If investigation 28.4 is performed on an open bench the lines of force do not represent the true field of the magnet but the combined field of the Earth and the magnet. You can plot the field of the magnet alone by performing the experiment inside a large flat biscuit tin. The tin shields the magnet from the effects of the Earth's field.

Figure 28.10 (overleaf) shows various magnetic fields. The arrows show the directions of the lines of force.

1 Where the lines of force are close together the field is strong and where they are well spaced out the field is weak.

2 The points marked X in Figs. 28.10(b), (c), (d), (f) and (g) are **neutral points**. At these points the compass needle does not set in any specific direction. They occur where the magnetic field intensities, which are vectors, cancel each other and leave no resultant force on the compass needle.

Note The lines of force for a magnetic field can never cross or intersect each other.

Two very important magnetic fields are

1 The **uniform magnetic** field in which the lines of force are parallel straight lines an equal distance apart;

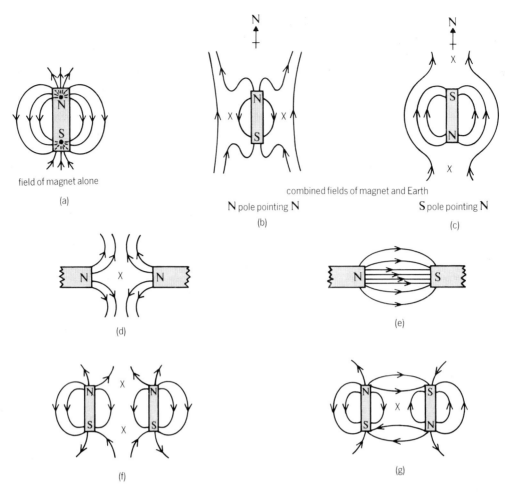

field of magnet alone

(a)

combined fields of magnet and Earth

N pole pointing N

(b)

S pole pointing N

(c)

(d)

(e)

(f)

(g)

28.10 Combined magnetic fields (in parts (d) to (g) only the fields between the magnets are shown)

2 the **radial field** in which the lines of force spread out from a point rather like the radii of a circle.

Magnetic material affects any magnetic field in which it is placed. The lines of force are drawn towards the magnetic material as shown in Fig. 28.11. If the magnetic material is an iron ring (Fig. 28.11c), no line of force penetrates inside the ring and a compass needle placed inside the ring does not set in any fixed direction. Thus a hollow box made of magnetic material may be used to screen instruments from magnetic effects.

28.4 Making magnets

Domains in a magnetic material behave rather like compass needles and align themselves along the magnetic field. Hammering a steel rod tends to magnetise it, particularly if it is held along the Earth's magnetic field. The domains are disturbed by the banging and line up in the direction of the magnetic field. Heating a steel rod to a high temperature and allowing it to cool slowly in the Earth's magnetic field has the same effect. However if the hot steel rod is

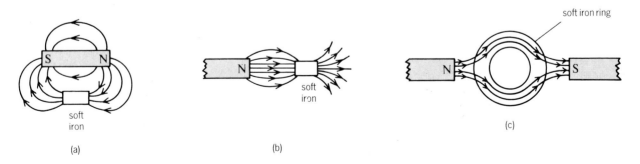

(a)

(b)

(c)

28.11 Lines of force crowd into magnetic materials

plunged into cold water so that the cooling is rapid, the domains set haphazardly, and the magnetism is lost.

Most steel objects contain a certain amount of magnetism. Ships are usually magnetic since the hammering and welding involved in their construction tend to align the domains along the Earth's magnetic field.

One way of making a magnet must be to align the domains. You can make a strip of steel watch spring into a magnet by stroking it with a permanent magnet. It is essential always to stroke in the same direction (Fig. 28.12). Stroking backwards and forwards along the spring will not succeed. The end of the spring where the S-pole finishes stroking is a N-pole: the end where the stroking finishes is always of opposite polarity to the stroking pole.

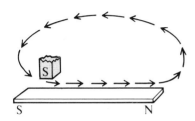

28.12   Magnetisation by stroking

If you stroke an ordinary iron nail in the same way it does not become a magnet. Although the domains in the iron are aligned when the stroking magnet is present, they revert to their normal position when it is removed. This shows that steel is suitable material for a permanent magnet but iron is not.

If you break the magnetised watch spring in the middle you are left with two separate magnets. Continued breaking produces more magnets. The inference is that no matter how small the piece of watch spring produced, it will be a magnet. This supports the domain theory of magnetism.

The hammering, heating and stroking methods are not suitable for making permanent magnets. They are far too unreliable and do not produce strong magnets. Electrical methods are better both for magnetisation and demagnetisation and so these are usually the expected answers to examination questions.

28.5   Magnetic effect of an electric current

This effect was first demonstrated by the Danish physicist Oersted in 1820.

Investigation 28.5   To demonstrate the magnetic effect of an electric current

The apparatus used in this investigation is shown in Fig. 28.13. One side of a large rectangular-shaped coil, consisting of six to ten turns of thick insulated copper wire, passes through the centre of a horizontal Perspex sheet which is supported on four pillars. The terminals of the coil are situated in the centre of the side opposite the hole and are connected via a rheostat and ammeter to a d.c. supply. Thus the current in the wire may be adjusted.

Place the coil so that its plane is in the magnetic meridian, i.e. pointing S–N. Hold a compass needle over the horizontal top side of the coil, and check that it points to the north. Then switch on the current. The compass needle is deflected. As you increase the magnitude of the current the size of the deflection increases. When you place the needle below the wire the deflection is in the opposite direction. Next reverse the direction of the current. You will find that this reverses the directions of the deflections. Figure 28.13(b) summarises what happens.

Now arrange a sheet of paper on the Perspex table so that the vertical side of the coil passes through a hole in the centre of the paper. Use plotting compasses to determine the lines of force round the vertical wires. These lines form a series of concentric circles with the wire as their centre (Fig. 28.13c). The direction of the lines of force is indicated in the diagram by the arrows. Reversing the current reverses the direction of the lines of force. Here again the Earth's field has an effect, but if a large current is used the effect is not so obvious.

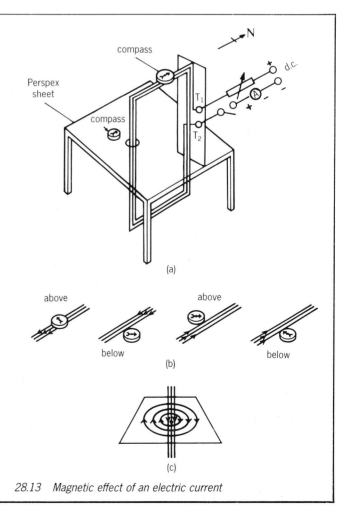

28.13   Magnetic effect of an electric current

More quantitative experiments will show that the field strength is proportional to the current, and inversely proportional to the distance from the wire.

Maxwell's Corkscrew Rule

This rule relates the direction of the magnetic field to the direction of the current and states: **imagine a right-handed person screwing a corkscrew along the wire in the direction of the current; then the motion of the thumb gives the direction of the lines of force.** The examples of investigation 28.5 agree with this rule.

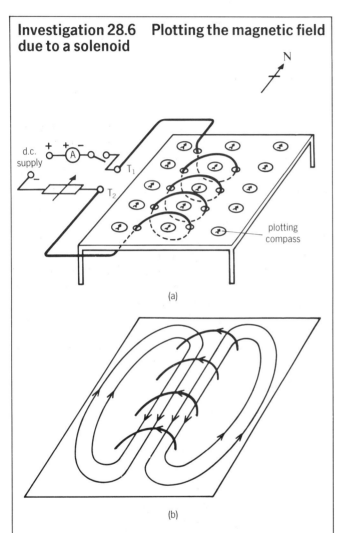

Investigation 28.6 Plotting the magnetic field due to a solenoid

(a)

(b)

28.14   Magnetic field due to a solenoid

Coil a length of insulated thick copper wire through a horizontal sheet of cardboard or Perspex as shown in Fig. 28.14(a). Connect the ends of the coil to a d.c. supply through a rheostat and ammeter. Switch on the supply and use plotting compasses to plot the magnetic field. Check that reversing the direction of the current reverses the direction of the field. The field is shown in Fig. 28.14(b). The lines of force inside the coil are parallel straight lines. Outside the coil the field is similar to that of a bar magnet. As you can see, the lines of force obey the corkscrew rule.

anticlockwise   clockwise

28.15   Polarity of a coil

An easy way to remember the polarity of the coil is shown in Fig. 28.15. To use it you must always look at the coil end on. If the current flows around the end in an anticlockwise direction, that end of the coil is a N-pole, and if it flows in a clockwise direction that end is a S-pole. A further aid comes from drawing letters N and S with the arrows on the ends of the letters denoting the current directions.

A flat circular coil may be regarded as a magnetic disc with the N-pole and S-pole very close together. Two flat circular coils together produce a uniform magnetic field, and this is a very important use. Two identical coils are placed parallel to each other with the current flowing in the same direction in each coil. They are separated by a distance equal to their radius (Fig. 28.16). In the space between the coils the magnetic field is uniform. These coils are known as **Helmholtz Coils**, and are used in the study of the motion of charged particles in a uniform magnetic field.

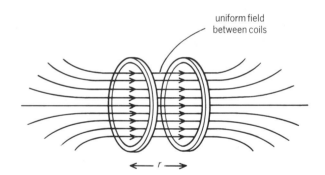

uniform field
between coils

28.16   To produce a uniform magnetic field

Further experiments may be performed with a long coil of wire or **solenoid**. You can make a simple solenoid by winding a length of insulated copper wire around a pencil. Pass a charge through the coil and then bring it near to a pivoted compass needle (Fig. 28.17). The N-pole is repelled by the end of the coil in which the charge flows in an anticlockwise direction and attracted by the end in which it flows in a clockwise direction. This verifies Maxwell's Corkscrew Rule.

A solenoid through which charge is flowing is known as an **electromagnet**. If you push a long soft iron rod inside the coil the magnetic effect is considerably enhanced. The field inside the coil may become as much as a thousand times greater.

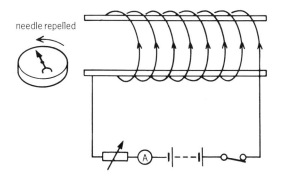

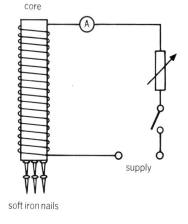

28.17   *Polarity of a solenoid*

28.18   *Electromagnet*

Investigation 28.7   Experiments with a solenoid

Place unmagnetised cylinders of iron, steel and other materials of the same size inside identical coils or solenoids which are each connected to a circuit containing a rheostat and ammeter and either a d.c. or a.c. supply. Use the coils to pick up magnetic materials such as nails or soft iron bars of equal mass. The number of bars picked up is a measure of the strength of the electromagnet. Devise experiments which demonstrate the following.

1   The strength of the electromagnet is proportional to the magnitude of the electric current.

2   The strength of the electromagnet increases with the number of turns of wire per unit length.

3   Under identical conditions an electromagnet with an iron core is a stronger magnet than an electromagnet with a steel core and will pick up a larger mass of magnetic material.

4   When the current is switched off quite a lot of material remains adhering to the electromagnet with the steel core but none remains on the electromagnet with the iron core. This indicates that steel retains its magnetism much better than iron.

5   A coil without a core only picks up a small amount of magnetic material. Inserting cores made of materials such as copper, brass, aluminium, wood etc. does not increase the mass of magnetic material picked up. This indicates that these substances do not increase the magnetic field, and are useless as cores for electromagnets.

Exercise 28.1

Why is iron suitable as the core for an electromagnet while steel is not?

Some alloys, e.g. stalloy, are more suitable than soft iron as an electromagnet's core. These are used in electromagnets, generators, motors, transformers etc.

A sixth point may be tested by connecting the circuit in Fig. 28.18 to an a.c. supply. This shows that an electromagnet works just as well with alternating current as it does with direct current. The polarity changes 50 times per second, but the material is attracted whatever the polarity.

Figure 28.19 shows a two-pole electromagnet. It is important to wire the electromagnet in such a way that a N-pole and a S-pole are produced. Two N-poles or two S-poles would not be very efficient. A two-pole electromagnet is more efficient than a single pole because when the magnetic material is attached, the lines of force follow a closed path as shown by the dotted lines.

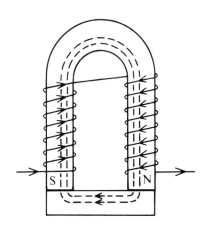

28.19   *Horseshoe electromagnet*

28.6 Uses of electromagnets

There are numerous uses of electromagnets apart from the obvious one of picking up large quantities of magnetic material and transferring it from one place to another. A few will be described briefly here.

Electric bell

Figure 28.20 shows an electric bell. The soft iron cores are wound so that they have opposite polarity. The soft iron armature is attached to the steel spring. When the key is depressed the charge flows; the soft iron cores become magnets and attract the armature, thus ringing the bell. As contact is broken the armature moves towards the magnet at C and the current is automatically switched off. The soft iron bars lose their magnetism and the armature is no longer attracted. The steel spring causes the armature to spring back and remake contact at C. This switches on the current and the cycle is repeated. Steel cores would be useless since they would not lose their magnetism when the circuit was broken and so the armature would remain attracted.

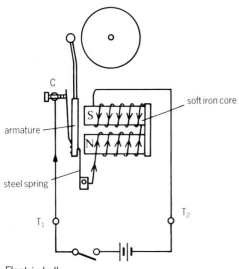

28.20   Electric bell

Ding-dong door bell chimes

Figure 28.21 shows the circuit of these two-tone chimes. When the switch is closed a current flows in the coil. A magnetic field is set up inside the coil which attracts the soft iron collar fixed to the bobbin. The bobbin moves to the right to strike the right-hand metal plate. This produces the 'ding' sound. Most of the kinetic energy of the bobbin is given to the coil spring as potential energy as it becomes compressed against the side of the magnetic coil. The bobbin stays to the right for as long as charge flows through the coil, but when the current is switched off the magnetic field collapses. There is now no force pulling the bobbin to the right so the potential energy stored in the spring

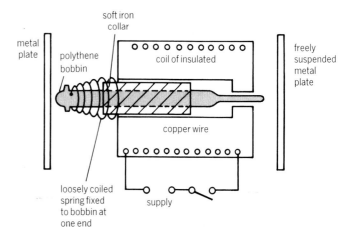

28.21   Door bell chimes

causes the bobbin to move quickly to the left. It then strikes the left-hand metal plate, producing the 'dong' sound. This gadget works because the iron collar becomes an induced magnet and is attracted into the coil.

Telephone earpiece

The horseshoe-type magnet inside the earpiece is formed by placing two soft iron rods on a permanent magnet. Coils are wound round the soft iron rods to make an electromagnet (Fig. 28.22). The permanent magnet ensures that the diaphragm, made of a magnetic alloy, is in a state of permanent tension. As the current through the coils varies the strength of the electromagnet varies and thus the force on the diaphragm varies. The current varies at the same rate as the voice, and thus the sound is reproduced.

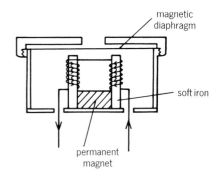

28.22   Telephone earpiece

Magnetic relay

This device uses one circuit to switch on another. When the key is depressed a current is set up in the solenoid which magnetises the soft iron core, and attracts the iron armature B (Fig. 28.23). The contacts at C close and the current in the secondary circuit is switched on. Relays are widely used in telephone exchanges. They may also be used to control circuits

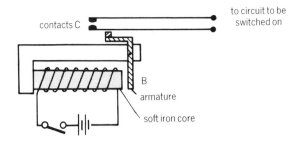

contacts C

to circuit to be switched on

B

armature

soft iron core

28.23 *Magnetic relay*

carrying higher currents. Only a small current is needed in the solenoid to energise the soft iron bar and so switch on another circuit in which a much higher current is carried, e.g. in a lift. This protects the operator from direct contact with the high current circuit.

28.7 Permanent magnets

Investigation 28.8 To make a permanent magnet

Place a steel bar inside a long solenoid which is connected to a d.c. supply (Fig. 28.24). Switch the current on and off. When you remove the bar it is a strong permanent magnet.

d.c. supply

28.24 *Making a permanent magnet*

The strong uniform magnetic field inside the solenoid aligns the domains in the direction of the magnetic field. Thus the N-pole of the magnet is at the N end of the solenoid. The long solenoid is used so that it is not necessary to use a very large current. However, the current should be large enough to ensure that all the domains are aligned. This means that the magnet will be as strong as it possibly can be. Direct current is used so that the polarity of the magnet is known. Alternating current can be used, but it has the disadvantage that the polarity of the magnet is not known and the strength of the magnet depends upon the position in the a.c. cycle when the current was switched off.

Demagnetisation

Sometimes it is necessary to demagnetise a steel rod completely. The best method is to use the solenoid in Fig. 28.24 connected this time to an alternating current (a.c.) supply. Hold the magnet in the solenoid and switch on the current. With the current *still switched on*, pull out the rod along the axis of the solenoid in an east–west direction until it is a good distance away. The magnet becomes demagnetised because the domains alter their alignment fifty times each second and, as the rod gets further away from the solenoid, the magnetic field becomes weaker and weaker until it is not strong enough to align the domains. Thus they set in a haphazard manner and the rod is demagnetised. The same effect is produced if the steel rod is left in the solenoid while the current is reduced to zero. An a.c. current is essential for both methods.

Types of magnet

Figure 28.25 shows different types of permanent magnets. Bar magnets (Fig. 28.25a) may be either rectangular bars or cylindrical rods. When not being

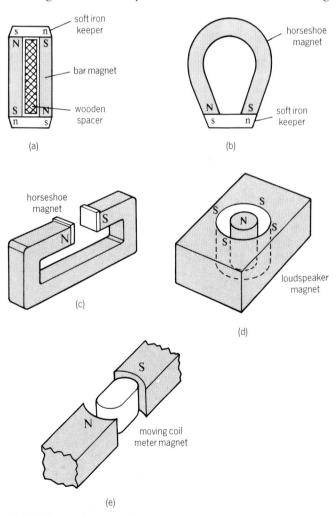

28.25 *Types of permanent magnet*

used they are best stored with soft iron keepers across their ends. This ensures that there is a continuous magnetic field linking the magnets and keepers and helps to keep the domains aligned. Two different types of horseshoe magnet are shown in Figs. 28.25(b) and (c). The loudspeaker magnet (Fig. 28.25d) has a central N-pole surrounded by a S-pole and produces a radial field. At the other end there is a S-pole surrounded by a N-pole. The moving-coil meter magnet (Fig. 28.25e) has a curved N-pole and S-pole with a soft iron cylinder between them. This also produces an approximately radial field.

Questions

Questions 1–4

In the diagram XY is a solenoid of insulated wire wound on a cardboard tube. PQ is a soft iron cylinder.

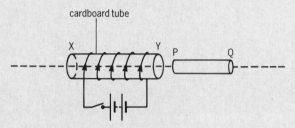

Q1 The current is switched on and is in the direction indicated by the arrows. Which of the following pairs of poles is correct?

   A X is north and P is north.
   B X is north and P is south.
   C Y is north and P is north.
   D Y is south and P is south.
   E X is south and Y is north. *(L)*

Q2 The magnetic field lines in the middle of the solenoid are

   A circles.
   B spirals.
   C of no simple shape.
   D parallel to the axis of the tube.
   E perpendicular to the axis of the tube. *(L)*

Q3 If the soft iron cylinder is free to move along the dotted line it will come to rest

   A beyond.
   B when P reaches Y.
   C further away from Y.
   D when P reaches X.
   E in the middle of XY. *(L)*

Q4 The initial force between the cylinder and the solenoid would be much greater if the cardboard tube were replaced by one made from

   A plastic   **B** aluminium
   C copper   **D** brass
   E steel *(L)*

Q5 The strength of the magnetic field between the poles of an electromagnet would be unchanged if the

   A current in the electromagnet windings were doubled.
   B direction of the current in the electromagnet windings were reversed.
   C distance between the poles of the electromagnet were doubled.
   D material of the core of the electromagnet were changed.
   E number of turns in the electromagnet windings were doubled. *(L)*

Q6 Each of the diagrams below shows two iron-cored solenoids carrying an electric current. In which of the diagrams is the effect of the force between the solenoids NOT correctly marked?

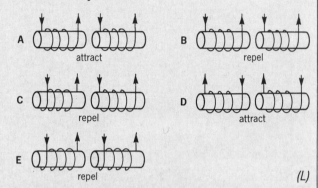

(L)

Q7 Describe how you would magnetise a small steel rod, using (i) a permanent magnet, (ii) a solenoid.

   Draw diagrams showing the magnetic field produced by (i) two bar magnets with North-poles facing each other, (ii) a straight wire carrying a direct current, and (iii) a solenoid carrying a direct current. *(W)*

Q8 Draw a large, clearly labelled, diagram of an electric bell and explain how it works, using a battery of dry cells as a source.

   A careless person wires the bell circuit with the switch in parallel with the source. Comment on what might happen. *(S)*

Q9 Given an unmagnetised steel bar, how would you test experimentally that it is unmagnetised? Describe how you would then use a solenoid, a d.c. supply, and other apparatus

   (i) to test that there is a limit to the strength of the magnet that can be made by magnetising the steel bar,
   (ii) to find a relation between the direction of the current in the turns of the solenoid and the polarity of the magnetised steel.

   A steel bar is inside a solenoid which carries a current sufficient to magnetise the steel fully. State the effect, on the magnetism of the bar, of switching off the current and then gradually increasing the current to its previous value but in the opposite direction.

   Describe briefly any **one** method of demagnetising a magnetised steel bar.

Q10 Draw diagrams to show the magnetic field due to a direct current flowing in (a) a solenoid, (b) a straight wire. Each diagram should show the magnetic field in only one plane. Show clearly the directions of the current and of the lines of force.

   Describe how you would use iron filings to show the

magnetic field in a horizontal plane close to a U-shaped magnet placed with the U-shaped section horizontal.

Explain how it is that the iron filings (initially unmagnetised) show the pattern of the magnetic field. Give reasons why, if the magnet is a very strong one, many of the filings cluster round the poles and some groups of the filings stand up nearly vertically. *(C)*

Q11 The diagram shows a conductor in which an electric current flows vertically down through a piece of horizontal card, and then back up. The two sections of the conductor are seen to repel each other.

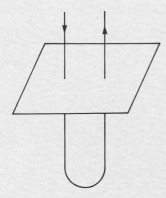

(a) With the help of a diagram, describe how you would plot a line of the magnetic field on the card.

(b) Sketch the magnetic field which could be plotted on the card around both sections of the conductor. Use your sketch (or an alternative argument) to explain why the two sections repel each other.

(c) The force of repulsion between the two sections is small. What changes could be made to increase it? *(O)*

Q12 *This question is about magnetic fields and an electromagnetic switch.*

(a) (i) Describe how you would show experimentally the shape and direction of the magnetic field lines in a horizontal plane around a vertical wire connected to a d.c. source.

(ii) Draw a diagram showing clearly the direction of the current and the direction of the magnetic field lines.

(iii) If a.c. were used in place of d.c., what effect would this have on your experiment? Give a reason.

(b) The diagram shows a small plotting compass placed between two strong magnets. The tip of the arrow represents the N pole of the compass.

(i) What is the polarity of the end C of the right hand magnet?

(ii) Draw a diagram of the magnets only as seen from above and sketch the magnetic field lines in the region between B and C.

(c) The diagram shows a model circuit breaker designed to switch off the current in a circuit when it becomes excessive. The current enters the circuit breaker at T_1,

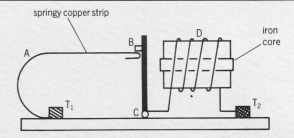

passes along the copper strip A, the iron armature BC, the coil D, and leaves at terminal T_2. The iron armature BC is pivoted at C.

(i) Describe how the circuit breaker works.

(ii) State the effect on the operation of the circuit breaker of each of the following changes. Give a reason in each case.

(1) The removal of the iron core from the coil.

(2) The use of a.c. instead of d.c. *(L)*

Q13 (a) Two strong bar magnets with poles at the ends of each bar are placed parallel and adjacent to one another so that they form the opposite sides of a square.

(i) How could you quickly demonstrate the shape of the force field that exists in the region between the magnets?

(ii) Draw a diagram of the shape of this force field, marking the North-seeking poles of both magnets. State whether the magnets experience forces of attraction or repulsion in this arrangement.

(iii) One of the bar magnets is now turned, end for end. Draw a diagram of the shape of the magnetic force field you would now expect to obtain and identify the North-seeking pole of each magnet. Do the magnets experience forces of attraction or repulsion in this field? *(L)*

Q14

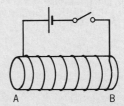

An unmagnetised steel rod is placed in a solenoid connected as above, and the current is switched on. After a short time the current is switched off and the rod is removed from the solenoid. Each end of the rod is then brought up to the North-seeking pole of a compass.

The entire procedure is then repeated using an initially unmagnetised soft iron rod.

(i) Describe and account for the changes which occur in each of the rods when they are placed in the solenoid and the current is switched on.

(ii) Describe and account for the behaviour of the North-seeking pole of the compass when the ends of each of the rods are then brought up in turn to it.

(iii) Which rod would be suitable to make the magnet of a small electric motor and which would be suitable to make the core of a relay? Give a reason for each choice. *(L)*

29 Electromagnetism

29.1 Force on a current-carrying conductor in a magnetic field

When a steel or wooden ruler is bent a tension is set up inside the steel or wood, so that when the ends of the ruler are released they spring back into their original positions. Magnetic lines of force are similar: when they are curved they act as though they are under tension and tend to straighten. The strength of a magnetic field is measured by the number of lines of force crossing perpendicular to a unit area. The stronger the magnetic field the larger the number of lines of force per unit area. In a uniform field the lines of force are parallel to each other, and the number per unit area is constant.

Imagine a wire running perpendicularly through the paper with the current directed into the paper. The magnetic field produced by the current alone is shown in Fig. 29.1(a). Although the lines of force are curved they are symmetrical around the wire. The number of lines of force per unit area around the wire depends upon the strength of the current. The stronger the current the greater the number of lines of force per unit area, or the greater the **magnetic flux density**. Figure 29.1(b) shows a uniform magnetic field. When the wire is placed in the centre of the uniform magnetic field there is a reaction between the two fields of magnetic force. On the right of the wire the two fields

are acting in the same direction and the resultant field strength is obtained by adding the two strengths together. On the left of the wire the fields act in opposite directions and the resultant field strength is the difference between the two strengths. Behind and in front of the wire the fields are not parallel. The combined magnetic field is shown in Fig. 29.1(c). There is a strong curved field to the right of the wire, and a weak field to the left. The lines of force act as if they are under tension and tend to straighten. Consequently there is a force on the wire directed from the strong field to the weak field, and if the wire is free to move it moves from right to left in the direction shown by the arrow.

The force on the wire depends upon the strengths of the two magnetic fields. Thus a force may be increased

(a) by increasing the current in the wire;
(b) by increasing the strength of the uniform field.

There is always a force on a current-carrying wire when it is placed *perpendicular* to any magnetic field. It is not necessary for the field to be uniform. However, a uniform field is easier to study.

If the current-carrying wire runs *parallel* to the magnetic field there is *no force* on the wire. The magnetic fields are perpendicular to each other and the resultant field is symmetrical with respect to the wire. Thus there is no resultant force on the wire.

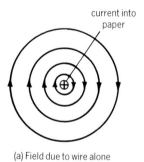

current into paper

(a) Field due to wire alone

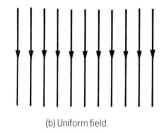

(b) Uniform field

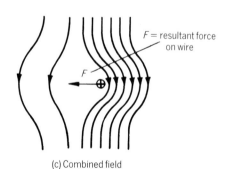

F = resultant force on wire

(c) Combined field

29.1 Force on a current-carrying conductor in a magnetic field

Investigation 29.1   To show force on a wire carrying a current in a magnetic field

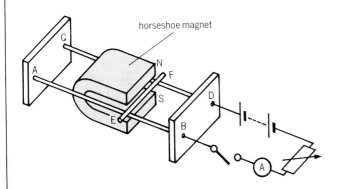

horseshoe magnet

29.2   Demonstration of the force on a current-carrying conductor

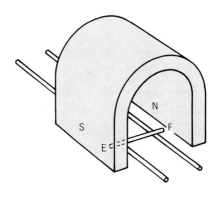

29.3   Force on a conductor parallel to a magnetic field

The apparatus used in this investigation is shown in Fig. 29.2. Two parallel horizontal copper rods AB and CD are supported by end boards and connected to terminals, which in turn are connected to the external circuit. EF is another copper rod which rests on AB and CD. Close the switch so that charge flows in the circuit. There is no movement of EF. Now switch off the current and place a strong horseshoe magnet between AB and CD so that EF is between the poles of the magnet. Close the switch again so that charge flows. EF rolls to the right. Note that the current direction is from F to E. If you reverse the terminals connecting B and C to the external circuit the current direction is from E to F and EF rolls to the left.

Note   EF is *not* attracted to the poles of the magnet but moves in such a way as to 'cut' the magnetic flux lines, i.e. it moves at right angles to the magnetic field. If you adjust the rheostat so that the current is increased, the rod moves more quickly because it experiences a larger force.

Replace the magnet with a larger magnet placed over AB and CD as shown in Fig. 29.3. Switch on the current. EF does not move, whatever the direction of the current, because the rod and hence the current are parallel to the magnetic field. Thus there is no force on the rod. If the rod moves it does not 'cut' any lines of force.

It is not essential that the rod is perpendicular to the magnetic field. Movement occurs if there is some component of the magnetic field perpendicular to the current. This may be shown by re-adjusting the position of the magnet in investigation 29.1, so that the copper rod is at an angle to the magnetic field. However, the movement will be a maximum (i.e. the force on the rod is greatest) when the current and the magnetic field are at right angles to each other.

Fleming's Left-hand Rule

The rule for deciding the direction of motion of the rod is **Fleming's Left-hand Rule** shown in Fig. 29.4. (Do not confuse this with the right-hand rule which determines the direction of the induced electromotive force. The left-hand rule is sometimes called the motor rule and an easy way to remember this is that in the United Kingdom motorists drive on the left-hand side of the road.) The rule states **'if the thumb, first and second fingers of the left hand are held at right angles to each other, then if the first finger represents the direction of the magnetic field and the second finger the direction of the current, the thumb represents the direction of the motion'.**

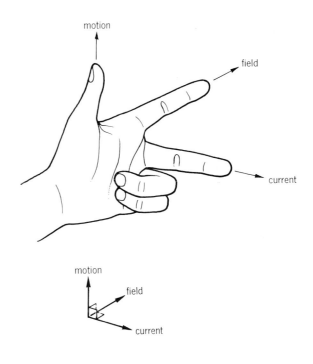

29.4   Fleming's Left-hand Rule

Moving coils

Apply Fleming's Left-hand Rule to the coil ABCD suspended between the poles of a strong horseshoe magnet (Fig. 29.5a). When the fields are combined there is a force in one direction on one side of the coil and an equal force in the opposite direction on the other side (Fig. 29.5b). Thus a **couple** (an electromagnetic couple) is exerted on the coil, and it rotates. Using Fleming's Left-hand Rule, you can work out that AD moves into the paper and BC moves out of the paper. The coil rotates until it is perpendicular to the magnetic field. Then the forces *f* on AD and BC, although still in opposite directions, are acting along the same straight line (Fig. 29.5c). Thus there is no couple and no turning effect, and the coil does not rotate. The couple on the coil varies from its maximum when the plane of the coil is parallel to the magnetic field to zero when the plane of the coil is perpendicular to the magnetic field.

Now consider the top and bottom of the coil, AB and CD. Initially they are parallel to the field and so there is no force on them. As the coil turns they become perpendicular to the field, but the forces acting on them are vertical and so do not affect the rotation of the coil.

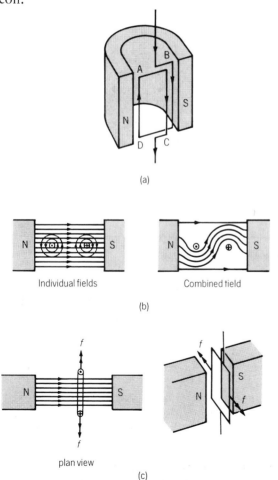

(a)

(b)

Individual fields   Combined field

(c)

plan view

29.5   Force on a coil in a magnetic field

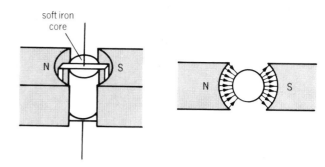

29.6   Coil in a radial magnetic field

In the simple arrangement shown in Fig. 29.5 the coil rotates but the value of the electromagnetic couple decreases as the plane of the coil becomes more nearly perpendicular to the field. The couple would be approximately constant if the plane of the coil were always parallel to the magnetic field. This is achieved by making the pole pieces of the magnets curved to give a radial field (Fig. 29.6). A soft iron core between the curved pole pieces increases the magnetic field strength. The stronger the magnetic field the larger the couple for a given current in the coil.

Perhaps a more simple way of understanding the rotation of a coil in a magnetic field is to remember that as soon as the current is switched on the coil becomes a magnet. If it is free to move it rotates until the S-pole of the coil is opposite to the N-pole of the magnet and vice versa. In Fig. 29.5(a) the current in the coil is clockwise so that the front face of the coil is a S-pole and the back face a N-pole. Thus the coil rotates in a clockwise direction.

29.2   Forces between currents

Investigation 29.2 shows that currents in the same direction attract, and currents in opposite directions repel.

The ampere

The force exerted between the currents is used as the basis for the definition of the **ampere**. The ampere is defined as **that current which produces a force of 2×10^{-7} newton per metre in a vacuum between two parallel infinitely long conductors of negligible cross-sectional area 1 metre apart when each conductor carries the same current.**

Current balance

Figure 29.8 shows a current balance. A and B are two fixed coils, and C is a movable coil. Coil C is attached to a long arm which is pivoted at P. The weight M helps to counterbalance C. When no current flows the arm carrying C is horizontal and both the pointer and rider X are at zero positions on the scales. When the

Investigation 29.2   To demonstrate the force between two parallel conductors carrying currents

Connect two strips of metallic foil to an external circuit so that the same current passes in the same direction in each strip. Stand the strips parallel to each other as in Fig. 29.7(a). Switch on the current. The two strips move towards each other (Fig. 29.7b). This occurs because the magnetic fields between the strips are in opposite directions. Consequently the combined field between the strips is less than that outside, and the strips are pushed together. Reconnect one strip so that current flows along it in the opposite direction. Now the fields between the strips are in the same direction (Fig. 29.7c). The combined field between the strips is now greater than that outside and it forces the strips apart. If you increase the strength of the current the forces of attraction and repulsion increase.

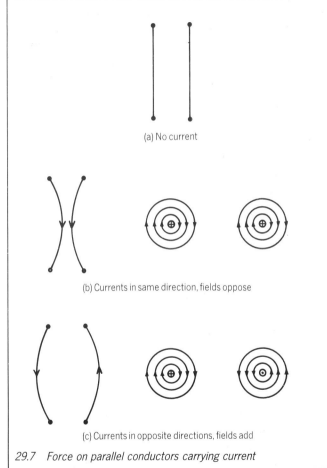

(a) No current

(b) Currents in same direction, fields oppose

(c) Currents in opposite directions, fields add

29.7   Force on parallel conductors carrying current

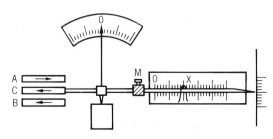

29.8   Current balance

current is switched on it passes in the same direction in B and C and in the opposite direction in A. Thus C is repelled by A and attracted by B and as a result moves downwards. The rider X is moved until the pointer again reads zero. The force on the coil C can then be calculated.

29.3   Moving-coil measuring instruments

When a current passes through the coil in Fig. 29.5 the coil always sets at right angles to the magnetic field no matter what the strength of the current. This is because the only couple acting on the coil is the electromagnetic couple, and there is no opposing couple. The strength of the current affects only the speed with which the coil moves. However, by including springs which provide a mechanical couple to oppose the electromagnetic couple, the arrangement can easily be made into an instrument which measures current.

Moving-coil galvanometer

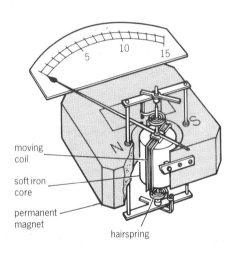

moving coil

soft iron core

permanent magnet

hairspring

29.9   Moving-coil galvanometer

A moving-coil galvanometer is shown in Fig. 29.9. It consists of a coil of many turns of enamelled copper wire wound onto an aluminium former. This moves round a soft iron core placed between the curved pole pieces of a strong magnet. Thus the coil moves in a radial magnetic field. The coil is mounted on jewelled bearings, and its motion is controlled by two hairsprings. When the coil carries a current an electromagnetic couple is set up which causes the coil to rotate. The value of the electromagnetic couple depends upon:

   (a) the strength of the current,
   (b) the number of turns in the coil,
   (c) the cross-sectional area of the coil,

(d) the strength of the magnetic field.

It does *not* depend upon the angle through which the coil has turned. In effect the only variable in a particular instrument which affects the couple is the strength of the current.

The coil is brought to rest when the mechanical couple exerted by the hairsprings is equal and opposite to the electromagnetic couple. This mechanical couple is proportional to the angle through which the coil has turned. It follows that the angle at which the coil comes to rest is proportional to the current. Thus the divisions on the scale are equally spaced. When the current is switched off the electromagnetic couple becomes zero, and the mechanical couple returns the coil to its equilibrium position. If a centre-reading galvanometer is required, the zero is placed in the centre of the scale, and the pointer is set to this position. Current can then pass in either direction through the instrument.

Note This does not mean that the galvanometer can be used to measure alternating current. The frequency of the alternating current is much greater than the frequency at which the coil can oscillate, and the galvanometer just records the average value of the alternating current, which is zero.

If the instrument is to read in one direction only the zero is put at the end of the scale and the pointer is adjusted to that mark when the coil is in its rest position.

(**Note** The rest position of the coil is the same whether the instrument is centre-reading or direct.) It is essential that the positive terminal on a direct-reading instrument is connected to the positive terminal of the battery. Otherwise the instrument may be damaged as the coil tries to rotate in the opposite direction.

On p.304 a mirror galvanometer was used to measure very small currents. This instrument is a moving-coil galvanometer, but with a different type of suspension. Instead of being pivoted the coil is suspended by a phosphor-bronze strip to which a mirror is attached (Fig. 29.10a). Below the coil is a loosely coiled spring. This, together with the phosphor-bronze strip, provides the restoring couple. There is no physical pointer. A beam of light falls onto the mirror and is reflected to give a spot of light (with a central mark) on a scale (Fig. 29.10b). In the rest position the spot is on the zero mark. When the coil turns, the mirror turns through the same angle, but the reflected beam turns through twice the angle. Thus, depending upon the distance of the lamp and scale from the mirror, a small deflection of the mirror can give quite a large deflection of the spot of light. At one time the lamp and scale were separate from the galvanometer, but it is now common practice to build them into the instrument.

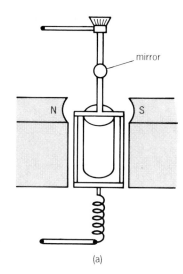

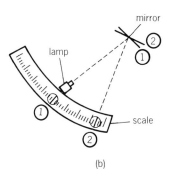

29.10   *Mirror galvanometer*

Ammeters and voltmeters

An ammeter measures current and must be put into the circuit in series so that the current to be measured has to pass through it. Including it into the circuit should not alter the current which it is supposed to measure.

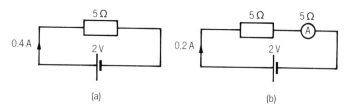

29.11   *Place of an ammeter in a circuit*

The circuit in Fig. 29.11(a) has no ammeter in it. Using Ohm's Law it is seen that the current in the circuit is given by

$$I = \frac{V}{R}$$
$$= \frac{2 \text{ V}}{5 \text{ }\Omega}$$
$$= 0.4 \text{ A}$$

Suppose an ammeter having a resistance of 5 Ω is put into this circuit to measure the current (Fig. 29.11b). The total resistance R_1 is now 5 Ω + 5 Ω = 10 Ω and the new current is

$$I_1 = \frac{V}{R_1}$$
$$= \frac{2\ \mathrm{V}}{10\ \Omega}$$
$$= 0.2\ \mathrm{A}$$

Thus introducing this ammeter would half the current in the circuit. Obviously this is an extreme example, but if the ammeter resistance were only 0.5 Ω the reduction in the current would still be too large to be tolerable. If the current is to remain unaffected by the inclusion of the ammeter then the ammeter's resistance must be very small – ideally zero.

A voltmeter is used to measure the potential difference between two points in a circuit, so obviously it should be placed in parallel with whatever is between the points. Including the voltmeter in the circuit must not alter the potential difference it is supposed to measure.

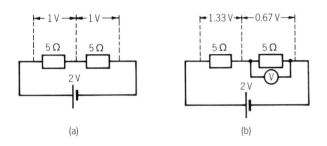

(a) (b)

29.12   Place of a voltmeter in a circuit

The potential drop across each of the 5 Ω resistors in Fig. 29.12(a) is given by

$$V = 5\ \Omega \times 0.2\ \mathrm{A}$$
$$= 1.0\ \mathrm{V}$$

If a voltmeter with a resistance of 5 Ω is connected in parallel with the second resistor, then the combined resistance of this part of the circuit is now 2.5 Ω. Thus the total resistance of the circuit is 5 Ω + 2.5 Ω = 7.5 Ω, and the potential difference between the ends of this resistor falls to 0.67 V. Again this is an extreme case, but the error, which occurs because the resistance of the voltmeter is of the same order as the resistors in the circuit, is not tolerable. The inclusion of the voltmeter will not alter the total resistance of the circuit if the voltmeter has a very high resistance — ideally an infinite resistance.
(**Note**   If a very large resistor is connected in parallel with a small resistor, the total resistance of the combination for all practical purposes is that of the small resistor.)

The rules for ammeters and voltmeters are:
1 An ammeter should have a very small resistance and be connected in series.
2 A voltmeter should have a very large resistance and be connected in parallel.

Conversion of meters

There is little difference between a moving-coil ammeter, and a moving-coil voltmeter. The movement is the same for both; they differ only in the way they are connected and the type of resistor used with them.

A milliammeter with a resistance of 40 Ω which gives a full scale reading of 5 mA can be used as an ammeter if it is modified by putting a suitable small resistor in parallel across its terminals. This resistor is known as a **shunt** because it diverts most of the current away from the delicate coil of the meter.

Example

What value shunt is needed to convert a milliammeter whose resistance is 40 Ω and reads 0–5 mA into an ammeter reading 0–5 A?

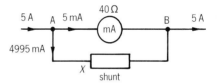

29.13   Changing a milliammeter into an ammeter

First draw a diagram like that in Fig. 29.13. A and B are the terminals of the milliammeter and only 5 mA (0.005 A) can pass through without damaging the instrument. Thus 5000 − 5 = 4995 mA must pass through the shunt of resistance X. The potential difference is the same, whichever path the current takes between A and B. Hence using Ohm's Law:

$$5\ \mathrm{mA} \times 40\ \Omega = 4995\ \mathrm{mA} \times X$$

$$X = \frac{5 \times 40}{4995}\ \frac{\mathrm{mA}\,\Omega}{\mathrm{mA}}$$

$$= 0.004\,004\ \Omega$$

This is a very small resistance. The resistance of the converted ammeter (combined resistance of the shunt and milliammeter in parallel) will be 0.004 Ω which will not affect a circuit in which the current may be as much as 5 A. By using other shunts the milliammeter may be used for different ranges of current.

Exercise 29.1

Find the values of the shunts necessary to convert the milliammeter into an ammeter reading (a) 0–15 A and (b) 0–30 A.

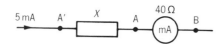

29.14 *Changing a milliammeter into a voltmeter*

The milliammeter can also be converted into a voltmeter. This time a high resistance must be connected in *series*, and the end of the resistor remote from the instrument will become the new terminal A′ (Fig. 29.14).

Example

Find the value X of the resistor which must be connected in series to convert a milliammeter reading 0–5 mA into a voltmeter reading 0–5 V.

The potential difference between A′ and B must be 5 V. The current cannot exceed 5 mA. The total resistance between A′ and B = $(X + 40)$ Ω. Hence, using Ohm's Law,

$$5 \text{ mA} (X + 40) \, \Omega = 5 \text{ V} = 5000 \text{ mV}$$

$$X + 40 = \frac{5000}{5} \frac{\text{mV}}{\text{mA}}$$

$$= 1000 \, \Omega$$

$$X = 1000 - 40$$

$$= 960 \, \Omega$$

Although this is a fairly large resistor the instrument will not be a good voltmeter. It is desirable for the resistance of a voltmeter to be 1000 Ω per volt, or preferably 10 000 Ω per volt.

Exercise 29.2

Calculate the resistors necessary to convert the milliammeter in the example into an instrument reading (a) 0–15 V and (b) 0–30 V.

Alternating-current instruments

The moving-coil ammeter does not measure a.c. but may be adapted to do so by connecting a **rectifier** in series. This ensures that the charge only flows one way through the instrument. The **moving-iron ammeter** is an instrument which measures a.c. directly. A simplified version is shown in Fig. 29.15. A is a fixed iron bar and B an iron bar which can move. B is attached to a pointer and its movement is controlled by a hairspring. Both bars are inside a coil (short solenoid). When a current passes through the coil both bars become magnetised with their N-poles at the same ends. Thus they are repelled along their length. B moves away from A and the pointer moves over the scale. The strength of each magnet depends upon the strength of the current and thus the force of repulsion between them is proportional to the (current)². This makes the scale uneven. The divisions start very close

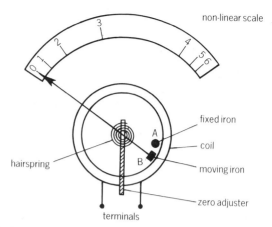

29.15 *Moving-iron ammeter*

together and then get wider apart. They are close together again at the other end of the scale. As similar poles are always at the same ends of bars A and B, the direction of the current does not matter. Moreover, it makes no difference if the current continually changes direction. This instrument is not suitable for measuring small (or very small) currents, but it is very useful for large currents.

29.4 Moving-coil loudspeaker

The moving-coil loudspeaker works due to the force exerted upon a current-carrying conductor in a magnetic field. The magnet is a ring magnet as shown in Fig. 29.16 and the coil is wound round a former attached to a paper cone. The coil slips over the centre pole of the magnet. When a current is in the coil in the magnetic field it experiences a force. The strength of the force depends upon the strength of the current and thus it fluctuates as the current varies. When there is no current the paper cone springs back to its original position. The vibration of the cone as the current in the coil varies causes a sound of the same frequency to be transmitted through the air.

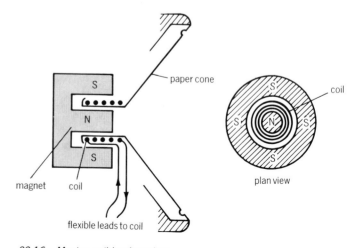

29.16 *Moving-coil loudspeaker*

29.5 Motors

Direct-current motor

The coil in the moving-coil galvanometer rotates until the plane of the coil is perpendicular to the magnetic field, i.e. until the S-pole of the coil is opposite the N-pole of the magnet. If some means can be found to change the direction of the current at this point, the polarity of the coil will change and it will continue to rotate. Its momentum will carry it slightly beyond the rest position and the pole, which is now a N-pole, will be repelled by the N-pole of the magnet. Thus for continuous motion it is necessary to change the direction of the current in the coil after every half revolution, i.e. when the plane of the coil is perpendicular to the magnetic field. This is achieved by connecting the ends of the coil to a **split-ring commutator** (Fig. 29.17). This consists of two half cylinders of copper attached to a cylinder of insulator so that there is a gap between the copper at both top and bottom. Each end of the coil is connected to one half of the copper cylinder, arranged so that the split in the commutator is perpendicular to the plane of the coil. Thus when the coil is vertical the split in the commutator is horizontal. The current is led in and out of the coil by carbon blocks or strips or metal. These are known as **brushes**.

Fig. 29.17 shows a simple motor. When the switch is closed the coil rotates in an anticlockwise direction. When the coil is vertical its momentum carries it forward. The split in the commutator is now slightly past the horizontal and the direction of the current is reversed. Thus the coil continues to rotate.

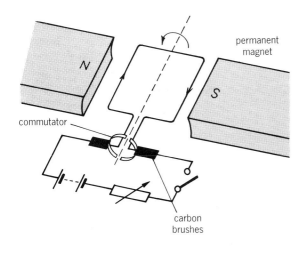

29.17 D.c. electric motor

Back e.m.f.

As soon as the coil of the motor starts to rotate it behaves like a **dynamo**, and an induced e.m.f. is set up which opposes the applied e.m.f. This is known as the **back e.m.f.** The resistance of the armature coil of a motor is very small and if a large e.m.f. were to be applied directly to it, the large current produced may cause the armature coil to burn out. A **starter resistance** is used in series with the motor so that the original current is reasonably small. As the motor speeds up and the back e.m.f. begins to take effect the value of the starter resistance is reduced. When the motor is running freely the difference between the applied e.m.f. and the back e.m.f. is equal to the current in the armature coil × the resistance, i.e.

$$E \text{ applied} - E \text{ back} = IR$$

When a motor slows down the back e.m.f. decreases. This causes the current to increase, and so the torque on the armature coil increases and the motor speeds up. Thus the back e.m.f. acts as a regulator and the motor runs at constant speed.

Working motors

A working motor is more complicated than the simple model described above, for the following reasons:

1. Instead of a single coil there is a large number of coils, and a large number of sectors on the commutators. This ensures smoother running.
2. The coils are wound round the core which is made up of thin laminations of a strong magnetic alloy. The laminations are insulated from each other. The whole of the rotating system is called the **armature** and the moving coil is known as the **armature coil**.
3. Instead of a permanent magnet, an electromagnet provides the magnetic field. The coil used to excite the electromagnet is known as the **field coil**.

The purpose of an electric motor is to convert electrical energy into mechanical energy. There are different types of motor, depending upon how the coils in the motor are wound.

Series-wound motors Here the field coil is in series with the armature coil and so the current is the same in both coils. Since the torque on the armature depends upon the (current)^2 (I^2), there is a large initial torque. These motors are very useful as starter motors in trains, cars, etc.

Shunt-wound motors As the name implies, the field coil and the armature coil are in parallel. The current in the field coil stays constant, and the current in the armature coil varies depending upon the speed of the motor. Due to the back e.m.f. the motor is more or less self-regulating and will run at constant speed. These motors are used to drive machines such as lathes in factories, and are used in vacuum cleaners, refrigerators etc., in the home.

Compound-wound motors These motors are a combination of the other two types and attempt to retain the advantages of both.

Example

A motor rated at 750 W drives a pump which pumps 300 litre water per minute from a well to a channel 4 m above the surface of the well. Calculate the efficiency of the motor and account for some of the lost energy.

Input = $750 \, \text{J s}^{-1}$; density of water is $1000 \, \text{kg m}^{-3}$ so the mass of 300 litre is 300 kg.

Work done in raising the water

$$= mgh$$
$$= 300 \, \text{kg} \times 10 \, \text{m s}^{-2} \times 4 \, \text{m}$$
$$= 12\,000 \, \text{kg m}^2 \, \text{s}^{-2}$$
$$= 12\,000 \, \text{J}$$

This work is done in 1 minute = 60 s, so output = $12\,000 \, \text{J}/60 \, \text{s} = 200 \, \text{J s}^{-1}$.

$$\text{Efficiency} = \frac{\text{work output}}{\text{work input}} = \frac{200 \, \text{J s}^{-1}}{750 \, \text{J s}^{-1}}$$
$$= \frac{4}{15}$$
$$= 0.266$$

$$\text{Percentage efficiency} = 26\tfrac{2}{3}\%$$

Some causes of loss of energy are:

1 kinetic energy of the moving parts;
2 kinetic energy of the water (it has kinetic energy, as well as potential energy when it reaches the top);
3 heat produced in the windings and bearings;
4 sound produced.

Power of a motor

The power output of a small motor can be measured by allowing it to raise a mass through a given height. The motor drives a shaft around which a string, attached to the mass, is wound. The mass is adjusted until the motor raises it at more or less constant speed. Then the time (t) for the mass to rise through a measured height (h) is taken.

$$\text{Power output} = \frac{m\,g\,h}{t} \text{ W}$$

where m is in kg, h is m and t is s.

29.6 Force on a charged particle

So far only the force on a wire carrying moving charge has been considered. However any charged particle which is moving creates its own magnetic field and is affected when it moves through another magnetic field. There is a force on it just as there is on the charge in a wire, and Fleming's Left-hand Rule again applies. However, you must remember that this rule refers to conventional current direction and a beam of electrons moves in the opposite direction to the conventional current. Figure 29.18 shows a beam of electrons passing into a magnetic field which is directed into the paper. You can see the direction in which the beam is deflected. When inside the magnetic field the force on the charged particle is always perpendicular to the direction of motion. Thus its path in the magnetic field is an arc of a circle.

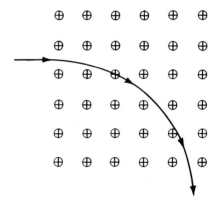

29.18 Path of a charged particle in a magnetic field

It was shown on p.326 that two parallel coils of wire carrying a current (Helmholtz coils) could be used to produce a uniform magnetic field. Figure 29.20 shows the effect of passing a beam of electrons through a uniform magnetic field. Electrons liberated from the filament are focussed and accelerated by the cylindrical anode, and emerge as a narrow beam. When they enter the uniform magnetic field the force on the electrons is constant (if they have the same speed) and perpendicular to the direction of motion, so they move in a circular path. There is a small quantity of hydrogen in the tube, and the path shows up as a coloured circle. Measurements may be taken from which the ratio of the charge on the electron to its mass may be determined.

The fact that high-speed charged particles move in a circular path when in a uniform magnetic field has useful applications. Positively charged particles need to be accelerated to very high speeds before they can penetrate atomic nuclei, because of the very strong repulsive forces between the charged particle and the nucleus. One way of achieving this is to place the source of the particles inside an evacuated box. This flat circular box is in two halves, diameters AB and

Investigation 29.3 To determine the path of a charged particle in an electric and magnetic field

Any of the cathode beam tubes readily available, e.g. a Thomson Tube (Fig. 29.19) can be used. Electrons are released from the filament in the tube. The cylindrical anode is at a high positive potential with respect to the filament and attracts and focusses the electrons into a flat beam. Their path is shown on the fluorescent screen. If a high d.c. voltage is put across the deflection plates, the beam is bent towards the positive plate, showing that the charge is negative.

You can create a strong magnetic field at the point where the beam leaves the anode by putting the N-pole of one magnet on one side of the tube and the S-pole of a second magnet on the other. The beam of electrons is deflected in a direction that is found to agree with Fleming's Left-hand Rule. Like wires carrying currents, charged particles are not deflected when they move parallel to a magnetic field.

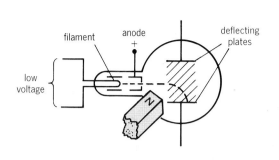

29.19 Cathode-beam tube

CD, which are slightly separated. AB and CD have a strong alternating electric field between them, and this is synchronised so that when the particles pass from AB to CD or from CD to AB they are accelerated. The strong magnetic field makes them move in a circular path and as their speed increases the radius of their path increases. Eventually, when the speed is fast enough, the particles emerge at the circumference and proceed to the target (Fig. 29.20).

One way in which nuclear energy may be obtained in the future is by making protons fuse together to form other nuclei. This happens in the Sun and is known as nuclear fusion. The very high temperatures required would vapourise any container. The charged particles are kept away from the walls of the container by using very strong magnetic fields which keep them in circular paths.

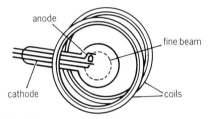

29.20 Accelerating a charged particle

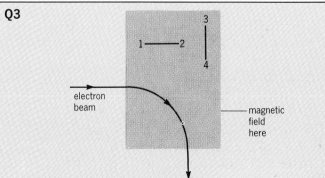

29.21 Helmholtz tube

Questions

Q1 Which one of the following modifications would increase the sensitivity of a moving-coil milliammeter?
 A Using a smaller coil.
 B Using fewer turns of wire on the coil.
 C Using a less heavy coil.
 D Using a weaker magnet.
 E Using weaker hair-springs. *(C)*

Q2 (a) Draw diagrams to show the shape and direction of the magnetic field produced by a steady current flowing in
 (i) a straight wire,
 (ii) a solenoid.
 In each case show the direction of the current.
 (b) Describe a simple experiment to demonstrate that a force acts on a current carrying wire when it is placed at right angles to a magnetic field.
 (c) With the aid of a diagram explain the operation of a loudspeaker when it is playing a single musical note. *(C)*

Q3

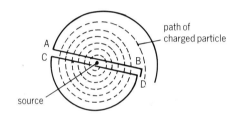

The diagram shows the path of a beam of electrons. The shading represents the area where a magnetic field is acting.
 The magnetic field must be acting
 A in direction 1 to 2 B in direction 2 to 1
 C in direction 4 to 3 D in direction 3 to 4
 E into the plane of the paper *(L)*

341

Q4 (a) Draw a labelled diagram to show the structure of a simple moving coil ammeter or galvanometer which could be used to measure direct current. Indicate on your diagram the relation between the direction of the current in the coil and the direction of its rotation.

(b) An ammeter has a resistance of $10\,\Omega$ and gives a maximum scale reading for a current of 30 mA. How could it be converted into an ammeter reading up to 3.0 A?

(L)

Q5 Describe an experiment which may be performed to demonstrate the interaction between a conductor carrying a direct current and a magnetic field produced by a bar, or horseshoe, magnet.

State and explain the law used to predict the relationship between the directions of the force experienced, the magnetic field and the (conventional) current flow.

Explain the construction and working of a simple d.c. motor.

(W)

Q6 In a moving coil galvanometer, the current to be measured passes through a rectangular coil of insulated wire, pivoted so that it can rotate in the *radial magnetic field* between the poles of a permanent magnet. Spiral hairsprings at each end of the axis of the coil exert a 'spring balance' effect.

(a) Draw a diagram showing the radial magnetic field, as it is obtained between the curved pole pieces of a permanent magnet with the help of a soft iron core.

(b) Explain why the coil rotates about its axis when a current passes through it, and why it settles in a definite position for a given value of the current.

(c) Why does this steady deflection of the coil depend on the number of turns on the coil as well as the strength of the current?

(d) What would you expect to observe if the galvanometer were connected in series in a circuit which carried a very low frequency (say 0.2 Hz) alternating current?

(e) What would you expect to observe if the 0.2 Hz circuit included a rectifier, as in the diagram?

(f) What would you expect to observe in (*d*) and (*e*) if the source was the usual 50 Hz low-voltage laboratory supply? Explain.

(O)

Q7 Draw a circuit diagram showing how a 10 V d.c. electric motor may be operated at the correct p.d. using a 12 V battery. Include in you circuit meters to measure the current passing through the motor and to check the p.d. across it.

In an experiment to measure the efficiency of the above motor the current was 3 A and a mass of 6 kg was lifted vertically through 2 m in 5 s. How much energy was supplied to the motor in this time? How much potential energy did the mass gain? Calculate the efficiency of the motor.

Draw a labelled sketch of part of the motor to show how current from the circuit is passed through the rotating coil.

(S)

Q8 (a) Describe a simple experiment to show that a force acts on a current-bearing wire when suitably placed in a magnetic field. Show clearly the directions of current, force and magnetic field.

(b) Draw a labelled diagram to show how a radial magnetic field may be produced and explain its importance either in a moving coil galvanometer or some other instrument or apparatus.

(c) A moving coil galvanometer gives a full scale deflection of 5 mA and it has resistance $10\,\Omega$. Show how a resistor should be connected to convert the meter into a voltmeter reading to 50 V. Calculate the value of this resistor and say why a good voltmeter should have a high resistance.

(S)

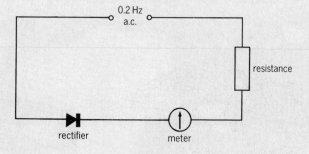

30 Electromagnetic induction

30.1 Inducing an e.m.f. using a magnet

In Chapters 28 and 29 the creation of a magnetic field by a moving charge and the effect on a charge of moving it in a magnetic field were considered. This chapter looks at the effect of a changing magnetic field on a stationary charge.

Investigation 30.1 leads to two broad conclusions:

1 When lines of force are cut by a wire, or when the magnetic field inside a coil changes, charge flows.
2 The rate of flow of charge depends upon the speed with which the changes occur.

There is no source of electromotive force, e.g. a cell, in the circuit, but electromotive force is necessary for charge to flow. Therefore a change in the magnetic field around a wire causes an electromotive force to be induced in the wire.

30.2 The direction and magnitude of an induced e.m.f.

A preliminary experiment can be undertaken to relate the polarity of the coil to the direction of the deflection.

Investigation 30.1 To induce an e.m.f. in a wire

Connect the copper wire AB to a sensitive centre-reading galvanometer (the mirror-type is ideal) and place it between the poles of a powerful horseshoe magnet (Fig. 30.1). Confirm the following observations:

1 When AB is at rest there is no movement of the spot on the galvanometer.
2 When AB is moved horizontally into the magnet the spot deflects from the centre position, but when AB stops moving the spot returns to the rest position.
3 When AB moves out of the magnet the spot on the galvanometer moves in the opposite direction.
4 The same results can be achieved by keeping the wire stationary and moving the magnet forwards and backwards.

5 The distance moved by the galvanometer spot (or needle) depends upon the speed of motion. A larger deflection is produced by a quick movement than by a slow one. A very slow movement scarcely produces a deflection.
6 Moving the wire up or down towards the N-pole or S-pole of the magnet does not cause a deflection.

You will obtain larger deflections if you use a small coil instead of a straight wire. Try the same experiments that you performed with the straight wire and then try rotating the coil. Rotating it quickly through 90° produces quite a large deflection; rotating through 180° produces a much larger deflection.

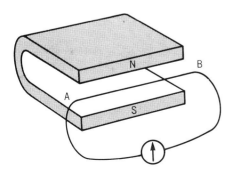

30.1   Induced e.m.f. in a wire

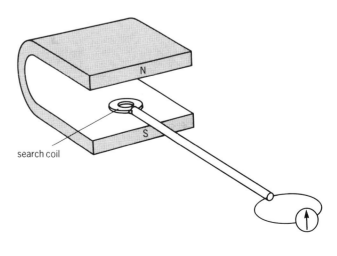

search coil

30.2   Induced e.m.f. in a search coil

Investigation 30.2   To induce an e.m.f. in a coil

Connect the ends of a large coil to a centre-reading galvanometer. Move a bar magnet in and out of the coil (Fig. 30.3). Ascertain the following results:

1 When the N-pole is moved into the coil there is a deflection in one direction; when it is removed there is a deflection in the opposite direction.
2 When the experiment is repeated using a S-pole instead of a N-pole the deflections are in the opposite directions.
3 The magnitude of the deflections increases as the speed of the moving magnet increases.
4 There is no deflection when the magnet is stationary inside the coil.
   Note This is very important in that it shows that a magnetic field inside a coil is not alone sufficient to induce an electromotive force. **The magnetic field must be changing.**

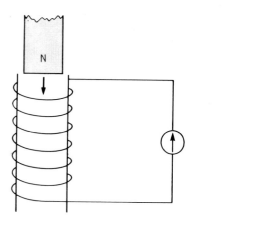

30.3   Induced e.m.f. in a coil

Investigation 30.3   To discover the direction of the induced e.m.f.

Connect a coil to a battery, rheostat, switch, and the centre-reading galvanometer (Fig. 30.4). Check that the deflection is to the right with the current direction as shown in Fig. 30.4, i.e. the top of the coil is a S-pole. (If it is not obvious which way the coil is wound the polarity may be checked using a compass needle.) Remove the rheostat, switch and cell from the circuit and put the N-pole into the coil. The deflection on the galvanometer is to the *left*. Thus the top of the coil is a N-pole, and tends to repel the magnet. When you pull the N-pole out of the coil the deflection is to the *right*, making the top of the coil a S-pole, and thus attracting the receding N-pole.

From these observations you can deduce the direction of the e.m.f. induced in the coil.

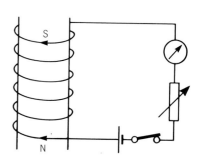

30.4   Direction of induced e.m.f.

Lenz's Law

Lenz's Law describes these observations. It states 'the **direction of the induced electromotive force acts in such a way as to oppose the action which produces it**'.

Fleming's Right-hand Rule

By doing a preliminary experiment similar to investigation 30.3 the direction of the induced e.m.f. in the wire in Fig. 30.1 may be related to the motion. You will find that it obeys Fleming's Right-hand Rule which states '**if the thumb, first and second fingers of the right hand are held mutually perpendicular, then if the thumb represents the direction of motion and the first finger the direction of the magnetic field, the second finger represents the direction of the induced electromotive force**.'

Here again the importance of 'mutually perpendicular' must be stressed. An electromotive force is *not* induced if the wire moves parallel to the magnetic field, an e.m.f. is only induced if there is a component of the motion perpendicular to the magnetic field. Obviously the magnitude of the induced electromotive force is greatest when the motion is perpendicular to the magnetic field.

Faraday's Law

The third law dealing with the production of an induced electromotive force is Faraday's Law. This states '**the magnitude of the induced electromotive force is proportional to the rate of change of magnetic flux linkages**'. A single line of force passing through a single-turn coil constitutes one **magnetic flux linkage**. Two lines of force passing through a single-turn coil constitute two flux linkages. This is equivalent to one line of force passing through a two-turn coil. So the number of flux linkages is the number of lines of force multiplied by the number of turns in the coil, or the magnetic field × the number of turns in the coil. (**Note** The magnetic field is the field strength (number of lines of force per unit area) × area of cross-section of the coil.

The law refers to the 'rate of change of magnetic flux linkages', implying that the time taken for a given change in magnetic field is very important. For example, if it takes t s to reduce the magnetic field in a given coil to zero, the electromotive force produced will only be half as great as that produced if the magnetic field is reduced to zero in $\frac{1}{2}t$ s. Also if two coils have the same magnetic field strength but one coil has twice as many turns as the other, then the induced electromotive force in this coil will be twice as large as that induced in the first coil (as long as the time taken to reduce the magnetic field to zero in each coil is the same).

$$\text{induced e.m.f.} = -\frac{\text{change in magnetic flux linkages}}{\text{time}}$$

The negative sign gives the direction of the induced e.m.f. It will be such that it opposes the change producing it.

Example

If the magnet in Fig. 30.3 is dropped right through the coil, N-pole first, what will happen to the galvanometer needle? Explain your answer.

(a) The needle will first deflect to the left because the top of the coil becomes a N-pole and the bottom a S-pole.

(b) When the magnet is in the middle of the coil there will be no deflection.

(c) When the magnet falls out of the coil, the bottom of the coil will be a N-pole to attract the S-pole which is moving away, so the needle will deflect to the right. This deflection will be larger than that in (a) because the magnet is moving faster.

(d) As the magnet moves further away the deflection returns to zero as the magnetic field becomes weaker.

30.3 Generating electricity

Alternating-current generator

The ability to produce an electromotive force by changing the magnetic field inside a coil is used to generate electricity. The apparatus used is similar to that in Fig. 30.5. The coil CDEF rotates between the poles of a horseshoe magnet and an electromotive force is induced. Charge does not flow unless the ends of the coil are connected to an external circuit (resistor). The current is taken to the external circuit by slip rings A_1 and A_2 which are made of copper. A_1 is connected to the side CD of the coil and A_2 to the side EF. A_1 is always in contact with the brush B_1 and A_2 with the brush B_2. When the side CD moves upwards Fleming's Right-hand Rule shows that the

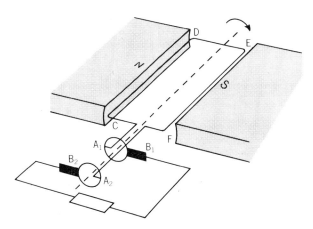

30.5 Alternating current generator

direction of the current is from C to D and E to F. Thus the current enters the circuit at B_1 and leaves at B_2. Half a revolution later FE will be in the position previously occupied by CD and the current direction is reversed, i.e. it is from F to E and D to C. The current now enters the circuit at B_2 and leaves at B_1. Thus the direction of the induced electromotive force and the current changes every half revolution.

These vary not only in direction, however, they also vary in magnitude. The graph of electromotive force against time is shown in Fig. 30.6 and represents three revolutions of the coil. The maximum value of the electromotive force E_o is known as the **peak value**. The time taken for one revolution T is called the **period**, whilst f, the frequency, is the number of revolutions per second. Hence

$$f = \frac{1}{T}$$

The domestic electricity supply has a frequency of 50 hertz, which means that the generator makes fifty revolutions each second. The graph of current against time has the same shape as that of electromotive force against time, but the magnitude of the current depends upon the resistance of the external circuit.

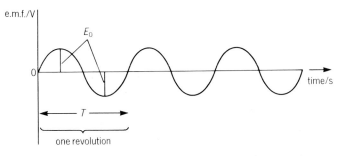

30.6 Graph of induced e.m.f. against time

It is useful to know the positions of the coil that correspond to various points on the graph. These are shown in Fig. 30.7 (assume that the coil is viewed end-on). The induced electromotive force is a maximum when the coil is horizontal and a minimum when the

345

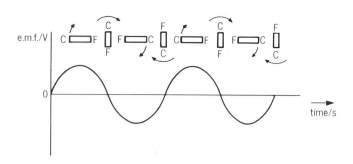

30.7 Positions of coil relating to induced e.m.f.

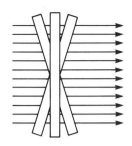

30.8 Flux linkages in a coil

Example

What would be the effect on the output of an alternating-current generator of (a) doubling the number of turns on the coil and (b) keeping the number of turns on the coil constant and doubling the number of revolutions per second? Draw graphs to illustrate your answer.

(a) Doubling the number of turns would double the induced e.m.f., but would not affect the frequency (Fig. 30.9b).

(b) Doubling the number of revolutions per second doubles the frequency (Fig. 30.9c). It also doubles the induced e.m.f. because the angular speed is doubled and thus the rate at which the flux linkages are cut is doubled.

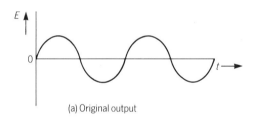

(a) Original output

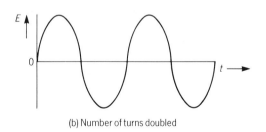

(b) Number of turns doubled

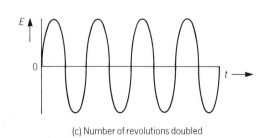

(c) Number of revolutions doubled

30.9 Graphs of e.m.f. from an a.c. generator

coil is vertical. This often confuses students, because the coil has the maximum number of lines of force passing through it when it is vertical, and hence the maximum number of flux linkages. However it is not the *number* of flux linkages which determines the induced electromotive force, but the *rate* at which the number of flux linkages changes. From Fig. 30.8 you can see that there is very little change in the number of flux linkages when the coil is near the vertical position and consequently no, or very little induced electromotive force. Another way of looking at the problem is to consider the sides CD and EF of the coil which are responsible for the induced electromotive force. When the coil is horizontal sides CD and EF are moving perpendicular to the magnetic field and so the induced electromotive force is a maximum; when the coil is perpendicular to the field sides CD and EF are moving parallel to the magnetic field and so the induced electromotive force is zero.

Direct current generator

Alternating current is always produced by a rotating coil, but this output can easily be converted to d.c. by changing the method of taking out the current. A splitting-ring commutator (Fig. 30.10), as in the d.c. motor, (p.339) is used instead of slip rings. As before, the split in the commutator is perpendicular to the plane of the coil. This means that when the coil is vertical the commutator split is horizontal. The sides of the coil are connected to different brushes for each half revolution and the change takes place when the induced electromotive force is zero. Thus B_1 is always connected to the side of the coil which is moving upwards, and B_2 to the side which is moving downwards, and the current always enters the circuit at B_1 and leaves at B_2. Figure 30.11(a) shows the graph of e.m.f. against time produced with the commutator. The current is **pulsating d.c.** With two coils set at right angles on the armature and four segments on the commutator the smoother output shown in Fig. 30.11(b) is obtained.

In working generators many coils are wound on armatures and the magnets are electromagnets. The following important points highlight the similarities between motors and generators.

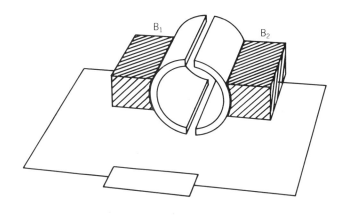

30.10 *Split-ring commutator*

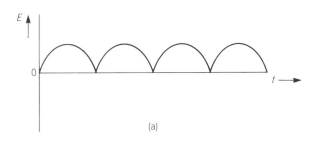

(a)

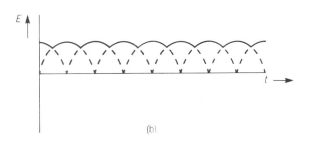

(b)

30.11 *Graphs of e.m.f. against time for a d.c. generator*

1 *There is no structural difference between a d.c. motor and a d.c. generator*, and the same machine can be used for either purpose. In a motor electrical energy is used to rotate the armature, and the rotating armature is used to produce mechanical work. In a generator, mechanical energy is used to rotate the armature and the rotating armature produces electrical energy.

2 *It is not essential to have a rotating coil in a generator.* In some generators the coils are fixed and a magnet rotates between them. The only essential is that the magnetic field inside the coil or coils should change in a regular manner. Sometimes it is more convenient to move the magnet, because brushes and slip rings are not needed if the coil does not move. In a bicycle dynamo a circular magnet is made to spin inside an iron core on which a coil is wound.

3 Since there is no structural difference between a motor and a generator, *a motor acts like a generator when the armature rotates.* (This was explained in Chapter 29, p.339.)

4 *There is a motor effect in a dynamo similar to the dynamo effect in a motor.* When the dynamo is giving current, forces act on the sides of the coil which oppose the motion and tend to slow down the rotating coil.

30.4   Inducing an e.m.f. using two coils

Induction coil

Investigation 30.4   To induce an e.m.f. in a coil using a second coil

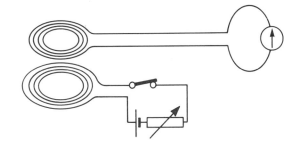

30.12   *Induced e.m.f. between two coils*

Connect the first coil to a centre-reading galvanometer and place it parallel and just above the second coil. Connect the bottom coil to a battery, rheostat and switch (Fig. 30.12). Close the switch in the bottom circuit. The galvanometer needle swings sharply to one side and then quickly returns to zero. There is no deflection when the key remains closed. Now open the switch. The galvanometer needle swings sharply in the other direction and again quickly returns to zero. If you move the slider on the rheostat backwards and forwards when the switch is closed, the galvanometer needle flickers from side to side.

From this investigation you can conclude that when the current in one circuit changes, a current is induced into the other circuit. Changing the current in the bottom coil changes the magnetic field it produces, and hence changes the magnetic flux linkage with the top coil. Thus an electromotive force is induced in the top coil. Putting a soft iron bar through the two coils considerably enhances the effect as the magnetic field strength is multiplied by a factor of about one thousand.

An arrangement of two coils can be used to generate current. In the **induction coil** (Fig. 30.13) there are two fixed coils and the current in one is varied to induce an e.m.f. in the other. The inner coil A which carries the current is known as the **primary coil.** It consists of a relatively few turns of thick insulated copper wire

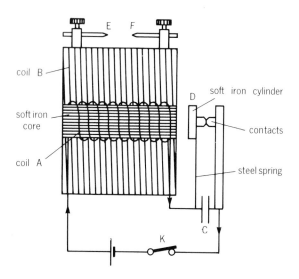

30.13   Induction coil

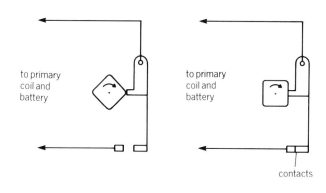

30.14   Contact breaker in car ignition system

wound round a soft iron core (a bundle of soft iron wires). The outer coil B, known as the **secondary coil**, is wound outside coil A and consists of many thousands of turns of fine insulated copper wire ending at E and F. When the switch K is closed a current is set up in coil A and the soft iron core becomes a magnet. This attracts the soft iron cylinder D and the contacts are opened, thus switching off the current. The core loses its magnetism, D springs back and contact is remade. As a result the current is continually made and broken, the magnetic field inside coil B continually changes and a large e.m.f. is induced into B. It may be large enough to make a spark in the air between points E and F.

The very small voltage in the primary is stepped up to several thousand volts in the secondary. The current in the secondary is very small indeed, because the total energy cannot be increased. At the best, assuming an efficiency of 100%,

energy in secondary = energy in primary
$$V_s I_s t = V_p I_p t$$
$$V_s I_s = V_p I_p$$

where the suffix p represents primary and s secondary. It follows that if the secondary voltage is several thousand times greater than the primary voltage, then the secondary current must be several thousand times smaller than the primary current.

The capacitor C in the circuit serves two useful purposes. It cuts down sparking at the contacts and lessens the time during which the circuit breaks. Thus a very large e.m.f. is induced when the contacts break and this is the output e.m.f. The current produced is intermittent d.c.

Induction coils were once used to produce the high voltages necessary to energise such things as spark discharge and X-ray tubes. These are now energised by transformers and rectifiers. However the induction coil still has a very valuable and common use in the ignition system of motor cars, where it produces the high voltage necessary to make a spark across the points of the sparking plug. The contact breaker is rather different from that shown in Fig. 30.13. In a four-cylinder engine the contact breaker is a rotating four-sided cam (Fig. 30.14). When the contact breaker is in contact with the flat side of the cam the contacts are closed, but when an edge comes round the contacts open, the current is switched off and a spark is produced. This spark is produced four times during each revolution of the cam, and the distributor ensures that the spark occurs in turn in each cylinder at the end of the compression stroke.

30.5   Transformers

The most common and useful application of the production of an induced e.m.f. in one coil by varying the current in another is the transformer. The transformer depends on the use of alternating current. The centre of a transformer consists of a laminated core of magnetic material which is easily magnetised and demagnetised, but becomes a very strong magnet. Around this is wound a primary coil, and around the primary coil is wound a secondary coil. It is easier to show the two coils separately, as in Fig. 30.15.

When an alternating e.m.f. is applied to the primary coil an alternating magnetic field is produced in the core. This in turn passes through the secondary coil and induces an alternating e.m.f. in it. Since the magnetic field in each coil is the same, it follows that the e.m.f. in each coil is proportional to the number of turns in the coil. Hence

$$\frac{V_s}{V_p} = \frac{N_s}{N_p}$$

where V_p = primary voltage, V_s = secondary voltage, N_p = primary turns, N_s = secondary turns. If $N_s > N_p$

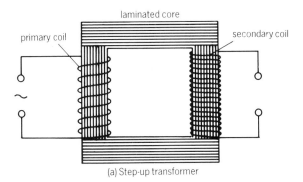

(a) Step-up transformer

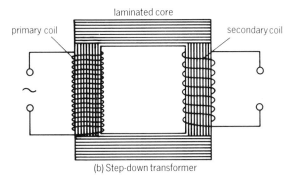

(b) Step-down transformer

30.15   Transformers

then $V_s > V_p$ and the transformer is called a **step-up transformer**. When $N_s < N_p$ it follows that $V_s < V_p$ and it is called a **step-down transformer**. Note that the terms 'step-up' and 'step-down' apply only to the voltages or electromotive forces. The amount of energy cannot be stepped up or down. At best, as with the induction coil, as much energy can be obtained from the secondary as is put into the primary, i.e. the efficiency of the transformer is 100%. This theoretical efficiency cannot be obtained in practice, although the transformer is a very good machine with an efficiency in the region of 90%. As for the induction coil (assuming a theoretical efficiency of 100%),

$$V_s I_s = V_p I_p$$
$$\frac{V_s}{V_p} = \frac{I_p}{I_s}$$

It follows that if the voltage is stepped up, the current is stepped down and vice versa. If a high voltage is required a step-up transformer is used, whereas if a high current is required a step-down transformer is used. The latter gives a high current at a low voltage which is often preferable to using the mains voltage to give a high current.

Investigation 30.5   To demonstrate Lenz's Law

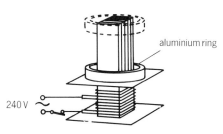

(a) Demonstration of Lenz's Law

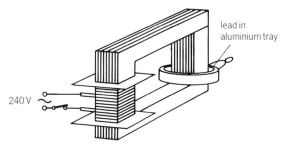

(b) Demonstration of electric furnace

30.16   Uses of transformers

Place a coil of 400 turns of insulated copper wire at the bottom of a long laminated core of magnetic material (Fig. 30.16a). Connect the coil to the 240 V mains and place an aluminium ring on top of it. Close the switch. The aluminium ring is projected high into the air. If you place your hand on top so that the ring cannot fly off, it remains in the dotted position. When the current is switched off the ring falls down.

This can be explained by Lenz's Law. The ring is a single-turn coil, and when a current is induced into it, the direction of the current is such that the bottom face of the ring is the same polarity as the top face of the coil, and repulsion occurs. The ring gets quite hot, indicating that it is carrying quite a large current.

The large current produced in a single-turn secondary can be demonstrated with the apparatus in Fig. 30.16(b). The secondary

is a circular aluminium tray into which molten lead has been poured and allowed to solidify. The current in the primary is switched on and after two or three minutes the lead in the aluminium container melts. If there are 400 turns in the primary, the secondary voltage is only about 0.6 V, but the current, which is 400 times as large as the primary current, is considerable. For this experiment to succeed, the top bar of the core must be firmly clamped to form a closed ring. If the top bar is merely laid on to the remainder of the core, the lead does not melt. It is essential that there is no air gap, however small, or the magnetic flux through the secondary is considerably reduced, thus drastically reducing the efficiency of the transformer.

This apparatus forms the basis of the electric furnace.

Fairly simple but effective experiments can be performed with the transformer kits available.

Eddy currents

An aluminium vane is allowed to oscillate between the poles of a powerful electromagnet as in Fig. 30.17. When the electromagnet is switched off the vane swings quite freely, but when the electromagnet is switched on the vane comes to rest very quickly. If the solid vane is replaced by a serrated vane and the experiment repeated, it is found that switching on the

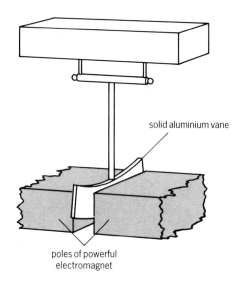

solid aluminium vane

poles of powerful electromagnet

serrated vane

30.17 Eddy currents

electromagnet makes little difference to the swinging vane. In the solid vane a large current is induced (**eddy current**) because the metal is moving at right angles to the magnetic field. This induced current generates a magnetic field which opposes the applied magnetic field and so has a large braking effect. The induced e.m.f.s in each part of the serrated vane are much smaller because of the much smaller area and also the resistance of each small segment is higher, so the induced eddy currents are small and have only a very small effect on the vane's motion.

On p.335 you read that the coil in the moving-coil galvanometer is wound on a metal former. When this former moves in the magnetic field quite a large current is induced into it and this opposes the motion of the coil. Hence the coil and pointer come to rest immediately and do not oscillate.

Causes of loss of efficiency in a transformer

1 *Flux leakage* It is essential that all the flux generated by the primary passes through the secondary. This is best achieved by winding the primary on top of the secondary and having a 'closed' iron core.
2 *Loss due to heating effect of eddy currents (iron losses)* The metal core is a conductor and the magnetic field varies continually. Hence an e.m.f. and consequently a current are induced in it. If the core is solid it acts in effect as a secondary of one turn and a very large current is induced. The heating effect is proportional to the square of the current and is therefore quite large. The effect is very considerably reduced by using a bundle of fine wires or thin metal stampings (laminations) insulated from each other. Then the current induced in each is very small and there is only a small heating effect.
3 *Copper losses* These represent the energy lost by heating of the wire in both the primary and secondary coils ($\propto I^2 R$).
4 *Hysteresis losses* The magnetic field in the core is in one direction 50 times each second and in the opposite direction 50 times each second. Consequently the domains are continually changing their alignment. The energy needed to effect this is taken from the input energy.

Uses of transformers

The transformer has many uses. Step-up transformers are used in power packs, TV sets, X-ray tubes etc. When a d.c. voltage is required a rectifier is used across the output. Step-down transformers are used where a large current is required, e.g. for electric furnaces, welding etc. They have the advantage that the output voltage is small. They are also used for lights, small motors etc. where a large output is not required.

30.6 Transmission of electricity

Electricity is transmitted from one part of the country to another by the **grid system** and is carried by the pylons and wires strung out across the countryside. The generator at the power station produces electricity in three phases. This simply means that three separate coils on the armature produce e.m.f.s of the same frequency and peak value, but the peaks do not coincide (Fig. 30.18). At the power station the electricity is generated at 25 000 V and then transformers are used are used to step it up to 132 000 V. Each phase is stepped up to this value. The pylons carry four wires: the one connecting the tops of the pylons is the earth or neutral wire and each of the others carries a separate phase. The voltage is stepped up to this high value so that the current is comparatively small, resulting in a small heat loss ($\propto I^2 R$). Also thinner cable can be used with this current, giving a considerable saving in cost. At local sub-stations the voltage is stepped down again and a further stepping-down to 240 V occurs before the electricity enters a house.

Normally only one phase is carried into a house. During a power cut the electricity may be off down one side of a street but not down the other, because different phases are used. All three phases are connected into industrial premises where three-phase motors are used.

In bad weather conditions, e.g. during gales or

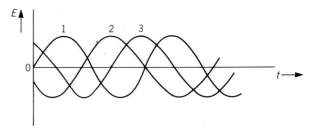

30.18 Three-phase e.m.f.

heavy snowstorms, power cables may snap and be brought to the ground. They should be left severely alone.

Alternating current and direct current

Direct current was used at one time, but alternating current is now preferred. Its great advantage is that it can be stepped up and down much more easily. Direct current cannot be used with a transformer because a changing magnetic field is required. To step up d.c. voltages is quite a complicated process. To step it down involves using resistors in series and a considerable amount of energy is lost as heat.

Example

Why is it quite safe for birds to perch on overhead power cables, but it is very dangerous for a person standing on the ground near the overhead cables to fly a kite?

A bird perching on a cable has both claws on the cable and therefore they are at the same potential. Thus no charge flows through the bird. The string from the kite may come into contact with one or more of the overhead cables. What happens then depends upon the conducting properties of the string. It may either short-circuit two cables or may connect one cable to the ground through the person flying the kite, when the high voltage may kill him.

Example

A person decides to run a 12 V 48 W lamp off a 120 V d.c. supply. Find the value of the resistor which is needed and calculate the heat lost in this resistor.

$$\text{potential difference across resistor} = 120\,\text{V} - 12\,\text{V}$$
$$= 108\,\text{V}$$

$$\text{current through lamp } I = \frac{W}{V} = \frac{48\,\text{W}}{12\,\text{V}}$$
$$= 4\,\text{A}$$

$$\text{value of resistor } R = \frac{108\,\text{V}}{4\,\text{A}}$$
$$= 27\,\Omega$$

Thus a 27 Ω resistor is needed in series with the lamp.

$$\text{heat lost in resistor} = I^2 R = 4\,\text{A} \times 4\,\text{A} \times 27\,\Omega$$
$$= 423\,\text{W}$$

Thus about nine times as much energy is dissipated in the resistor as in the lamp.

Questions

Q1 Each one of the following changes will increase the e.m.f. in a simple generator **except**
A increasing the number of turns in the armature coil.
B winding the coil on a soft iron armature.
C increasing the size of the gap in which the armature turns.
D increasing the speed of rotation.
E using a stronger field magnet.   *(AEB)*

Q2 The North pole of a long bar magnet was pushed slowly into a short solenoid connected to a galvanometer. The magnet was held stationary for a few seconds with the North pole in the middle of the solenoid and then withdrawn rapidly. The maximum deflection of the galvanometer was observed when the magnet was
A moving towards the solenoid.
B moving into the solenoid.
C at rest inside the solenoid.
D moving out of the solenoid.
E moving away from the solenoid.   *(AEB)*

Q3 A transformer which is 80% efficient gives an output of 10 V and 4 A. What is the input power, in W?

A 25 **B** 32 **C** 40 **D** 50 **E** 200 *(AEB)*

Q4

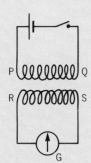

PQ and RS are two insulated coils placed near to each other as shown in the diagram. PQ is connected to a battery through a switch. RS is connected to a sensitive galvanometer G. When the switch is closed and kept closed, the pointer of the galvanometer

A is unaffected.

B registers a momentary deflection and quickly returns to zero.

C registers a steady deflection to one side.

D registers a deflection to one side and slowly returns to a lower steady reading on the same side.

E oscillates about the zero point. *(L)*

Q5 (a) Draw a clear diagram of an a.c. generator which could be used to light a lamp. Show clearly how the current is led to the external circuit. By means of a sketch graph, show how this current varies with time. Indicate the position of the rotating part of the generator when the current is maximum.

Explain briefly how this output current could be rectified (without alteration to the structure of the generator).

(b) Describe, by means of a clear labelled diagram, the structure of a meter suitable for measuring a.c. *(S)*

Q6 (a) State **two** laws of electromagnetic induction, one law relating to the size of the induced e.m.f. (Faraday's law) and the other relating to its direction (Lenz's law).

Describe a simple experiment which illustrates the truth of **one** of these laws. Explain how the law can be deduced from the observations made in the experiment.

(b) Draw a diagram showing the main components of a simple a.c. generator. Briefly describe how the generator works and explain why it produces alternating current. Trace the energy changes taking place in the generator and the load to which it is supplying current. *(JMB)*

Q7 Draw a clearly labelled diagram to show the structure of a transformer suitable for operating a 24 V 48 W lamp from the 240 V mains supply. Assuming the efficiency of the transformer to be high, what current would be supplied from the mains?

If the mains frequency is 50 Hz, show, by means of a labelled sketch graph, how the output p.d. from the above transformer varies with time. Describe briefly how you would use a cathode ray oscillograph to display a trace of this output.

Why is it not advisable to connect a d.c. supply across the input of such a transformer? *(S)*

Q8 (a) In this country, electrical energy is distributed by the National Grid system which transmits alternating current at very high voltage.

Explain why (i) a very high voltage is necessary; (ii) alternating current is used.

(b) A generator capable of producing 100 kW is connected to a factory by a cable with a total resistance of 5 ohm. If the generator produces the power at a potential difference of 5000 V, (i) what would be the maximum current in the cable; (ii) what would be the maximum power available to the factory? *(JMB)*

Q9

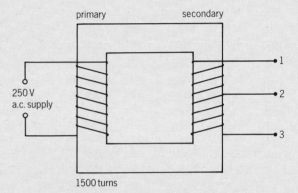

(a) The diagram shows a voltage step-down transformer connected to a 250 V a.c. supply. When a 5 ohm resistor is connected between terminals 1 and 2, the current flowing in the resistor is 0.5 A, and when the same resistor is connected between terminals 2 and 3 the current is 1.0 A. Assuming that the transformer is 100% efficient, calculate

   (i) the potential difference between terminals 1 and 2.

   (ii) the potential difference between terminals 2 and 3.

   (iii) the number of turns on the secondary coil between terminals 1 and 2.

   (iv) the number of turns on the secondary coil between terminals 2 and 3.

   (v) the potential difference between terminals 1 and 3.

   (vi) the current which would flow in the 5 ohm resistor when connected between terminals 1 and 3.

(b) In practice, the potential difference between any two of the terminals is less than calculated in (a). State why this is so and explain how the difference is kept to a minimum in a modern transformer.

(c) (i) Briefly describe how a cathode ray oscilloscope could be used to compare the voltage output from terminals 1 and 2 with the output from terminals 2 and 3 of the transformer shown in the diagram.

   (ii) On the same axes, sketch **two** graphs of the traces seen on the oscilloscope, one for terminals 1 and 2, and another for terminals 2 and 3, indicating clearly the relative sizes and frequencies of the two outputs. *(JMB)*

31 Thermionic diode valves, the cathode-ray oscilloscope and deflection tubes

31.1 Thermionic diode valves

A **diode valve** is a simple electron tube. If the electron beam is produced by the emission of electrons from the surface of a heated metal it is called **thermionic**. A **thermionic diode valve** consists of a cathode (or a cathode with a separate heater) and an anode that have been sealed into an evacuated glass envelope. There are two types of thermionic (heat emission) diodes: those whose cathode is directly heated and those with an indirectly heated cathode. These diodes are shown symbolically in Fig. 31.1. In the type with a directly heated cathode a piece of tungsten wire serves as both the heater and the cathode supplying electrons (negative charges) to the cylindrical nickel anode surrounding it in the evacuated space within the glass envelope. In the diode with an indirectly heated

cathode (Fig. 31.2) the tungsten wire heater (Fig. 31.2a) is surrounded by a hollow nickel cylinder (Fig. 31.2b) coated with oxides of barium or strontium, which is in turn surrounded by a nickel anode (Fig. 31.2c). The whole arrangement is sealed into the evacuated glass envelope.

The valve can be controlled in two ways: by varying the heater voltage V_h or by varying the anode voltage V_a.

Varying the heater voltage

When the cathode is heated by the heater operated at 2 V, electrons (e^-) are emitted from the oxides on the cathode. These form a cloud around the cathode, which itself becomes positive due to the loss of negative charges (Fig. 31.3a). Thus a 'cloud' of electrons e^- called the **space charge** gather in the region

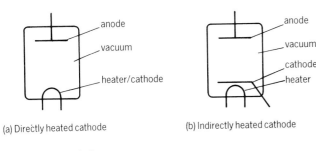

(a) Directly heated cathode   *(b) Indirectly heated cathode*

31.1   Diode symbols

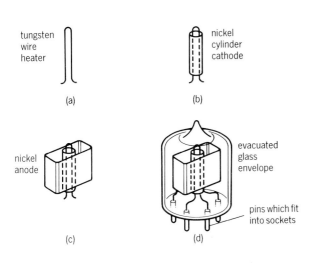

(a)   *(b)*

(c)   *(d)*

31.2   Diode valve with indirectly heated cathode

31.3   Space charge increases with increase in heater voltage

353

of the cathode. Increasing the heater voltage to 4 V and then 6 V raises the temperature of the heater and thus increases the size of the space charge (Figs. 31.3b and c). At each given heater voltage there is an equilibrium of charges escaping from the cathode and charges attracted back to the cathode by its slight positive potential. A very sensitive microammeter connected between the anode and the cathode can detect an extremely small current known as the Edison current, produced because those electrons with sufficient k.e. cross the gap and reach the anode.

Varying the anode voltage

When the heater voltage is fixed, producing a steady space charge, the flow of electrons (electric current) to the anode depends on the potential difference V_a between the anode and the cathode (Fig. 31.4). When the anode is at a negative potential with respect to the cathode (or $V_a = 0$) no current flows through the valve. However, when the anode is positive, electrons are accelerated across the gap between the cathode and the anode. Increasing the value of V_a increases the rate of flow of the electrons (current) through the valve. The anode current I_a increases as the anode potential is increased from zero to a certain value and thereafter remains almost at a constant value called the **saturation current I_s** (Fig. 31.5).

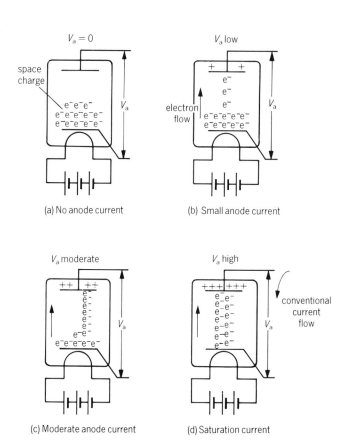

(a) No anode current (b) Small anode current

(c) Moderate anode current (d) Saturation current

31.4   Effect of varying the anode voltage

Investigation 31.1   To determine the I_a/V_a characteristics of a thermionic diode

Connect the circuit as shown in Fig. 31.6. Make a preliminary investigation to ensure saturation current can be reached for different values of heater voltage V_h. Switch on the heater supply (battery A) and adjust the potentiometer R_1 until a suitable voltage V_h is applied to the heater. Switch on the battery B and adjust the potentiometer R_2 until a small potential difference V_a

is applied between the anode and the cathode of the valve. Adjust the potentiometer R_2 to obtain a series of readings of I_a and V_a recorded on the milliammeter and voltmeter respectively. Draw up a table of results like Table 31.1 and record values of I_a and V_a for the known value of V_h. Repeat the procedure for two more values of V_h. Plot a graph of anode current I_a against anode voltage V_a for each value of V_h. A typical graph of the results is shown in Fig. 31.7.

Table 31.1   Table of results for investigation 31.1

I_a/mA	0							
V_a/V	0							

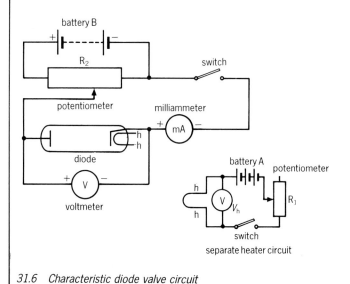

31.6   Characteristic diode valve circuit

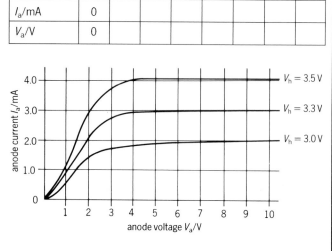

31.7 I_a/V_a characteristics of a thermionic diode

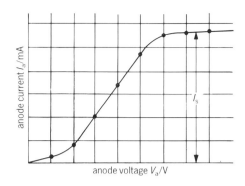

31.5 *Saturation current of a thermionic diode*

31.2 Cathode-ray oscilloscope

A cathode-ray oscilloscope (Fig. 31.8) is an instrument which displays electrical signals. As in the diode valve, a heater H (of tungsten wire) operated by 6.3 V across its ends heats a cathode C which emits electrons. These are accelerated through a vacuum towards a positive anode. They pass through the anode and travel down the evacuated tube until they strike a fluorescent screen. The movement of the electrons can be controlled by varying the potential applied to (a) the grid G, (b) the anodes A_1 and A_2, and (c) the X-plates and the Y-plates.

The grid G carries a negative potential with respect to the cathode and thus repels the electrons emitted from the cathode C. A strong repulsion force (large negative potential) means that few, if any, electrons are able to reach the fluorescent screen. A weak repulsion force (lesser negative potential) allows many electrons to reach the fluorescent screen where they produce a bright spot. When the grid is made less negative a greater number of electrons reach the screen giving a brighter spot. However, when the grid is made more negative, fewer electrons reach the screen and so

the spot becomes less bright and may even disappear. Since the grid is at a negative potential with respect to the cathode it also prevents negative electrons in the beam from repelling each other outwards and thus has a pre-focussing effect. The rheostat which controls the grid potential is called the **brightness** or **brilliance control**.

Anode A_1, which is usually in the shape of a metal disc, and anode A_2, in the shape of a metal cylinder, both have a hole in the centre for the beam to pass through. They are maintained at positive potentials which are high with respect to the potential of the cathode. The electrons are accelerated to very high velocities (one-tenth of the speed of light) by the positively charged anodes. Although the electrons have a very small mass they are accelerated to such high velocities that they have sufficient kinetic energy ($\frac{1}{2}mv^2$) to emit light when they strike the fluorescent screen. Since electrons will be slowed down by collisions with air molecules and cause ionisation of any gas present, all the air must be evacuated from the tube so that the electrons can travel freely along the whole length of the tube. Anode A_2 is operated at a higher potential than anode A_1 and, by varying the potential *difference* between the anodes, the electron beam can be focussed to give a small spot on the fluorescent screen. The anode A_2 is earthed (zero potential), thus making all the other potentials negative. Since these are inaccessible the terminals and connections are safe. The rheostat which enables the positive potential applied to A_1 to be varied is known as the **focus control**. (Correct focussing is achieved in practice by adjusting the brightness and focus controls in turn.)

A **deflecting system**, consisting of two pairs of parallel plates X and Y set inside the tube enables the spot to be moved to any point on the screen. The horizontal Y-plates can deflect the spot vertically up and down while the vertical X-plates can deflect the

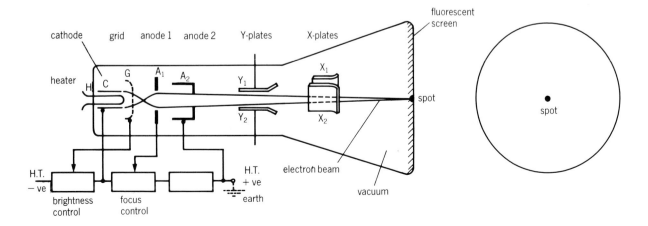

31.8 *The structure of the cathode-ray oscilloscope*

355

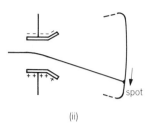

(ii)

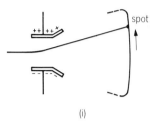

(i)

(a) Vertical deflection (side elevation)

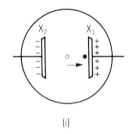

(i)

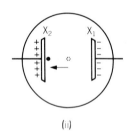

(ii)

(b) Horizontal deflection (front elevation)

31.9   Effects of X and Y deflecting plates

spot horizontally from side to side. When a potential difference is applied across the Y-plates with Y_1 positive and Y_2 negative the negative electrons will be deflected upwards (Fig. 31.9a(i)). Alternatively, if Y_1 is negative and Y_2 positive, the electrons will be deflected downwards (Fig. 31.9a(ii)). If a potential difference is applied across the X-plates with X_1 positive and X_2 negative (Fig. 31.9b(i)), the electrons will be deflected to the right. If X_1 is negative and X_2 positive (Fig. 31.9b(ii)), the electrons will be deflected to the left. The size of the deflection depends on the size of the potential difference between the plates concerned.

The screen at the end of the tube is coated with a thin layer of a fluorescent salt such as zinc orthosilicate (giving a bluish-white colour when the electrons strike), zinc phosphate or sulphate (giving a green colour) or calcium tungstate (giving a blue colour).

The cathode-ray oscilloscope as a voltmeter

The cathode-ray oscilloscope can be used as either an a.c. or a d.c. voltmeter.

Investigation 31.2   To use the cathode-ray oscilloscope as a d.c. voltmeter

Set the a.c./d.c. switch to d.c., the volts/cm to 2 and check that the timebase is switched off. Switch on the oscilloscope and adjust the brightness and focus controls to give a small, bright spot in the centre of the screen using the X and Y shift controls if necessary. Set up the circuit as shown in Figure 31.10(a).

Switch on the d.c. supply and adjust the potentiometer so that the voltmeter records 2 V, 4 V, 6 V and 8 V. Measure the deflection d in millimetre for each voltage. The typical set of results in Table 31.2 gives the graph shown in Fig. 31.10(b). Using this graph, a given deflection d in millimetre can be converted to the corresponding voltage.

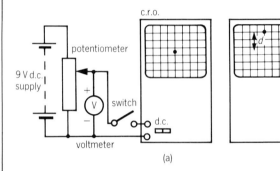

(a)

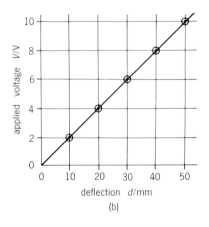

(b)

31.10   Cathode-ray oscilloscope as a d.c. voltmeter

Table 31.2   Table of results for investigation 31.2

V/V	0	2	4	6	8
d/mm	0	10	20	30	40

Repeat the experiment with the timebase switched on. A straight horizontal line is produced instead of the spot but the recorded deflections remain the same.

Investigation 31.3   To use the cathode-ray oscilloscope as an a.c. voltmeter

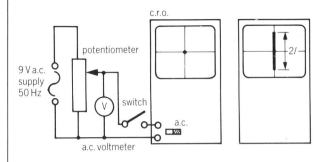

31.11   Cathode-ray oscilloscope as an a.c. voltmeter

Connect up the circuit as shown in Fig. 31.11.
(**Note**   An a.c. voltmeter must be used with the 9 V a.c. supply.) Set the a.c./d.c. switch on the cathode-ray oscilloscope to a.c. and make sure the timebase is off. When the supply is switched on, the spot moves up and down rapidly to give a line trace. Using the potentiometer set the voltage at 2 V, 3 V, 4 V, 5 V and 6 V as recorded by the a.c. voltmeter and measure and record the length 2*l* of the corresponding lines.

Note   The a.c. voltmeter records the root-mean-square (r.m.s.) voltage $V_{r.m.s.}$ while the line trace 2*l* on the oscilloscope represents twice the peak voltage V_p (see below). The root-mean-square voltage $V_{r.m.s.}$ is related to the peak voltage V_p by the relationship $V_{r.m.s.} = V_p/\sqrt{2}$.

An alternating voltage is one whose value is always changing direction with time, and the simplest form is the **sinusoidal voltage** (Fig. 31.12). The root-mean-square power of this supply is the effective mean power of an a.c. supply.

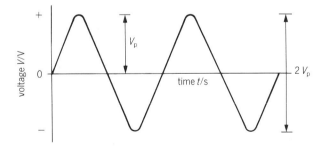

31.12   Sinusoidal alternating voltage

To find the power *P* consumed in a resistor of *R* Ω you should not use the equation $P = V_p^2/R$ because there are times when *V* = 0, and indeed the voltage varies between 0 V and V_p. Instead you should take the average power of 0 and V_p^2/R, i.e. $\frac{1}{2}V_p^2/R$. The root-mean-square voltage $V_{r.m.s.}$ is equivalent to the steady d.c. voltage which would dissipate the same

power *P* in the same resistor R. Now $P = V_{r.m.s.}^2/R$ and equating values for power, gives

$$\frac{V_{r.m.s.}^2}{R} = \frac{1}{2}\frac{V_p^2}{R}$$

$$V_{r.m.s.}^2 = \frac{1}{2}V_p^2$$

$$V_{r.m.s.} = \frac{V_p}{\sqrt{2}}$$

$$V_{r.m.s.} = 0.707\,V_p$$

Simple use of the timebase

If the X-shift control is adjusted so that the spot moves to the left of the screen, and the timebase is switched to 1 ms cm^{-1}, a horizontal line trace is produced. The voltage applied to the X-plates is such that the spot moves at uniform speed across the screen and then flies back very quickly to repeat the motion over and over again. When the frequency of the timebase is 50 Hz, equal to the frequency of the 50 Hz voltage applied to the Y-plates, the trace in Fig. 31.13(b) is obtained. The spot moves both horizontally and vertically, as shown in Fig. 31.14. In $\frac{1}{50}$ s the spot makes one horizontal sweep (Fig. 31.14a) and one vertical oscillation (Fig. 31.14b). When these two movements of the spot occur simultaneously the sinusoidal trace shown in Fig. 31.14(c) is obtained. This trace is drawn 50 times per second and always at the same place on the screen.

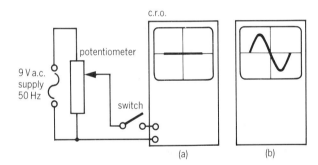

31.13   Simple use of the timebase

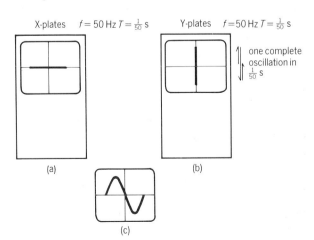

31.14   Trace produced when timebase frequency is equal to input frequency

357

Wave traces and use as a timer

The cathode-ray oscilloscope is able to give a visible demonstration of vibrations. It can also be used as a sensitive timing device. If a person sings into a microphone connected to the oscilloscope, a trace similar to that in Fig. 31.15(a) can be obtained when the timebase is on. Figure 31.15(b) shows the kind of traces that would appear if the same note is sounded on a tuning fork, violin and piano respectively. The difference in character of the traces is due to the overtones in the case of the violin and piano. This gives the notes their characteristic **quality** or **timbre** which enables the listener to identify the 'instrument' being sounded. The photographs show famous instrumentalists with the wave traces associated with their instruments.

The oscilloscope can be used as a timer. The microphone is attached to the oscilloscope and turned to face a hard smooth wall. If a sharp noise is made, this noise registers as the first trace on the oscilloscope while the sound reflected off the wall registers as a

(a)

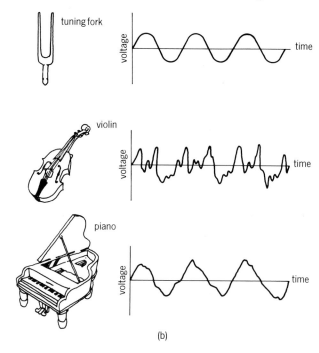

(b)

Yehudi Menuhin (violin)   Louis Armstrong (trumpet)   Acker Bilk (clarinet)

31.15   Musical sounds as wave traces

smaller trace further along the screen as shown in Fig. 31.16. With the timebase at a known setting, e.g. 2 ms cm, a distance of x cm^{-1} between the two traces represents a time of $2x$ ms. Therefore the distance between the two traces, measured in centimetre, can be converted into a time value using the accurate timebase setting. These timebase settings can range from 100 ms cm^{-1} to 1 μs cm^{-1}. The measured time t could be used to calculate the speed of sound in air in the laboratory because it is the time taken for the sound to travel from the microphone to the wall and back, i.e. a distance of $2d$. Hence the speed of sound can be calculated from $2d/t$.

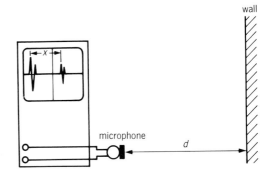

31.16   Cathode-ray oscilloscope as a timer

Investigation 31.4   To demonstrate half-wave rectification

Connect the a.c. supply directly to the oscilloscope and switch on. Adjust the timebase until two or three complete sine traces appear on the screen (Fig. 31.17b). Connect the circuit as shown in Fig. 32.17(a). When alternating voltage is applied across the anode and the cathode of the diode, the anode is alternatively positive and then negative. During the positive half of the cycle the anode conducts current (attracts electrons across the diode valve) and establishes a potential difference across the resistor R and the Y-plates. The shape of the trace on the screen imitates the shape of the applied a.c. voltage. For the second half of the cycle the anode is negative and cannot conduct, therefore no potential difference appears across R. During this period the trace on the screen is a horizontal line representing zero volt. When the cycle is repeated the valve again conducts when the anode is positive and does not conduct when it is negative. The complete trace is shown in Fig. 31.17(c).

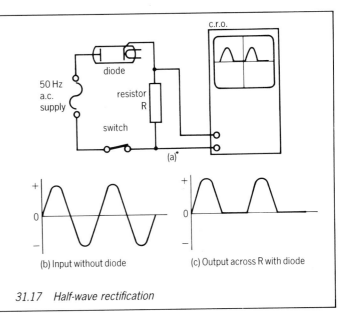

31.17   Half-wave rectification

Investigation 31.5   To demonstrate full-wave rectification

Connect a transformer with a centre-tapped secondary coil to two diode valves as shown in Fig. 31.18(a). When an a.c. voltage is applied to the primary coil the output across the load resistor R will be pulsating d.c. (Fig. 31.18b). First one diode conducts and then, when the polarity of the supply is reversed, the other diode conducts, and so on. The half wave normally lost when using a single diode is utilised when two diodes are used. A double diode usually replaces the two separate diodes in this circuit. It has two anodes and a common cathode and heater.

If you add a capacitor C to the circuit between the points X and Y the voltage output is **smoothed**. As the alternating voltage falls from its peak value the charged capacitor discharges, so maintaining the voltage. The wave trace produced when a high-value capacitor is used is shown in Fig. 31.18(c). The presence of the charged capacitor prevents the voltage falling to zero (Fig. 31.18b).

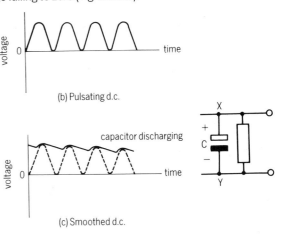

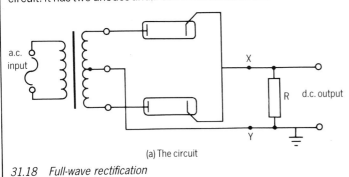

(a) The circuit

31.18   Full-wave rectification

359

31.3 Cathode rays

Magnetic deflection of cathode rays to show they carry negative charge

Cathode rays are known to travel towards the screen of a cathode-ray tube or oscilloscope. When the N-pole of a bar magnet is brought towards the screen, as in Fig. 31.19(a), (b) and (c), the spot is deflected as shown. Fleming's Left-hand Rule (to the field, current and motion) does not, at first, seem to apply. However, it would do so if the current flow were into the plane of the paper in Fig. 31.19. This implies that the charges flowing towards the reader have the opposite sign to that of conventional (positive) current. Hence cathode rays must be negatively charged.

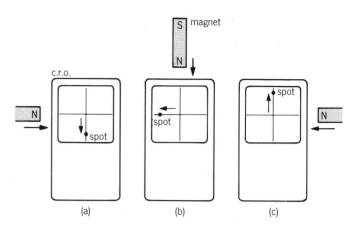

31.19   Magnetic deflection of cathode rays

Exercise 31.2

Repeat the above demonstration using the S-pole of the magnet. Draw diagrams to show the deflection of the spot.

Investigation 31.6   To demonstrate electrostatic and magnetic deflection of cathode rays

(a) Electrostatic deflection   Set up the apparatus shown in Fig. 31.20. A hot wire cathode and anode are used to produce and accelerate a beam of electrons (cathode rays) through a tube that contains gas at a very low pressure. The gas is present so that the path of the moving electrons can be seen. The gas molecules are excited when the electrons collide with them during their motion in the tube. Since the heater/filament is white-hot a horizontal ray of white light is always visible along the axis of the tube. The path of the electrons is visible as a red/blue trace in the tube. Switch on the 0–1 kV d.c. supply, so that a potential difference is applied between the Y-plates with Y_1 positive and Y_2 negative. The narrow beam of electrons is bent into a parabolic arc in the region between the two plates. When the beam leaves the region between the plates it continues in a straight line.

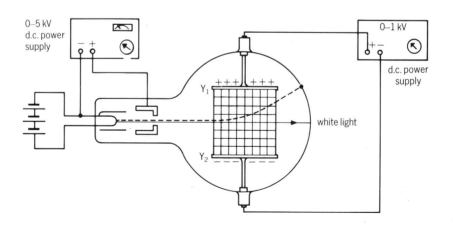

31.20   Demonstration deflection tube

— continued

Exercise 31.3

Reverse the connections to the 0–1 kV d.c. power supply on the cathode ray tube shown in Fig. 31.20. Draw a diagram like Fig. 31.20 with Y_1 negative and Y_2 positive and show the deflection of the electron beam.

(b) **Magnetic deflection** Apply a uniform magnetic field at right angles to the beam of electrons which are deflected downwards as shown in Figure 32.21(a) above. The magnetic field is produced by two parallel coils carrying equal currents and placed as shown in Fig. 31.21(b). Applying Fleming's Left-hand Rule (see Fig. 31.21c) requires the conventional current flow to be into the plane of the paper. However, it is known that the charged particles are moving *out* of the plane of the paper. Therefore these charged particles must carry a negative charge.

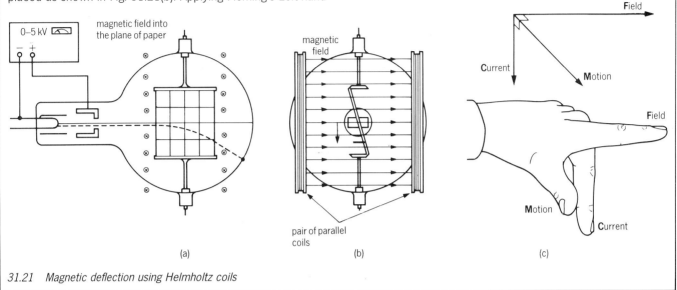

31.21　*Magnetic deflection using Helmholtz coils*

Exercise 31.4

If the current in the coils is reversed as in Fig. 31.21, the magnetic field is reversed. Draw a diagram like Fig. 31.21(a) to show how the beam is deflected when the magnetic field is out of the plane of the paper.

The apparatus in Fig. 31.22 can be used to show that the cathode rays are negatively charged particles. A beam of particles is accelerated by operating the anode at a high potential. The beam passes straight down the centre of the tube and strikes the fluorescent screen. When a magnetic field is applied perpendicular to and out of the plane of the paper the beam is deflected upwards. The strength of the magnetic field can be adjusted so that the beam strikes the Faraday cylinder which is connected to a leaf electroscope. Charges are collected by the cylinder and cause the leaf of the electroscope to deflect. Testing the electroscope shows that the charge is negative. Hence the beam consists of negative particles.

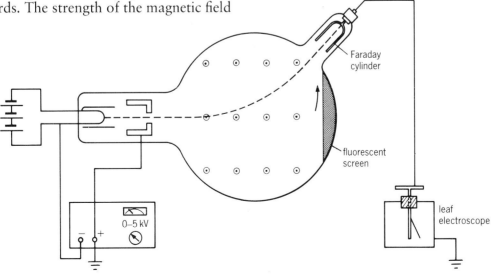

31.22　*Cathode rays are composed of negatively charged particles*

Questions

Q1 By thermionic emission is meant the emission by an incandescent filament of
A electrons.   **B** heat.   **C** ions.
D infrared radiation.   **E** light.   *(L)*

Q2 (a) What is meant by thermionic emission?
Explain with a circuit diagram the use of a thermionic diode to rectify alternating current.
(b) Explain how you would use a cathode ray oscillograph complete with the time base (i) to compare two d.c. potential differences, (ii) to demonstrate the variation with time of an alternating potential difference.
In each case sketch the result obtained.   *(JMB)*

Q3 Write down **four** properties of electron streams (cathode rays). With the aid of labelled diagrams, describe the construction and explain the action of a simple cathode ray tube. Briefly explain how you would use this simple cathode ray tube, complete with time base, to demonstrate the variation of an alternating voltage with time.
Sketch the kind of trace you would expect to observe on the screen.   *(W)*

Q4 (a) Sketch the layout of the following components in a cathode ray oscilloscope and label them: (i) evacuated envelope, (ii) heated cathode, (iii) accelerating anode, (iv) X deflection plates, (v) Y deflection plates, (vi) screen.
(b) The time base of a cathode ray oscilloscope makes the spot move across the screen horizontally at a constant speed and fly back again repeatedly.
(i) Give two reasons for making the spot move in such a way.
(ii) Explain, without including details of the circuits required, how this motion of the spot is achieved.
(c) How may the brightness of the trace on the screen of a cathode ray oscilloscope be increased?
(d) Sketch the appearance of the trace on the screen of a cathode ray oscilloscope when a sinusoidally alternating p.d. of frequency 1 kHz is applied to the Y plates and the time base is (i) switched off, (ii) switched on with a time sweep of one millisecond.   *(O & C)*

Q5

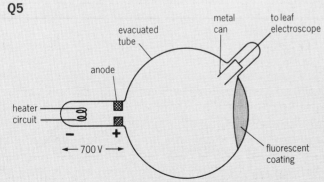

Assuming that the particles produced in the tube shown are negatively charged, describe where you would place a magnet in order to deflect them into the metal can, which is connected to the cap of a leaf electroscope.

State what you would observe from when the magnet was first used, and describe briefly a final check that could be made to show that the charge was negative.
(L part question)

Q6

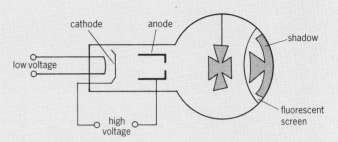

The diagram shows a simple form of cathode ray tube (known as a Maltese–Cross tube) which produces a sharp shadow of a cross on a fluorescent screen.
(a) Explain what is meant by cathode rays and how they are produced.
(b) State the properties of cathode rays, mentioning similarities and differences compared with light.
(c) Draw a diagram to show how two plane circular coils carrying current (Helmholtz coils) could be used to deflect the shadow on the screen downwards. By means of labels on your diagrams, or otherwise, explain how the deflection is produced.   *(O part question)*

Q7 (a) Three components of a simple cathode-ray tube are a tungsten resistance wire, R, a cylinder, S, and a pair of parallel plates, T and U.
(i) State two other important features of the tube if it is to be capable of detecting a beam of cathode rays.
(ii) Draw a labelled sketch showing clearly the position of each component in the tube.
Explain carefully
(iii) why tungsten is a good material for R,
(iv) what you would do and observe when using the plates T and U to determine the sign of the charge on the particles emitted by R,
(v) whether you would expect any difference in what you would observe in (iv) if R were replaced by resistance wire of a metal other than tungsten,
(vi) why S is maintained at a high positive potential relative to R.
(b) The cylinder S is removed and R is replaced by a radioactive source, X, which emits a parallel beam of alpha and beta particles. Explain carefully
(vii) what you would expect to observe when using T and U to determine the sign of the charge on the particles emitted by X,
(viii) the difference in the origin of these particles and those emitted in the simple cathode ray tube in (a).   *(L)*

32 Semiconductors, diodes, transistors and operational amplifers

32.1 Semiconductors

In electrical terms, the difference between a metal and a non-metal is that the metal can conduct electricity, i.e. allow electrons to 'drift' through its structure. The metals (shown on the left-hand side of the 'part' Periodic Table in Fig. 32.1) all conduct electricity (and incidentally, also heat) very well. They do this because the electrons in their outer shell (the **valence shell**) leave the atom and 'wander' freely through the lattice structure of the atoms. When a potential difference (or a temperature gradient) is applied to the metal innumerable electrons are freed from their atoms and are available to conduct electricity (or heat energy). The non-metals (or non-conductors) are shown on the right-hand side of the Periodic Table in Fig. 32.1. They are usually discrete molecules without loosely held electrons and, consequently, they do not conduct electricity (or heat). Not all elements can be classed easily as metal (conductor) or non-metal (insulator). There are a number of elements with metal-like lattices in which the electrons are not totally free to wander. These elements are called **metalloids** and come between the elements that are obviously metals and those that are obviously non-metals. They are shaded in Fig. 32.1. Of these, silicon (Si) and germanium (Ge) are useful as semiconductors because their metalloid character is most prevalent at room temperatures.

As the name implies, a **semiconductor** has some electrons in its lattice (it *must* be a solid) that are more tightly held than in a metal, but less tightly than in a non-metal. Raising the temperature of a

3 Li 6.94	4 Be 9.01	5 B 10.81	6 C 12.01	7 N 14.0	8 O 16.0	9 F 19.0	10 Ne 20.18
11 Na 22.99	12 Mg 24.31	13 Al 26.98	14 Si 28.09	15 P 30.97	16 S 32.06	17 Cl 35.45	18 Ar 39.95
19 K 39.10	20 Ca 40.08	31 Ga 69.72	32 Ge 72.6	33 As 74.92	34 Se 79.0	35 Br 79.9	36 Kr 83.8
37 Rb 85.47	38 Sr 87.62	49 In 114.82	50 Sn 118.7	51 Sb 121.8	52 Te 127.6	53 I 126.9	54 Xe 131.3
55 Cs 132.91	56 Ba 137.3	81 Tl 204.4	82 Pb 207.2	83 Bi 208.98	84 Po 209	85 At 210	86 Rn 222

32.1 Simplified Periodic Table

semiconductor causes these electrons to shake loose and thus the ability of a semiconductor to conduct increases with temperature. When cold, semiconductors have no free electrons to act as charge carriers, but at room temperature a few electrons are freed by thermal agitation and hence slight conduction of electricity can occur.

An atom of silicon consists of a nucleus containing fourteen protons and fourteen neutrons surrounded by a cloud of fourteen electrons. The fourteen electrons are imagined to be distributed in three shells containing two, eight and four electrons respectively (Fig. 32.2a). The stability of an element depends on the

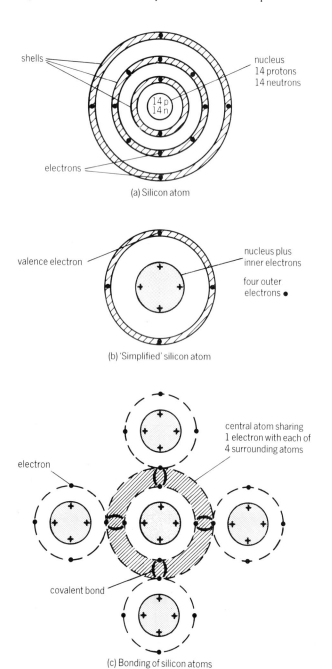

(a) Silicon atom

(b) 'Simplified' silicon atom

(c) Bonding of silicon atoms

32.2   The silicon atom and covalent bonding

number of electrons in the outer shell; the most stable structures have eight outer electrons. Silicon has four outer electrons in its valence shell (Fig. 32.2b). This atom should gain (or more correctly share) four electrons in its outer shell to reach the next most stable structure. Figure 32.2(c) shows a simplified atom of silicon surrounded by four other atoms. Each of the four surrounding atoms shares one electron with the central atom, which thus appears to have a stable outer shell of eight electrons. Each of the four original electrons forms what is called a **covalent bond** with one electron from a surrounding atom. Therefore, pure silicon has all the outer, valence electrons in its atoms linked by covalent bonds; there are no free electrons and so pure silicon is a good insulator. However, a slight rise in temperature 'breaks' some of the bonds, by increasing the kinetic energy of the electrons until they have sufficient energy to break loose. These electrons are free to move and hence constitute an electric current.

p-type and n-type material

Another way of increasing the conductivity of silicon is to add minute but carefully controlled amounts (e.g. 1 part per 10^{12}) of an impurity. This is called **doping** and the nature of the doping element determines whether the silicon becomes **p-type** (positive type) or **n-type** (negative type). Elements which have **three** valence electrons in the outer shells of their atoms, e.g. aluminium, boron, gallium or indium, give p-type properties to the silicon. These atoms, which do not give an electron to a covalent bond, are known as **acceptor atoms**. The acceptor atom shown in Fig. 32.3(a) has seven electrons in its outer shells. If the gap or 'hole' is filled by one electron the structure of the shell becomes stable. This positive 'hole' readily accepts electrons which may be moving in the silicon. However, the electrons move from atom to atom, and an electron which moves into the 'hole' must leave a 'hole' in the atom it has come from. Therefore the positive 'hole' *appears* to move through the material in the opposite direction to the electron movement.

Note   Although *the positive 'hole' does not really exist* it is a useful model at this level. It is analogous to a row of ten chairs being occupied by nine children, leaving one empty chair at, say, the right-hand end. If the child next to the empty chair moves to fill it, the empty chair *appears* to move one place to the left. If now each child in turn moves to the right to fill the empty chair, the empty chair will finally appear at the extreme left of the row. In this analogy the children represent electrons and the empty chair represents the 'hole'.

Elements which have five electrons in the outer shells of their atoms, e.g. phosphorus, arsenic or antimony, give n-type properties to the silicon. These

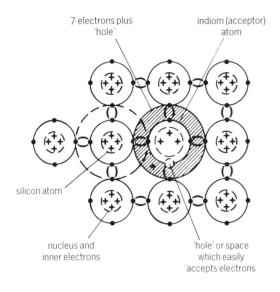

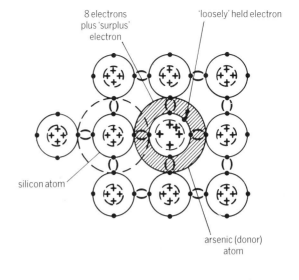

7 electrons plus 'hole'

indiom (acceptor) atom

silicon atom

nucleus and inner electrons

'hole' or space which easily accepts electrons

8 electrons plus 'surplus' electron

'loosely' held electron

silicon atom

arsenic (donor) atom

(a) p-type

(b) n-type

32.3   p-type and n-type silicon

atoms are called **donor atoms**, and each forms covalent bonds with *four* surrounding atoms of silicon. One of the donor atom's outer electrons is held very loosely by the protons in the nucleus (Fig. 32.3b). This electron can easily be detached by thermal energy or by a small potential difference applied to the silicon.

The atoms of the impurity increase the conductivity of the silicon by providing a majority of positive charge carriers ('holes') in the p-type silicon and a majority of negative charge carriers (electrons) in the n-type silicon. It must be stressed that **both p-type and n-type silicon are electrically neutral**. Each atom of silicon or impurity has an equal number of electrons and protons and hence is electrically neutral. However, the 'doped' material has the ability to accept electrons easily from certain surrounding atoms or to release electrons easily to the atoms of the semiconductor.

Note A common *mistake* is to refer to p-type material as being 'positively charged' and n-type material as being 'negatively charged'.

32.2   Semiconductor diodes

The p–n junction

A **p–n junction** consists of a piece of p-type silicon and a piece of n-type silicon 'joined' together and acts as a **rectifier**, i.e. allows current to flow in one direction only. The junction is formed by processing a single crystal of silicon so that there is an abrupt change in doping from acceptor to donor type at some plane surface within the crystal. When the junction is formed, electrons from the n-type region move across

the junction to fill some of the 'holes' in the p-type region. This makes the p-type silicon negatively charged and leaves a net positive charge on the n-type silicon (Fig. 32.4a, overleaf). This charge movement takes place only in the immediate vicinity of the junction and the mechanism is analogous to gaseous diffusion (p.18), i.e. a flow from a region of high concentration to one of low concentration. It is also analogous to contact potential when two dissimilar metals are joined (p.162). At the same time, 'holes' from the p-type region appear to move across the junction to the n-type region where they are filled by some electrons, producing a net positive charge in the n-type region and leaving a net negative charge in the p-type region (see Fig. 32.4a).

Figure 32.4(b) shows the build-up of negative and positive charges on opposite sides of the boundary in the region known as the **depletion layer**. The depletion layer is a very narrow region which has lost all its available free electrons and 'holes' (all 'holes' have been filled by an electron) and thus behaves almost like pure silicon, i.e. with high resistivity. Any further movement of charges across the boundary in the depletion layer will be repelled by the charges in the layer. The layer of negative charge in the p-type region will prevent the majority charge carriers from the n-type region (the electrons) from crossing the boundary. Similarly, the positive charge 'layer' in the n-type region will prevent the majority charge carriers from the p-type region (the 'holes') from crossing the boundary in the opposite direction. Thus a potential difference, known as the **barrier potential** (of about 0.1 V), is set up in the depletion layer. In its normal state a p–n junction delivers no current since the charges are in equilibrium.

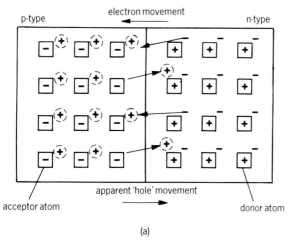

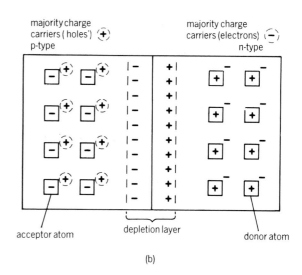

(a)

(b)

32.4   p–n junction

Using the p–n junction

The p–n junction can be operated in one of two modes, **reverse biased** or **forward biased**, depending on the direction in which the current flows. If an external applied voltage is connected to the p–n junction so that the positive of the cell is connected to the n-type region and the negative of the cell to the p-type region (as in Fig. 32.5), the applied voltage *increases* the barrier potential. Hence it is more difficult for the majority charge carriers from the p-type and n-type silicon ('holes' and electrons respectively) to cross the depletion layer and hence no current flows. This is a reverse-biased p–n junction. There is, however, a very small reverse current (the **intrinsic current**) of a few microamperes due to the intrinsic conductivity of the silicon, and this can be detected by a sensitive microammeter. The very small intrinsic current increases with temperature and reverse voltage for semiconductor diodes.

If an external voltage, greater than the barrier potential, is connected to the p–n junction such that the positive of the cell is connected to the p-type region and the negative to the n-type region (Fig. 32.6), the *internal* barrier potential is overcome and a 'forward' current can flow across the **forward-biased** p–n junction. Now the p-type region has a positive potential with respect to the n-type region and hence electrons flow across the depletion layer from the n-type region and 'holes' move to the n-type region, releasing a relatively 'large' forward current. This current swamps any intrinsic current, which is therefore ignored.

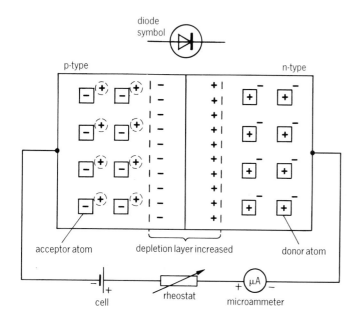

32.5   Reverse biased p–n junction

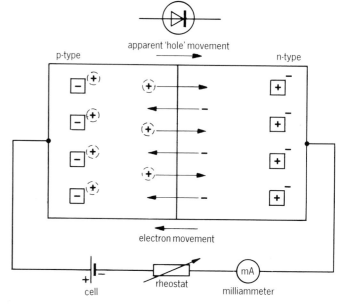

32.6   Forward biased p–n junction

Investigation 32.1 To determine the current/voltage characteristics of a semiconductor diode

Connect the circuit as shown in Fig. 32.7(a) so that the diode is forward biased, i.e. positioned for the easy flow of current. Switch on the supply and vary the potential difference V_F across the diode by using the rheostat as a potentiometer. Record several pairs of readings of forward current I_F and potential difference V_F using the milliammeter and voltmeter respectively.

To apply a reverse bias to the diode simply remove the diode from the circuit and replace it in the 'reverse' direction as indicated in Fig. 32.7(b). The milliammeter must be changed to a microammeter so that the very small intrinsic current readings

I_R can be measured as the potential difference V_R is varied. The readings can be recorded in a table of results similar to Table 32.1, and a graph of the readings drawn. A typical characteristic curve for a silicon diode is shown in Fig. 32.8.

Table 32.1 Table of results for investigation 32.1

Forward voltage V_F/V	Forward current I_F/mA	Reverse voltage V_R/V	Reverse current $I_R/\mu A$

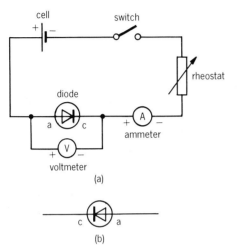

(a)

(b)

32.7 Semiconductor diode characteristics

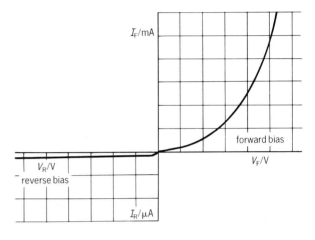

32.8 Characteristic curve for a silicon diode

Note A current flowing in the diode will cause a heating effect which will lead to a greater intrinsic current. This could, if not controlled, irreparably damage the diode.

Figure 32.9 shows what happens to a lamp when the diode is connected in series to a d.c. supply. In Fig. 32.9(a) the diode is forward biased and so it conducts and the lamp lights. In Fig. 32.9(b) it is reverse biased, does not conduct electricity, and so the lamp does not light. Figure 32.10 shows the rectification action of a diode when an **a.c.** supply is used.

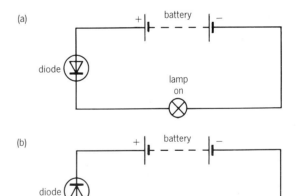

32.9 Effect of a diode in a d.c. circuit

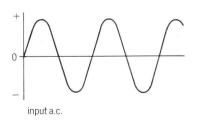

input a.c.

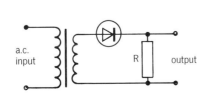

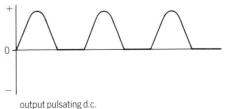

output pulsating d.c.

32.10 Half-wave rectification by a silicon diode

Semiconductor diodes are usually of the junction type or the point contact type. The point contact type are usually made of germanium while the junction type and most other diodes are made of silicon. A diode which is increasingly used for display purposes is the light-emitting diode (l.e.d.).

Bridge rectifier

Four diodes can be connected in a bridge network across the secondary coil of a transformer, as shown in Fig. 32.11. This gives **full-wave** rectification, i.e. pulsating d.c. output for either the positive or negative cycle of the input voltage. At any given time one pair of diodes conduct while the other pair does not. You should verify that if X is positive and Y is negative the pair of diodes D_2 and D_4 conduct, while diodes D_1 and D_3 conduct when the potential at X and Y is reversed. The current through R_L is the same in both cases.

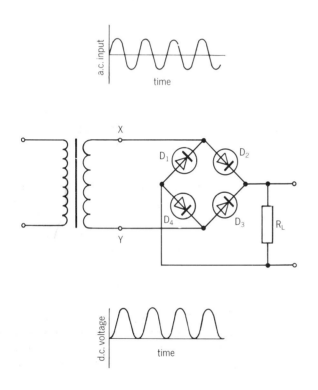

32.11   Bridge rectifier circuit

32.3   Transistors

The transistor is a very important device which is at the heart of all electronic circuits. It may be connected in the circuit as a separate device or in integrated form on a **chip**. There are two forms of transistor: the **junction (bipolar) transistor** and the **field effect transistor** (f.e.t.). In this text only the junction transistor will be considered.

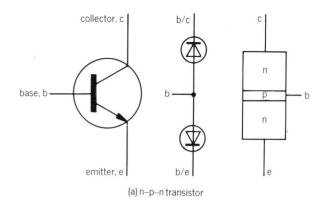

(a) n–p–n transistor

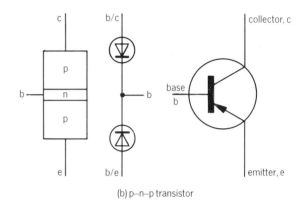

(b) p–n–p transistor

32.12   Transistor symbols

A junction transistor consists of two p–n junctions back to back. This 'sandwich' structure can have either p-type or n-type material as the 'filling' in the middle section, as shown in Fig. 32.12. This type of transistor has three connections called the emitter **e**, the base **b** and the collector **c**; the base is the 'filling' in the sandwich and is only a few microns thick. The arrow on the electrical circuit symbol on the emitter lead indicates the direction of flow of conventional current (i.e. of positive charges or 'holes'); of course, electrons flow in the opposite direction. Thus the arrow always points towards the n-type material. Figure 32.13 shows diagrams of the leads from a transistor.

To operate a transistor the base terminal must be connected so that one of the p–n junctions becomes forward biased, i.e. a potential is applied to it so that it conducts. The other p–n junction is reverse biased, i.e. it does not conduct (see Fig. 32.14). At the emitter/base junction the depletion layer is reduced because it is forward biased, while the depletion layer at the collector/base junction is increased. This results in a small base current I_b from base to emitter and a relatively much larger collector current I_c between the

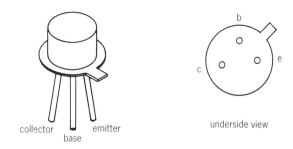

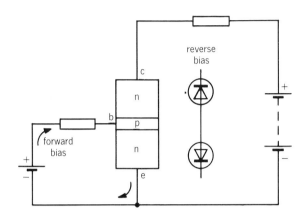

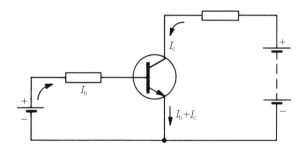

32.13   Transistor leads

32.14   Biasing a transistor

collector and the emitter. From Kirchhoff's First Law (p.297), it should be obvious that the emitter current $I_e = I_b + I_c$.

Exercise 32.1

Redraw Fig. 32.14 with a p–n–p transistor. State how the batteries are connected and how the current flows through the transistor.

The transistor as current amplifier

Although the two separate batteries in Fig. 32.14 bias each p–n junction correctly, this is not necessary.

Figure 32.15 shows an n–p–n transistor connected in the **common emitter mode** with a lamp L_1 in the collector/emitter circuit and a lamp L_2 with a resistor R (typically 1 kΩ) in the base/emitter circuit.

Note   The base connection of all transistors must be connected to the collector through a current-limiting resistor to protect the transistor from damage and ensure the correct potential at the base. The collector of an n–p–n transistor is connected to the positive of the battery while that of a p–n–p transistor would be connected to the negative of the battery.

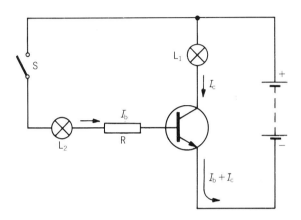

32.15   A n–p–n transistor in common emitter mode (the arrows show the direction of the conventional current)

When the switch S is closed the lamp L_1 lights up but L_2 does not light up. A small current *is* flowing through L_2 but it is too small to make the lamp glow. This can be demonstrated by unscrewing the lamp L_2—L_1 will immediately go out because there is a break in the base circuit. Replacing the lamp L_2 will 'switch on' a small base current I_b (say 0.5 mA) which, in turn, allows a larger collector current I_c (say 50 mA) to flow in the lamp L_1 which glows brightly. Small changes in the base current control 'large' changes in the collector current, and so the transistor acts as a current amplifier. Current gain h_{FE} is the ratio I_c/I_b; in the above example h_{FE} is 100.

The transistor as a switching device

A transistor can be used as a switching device. Anything which can 'switch on' a small base current to a transistor will release a larger collector current to operate a lamp, loudspeaker or relay. The relay could, in turn, operate a bell or a motor, etc. Transducers (devices for changing energy from one form to another) such as photocells, thermistors and microphones can be used to produce small electric currents from light, heat and sound respectively. The two methods of biasing the transistor, with a cell as in Fig. 32.14 or with a single resistor as in Fig. 32.15, are

369

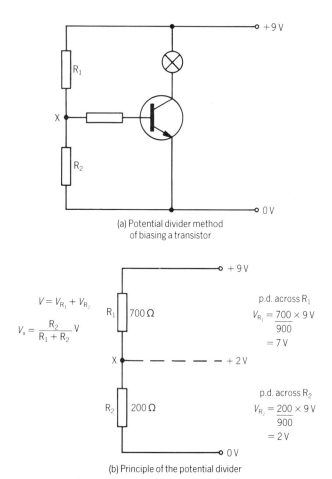

(a) Potential divider method
of biasing a transistor

$V = V_{R_1} + V_{R_2}$

$V_x = \dfrac{R_2}{R_1 + R_2} V$

R_1 | 700 Ω

X .... + 2 V

R_2 | 200 Ω

p.d. across R_1
$V_{R_1} = \dfrac{700 \times 9\,V}{900}$
$= 7\,V$

p.d. across R_2
$V_{R_2} = \dfrac{200 \times 9\,V}{900}$
$= 2\,V$

(b) Principle of the potential divider

32.16   The potential divider method of biasing a transistor

replaced in practical circuits by the potential divider method shown in Fig. 32.16(a). Here the two resistors are carefully chosen so that the correct bias voltage is applied to the base. By choosing suitable values for R_1 and R_2 the potential at X can be adjusted to switch on the transistor. A simple numerical example illustrating the principle of the potential divider is shown in Fig. 32.16(b).

Figure 32.17 shows simple circuits of a light-operated switch and a heat-operated switch. In Fig. 32.17(a) a light-dependent resistor (l.d.r.), e.g. an ORP 12, whose resistance varies with the intensity of illumination falling on it, replaces the resistor R_2 in the potential divider. The l.d.r's resistance varies from about 10 MΩ in total darkness to about 150 Ω in bright light. With the ORP 12 covered or in darkness the potential at the base terminal of the transistor is high enough for the transistor to conduct and hence light the lamp. When a light shines on the ORP 12 the potential at the base falls and the lamp is off. This circuit can be used to operate a parking light for a car so that it lights at dusk. If R_1 and ORP 12 are interchanged the circuit can operate as a burglar alarm triggered by light from a burglar's torch or when room lights are turned on. In both versions of this circuit the fixed resistor R_1 could be replaced by a variable

resistor (usually 10 kΩ or more) to enable the sensitivity of the circuit to be adjusted to varying conditions.

In the heat-operated-switch circuit (Fig. 32.17b), a thermistor replaces R_1 and a variable resistor is included at R_2. This circuit can be used as a simple fire alarm. When heat is applied to the thermistor its resistance falls, so switching on the transistor. This energises a relay coil which closes the contacts to ring a bell.

Note   A diode D must be connected across the relay

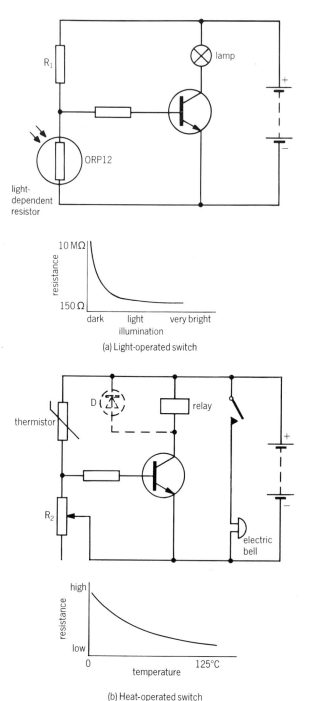

(a) Light-operated switch

(b) Heat-operated switch

32.17   Light- and heat-operated switches

coil, as shown, to protect the transistor from surges which occur when the transistor is turned off. The thermistor is of the type whose resistance decreases as the temperature increases (see the graph in Fig. 32.17b). Typical values of the change in resistance for thermistors over the temperature range 25 °C to 125 °C are 4 kΩ to 200 Ω, 1 kΩ to 36 Ω or even 380 Ω to 30 Ω, depending on which type is used. If the thermistor and the variable resistor are exchanged in the circuit the bell will ring when the temperature falls to a low predetermined value. The fire alarm has become a frost warning device which would be suitable as a sensor in a greenhouse to warn the gardener of the onset of frost.

A rain sensor (or moisture probe) can be made from two bare copper wires (or strips on a veroboard). The two wires (or strips) are separated by a small gap but if rain (or moisture) bridges the gap some conduction can take place. With the rain sensor at R_1 in the circuit in Fig. 32.16, the lamp will light when rain falls on it but will stay off when it is dry.

Time-delay circuit

If resistor R_2 in Fig. 32.16(a) is replaced by a capacitor the circuit will form a simple time-delay circuit, i.e. a time switch. Figure 32.18 shows a simple 'on/off' time-delay circuit. When the switch is in the off position a fully charged capacitor will discharge with time as shown in sketch graph (a). When the switch is in the 'on' position the voltage (potential) on the capacitor rises with time as shown in sketch graph (b). When the potential of the base reaches the required level the transistor is 'switched on' and the lamp lights.

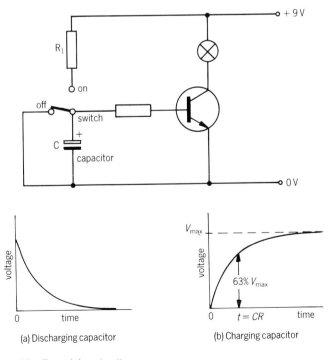

32.18   Time-delay circuit

Practical applications of this type of circuit would be in egg-timers and photographic timers. A timing device could be used to switch off a light after a preset time interval , say, after a person leaves a room. A time delay connected to a relay could close a door or a valve after a preset interval of time.

The time taken for the voltage of a capacitor to rise to 63% of its maximum voltage is known as the **time constant** (see Fig. 32.18b). The time constant t in second for a resistor and capacitor connected in series is given by $t = CR$ where C = capacitance in farad and R = resistance in ohm.

32.4   The transistor as an amplifier

Current amplification

An amplifier is a device that magnifies the input. Electronic amplifiers magnify small input signals and produce larger output signals. The input might be a current or a voltage. Earlier it was shown that a small base current I_b controls a much larger current I_c from collector to emitter through the transistor, and $I_e = I_c + I_b$. Since a small change in base current controls a larger change in current from the collector to the emitter, the transistor operates as a **current amplifier**. Also the d.c. current gain equals the ratio of the steady collector current to the steady base current $h_{FE} = I_c/I_b$.

The amplifying action of a transistor can be demonstrated using the circuit shown in Fig. 32.19. A variable resistor is used to vary the current into the base, and so the collector current also varies. Note the fixed resistor which prevents the base current from becoming large enough to damage the transistor. The changing values of base and collector currents show that a change in current is amplified by the transistor. For a transistor with changing direct currents, the current gain h_{FE} is defined as

$$h_{FE} = \frac{\text{change in collector current}}{\text{change in base current}} \quad \frac{\Delta I_c}{\Delta I_b}.$$

Typical figures for a BC 108 transistor could be that a change in base current from 10 μA to 60 μA produces

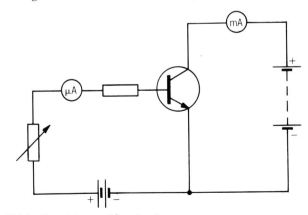

32.19   Transistor amplifier circuit

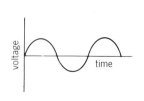 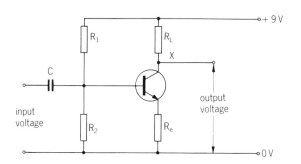 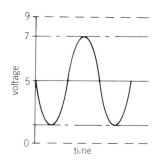

32.20 Voltage amplification

a change in collector current from 5 mA to 25 mA. The current gain

$$h_{FE} = \frac{\Delta I_c}{\Delta I_b}$$

$$= \frac{(25 - 5) \times 10^{-3} \; \cancel{A}}{(60 - 10) \times 10^{-6} \; \cancel{A}}$$

$$= 400$$

Note that both currents are in phase throughout the changes.

Voltage amplification

Amplifiers are normally used to provide voltage amplification rather than current amplification. Practical examples of the use of a transistor as a voltage amplifier are in an intercom (or baby alarm) and a radio. By inserting a **load resistor** in the collector lead of the transistor circuit, voltage amplification can be achieved. If a changing voltage is applied to the base of a transistor a changing base current is produced which will be amplified by the transistor. The amplified output current passing through the load resistor will produce a magnified changing output voltage. Using the different values of load resistor enables the magnitude of the output voltage to be varied.

A simple one-transistor amplifier is shown in Fig. 32.20. Two resistors R_1 and R_2 act as a potential divider to produce the correct bias for the base of the transistor. R_L is the load resistor across which the output voltage will be produced and the resistor R_e is used to give the correct bias for the emitter. The capacitor C has been added to the base circuit because it blocks d.c., i.e. the insulator between the two plates of the capacitor does not let direct current flow through it. However, a capacitor does allow a.c. voltages to 'pass' through it. Hence the capacitor C will allow an a.c. signal through the input while blocking any d.c. component of the signal which would affect the bias of the transistor. Capacitor C is known as a **coupling capacitor**. A small a.c. voltage fed to the base of the transistor via the coupling capacitor will be amplified at load resistor (output). Note that the magnified output voltage is inverted (180 ° out of phase) with respect to the input voltage. An increase in base current will cause an increase in the collector

current which in turn causes an increase in the *potential difference* across R_L. This results in a lowering of the potential at X. Therefore an increase in the input voltage V_i produces a decrease in the output voltage V_o. Voltage amplification is defined as the ratio of the change in output voltage to the change in input voltage, i.e. $\Delta V_0/\Delta V_2$.

Investigation 32.2   To make a simple radio receiver

Make a simple coil by winding about 100 turns of fine insulated copper wire onto a ferrite rod. Connect the coil to a 500 pF variable capacitor, and use a long piece of wire as an aerial. The receiver circuit is shown in Fig. 32.21(a). When the earphone is connected to AB you can 'tune in' local radio stations by varying the 500 pF tuning capacitor. A single-stage transistor amplifier, shown in Fig. 32.21(b), can be added to AB in place of the earphone so that the stations can be heard more clearly. Note that the first circuit has no power supply other than that carried by the radio waves.

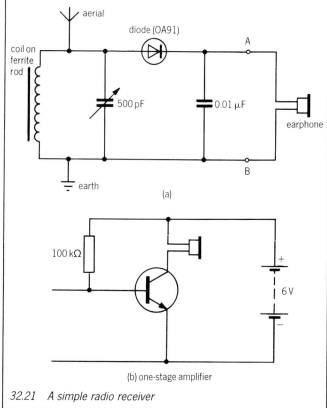

32.21   A simple radio receiver

32.5   The operational amplifier

An amplifier is a device which is used to increase the amplitude of a small alternating voltage without distortion. An **operational amplifier** operates as soon as it is connected, without another power supply. One form of operational amplifier (the 741 Op Amp) is shown in Fig. 32.22. The 741 Op Amp is an 8-pin dual-in-line (DIL) package and contains a silicon chip which has a complete linear amplifier circuit of about twenty transistors, eleven resistors and a capacitor. This section concentrates on what the circuit can do and how to use the device.

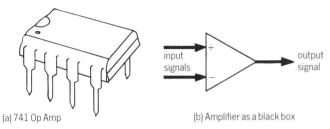

(a) 741 Op Amp   (b) Amplifier as a black box

32.22   Operational amplifier

The amplifier has two input terminals and an output terminal. Input signals to the operational amplifier are input voltages whilst the output signal is an output voltage (Fig. 32.23). The amplification operation is performed on the *difference* between the two input voltages, hence it is termed a **differential amplifier**.

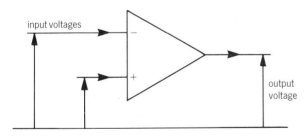

32.23   Amplifier inputs and outputs

The operational amplifier has one output terminal and two input terminals. The terminal for the **inverting input** is marked −, that for the **non-inverting input** is marked +, as shown in Fig. 32.24. A further terminal is connected to the positive polarity of the supply and another to the negative polarity of the supply.

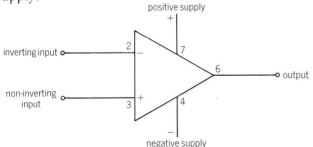

32.24   Circuit diagram symbol for an operational amplifier

There are eight terminals, or pins, numbered 1 to 8 in an anticlockwise direction starting with pin 1 nearest to the indentation or dot on the surface of the amplifier (Fig. 32.25). Supply voltages should not exceed +18 V on the positive rail and −18 V on the negative rail.

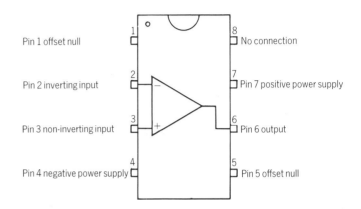

32.25   Pin connections for the 8-pin DIL 741 OP Amp

Voltage gain

The amplifying property is measured by the voltage gain of the amplifier, which is the ratio of the change in output voltage to the change in input voltage.

$$\text{voltage gain } A_v = \frac{\text{change in output voltage}}{\text{change in input voltage}} = \frac{\Delta V_{\text{out}}}{\Delta V_{\text{in}}}$$

When a 10 mV change in input voltage produces a 1 volt change in output voltage the voltage gain is 100.

$$\text{voltage gain } A_v = \frac{1.0 \ \cancel{V}}{0.01 \ \cancel{V}} = 100$$

When the change in output voltage is directly proportional to the change in input voltage the amplifier is called a **linear amplifier**. Ideally, the 741 Op Amp should give the graph shown in Fig. 32.26(a). However, in practice it is not quite linear, as shown in Fig. 32.26(b). When a certain input voltage is reached there will be no further rise in the output voltage; the amplifier is then said to be **saturated**.

When the 741 Op Amp is connected in a circuit without external feedback resistors, as shown in Fig. 32.27, the voltage gain is high, about 10 000, and is called the **open-loop gain**. The input and output voltages are measured with respect to the earth (or ground) rail. When both the inverting and non-inverting inputs are used it is the voltage difference $(V_2 - V_1)$ between the input terminals which is being

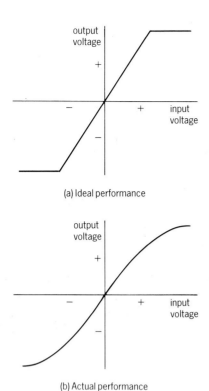

(a) Ideal performance

(b) Actual performance

32.26   Performance of the 741 Op Amp

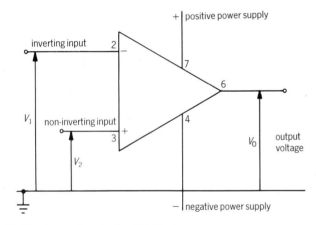

32.27   Connections to the 741 Op Amp

amplified and appears as an output voltage. Thus

$$A_v = \frac{V_{out}}{(V_2 - V_1)}$$

or $V_{out} = A_v(V_2 - V_1)$ where A_v is the open-loop gain. When operating like this the 741 Op Amp is said to be functioning as a **differential amplifier**.

Assuming the open-loop gain of a 741 Op Amp is 10 000, $V_2 = 5.1$ mV and $V_1 = 5$ mV, the output voltage V_{out} is given by

$$V_{out} = A_v(V_2 - V_1)$$
$$= 10\ 000 \times \frac{(5.1 - 5)}{1000}\ V$$
$$= 10 \times 0.1\ V$$
$$V_{out} = 1\ V$$

374

Used on open loop the 741 Op Amp is not very stable. By using a **feedback resistor** R_f (see Fig. 32.28), the overall voltage gain is reduced but it can be accurately controlled. A fraction of the output voltage is fed back through the resistor to the negative input terminal. This negative feedback modifies the voltage gain of the 741 Op Amp which is said to be operating on **closed-loop** amplification.

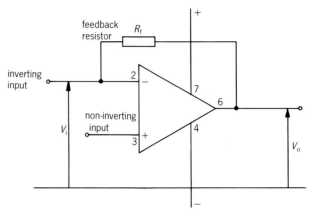

32.28   Feedback resistor

Connecting the non-inverting input terminal to earth, as in Fig. 32.29, and applying the input signal via R_{in} to the inverting input terminal gives a phase inversion. Thus an increasing positive voltage at the input becomes an increasing negative voltage at the output; hence pin 2 has a minus sign ($-$) against it.

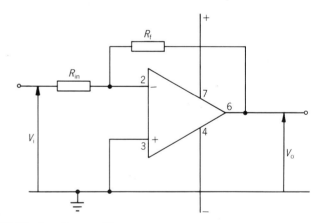

32.29   Inverting amplifier

When operating like this the 741 Op Amp is said to be functioning as an **inverting amplifier**. The voltage gain of an inverting amplifier is given by voltage gain $A_v = -R_f/R_{in}$, the minus sign indicating the phase inversion. If $R_f = 10$ kΩ and $R_{in} = 500$ Ω then the voltage gain A_v is given by

$$A_v = -\frac{10\ 000}{500}\ \frac{\Omega}{\Omega}$$
$$A_v = -20$$

This is an amplification of 20 with a phase inversion.

The 741 Op Amp requires two power supplies and

the amplification is limited by the power supplies. Common input and output voltages are measured with respect to the earth rail which is connected to the centre tapping of the power supply. Two 9 V batteries are shown in Fig. 32.30 and the maximum power supply that can be used is $\pm$ 18 V. If $R_f = 10\ \text{k}\Omega$ and $R_{in} = 1\ \text{k}\Omega$ then $A_v = V_{out}/V_{in} = - R_f/R_{in} = - 10$.

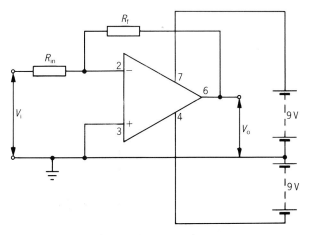

32.30   Inverting amplifier with power supplies

Investigation 32.3   To discover the amplification of an inverting amplifier

Connect a signal generator set at a suitable frequency and a double beam oscilloscope to the 741 Op Amp as shown in Fig. 32.31. This will display the input and output voltages. Measure the amplitude of the input and output voltages to show that the output is 10 times the input and the phase is inverted. If you investigate the voltage gain for different frequencies you will find that the gain depends on the frequency.

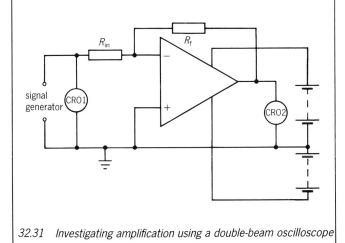

32.31   Investigating amplification using a double-beam oscilloscope

---

If the inverting input terminal of the 741 Op Amp is connected to earth and the input signal is applied to the non-inverting input (Fig. 32.32), the output signal is in phase with the input signal, i.e. an increasing positive voltage at the input appears as a magnified increasing positive voltage at the output.

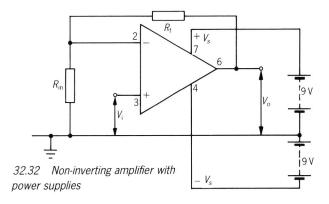

32.32   Non-inverting amplifier with power supplies

Investigation 32.4   To measure small e.m.f.s using an amplifier

When a thermocouple of copper and constantan is heated at one junction while the other junction is in ice, thermoelectric e.m.f.s in the range 2–10 mV are produced. Connect the thermocouple to the input as shown in Fig. 32.33. When $R_f = 100\ \text{k}\Omega$ and $R_{in} = 1\ \text{k}\Omega$ the voltage gain $A_v = R_f/R_{in} = 100\ \text{k}\Omega/1\ \text{k}\Omega = 100$.

Thus a 1 V voltmeter connected to the output will register the millivolt e.m.f.s of the thermocouple as 0.2–1.0 V. Take readings of thermoelectric e.m.f.s for different temperatures and plot a graph of thermoelectric e.m.f. against temperature to show the non-linear relationship.

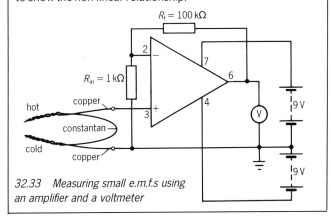

32.33   Measuring small e.m.f.s using an amplifier and a voltmeter

32.6   Digital systems

Digital electronics has had a great impact on society — it has given rise to calculators, digital watches and, most importantly, microcomputers. A digital system is concerned only with the presence (high or 1) or absence (low or 0) of a voltage or p.d. Since only two levels are used (1 and 0) the system is called a **binary system**. The simple switch used to turn on a room light is an example of a 'digital system' because the switch is either on or off; the voltage across the bulb is either high (light is on) or low (light is off).

Switching and logic

It is possible to deal with switching and logic circuits, the basis of electronics, without using the specific transistor circuits given earlier in this chapter. Certain principles apply regardless of the individual components that are used in a circuit, e.g. the principle of the potential divider (see page 370). Most electronic circuits operate on a low voltage supply (often 5 V). An output voltage of either 5 V (logical 1) or 0 V (logical 0) can be obtained when R_2, a resistor in Fig. 32.16, is replaced with a 'switch' or device which has an effective resistance of infinity (open) or zero (closed). Since logic circuits operate on 5 V (TTL chips) or 3–15 V (CMOS chips) and deliver only small currents (mA) the filament lamps used in the transistor circuits will be of no use as an indicator lamp. What is required is an indicator light which operates on low current (at low voltage). The **light emitting diode** (l.e.d.) is just such an output transducer which converts electrical energy into light energy. The l.e.d. needs a current-limiting resistor connected in series just as the base connection of a transistor needed a current-limiting resistor to protect it from damage (see page 369).

Note the symbol for the l.e.d. in Fig. 32.34 and that the current (conventional) flows in the foward biased condition from the anode to the cathode (from left to right in the diagram).

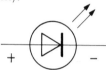

32.34 L.e.d. symbol

Example

The voltage drop across a lit l.e.d. is 2 V and the current through it should be limited to 20 mA (Fig. 32.35). Calculate the value of the limiting resistor R placed in series with the l.e.d.

$V = (5 - 2)\,V \quad I = 0.02\,A \quad R = ?\,\Omega$

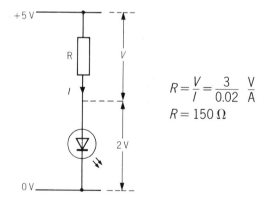

$$R = \frac{V}{I} = \frac{3}{0.02}\;\frac{V}{A}$$
$$R = 150\,\Omega$$

32.35 Limiting resistor for l.e.d.

If the supply voltage through the l.e.d. in Fig. 32.35 is changed to 9 V, show that the protective resistor must now be 350 Ω.

L.e.d.s emit coloured light, e.g. red, green or yellow. The maker's instructions give the 'safe' values of the voltage V_f (5 V, 2 V or 1.4 V) and the current I_f (40 mA, 20 mA or 10 mA) to be used. If you know this information and the value of the supply voltage, you should be able to work out the appropriate limiting resistor. (It is often about 200 Ω.)

Exercise

An l.e.d. with a specification $V_f = 3$ V and $I_f = 15$ mA is to be used on a 6 V supply. What value of limiting resistor must be used?

Seven-segment display Many watches and calculators use seven l.e.d.s arranged so that any number from 0 to 9 can be formed when the correct combination of l.e.d.s is lit. Seven switches, plus one for the decimal point (d.p.), are shown in the model circuit in Fig. 32.36. Note the protective resistor in series with each l.e.d.

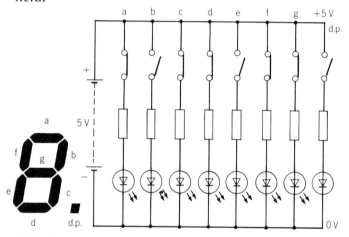

32.36 Seven-segment display

What number is formed when switches a, c, d, f and g are closed and switches b and e are open?

Switches

In electronics, switching can be done by using rocker switches, push switches, reed switches, relays and even by using transistors as switches. **Reed switches** contain two or three iron strips (reeds) inside a sealed glass tube. They are operated by a permanent magnet or an electromagnet. As in the case of a relay (see page 328), the contacts may be normally open (NO), normally closed (NC) or operate as a change-over (CO) switch. A burglar alarm can be made with a reed switch buried in the frame of a door or window and a magnet buried in the top of the door or window directly beneath it. When the door or window is opened the magnet which has been holding the NC contacts open moves away, allowing the contacts to close and set off the alarm bell.

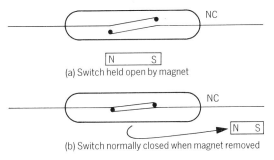

(a) Switch held open by magnet

(b) Switch normally closed when magnet removed

32.37 Reed switch and magnet

Relays are used to interface (join) a low voltage (safe) supply and a 'high' voltage (dangerous) supply. A small voltage (say 5 V) applied to the coil of a relay can switch on or off another circuit without any direct electrical connection between them. A small current flowing in the coil is enough to magnetize it so that it operates the contacts. For example, the small current in the transistor switch, shown in Fig. 32.17(b), controls the relay (NO) which switches on a larger current to the bell. A small current through the ignition switch of a car operates a relay which sends a very large current to the starter motor. In this sense the relay acts as a mechanical current amplifier. A low voltage relay could be used to operate a 240 V motor as shown in Fig. 32.38.

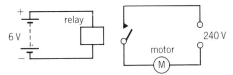

32.38 A relay as a current amplifier

Relays are often used to interface low voltage integrated circuits (ICs) with mains-operated devices.

Logic circuits

Digital electronics is based on the use of **logic circuits**. These are the circuits used to add, subtract, multiply and divide in calculators and computers although there are many other applications. The **'switch'** is the basic building block of all logic circuits. It is the combination of 'switches' which produces the many different functions that digital electronics circuits can perform.

To understand the systems approach to digital electronics, start by looking at some simple switching circuits. The 'switch' and the l.e.d. shown in Fig. 32.39 is a system which works according to a set pattern; simply close the switch and the l.e.d. lights, open the switch and the l.e.d. goes off. Any of the 'switches' mentioned earlier will do instead of the switch shown in the diagram. Here a 'switch' means any device which puts a low voltage (p.d.) of 0 V across the output (l.e.d. and resistor), in which case the l.e.d. does not light; or it puts a high voltage (p.d.) of 5 V across the output, in which case the l.e.d. lights.

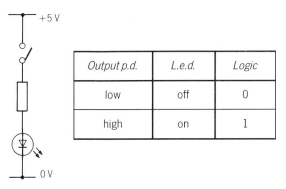

Output p.d.	L.e.d.	Logic
low	off	0
high	on	1

32.39 A simple digital system

The switch is simply open or closed; the l.e.d. is either off or on. The voltage is either low (think of this as 0) or high (think of this as 1); the voltage is either 0 V or 5 V and never has any value in between. Hence the output of the system can be described as either logic 1 (high voltage, l.e.d. on) or logic 0 (low voltage, l.e.d. off). The table alongside the circuit in Fig. 32.39 shows this information very simply. Since the system uses the digits 0 and 1 as its logic symbols it is known as a **digital** system. Since it uses only two digits it is also called a **binary** system.

Two-state systems

Figure 32.40 shows two push switches (remember — any type of switch will do) in series with an l.e.d. and its protective resistor. The switches A and B are **inputs** of the system and each can have only one of two states: either open or closed. The **output** of the system, the l.e.d., also has only two possible states: either on or off. Now there are four combinations of the input (shown in the table in Fig. 32.40) but only one of these lights the l.e.d., i.e. when both switches are closed.

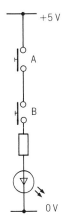

	Switch		Lamp
	A	B	
	open	open	off
	open	closed	off
	closed	open	off
	closed	closed	on

32.40 Two-state system

In the system shown in Fig. 32.41, the l.e.d. will light only when the output potential at Q is 9 V and so the p.d. across the led. and resistor is $(9 - 0) = 9$ V. Again both 'switches' A and B must be closed to provide the 'high' potential to light the l.e.d.

377

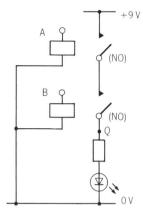

32.41 Two-state relay system

The relay coils A and B will only operate properly, i.e. close the contacts, when the p.d. across them is 'high', e.g. 5 V for a small relay. In electronics it is standard convention to refer all potentials to the 0 V supply rail. When the relay is +5 V with respect to the 0 V supply rail the coil will energize sufficiently to close the contacts. If the input potential to either A or B is less than 5 V then the contacts will not close and the output at Q will remain at 0 V. In this case a potential above 5 V is defined as logic 1 (high) and one below 5 V as logic 0 (low). The overall behaviour of the circuit or system can be described as:

Q is 1 when A **AND** B are both 1; otherwise Q is 0.

The system acts as a **logic gate,** in this case a combination of switches whose output is considered 'on' when the output voltage is high (1) and 'off' when the output voltage is low (0). Such an arrangement is called a gate because only under certain conditions does the output 'open up' like a gate to let the signal flow through. Instead of writing open, closed, on or off as before, the four combinations can be shown in a **truth table** using logic symbols, as shown in Table 32.2.

A truth table describes all the possible combinations of inputs and the corresponding output decisions for a particular logic gate or combination of gates. It shows how an electrically controlled circuit can 'make decisions'. The state of the inputs to the circuit decides what the output will be. Any system which has the truth table shown in Table 32.2 is known as an AND gate. AND gates can be constructed using push switches, reed switches, relays or transistors; or they can be bought as a logic chip or integrated circuits (ICs). A number of other important gates (two-state systems which process signals according to certain combinations of inputs) can be bought mounted on circuit boards which can be linked together to build electronic circuits. Knowledge of the construction of IC logic gates is not required; however, you should know how each gate performs as shown by its truth table and how the gates can be used as 'building blocks' in a circuit.

The three basic logic gates are the AND gate, the OR gate and the NOT gate. Any other logic system can be built from these three logic gates. The symbol and truth table for each gate should be learnt.

AND gate This gate gives an output high, logic 1, when the input A AND the input B are both high (see Fig. 32.42). Logic level 0 is usually interpreted as being at 0 V while logic level 1 is at the positive rail voltage of about 5 V. (TTL logic chips operate on a stabilized 5 V d.c. supply.)

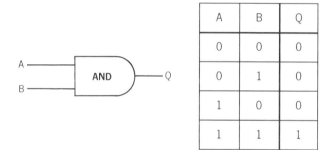

A	B	Q
0	0	0
0	1	0
1	0	0
1	1	1

32.42 *Symbol and truth table for* **AND** *gate*

Ideally, logic 1 is 5 V and logic 0 is 0 V with no values in between. In practice for IC logic gates, any voltage between 2 V and 5 V will be logic 1 and any voltage between 0.8 V and 0 V acts as logic 0. Note that the symbol for an AND gate does not need the word AND written in it but in this chapter the name of the gate will be added to help the reader.

OR gate This can be regarded as two 'switches' A and B connected in parallel (Fig. 32.43). If either A OR B OR both switches are closed the l.e.d. will light. This gate gives an output high, logic 1, when one or other of the inputs is high (1) or when both inputs are high (1).

NOT gate This gate can be illustrated using a relay with normally closed contacts (Fig. 32.44). When the input voltage is low, the l.e.d. lights. When the input voltage is high the contacts open and the l.e.d. goes off. A NOT gate acts as an **inverter**, that is, it changes a low (0) input into a high (1) output and vice-versa.

Table 32.2   Truth table for AND gate

Inputs		Output
A	B	Q
0	0	0
0	1	0
1	0	0
1	1	1

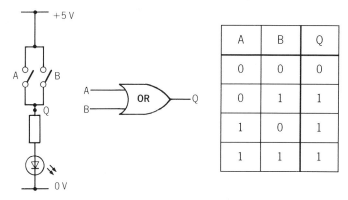

32.43 *Circuit, symbol and truth table for* **OR** *gate*

A	B	Q
0	0	0
0	1	1
1	0	1
1	1	1

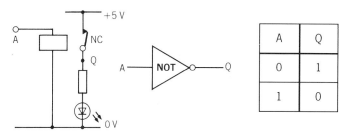

32.44 *Circuit, symbol and truth table for* **NOT** *gate*

A	Q
0	1
1	0

Example: Analysis of a logic system

Find the logical output Q in the systems shown in Fig. 32.45.

First the intermediate inputs C and D need to be worked out and applied as the inputs to the **OR** gate. The truth table for the system shown in Fig. 32.45(a) has been completed. (The reader can complete the table for the system shown in Fig. 32.45(b).

The output at C is an inverted version of the input; 1 replaces 0 and 0 replaces 1 in column C. The output D obeys the truth table for an AND gate; D is only 1 when both A AND B are 1; otherwise D is 0. The inputs C and D to the **OR** gate control the output Q which is high (1) when either C OR D is high (1) or both are high (1).

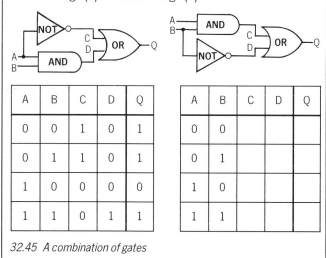

A	B	C	D	Q
0	0	1	0	1
0	1	1	0	1
1	0	0	0	0
1	1	0	1	1

A	B	C	D	Q
0	0			
0	1			
1	0			
1	1			

32.45 *A combination of gates*

Two further gates need to be studied; the NAND gate and the NOR gate.

NAND gate The NAND gate (or AND–NOT gate) has an output high, logic 1, when input A AND input B are NOT both high (see Fig. 32.46). It can be shown (see Fig. 32.47) that the NAND gate behaves like an AND gate linked to a NOT gate. The output of a NAND gate is the inverted output of an AND gate.

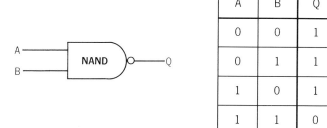

A	B	Q
0	0	1
0	1	1
1	0	1
1	1	0

32.46 *Symbol and truth table for* **NAND** *gate*

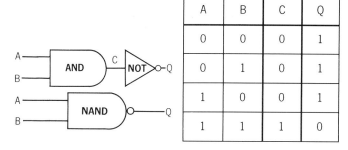

A	B	C	Q
0	0	0	1
0	1	0	1
1	0	0	1
1	1	1	0

32.47 **NAND** *gate =* **AND–NOT** *gates*

NOR gate The NOR gate (or OR–NOT gate) has an output high, logic 1, when neither input A NOR input B is high (Fig. 32.48).

Note how the small circle at the output end of a gate symbol denotes the inverting or **NOT** symbol.

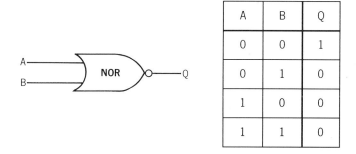

A	B	Q
0	0	1
0	1	0
1	0	0
1	1	0

32.48 *Symbol and truth table for* **NOR** *gate*

Exercise

By drawing the truth table show that an OR gate linked to a NOT gate is equivalent to a NOR gate.

Electronic modular boards can be bought which link together to form a required circuit. The electronic components are mounted on small boxes and a typical set includes: power connection unit, input voltage unit, light-sensing unit, switch unit, rain-sensing unit, sound-sensing unit, temperature-sensing unit, magnetic switch unit, bulb unit, buzzer unit, relay switch unit, solenoid unit, motor unit, AND gate, NAND gate, OR gate, NOR gate, inverting amplifier, non-inverting amplifier, difference amplifier, comparator, summer, transistor switch, transducer driver, inverter, latch, pulse generator and counter display unit. The method of linking such boards together is shown in Fig. 32.49 where the boards are arranged to test the truth table for an **AND** gate.

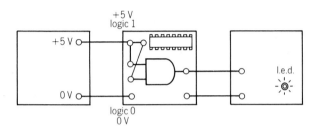

32.49 Connecting logic boards

Exercise

Explain why the l.e.d. in the circuit in Fig. 32.50 only glows when the thermistor has a very low value of resistance.

  What is the purpose of the resistor R? Calculate the value of R assuming the output voltage of the **NOR** gate is 9 V. The maker's recommended current and p.d. are $I_f = 20\,mA$, $V_f = 1.4\,V$.

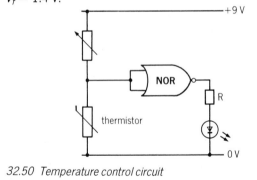

32.50 Temperature control circuit

Note that the **NOR** gate connected as shown in Fig. 32.50 behaves as a **NOT** gate.

A light-dependant resistor (l.d.r.) is an input transducer which converts light energy into electrical energy when placed in a potential divider (see p. 370). If an l.d.r. is part of a potential divider network, the variations in resistance will result in a variation in potential which can be used as a logic signal.

If the l.d.r. has a resistance of 2 kΩ then there is a 3 V p.d. across both the resistor and the l.d.r. When the l.d.r. is in the dark its resistance is very high (MΩ) so the potential at A (input to **NOT** gate) is well above 3 V (high or logic 1) and the output is logic 0; hence the l.e.d. is off. When a bright light shines on the l.d.r.

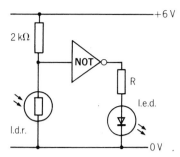

32.51 Light control circuit

its resistance is very low (100 Ω) and so the potential at A is well below 3 V or logic 0, and the output from the NOT gate is logic 1; hence the l.e.d. glows. If a logic gate is required to do more than make an l.e.d. glow then a relay can be used as a power amplifier as stated on page 300.

Exercise

Describe the operation of the circuit in Fig. 32.51 when the 2 kΩ resistor and the l.d.r. are interchanged.

The circuit in Fig. 32.52 shows how a d.c. motor can be controlled by logic gates so that its rotation, forward or reverse, can be altered.

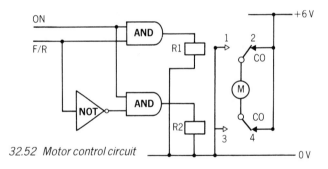

32.52 Motor control circuit

When the ON/OFF input is logic 1, the relay R2 causes the contacts to change over (4 to 3), hence the motor rotates. When the FORWARD/REVERSE input is logic 1 the relay R1 changes the contacts from 2 to 1 while the contacts at R2 change from 3 to 4. This reverses the current through the motor, hence its direction of rotation is reversed.

The bistable latch A pair of cross-coupled NAND gates form a **bistable latch**, as shown in Fig. 32.53. (This may also be called a flip-flop.) If A and B are both logic 1 the outputs at both Q and $\overline{Q}$ are logic 1 and the bistable holds its state. If A is changed to logic 0 (B remaining 1) the output 'flips' over, i.e. Q is 1; $\overline{Q}$ is 0.

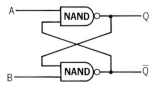

32.53 Bistable latch

The outputs do not change when A is returned to logic 1. If B is then changed to logic 0, the output 'flops' back to give Q at 0 and $\overline{Q}$ as 1. Returning B to logic 1 has no effect. The circuit remains latched in one of its two stable states (hence the term bistable) depending on which of the inputs A or B was last at a low voltage, logic 0. The bistable forms the basis of memory circuits which with additional logic can be used in binary counters.

A model set of traffic-lights with a pair of red and green lights only can be constructed using a bistable or flip-flop as shown in Fig. 32.54. Starting with the green light on and the red light off, momentarily press the switch S1. The green light goes off and the red light comes on. Flick the switch S2; the green light comes on and the red light goes off. The switches could be pressure switches, reed switches or electronically controlled time-delay switches which operate in a given time interval and sequence. This and other circuits can be adapted for use as a burglar alarm.

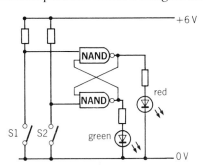

32.54 Model traffic lights

Example

Three NAND gates connnected as shown in Fig. 32.55 act as an OR gate.

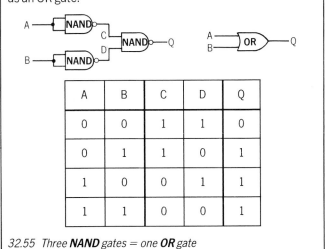

A	B	C	D	Q
0	0	1	1	0
0	1	1	0	1
1	0	0	1	1
1	1	0	0	1

32.55 Three **NAND** gates = one **OR** gate

Exercise

If a fourth NAND gate is added to Q (with second input E), show that the resultant gate is a NOR gate.

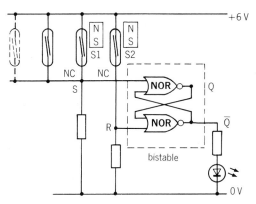

32.56 Burglar alarm

A pair of cross-coupled NOR gates can also behave as a bistable latch as in the burglar alarm circuit in Fig. 32.56. When S and R are both logic 0 and ouputs Q and $\overline{Q}$ are 1 and 0 respectively. When S goes from logic 1 to logic 0 the bistable changes over to give Q as 0 and $\overline{Q}$ as 1. Returning S to logic 0 has no effect on Q or $\overline{Q}$. When R changes from logic 1 to logic 0 the bistable changes over again to give Q as 1 and $\overline{Q}$ as 0. Returning R to logic 0 has no effect on Q and $\overline{Q}$. Switch S2 is the reset switch because it allows R to go high, logic 1. Switch S1 controls the input at S (0 V or 6 V). When S goes logic 1, even temporarily, the l.e.d. remains lit, i.e. even when S1 opens. The l.e.d. can only be switched off by the reset switch S2, i.e. when R is momentarily raised to 6 V (logic 1). If a sound output is required the relay circuit shown in Fig. 32.57 should be connected between $\overline{Q}$ and the 0 V rail. The bistable 'seems' to be able to 'remember' which input was connected to +6 V, logic 1. It is called bistable because it is stable in either of two states and it is 'latched' because it stays in the state in which it was last put. The series of switches to the left of S can be placed in doors and windows and each will operate the alarm.

Light operated alarm A two-way switch enables the circuit in Fig. 32.57 to be switched off regardless of the light level on the l.d.r. When the switch is up, R is 5 V, logic 1, so $\overline{Q}$ is logic 0 whatever the value of the potential at S. When the switch is in the down position, a momentary flash of light on the l.d.r. will send the input S to logic 1 which activates the buzzer continuously even when the light level reduces again to make S logic 0.

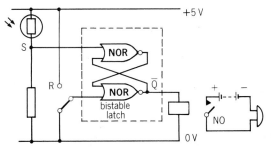

32.57 Light operated burglar alarm

Questions

Q1 Which of the following does **not** give **p**-type properties to a semiconductor when used as a doping agent?
A aluminium **B** antimony **C** boron
D gallium **E** indium

Q2 Describe how you would carry out an experiment to plot a voltage/current characteristic for a diode (either p–n or thermionic type). Draw a clear diagram of the circuit, as well as showing a typical characteristic. *(S part question)*

Q3 (a) (i) Describe the current–voltage characteristic of a p–n junction diode, illustrating your answer with a sketch-graph. (ii) Draw a circuit diagram showing the use of a diode in a half-wave rectifier circuit. Sketch the input and output waveforms.

(b) (i) Give a block diagram to show the relation between the main parts of a burglar alarm which is set off when an intruder breaks an infrared light beam. (ii) Draw a transistor switching circuit that could be used for this purpose. (iii) Explain how the circuit operates. *(O)*

Q4

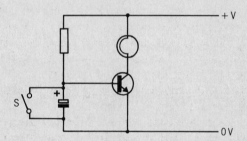

The diagram shows the circuit of a time delay switch.

(a) To which lead of the transistor is (i) the lamp connected? (ii) the 0 V line connected? (iii) the bottom of the resistor connected?

(b) State the approximate potential difference between the base and the emitter of a silicon transistor needed to switch the transistor on.

(c) With switch S open, the lamp lights some time after the battery is connected. Explain why this happens.

(d) State **two** ways by which the time delay may be increased.

(e) Switch S may be used to switch the lamp off so that the circuit may be used again. Explain how the switch achieves this.

(f) Draw the circuit diagram of a circuit which will switch a lamp **off** after a given delay period.

(g) How may this time delay be made variable? *(L)*

Q5 The circuit shown is of a power supply designed to provide a 12 volt d.c. output. The resistor, R, represents the load on the power supply.

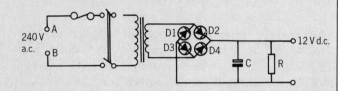

(a) Which of the two mains leads, labelled A and B, is the live? Give a reason for your choice.

(b) What kind of transformer is used in this circuit, step-up or step-down?

(c) If the potential difference across the secondary of the transformer is 12 volts, calculate the turns ratio of the transformer.

(d) Draw the traces you would expect to see on an oscilloscope (i) across the secondary of the transformer. (ii) across the resistor R when the capacitor C is removed.

(e) The four diodes, D1 to D4, make up a bridge rectifier. By considering one complete cycle of alternating voltage, explain how the bridge rectifier performs its task. You may begin as follows: 'During the first half cycle current flows through . . .'

(f) What is the purpose of the capacitor C?

(g) How would the capacitor affect the trace obtained across the resistor R? Draw a diagram of the modified trace.

(h) If the resistance of the load is reduced it will draw more current from the power supply. How will this affect the trace you have just drawn? Is this power supply very suitable for providing current for loads with very low resistance? Give reasons to support your answers. *(L)*

33 Radioactivity

33.1 The discovery of radiation

One of the most exciting and far-reaching events in the history of Physics was the discovery of radioactivity. Up to the last decade of the nineteenth century atoms of different elements were thought to be small solid particles which were indivisible. In the first decade of the twentieth century the model changed to a positively charged nucleus surrounded by a cloud of negatively charged electrons. The nuclei of individual atoms are now thought to consist of different numbers of the same two fundamental particles, the **proton** and the **neutron**. This nucleus is still believed to be surrounded by electrons, which, it is thought, can exist in different energy levels.

Work on the discharge of electricity through gases led to the discovery of **X-rays** by Röntgen in 1895. It was found that X-rays could travel through opaque materials and fog photographic plates. They could also cause **fluorescence**, as could ultraviolet light. When electromagnetic radiation falls on certain substances, these substances give off radiation of a different (longer) wavelength. If this radiation is in the visible part of the spectrum the substance glows or fluoresces. Fluorescence differs from reflection because the radiation that is given out has a different wavelength from the incident radiation. The wavelength of the reflected radiation is the same as that of the incident radiation.

When X-rays fall on certain uranium salts they fluoresce, emitting visible light. Becquerel wondered whether this process could happen in reverse, i.e. sunlight could cause the uranium salt to emit X-rays.

To test this he wrapped a photographic plate in opaque paper so that it was protected from the sunlight, placed a uranium salt on the paper and put them both in the sunlight. He assumed that, since the plate was fogged, X-rays were produced. Fortunately he also found that the photographic plate was fogged if the photographic plate with the uranium salt upon it were placed in a closed drawer. Since no light could enter the drawer he deduced that the uranium salt was emitting the radiation which passed through the protective covering and fogged the plate.

This is an example of an experiment for which a control would have been very valuable. Had the same quantity of uranium salt been placed on different photographic plates which were subjected to different amounts of incident light, it would have been immediately obvious that the fogging of the plates was independent of the incident light.

One of the properties of the radiation given off by the uranium salt is that it ionises the air. This may be demonstrated by using a spark counter.

Another method of showing the ionising properties of radiation is by charging two identical gold leaf electroscopes to give a full scale reading (Fig. 33.2). When a radium source is brought above one of them the leaf collapses, whereas the other (control) remains deflected. If the charges on the electroscopes are made the opposite sign the effect is just the same. This indicates that the discharge is due to ionisation of the air above the plates. The radium produces positive and negative ions in the air. When the electroscope is negatively charged the positive ions drift towards it and combine with the negative charges on the

---

Investigation 33.1   To demonstrate ionisation by radiation

Place a bare metal wire supported by insulators just above an earthed metal plate in a block of insulator (Fig. 33.1). Connect the wire to the positive terminal of a power pack and the metal plate to the negative terminal. Adjust the potential difference between the wire and the plate until sparks pass between the wire and the plate, then reduce the p.d. until sparks just cease to pass. When you bring a radium source near the apparatus, the air between the wire and the plate becomes ionised and sparks pass.

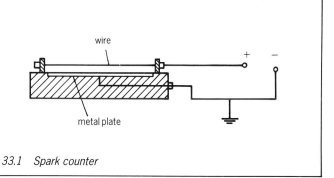

33.1   Spark counter

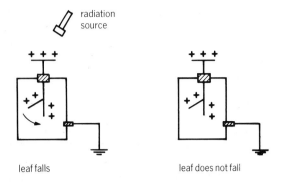

radiation source

leaf falls   leaf does not fall

33.2 Discharging leaf electroscope with a radiation source

electroscope plate. This reduces the potential of the electroscope so that the leaf falls. If the electroscope is positively charged the negative ions drift to the plate, with the same result.

Marie and Pierre Curie became very interested in the work of Becquerel. They put various substances into **ionisation chambers** to test whether they were radioactive. The principle of the ionisation chamber is shown in Fig. 33.3. The chamber contains two plates and the radioactive source may be placed on the bottom plate or introduced through the side of the chamber. The top plate is at a high positive potential, and the bottom plate is earthed. The air in the chamber is ionised by the source and a small current flows. This current may be measured by an electrometer, and the strength of the current is a measure of the activity of the source. It was found that uranium salts were radioactive, as also were substances containing thorium. Pitchblende, an ore of uranium, was very active and the Curies succeeded in isolating two new elements, polonium and radium, which were both extremely radioactive.

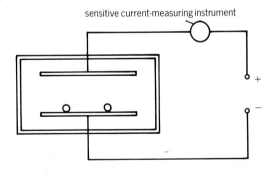

sensitive current-measuring instrument

+

−

33.3 Ionisation chamber

33.2 Types of radiation

Experiments which were performed to identify the radiations emitted from the radioactive substances may be found elsewhere. Three different types of radiation were identified and were named alpha (α) particles, beta (β) particles, and gamma (γ) rays.

Alpha particles

These are the most massive form of radiation, and have been identified as helium nuclei. They have a mass of 4 atomic mass units (a.m.u.) and a charge of $+2e$. [1 a.m.u. $= 1.66 \times 10^{-27}$ kg and $e = 1.60 \times 10^{-19}$ C]. Although they cause intense ionisation, they have a very small range of only a few centimetre (usually less than 5 cm) in air at normal atmospheric pressure, and are stopped by the human skin or a sheet of ordinary paper. They collect two electrons and become atoms of neutral helium gas.

$$\underset{\text{α-particle electrons}}{{}_2^4\text{He}^{2+} + 2e^-} = \underset{\text{helium atom}}{{}_2^4\text{He}}$$

All α-particles emitted by a particular radioactive source usually have the same energy (i.e. they are monoenergetic). Sometimes two sets with different energies are emitted. Since they are charged particles, α-particles can be deflected by both magnetic and electric fields. The speed with which they are emitted is of the order of one-twentieth the speed of light.

Beta particles

These are negatively charged particles with a charge of $-e$. Their mass is the same as that of the electron found in the outer orbits of the atom, namely about 0.0005 a.m.u., and they can be identified as fast-moving electrons. There are wide variations in their speeds, but the average is about half the speed of light. Since beta particles have a wide range of speeds they have a wide range of kinetic energies. As they are much smaller than α-particles, they have much less ionising power. They have a range of several metres in air and can penetrate a few millimetre of aluminium. They are easily deflected by magnetic and electric fields.

Gamma rays

These radiations are very penetrating and can pass through several centimetres of lead. They only produce very weak ionisation. Since they are not charged they cannot be deflected by electric or magnetic fields. Experiments have led to the conclusion that they are electromagnetic radiation of very short wavelength. This wavelength can be estimated by diffracting them through crystals. They travel with the speed of light.

Figure 33.4 shows a common but rather misleading diagram. It depicts α-, β- and γ-rays emitted from a source situated in a magnetic field and shows how they are deflected. This effect is not reproducible in the

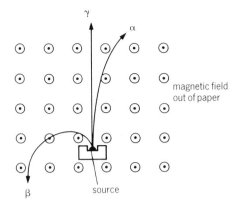

33.4 Deflection of α -, β- and γ -rays — a misleading diagram

laboratory, as a little thought will confirm. Since the magnitude of the charge on the alpha particle is twice that on the beta particle, the alpha particle will experience a force twice as large as that experienced by a beta particle in the same magnetic field. The forces on these particles are in opposite direction. However, the mass of the alpha particle is approximately 8000 times as large as that of the beta particle. Consequently the acceleration of an alpha particle in a direction perpendicular to its path is 4000 times as small as that of a beta particle. Thus a magnetic field which is strong enough to deflect the α-particles will bend the β-particles into such tight circles that they may not emerge from the lead chamber. Most school laboratories have magnets which are quite capable of deflecting β-particles, but they are unlikely to have any which will deflect α-particles.

33.3 The atom

Protons

The proton has a mass of approximately 1 a.m.u. and a charge of $+e$. It is the hydrogen nucleus. The charge is equal and opposite to that on the electron, and its mass is approximately two thousand times as large.

When α-particles bombard nitrogen, protons are emitted. Since the proton is smaller than the α-particle it has greater penetrating power. It can be deflected by both magnetic and electric fields, because it is electrically charged.

Neutrons

The neutron was discovered in 1930 when α-particles were made to bombard beryllium. Penetrating radiation was emitted which would pass through quite large thicknesses of lead (about 10 cm). This radiation could not be deflected by an electric or magnetic field, so it was concluded that it had no charge. The energies involved made it very unlikely that it was electro-magnetic radiation. Further experiments showed that its mass was approximately the same as the mass of the proton.

Structure of the atom

After the discovery of the neutron it was suggested that the nuclei of atoms were made up of protons and neutrons. Protons and neutrons are sometimes referred to as **nucleons**. Thus the atom was thought to consist of a central nucleus of protons and neutrons surrounded by negatively charged electrons which could exist in specified energy levels. Since the atom is **electrically neutral**, the number of electrons surrounding the nucleus must be equal to the number of protons in the nucleus. (Electrically neutral means that the particle either carries no charge at all or carries equal quantities of positive and negative charges so that any forces (magnetic or electric) produced will be equal and opposite and will cancel.) Practically all the mass of the atom is contained in the nucleus. The diameter of the nucleus is about 10^{-15} m and that of the whole atom about 10^{-10} m. It is clear that so-called solids contain very large amounts of empty space!

Figure 33.5 represents atoms of hydrogen $^1_1$H, helium $^4_2$He, carbon $^{12}_6$C, and oxygen $^{16}_8$O. The *upper number A* (4 for helium) is the **nucleon number**, formerly called the mass number, and is the number of

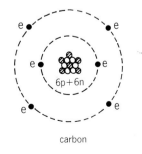

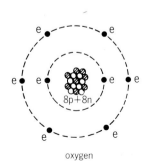

33.5 Structure of atoms

nucleons (protons plus neutrons) in the nucleus. The *lower* number Z (2 for helium) is the **proton number**, formerly called the atomic number, and is the number of protons (positive charges) in the nucleus. This will also be the number of electrons outside the nucleus. $A - Z$ is equal to the number of neutrons in the nucleus. Using this notation the particles are represented as follows: alpha $_2^4\text{He}$, beta $_{-1}^0\text{e}$, proton $_1^1\text{H}$, and neutron $_0^1\text{n}$. Gamma rays have neither mass nor charge, but do possess energy because they are electromagnetic waves.

Isotopes

With the exception of hydrogen, the number of protons in each nucleus in the atoms in Fig. 33.5 is the same as the number of neutrons. This is not always so, e.g. the heavier elements contain more neutrons than protons in the nucleus. Indeed, an individual element can exist in different forms. All the particles in Fig. 33.6 have the same number of protons in the nucleus and the same number of outer electrons. Since the chemical properties of an element depend upon the number of outer electrons, they are all particles of the same element, namely oxygen. However, each has a different nucleon number. They are called **isotopes** of oxygen. Isotopes are substances with identical proton numbers but with different nucleon numbers and cannot be separated chemically. They can be separated physically if they are first ionised and then deflected in a strong magnetic field (using a mass spectrograph). Since their charges are the same they experience the same force, but because their masses are different they are deflected by different amounts. Normal substances are often made up of a mixture of isotopes.

33.4 Radioactivity

Radioactivity is the **spontaneous random emission of particles from within the nucleus of the atom.** *Spontaneous random* means that the particles are emitted in bursts at irregular intervals with no set pattern and are emitted in any direction. The number emitted per second varies between very wide limits. This process is unique in that the particles are emitted without any energy having been given to the atom. Thus energy is obtained without energy being introduced, and so the atom itself is a source of energy. The atom is not the same after the emission of the particles. It has changed into an atom of another substance which may be **unstable** (will undergo further disintegration) or **stable** (will not emit any more particles). A permanent change has taken place. Unlike chemical reactions (changes) it is not possible to control this change. Neither is it possible to reverse it. Changing the temperature changes the rate at which a chemical reaction takes place. It does not change the rate at which a radioactive substance decays. Radioactive decay is independent of temperature, pressure or chemical combination.

As mentioned earlier, different radioactive emissions have different **penetrating powers**. The more massive a particle the greater the chance that it collides with other particles, and the less likelihood that it will travel far. The chances of a collision also depend upon the number of particles per unit volume and the size and charge of the individual particles. When a positively charged particle comes near to a positively charged nucleus it is repelled, avoiding a collision. An uncharged particle is not deflected unless it actually strikes a nucleus. Thus, although neutrons and protons have the same mass, neutrons are more penetrating because they have no charge.

Figure 33.7 shows a stream of radiation falling on to a plate. The plate in Fig. 33.7(a) is thin and a fair amount of radiation gets through, while much less radiation passes through the thicker plate in Fig. 33.7(b). Some of the radiation which does not pass through the plate is reflected and some is absorbed.

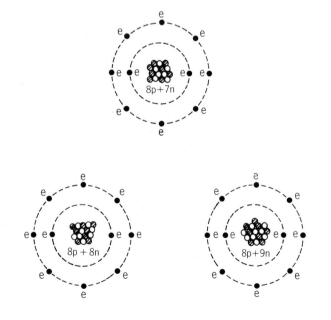

33.6 Isotopes

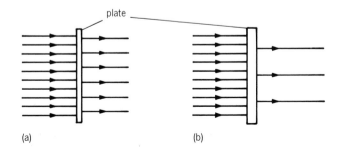

33.7 Penetration of radiation

Radioactive disintegration

When an α-particle is emitted by a nucleus, the mass of the nucleus decreases by 4 units and the charge by 2 units. Radium-226 decays with the emission of an α-particle to form an inert gas radon ($^{222}_{86}\text{Rn}$). The transformation is given by

$$^{226}_{88}\text{Ra} - {}^{4}_{2}\text{He} = {}^{222}_{86}\text{Rn}$$

Both the mass ($226 - 4 = 222$) and the charge ($88 - 2 = 86$) must be conserved.

Radon is unstable and also decays with the emission of an α-particle:

$$^{222}_{86}\text{Rn} - {}^{4}_{2}\text{He} = {}^{218}_{84}\text{Po}$$

Radium emits γ-rays as well as α-particles but the emission of γ-rays has no effect on the charge or on the mass of the nucleus. During the emission of α-particles or β-particles the nucleus is rearranged with a decrease in energy; the surplus energy is given off in the form of γ-rays. Polonium-218 is also an α-particle emitter.

$$^{218}_{84}\text{Po} - {}^{4}_{2}\text{He} = {}^{214}_{82}\text{Pb}$$

So far only α-particle emission has been considered. When a β-particle is emitted there is effectively no change in the mass of the nucleus because the mass of the β-particle is so very small. However, the charge increases by one unit. Lead-214 decays with the emission of a β-particle.

$$^{214}_{82}\text{Pb} - {}^{0}_{-1}\text{e} = {}^{214}_{83}\text{Bi}$$

The equation for charge is $82 - (-1) = 82 + 1 = 83$. But the nucleus is supposed to be made up of protons and neutrons only, so how can a β-particle be emitted? A neutron in the nucleus has changed into a proton by emitting an electron. This leaves one more proton and one fewer neutron in the nucleus. Thus the nucleon number does not change, but the proton number increases by one.

What must happen for the unstable isotope of lead $^{214}_{82}\text{Pb}$ to change into stable lead $^{206}_{82}\text{Pb}$? Since both substances are lead, the number of protons in the nucleus must stay the same. Stable lead contains eight fewer neutrons, but neutrons are not emitted in natural radioactive decay. Thus in order to keep the charge constant and decrease the mass by eight units, a total of two α-particles and four β-particles must be emitted. The complete change is shown by

$$^{214}_{82}\text{Pb} - {}^{0}_{-1}\text{e} \rightarrow {}^{214}_{83}\text{Bi} - {}^{0}_{-1}\text{e} \rightarrow {}^{214}_{84}\text{Po} - {}^{4}_{2}\text{He} \rightarrow$$

$$^{210}_{82}\text{Pb} - {}^{0}_{-1}\text{e} \rightarrow {}^{210}_{83}\text{Bi} - {}^{0}_{-1}\text{e} \rightarrow$$

$$^{210}_{84}\text{Po} - {}^{4}_{2}\text{He} \rightarrow {}^{206}_{82}\text{Pb}$$

($^{214}_{82}\text{Pb} - {}^{0}_{1}\text{e} = {}^{214}_{83}\text{Bi}$. $^{214}_{83}\text{Bi}$ then emits an electron (β-particle) to become $^{214}_{84}\text{Po}$, which emits an α-particle, and so on.)

When radium-226 decays to form stable lead, three isotopes of polonium, two of bismuth, and three of lead are formed. All the isotopes of polonium emit α-particles whilst those of bismuth and lead emit β-particles. In the whole transformation five α-particles and four β-particles are emitted, causing the nucleon number to decrease by 20 and the proton number to decrease by 6.

Conservation of momentum

The Principle of Conservation of Momentum applies to nuclear decay. When an α-particle is emitted in one direction the nucleus recoils in the opposite direction. If the α-particle is emitted as shown in Fig. 33.8 then

momentum before emission = momentum after emission
$$M \times 0 = (M - m)\,v + m\,(-V)$$
$$0 = (M - m)\,v - mV$$
$$mV = (M - m)\,v$$

where M = mass of original nucleus; m = mass of α-particle; V = velocity of α-particle; v = velocity of residual nucleus.

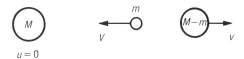

33.8   Conservation of momentum in nuclear decay

Half-life

Radioactive decay is a random process and different radioactive substances decay at different rates. The time taken for the number of particles emitted per unit time to drop top half of its original value is known as the **half-life** of the substance. In this time half of the atoms of the original material will have given off radioactive particles and changed into another substance. This new substance may or may not be unstable.

Suppose a sample of radioactive material is emitting 1056 particles per minute and has a half-life of 5 days. Table 33.1 shows that the rate of emission halves every five days. A graph of particles emitted per minute against time in days may be plotted and a smooth curve drawn through the points. From this graph the rate of emission at any other time, e.g. after seven days, may be determined.

Table 33.1   Rate of radioactive decay

Particles emitted per minute	Time/ days	Fraction of radioactive nuclides remaining
1056	0	1
528	5	$\frac{1}{2}$
264	10	$\frac{1}{4}$
128	15	$\frac{1}{8}$
64	20	$\frac{1}{16}$
32	25	$\frac{1}{32}$

A *very misleading and ambiguous* definition of half-life is that it is the time taken for the mass of radioactive substance to decrease to half the original mass. This gives the false impression that the substance is fading away. The total number of atoms in the sample does *not* alter, only the number of them that are radioactive. This means that the total mass of the sample stays almost constant. The **daughter products** (a daughter product is the element produced when a radioactive particle is emitted) do not separate from the original substance. Suppose the example in Table 33.1 is one of β-particle emission, and the original mass is 1 g. After 5 days the mass of the sample is still approximately 1 g but only half of it is the original radioactive element. After 25 days the mass of the sample is still approximately 1 g but only $\frac{1}{32}$ g is still radioactive. (This assumes that the daughter product produced is stable.)

Determining the half-life of a substance may be complicated by the presence of daughter products which are also radioactive. Radium emits α-particles and γ-rays, but daughter products are produced which emit β-particles. Thus a radium source may be regarded as emitting all three types of radiation.

Half-lives vary considerably. A few half-lives are given in Table 33.2.

Table 33.2 Half-lives

Element	Half-life
thorium	10^{10} years
radium	1620 years
bismuth (210)	5 days
polonium (218)	3 minute
polonium (214)	10^{-6} second (one millionth of a second)

33.5 Radioisotopes

Naturally occurring radioactive substances have high nucleon numbers. It is possible to make artificial radioactive substances by bombarding lighter nuclides with α-particles, protons or neutrons. The radioactive substances produced in this manner are known as **radioisotopes**.

Note A nuclide is any species of atom of which each atom has an identical proton number and also an identical nucleon number. Different nuclides which have the same proton number (but different nucleon numbers) are called **isotopes** (isotopic nuclides).

The first radioisotope was an unstable isotope of phosphorus. It was produced in 1934 by bombarding aluminium with α-particles.

$$^4_2\text{He} + ^{27}_{13}\text{Al} = ^{30}_{15}\text{P} + ^1_0\text{n}$$

Phosphorus-30 was produced, together with a neutron. Notice that on each side of the equation the sum of the nucleon numbers is 31 and the sum of the proton numbers is 15. Phosphorus-30 decays by ejecting a **positron** and has a half-life of about 3 minutes.

The positron has not been mentioned before because it does not occur in natural radioactivity. It has a mass equal to that of the electron, and a positive charge which is equal and opposite to that on the electron. It is denoted by ^0_1e.

When magnesium is bombarded by neutrons a radioisotope of sodium is formed. The reaction is

$$^{24}_{12}\text{Mg} + ^1_0\text{n} = ^{24}_{11}\text{Na} + ^1_1\text{H}$$

The sodium decays with the emission of a β-particle:

$$^{24}_{11}\text{Na} - ^{\ 0}_{-1}\text{e} = ^{24}_{12}\text{Mg}$$

Details of the technique involved in producing radioisotopes may be found elsewhere. The important point is that it is now possible to produce any radioisotope. Most of those produced have short half-life periods. This is very important because the activity and hence the danger from radioactive emissions does not last very long.

Uses of radioisotopes

All isotopes of a substance have the same chemical properties and behave in an identical manner. The advantage of a radioisotope is that its position can be detected very easily by the radiation which it emits.

Example

Describe an experiment to determine the rate at which a certain chemical is taken up by a plant.

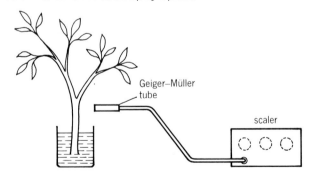

33.9 Detecting radiation in a plant

The plant is placed in water as shown and a radiation detector (Geiger–Müller counter and scaler) is placed near various parts of the stem, starting from the water level and moving upwards. This determines the level of the background radiation. The chemical containing a small trace of its radioisotope is then stirred into the water. The Geiger–Müller counter is placed near various parts of the plant at regular intervals. A large increase in the count rate at a certain point on the plant indicates that the chemical has reached that point. A graph of distance up the plant against time can be plotted.

Radioisotopes can also be used to estimate the amount of wear in bearings. If the radioisotope is impregnated into the bearings, the fine bearing filings are radioactive and are carried away by the oil. If a sample of the oil containing the filings is tested for radioactivity, the amount of wear can be estimated from the results.

Leaks in pipes may be traced by introducing a small quantity of a radioisotope into the fluid in the pipe. A radiation detector can be used to determine where the radioisotope is escaping.

Cobalt-60 is an unstable radionuclide with a half-life of 5.23 years. It is produced by bombarding cobalt-59 with neutrons:

$$^{59}_{27}\text{Co} + ^{1}_{0}\text{n} = ^{60}_{27}\text{Co}$$

Cobalt-60 emits high energy γ-radiation. This is used in cancer therapy instead of the more elaborate high energy X-radiation. It can also be used to examine welds for cracks. The source has to be shielded properly, but has the great advantage over X-rays that it is much more portable and needs no power supply.

Radio phosphorus P-32 and radio iodine I-131 are among many artificial radionuclides used as tracers. Compounds containing small proportions of the radioactive isotope along with the stable isotope are used so that the path of the element in the body of a plant, animal or human being can be followed. The position of the radioactive isotope in the body can be detected from outside the body by the radiation which it emits. This allows some medical diagnosis about internal organs to be made without surgery.

Radioisotopes are widely used in industry, e.g. to check that the thickness of a material being produced is constant. As the material passes between the radioactive source and a counter, any variation in thickness causes a change in the count rate (if the thickness decreases, the count rate increases) and irregularities can be pinpointed (Fig. 33.10).

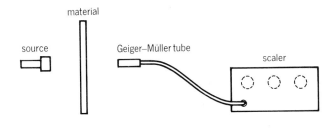

33.10 Checking the thickness of material using a radioactive source

Natural radioactive isotopes

There are a small number of radioisotopes of low proton number which occur naturally. They are produced by bombardment by radiation from outer space (cosmic rays). The most well known of these is radioactive carbon-14, which is produced when nitrogen is bombarded by neutrons.

$$^{14}_{7}\text{N} + ^{1}_{0}\text{n} = ^{14}_{6}\text{C} + ^{1}_{1}\text{H}$$

Carbon-14 decays with the emission of a β-particle, and reverts to nitrogen.

$$^{14}_{6}\text{C} - ^{0}_{1}\text{e} = ^{14}_{7}\text{N}$$

Carbon-14 has a long half-life of about 5600 years. It is reasonable to assume that equilibrium has been reached between the rate at which carbon-14 forms in the atmosphere and the rate at which it decays, and that the amount of it in the atmosphere is constant. Some of it is taken in by living plants and animals. When the plant or animal dies fresh carbon is no longer taken in and the carbon-14 which is present decays. Thus the length of time a specimen has been dead may be determined by the activity of the carbon-14 which remains in it. Carbon-dating has therefore become an important tool for archaeologists and anthropologists.

33.6   Nuclear stability

Binding energy

The nucleus is made up of neutrons and protons. What causes them to stick together? Why do the protons not repel each other?

Surprisingly, the mass of the nucleus is less than the sum of the masses of the individual protons and neutrons which make up the nucleus. The lost mass (**mass defect**) has been changed into the energy necessary to bind the nucleus together. Suppose the mass defect is Δm. Then the energy binding the nucleus together is given by

$$\Delta E = \Delta m \times c^2$$

where c is the speed of light.

If ΔE is divided by the number of nucleons in the nucleus, then the binding energy per nucleon is obtained. The higher this value is the more stable is the nucleus.

Stable nuclides

Since the positive protons in the nucleus repel each other, neutrons are required to bind the nucleus together. For lighter elements the number of protons and neutrons are approximately equal. As the number of protons increases the force required to hold the nucleus together increases to such an extent that more neutrons are required and the ratio of neutron/proton is greater than one. For heavier elements the number of neutrons in the nucleus is approximately one and a half times the number of protons.

Unstable nuclides

Whenever a β-particle is emitted a neutron is lost and a proton gained. Therefore the neutron/proton ratio is reduced by β-radiation.

When an α-particle is emitted the nucleus loses two protons and two neutrons. Since there were originally more neutrons than protons it follows that the neutron/proton ratio is increased.

Thus if the neutron/proton ratio is higher than the stability ratio a β-particle is emitted to bring it nearer to the stability ratio. When the neutron/proton ratio is lower than the stability ratio an α-particle is emitted to raise the ratio and bring it nearer to the stability ratio.

Nitrogen $^{14}_{7}$N is stable and the neutron/proton ratio is 1. When it is bombarded by neutrons $^{14}_{7}$N $+ ^{1}_{0}$n $= ^{14}_{6}$C $+ ^{1}_{1}$H. Thus carbon $^{14}_{6}$C is formed and the neutron/proton ratio is 8/6, which is greater than 1. Carbon-14 then emits a β-particle to form the stable $^{14}_{7}$N, the equation being $^{14}_{6}$C $- ^{0}_{-1}$e $= ^{14}_{7}$N.

33.7 Radioactivity and humanity

Nuclear fission

Heavy unstable nuclides can be broken up to produce energy in a process called nuclear fission. When uranium decays naturally α-particles and β-particles are emitted. However, when uranium-235 is bombarded by neutrons it forms uranium-236. Uranium-236 is unstable and breaks down, splitting into two large particles and emitting three neutrons.

$$^{235}_{92}U + ^{1}_{0}n \rightarrow ^{236}_{92}U \rightarrow ^{141}_{56}Ba + ^{92}_{36}Kr + ^{1}_{0}n + ^{1}_{0}n + ^{1}_{0}n$$

When the exact masses of the final products are added together, the sum is found to be appreciably less than the sum of the exact masses of the uranium-235 and the original neutron. This difference in mass Δm appears as energy given by

$$\Delta E = \Delta mc^2$$

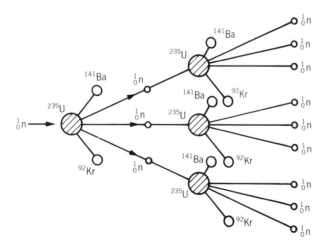

33.11 Nuclear fission

Another important point arises. The three neutrons released may collide with other nuclides, splitting them in turn. The nine neutrons formed may then split nine other nuclides and so on (Fig. 33.11). In this way a chain reaction may occur, and as a result the quantity of energy released may be very large. A few kilogram of uranium can produce as much heat energy as thousands of tonnes of coal.

This energy may be released in an uncontrolled manner, e.g. in an atomic bomb. Not only is the quantity of normal energy released (heat energy, blast etc.) very large indeed, but damaging radiations are also released which have both short-term and long-term effects.

The energy may also be released in a controlled manner, e.g. in a nuclear power station. Here boron steel rods, which absorb two out of every three of the neutrons emitted, are introduced and allow the reaction to continue at a steady rate (see Fig. 33.12). The heat energy released is used to drive steam turbines and produce electric power.

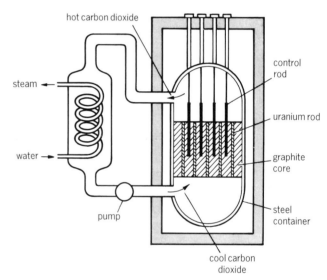

33.12 Nuclear reactor

Nuclear fusion

When lighter nuclides fuse together in a process called nuclear fusion, energy is produced and mass is lost. For example, two atoms of heavy hydrogen may fuse together to form helium and a neutron:

$$^{2}_{1}H + ^{2}_{1}H = ^{3}_{2}He + ^{1}_{0}n$$

The sum of the exact masses of the helium atom and the neutron is less than the sum of exact masses of the two heavy hydrogen atoms. This lost mass is released as energy. It is thought that the Sun's energy is produced by nuclear fusion. The two heavy hydrogen atoms must move with great speed in order to overcome the strong repulsive forces between the positively charged nuclei. The very high temperatures required for fusion reactions would melt any known material. Therefore the atoms are held in a plasma (hot ionised gas) in an intense magnetic field so that they do not touch the walls of the container. It has not yet been possible to produce a controlled reaction, but in future this problem may well be overcome. An uncontrolled fusion reaction has been produced in the hydrogen bomb.

Dangers of radiation

The first and only time atomic bombs were used in war was in 1945 when Hiroshima and Nagasaki were devastated. Widespread destruction and damage were produced immediately by the blast. Some of the damage caused by the emitted radiation became evident within days, but some did not become evident until years after the event. Some of the effects on humans of exposure to large doses, or prolonged small doses, of radiation are

(a) burns;
(b) leukaemia (cancer of the blood);
(c) sterility (inability to produce children);
(d) some children born with serious abnormalities;
(e) damage to the blood may lower resistance to normal diseases.

Safety precautions

The growth and use of radioactive products has increased considerably since about 1930. Radioactive sources have become part of normal school equipment and although the sources are very weak, it is essential to take stringent safety precautions.

1 The sources should only be handled by the forceps provided and never touched by hand.

2 They should never be pointed towards a person.
3 Food should not be taken where the sources are being used, because it may become contaminated.
4 Never smoke near a radioactive source.
5 The user should wear rubber gloves, and hands should be washed after the sources have been put away safely.

In places where the quantities of radioactive materials used are greater, special clothing is worn and photographic emulsions or some means of monitoring the radiation are used. α-particles cause intense ionisation but they are easily absorbed by protective clothing. Thus they are not likely to do much damage unless they enter the body on contaminated food etc. They will then do a lot of damage because they have been absorbed internally. β-particles have a greater range, but they too are easily absorbed and a Perspex screen may be used as protection. Again, they will do more damage if taken internally. γ-rays are most dangerous because of their high penetrating power, and great care should be taken when they are used.

Radioisotopes increase the level of radiation, but the effects can be minimised by using those with a fairly short half-life. This period should be long enough to do what is required, but short enough for the level of radiation to become very low soon afterwards.

Radioactive waste

Waste products from nuclear power stations etc. are becoming a serious problem. They should be put where the radiation can do no harm. Unfortunately there is no way of stopping a radioactive nucleus from emitting radiation.

Questions

Q1 An atom of lithium contains 3 electrons, 3 protons and 4 neutrons. Its nucleon number (atomic mass number) is
A 3　**B** 4　**C** 6　**D** 7　**E** 10　　　*(AEB)*

Q2 A nucleus consists of 90 protons and 144 neutrons. After emitting two beta particles followed by an alpha particle this nucleus will have
A 85 protons and 140 neutrons
B 87 protons and 140 neutrons
C 90 protons and 140 neutrons
D 90 protons and 142 neutrons
E 96 protons and 142 neutrons　　　*(C)*

Q3 A piece of cobalt is known to be a source of radiation. The radiation is detected by a suitable device. When a piece of lead 20 millimetres thick is used as an absorber between the source and the detector a response is still recorded. The radiation is
A alpha particles　**B** beta particles
C gamma rays　**D** high speed cobalt atoms
E high speed cobalt nuclei　　　*(L)*

Q4 In an experiment to measure the half-life of a radioactive element the following results were obtained.

Count rate/counts per minute	1 000	250	125
Time/seconds	0	110	160

(a) State clearly what is meant by the half-life of a radioactive element.
(b) From the results in the table calculate
　(i) **two** different values for the half-life of the element and
　(ii) the average half-life of the element.　　*(JMB)*

Q5 (a) What changes in the mass and charge of the nucleus of an atom take place if it emits (i) an α-particle, (ii) a β-particle, (iii) a γ-ray?
(b) Explain how it is possible for atoms of different elements to have the same mass numbers.
(c) Describe an experiment for finding the half-life of a radioactive material. Indicate how the result is obtained from the observations.

(d) If the half-life of thoron is 52 s, how long will it take for the activity of thoron sample to be reduced to $\frac{1}{32}$ of its initial value? *(O)*

Q6 In an experiment to determine the half-life of radon-220 ($^{220}_{86}$Rn) the following results were obtained, after allowing for the background count:

Time/s	0	10	20	30	40	50	60	70
Count rate/s^{-1}	30	26	23	21	18	16	14	12

(a) By plotting the count rate (vertically) against the time (horizontally), determine the half-life of $^{220}_{86}$Rn. Show clearly on your graph how you obtain your answer.

(b) (i) What is the origin of the background count?
   (ii) How is the background count determined?

(c) $^{220}_{86}$Rn emits α-particles.
   (i) What is an α-particle?
   (ii) When $^{220}_{86}$Rn emits an α-particle it becomes an isotope of the element polonium (Po). Write an equation to represent this change.

(d) When carrying out experiments with radioactive sources, students are instructed that
   (i) the source should never be held close to the human body,
   (ii) no eating or drinking is allowed in the laboratory.
   Why is it important to follow these instructions? *(L)*

Q7 A certain nuclide F decays by emission of a β-particle to form a daughter product G. The half-life of F is 20 s.

(a) Name two types of particles which form the nucleus of the nuclide F.

(b) How does the nucleus of G differ from the nucleus of F?

(c) How long would it take for three-quarters of a sample of F to decay?

(d) What effect, if any, would it have on the rate of decay of F to raise its temperature to 100 °C. Explain.

(e) The daughter product G subsequently decays by α-emission to form nuclide H. How does the atomic number of nuclide H compare with that of nuclide F? *(O)*

Q8 Radon is a radioactive element which may be represented by $^{222}_{86}$Ra.

(a) State the meaning of the numbers 222 and 86.
   Radon disintegrates with the emission of an α-particle to form a different element.

(b) How may this element be represented?

(c) What are the constituents of the nucleus of this element? The element which has been formed from radon is an isotope of polonium.

(d) In what ways will the nuclei of other isotopes of polonium differ from the nucleus of the element formed from radon?

(e) Radon disintegrates with a half-life of 3.8 days. How long will it take for the number of emissions per second of a sample of radon to be reduced to 25% of the original value? Show how you obtain your answer. *(C)*

Q9 (a) Give two properties, in each case, of alpha, beta and gamma radiation.

(b) Explain what is meant by the *half-life* of radioactive substance.

(c) The number of particles counted per second from a certain sample of a material, which radiates alpha-particles, is recorded regularly for a period of time. The measurements are given below. Use these figures to determine the half-life of the material.

Time/hours	0	1	2	3	4
Number per second	500	305	186	118	62

(d) Explain the meaning of the terms *isotope, proton number* and *nucleon number*.
   Thorium 227 (atomic number 90) decays by alpha-emission to an isotope of Radium. Give the atomic number and atomic mass number of the Radium isotope formed. *(O & C)*

Q10 (a) A nitrogen nuclide is written as $^{14}_{7}$N. What information about the structure of the nitrogen atom can be deduced from this symbol for the nuclide?

(b) A nuclide whose symbol is $^{16}_{7}$N is an isotope of nitrogen. In what way is an atom of this type of nitrogen different from the atom in (a)?

(c) The nuclide $^{16}_{7}$N decays to become an oxygen nuclide by emitting an electron. Write down an equation to show this process.

(d) The half-life of the nuclide $^{16}_{7}$N is 7.3 s. What does this mean? A sample of this type of nitrogen is observed for 29.2 s. Calculate the fraction of the original radioactive isotope remaining after this time. *(C)*

Q11 (a) Explain what is meant by the spontaneous nature of radioactive decay.

(b) Explain what is meant by *half-life* and how the concept depends on the random nature of radioactive decay.

(c) A sample of a certain nuclide which has a half-life of 1500 years has an activity of 32 000 counts per hour at the present time.
   (i) Plot a graph of the activity of this sample over the period in which it will reduce to $\frac{1}{16}$ of its present value.
   (ii) If the sample of the nuclide could be left for 2000 years, what would be its activity then? *(O)*

34 Simple experiments in radioactivity

34.1 Detecting radioactivity

The ionising properties of α-particles, β-particles and γ-rays (see p.384) are used in the detecting and counting of the radiations.

Geiger–Müller tube

The apparatus used to measure radiation is the Geiger–Müller tube. It consists of a metal tube, the outside of which is earthed. A metal wire runs down the centre of the tube and the wire and tube are connected to terminals through the insulated stopper. The wire is maintained at a positive potential of 400–450 V. A very thin mica window, which allows the radiation to pass through quite easily, closes the end of the tube. Inside the tube is argon containing a trace of bromine, and the pressure is about $\frac{1}{7}$ of the atmospheric pressure. There is quite an intense electric field between the wire and the outside tube. When a radioactive particle enters through the mica window, ionisation is produced in the gas, and there is an electrical discharge between the wire and the tube. This electrical impulse produces a voltage across the resistor R which is amplified and recorded on a **scaler**. The scaler usually contains the voltage supply for the tube, amplifier and counter. The digital counter records the number of ionisations and hence the number of radiations entering the tube.

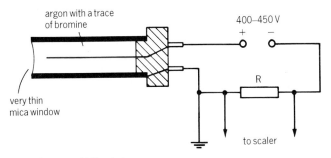

34.1 Geiger – Müller tube

Background radiation

When the apparatus is set up in position for an experiment with radioactive sources, the counter starts to count before the radioactive source is brought near. This is known as the **background count** and is due to **background radiation** which is always present. A number of sources contribute to the background radiation. These may be:

(a) cosmic radiation from outer space;
(b) radiation from the Sun;
(c) rocks in the earth which contain traces of radioactive substances;
(d) naturally occurring radioisotopes;
(e) artificial radioisotopes;
(f) products made from nuclear explosions, e.g. strontium-90 which has a half-life of 28 years.

If you point the dial of a luminous watch towards the end of the tube the count rate increases considerably.

Table 34.1 shows the number of counts of background radiation each minute for a period of ten minutes. Notice that the count rate

(a) varies considerably showing the random nature of the radiation;
(b) is small;
(c) has an average of about 20 counts/minute.

There is no need to count every minute separately when determining the background count, average count per minute can be found from the total count over the ten-minute interval. The average background count must be taken in all experiments involving measurements in radioactivity. In accurate work it is usual to find the average background count both before starting and after finishing the experiment. The average of these two is taken and subtracted from readings taken during the experiment.

Table 34.1 Measuring background radiation

time interval/min	1	2	3	4	5	6	7	8	9	10
number of counts	22	12	16	32	10	26	15	13	23	29

34.2 Determining the penetrating power of different radiations

Various kits are available which may be used for experiments on radioactivity. The essential requirements are:

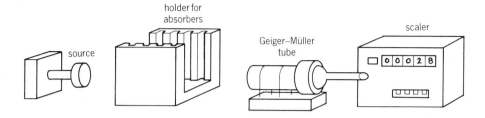

34.2 Apparatus for determining penetrating power of radiation

(a) long metal tongs to handle the sources;
(b) a source holder, which may be a Perspex sheet with a hole in the middle, into which the source may be placed;
(c) a set of absorbers consisting of paper, aluminium sheets of various thicknesses, and sheets and blocks of lead of different thicknesses;
(d) a holder on which the absorbers may be placed or into which they may be slotted;
(e) a holder for the G.M. (Geiger–Müller) tube;
(f) a set of radioactive sources.

The following sources may be available:

1 plutonium-239 or americium-241 for α-particles only;
2 strontium-90 for β-particles only;
3 cobalt-60 for γ-rays only;
4 radium-226 for α-particles, β-particles and γ-rays together.

The general arrangement of the apparatus is shown in Fig. 34.2.

Precautions

When the sources are not in use they should be kept in the special lead-lined boxes provided. These boxes in turn are kept in a small lead-lined cupboard or safe which can be securely locked and is well away from any working or well-frequented area. A source should not be left lying in its holder on a bench whilst another source is used, but should be replaced in its box and the lid closed. Neither should a source be left in a holder after readings have been taken. **Under no circumstances should a source be placed in a pocket.**

The sources are of low strength, but the number allowed in one establishment is limited. The total strength of all the sources together must be below a certain value.

The following investigations should be performed by your teacher.

Investigation 34.1   To measure the range of α-particles in air

Place the G.M. tube in its holder, connect it to the scaler, and take the average background count. Then place the source, plutonium-239, in front of the G.M. tube and quite close to it (Fig. 34.3). A large count rate, say 1500/min, is observed. Then gradually pull the source holder away from the tube, taking care to keep both source holder and the window of the tube in line.

When the holder is a certain distance from the tube, say 4 cm, the count rate drops suddenly to the background count. This indicates that the range of α-particles in air at normal atmospheric pressure is approximately 4 cm. Return the source quite close to the tube and place a sheet of paper between the source and the tube (Fig. 34.4). The count rate falls to the background count, indicating that a sheet of paper is sufficient to absorb the α-particles.

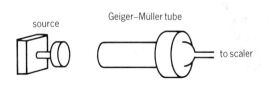

34.3 Range of α-particles in air

34.4 Absorption of α-particles by paper

Investigation 34.2 To measure the range of β-particles in air

First measure the background count. Then place the source, strontium-90, at the end of a metal tube with a slit in the end (a collimating tube) which cuts down the divergence of the β-particles and gives a more-or-less parallel beam. You will find that there is still a large count rate when you move the source a considerable distance from the G.M. tube. This indicates that β-particles have a long range in air.

Now place the source about 15 cm from the G.M. tube and set up the apparatus as in Fig. 34.2. Place different absorbers in the slots in the box and note the count rate with each. Paper has practically no effect on the count rate, and the β-particles pass through thin sheets of aluminium, although there is a fall in the count rate. When the thickness of the aluminium reaches about 4 mm the count rate drops to the background count. A much thinner sheet of lead produces the same effect. Thus aluminium 4 mm thick completely absorbs β-particles.

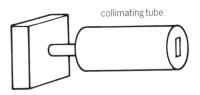

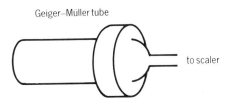

34.5 *Range of β-particles in air*

Investigation 34.3 To demonstrate the deflection of β-particles

First measure the background count. Then place a strong horseshoe magnet at the exit of a collimating tube with a strontium-90 source (Fig. 34.6). The count rate on a G.M. tube held in position 1 falls almost to the background count. Move the tube in a clockwise direction in a horizontal plane until you reach a point, position 2, when the count rate rises to almost the same value as in investigation 34.2. This indicates that the β-particles are deflected by the magnetic field. When you move the G.M.

tube in an anti-clockwise direction from position 1 there is no increase in the count rate. The direction of the deflection indicates that the β-particles are negatively charged.

Replace the strontium-90 by plutonium-239 and attempt to deflect the α-particles in the same way. This is not successful because the range of the α-particles in air is far too small to make the experiment viable. Also the deflection of the α-particles would only be 1/4000 of the deflection of the β-particles (p.385).

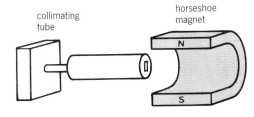

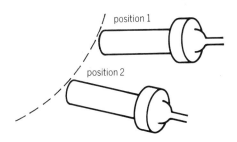

34.6 *Deflection of β-particles by magnetic force*

Investigation 34.4 To measure the intensity and absorption of γ-rays

Using the cobalt-60 source without a tube to collimate the beam, follow the procedure of investigation 34.1. When the source is moved away from the G.M. tube the count rate falls. This is not because the γ-rays do not penetrate the air, but simply because they spread out like any other electromagnetic radiation. Measure the distance d of the source from the end of the G.M. tube and record the count rate for several distances. Draw up a table like Table 34.2 and plot a graph of corrected count rate against $1/d^2$. This proves to be a straight line through the origin, indicating that the intensity of the radiation is inversely proportional to the square of the distance from the source.

Now arrange the apparatus as shown in Fig. 34.2 and place lead sheets of different thicknesses in the holder. Draw up a table like Table 34.3 and plot a graph of corrected count rate against thickness of lead (Fig. 34.8).

Table 34.2 Table of results of demonstration to show the intensity of γ-rays

Distance d/m	Count rate/min	Background count rate	Corrected count rate	d^2	$1/d^2$

Table 34.3 Table of results of a demonstration to show the absorption of γ-rays by lead

Count rate/min	Background count rate	Corrected count rate	Thickness of lead/cm

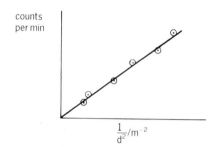

34.7 Inverse Square Law for γ-rays

34.8 Absorption of γ-rays by lead

Investigation 34.5 To identify the radiation from radium-226

First measure the background count. Then place a radium-226 source in the source holder and stand it less than 4 cm from the window of the G.M. tube. A very large count rate is observed. If you place a sheet of paper between the source and the G.M. tube the count rate drops considerably. However, the lowered count rate is still large and well above the background count. The reduction in the count rate caused by inserting the sheet of paper indicates that α-particles are being emitted by the source.

The fact that the count rate is still large indicates that other types of radiation are present.

Now replace the paper with a sheet of aluminium 4 mm thick. This causes the count rate to fall by a further large amount, indicating the presence of β-particles which are stopped by 4 mm of aluminium. The count rate is still considerably higher than the background count, and this indicates that γ-rays are also emitted. Thus you can conclude that radium-226 emits α-particles, β-particles and γ-rays.

Example

A source is placed 20 cm in front of a G.M. tube and scaler. The average background count is 25 per minute. The initial count is 2125 per minute. When a sheet of paper is placed between the source and the G.M. tube near the G.M. tube, the count for the next minute is 2100. A sheet of aluminium 5 mm thick replaces the paper and the count rate becomes 1980. Finally when the aluminium is replaced by a block of lead 5 cm thick the count rate drops to 40. What may be deduced from these readings?

1 Nothing can be deduced from the reading after the sheet of paper has been inserted. The air between the source and the G.M. tube absorbs any α-particles which may be emitted so the sheet of paper can have no further effect.

The difference between the readings is due to the random nature of the emission. Thus it is not possible to say whether or not α-particles are emitted.

2 There are definitely no β-particles present. If there were the count rate would be much lower after the introduction of the aluminium sheet. The small drop in the count rate is probably due to a slight absorption of γ-rays.

3 The presence of γ-rays is indicated by the large fall in count rate when the lead is inserted. The final count of 40 per minute is due to the variation in background radiation.

34.3 Measuring the half-life of thoron

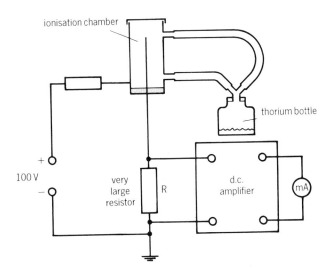

34.9   Measuring the half-life of thoron

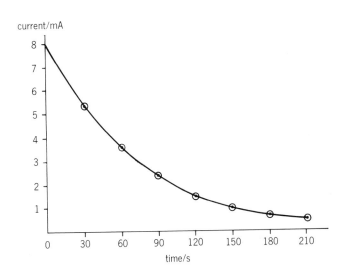

34.10   Graph showing the half-life of thoron

Thoron is a sensible substance to use for measuring half-life in a school laboratory. Thoron can be separated from its parent element, and there is no daughter element to complicate the experiment. It has a short half-life and can be replenished easily. The thorium salt in the polythene bottle emits thoron gas which mixes with the air in the bottle. When the apparatus, shown in Fig. 34.9, is set up, the clips on the rubber tubing attached to the bottle are opened. The bottle is squeezed several times and a mixture of air and thoron is pumped into the ionisation chamber. The clips are then closed. Readings of the milliammeter are taken at half-minute intervals. These values are of the amplified current and are much larger than the actual ionisation current. This does not matter when finding the half-life, because all the readings are the actual ionisation current multiplied by the same factor. Table 34.4 gives sample readings and the corresponding graph of milliammeter reading against time, with the smoothest possible curve drawn through the points, is shown in Fig. 34.10. A number of values of the half-life is taken from the graph and the average value of the half-life is found.

Note The starting point on the graph is not important when finding the half-life. All that is required is to note the time on the graph when the

Table 34.4   Sample readings when measuring the half-life of thoron

time/s	0	30	60	90	120	150	180	210
current/mA	8.00	5.35	3.50	2.55	1.55	1.10	0.75	0.50

Example

When a source is placed in front of a G.M. tube and scaler, the initial count rate after the background count has been deducted is 4000. After twenty minutes the count rate after deduction of the background count is 125. What is the half-life of the source?

It is necessary to find out how many half-lives there are in 20 minute, remembering that the count rate halves during each half-life. Thus

    1st half-life count rate falls from 4000 to 2000
    2nd half-life count rate falls from 2000 to 1000
    3rd half-life count rate falls from 1000 to 500
    4th half-life count rate falls from 500 to 250
    5th half-life count rate falls from 250 to 125

Thus the activity has halved five times during the 20-minute interval and the half-life is 4 minute.

A second method of doing this example is given below.

$$\text{Original count rate } A_o = 4000$$
Suppose number of half-lives $= n$
$$\text{Final count rate } A_n = 125$$

$$\frac{A_o}{A_n} = 2^n$$

$$\frac{4000}{125} = 2^n$$

$$32 = 2^n$$

$$2^5 = 2^n$$

$$5 = n$$

$$\text{Half-life of thoron} = \frac{20}{5}$$

$$= 4 \text{ min}$$

current is at a certain value, and then note the time when the current is at half this value. The difference between these two times is the half-life.

Table 34.5 shows a series of readings taken from the curve. From these the average value of the half-life of thoron is found to be 54 s.

Table 34.5   Calculating the half-life of thoron

	1st	2nd	1st	2nd	1st	2nd	1st	2nd	1st	2nd
current readings/ mA	8.00	4.00	7.00	3.50	6.00	3.00	5.00	2.50	4.00	2.00
time/s	0	51	8	63	20	75	33	89	51	104
half-life/s	51		55		55		56		53	

Although thoron is a gas and emits α-particles it can be used with safety. It is not likely to escape from the ionisation chamber, and the half-life is so short that the activity becomes very slight after a few minutes.

34.4   Cloud chambers

The path or **track** of an ionising radiation can be made visible by using a **cloud chamber**. A track is the path taken by a particle. A cloud chamber contains a supersaturated vapour in a dust-free atmosphere. When radiation passes through the chamber a string of ions is formed. These serve as condensation nuclei, and the supersaturated vapour condenses upon them so that the path shows up as a vapour trail. The condensed vapour must be removed fairly rapidly or else the cloud chamber becomes full of vapour and it is impossible to observe individual tracks. A strong electric field inside the chamber removes the ions (and hence the condensed vapour) soon after they are formed.

Wilson cloud chamber

The vapour in the Wilson cloud chamber is made supersaturated by allowing the gas to expand and hence cool. The base plate A (see Fig. 34.11) is a circular metal plate with a hole in the centre. From this hole a tube leads to a pump (which may be a cycle

pump with the washer reversed) for pumping out the air. Fixed just above A is another metal plate B and on top of this is a black felt pad. The pad is black so that the white vapour tracks may be seen more easily. A Perspex dome fits over A, and the source holder S passes through the top of the dome. A metal ring C is attached inside the dome, and the electric field is applied between C and A. Before the dome is placed on A the black felt pad is soaked with alcohol, so that the chamber contains a mixture of alcohol vapour and air. When the pump is given a sharp pull, the pressure in the chamber is reduced, consequently the air and vapour expand. The resulting cooling causes the vapour to become supersaturated, and white tracks of condensed vapour can be seen emanating from the source.

Diffusion cloud chamber

The diffusion cloud chamber also consists of a Perspex dome resting upon a black-coated metal plate (Fig. 34.12). Inside the top of the Perspex cylinder is a ring of sponge or felt which has been soaked with alcohol. The source holder also fits into the side of the dome. Below the metal plate is a chamber which can be screwed onto the plate. This chamber contains a sponge on which a layer of solid carbon dioxide is placed. When the chamber is screwed onto the base plate, the solid carbon dioxide is in contact with the base plate, and so a steep temperature gradient is formed between the top of the Perspex dome and the metal plate. This causes a layer of supersaturated alcohol vapour to be formed. The electric field is produced electrostatically by rubbing the top of the Perspex dome with a dry cloth. When the source is introduced the tracks can be seen very clearly.

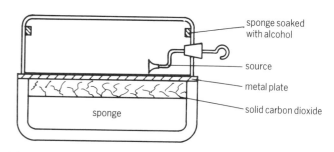

34.12   Diffusion cloud chamber

Cloud chamber tracks

Some typical cloud chamber tracks are shown in Fig. 34.13. Figure 34.13(a) shows the tracks of mono-energetic α-particles. The tracks of α-particles are straight and thick, showing little or no deviation and intense ionisation. They are all approximately the same length, indicating that they are emitted with the same energy.

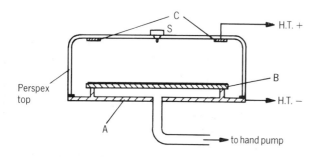

34.11   Wilson cloud chamber

The tracks in Fig. 34.13(b) are also those of α-particles. However, they are of two different lengths indicating that two sets of particles with different energies were emitted.

Figure 34.13(c) shows the tracks of high energy β-particles. They are thin but more or less straight. The tracks are thinner than those of α-particles because they make ionising collisions much less frequently, and so there are fewer condensation nuclei.

β-particle tracks are normally thin and tortuous (see Fig. 34.13d) because the particles are easily deflected and cause little ionisation.

Figure 34.13(e) indicates what may happen when γ-rays pass through a cloud chamber. The path of the γ-ray may be inferred. γ-rays do not produce tracks, but they may collide with an electron in the shell of an atom, giving sufficient energy to this electron to enable it to cause ionisation and produce its own short track.

Thus a number of short thin tracks are seen starting from the same straight line. This line is the path of the γ-ray.

Uses of cloud chamber tracks

The tracks produced from a source in a cloud chamber give a quick indication of the type of radiation which is being emitted. An observer would be very lucky to see any unusual track in a cloud chamber. The probability of seeing an α-particle collide with another nucleus is very small. However, if continuous photographs are taken and studied at leisure, the occasional collision may be detected. It is possible to see the odd collision in this way when the cloud chamber is filled with nitrogen and an α-particle source is used.

Figure 34.14 shows one such collision. The α-particle tracks are straight, and the shortened one shows a collision between an α-particle and a nitrogen nucleus.

$$ {}^{14}_{7}N + {}^{4}_{2}He = {}^{17}_{8}O + {}^{1}_{1}H $$

The short thick track is that of ${}^{17}_{8}O$, the long thin track is that of the emitted proton.

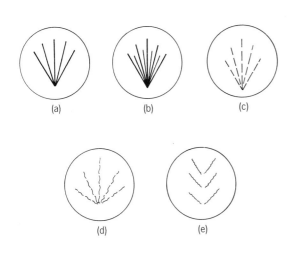

34.13 Cloud chamber tracks

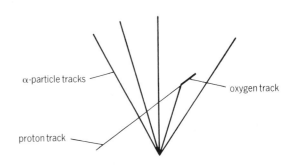

34.14 Tracks of a collision in a cloud chamber

Questions

Q1

A radioactive source is placed in front of a detector as shown in the diagram, and a high count rate is observed. When a sheet of paper X is lowered between the source and detector, there is a reduction in the count rate. When an aluminium sheet Y is lowered next to X, there is practically no further reduction in the count rate. The radiation is most likely to be

A alpha radiation only.
B alpha radiation only.
C a mixture of alpha and beta radiation.
D a mixture of beta and gamma radiation.
E a mixture of alpha and gamma radiation.   (L)

Q2 Various sheets are placed between a radioactive source and a detector which is capable of indicating the presence of alpha, beta or gamma emissions. The following observations are recorded.

Material of sheets	Effect on the count rate
Paper	Slight drop
Paper + aluminium	No further drop
Paper + aluminium + lead	A further slight drop

The emissions from the source are
A gamma only. B beta and gamma. C alpha and beta.
D alpha and gamma. E alpha, beta and gamma.   (L)

Q3 Certain atoms emit gamma radiation because
A they have a large nucleon number.
B their nuclei emit electrons.
C their nuclei contain protons and neutrons.
D their nuclei are unstable.
E their nuclei are at a high temperature.   (L)

Q4 Describe the mode of action of any **one** type of nuclear radiation detector.

A nuclear radiation detector is connected to a scaler which counts the number of particles detected. The scaler indicates 12 counts during a period of one minute. During two subsequent periods of one minute the scaler indicates 11 and 15 counts.

When a source of radioactive material is placed near the detector, the counts over three periods of one minute are: 1480, 1508 and 1496.

A piece of thick paper is placed between the source and detector and the counts reduce to 1216, 1226 and 1230 over one-minute periods.

Finally, when a sheet of lead 5 mm thick is placed between the source and detector the counts are 13, 11 and 14 over one-minute periods.

(i)   Why is a count obtained without the source?
(ii) Why do the counts obtained in any group differ?
(iii) Which of the three types of radiation, α, β and γ, are emitted by the source?   *(O & C)*

Q5 State the changes that take place in the nucleus of an atom of a radioactive source when an α-particle is emitted. Illustrate your answer by an equation for the emission of an α-particle from the nuclide $^A_Z X$.

The arrangement illustrated in the diagram is set up and a ratemeter is connected to the detector.

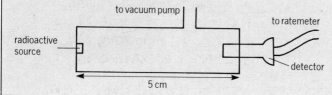

A low count rate is observed on the ratemeter when the pressure of the air in the vessel is atmospheric. As the air is pumped out, the count rate rises to a maximum value of 2000 per second.

The experiment is repeated six hours later. Similar observations are made except that the maximum count rate observed is only 250 per second.

(a) Identify the radiation emitted from the source, explaining fully how you reach your conclusion.
(b) Calculate a value for the half-life of the radioactive source. Indicate, with a reason, whether or not the half-life is affected by variations in air pressure.

Suggest reasons why
(i) α-particles produce much denser tracks in a cloud-chamber than do β-particles.
(ii) β-particles are much more readily deflected by an electric field than are α-particles.   *(C)*

Q6 A Geiger–Müller tube attached to a scaler is placed on a bench in the laboratory. Over three consecutive minutes the scaler reads 11, 9 and 16 counts per minute. When a radioactive source is placed near to the Geiger–Müller tube the counts over three consecutive minutes are 1310, 1270, and 1296 per minute. When a piece of thick paper is placed between the source and the tube the counts are 1250, 1242, and 1236 per minute. When the paper is replaced by a sheet of aluminium 2 mm thick the counts are 13, 12 and 11 per minute.

(i)   Why is there a reading when no source is present?
(ii) Why do the three readings in any one group differ?
(iii) What can be deduced about the nature of the emission?

Give reasons for your answer.   *(L)*

Answers

Introduction

Q1 1.08 mm, 86 $\pm$0.5 mm

Q2 3.2 (3.16) (no unit)

Q3 9.5 g, 360 g. (Make sure you have not plotted the graph the wrong way round.)

Q4 0.5 kg m^{-3}

Q5 +2.5 m s^{-2}

Q6 $R_o = 5.0 \pm 0.1\ \Omega$, $\theta = 41\ ^\circ C$, 0.05 $\Omega\ ^\circ C^{-1}$

Q7 (4.2, 30), $v = 0$ m s^{-1}, $t = 3.25$ s

Q8 (a) 8.7 m, (b) 5.0 m, (c) 60°

Q9 4.5 s (4.47 s), -20.0 m s^{-1}

Q10 -5.0 m s^{-2}

Q11 $L = 6$ m, 36 m^2

Q12 0.81 (no unit). (Make sure you have not plotted the graph the wrong way round.)

Q13 Intercept = $-0.5\ \Omega^{-1}$

Q15 (a) Average mass = mass 100 ball-bearings/100.
(b) Average diameter $\approx$ diameter of 10 ball-bearings/10.
(c) Measure diameter several times at one place and in several different places and average the result.

Chapter 1

Q1 A

Q2 C

Q3 E

Q4 B

Q6 (i) Proton, neutron, electron (ii) electron (iii) neutron

Q8 1.6×10^{-5} cm

Q9 2.0×10^{-6} mm

Q10 (a) 2.0×10^{-6} kg, (b) 2.5×10^{-9} m^3, (c) 1.25×10^{-8} m, (d) 0.4 m^2

Q11 10×10^{-6} mm

Q13 (d) 0.03 m^2 (f) 5.6×10^{-9} m

Q14 1.6×10^{-6} mm

Chapter 2

Q1 C

Q2 D

Q3 C

Q4 E

Q5 B

Q6 C

Q7 2.15 cm

Q8 1.0 mm, 18.7 mm, 17.7 mm

Q9 (a) 3.46 mm (b) 7.98 mm (c) 12.69 mm; (a) 2 (b) 2 (c) 1

Q10 (b)(i) 1.3 g cm^{-3} (ii) 64.1 cm^3

Q11 8.5 g cm^{-3}

Q12 (a) 2.25 mm (b) 0.9 g cm^{-3}

Q13 1.056 g cm^{-3}; volume of solution = volume of water

Q14 11.4, 11 400; 8.0, 8000; 13.6, 136 000; 125, 0.5; 97, 19 400; 100, 800; 20 000, 0.0012

Q16 (a) 3.5 cm^2 (b) 165.9 g

Q17 0.012 m^3, 12.0 kg. 0.008 m^3, 2400 kg m^{-3}

Q18 5.767×10^{24} kg

Chapter 3

Q1 B

Q2 E

Q3 C

Q4 C

Q8 (a) 0–4.0 N (b) 1.5 N

Q10 (a) 54 mm (b) 40 N upward, $3\frac{1}{3}$ m s^{-2}

Q11 4.5 N, length of spring 13.0 cm $\pm$0.8 cm

Q12 (a) 0.25 N (b) 90 mm (c) 12 N upwards (e) 0.8 J

Q13 (a)

F/N	0	2	4	6	8
e/m	0	0.006	0.012	0.018	0.024

(c) Yes (d) 5 N, 0.0375 J (e) oscillates about 0.012 m $\pm$0.003 m

Q14 (a) 100 g (b) Weight = 1 N; apparent weight = 0.36 N (c) 0.68 N

Q15 (b) 2000 N downwards (c) 1.5 m s^{-2} upward

Chapter 4

Q1 E

Q2 C

Q3 E

Q4 A

Q5 1088 m

Q9 99 960 Pa

Q10 (b)(i) 160 N (ii) 80 000 Pa (iii) 80 000 Pa (iv) 24 000 N upward (v) 600

Chapter 5

Q1 D

Q2 E

Q3 D

Q4 C

Q5 C

Q6 C

Q7 A

Q8 D

Q9 5 m s^{-2}

Q10 $a = -0.9$ m s^{-2}, $t = 6\frac{2}{3}$ s

Q11 $a = 80$ m s^{-2}, $s = 576$ km

Q12 $-60\,\mathrm{m\,s^{-2}}$
Q13 $a = 1\,\mathrm{m\,s^{-2}}$, $v = 25\,\mathrm{m\,s^{-1}}$
Q14 (a) $\frac{10}{11}\,\mathrm{m\,s^{-1}}$ (b) $1000\,\mathrm{N}$ (c) $55\,\mathrm{m}$
Q15 (a) $v = 10\,\mathrm{m\,s^{-1}}$ (i) at 'origin' (ii) $+20\,\mathrm{m}$ from 'origin'
  (b) $1\,\mathrm{m\,s^{-1}}$, $0.5\,\mathrm{m\,s^{-1}}$
  (c) (i) $+1\,\mathrm{m\,s^{-2}}$ (ii) $-2\,\mathrm{m\,s^{-2}}$ (iii) $6\,\mathrm{m}$
  (d) (i) $115\,\mathrm{m}$ (ii) $11.5\,\mathrm{m\,s^{-1}}$
  (e) (i) $+0.8\,\mathrm{m\,s^{-2}}$ (ii) $-0.8\,\mathrm{m\,s^{-2}}$ (iii) $200\,\mathrm{m}$ (iv) $5\,\mathrm{m\,s^{-2}}$
Q16 (a) uniform acceleration (b) acceleration doubled
  (c) uniform velocity
Q17 (b) (i) $1\frac{1}{3}\,\mathrm{m\,s^{-2}}$ (ii) $225\,\mathrm{m}$
Q18 (a) $-1.5\,\mathrm{m\,s^{-2}}$ (b) $1125\,\mathrm{m}$

Chapter 6

Q1 D
Q2 C
Q3 D
Q4 B
Q5 $4\,\mathrm{m\,s^{-2}}$, $3\,\mathrm{m\,s^{-2}}$
Q6 $0.1\,\mathrm{m\,s^{-2}}$
Q7 (a) ascending at $2\,\mathrm{m\,s^{-2}}$ (b) descending at $4\,\mathrm{m\,s^{-2}}$
Q8 (a) $700\,\mathrm{N}$ (b) $805\,\mathrm{N}$ (c) $700\,\mathrm{N}$ (d) $0\,\mathrm{N}$
Q9 $0.05\,\mathrm{N}$, uniform velocity $0.2\,\mathrm{m\,s^{-1}}$
Q10 $4 \times 10^5\,\mathrm{N}$
Q11 $0.2\,\mathrm{m\,s^{-1}}$
Q12 First ball $0\,\mathrm{m\,s^{-1}}$; second ball $0.2\,\mathrm{m\,s^{-1}}$; both momentum
  and kinetic energy conserved
Q13 (i) $40\,\mathrm{N\,s}$ (ii) $40\,\mathrm{N\,s}$ $(5v)$ (iii) $8\,\mathrm{m\,s^{-1}}$
Q14 C
Q15 (i) $4\,\mathrm{s}$ (ii) $40\,\mathrm{m\,s^{-1}}$ (iii) $4000\,\mathrm{J}$
Q16 (a) $2.5\,\mathrm{N}$ (b) $5\,\mathrm{m\,s^{-2}}$ (c) $0.625\,\mathrm{m}$
Q17 (i) $0.125\,\mathrm{m\,s^{-2}}$ (ii) $112\,500\,\mathrm{J}$ (iii) $15\,000\,\mathrm{N\,s}$
Q18 (a) $5\,\mathrm{m\,s^{-1}}$ (b) $0.4\,\mathrm{N\,s}$ (c) $1.0\,\mathrm{J}$ (d) $0.2\,\mathrm{J}$
Q19 (a) (i) $0\,\mathrm{N\,s}$ (ii) $0\,\mathrm{N\,s}$ (b) $\sqrt{5}\,\mathrm{N\,s}$ (c) $10\sqrt{5}\,\mathrm{m\,s^{-1}}$

Chapter 7

Q1 E
Q2 D
Q3 A
Q4 D
Q5 D
Q6 B
Q7 B
Q8 D
Q9 B
Q10 $7.9\,\mathrm{N}$ at $19°$ S of W
Q11 $17.3\,\mathrm{N}$ at $14°$ to $11\,\mathrm{N}$ force, $12.5\,\mathrm{m\,s^{-2}}$
Q12 (a) $4500\,\mathrm{N}$ at $39°$ to $2500\,\mathrm{N}$ force (c) $0.36\,\mathrm{m\,s^{-2}}$
Q13 (b) (i) $3464\,\mathrm{N}$ (ii) $2000\,\mathrm{N}$
Q14 (a) (i) $40\,\mathrm{m\,s^{-1}}$ (ii) $80\,\mathrm{m}$ (c) $40\sqrt{2}\,\mathrm{m\,s^{-1}}$ at $45°$
Q15 (a) $0.5\,\mathrm{N}$ (b) $0.5\,\mathrm{m\,s^{-2}}$ (c) $1\,\mathrm{J}$, $\sqrt{2}\,\mathrm{N\,s}$
Q16 (a) $6\,\mathrm{s}$ (b) $6\,\mathrm{s}$ (c) $9\,\mathrm{m}$ (d) $2.5\,\mathrm{m\,s^{-1}}$ at $53°$ to bank
Q17 $20\,\mathrm{m\,s^{-1}}$

Chapter 8

Q1 E
Q2 D
Q3 A
Q4 B
Q5 (a) $100\,\mathrm{N}$, $900\,\mathrm{N}$, $0.4\,\mathrm{m}$ from support ($0.2\,\mathrm{m}$ from end)
Q6 $11.25\,\mathrm{N\,cm}$, $52.5\,\mathrm{cm}$ graduation
Q7 $50\,\mathrm{cm}$
Q8 (b) $60\,\mathrm{kg}$
Q9 $80\,\mathrm{cm}$, 0.75
Q10 A
Q12 $0.6\,\mathrm{m}$
Q14 $0.7\dot{3}$, $60\,\mathrm{W}$
Q15 (ii) 4 (iii) $320\,\mathrm{J}$, $200\,\mathrm{J}$ (iv) 0.625

Chapter 9

Q1 E
Q2 A
Q3 B
Q4 D
Q5 C
Q6 B
Q7 B
Q8 $4.25\,\mathrm{kW}$
Q9 $2500\,\mathrm{N}$
Q11 $150\,\mathrm{kW}$
Q13 $1.8\,\mathrm{m\,s^{-1}}$
Q14 (a) $1400\,\mathrm{J}$ (b) $1800\,\mathrm{J}$ (c) work done against frictional forces
Q15 $4.8\,\mathrm{J}$, $4.9\,\mathrm{m\,s^{-1}}$. $2.4\,\mathrm{J}$

Chapter 10

Q1 C
Q2 E
Q3 E
Q4 E
Q5 C
Q6 $5\,\mathrm{kW}$
Q7 $249\,°\mathrm{C}$
Q9 $39.2\,\mathrm{kJ\,min^{-1}}$
Q11 $480\,\mathrm{J\,kg^{-1}\,K^{-1}}$

Chapter 11

Q1 D
Q2 D
Q3 A
Q4 C
Q5 $2.14 \times 10^5\,\mathrm{Pa}$
Q6 $62\,\mathrm{cm^3}$
Q7 (b) $750\,\mathrm{K}$ or $477\,°\mathrm{C}$
Q10 $1720\,\mathrm{mm\,Hg}$
Q11 2.6
Q13 $3.\dot{3}\,\mathrm{mm^3}$

Chapter 12

Q1 C
Q2 D
Q3 D
Q8 20.0088 m
Q9 9.9978 m
Q10 469.5 °C
Q11 $20 \times 10^{-6}\,\text{K}^{-1}$

Chapter 13

Q1 D
Q2 D
Q3 E
Q4 B
Q5 C
Q12 $-12.5\,°\text{C}$
Q14 135 °C
Q16 $2\,\Omega$

Chapter 14

Q1 B
Q2 C
Q3 D
Q4 30.37 kJ
Q5 30 g or 0.03 kg
Q6 (c) 2000 s (d) rate of heat loss = 8 W = rate of supply of heat
Q7 $804\,\text{J s}^{-1}$, $321\,600\,\text{J kg}^{-1}$
Q8 (i) $168\,\text{g min}^{-1}$ $(2.8\,\text{g s}^{-1})$ (ii) 19.6 W
Q9 $2\,240\,000\,\text{J kg}^{-1}$
Q10 (c) 349 000 J
Q12 (a) $17 \pm 1\,°\text{C}$ (b) $4800\,\text{J kg}^{-1}\,\text{K}^{-1}$
Q14 $75\frac{1}{3}$ min (a) (i) 1.05 kW (ii) 7 min

Chapter 15

Q1 C
Q2 E
Q3 B
Q4 C
Q5 C
Q6 E
Q9 4.5 m
Q11 E
Q12 0.05 m
Q17 25 mm
Q18 $v = +32\,\text{cm}, u = +32\,\text{cm}, f = +16\,\text{cm}$

Chapter 16

Q1 E
Q2 (b) (ii) $n = 1.414$
Q3 $n = 1.73$
Q6 $n_\text{g} = 1.5$
Q7 (a) $c = 48.6°$ (b) $n_\text{w} = 1.3$
Q8 (i) $c = 48.6°$ (ii) 40° (iii) 0.6 m

Chapter 17

Q1 C
Q2 D
Q3 A
Q4 E
Q5 $n_\text{w} = 1.3\dot{3}$
Q6 31.66°
Q9 $\lambda = 250$ m
Q11 (d) $f = 200$ kHz

Chapter 18

Q1 D
Q2 C
Q3 A
Q4 D
Q5 B
Q7 $v = +6\frac{2}{3}\,\text{cm}, 1\frac{2}{3}\,\text{cm}$
Q9 (a) $u = +7.5$ cm
Q11 (c) $u = +45\,\text{cm}, m = +2.0\times$
Q12 $v = -7.5\,\text{cm}, 5.0\,\text{cm}$
Q13 10 cm on opposite side of lens; 2 cm high; real

Chapter 19

Q1 C
Q2 E
Q3 D
Q4 D
Q5 $\frac{2}{5}$ m from object. $f = \frac{8}{25}$ m
Q6 1.45
Q8 (b) $7\frac{1}{7}$ cm, 24.5 mm
Q9 1.5 cm high, virtual, magnified $(+3\times)$, erect
Q14 -10.5 cm
Q15 (a) (i) $+20$
Q17 6 cm
Q18 (d) 22 cm
Q19 (b) $4\frac{4}{49}$ cm

Chapter 20

Q1 C
Q2 D
Q3 E
Q4 D
Q5 D
Q6 B
Q7 E
Q8 B
Q10 A
Q11 D
Q12 B
Q13 (b) 250 Hz, 1.32 m
Q14 $16\,\text{cm s}^{-1}$
Q16 (a) $3 \times 10^8\,\text{m s}^{-1}$ (b) 240 m
Q17 (a) (i) 500 Hz (ii) 0.68 m
Q18 500 Hz, beats $f = 2$ Hz

Chapter 21

Q1 D
Q3 (a) (ii) 680 Hz
Q4 (b) (ii) 400 Hz (iii) 0.85 m
Q5 (iii) 320 Hz

Q6 $340 \, \text{m s}^{-1}$

Q7 (ii) $350 \, \text{m s}^{-1}$ (iii) 500 Hz, pitch is 1 octave higher

Q8 $0.\dot{6} \, \text{m}, 0.\dot{3} \, \text{m}$, pitch is 1 octave higher

Chapter 22

Q1 E

Q3 A

Q4 D

Q5 $1.18 \times 10^{-3} \, \text{m}$

Q9 (b) (ii) 0.013 m,   (iii) $6.5 \times 10^{-7} \, \text{m}$

Chapter 23

Q1 D

Q2 D

Chapter 24

Q1 A

Q2 E

Q3 D

Q4 C

Q7 D

Q9 (b) (ii) $7.5 \, \mu\text{F}$

Q10 $60\,000 \, \text{V m}^{-1}$

Chapter 25

Q1 C

Q2 $8 \, \text{V}, \frac{2}{3} \, \text{A}, 24 \, \text{W}$

Q3 (i) $13 \, \Omega$ (ii) 0.2 V, 0.65 V

Q4 (i) A 'bright', B 'dim' (ii) A 0.3 A, B 0.15 A (iii) A 0.6 A, B 0.15 A

Q5 (a) $4 \, \Omega$ (c) (i) $\frac{1}{2}$ (ii) $\frac{2}{1}$ (iii) $\frac{2}{1}$

Q7 (iii) $1\frac{1}{3} \, \text{A}, \frac{2}{3} \, \text{A}, \frac{2}{3} \, \text{A}$ (iv) 8 V, 4 V, 4 V   (v) 16 W

Chapter 26

Q1 D

Q2 E

Q3 C

Q4 (i) $1 \, \Omega$ (ii) 150 J

Q5 (i) $8 \, \Omega$ (ii) $6 \, \Omega$; 2 V

Q6 (i) $20 \, \Omega$ (ii) $9 \, \Omega$ (iii) 0.5 A
   (iv) 0.1 A; resistance should be very high

Q7 (i) 1.2 A   (ii) 5.4 V   (iii) 4.32 J

Q8 (a) 3.6 V   (b) 24 C   (c) 4.2 V   (d) 72 J

Q9 (a) $4 \, \Omega$ (b) 1.2 V   (c) 0.3 A   (d) 1.44 V   (e) 1.8 A

Q10 (b) (i) 1.97 A, $R_1 = 6 \, \Omega$ (ii) $0.2 \, \Omega$ (iii) 60 A

Q11 $X = 30 \, \Omega, E = 1.5 \, \text{V}; 3 \, \text{A}$

Q12 $E = 2 \, \text{V}, r = 1 \, \Omega$

Chapter 27

Q1 A

Q2 D

Q3 D

Q4 A

Q5 $19.2 \, \Omega$ (i) 12 A   (ii) 115.2 W

Q6 $3.6 \, \Omega, 2.4 \, \Omega$; 14.4 W, 9.6 W

Q7 5 kW h, 30p, 40 A

Q9 (i) 3.05 kW   (ii) 12.2 A   (iii) 43 920 kJ

Chapter 28

Q1 A

Q2 D

Q3 E

Q4 E

Q5 B

Q6 E

Q12 (b) (i) N

Chapter 29

Q1 E

Q3 E

Q4 (b) $0.101 \, \Omega$ resistor in parallel with meter

Q7 150 J, 120 J, 80%

Q8 (c) $9990 \, \Omega$ in series

Chapter 30

Q1 C

Q2 D

Q3 D

Q4 B

Q8 (i) 20 A   (ii) 98 kW

Q9 (a) (i) 2.5 V   (ii) 5 V   (iii) 15   (iv) 30   (v) 7.5 V   (vi) 1.5 A

Chapter 31

Q1 A

Chapter 32

Q1 B

Q5 (c) 20 : 1

Chapter 33

Q1 D

Q2 C

Q3 C

Q4 (b) (i) 55 s, 50 s,   (ii) 53.3 s

Q5 (d) 260 s

Q6 (a) 53 ± 1 s   (c) (ii) $^{220}_{86}\text{Rn} = {}^{4}_{2}\text{He} + {}^{216}_{84}\text{Po}$

Q7 (c) 40 s

Q8 (b) $^{218}_{84}\text{Po}$ (c) 84 p, 134 n   (e) 7.6 days

Q9 (c) 1.4 h   (d) $^{223}_{88}\text{X}$

Q10 (c) $^{16}_{7}\text{N} - {}^{0}_{-1}\text{e} = {}^{16}_{8}\text{O}$ (d) $\frac{1}{16}$

Q11 (c) (ii) 1290 ± 20 counts per hour

Chapter 34

Q1 E

Q2 D

Q3 D

Q4 (iii) α and β

Q5 (a) α (b) 2 h

Q6 (iii) β

Index